OXFORD EARLY CHR

General Editors

Gillian Clark   Andrew Louth

THE OXFORD EARLY CHRISTIAN STUDIES series includes scholarly volumes on the thought and history of the early Christian centuries. Covering a wide range of Greek, Latin, and Oriental sources, the books are of interest to theologians, ancient historians, and specialists in the classical and Jewish worlds.

Titles in the series include:

The *Consolation* of Boethius as Poetic Liturgy
Stephen Blackwood (2015)

The Theological Anthropology of Eustathius of Antioch
Sophie Cartwright (2015)

The Song of Songs and the Fashioning of Identity in Early Latin Christianity
Karl Shuve (2016)

The Greek *Historia Monachorum in Aegypto*
Monastic Hagiography in the Late Fourth Century
Andrew Cain (2016)

The Demonic in the Political Thought of Eusebius of Caesarea
Hazel Johannessen (2016)

Enchantment and Creed in the Hymns of Ambrose of Milan
Brian P. Dunkle, SJ (2016)

Social Justice and the Legitimacy of Slavery
The Role of Philosophical Asceticism from
Ancient Judaism to Late Antiquity
Ilaria L. E. Ramelli (2016)

Making Amulets Christian
Artefacts, Scribes, and Contexts
Theodore de Bruyn (2017)

Isaac of Nineveh's Ascetical Eschatology
Jason Scully (2017)

The Roman Martyrs
Introduction, Translations, and Commentary
Michael Lapidge (2017)

Liturgy and Byzantinization in Jerusalem

DANIEL GALADZA

OXFORD
UNIVERSITY PRESS

OXFORD
UNIVERSITY PRESS

Great Clarendon Street, Oxford, OX2 6DP,
United Kingdom

Oxford University Press is a department of the University of Oxford.
It furthers the University's objective of excellence in research, scholarship,
and education by publishing worldwide. Oxford is a registered trade mark of
Oxford University Press in the UK and in certain other countries

Published in the United States of America by Oxford University Press
198 Madison Avenue, New York, NY 10016, United States of America

British Library Cataloguing in Publication Data
Data available

Library of Congress Cataloging in Publication Data
Data available

ISBN 978–0–19–881203–6 (Hbk.)
ISBN 978–0–19–884353–5 (Pbk.)

Preface and Acknowledgements

This book examines how the liturgical worship tradition of the tumultuous region of Jerusalem and Palestine changed under Byzantine influence during the complex time of transition from late antiquity to the medieval period. Before starting, certain technical details need to be explained, and those who made this work possible deserve to be acknowledged.

All quotations of Scripture follow the Septuagint numbering and, unless otherwise stated, English translations are from the Revised Standard Version (RSV). Quotations from texts in ancient languages, especially from Greek and Georgian, are included: they give the reader access to texts that are often difficult to find. Quotations in the body of the present work are always translated into English. Unless otherwise indicated, accents and breathing marks in Greek texts from manuscript sources are corrected to conform to current scholarly and editorial norms. In the case of Georgian, texts are transcribed in modern Georgian script (მხედრული, *mxedruli*, 'cavalry'), and technical terms or brief phrases are transliterated. For all languages I follow the Romanization tables of the Library of Congress. For Syriac, Arabic, and Armenian I have relied on translations and I present technical terms in transliteration. In bibliographical references the names of authors are always given in Latin characters, either in the form they themselves employ (e.g. A. M. Pentkovsky) or—in those instances where the name does not possess a conventional Latin form—according to the Romanization system of the Library of Congress (e.g. A. A. Dmitrievskii).

Regarding sources, I have attempted to use the most up-to-date shelf marks for each manuscript, although the system here renders the location name of each library in English rather than in Latin or another language. For example, it gives *Vatican* instead of *Vaticanus* (*Vat.*) and *Sinai* instead of *Sinaiticus* (*Sin.*). The same goes for the name of the language used in a manuscript: the adjective is 'Greek' (*Gr.*) instead of *graecus* (*gr.*), 'Georgian' (*Geo.*) instead of *ibericus* (*iber.*), 'Syriac' (*Syr.*) instead of *syriacus*, and 'Arabic' (*Ar.*) instead of *arabicus*. Each time a manuscript's shelf mark is given, the date of the manuscript (either the century or the year) is also given in parentheses, so that the reader need not remember the dates of every source cited.

This book, originally prepared as a doctoral thesis at the Pontifical Oriental Institute in Rome and defended in 2013, would never have been completed without the generous help of others. First of all, I wish to express my deep gratitude to Fr Robert F. Taft, SJ, for his mentorship and for suggesting, during a visit to Rome in May 2008, what became the topic of my dissertation. Stefano

Parenti, my doctoral advisor (*Doktorvater*), and Elena Velkovska were like surrogate parents during my time in Rome and I thank them for their kindness, hospitality, patience, and encouragement. Thanks are also due to members of the dissertation committee, Archbishop Boghos Levon Zekiyan of Istanbul and Basilius J. Groen, for providing comments and suggestions for revisions. My sincere thanks to the Congregation for the Eastern Churches for a scholarship that enabled me to live and pray with the students of the Pontificio Collegio Russicum and to study at the Pontifical Oriental Institute. Special thanks are due to Daniel Černý, Gabriel Radle and Nina Glibetić, Fr Germano Marani, SJ, and Fr Andrew Summerson, with whom I spent countless hours in discussion; and to my professors, Fr Luca Pieralli for Greek palaeography and Gaga Shurgaia for ancient Georgian. The Trustees of Harvard University granted me, during the academic year of 2011–12, a junior fellowship in Byzantine Studies at the Dumbarton Oaks Research Library and Collection in Washington, DC, where I learned much from the director of Byzantine Studies, Margaret Mullett, as well as from Johannes Pahlitzsch, Divna Manolova, Nebojša Stanković, Nikos Tsivikis, and Jeff Wickes. During that year Scott F. Johnson and Jack Tannous became true mentors. Without these scholarships, the moral support of those who offered them, and the friendship of those with whom I worked, I could not have written this book.

A study of liturgy's history would be impossible without access to sources. I am extremely grateful to Archbishop Damianos of Sinai and Fr Justin of the Monastery of St Catherine on Mount Sinai for allowing me to visit the monastery and to study in its library. Particular thanks go to Fr François Gick, SJ, librarian of the Pontifical Oriental Institute, Byzantine Studies librarian Deborah Brown at Dumbarton Oaks, Fr Antoine Lambrechts, librarian of the Monastery the Holy Cross in Chevetogne, and the librarians of the Vatican Apostolic Library in Rome, those of the Microfilm Reading Room at the Library of Congress, Washington, DC, and those of the many libraries at the University of Vienna.

Revisions to this book began during my transition from the life of a student to the working world, under the guidance of Bishop Borys Gudziak of Paris and Hans-Jürgen Feulner at the University of Vienna. Members of the North American Academy of Liturgy 'Problems in the Early History of the Liturgy' Seminar Group and members of the Society of Oriental Liturgy painstakingly read parts of the manuscript and offered invaluable comments and suggestions. Among them, I wish to thank particularly my friends and colleagues Harald Buchinger, Stig Frøyshov, Sr Vassa Larin, Fr Thomas Pott, Vitaly Permiakov, Fr Alexander Rentel, and Fr Damaskinos Olkinuora, who read various drafts and offered invaluable comments, corrections, and suggestions for improvement. I also wish to thank Fr Stefanos Alexopoulos and Alexander Lingas for the important improvements they suggested; Heinzgerd Brakmann, Predrag Bukovec, Sysse Engberg, Joseph Patrich, Claudia Rapp, and Daniel

Seper for discussion of specific questions addressed here; and Brouria Bitton-Ashkelony, Elizabeth S. Bolman, Cecilia Gaposchkin, Derek Krueger, and Iris Shagrir for providing opportunities at conferences where I could discuss aspects of this book and receive feedback. Sincere thanks go to all the editors at Oxford University Press who diligently worked on this book and to Ivanka Galadza for preparing and drawing the maps and plans in Appendix 2. God knows the names of all those who helped me in the process of researching, writing, and revising this book but whom I have forgotten to mention here. May he reward them all abundantly. All remaining errors are my own.

Finally, I wish to thank my family, in particular Fr Roman and Irene Galadza, Ivanna Hanushevsky, my sisters Marika and Ivanka, and my parents, Fr Peter and Olenka, for their love.

Contents

List of Tables   xi
Abbreviations   xiii

Introduction   1

PART I. LITURGY AND CONTEXT

1. Liturgy in Byzantine Jerusalem   29

2. The Historical Contexts of Byzantinization   73

PART II. BYZANTINIZATION OF THE LITURGY OF ST JAMES, THE CALENDAR, AND THE LECTIONARY

3. The Liturgy of St James   157

4. The Liturgical Calendar of Jerusalem   220

5. The Lectionary of Jerusalem   300

    Conclusion: Worship in Captivity   350

Appendix 1: Liturgical Manuscripts   359
Appendix 2: Maps and Plans   388
Glossary   393
Bibliography   397
Online Resources   419
Index of Biblical References   421
Index of Manuscript References   427
General Index   431

List of Tables

1.1. Structure of the Eucharist in the fifth mystagogical catechesis   41

1.2. The eucharistic synaxis in the Armenian lectionary   48

1.3. The eucharistic synaxis in the Georgian lectionary   51

1.4. The Divine Liturgy in Constantinopolitan sources   65

3.1. Manuscripts of the Liturgy of St James   177

3.2. Structure of the Liturgy of the Word of St James   180

3.3. *Propsalmon* in *Sinai Gr. 212* (9th cent.)   195

3.4. Structure of the Liturgy of the Eucharist of St James   202

3.5. Structure of the anaphora of St James   210

3.6. Hymnography at the transfer of the gifts in the Liturgy of St James   218

4.1. Comparison table of liturgical calendars   237

4.2. Major feasts of Christ   238

4.3. Feasts of the Theotokos   250

4.4. Commemorations of St John the Baptist   256

4.5. Commemorations of St James the Brother of the Lord   263

4.6. Commemorations of St Stephen the Protomartyr   266

4.7. Joint commemorations of New Testament figures   270

4.8. Joint commemorations of Old Testament figures   272

4.9. Monastic saints   274

4.10. St Athenogenes   277

4.11. Local Palestinian saints   278

4.12. Saints from beyond Palestine   280

4.13. New Martyrs   285

4.14. The Precious Cross   289

4.15. The Ark of the Covenant   290

4.16. Church buildings   293

4.17. Church councils   296

4.18. Classification of liturgical calendars   298

5.1. Gospels for Bright Week   310

5.2. Gospels for Bright Week and the resurrectional Gospels   311

5.3. Comparative table of Sunday cycles   313

5.4. Gospels from the cycle of John   316

5.5.   Gospels from the cycle of Matthew   319

5.6.   Gospels from the cycle of Mark   321

5.7.   Gospels from the cycle of Luke   323

5.8.   Gospels for Great Lent   324

5.9.   Gospels for Holy Week   328

5.10. Epistles for Pascha and Bright Week   332

5.11. Sunday Epistle cycles in Constantinople   334

5.12. Epistles for Great Lent   335

5.13. Old Testament readings for Holy Week   341

5.14. Readings for general commemorations   344

5.15. Weekday readings   346

Abbreviations

AASS	*Acta sanctorum*. Antwerp/Paris/Rome/Brussels: Société des Bollandistes, 1643–1925
AB	*Analecta Bollandiana*
AL	*Le Codex Arménien Jérusalem 121*, vol. 2: *Édition comparée du texte et de deux autres manuscrits*, ed. by Athanase Renoux. PO 36.2. Turnhout: Brepols, 1971
BAS	Liturgy of St Basil the Great
BBGG	*Bollettino della Badia Greca di Grottaferrata*
BELS	Bibliotheca 'Ephemerides Liturgicae': Subsidia
BHG	Halkin, François. *Bibliotheca hagiographica graeca*, 3 vols. SH 8a. Brussels: Société des Bollandistes, 1957
BHGna	Halkin, François. *Novum Auctarium Bibliothecae hagiographicae graecae*. SH 65. Brussels: Société des Bollandistes, 1984
BK	*Bedi Kartlisa: Revue de Kartvélologie*
BMFD	*Byzantine Monastic Foundation Documents*, 5 vols, ed. by John Thomas and Angela Constantinides Hero. Dumbarton Oaks Studies 35. Washington, DC: Dumbarton Oaks Research Library, 2000
BS	*Bibliotheca sanctorum*, 12 vols, ed. by Filippo Caraffa et al. Rome: Istituto Giovanni XXIII della Pontificia Università Lateranense, 1969
BZ	*Byzantinische Zeitschrift*
CCCM	Corpus Christianorum, Continuatio Mediaevalis
CCSG	Corpus Christianorum, Series Graeca
CCSL	Corpus Christianorum, Series Latina
CHR	Liturgy of St John Chrysostom
CPG	*Clavis patrum graecorum*, 5 vols, ed. by Maurice Geerard et al. CCSG. Turnhout: Brepols, 1974–2003
CPL	*Clavis patrum latinorum*, 3rd edn, ed. by Eligius Dekkers et al. CCSL. Steenbrugge: Abbatia Sancti Petri, 1995
CSCO	Corpus Scriptorum Christianorum Orientalium
DACL	*Dictionnaire d'archéologie chrétienne et de liturgie*, ed. by Fernand Cabrol and Henri Leclercq. Paris: Letouzey et Ané, 1907–1953
DOP	*Dumbarton Oaks Papers*
GEDSH	*Gorgias Encyclopedic Dictionary of the Syriac Heritage*, ed. by Sebastian P. Brock, Aaron M. Butts, George A. Kiraz, and Lucas Van Rompay. Piscataway, NJ: Gorgias Press, 2011

xiv

Abbreviations

GL	*Le grand lectionnaire de l'Église de Jérusalem (V^e–VIIIe siècle)*, ed. by Michel Tarchnischvili. CSCO 188–9, 204–5. Louvain: Secrétariat du CSCO, 1959–60
HagPRES	Hagiopolite Liturgy of the Presanctified Gifts (of St James)
JAS	Liturgy of St James
JTS	*Journal of Theological Studies*
Mansi	Mansi, Johannes Dominicus. *Sacrorum Conciliorum nova et amplissima collectio*, 53 vols. Florence: Antonius Zatta Veneti, 1759–98
Mus	*Le Muséon: Revue d'études orientales*
NGDMM	*New Grove Dictionary of Music and Musicians*, 2nd edn, ed. by Stanley Sadie. London: Macmillan, 2001
ΝΣ	*Νέα Σιών. Ἐκκλησιαστικὸν περιοδικὸν σύγγραμμα* (Jerusalem)
OC	*Oriens Christianus: Hefte für die Kunde des christlichen Orients*
OCA	Orientalia Christiana Analecta
OCP	*Orientalia Christiana Periodica*
ODB	*The Oxford Dictionary of Byzantium*, 3 vols, ed. by Alexander P. Kazhdan, Alice-Mary Talbot, Anthony Cutler, Timothy E. Gregory, and Nancy P. Ševčenko. New York: Oxford University Press, 1991
OLA	Orientalia Lovaniensia Analecta
PG	Patrologia Graeca
PL	Patrologia Latina
PLP	*Prosopographisches Lexikon der Palaiologenzeit*, ed. by Erich Trapp and Christian Gastgeber. CD-ROM version. Vienna: Verlag der Österreichischen Akademie der Wissenchaften, 2001
PmbZ	*Prosopographie der mittelbyzantinischen Zeit: 2. Abteilung (867–1025)*, 8 vols, ed. by Friedhelm Winkelmann, Ralph-Johannes Lili, Claudia Ludwig, Thomas Pratsch, Beate Zilke et al. Berlin: De Gruyter, 2013
PO	Patrologia Orientalis
POC	*Proche-Orient Chrétien*
ППС	*Православный Палестинскій Сборникъ* (1881–1916, 1992–)
PRES	Liturgy of the Presanctified Gifts
ПС	*Палестинский Сборник* (1954–1990)
ПУЦТ	*Православное Учение о Церковных Таинствах. V Международная Богословская Конференция Русской Православной Церкви. Москва, 13–16 ноября 2007 г*, 3 vols. Moscow: Синодальная библейско-богословская комиссия, 2009
ПЭ	*Православная Энциклопедия*, vols 1–, ed. by Sergei L. Kravets et al. Moscow: Церковно-научный центр «Православная Энциклопедия», 2000–
REB	*Revue des études byzantines*

RHE	*Revue d'histoire ecclésiastique*
RSBN	*Rivista di studi bizantini e neoellenici*
SC	Sources chrétiennes
SH	Subsidia Hagiographica
ST	Studi e Testi (Vatican City)
SVTQ	*St Vladimir's Theological Quarterly*
ΘHE	Θρησκευτικὴ καὶ Ἠθικὴ Ἐγκυκλοπαιδεία, 12 vols. Athens: Ath. Martinos, 1962–8

Introduction

The purpose of this study is to investigate the Christian liturgy of Jerusalem and to understand how its indigenous rite was supplanted by another liturgical tradition, the Byzantine rite. This process occurred after the Arab conquest, in particular between the eighth and the thirteenth centuries.

In the Byzantine rite today, hymnography paints a picture of teachings that flow from Sion, 'the Mother of all the Churches of God', like a river, gushing forth grace to the whole world.[1] Other Byzantine rite hymns sing of Jerusalem and Sion rejoicing and of people from all the ends of the earth gathering around Jerusalem as its children.[2] Jerusalem's geography and topography were so intimately connected to the life of Christ in the New Testament and to events recounted in the Old Testament, not to mention the life of the early church, that places where these events happened were called 'holy sites'. Jerusalem thus became 'the Holy City' (ἁγία πόλις) and its residents, bishops, hymns, and liturgy were called 'Hagiopolite', in the singular, *hagiopolitēs* (ἁγιοπολίτης or ἁγιοπολιτικός), which meant 'of the holy city' in ancient Greek.[3] Consequently, Jerusalem has left its mark on the high points of the liturgical year, from the paschal Triduum through Pentecost to Palm Sunday. This is because Jerusalem's cathedral—the Church of the Holy Sepulchre, also known as the Church of the Anastasis (the Church of the Resurrection)— welcomed throngs of pilgrims, led them into prayer before they returned home, and, to varying degrees, introduced elements of Hagiopolite practice

---

[1] See Δόξα. Ἦχος πλ. β΄. Ἀνατολίου Τὰ θεῖα ἐποπτεύων, Χριστοῦ τῆς σοφίας…ὅθεν ἐκ Σιὼν ὡς ποταμὸς τῆς χάριτος ἐξῆλθες, τὰ σὰ ἐκβλύζων ἔνθεα δόγματα εἰς τὴν σύμπασαν κτίσιν. Tone 6 *doxastikon* at the *aposticha* of vespers for the Holy Apostle Thomas on October 6. Follieri, *Initia hymnorum* IV, 6.

[2] Ἆρον κύκλῳ τοὺς ὀφθαλμούς σου Σιὼν καὶ ἴδε· ἰδοὺ γὰρ ἤκασί σοι, θεοφεγγεῖς ὡς φωστῆρες, ἐκ δυσμῶν καὶ βορρᾶ, καὶ θαλάσσης, καὶ ἑῴας τὰ τέκνα σου ἐν σοὶ εὐλογοῦντα, Χριστὸν εἰς τοὺς αἰῶνας. Troparion, Ode 8, Canon of Pascha. Follieri, *Initia hymnorum* I, 176.

[3] Trapp, *Lexikon zur byzantinischen Gräzität*, 8–9. For a discussion of the meaning of this term as it relates to musical manuscripts, see Jørgen Raasted, *The Hagiopolites: A Treatise on Musical Theory* (Cahiers de l'Institut du Moyen-âge grec et latin 45, Copenhagen: Université de Copenhague, 1983), 10. Raasted speculates that the term 'Hagiopolites' was adopted in later musical treatises from earlier books, such as the Tropologion.

into their own worship. Pilgrims who decided to stay and dedicate their lives to God joined many of the outlying monasteries, such as Mar Sabas Lavra in the Judean desert and the more distant Monastery of St Catherine on Mount Sinai. In turn, these monastic centres became formative in the liturgical tradition known today as 'the Byzantine rite'.

But the story of Byzantine liturgy is a tale of *two* cities and several monasteries;[4] the other city is Constantinople. Despite Jerusalem's influence on the liturgical practices of all of Christendom, the imperial capital of Constantinople—'the City'—became a rising force, eventually spreading its influence even to Jerusalem. Constantinople's cathedral, Hagia Sophia, and its monasteries, such as the Stoudios Monastery, rose to such prominence that they became important liturgical centres, while Jerusalem, the centre of Christianity, was eventually relegated to the periphery as far as Byzantine liturgy is concerned.

The dialectic between centre and periphery has been examined in various disciplines, including within the study of Byzantium. Geographically broad, the 'Byzantine periphery' includes southern Italy, the Balkans, Cappadocia, Cyprus, Syria, and Palestine and moves increasingly eastward to encompass other regions, such as Mesopotamia, Persia, Georgia, Armenia, and the Arabian Peninsula. Byzantine art historians and archaeologists have observed that, despite certain regional characteristics in the periphery, monumental architecture and painting, for example, almost inevitably reveal dependence on metropolitan forms from the centre.[5] The methodological framework of 'interlocking societies' applied to art historical studies has challenged an enduring hierarchal relationship between the Constantinopolitan centre and its peripheries within the Byzantine commonwealth, pointing to 'multi-faceted dynamics of cultural exchange'.[6] For example, Byzantine literature displays a dependence of the capital on the periphery. In the ninth century, after a period of decline, the consolidation of resources stimulated a revival of Greek literary culture. What may come as a surprise is that most of this periphery, particularly Palestine, was outside the Byzantine empire at that time, and yet it was this region that had preserved texts of Eusebius of Caesarea (*c*.260–339/40) and transmitted them to Constantinople. Palestinian churchmen also revived

[4] Taft, *Byzantine Rite*, 56–60.

[5] See Annabel Jane Wharton, *Art of Empire: Painting and Architecture of the Byzantine Periphery: A Comparative Study of Four Provinces* (University Park, PA: Pennsylvania State University Press, 1988).

[6] Elena N. Boeck, *Imagining the Byzantine Past: The Perception of History in the Illustrated Manuscripts of Skylitzes and Manasses* (Cambridge: Cambridge University Press, 2015), 10–13, here 11. The method is based on Richard Fowler and Olivier Hekster, 'Imagining Kings: from Persia to Rome', in *Imaginary Kings: Royal Images in the Ancient Near East, Greece and Rome*, ed. by Olivier Hekster and Richard Fowler (Stuttgart: Steiner, 2005), 9–38, here 35.

certain Greek poetic metres and developed genres of Greek liturgical hymn-ography, which then made their way to Constantinople.[7]

Ecclesiastical and liturgical histories challenge the accepted dynamics of centre and periphery and reveal that the concept of periphery depends upon one's perspective. The five patriarchal sees known as 'the pentarchy', selected as much for their crucial role and influence in the formative years of the early Christian church as for their political and economic importance, are a case in point. Within this hierarchal arrangement, Constantinople found itself in second place after Rome. Canonists and patristic authors later considered all five patriarchal sees equal, putting Constantinople and Rome on the same level with the three eastern patriarchates of Alexandria, Antioch, and Jerusalem.[8] Just like their politics, the liturgy of each of these patriarchates was also local. Over time, their local theology and politics moved beyond these local origins to influence the broader tradition. Nevertheless, both had local points of departure.[9] With this focus on local history and from the vantage point of liturgy, the periphery of one centre can become the centre of yet another periphery.[10]

Applying this analogy of centre and periphery in order to compare Constantinople and Jerusalem is not intended to be didactic or moralizing, even if early church authors created some antagonism between the two cities. For them, Jerusalem could be both the earthly dwelling of Jesus immersed in the history of the Bible and a tourist trap, while Constantinople appeared at once as the imperial capital of a new Christian empire and as the symbolic source of pagan Hellenistic philosophy which swamped the Gospel message. Each city had its own patriarch; its own cathedral, where the patriarch presided over services that influenced the rites and practices of all other churches in that city; its own topography, which determined how processions would develop throughout the city; and its own ascetic heroes and monastic centres, which later would dominate the cathedral rite and replace it with a monastic one. Liturgical historians have even found parallels in the history of the two cities, dividing them into early, middle, and late periods. But, just as projecting the historical breaks and ruptures of the West onto the East is unacceptable, so, too, the history of Constantinople is not that of Jerusalem. The Holy City's captivity

---

[7] Mango, 'Greek Culture in Palestine'.

[8] See Council of Chalcedon, canon 28, in *Decrees of the Ecumenical Councils*, vol. 1, ed. by Norman P. Tanner, SJ (London: Sheed & Ward, 1990), 99–100; John Meyendorff, *Imperial Unity and Church Divisions: The Church 450–680 AD* [*sic*] (The Church in History 2, Crestwood, NY: St Vladimir's Seminary Press, 1989), 54–9; Aristeides Papadakis, 'Pentarchy', in ODB 3, here 1625–6; Price and Gaddis, *Acts*, 1–85.

[9] Taft, *Concluding Rites*, 439 and 788.

[10] For more on this question, see Parenti, 'Towards a Regional History', originally published in Russian as Stefano Parenti, 'К вопросу об истории локальных традиций чинов таинств по византийскому Евхологию', ПУЦТ, vol. 3, 332–45.

to Persian (614–28), Arab Islamic (638–1099), and crusader (1099–1187) forces is simply the political context of its liturgical captivity to the foreign Constantinopolitan liturgical tradition.[11]

Previous attempts to periodize the liturgical history of Jerusalem, most notably by Miguel Arranz (1930–2008) and Aleksei Pentkovsky, sought parallels between the evolution of worship in Constantinople and in Jerusalem and divided their liturgical history into corresponding periods on the basis of significant events in each city's history. Arranz proposed the Persian invasion of Jerusalem on 5 May 614 and the destruction of the Church of the Anastasis by Fatimid Caliph al-Ḥākim bi ʿAmr Allāh (r. 996–1021) on 28 September 1009 to be cataclysmic events that immediately disrupted liturgical practice and ushered in a new type of liturgy.[12] Pentkovsky focused more on the destruction of the Anastasis in 1009 and on how this affected the loss of Jerusalemite usages in favour of Constantinopolitan liturgy.[13] While such significant 'threshold' dates can be useful, closer examination of the historical and archaeological evidence has shown that these historical frameworks require nuancing.[14] In a similar vein, drawing direct parallels between Jerusalem and Constantinople is not always possible; and the purpose of comparing these two traditions should be not to find a liturgical 'golden age' of one or the other city, but to understand how the two liturgical traditions interacted and how it is that one could have caused the extinction of the other.[15]

BYZANTINIZATION

Put bluntly, 'the Byzantine Rite is a mongrel'.[16] Like in the Roman rite and, indeed, in most great cultural traditions, the synthesis of various liturgical elements from the Eastern Mediterranean led to the birth of something new.

---

[11] For introductions to Jerusalem's topography, see Hugues Vincent and Félix-Marie Abel, *Jérusalem: Recherches de topographie, d'archéologie et d'histoire*, vol. 2: *Jérusalem nouvelle* (Paris: Librarie Victor Lecoffre, 1914); Abel, 'Jérusalem'; Ute Wagner-Lux and Heinzgerd Brakmann, 'Jerusalem I (stadtgeschichtlich)', *Reallexikon für Antike und Christentum* 17 (1996), 631–718; 'Иерусалим', ПЭ 21, 397–445; K. A. Panchenko, 'Иерусалимская православная церковь', ПЭ 21, 466–76.

[12] Arranz, 'Grandes étapes'; M. Canard, 'al-Ḥākim Bi-amr Allāh', *Encyclopaedia of Islam* 3, 76–82, especially 77–8 for a list of al-Ḥākim's policies towards Christians.

[13] Pentkovsky, 'Богослужебные уставы'.

[14] Galadza, '"Les grandes étapes de la liturgie byzantine" de Miguel Arranz'.

[15] For a reflection on the idea of 'golden ages' of liturgy, see A. M. Triacca, 'Sviluppo-evoluzione, adattamento-inculturazione? Iniziali riflessioni sui passaggi dalla "Liturgia romana pura" alla "Liturgia secondo l'uso della Curia Romana"', in *L'adattamento della liturgia: Metodi e modelli* (Analecta Liturgica 19/Studia Anselmiana 113, Rome: Pontificio Ateneo S. Anselmo, 1993), 61–116, here 77.

[16] Taft, *Hours*, 273.

Writing of the Roman liturgical tradition, Cyrille Vogel (1919–82) states that the process of the evolution of the Roman rite was one of 'osmosis, amalgamation, and hybridization; liturgies were never simply substituted for one another; they influenced and modified one another, and even the dominant Roman liturgy issued from the process changed and enhanced'.[17] Were it not for the word 'Roman', the Byzantine liturgical scholar would be content to apply the same statement to the development of the Byzantine rite. For this reason, the statement that 'Byzantine liturgy, as it is known and practiced today, originates in the synthesis between the Palestinian monastic tradition and the Constantinopolitan cathedral tradition'[18] is less than satisfying for those who examine liturgical manuscripts; it requires qualification. Although this assertion paints a clear picture of the synthetic nature of the Byzantine rite, this synthesis is more than the simple fusion of a Constantinopolitan cathedral Euchologion with a Palestinian monastic Horologion in two stages; its nature is more complex.[19] Jerusalem and Constantinople had each its own cathedral with its own liturgies, as well as multiple monastic centres that made an impact on the city's and the patriarchate's liturgy.[20] Each city had its own eucharistic liturgy, contained in an Euchologion, its own Liturgy of the Hours, its own calendar, and its own lectionary, all of which, together, formed a coherent system that can be called a local 'rite'. Because of the complexity of the development, over time, of the Liturgy of the Hours in the Horologion and of the eucharistic liturgies in the Euchologion, liturgical Byzantinization is more clearly visible in the liturgical calendar and lectionary, which were distinct in Jerusalem and Constantinople and could be distinguished from liturgical manuscripts from the eighth century onwards. For this reason, the liturgical Byzantinization of the calendar and lectionary of Jerusalem is the focus of this book.

On the basis of this and of what follows, my definition of 'liturgical Byzantinization' is: the process of making liturgical practices conformable to those of the Great Church of Constantinople, at the expense and to the detriment of local, in this case Hagiopolite, liturgical practices. The term 'Byzantinization' is preferred here to the term 'Constantinopolization' because the latter fails to recognize the synthetic nature of the Byzantine rite's liturgical

---

[17] Cyrille Vogel, *Medieval Liturgy: An Introduction to the Sources*, rev. and trans. by William G. Storey and Niels Krogh Rasmussen, OP (Washington, DC: Pastoral Press, 1986), 3.

[18] Pott, *Byzantine Liturgical Reform*, 153, based on Taft, *Byzantine Rite*, 58.

[19] Taft, *Byzantine Rite*; Pott, *Byzantine Liturgical Reform*, 122–3 and 153.

[20] For the distinction between these liturgical centres, see Elena Velkovska, 'Система на византийските и славянските богослужебни книги в периода на възникването им', in *Medieval Christian Europe: East and West. Tradition, Values, Communications*, ed. by Vassil Gjuzelev and Anisava Miltenova (Sofia: ИК „Гутенберг", 2002), 220–36, esp. 220–1. For more on the distinctions between cathedral and monastic liturgy, see the first two sections in Chapter 1 here.

practices, which were themselves often highly influenced by Jerusalem and Palestine. The justification for this distinction between the two terms should become clear in the following chapters, as will the fact that liturgical Byzantinization was not a process that occurred overnight or was completed in one fell swoop. Hagiopolitan and Constantinopolitan liturgical practices existed together in Palestine for some time, until Byzantinization displaced authentic local practices.

Nevertheless, the contemporaneous presence and awareness of more than one liturgical rite, or even the parallel coexistence of several distinct liturgical rites and traditions in the same city or ecclesiastical region, is not a unique characteristic of Jerusalem and Palestine but a phenomenon evident in various other historical contexts. In the fifth century the often cited exchange between St Ambrose of Milan (*c*.340–97) and St Augustine of Hippo (354–430) concerning fasting, summarized in English as 'when in Rome, do as the Romans', refers specifically to conflicts between fasting practices in Rome and Milan that Augustine was attempting to understand and reconcile.[21] From the eighth century onwards, southern Italian liturgical manuscripts reveal the presence of Hagiopolitan and Constantinopolitan prayers, mixed with local prayers from southern Italy.[22] During the ninth, tenth, and eleventh centuries, the Franks exerted a significant liturgical influence on Rome, causing the adoption of various prayers and liturgical elements by popes; these were to form what would become known as the Roman rite.[23] Much later, in the seventeenth century, Roman influence on the Orthodox and Uniate Ruthenians in the Polish–Lithuanian commonwealth flooded the region with liturgical practices of the Roman rite that resulted in the 'Latinization' of many aspects of the Slavic Orthodox liturgy.[24] These varied examples show that the local character

---

[21] *Cum Romam venio, ieiuno sabbato; cum his sum, non ieiuno. Sic etiam tu, ad quam forte Ecclesiam veneris, ejus morem serva, si cuiquam non vis esse scandalo, nec quemquam tibi* ('When I visit Rome, I fast on Saturday; when I am here [*sc.* in Milan], I do not fast. On the same principle, do you observe the custom prevailing in whatever Church you come to, if you desire neither to give offense by your conduct, nor to find cause of offense in another's'). St Augustine of Hippo, *Ad Inquisitiones Ianuarii, Epistola LIV*, II.18, in PL 33, col. 201 = CPL 262.

[22] For example, Εὐχὴ λεγομένη ἐν τῷ διακονικῷ μετὰ τὴν λειτουργίαν τοῦ ἁγίου Ἰακώβου, in *Barberini Gr. 336* (8th cent.). See Parenti and Velkovska, *Barberini 336*, 242 (§ 277.1). See also Jacob, 'Messanensis gr. 177', 124–5; Jacob, 'La tradition manuscrite', here 114–21 and 137–8; Parenti, *A oriente e occidente di Costantinopoli*, 149–215; Elena Velkovska, 'La liturgia italo-bizantina negli eucologi e lezionari del Nuovo Testamento della "scuola niliana"', in *Il monachesimo d'Oriente e d'Occidente nel passagio dal primo al secondo millennio: Atti del Convegno Internazionale, Grottaferrata, 23–25 settembre 2004* (Ἀνάλεκτα Κρυπτοφέρρης 6, Grottaferrata: Monastero Esarchico, 2009), 215–55, esp. 232–40 and 253–5.

[23] Baumstark, *Comparative Liturgy*, 6–7; Enrico Cattaneo, *Il culto Cristiano in occidente: Note storiche* (BELS 13, Rome: Edizioni Liturgiche, 1978).

[24] Laurence Daniel Huculak, OSBM, *The Divine Liturgy of St John Chrysostom in the Kievan Metropolitan Province during the Period of Union with Rome (1596–1839)* (Analecta OSBM, Rome: P. P. Basiliani, 1990); Peter Galadza, 'Seventeenth-Century Liturgicons of the Kievan Metropolia

of the liturgy was often disrupted throughout the course of history, so that those who worshiped according to one liturgical tradition were forced to reconcile foreign aspects of liturgy—aspects that came from other liturgical centres—with their own.

For Jerusalem, awareness of the diverse liturgical traditions upheld by Christians in Palestine and the presence of two or more liturgical rites within liturgical manuscripts are of extreme importance for our understanding of the phenomenon of Byzantinization. Foreign pilgrims to Jerusalem often brought with them their liturgical traditions, and these existed side by side with the local liturgy. For example, the *Life of Peter the Iberian* recounts how Gerontius, priest and archimandrite of the Mount of Olives in the fifth century, served several liturgies according to different traditions:

> When he had been appointed simultaneously as priest and as abbot of the holy Mount of Olives and of the monasteries on it, often he would celebrate three gatherings of the divine service in a single day, and especially on the holy Sunday: one on the holy mountain, and one in the monastery for men, and again one in the monastery for women. On the remaining days, he celebrated daily a gathering and a private service for the blessed Melania according to the custom of the Church of Rome.[25]

Monastic liturgical Typika in Palestine make reference to contemporaneous, twelfth-century usage alongside practices 'from the old type' (ἐξ ἀρχαίου τύπου).[26] Whether this refers to the Stoudite and Sabaite synthesis or to an internal liturgical reform is unclear.[27] What is clear, however, is that those who celebrated the liturgies and participated in the services in Jerusalem were aware of other liturgical practices, and often also aware that these had a foreign origin.

Foreign provenance immediately suggests some kind of a liturgical centre of origin, such as Hagia Sophia or Stoudios Monastery. In such a model, Byzantinization could be explained through the concept of 'diffusionism',[28] whereby Constantinopolitan liturgical practice would have been unilaterally

---

and Several Lessons for Today', SVTQ 56 (2012), 73–91; Maria Takala-Roszczenko, *The 'Latin' within the 'Greek': The Feast of the Holy Eucharist in the Context of Ruthenian Eastern Rite Liturgical Evolution in the 16th–18th Centuries* (Joensuu: University of Eastern Finland, 2013).

[25] See Horn and Phenix, *Lives*, 62–3. The liturgical practices may have actually been those of North Africa and not Rome.

[26] *Sinai Gr. 1096* (12th cent.), fol. 153; Dmitrievskii, *Описание* III, 58. For other sources that show clear awareness of two or more liturgical orders, see Appendix 1.

[27] A. M. Pentkovsky, 'Иерусалимский устав', ПЭ 21, 504–6. See also the section 'Stoudite Monastic and Liturgical Reforms' in Chapter 2 here.

[28] Alfred L. Kroeber, 'Stimulus Diffusion', *American Anthropologist* 42 (1940), 1–20; Victor H. Mair, 'Diffusion, Cultural', in *New Dictionary of the History of Ideas*, vol. 2, ed. by Maryanne Cline Horowitz (Detroit: Thomson Gale, 2005), 587–8. For this theory from the perspective of liturgical studies, see Aldo Natale Terrin, 'Anthropologie culturelle', in *Dictionnaire encyclopédique de la liturgie*, vol. 1, ed. by Domenico Sartore and Achille M. Triacca, rev. by Henri Delhougne (Turnhout: Brepols, 1992), 55–69, especially 57.

exported and adopted in Jerusalem and its environs. Such an explanation, however, must not overlook the fact that each of the liturgical sources examined in this study is unique and is 'Byzantinized' in a different way. Many show awareness of two—or more—liturgical traditions, and resolve the incongruities and discord of the synthesis of each of these liturgical practices in their own unique way. Thus the concept of diffusion can only be helpful if it acknowledges the multidirectional and interwoven nature of the process of Byzantinization and the dialectic between various centres and their respective peripheries.

By its very nature, the investigation of the influence of Constantinople on Jerusalem is comparative. And, because the central question of this book has a liturgical focus, the principal method of approach is also liturgical, that of 'comparative liturgical studies'. This method, pioneered by Anton Baumstark (1872–1948), can be summarized as an investigation of primary liturgical sources across traditions, in their original languages and in context, by individuating their possible genetic and structural relationships.[29] Comparison of these sources results in either differences or agreements that must then be explained by recourse to history. Preconceived notions must be excluded at all costs, in order that the data be respected.[30]

Speaking of liturgy, Baumstark points out that its subject matter belongs to theology but the procedures and methods used to investigate it must be critical and scholarly.[31] Thus the method of comparative liturgical studies 'is of necessity an empirical one; for it is only by setting out from exact results and precise observations that right conclusions will be reached. The scrupulous establishment of the factual *data* underlying the problems should precede every attempt at explanation.'[32] Despite this empirical approach, Baumstark certainly does not exclude a theological understanding of liturgy.[33] In fact, Robert F. Taft notes that the historical, practical, and theoretical aspects arising from the 'laws' of the comparative method reveal the inseparable nature of liturgy and theology, since 'origins, meaning, [and] practice go hand in hand'.[34] While this method is text-based and historical, its fruits can ultimately identify the organic rhythm and theology of prayer.[35]

---

[29] See Gabriele Winkler and Robert F. Taft, SJ, 'Introduction', in *Liturgy Fifty Years after Baumstark*, 14–16.

[30] Baumstark, *Comparative Liturgy*, 3.   [31] Ibid.   [32] Ibid.

[33] Ibid., 8; Fritz West, *The Comparative Liturgy of Anton Baumstark* (Alcuin/GROW Joint Liturgical Studies 31, Nottingham: Grove Books, 1995), 34.

[34] Robert F. Taft, SJ, 'Anton Baumstark's Comparative Liturgy Revisited', in *Liturgy Fifty Years after Baumstark*, 191–232, here 232. Winkler and Taft note that the German term by which Baumstark describes the method of *Vergleichende Liturgiewissenschaft* is *Gesetzmäßigkeiten*, which is better translated as 'legality' or 'legitimacy'. See Gabriele Winkler and Robert F. Taft, SJ, 'Introduction', in *Liturgy Fifty Years after Baumstark*, 9–29, here 16.

[35] Robert F. Taft, SJ, 'Anton Baumstark's Comparative Liturgy Revisited', in *Liturgy Fifty Years after Baumstark*, here 196.

The method of analysis of structural units in liturgy developed by Taft is an extension of Anton Baumstark's methods in comparative liturgical studies. After the initial process of gathering data, the information is sorted, identified, and hypothetically reconstructed into individual structures and units. Such analysis is important because liturgies do not grow evenly; their individual elements 'possess a life of their own'.[36] Likewise, the method of structural analysis is useful insofar as it allows one to see the common elements from a variety of primary sources. In the present study, for example, apart from the early lectionaries, such as the AL and the GL, no one source of Hagiopolite liturgy contains all the elements of the Liturgy of the Word of JAS. However, having established their Hagiopolitan origin, it is possible to recreate the structure of the Liturgy of the Word from the various elements contained in each of these sources.

It is important to note that even the most faithful promoters of the comparative method are aware that this method is 'only a convenient device', which, because of the inability to distinguish between hypothesis and historical reality, at times must be abandoned.[37] Taft admits that this is not '*the* method for studying liturgy, nor even *an* organic, complete methodology'.[38] Nevertheless, insights that this method can give into the evolution of liturgical texts, scriptural pericopes, prayers, hymnography, and hagiography will be employed here to the extent that they are useful.

The presence of two parallel liturgical practices, and the ultimate loss of one of them, lead to the question of a liturgical reform. Writing specifically of the Hagiopolitan liturgical calendar, Joseph-Marie Sauget (1926–88) calls the change of its commemorations through Byzantinization a 'liturgical reform, in the modern sense of the expression', and laments that there is no documented historical information on this process to explain why it occurred and what motivated it.[39] Thomas Pott has defined liturgical reform as 'any active and deliberate intervention by man that presents itself as a change in the form of the liturgy'.[40] This definition certainly fits with the changes effected by

---

[36] 'The Structural Analysis of Liturgical Units: An Essay in Methodology', in Taft, *Beyond East and West*, here 193.

[37] Bernard Botte, OSB, 'Foreword to the Third Edition', in Baumstark, *Comparative Liturgy*, here ix. See also Gabriele Winkler and Robert F. Taft, SJ, 'Introduction', in *Liturgy Fifty Years after Baumstark*, here 11–13. Winkler and Taft point out the paradox that Baumstark, an expert in Christian cultures, was a Nazi sympathizer; and they observe that such a paradox reveals the 'obscurity of the human psyche, which permits intellectual prowess and generosity of mind to stand side by side with the abysses of human failure'.

[38] 'The Structural Analysis of Liturgical Units: An Essay in Methodology', in Taft, *Beyond East and West*, here 187–8.

[39] *Nous restons jusqu'ici privés d'une information documentée à propos d'une réforme liturgique, au sens moderne de l'expression, dans l'Église melkite, à laquelle nous pourrions avec certitude attribuer cette modification du calendrier.* Sauget, *Synaxaires Melkites*, 176.

[40] Pott, *Byzantine Liturgical Reform*, 83.

liturgical Byzantinization upon the Orthodox patriarchate of Jerusalem. While Pott's study has attempted to discern the intention of liturgical reform,[41] this is more difficult in the present case because no authors between the eighth and thirteenth centuries explained why the change occurred, what its motivation might have been, or whether they were even aware that a change of the liturgical tradition of Jerusalem had occurred at all. As already noted, Christians in late antiquity and during the Byzantine period were aware of different forms of worship and generally respected the liturgical tradition of Jerusalem. However, with regard to any intention behind the change, there is only silence. Theories by modern liturgical scholars, such as the explanation that liturgical Byzantinization was a response to iconoclasm, seem simplistic because they do not explain why certain liturgical practices were adopted or abandoned and because they are often based on outdated historical information.[42]

As this study focuses on changes to the calendar and lectionary, I am dealing with changes that would have been noticeable to the average person attending a liturgical service—or 'liturgy from the bottom up'.[43] Textual changes to the presbyteral prayers in the eucharistic liturgy between JAS, BAS, or CHR would not have been immediately noticeable to anyone other than the presider praying these anaphoral prayers, especially since many of them were already recited inaudibly by the eighth century.[44] What would have been more noticeable is a change from JAS to BAS or CHR, as well as changes to texts or hymns read or sung aloud in church, for example scriptural readings, psalmody, or hymnody. Any change to their order, or to the dates

---

[41] See especially the chapter on the Stoudite liturgical reform in ibid., 115–51.

[42] See Anton Baumstark, 'Denkmäler der Entstehungsgeschichte des byzantinischen Ritus', *Oriens Christianus* 24 (1927), 1–32.

[43] See Taft, *Through Their Own Eyes*.

[44] This is evidenced by various comments by patristic authors, as well as by the rubric 'μυστικῶς' in the earliest Euchologies, such as *Barberini Gr. 336* (8th cent.). For more on this question, see Cyril Quatrone, 'The Celebrant: Priest or Pastor: An Investigation of the Mystical Prayers of the Divine Services of the Holy Catholic and Apostolic Orthodox Church', *Orthodox Life* 4 (1996), 17–41; G. N. Filias, Ὁ Τρόπος Ἀναγνώσεως τῶν Εὐχῶν στὴ Λατρεία τῆς Ὀρθοδόξου Ἐκκλησίας (Athens: Ἐκδόσεις Γρηγόρη, 1997); Robert F. Taft, SJ, 'Questions on the Eastern Churches: Were Liturgical Prayers Once Recited Aloud?', *Eastern Churches Journal* 8.2 (2001), 107–13; David M. Petras, 'The Public Recitation of the Presbyteral Prayers', *Eastern Churches Journal* 8.2 (2001), 97–106; Panagiotis Trembelas, 'The Hearing of the Eucharistic Anaphora by the People', trans. by David Petras, *Eastern Churches Journal* 8.2 (2001), 81–96—originally published in French in the volume *1054–1954: L'Église et les Églises: Études et travaux sur l'unité chrétienne offerts à Dom Lambert Beauduin*, vol. 2 (Collection Irénikon, Chevetogne: Collections de Chevetogne, 1955), 207–20; Robert F. Taft, SJ, 'Was the Eucharistic Anaphora Recited Secretly or Aloud? The Ancient Tradition and What Became of It', in *Worship Traditions in Armenia and the Neighbouring Christian East*, ed. by Robert R. Ervine (Crestwood, NY: St Vladimir's Seminary Press, 2006); Gregory Woolfenden, 'Praying the Anaphora: Aloud or in Silence?', SVTQ 51.2/3 (2007), 179–202. For a more recent examination of this question, see Derek Krueger, *Liturgical Subjects: Christian Ritual, Biblical Narrative, and the Formation of the Self in Byzantium* (Philadelphia: University of Pennsylvania Press, 2014), 106–29 (Chapter 4: 'Eucharistic Prayers: Compunction and the History of Salvation').

of celebrating a feast with potential connections to the seasons of the year or to agricultural practices, would immediately elicit a response even from a passive observer. Despite numerous studies of archaeology and architecture in the Holy Land, it is still unknown whether Byzantinization affected church architecture or the internal arrangement of liturgical objects within churches, and whether this would in turn have affected liturgical rites and been apparent to observers. Thus the main sources for the study of the Byzantinization of the liturgy are textual, in the form of liturgical manuscripts and literary accounts, rather than architectural or archaeological remains.

THE HISTORY OF THE QUESTION OF BYZANTINIZATION

Many authors have touched upon the liturgical Byzantinization of the eastern patriarchates but, to date, there has been no systematic study of this question. Every history has its own history, as does that of the study of the liturgical Byzantinization of Jerusalem.

An article by Gregor Hohmann is emblematic of the type of scholarship that has tried to resolve, or at least to address, the question of the liturgical Byzantinization of the eastern patriarchates.[45] Rarely straying beyond the seventh century, relying only on secondary sources, and conflating the post-Chalcedonian Melkites with the Melkites of the post-eighteenth-century Greek Catholic Church,[46] such scholarship only skims the surface of the matter at hand. Similarly, Placide de Meester (1873–1950) asserted that, towards the end of the thirteenth century, the exiled patriarchs of Alexandria, Antioch, and Jerusalem 'began to return to their respective sees and definitively established the Byzantine rite there among the Melkites'.[47] Such conclusive statements come unaccompanied by any references to historical sources that might justify or explain their authors' conclusions but are, unfortunately, repeated

---

[45] Gregory Hohmann, 'Loyalty to the Emperor and Change of Rite: What Induced the Melkite Church to Exchange the Syrian for the Byzantine Tradition', *Harp* 13 (2000), 49–56; Gregor Hohmann, 'Der Rituswechsel der Melkiten: Was hat die melkitische Kirche veranlaßt, die syrische gegen die byzantinische Tradition einzutauschen?', in *'Wachsam in Liebe': Eine Festgabe zum 75. Geburtstag Seiner Seligkeit Patriarch Gregorios III.*, ed. by Michael Schneider (Kisslegg: Fe-Medienverlag, 2008), 175–84.

[46] See Ignace Dick, *Les Melkites: Grecs-orthodoxes et grecs-catholiques des patriarcats d'Antioche, d'Alexandrie et de Jérusalem* (Turnhout: Brepols, 1994). For more on the Melkites and the use of this term, see the section 'Melkites: A Subgroup?' in Chapter 2 here.

[47] *Vers la fin du XIIIe siècle, ils commencèrent à retourner à leur siège respectif et ils y établirent définitivement le rite byzantin parmi les melkites.* Placide De Meester, OSB, 'Grecques (Liturgies)', DACL 6.2:1591–1662, here 1608.

elsewhere.[48] Placing the source of Byzantinization during the period of exile
of the eastern patriarchs is most likely due to the extant correspondence
between exiled Patriarchs Theodore Balsamon of Antioch (1186–1203) and
Mark III of Alexandria (*c*.1195). Nevertheless, their debates on the celebration and use of JAS and of the Liturgy of St Mark are among the first signs of
an awareness of liturgical Byzantinization as being in effect.[49]

The question of Byzantinization, however, does not begin here. Unlike
many centres of Christian worship, primary sources describing the liturgical
tradition of Jerusalem and Palestine are still extant from the earliest centuries
of Christianity. Their rediscovery in the nineteenth and twentieth century
raised questions and pointed liturgical scholars of the last century towards the
lost liturgical tradition of Jerusalem. These students of liturgy can be grouped
into three categories: pre-revolutionary Russian scholars, liturgical scholars in
the West, and scholars—or, perhaps more accurately, inheritors—of the
Hagiopolite liturgical tradition from within the Jerusalem patriarchate itself.

The Russian presence in the Holy Land during the nineteenth and twentieth
centuries in the guise of the Orthodox Imperial Palestinian Society and of the
Russian Ecclesiastical Mission in Jerusalem led by Archimandrite Antonin
Kapustin (1817–94) also encouraged research and scholarship on the Holy
City and its liturgy.[50] One of the foremost representatives of the Russian pre-
revolutionary school of liturgy was Nikolai Krasnosel'tsev (1845–98).[51] In his
1895 review of Aleksei Dmitrievskii's (1856–1929) book on the services of
Holy Week and Pascha in Jerusalem in the ninth and tenth centuries,[52]
Krasnosel'tsev concludes that 'the influx of new liturgical material from

[48] For example, the claim is repeated as conclusive in a general introduction to the topic of
eastern Christianity: *Fu allora che il successore del patriarca gerosolimitano ritornò nella sua sede,
avendo ormai acquisito nella capitale dell'Impero romano d'Oriente il rito bizantino* ('It was at
this time that the successor of the Jerusalemite patriarch returned to his see, having already by
then acquired the Byzantine rite in the capital of the Eastern Roman Empire'). *Le antiche Chiese
orientali: Storia e letteratura*, ed. by Paolo Siniscalco (Rome: Città Nuova, 2005), 56.

[49] Swainson, *Greek Liturgies*, xxix–xxxi. For more on their correspondence, see also the
section 'Theodore Balsamon and the Rite of Constantinople' in Chapter 2 here.

[50] See *Православный Палестинскій Сборникъ* (ППС; 1881–1916, 1992–), which was
renamed *Палестинский Сборник* (ПС; 1954–1990) during the Soviet era. See also Archimandrite Avgustin (Nikitin), *Русское православие на Святой Земле* (Yekaterinburg: Русская
Духовная Миссия в Иерусалиме, 2016). Russian scholars have recently pointed to the presence
of Hagiopolite liturgical practices in Slavic liturgical books through commemorations in calendars and in hymnography. See Olga V. Loseva, 'Праздники святогробского типикона в
русских календарях XI–XII веков', ППС 100 (2003), 132–41; Roman N. Krivko, 'Славянские
служебные минеи как источник по византийской гимнографии', *Христианский Восток* 6
(*XII*) (2013), 378–90.

[51] Nikolay Sokolov, 'Мелкія Замѣтки и Извѣстія: † Николай Ѳомичъ Красносельцевъ',
Византийскій Временникъ 5 (1898), 819–30.

[52] Dmitrievskii, *Богослуженіе страсной и пасхальной седмицъ*; Sergei I. Akishin, 'Дми-
триевский, Алексей Афанасьевич', ПЭ 15, 429–38.

Byzantium…which reached particularly broad development under the reign of Constantine Porphyrogennetos' caused the redaction, in the tenth century, of older material in the codex *Hagios Stavros Gr. 43* (1122), known as the Typikon of the Anastasis.[53] Aleksei Pentkovsky suggests that this is perhaps the first time when this phenomenon is attributed to direct Byzantine influence.[54] Later works by Dmitrievskii, Bertonière, Arranz, and Pentkovsky further developed this observation.[55] They identified the year 1009, in which the Church of the Anastasis in Jerusalem was destroyed by Caliph al-Ḥākim, as the crucial turning point for Hagiopolite liturgy, comparable to 1204—the year of the sack of Constantinople by the Fourth Crusade—in its impact on the liturgy of Constantinople. For these authors, the main evidence of Byzantinization was to be found in the Liturgy of the Hours, most notably in changes to its structure. Although they had access to few of the sources known today and their contextualization of these liturgical manuscripts within historical frameworks requires nuance, these scholars were able to arrive at conclusions that are, for the most part, being confirmed today by numerous newly discovered Hagiopolitan liturgical sources.

The edition of the Jerusalem kanonarion produced in 1912 by the Georgian priest and scholar Kornelii Kekelidze (1879–1962) was one of the first texts from the wealth of the Georgian liturgical heritage that was made accessible to scholars in the West.[56] Keenly aware of the importance of Georgian manuscripts for the study of liturgy in Jerusalem, Kekelidze desired to publish the rich hymnography of tenth-century Jerusalem in Georgian sources, as Cardinal Jean-Baptiste Pitra (1812–89) had done for Greek hymnography.[57] Yet Kekelidze and other scholars of the Russian empire would have to wait for another generation. The evils of twentieth-century Soviet and Nazi totalitarianism also devastated liturgical scholarship: churches and seminaries were closed and destroyed, academies and libraries were liquidated, and scholars were forced to abandon studies related to Christianity—or suffer the consequences. Russian scholar Vladimir Beneshevich (1874–1938)[58] and Georgian

---

[53] *Пересмотръ этотъ и обусловленное имъ преобразованіе старой редакціи вызваны были, повидимому, наплывомъ новаго литургическаго матеріала изъ Византіи и совершались вообще подъ вліяніемъ византійской литургической литургической практики, которая при Константинъ Багрянородномъ получила особенно широкое развитіе.* Krasnosel'tsev, 'Review', 641–2. For more on this manuscript, see the section 'Hagiopolitan Patriarchs in Exile' in Chapter 2 and Appendix 1 in this book.

[54] See Pentkovsky, 'Богослужебные уставы', here 78 n. 33.

[55] Dmitrievskii, *Древнѣйшіе Патріаршіе Типиконы*; Bertonière, *Easter Vigil*, esp. 12–18; Arranz, 'Grandes étapes'; Pentkovsky, 'Богослужебные уставы'.

[56] Gérard Garitte, 'Bibliographie de K. Kekelidze († 1962)', Mus 76 (1963), 443–80.

[57] C. Bailey, 'Pitra, Jean Baptiste', in *New Catholic Encyclopedia*, vol. 11, ed. by Berard L. Marthaler et al., 2nd edn (Detroit, MI/Washington, DC: Thomson-Gale/Catholic University of America, 2003), 365–6. See Kekelidze, *Канонарь*, 28.

[58] Lora A. Gerd and Iaroslav N. Shchapov, 'Бенешевич, Владимир Николаевич', ПЭ 4, 619–21.

hieromonk and philologist Grigol Peradze (1988–42)[59] died respectively at the hands of Soviets and Nazis, and both have since come to be venerated in the Orthodox Church.

The closure of ecclesiastical schools and the censure of religious studies in the Soviet Union shifted the centre of liturgical studies westward. A little more than a decade after Dmitrievskii's *Древнѣйшіе Патріаршіе Типиконы* (*The Most Ancient Patriarchal Typika*), Cyril Korolevsky (1878–1959), born Jean François Joseph Charon,[60] wrote a lengthy article on the liturgy in the Melkite patriarchates of Alexandria, Antioch, and Jerusalem, already noting the 'adoption' of Byzantine practices in the subtitle to its first part.[61] Korolevsky observed that the adoption of the Byzantine rite 'was more or less complete by the eleventh century with regard to the office' but 'the Liturgy of St James continued to be celebrated there and did not disappear altogether until the thirteenth century'.[62] This statement relied on an article on West Syrian liturgy by Gustav Bickell (1838–1906).[63] Due to lacunae in the liturgy of Jerusalem, Korolevsky was forced to fill in the gaps with information from Antioch or Alexandria, thereby conflating certain liturgical practices that were local to one or another of the three eastern patriarchates. Joseph Nasrallah (1911–93) greatly expanded on Korolevsky's work with his multivolume *Histoire du mouvement littéraire dans l'Église Melchite du Ve au XXe siècle*, which features numerous sections on liturgy in the greater historical and cultural context of Palestine and Syria under Muslim occupation. In addition, his article dedicated to the liturgy of the Melkite patriarchates at the height of Byzantinization is a significant contribution to this topic, identifying key

---

[59] Henryk Paprocki, 'L'Archimandrite Grigol Peraӡe (1899–1942)', *Revue des études géorgiennes et caucasiennes* 4 (1988), 198–230; Henryk Paprocki, 'Tbilissi: Le père Grigol Peradze canonisé', *Service Orthodoxe de Presse* 203 (1995), 11–12. Peradze's death at Auschwitz on 6 December 1942 has become the date of commemoration of his martyrdom.

[60] Cyrille Korolevskij, *Kniga Bytija Moego (Le Livre de ma vie): Mémoires autobiographiques*, 5 vols, ed. by Giuseppe M. Croce (Collectanea Archivi Vaticani 45, Vatican City: Archives Secrètes Vaticanes, 2007). Jean François Joseph Charon was a French Catholic priest and scholar who adopted the Byzantine rite in the Middle East, writing and working at the Congregation of the Eastern Churches in Rome under the adopted name Cyril Korolevsky. See Cardinal Eugène Tisserant, 'Biographie', in Cyrille Korolevskij, *Metropolite André Szeptyckyj, 1865–1944* (Rome: Opera Theologicae Societatis Scientificae Ucrainorum, 1964), vii–xxvi; Constantin Simon, SJ, *Pro Russia: The Russicum and Catholic Work for Russia* (OCA 283, Rome: Pontifical Oriental Institute, 2009), 205–10.

[61] See 'Première partie: Adoption du rite byzantin par les patriarcats melchites', in Charon, 'Le rite byzantin', 476. Much of this article was incorporated into his study on the history of the Melkite patriarchates. See Charon, *History of the Melkite Patriarchates*, especially vol. 3. Although this is a translation from the original French, the English version is more complete and updated, and will be relied upon here.

[62] [L]'*adoption du rite byzantin...était à peu près consommée au onzième siècle pour ce qui regarde l'office: la liturgie de S. Jacques continua cependant à y être célébrée et ne dut disparaître entièrement qu'à la fin du treizième.* Charon, 'Le rite byzantin', 494.

[63] Gustav Bickell, 'Die westsyrischen Liturgien', *Literarischer Handweiser* 86 (1869), 513–26. I thank Heinzgerd Brakmann for providing the full bibliographical information for this article.

primary sources for the further study of liturgical Byzantinization in Alexandria, Antioch, and Jerusalem.[64] Unlike the Russian school, Korolevsky and Nasrallah focused more on the absence or presence of JAS as a sign of Byzantinization, acknowledging that tracing changes in the Liturgy of the Hours is a more complicated question until the necessary liturgical manuscripts and sources have been properly catalogued and studied.[65]

Georgian scholars in the West greatly contributed to making available liturgical sources that were previously unknown. The most notable was Michael Tarchnishvili (1897–1958),[66] a Georgian Greek Catholic priest who produced a critical edition of the Georgian translation of the Jerusalem lectionary and other liturgical texts, accompanied by a Latin translation.[67]

Robert Taft has been one of the loudest voices in drawing attention to the phenomenon of 'liturgical Byzantinization' in the eastern Orthodox patriarchates of Alexandria, Antioch, and Jerusalem and in calling for further study of this matter.[68] Bringing together the contributions of pre-revolutionary Russian scholars and of liturgical 'schools' at Roman pontifical universities and institutes, Taft has identified the changes made to the Liturgy of the Hours, along with the abandonment of JAS, as decisive factors in Byzantinization, thereby underlining the importance of this process, its relevance to the study of the liturgy of Constantinople, and its significance for the development of the Byzantine rite.[69]

Recent studies in various fields both within and beyond liturgiology have contributed new information and approaches to our knowledge of Jerusalem in the first millennium after Christ, from late antiquity and the early middle ages (under Islamic rule) until the crusades. The discovery, in 1975, of manuscripts

---

[64] Nasrallah, 'Liturgie des Patriarcats melchites'. English translation: 'The Liturgy of the Melkite Patriarchs from 969 to 1300', in *Languages and Cultures of Eastern Christianity: Greek*, ed. by Scott Fitzgerald Johnson (Farnham: Ashgate, 2015), 507–32.

[65] *En particulier, l'aspect historique de cette question n'a pas été suffisament éclairé. Toutefois, nous présentons ici quelques documents relatifs à ce sujet dans l'espoir que des études plus poussées dans ce domaine viendront un jour nous donner une vue synthétique plus complète de l'évolution de la liturgie melchite* ('In particular, the historical aspect of this question has not been clarified sufficiently. Nevertheless, we present here several documents related to this subject in the hope that studies more advanced in this domain will one day give us a synthetic view of the evolution of Melkite liturgy that is more complete'). Nasrallah, *Histoire* II.1, 99–100. See also Nasrallah, 'Liturgie des Patriarcats melchites', 157–8; Charon, *History of the Melkite Patriarchates*, vol. 3.1, 25.

[66] Heinzgerd Brakmann, 'Tarchnišvili, Michael', in *Lexikon für Theologie und Kirche*, vol. 9, ed. by Walter Kasper, 3rd edn (Freiburg: Herder, 2000), 1266–7.

[67] See GL; Tarchnishvili, *Liturgiae ibericae antiquiores*.

[68] Taft, *Great Entrance*, 70–6, 120, 131–2, 261, 305; Taft, *Concluding Rites*, 230, 278, 283, 368, 412, 545, 572, 615, 633–4, 641–2; Robert F. Taft, 'Liturgy', in *The Oxford Handbook of Byzantine Studies*, ed. by Elizabeth Jeffreys with John Haldon and Robin Cormack (New York: Oxford University Press, 2008), here 608; Robert F. Taft, 'The Liturgical Enterprise Twenty-Five Years After Alexander Schmemann (1921–1983): The Man and His Heritage', SVTQ 53.2/3 (2009), 139–63, here 141 n. 6; Taft, 'Worship on Sinai', 151; Taft, 'Maximus', 253.

[69] Taft, *Byzantine Rite*, esp. 56–7.

referred to as 'new finds' (νέα εὑρήματα) at the Monastery of St Catherine on Mount Sinai has provided previously unknown sources, particularly Greek and Georgian, for the study of early Hagiopolitan liturgy, thus expanding our knowledge of worship in the Holy City before it yielded to Byzantine practice.[70]

THE PATRIARCHATE OF JERUSALEM TODAY

The twentieth century saw increased interest in Hagiopolite liturgical practices within the Jerusalem patriarchate as well. The journal *Νέα Σιών*, founded at the Holy Sepulchre in 1904,[71] flourished under Patriarch Timothy of Jerusalem (r. 1935–55) and provided systematic descriptions of Hagiopolite liturgical and theological works.[72] However, this study seems to have made no impact on liturgical practice in Jerusalem. The current calendar of the Greek Orthodox patriarchate of Jerusalem, the Ἁγιοταφιτικὸν Ἡμερολόγιον, shows complete faithfulness to the current common Byzantine calendar and no evidence of a return to original local practices. A clear sign of this state of things is that the main feast of the patriarchal throne is celebrated on the completely Byzantinized date of 23 October.[73]

Western interest in the Middle East, revived especially after the terrorist attacks in 2001 and the subsequent wars and violence in Iraq and Syria, has drawn attention to the continuing Christian presence in the Holy Land under Muslim occupation. This interest has also stimulated new studies on the identity of the Christians in the patriarchate of Jerusalem, their languages, and their ecclesiastical organization.[74] The Catholic Church has focused attention on the Middle East as well, responding with a special synod in

[70] Hierom. Gregorios Sinaites, 'Τὸ ἀρχειακὸν ὑλικὸν τῶν εὑρημάτων τοῦ ἔτους 1975 εἰς τὴν Ἰ. Μονὴν Σινᾶ', in *Paleografia e codicologia greca: Atti del II Colloquio internazionale (Berlino-Wolfenbüttel, 17–21 ottobre 1983)*, vol. 1, ed. by Dieter Harlfinger and Giancarlo Prato (Turin: Edizioni dell'Orso, 1991), 571–7; Frøyshov, 'Early Development', 140; Aleksidze et al., *Catalogue of Georgian Manuscripts*.

[71] *Νέα Σιών. Ἐκκλησιαστικὸν περιοδικὸν σύγγραμμα* (Jerusalem: Τυποῖς Ἱεροῦ κοινοῦ τοῦ παναγίου τάφου). See Nikolaos L. Foropoulos, '"Νέα Σιών"', *ΘΗΕ* 9, here 329.

[72] Patriarch Timothy of Jerusalem, 'Πνευματικὰ ἔργα τῆς Ἐκκλησίας Ἱεροσολύμων, ἄτινα ἐγένοντο ἀποδεκτὰ ὑπὸ τῆς ὅλης Ὀρθοδόξου Ἐκκλησίας', *ΝΣ* 43 (1948), 65–82, 129–44, 193–207, 257–72; *ΝΣ* 44 (1949), 3–16, 65–88, 129–45.

[73] Ἑορτὴ τοῦ Πατριαρχικοῦ Θρόνου ἐπί τῇ μνήμῃ τοῦ ἁγίου Ἰακώβου τοῦ Ἀδελφοθέου', *Ἁγιοταφιτικὸν Ἡμερολόγιον 2012 (βιβ')* (Jerusalem: Ἔκδοσις Ἱερὸν Κοινὸν τοῦ Πανάγιου Τάφου, 2012), 35. Thanks to the generosity of Archbishop Aristarchos of Konstantines, *archigrammateus* of the Patriarchal Office of Jerusalem, I gained access to the calendars from 2010, 2011, and 2012. For the Hagiopolitan commemoration of St James the Brother of the Lord, see section 'St James the Brother of the Lord' in Chapter 4 here.

[74] Griffith, 'The Church of Jerusalem and the "Melkites"'; Leeming, 'The Adoption of Arabic as a Liturgical Language'; Levy-Rubin, 'The Reorganisation of the Patriarchate of Jerusalem'; Alexander A. Tkachenko et al., 'Иерусалимская православная церковь', ПЭ 21, 446–500.

2010 and with an apostolic exhortation dedicated to the topic.[75] Orthodox
Churches outside the Middle East have made efforts to aid Christians in Syria
and Iraq. The plight of Christians in the Holy Land has also attracted the
attention of American media, which have presented reports on their difficulties in the current political climate.[76]

Although the Jerusalem patriarchate finds itself now within the independent state of Israel, its precarious position since the Arab occupation of 638 lasts
until today.[77] Tolerated but not supported by the state, the patriarch relies
financially on the Greek diaspora. Former patriarchs from the recent past,
such as Patriarch Irenaios (r. 2001–5), believed that the patriarchate was an
outpost of Greece in the Holy Land, which meant that the 'interests of the
Church were identified with those of the Greek nation'. This view is to some
extent endorsed by Israel, which would like to avoid the political implications
of the Arabization of the Jerusalem patriarchate—the second largest land-
owner in Israel, after the state itself.[78] Such a dependence on Greece suggests
that any divergence in Jerusalem from the common liturgical practice and
tradition of worldwide Orthodoxy—or at least from the Greek Orthodox
Church—would not be greatly welcomed, as it would open rifts between
Jerusalem and its 'diaspora'.

Despite potential resistance, the patriarchate of Jerusalem did show some
interest in its authentically local traditions at the beginning of the twentieth
century—an interest that was due in part to scholarly awareness of the ancient
liturgy of Jerusalem. On Saturday, 30 December 1900 (12 January 1901, new
style), Greek Orthodox Patriarch Damianos (r. 1897–1931) blessed Archbishop Epiphanius of Jordan to celebrate JAS in the church of the patriarchal
theological seminary of the Holy Cross.[79] The text of JAS that was used was
that of Archbishop Dionysius Latas (1832–94) of Zakynthos in western

[75] *The Catholic Church in the Contemporary Middle East: Studies for the Synod for the Middle East*, ed. by Anthony O'Mahony and John Flannery (London: Melisende, 2010); *Esortazione apostolica postsinodale: Ecclesia in Medio Oriente del Santo Padre Benedetto XVI ai patriarchi, ai vescovi, al clero, alle persone consacrate e ai fedeli laici sulla chiesa in Medio Oriente, comunione e testimonianza* (Città del Vaticano: L'Osservatore Romano, 2012).
[76] See especially Bob Simon, 'Christians of the Holy Land' (Season 44, Episode 31), *60 Minutes*, CBS (WUSA, Washington, DC), aired on 22 April 2012.
[77] For a general overview of the contemporary situation of the Jerusalem patriarchate, see Ronald Roberson, CSP, *The Eastern Christian Churches: A Brief Survey*, 7th edn (Rome: Edizioni Orientalia Christiana, 2008), 51–4.
[78] Sotiris Roussos, 'Diaspora Politics, Ethnicity and the Orthodox Church in the Near East', *Journal of Eastern Christian Studies* 61.1/2 (2009), 137–48. This was evident on 22 March 2017 during the ceremonies surrounding the restoration of the aedicule of the Anastasis, at which Alexis Tsipras, the prime minister of Greece, was present. See 'The Ceremony Marking the Completion of the Restoration Project of the Sacred Edicule of the Holy Sepulchre', *Jerusalem Patriarchate: Official News Gate*. At http://www.jp-newsgate.net/en/2017/03/22/31037 (accessed on 24 March 2017).
[79] Anagnostes, 'Chronique: La liturgie de saint Jacques à Jérusalem', *Echos d'Orient* 4 (1901), 247–8.

Greece, where the practice of celebrating JAS was revived in the nineteenth century.[80] Korolevsky lamented that the text was poorly printed and had an exorbitant price for the time. Nevertheless, he suggested that Greek Catholics also restore this liturgy, especially for the feast of the Apostle James on 23 October, after a more critical and scholarly edition of the text was prepared by liturgists, of course with the approval of the Holy See.[81] Since then, highly Byzantinized editions of JAS have been published and the celebration of the liturgy has become fashionable throughout the Orthodox and Byzantine rite Catholic worlds.[82] A quick search on the Internet shows that texts of JAS are now readily available in various languages, new music is being composed for the liturgy, and the latter is celebrated annually with great solemnity. In every instance there is an unfounded notion that the liturgy being celebrated is of greater antiquity than the normally celebrated CHR or BAS. For this reason, the celebrants remove all signs of what they perceive to be later developments in, or accretions onto, the liturgy: the altar is stripped of the tabernacle, clergymen remove their mitres or other head coverings, Communion is given to the laity separately under both kinds, without the use of a Communion spoon, and everything is 'restored' to its primitive simplicity.

All the while, a consistent ignorance of the authentic practices of Jerusalem prevails. This is best illustrated by the note on the reading from the Old Testament in an instructional booklet for JAS in the Russian Orthodox Church:

> Regarding the readings—the Epistle and Gospel are taken either of the day or of the commemoration being celebrated, or according to the direction of the celebrant. As regards the reading of the Old Testament, an appropriate reading may be selected, or a reading of the commemoration being celebrated, or, in the end, the reading may be chosen by the [priest or bishop] celebrating the service.[83]

The problem here is not the celebration of JAS, whose anaphoral prayers are truly better read and prayed in church than exclusively studied in a classroom, but the incomplete understanding of this liturgy, of how it is supposed to function within the current Byzantine rite, and the ignorance of the calendar

---

[80] Ἡ θεία λειτουργία τοῦ ἁγίου ἐνδόξου ἀποστόλου Ἰακώβου, τοῦ Ἀδελφοθέου, καὶ πρώτου ἱεράρχου Ἱεροσολύμων, ἐκδοθεῖσα μετὰ διατάξεως καὶ σημειώσεων ὑπὸ Διονυσίου Λάτα, ἀρχιεπισκόπου Ζακύνθου (Zakynthos: n.p., 1886), 71; Brakmann and Chronz, 'Eine Blume der Levante', 90–2.

[81] Charon, *History of the Melkite Patriarchates*, vol. 3.1, 24.

[82] For more on the various editions of JAS, see the section 'Editions of the Liturgy of St James' in Chapter 3 here.

[83] Относительно чтенія—то Апостолъ и Евангеліе берутся или рядовые дня или празднуемаго событія, или же по усмотрѣнію служашаго. Что касается чтенія Ветхаго Завѣта, то можно взять подходящую паремію, или же паремію празднуемаго событія, или же, наконецъ, предоставить выборъ чтенія совершающему службу. In Общія указанія относительно чтенія Св. Писанія и пѣнія на Литургіи Св. Апостола Іакова. Приложеніе къ служебнику Литургіи Св. Апост. Іакова (Ladomirova: Printing Press of the Venerable Job of Pochaev, 1938), 5.

and lectionary directly connected to JAS, whose hymns and scriptural readings were prescribed and not at the whim of the presiding clergy.

While the Orthodox patriarchate of Jerusalem seems content to preserve its Byzantinized traditions, voices from within the Melkite Greek Catholic Church have been calling for a return to ancient forms of Hagiopolite liturgy. One of the most prominent voices was that of Bishop Néophyte Edelby (1920–95), a member of the Cairo Circle of liturgical reformers in the Melkite Greek Catholic Church. He insisted upon 'a return to more ancient forms through the elimination of unpleasant additions that centuries of negligence and misunderstood piety have accumulated without any discernment'.[84] Among these 'unpleasant additions' (*surcharges disgracieuses*), Edelby identifies both Byzantinization and Latinization as problematic, insisting that the former is as detrimental to authentic Melkite liturgy as the latter, since Byzantinization of the liturgy, in his view, has made the 'glories of Melkite spiritual life' disappear.[85] Another Melkite liturgist involved in reform, one not as radical as Edelby and perhaps more aware of current scholarship in liturgiology, was Nicholas Antiba, who insisted that 'our Melkite Church is to stay in harmony with the other Byzantine Churches'—but must remain faithful above all to the Antiochene Byzantine tradition.[86] In the course of these debates the authors conflate the distinct liturgical traditions of Alexandria, Antioch, and Jerusalem, making them the basis of a common 'Antiochene' and Byzantine Melkite liturgical identity. Reference to the 'Antiochene Byzantine' tradition suggests that distinctions between what is authentically Antiochene—or, for that matter, Hagiopolitan—and what is Byzantine were not altogether clear to them. Likewise, none of these authors makes it clear whether or not their reforms envision a return to the original Hagiopolite calendar, lectionary, or eucharistic Divine Liturgy.

PARAMETERS OF RESEARCH

In order to address the question of liturgical Byzantinization more carefully, it is necessary to define the limits of this study. The ecclesiastical, geographical,

---

[84] [U]n retour vers des formes plus anciennes par l'élimination des surcharges disgracieuses que des siècles d'incurie ou de piété mal comprise ont accumulées sans discernement. Néophyte Edelby, 'Pour une restauration de la liturgie byzantine', *Proche-Orient Chrétien* 7 (1957), 97–118, here 98.

[85] Ibid., 113.

[86] Nicholas Antiba, 'Liturgical Renewal in the Greek Melkite Catholic Church', *Euntes docete* 46 (1993), 19–32, here 21 and 28. For previous changes to the liturgy of the Melkite Church, see Paul Bacel, 'Les innovations liturgiques chez les grecs melchites au XVIIIe siècle', *Échos d'Orient* 9 (1906), 5–10.

chronological, and linguistic limits are intended to concentrate attention on the specific question under study and to eliminate material irrelevant to it.

The focus here is on the liturgical practice of the Orthodox patriarchate of Jerusalem, that is, the ecclesial body of Christians who accepted the decisions of the fourth ecumenical council, held in Chalcedon in 451, and have remained in Communion with the patriarchate of Constantinople until the present day. No native, non-Chalcedonian church ever formed in Jerusalem, as it did in Alexandria and Antioch. In the latter two, the Coptic Orthodox Church and the Syrian Orthodox Church became respectively the local majority churches. In Jerusalem, Armenians were present from the fourth century but, due to their opposition to the Council of Chalcedon, their liturgical practices began to differ from those of the Orthodox patriarchate of Jerusalem.[87]

The territory of the patriarchate of Jerusalem, established in 451 and virtually unchanged until today, extends over Galilee, Mount Carmel, and Lake Hula in the north of Palestine, arches down to Mount Sinai in the south, and is bounded by the Mediterranean to the west and by the Jordanian plains and Arabian Desert to the east; it is a territory of approximately 600 by 100 km².[88] Since AD 390, this area encompassed the Roman administrative divisions or 'provinces' (*provinciae*) Palaestina I, Palaestina II, and Palaestina Salutaris (Palaestina III), which lasted well into the period of Islamic occupation, until the Arab conquest in 638, Palaestina Salutaris being abolished even later.[89]

Known as 'the colony Aelia Capitolona' (*colonia Aelia Capitolina*) since the time of its foundation by Emperor Hadrian after AD 130, Jerusalem was initially neither the political nor the ecclesiastical centre of the region. That honour had been reserved for the metropolis of Caesarea in Palestine, formerly within the patriarchate of Antioch.[90] With the Councils of Nicaea in 325 and of Chalcedon in 451, Jerusalem achieved independence and was finally

[87] For the relevance of Hagiopolitan liturgical sources to the Armenian liturgy, see Gabrielle Winkler, 'Ungelöste Fragen im Zusammenhang mit den liturgischen Gebräuchen in Jerusalem', *Handes Amsorya: Zeitschrift für armenische Philologie* 101.1/12 (1987), 303–15.

[88] Siméon Vailhé, 'L'Érection du Patriarcat de Jérusalem, 451', *Revue de l'Orient Chrétien* 4 (1899), 44–57, here 55; Levy-Rubin, 'The Reorganisation of the Patriarchate of Jerusalem', here 223–6. For maps of the city of Jerusalem and the territory of the Jerusalem patriarchate, see Appendix 2, sections 2 (Map of the City of Jerusalem, 4th–9th cent.) and 3 (Map of the Jerusalem patriarchate, 8th–9th cent.).

[89] Levy-Rubin, 'The Reorganisation of the Patriarchate of Jerusalem', here 197; Kenneth G. Holum, 'Palestine', in ODB 3, here 1563–4; Dauphin, *La Palestine byzantine*, 39–40; F. van der Meer and Christine Mohrmann, *Atlas of the Early Christian World*, trans. and ed. by Mary F. Hedlund and H. H. Rowley (London: Thomas Nelson and Sons, 1966), 15, 32; *An Historical Atlas of Islam*, ed. by Hugh Kennedy, 2nd rev. edn (Leiden: Brill, 2002), 20–4, 26b.

[90] Hugues Vincent, OP, and Félix-Marie Abel, OP, *Jérusalem nouvelle* (Paris: Lecoffre, 1926), 1–39. For more on Caesarea, see Marlia M. Mango and Kenneth G. Holum, 'Caesarea Maritima', in ODB 1, here 364; *Caesarea Reports and Studies: Excavations 1995–2007 within the Old City and the Ancient Harbor*, ed. by Kenneth G. Holum, Jennifer A. Stabler, and Eduard G. Reinhardt (Oxford: Achaeopress, 2008).

elevated to the status of patriarchate, the last of the pentarchy in precedence, thus establishing its influence over both the city of Jerusalem and the region of Palestine.[91] Referring to Jerusalem by its Latin name Aelia Capitolina, Canon 7 of the Council of Nicaea stated that, 'since there prevails a custom and ancient tradition to the effect that the bishop of Aelia [ἐν Αἰλίᾳ ἐπίσκοπον] is to be honoured, let him be granted everything consequent upon this honour, saving the dignity proper to the metropolitan'.[92] After 451, apart from the patriarch, there were three capital cities or metropolia in Caesarea, Scythopolis, and Petra, and sixty episcopal sees that were reorganized after the Arab occupation into twenty-five independent archbishoprics.[93]

Although once part of the Roman territories of Palestine, Sinai is no longer directly within the jurisdiction of the patriarchate of Jerusalem, having been granted autonomous status in 1575 by the patriarchate of Constantinople.[94] Sinai's proper liturgical practices, not always easily identifiable in the manuscript collection of the Monastery of St Catherine, remain outside the focus of this study.[95] Nevertheless, the importance of Sinai's library for the Hagiopolite liturgy cannot be understated; for not all manuscripts from Sinai are expressions of the Sinai liturgy. St Catherine's served as a repository for other Palestinian monasteries, such as Mar Sabas Lavra and the Lavra of St Chariton, to which Palestinian monks sent precious manuscripts for preservation.[96] Thus the fact that a manuscript is found today in a certain library has little bearing on its origin; as we shall see, 'books travel with their owners'.[97] The fact that the monastic population of Sinai was multiethnic complicates matters even further: the monastery's library has preserved liturgical sources that represent diverse traditions in various languages and from different periods.[98]

The limitations of this study do not permit me to investigate the practices of the patriarchates of Alexandria and Antioch, although research into the liturgical Byzantinization of these patriarchates and of the Church of Georgia will hopefully fill certain lacunae in the future, helping to clarify the mode of

---

[91] Vailhé, 'L'Érection du Patriarcat de Jérusalem, 451' (see n. 88), 50–5.

[92] See *Decrees of the Ecumenical Councils*, vol. 1, ed. by Norman P. Tanner, SJ (Washington, DC: Georgetown University Press, 1990), 9.

[93] Charon, *History of the Melkite Patriarchates*, vol. 3.1, 298–301; Levy-Rubin, 'The Reorganisation of the Patriarchate of Jerusalem', here 202–4.

[94] Alexander Kazhdan, 'Sinai', in ODB 3, here 1902–3; Alice-Mary Talbot, 'Catherine, Monastery of Saint', in ODB 1, here 392; Ronald Roberson, CSP, *The Eastern Christian Churches: A Brief Survey*, 7th edn (Rome: Edizioni Orientalia Christiana, 2008), 101–3; Σιναϊτικὰ Δίπτυχα 2011 (Athens: Ἔκδοσις ἱερᾶς αὐτονόμου καὶ αὐτοκρατορικῆς μονῆς θεοβαδίστου ὄρους Σινᾶ, 2011).

[95] Nasrallah, 'Liturgie des Patriarcats melchites', 165–8.

[96] Nasrallah, *Histoire* II.1, 63, 66.　　　[97] Taft, 'Worship on Sinai', 168.

[98] Nasrallah, *Histoire* II.1, 100; Stig Syméon Frøyshov, 'Les manuscrits de la bibliothèque du Sinaï: Archives du monde orthodoxe, trésor de la liturgie hiérosolymitaine', *Le Messager Orthodoxe* 148 (2009), 60–74.

transmission of Constantinopolitan liturgical material to the Jerusalem patriarchate.[99]

The phenomenon of Byzantinization in Jerusalem occurred roughly between the Arab conquest in 638 and the expulsion of the crusaders in 1187. These two events mark the chronological limits of my study: Jerusalem still celebrated its own local liturgy at the start of the eighth century, but by the beginning of the thirteenth the liturgy had become completely Byzantinized. This process, of course, did not happen in a uniform manner and the various elements that make up the Hagiopolitan liturgical tradition were influenced diversely. For example, JAS was still celebrated until the thirteenth century, while the calendar and lectionary of Jerusalem came under Constantinopolitan influence much earlier. Given the various stages of development, the tenth and eleventh centuries are of particular interest in that they witness the transitional character of Hagiopolite liturgy during the process of Byzantinization. Despite falling outside the chronological limits of my study, certain liturgical sources of the fourth through to the seventh centuries are crucial for better gauging the nature of Hagiopolite liturgy before its gradual disappearance and for establishing what can be considered to be 'authentic' or local expressions of it before Byzantinization. These liturgical sources will be introduced in Chapter 1.

Multilingualism has been present among the Christian populations of Palestine from the very start of Christianity at the Cross of Christ, when Pilate wrote the charge for Jesus' Crucifixion 'in Hebrew, Latin, and Greek' (Ἑβραϊστί, Ῥωμαϊστί, Ἑλληνιστί, John 19:20), and then at the events of Pentecost (Acts 2:1–42). Apart from these three languages, Syriac and Christian Palestinian Aramaic were spoken by the local population of Jerusalem and Palestine, Georgian and Armenian were common among pilgrims from the Caucasus, who established monastic colonies in the Holy Land and copied many liturgical manuscripts, translating them into their own tongues, and Arabic became the lingua franca after the Arab conquest. All these languages played an important role in the patriarchate of Jerusalem. With regard to the Chalcedonian liturgy, however, the most important languages, in order of precedence, are Greek, Georgian, Arabic, and Syriac. This study will focus on Greek and Georgian sources because of their direct connection to the primary liturgical centres of the Jerusalem patriarchate. Any future study of liturgical Byzantinization must, however, endeavour to examine these sources in all their original languages.

---

[99] For an initial bibliography on the Byzantinization of the Alexandrian patriarchate, see Charon, 'Le rite byzantin', 477–84; Nasrallah, 'Liturgie des Patriarcats melchites', 163–5; Aristeides Papadakis, 'Alexandria, Patriarchate of', in ODB 1, here 61; Martiniano P. Roncaglia, 'Melchites and Copts', *The Coptic Encyclopedia*, vol. 5, ed. by Aziz S. Atiya (New York: Macmillan, 1991), here 1583. For Antioch, see Korolevsky, *Christian Antioch*; Charon, 'Le rite byzantin', 485–94; Nasrallah, 'Liturgie des Patriarcats melchites', 156–9; Aristeides Papadakis, 'Antioch, Patriarchate of', in ODB 1, here 116–17.

ARRANGEMENT OF THE MATERIAL

As Eusebius wrote of his own history of the church, I, too, could say the same of this book on the liturgical Byzantinization of the patriarchate of Jerusalem:

> From the scattered hints dropped by my predecessors I have picked out whatever seems relevant to the task I have undertaken, plucking like flowers in literary pastures the helpful contributions of earlier writers, to be embodied in the continuous narrative I have in mind.[100]

New sources and studies make it possible to pluck items from the static pool of extant information in order to provide a new synthesis, generating a stream of investigation into the dynamic interactions between patriarchs, emperors, caliphs, and scribes in the process of the Byzantinization of Jerusalem's liturgy.

The book begins with a presentation of the most ancient descriptions of liturgical practices in Jerusalem during the Byzantine period (roughly, the fourth century to the seventh), along with criteria for distinguishing Hagiopolite liturgical sources (Chapter 1). More detailed descriptions of liturgical manuscripts after the eighth century are given in Appendix 1. Chapter 1 is followed by an analysis of the historical context of Byzantinization in Chapter 2, with close attention to multilingual environments in Palestine and contact between Jerusalem and Constantinople. Once the liturgical manuscripts are contextualized, the remainder of the book deals with the Liturgy of the Word of JAS in Chapter 3, the Hagiopolitan liturgical calendar in Chapter 4, and the lectionary of Jerusalem in Chapter 5.

One major problem in the arrangement of the chapters was the ordering between Chapter 4 and Chapter 5. The question of which came first—the calendar or the cycle of readings—is crucial to studies of the liturgical year. The oldest liturgical books of Jerusalem contain both a calendar and a lectionary and are arranged around the fixed liturgical cycle, beginning with Annunciation on 25 March or Nativity on 25 December, while scriptural readings and the hymnography of the movable cycle centred upon the principal feast of the Resurrection are inserted as a block within the fixed cycle.[101] Thus I have opted for studying the calendar first, and then the lectionary system.

---

[100] Ὅσα τοίνυν εἰς τὴν προκειμένην ὑπόθεσιν λυσιτελεῖν ἡγούμεθα τῶν αὐτοῖς ἐκεινοις σποράδην μνημονευθέντων, ἀναλεξάμενοι καὶ ὡς ἂν ἐκ λογικῶν λειμώνων τὰς ἐπιτηδείους αὐτῶν τῶν πάλαι συγγραφέων ἀπανθισάμενοι φωνάς, δι᾽ ὑφηγήσεως ἱστορικῆς πειρασόμεθα σωματοποιῆσαι. Eusebius, *Historia ecclesiastica*, 1.4. English translation from Eusebius, *The History of the Church from Christ to Constantine*, trans. by G. A. Williamson, rev. and ed. by Andrew Louth (London: Penguin, 1989), 2.
[101] For more on the structure of these liturgical sources, see the sections 'Eucharistic Liturgies' in Chapter 1, 'Manuscripts of the Liturgy of St James' in Chapter 3, 'The Structure and Characteristics of the Hagiopolite Liturgical Year' in Chapter 4, and 'Structures of the Jerusalem Lectionary: Gospel Cycles' in Chapter 5 in this book, together with Appendix 1.

In essence, this book is a study of the Hagiopolite liturgical year and of how it changed under external Byzantine liturgical influence during the period of the Islamic conquest of Jerusalem. The arrangement of the chapters and the approach to studying the liturgical year are adapted from an article of Aleksei Pentkovsky, who defines the basic parameters of the church Typikon, or the liturgical ordo, as comprising (1) non-scriptural sources[102] that distribute feasts, saints' memorials, and various other commemorations throughout the fixed and mobile cycles of the liturgical year; (2) the lectionary system, which appoints the selection and division of scriptural readings from the Old Testament and New Testament throughout the liturgical year; and (3) texts from the Euchologion, which consist of liturgical formularies and of parts of the Liturgy of the Hours. As Pentkovsky asserts, these parameters are the same for both cathedral and monastic worship, depending on regional and chronological indications.[103] As Stefano Parenti has noted, 'the Euchologion tells only a part of the history of Orthodox worship', which means that this liturgical book 'must also be compared with other books, otherwise one runs the risk of obtaining idealized paradigms far removed from historical reality'.[104]

This approach is not only useful for the study of liturgy; its arrangement also reflects the nature of liturgy itself. One begins with (1) the feast, event, or person being celebrated by the church, proceeding to (2) the word of God in the Scriptures that corresponds to that celebration, and this in turn prompts the church to (3) petition, ascend to, converse with, give thanks, and sacrifice to God through words and actions recorded in the Euchologion. This progression reflects the order of salvation history itself—the mystery of Christ, through which Jesus Christ revealed himself as the Son of God in the events of his incarnation, earthly life, and resurrection. The disciples understood this only in retrospect, when Christ 'interpreted to them in all the scriptures the things concerning himself' (Luke 24:27), and then recorded the events of Christ's life in the Gospels.[105]

The same disciples, to whom Christ had just explained his presence in the Scriptures, recognized him only 'in the breaking of the bread' (Luke 24:37)— that is, in the Eucharist. In his first letter to the Corinthians, Paul declares 'for as often as you eat this bread and drink the cup, you proclaim the Lord's

---

[102] Pentkovsky's first category is actually called 'menologion' ('Месяцеслов'); see Pentkovsky, 'Богослужебные уставы', here 70. Noret notes the inadequacy and ambiguity of this and similar terms in Byzantine studies; see Jacques Noret, 'Ménologes, Synaxaires, Ménées: Essai de clarification d'une terminologie', AB 86 (1968), 21–4. In order to avoid confusion, I use here the awkward term 'non-scriptural sources', until scholars agree on a better nomenclature.

[103] Pentkovsky, 'Богослужебные уставы', here 70.

[104] Parenti, 'Cathedral Rite', 450.

[105] See 'Postscript: A Premodern Faith for a Postmodern Era', in John Behr, *The Mystery of Christ: Life in Death* (Crestwood, NY: St Vladimir's Seminary Press, 2006), 173–81.

death" until he comes' (1 Corinthians 11:26), to which BAS adds 'and his resurrection',[106] showing that the full understanding of Scripture and of the events celebrated there comes in the liturgy.[107] John Behr points to 'the night in which [Christ] was given up' in the 'institution narrative' of CHR and the addition of the phrase 'or rather, gave himself up, for the life of the world'[108] as the moment and turning point at which a historical report becomes a theological reflection—where 'theology proper begins'.[109]

In this manner, understanding the liturgical calendar of the celebrations of the liturgical year in Jerusalem, the pericopes from Scripture that were read, and the response of the church in prayers and hymns leads to a theological understanding of Hagiopolite liturgy. This process of understanding can be compared with the theology of the Byzantine rite if one wishes to understand, further, the impact of liturgical Byzantinization on Hagiopolitan liturgical theology. Actual liturgical theology, however, arises from liturgical structures and does not get detached from them; it does not search for a symbolic interpretation of liturgy but for its meaning, which resides in the liturgy's structure. This structure, when it is in action, is the matrix for *theologia prima*.[110] Like it or not, pre-Byzantinized Hagiopolite liturgy has been lost and is no longer the liturgy of any Christian community today. Thus to speak of this liturgy in action and to understand its *theologia prima* is impossible. Although here in this book the purpose of re-creating Jerusalem's lost worship tradition from liturgical manuscripts is to understand a historical change observed over time, it is nevertheless possible to attempt to understand the *theologia secunda* of Hagiopolite liturgy in the period of Byzantinization. Because no Hagiopolitan liturgical commentaries exist after the sixth century, *theologia secunda* must be understood through structures of liturgical services, their scriptural readings, and the hymnography that draws out the meaning of these readings in their particular structures.

---

[106] ὁσάκις γὰρ ἂν ἐσθίητε τὸν Ἄρτον τοῦτον, καὶ τὸ Ποτήριον τοῦτο πίνητε, τὸν ἐμὸν θάνατον καταγγέλλετε, τὴν ἐμὴν Ἀνάστασιν ὁμολογεῖτε. Ἱερατικον (Athens: Ἀποστολικὴ Διακονία, 1962), 184.

[107] Although this phrase is not found in CHR, the addition of 'and his resurrection' in BAS completes our understanding of Scripture. For more on this question, see Robert F. Taft, SJ, '"This Saving Command" of the Chrysostom Anamnesis and the "Missing Command to Repeat"', *Studi sull'Oriente Cristiano* 6.1 (2002), 129–49.

[108] τῇ νυκτὶ ᾗ παρεδίδοτο, μᾶλλον δὲ ἑαυτὸν παρεδίδου ὑπὲρ τοῦ κόσμου ζωῆς'. *The Divine Liturgy of our Father among the Saints John Chrysostom*, trans. by Archimandrite Ephrem Lash (Oxfordshire: Greek Orthodox Archdiocese of Thyateira and Great Britain, 2011), 45.

[109] John Behr, *The Mystery of Christ: Life in Death* (Crestwood, NY: St Vladimir's Seminary Press, 2006), 31. Although this is irrelevant to the argument at hand, the reader should be aware that the phrase 'or rather gave himself up, for the life of the world' is not found in the earliest version of CHR and was added to CHR after Iconoclasm. See Jacob, *Formulaire*, 493.

[110] David W. Fagerberg, *Theologia Prima: What is Liturgical Theology?* 2nd edn (Chicago, IL: Hillenbrand, 2004), 41.

Thus, the goals of this book are to establish the sources that preserve Hagiopolite liturgy before, during, and after its Byzantinization; to present their historical context; and to investigate JAS, its presence, its transformation, and its decline, as well as changes to the liturgical calendar and lectionary of Jerusalem, in order to understand how and why Jerusalem lost its liturgical tradition.

Part I

Liturgy and Context

1

Liturgy in Byzantine Jerusalem

In order to be able to examine the changes to Jerusalem's liturgy that occurred during the process of Byzantinization, from the Arab conquest in the seventh century until the crusades in the twelfth, one should have at least a basic understanding of what the liturgy of Jerusalem was like in late antiquity—in the fourth, fifth, and sixth centuries, when Jerusalem and Palestine were still part of the Byzantine empire. The purpose of this chapter is to present the early sources for the Hagiopolite liturgy—both from the city of Jerusalem and from its outlying monasteries—and to contrast them to contemporaneous liturgical books and descriptions of liturgical services from Constantinople, as far as that is possible. Particular attention will be paid to the eucharistic liturgy of St James (JAS), the liturgical calendar, and the lectionary, which form the subject of subsequent chapters. With an explanation of the different local traditions in both patriarchal sees, it will be possible to trace Byzantine influence and foreign liturgical practices in Hagiopolite liturgical books examined later on.

The contrast between popular understandings of the early liturgy in Jerusalem and in Constantinople is expressed in the titles of two recent handbooks for students of the late antique liturgy in these two cities: Jerusalem is the earthly abode of Christ and his presence there influenced the city's liturgical rites in the early years of Christianity, while worship in Constantinople is described as heavenly and closely connected to the imperial authority that the Byzantine capital's liturgies carried.[1] Studies of Jerusalem's liturgy have often attempted to show continuity between the practices of that city in late antiquity and in later periods, and some have attempted to extend this continuity back to the times of the early church and Jewish–Christian practices.[2] Using the catechetical works of Cyril of Jerusalem, the travel journals of Egeria,

---

[1] Lester Ruth, Carrie Steenwyk, and John D. Witvliet, *Walking Where Jesus Walked: Worship in Fourth-Century Jerusalem* (Church at Worship, Grand Rapids, MI: William B. Eerdmans, 2010); Walter D. Ray, *Tasting Heaven on Earth: Worship in Sixth-Century Constantinople* (Church at Worship, Grand Rapids, MI: William B. Eerdmans, 2012).

[2] For criticisms of this view, see Taylor, *Christians and the Holy Places.*

and the Armenian and Georgian lectionaries of Jerusalem, it is possible to examine initiation rites, the celebration of the Eucharist, the daily office, and the liturgical year—particularly Theophany, Lent, Pascha, Pentecost—and to get a general overview of saints' commemorations.[3] Stig Frøyshov has lamented that, despite the 'the richness of the sources, the ancient liturgy of Jerusalem is still rather poorly known'. While no extensive general study of Jerusalem's early liturgy exists, no such study could be written until its major documents are edited or discovered by liturgiologists. Even the 1975 'new finds' of Sinai will take time to undergo scholarly investigation.[4]

Before moving on to the liturgical sources themselves, it is necessary briefly to review a few questions regarding the textual sources of the liturgy and their classification. Although the aim of every historian of liturgy must be 'to let the sources speak for themselves', manuscripts of the ancient Hagiopolite liturgy's books have suffered the ravages of time and are incomplete witnesses to liturgical rites and actions.[5] In many cases the manuscript sources are simply no longer extant. If one wishes to compensate for the missing testimonies of worship in Jerusalem, theological commentaries and pilgrimage accounts prove extremely useful. As John Baldovin notes,

> one of the most difficult tasks for the contemporary liturgical historian is to discern what various acts of worship meant to those who participated in them. After all, the true history of Christian worship is not contained in prayer texts or lectionaries or Typika alone as much as in the actual experience of Christians in different places and different eras.[6]

Thus, not only do theological commentaries and pilgrimage accounts supplement the information from liturgical manuscripts—they also bring them to life. What the authors of these commentaries and accounts describe or omit from their experiences of liturgical worship is telling: it suggests which rites and actions they considered to be the most significant ones. Nevertheless, such accounts are by their very nature subjective because, in the process of describing certain elements of liturgical prayer, they inevitably omit others. As a consequence, descriptions of liturgy are not to be taken as perfect outlines of the unfolding of a liturgical rite. Despite criticism about the factual reliability of such perspectives, Robert Taft rightly defends the 'ingenuousness' of eyewitness accounts. The liturgical scholar's task is to examine prescriptive liturgical books together with eyewitness accounts. One can gain insights

---

[3] Baldovin, *Liturgy in Ancient Jerusalem*; Bradshaw, *Search for the Origins*, 113–17.

[4] Frøyshov, 'The Georgian Witness', 228. For more on the liturgical manuscripts found in the Sinai 'new finds', see Appendix 1.

[5] Taft, *Through Their Own Eyes*, 30.

[6] John F. Baldovin, SJ, 'A Note on the Liturgical Processions in the Menologion of Basil II', in Εὐλόγημα: *Studies in Honor of Robert Taft, SJ*, ed. by Ephrem Carr, Stefano Parenti, Abraham-Andreas Thiermeyer, and Elena Velkovska (Rome: Sant'Anselmo, 1993), 25.

from the texts transmitted in liturgical manuscripts only by reading them along with their commentaries, which Taft considers an 'infallibly reliable resource—indeed, the only source—for what the one saying them thought'.[7] In other words, one cannot understand a liturgical rite by relying solely upon a liturgical book. Such eyewitness accounts or liturgical commentaries provide abundant information for the dating of early liturgical sources, namely the AL, the GL, and the *Iadgari*, and for understanding various developments to liturgical rites in Jerusalem. Since liturgical rites evolve, and thus contain many layers of prayers and texts accumulated over time, distinguishing the various strata within liturgical manuscripts in order to arrive at the most ancient elements can be a difficult, if not impossible, task. However, textual sources such as the eyewitness accounts of pilgrims or the catechetical mystagogies presented in this chapter generally preserve more faithfully the work of their authors as witnesses of liturgical practice in their own lifetime. How faithful liturgical manuscripts are as witnesses to the actual liturgical practice of the time in which they were copied—as opposed to reflecting some kind of ideal programme or being the fanciful composition of a scribe—cannot generally be verified. Paul Bradshaw has noted that liturgical texts are 'living literature' and one must approach them with caution when attempting to reconstruct patterns of early Christian worship. He rightfully censures those who take many of these texts at face value without considering them critically, accepting instead their authoritative-sounding statements as genuine and their confusing liturgical legislation as reflections of actual liturgical practice.[8] For the purposes of this study, all the liturgical sources examined in it are selected and analysed on the basis of knowledge about their provenance, context, dating, and content.[9] Even if one chooses to hold a sceptical position regarding the actual use of some of the liturgical manuscripts examined here—or be a 'splitter' rather than a 'lumper', according to the terminology popularized by Bradshaw within liturgical studies[10]—one must admit that they at least reflect an ideal of liturgical practice and usage that was prevalent among their respective scribes during the period in which they were copied. Certain signs, such as worn folios, Arabic marginal notes, and modifications to the text by later scribal hands point to the fact that many of the manuscripts consulted in this study were actually used.[11]

Regarding the classification of these liturgical texts—both manuscripts and eyewitness accounts—much ink has been spilled on the distinction between

---

[7] Taft, *Through Their Own Eyes*, 13–14 and 17.

[8] See Bradshaw, *Search for the Origins*, 1–20, for a critical examination of methodologies used in previous reconstructions of early Christian liturgy.

[9] For more on the criteria for selecting sources in this study, see the section 'Hagiopolite Liturgical Manuscripts in the Period of Byzantinization' in this chapter, as well as Appendix 1.

[10] Bradshaw, *Search for the Origins*, ix–x.

[11] For more information on these manuscripts, see their description in Appendix 1.

'cathedral' and 'monastic' liturgy.[12] This distinction was introduced into Byzantine liturgiology by Baumstark, who separated between everyday services, communal and private, that were obligatory for monks and less frequent communal services for the whole community. These two kinds of rites existed side by side in Jerusalem, monastic influence eventually expanding the cathedral *cursus* from one daily morning and one daily evening service to a multiplicity of daily offices, observed even by the laity.[13] Objections to the descriptor 'cathedral' have questioned the restriction of non-monastic prayer to cathedrals—a crucial point to consider for Jerusalem, where monks were present at the Church of the Anastasis from the fourth century on and later formed an influential monastic community at this church—de facto the cathedral of Jerusalem from a very early time. Nevertheless, 'cathedral' is preferable, since it was generally the bishop's church that was the centre of liturgical life in each local church. Liturgical sources show this on their own, clearly differentiating a 'cathedral' or 'ecclesiastical' rite (τάξις...τοῦ ἐκκλησιαστοῦ) from a 'monastic' rite (τοῦ τυπικοῦ) in books of the Typikon, Triodion, and Praxapostolos and in liturgical commentaries.[14]

Hagiopolitan sources themselves provide further distinctions. The tenth-century Horologion in codex *Sinai Geo. O. 34* applies the term 'public' (საჯრო, *saeroj*) to vespers, Communion (presanctified), nocturns, matins, and compline, while the remainder of the offices were intended for ascetic or urban monastic communities, such as the *spoudaioi* (οἱ Σπουδαῖοι) and Egeria's *monazontes* (οἱ Μονάζοντες) associated with the Jerusalem cathedral.[15] Yet diverse practices existed even among monastics, as witnessed by the visit of the Abbots Sophronius and John to Sinai.[16] These examples suggest that the distinction between 'cathedral' and 'monastic' liturgy is useful, but must be handled carefully and with some nuance when analysing the situation of the patriarchate of Jerusalem—a territory that included both urban and desert monastics, in constant interaction with the Holy City's cathedral.[17]

---

[12] For recent bibliography on this debate, see Robert F. Taft, SJ, 'Cathedral vs Monastic Liturgy in the Christian East: Vindicating a Distinction', BBGG (terza serie) 2 (2005), 173–219; Stig Symeon Ragnvald Frøyshov, 'The Cathedral–Monastic Distinction Revisited, Part I: Was Egyptian Desert Liturgy a Pure Monastic Office?', *Studia Liturgica* 37 (2007), 198–216.

[13] Baumstark, *Comparative Liturgy*, 111–13; Anton Baumstark, *On the Historical Development of the Liturgy*, trans. and annotated by Fritz West (Collegeville, MN: Liturgical Press, 2011), 140–6; Taft, 'Cathedral vs Monastic Liturgy' (see n. 12).

[14] Taft, *Hours*, 32; Taft, 'Cathedral vs Monastic Liturgy' (see n. 12), 206–16; George Guiver, *Company of Voices. Daily Prayer and the People of God* (New York: Pueblo, 1988), 53. For more on the cathedral of Jerusalem, see 'Stational Liturgy and the Topography of Jerusalem' in this chapter.

[15] Egeria, *Itinéraire*, § 24: 1 and 25: 6; Frøyshov, 'Early Development', 145.

[16] Longo, 'Narrazione'. See the section 'Monastic Liturgy in Byzantine Jerusalem and Palestine' in this chapter for an analysis of this text.

[17] See also Juan Mateos, 'The Origins of the Divine Office', *Worship* 41 (1967), 477–85, who suggests a tripartite division, namely cathedral, urban–monastic, and Egyptian monastic.

LITURGY AT THE CATHEDRAL OF JERUSALEM

Unlike in the case of the liturgy in other important early Christian centres, we have comparatively early and abundant knowledge of liturgical practices at the Holy Sepulchre in Jerusalem. This knowledge comes from the *Mystagogical Catecheses* attributed to Cyril of Jerusalem, from the travel diary of the pilgrim Egeria, and from lectionaries and hymnals extant today in Armenian and Georgian translation, their complete Greek originals having been lost.

Stational Liturgy and the Topography of Jerusalem

One of the notable elements of Jerusalem's cathedral worship was its 'stational' liturgy, which involved processions from one shrine or holy place to another—and seemed to be a novelty in its time, according to Egeria. The information Egeria provides makes it possible to recover the structure of the daily, fixed, and movable cycles at the Anastasis. Daily services included a morning service referred to as *matutinus* [*h*]*ymnus*,[18] which lasted from before cockcrow until after daybreak; shorter services at the sixth and ninth hours;[19] and evening prayer at the tenth hour, called *licinicon* or *lucernare*.[20] All of them presupposed the daily presence of the bishop for at least part of the service, and several services included a stational component in which the whole congregation processed from one part of the church building to another.

Examining the stational liturgies of Jerusalem, Constantinople, and Rome, John Baldovin has identified four characteristics common to all three liturgical centres. He defines stational liturgy as

> a service of worship [1] at a designated church, shrine, or public place in or near a city or town, [2] on a designated feast, fast, or commemoration, which is [3] presided over by the bishop or his representative and [4] intended as the local church's main liturgical celebration of the day.[21]

These four elements are also present in the early Hagiopolite Liturgy of the Hours, since elements of stational liturgy were an integral part of most services in Jerusalem's liturgy. Processions were limited neither to services beyond the walls of the Anastasis, since there was a 'great deal of movement around the buildings of the Golgotha Complex itself', nor to eucharistic liturgies, since

---

John Cassian, *De coenobiorum institutis* 3:1 (= PL 49:111–12), says that Palestinian and Mesopotamian monks imitated Egyptian models.

[18] Egeria, *Itinéraire*, § 24: 1–2 (= pp. 234–6 in Maraval's edn).
[19] Ibid., § 24: 3 (= pp. 236–8 Maraval).
[20] Ibid., § 24: 4–7 (= pp. 238–40 Maraval).
[21] Baldovin, *Urban Character*, 37. The numbering is mine.

processions also occurred as part of evening prayer.[22] The main elements of this system were likely well established by the time of Cyril of Jerusalem's death in 387.

Worship in Byzantine Palestine was centred on several urban churches and monastic centres. Of the three churches constructed by Constantine on important caves connected with the life of Christ, the primary place of worship and the one most frequently mentioned in Jerusalem's stational liturgy was the Anastasis complex built over a pagan temple on Golgotha, the spot where Christ was crucified.[23] The complex consisted of three parts: (1) at the west end, the Anastasis or Holy Sepulchre, which housed the tomb of Christ within a rotunda and had an exposed forecourt outside its east entrance;[24] (2) at the east end, the Martyrium[25] or Basilica, built over the place where the Cross of Christ was found, with its own exposed forecourt at its east entrance opening onto the *cardo maximus*; and (3) at the south end, the Cross between the Anastasis and the Martyrium.[26] The image of the tomb of Christ and the church complex began to appear on ampullae and its form was imitated throughout Christendom by pilgrims.[27] The Anastasis began to accumulate diverse traditions and the site became a 'goldmine for pilgrims'.[28] Its location was often confused and conflated with that of the site of the Jewish Temple, which was completely abandoned during the Byzantine period.[29] The original Anastasis complex, different in plan from the current Holy Sepulchre,[30] facilitated

---

[22] Ibid., 59, 83.

[23] See Eusebius, *Vita Constantini*, III, 25–43; *Eusebius Werke*, vol. 1, ed. by Ivar A. Heikel (Die Griechischen Christlichen Schriftsteller, Leipzig: Hinrichs'sche Buchhandlung, 1902), 91–6; Eusebius, *Life of Constantine*, ed. by Averil Cameron, trans. by Stuart George Hall (Oxford: Oxford University Press, 1999), 132–8. For a discussion of some of these churches, see Shalev-Hurvitz, *Holy Sites Encircled*.

[24] Corbo, *Santo Sepolcro*, vol. 1, 51–80; John Wilkinson, 'The Tomb of Christ: An Outline of Its Structural History', *Levant: Journal of the British School of Archaeology in Jerusalem* 4 (1972), 83–97.

[25] 'Martyrium' normally designates a church built over relics. In this case the relics are understood to be those of the true Cross in Eusebius, *Vita Constantini* 3: 30 (= PG 20: 1089–92). Verhelst, 'Lieux de station' II, 249–50 notes that 'Martyrium' can also designate a place commemorating a 'theophany'. See also Corbo, *Santo Sepolcro*, vol. 1, 103–14.

[26] Corbo, *Santo Sepolcro*, vol. 1, 81–102. For a plan of the Anastasis complex, see the section 'Plan of the Anastasis Complex, 4th, 11th, 12th cent.' in Appendix 2. The location of the baptistery is still debated. See Annabel Jane Wharton, 'The Baptistery of the Holy Sepulcher in Jerusalem and the Politics of Sacred Landscape', DOP 46 (1992), 313–25.

[27] Lieselotte Kötzsche, 'Das Heilige Grab in Jerusalem und seine Nachfolge', in *Kongress für Christliche Archäologie*, 272–90.

[28] Baldovin, *Liturgy in Ancient Jerusalem*, 8.

[29] Heribert Busse and Georg Kretschmar, *Jerusalemer Heiligtumstraditionen in altkirchlicher und frühislamischer Zeit* (Abhandlungen des Deutschen Palästinavereins, Wiesbaden: Harrassowitz, 1987), especially 81–111; Tracy Thorpe, *The Power of Silence: The Empty Temple Mount in Late Antique Jerusalem* (Unpublished doctoral thesis, Cambridge, MA: Harvard University, 2009).

[30] Abel, 'Jérusalem', DACL 7.2, here 2312.

internal stational liturgy and daily services that included processions from one part of the complex to another.[31]

Jerusalem stational processions also went to other churches in the Holy City and within the territory of the patriarchate. After the Holy Sepulchre, the Mount of Olives received the greatest attention from patrons who built churches in Jerusalem. Already in the time of Constantine, several churches were built here. The Imbomon (ἐν βωμῷ, *in monticulo*), whose name meant 'raised platform or hillock', was built on the traditional site of the Ascension on the Mount of Olives.[32] Another station often mentioned in the GL is the Church of the Apostles (ἀποστολεῖον or μαθητεῖον; աշակերտարան, *ashakertaran*; მოწაფეთა, *mocap'et'ay*), named thus from the tradition that Jesus had taught the apostles here.[33] The church was also the location for the celebration of the Mystical Supper according to Egeria[34] and of Pentecost according to Cyril of Jerusalem,[35] while the *Life of Peter the Iberian* seems to integrate Gethsemane with the Upper Room and the place of the Ascension.[36] The presence of several churches on the Mount of Olives and their multiple symbolic associations often confused pilgrims.[37]

Another holy site with many associated and competing traditions is the Church of Sion on the south-west hill of the old city. It is referred to as 'the cathedral of Jerusalem' in modern scholarship and was considered by the early Jerusalem church to be the seat of St James, the brother of the Lord and first bishop of Jerusalem; but these traditions developed much later, only after the time of Constantine. The Church of Sion gradually lost its status as the Holy City's cathedral, as the Anastasis complex began to acquire all the titles previously attributed to Sion.[38] The increased emphasis on the Holy Spirit after the First Council of Constantinople in 381 necessitated a more precise

---

[31] For more theoretical studies of the Anastasis complex and the importance of holy sites, see Jonathan Z. Smith, *To Take Place: Toward Theory in Ritual* (Chicago, IL: University of Chicago Press, 1987); Jonathan Z. Smith, 'Constructing a Small Place', and Evelyne Patlagean, 'Byzantium's Dual Holy Land', both in *Sacred Space: Shrine, City, Land*, ed. by Benjamin Z. Kedar and R. J. Zwi Werblowsky (New York: NYU Press, 1998), 18–31 and 112–26, respectively.

[32] Abel, 'Jérusalem', DACL 7.2, here 2325–6; Pringle, *Churches of the Crusader Kingdom*, vol. 3, 72–88; Verhelst, 'Lieux de station' II, here 261.

[33] AL 136–7; GL § 253, 260, 642, 919, 926, 938, 968, 974, 1062, 1068, 1083, 1108, 1182, 1229, 1327, 1346, 1387, 1414; Pringle, *Churches of the Crusader Kingdom*, vol. 3, 117–24; Verhelst, 'Lieux de station' II, here 247–8; Taylor, *Christians and the Holy Places*, 143–56.

[34] Egeria, *Itinéraire*, § 35: 2–3 (= pp. 278–81 Maraval).

[35] Cyril, *Pre-Baptismal Catechesis* 16:4, McCauley and Stephenson, *Works of Saint Cyril of Jerusalem*, 78.

[36] John Rufus' details are not clear. See Horn and Phenix, *Lives*, 196–7.

[37] Hanswulf Bloedhorn, 'Die Eleona und das Imbomon in Jerusalem: Eine Doppelkirchenanlage auf dem Ölberg?', in *Kongress für Christliche Archäologie*, 568–71.

[38] This is evidenced by a homily of St John of Damascus for the feast of Enkainia. See Michel van Esbroeck, 'Le discours de Jean Damascène pour la Dédicace de l'Anastasis', OCP 63 (1997), 53–98, here 56–8 and 72. See also Pringle, *Churches of the Crusader Kingdom*, vol. 3, 261–87; Bieberstein, 'Sion', 543–51; Bieberstein and Bloedhorn, *Jerusalem*, 1:177, 2:118–27.

localization of the descent of the Holy Spirit at Pentecost; hence, according to Klaus Bieberstein, the location of Mount Sion as the place of the pouring out of the Holy Spirit in the Old Testament (Joel 3:1–5) was connected to the tradition of the Upper Room (τὸ ὑπερῷον) in Acts 1:13.[39] Cyril of Jerusalem is the first to connect Sion with the Apostles, although he does not mention Pentecost explicitly.[40] Apart from its association with the room where the Apostles gathered at Pentecost, Sion came to be considered the location of the Cenacle of the Mystical Supper and of the foot washing, also held in an 'upper room' (ἀνάγιον), according to Mark 14:15 and Luke 22:12.[41] Sion also became the place of the Virgin's Dormition, although this association was first mentioned in the seventh century by Patriarch Sophronius, who connected Sion with the 'house of Mary, the mother of John, called Mark' in Acts 12:12.[42]

The history of the construction of the basilica is quite complex, as a result of conflicting accounts. The Church of Sion is mentioned as a station in the AL, and the GL even indicates that it was Archbishop John II of Jerusalem (r. c.386/7–417) who 'first built Sion'.[43] Given the contradictory evidence, it is difficult to say whether any pre-Constantinian Christian centres of worship survived, as some had previously suggested. Baldovin accepts such theories; but, due to lack of any archaeological evidence, both Bieberstein and Taylor question any traditions connected with the topography of the Sion Basilica before its construction in the fourth century.[44] The history of Yaḥyā al-Anṭakī mentions that the Church of Sion, called Ṣahyūn in Arabic, was dismantled in 1033 and its stones were used to rebuild the city walls of Jerusalem.[45]

The Church of the Nativity of Christ in Bethlehem was also a significant Constantinian foundation within the patriarchate. As in Jerusalem, the church attracted pilgrims from all of Christendom and served as a monastic centre, the most notable resident being St Jerome (d. 30 September 420). During the Byzantine period Bethlehem never had its own bishopric and was part of the immediate jurisdiction of the nearby patriarch of Jerusalem.[46] The Constantinian church was a five-aisled basilica with an octagonal structure built over

---

[39] Bieberstein, 'Sion', 546.

[40] Cyril of Jerusalem, *Prebaptismal Catechesis* 16–18 (= PG 33:917–1060); Taylor, *Christians and the Holy Places*, 210.

[41] Abel, 'Jérusalem', DACL 7.2, 2320–4; Verhelst, 'Lieux de station' II, here 253–4; Bieberstein, 'Sion', 546–8. Maraval notes in his edition that the connection with the mystical supper was later. See Egeria, *Itinéraire*, p. 278 n. 2.

[42] Sophronius, *Anacreontica* 20:13–17; CPG 7650; PG 87:3817–24; Herbert Donner, *Die anakreontischen Gedichte Nr. 19 und Nr. 20 des Patriarchen Sophronius von Jerusalem* (Heidelberg: Carl Winter, 1981), 14–15.

[43] 'ვინცვლად სიონ აღაშენა'. GL § 565.

[44] Baldovin, *Urban Character*, 45–6; Bieberstein, 'Sion'; Taylor, *Christians and the Holy Places*, 207–20.

[45] Yaḥyā al-Anṭakī, *History* III, 534–5.

[46] Levy-Rubin, 'The Reorganisation of the Patriarchate of Jerusalem', 203.

the cave of the Nativity and consecrated in 339. During the Samaritan revolt of 529, the church was burned and replaced by Emperor Justinian with a similar basilica form, but one with access to the cave for pilgrims.[47] The basic form of Justinian's restoration is visible today; thus the Church of the Nativity is the only late antique, pre-Islamic church to have survived intact until the present day. After the Arab conquest, the walls of the nave were adorned with mosaics depicting various biblical scenes and excerpts of doctrinal declarations from the first seven ecumenical councils explaining the two natures of Christ. The mosaics were restored in 1165 or 1169 by the joint patronage of King Amalric of Jerusalem (1163–74) and Emperor Manuel I Komnenos (1143–80).[48]

Other significant churches visited during Jerusalem's stational liturgy included important Marian shrines, such as the Nea Church, the Kathisma, and the Tomb of Mary in Gethsemane.[49] According to Procopius of Caesarea, the Nea Church was one of the most magnificent churches of Jerusalem; it was built by Justinian in 543 and held a major feast of the Theotokos on 20 November. But the church was damaged in 614 and was in ruins by the tenth century.[50] The *Life of Theodosios* by Cyril of Scythopolis notes that the Kathisma Church was built at a monastery on the road between Jerusalem and Bethlehem, at what is today known as Ramat Rahel, by the pious and influential woman Hikelia in the second half of the fifth century, although the location is already mentioned in the AL as a station for 15 August.[51] The Church of the Theotokos at Gethsemane was likely built around the time of the return of Patriarch Juvenal from Chalcedon after 451 and mentioned in

[47] Pringle, *Churches of the Crusader Kingdom*, vol. 1, 137–56, especially 137–40; Verhelst, 'Lieux de station' II, here 248; Beat Brenk, 'Der Kultort, seine Zugänglichkeit und seine Besucher', in *Kongress für Christliche Archäologie*, 69–122, here 90–6. For an examination of the pre-Constantinian traditions associated with the holy site, see Taylor, *Christians and the Holy Places*, 96–112.

[48] William Harvey, William R. Lethaby, Ormonde M. Dalton, Henry A. Cruso, and Arthur C. Headlam, *The Church of the Nativity at Bethlehem*, ed. by Robert Weir Schultz (London: Byzantine Research Fund, 1910), 31–51 and plates 10–12; Gustav Kühnel, 'Die Mosaiken und Säulemalereien der Geburtskirche in Bethlehem: Ein byzantinisches Ausschmückungsprogram der Kreuzfahrerzeit', in *XVI. Internationaler Byzantinistenkongress, Wien, 4.–9.10.1981: Résumés der Kurzbeiträge* (Vienna: Ernst Becvar, 1981), 10.2, n.p.; Pringle, *Churches of the Crusader Kingdom*, vol. 1, 141 and 154.

[49] See also Chapter 4, 'Church Buildings'.

[50] Procopius of Caesarea, *De aedificiis*, 5: 6, in *Procopius*, vol. 3, ed. by Karl Wilhelm Dindorf (Corpus Scriptorum Historiae Byzantinae 42, Bonn: Weber, 1838), 321–4; Yoram Tsafrir, 'Procopius and the Nea Church in Jerusalem', *Antiquité Tardive* 8 (2000), 149–64; Verhelst, 'Lieux de station' II, here 25 and 57–8; Schick, *Christian Communities of Palestine*, 332–3; Joan Taylor, 'The Nea Church', *Biblical Archaeology Review* 34: 1 (2008), here 50–9 and 82.

[51] AL, 354–5; *Life of Theodosios*, Chapter 1, in Schwartz, *Cyril of Scythopolis*, 236; Schick, *Christian Communities of Palestine*, 435–6; Rina Avner, 'The Kathisma: A Christian and Muslim Pilgrimage Site', *ARAM* 18/19 (2006-7), 541–57; Verhelst, 'Lieux de station' II, here 262–3; Shalev-Hurvitz, *Holy Sites Encircled*, 117–41.

pilgrim accounts from the sixth century onwards.[52] According to the GL, 23 October commemorated the church's 'Great Enkainia' (სატფ̇ურჲჲ ჻ოჿო, *satp'uri didi*) under Emperor Maurice (582–602)—presumably a restoration.[53] Despite the importance of processions to these churches and throughout the city as part of Jerusalem's liturgy, the most important—and earliest— witnesses of Hagiopolite liturgy come from the Church of the Holy Sepulchre.

The *Catecheses* of St Cyril of Jerusalem

The earliest extant Hagiopolite liturgical texts are catechetical sermons and commentaries from the cathedral of Jerusalem delivered by the Holy City's bishop in the fourth century. The catechetical sermons are attributed to St Cyril of Jerusalem, although both his authorship and the details of his life are disputed. Cyril served as bishop of Jerusalem from around early 349 until his death on 18 March 387.[54] He had a turbulent episcopal career, although the details depend on which sources one reads. Cyril's conflicts with Accacius of Caesarea stemmed in part from jealousy and rivalry between the mother see of Caesarea and its suffragan see, Jerusalem, and from Cyril's preoccupation with the status of Jerusalem, although recent examination of historical sources suggests that Cyril's depositions arose from his involvement in the Arian controversy rather than from purely political or personal motives.[55] Considered an opponent of classical Arianism but sympathetic to semi-Arianism, Cyril never used the term ὁμοούσιος in his catechetical lectures on the grounds that it was not found in Scripture.[56] Reliance on Scripture was a hallmark of Cyril's theology. Explaining the Creed, he stated, 'in regard to the divine and holy mysteries of the faith, not even a casual statement should be delivered without the Scriptures'.[57]

The 'Hagiopolitan Creed' appears to be at the root of Cyril's catechetical oeuvre, which comprises a *Procatechesis*, eighteen *Prebaptismal Catecheses* delivered in Constantine's Martyrium to those preparing for enlightenment

[52] Verhelst, 'Lieux de station' II, here 259–60 and 270; Shalev-Hurvitz, *Holy Sites Encircled*, 141–67.
[53] GL § 1320; Verhelst, 'Lieux de station' II, here 270; Walter Emil Kaegi and Anthony Cutler, 'Maurice', ODB II, 1318.
[54] The dates of Cyril's episcopacy are not agreed upon; McCauley gives 349–87, Cross 350–86, and Piédagnel *c.*350–87.
[55] Peter Van Nuffelen, 'The Career of Cyril of Jerusalem (*c.*348–87): A Reassessment', JTS 58 (2007), 134–46.
[56] Alois Grillmeier, SJ, *Jesus der Christus im Glauben der Kirche*, vol. 1: *Von der Apostolischen Zeit bis zum Kozil von Chalcedon (451)*, 3rd rev. edn (Herder: Freiburg, 1990), 459–60; Barry Baldwin, 'Cyril, Bishop of Jerusalem', ODB I, 571–2.
[57] Δεῖ γὰρ περὶ τῶν θείων καὶ ἁγίων τῆς Πίστεως μυστηρίων, μηδὲ τὸ τυχὸν ἄνευ τῶν θείων παδαδίδοσθαι γραφῶν. *Prebaptismal Catechesis* 4: 17 (= PG 33:476–7).

(φωτιζόμενοι) at Pascha, and five *Mystagogical Catecheses* at the Anastasis that explained the mysteries into which the neophytes had been newly initiated (νεοφώτιστοι).[58] The first four *Prebaptismal Catecheses* provide a 'short compendium' (συντόμῳ χρήσασθαι) of Christian faith and living, starting with the need to turn from sin to repentance in Baptism, then going on to events in the life of Christ.[59] Here Scripture, confirmed by a list of canonical writings read publicly in church, is Cyril's preferred source for explaining the doctrines he expounds.[60] The Creed itself, something to be learned word for word and guarded in one's heart, is not included in any of the catecheses, although it appears to have been recited to the φωτιζόμενοι at the end of the fifth lecture and then expounded in the following *Prebaptismal Catecheses*.[61]

That these lectures were delivered during Lent in preparation for baptism and in Easter Week after baptism is clear; how they were delivered is not. The pre-eighth-century lectionaries that will be discussed later in this chapter—namely the Armenian and Georgian lectionaries—mention a particular order and time in which the lectures were delivered.[62] This delivery was related to the duration of Lent, which was still developing at the time of Cyril.[63] Given the decline of the catechumenate after the seventh century and the development and spread of hymnography by the ninth, it is not surprising that the

---

[58] For a reconstruction of the text of the 'Hagiopolitan creed' on the basis of Cyril's lectures, see Heinrich Denzinger, *Enchiridion Symbolorum* (Freiburg: Herder, 1932), 7–10 (§ 9–12); McCauley and Stephenson, *Works of Saint Cyril of Jerusalem* I, 63–4 and 60–2 (in this order). For the text of the *Mystagogical Catecheses* I rely on Piédagnel's edition, accompanied by a French translation; for an English translation, see Cross, *Lectures on the Christian Sacraments*. Christian Palestinian Aramaic fragments of the *Catecheses* have been edited in Alain Desreumaux, *Codex sinaïticus Zosimi rescriptus: Description codicologique des feuillets araméens melkites des manuscrits Schøyen 35, 36, et 37 (Londres—Oslo)* (Lausanne: Éditions du Zèbre, 1997), 143–71.

[59] *Prebaptismal Catechesis* 4:3 (= PG 33:457).

[60] ἃς καὶ ἐν Ἐκκλησίᾳ μετὰ παρρησίας ἀναγινώσκομεν ('only the ones that we read openly in church'). Ibid., 4: 35 (= PG 33:497).

[61] Ibid., 5:12 (= PG 33:524, n. 4).

[62] AL, 94–9, 188–9; GL § 478–480, 485–7, 500–2, 507–9, 529–31, 536–8, 543–5, 550–2, 557–9. The most recent analysis of this question is Nicholas Russo, 'The Distribution of Cyril's *Baptismal Catecheses* and the Shape of the Catechumenate in Mid-Fourth-Century Jerusalem', in *A Living Tradition: On the Intersection of Liturgical History and Pastoral Practice. Essays in Honor of Maxwell E. Johnson*, ed. by David Pitt, Stefanos Alexopoulos, and Christian McConnell (Collegeville, MN: Liturgical Press, 2012), 75–100.

[63] See Piédagnel's analysis in *Mystagogical Catecheses*, p. 14; McCauley and Stephenson, *Works of Saint Cyril of Jerusalem*, vol. 1, 1; Jan Willem Drijvers, *Cyril of Jerusalem: Bishop and City* (Supplements of Vigiliae Christianae 72, Leiden: Brill, 2004), 57–8; Talley, *Liturgical Year*, 168–76; Bertonière, *Sundays of Lent*, 30–3; Harald Buchinger, 'Origenes und die Quadragesima in Jerusalem: Ein Diskussionsbeitrag', *Adamantius* 13 (2007), 174–217; Harald Buchinger, 'On the Early History of Quadragesima: A New Look at an Old Problem and Some Proposed Solutions', in *Liturgies in East and West: Ecumenical Relevance of Early Liturgical Development*, ed. by Hans-Jürgen Feulner (Austrian Studies of Liturgy and Sacramental Theology 6, Vienna: Lit Verlag, 2013), 99–117; Bradshaw and Johnson, *Origins of Feasts*, 89–113.

post-eighth-century manuscripts of Hagiopolite liturgy do not prescribe the reading of Cyril's lectures.[64]

Apart from difficulties in dating Cyril's lectures and in knowing exactly when they were delivered, the manuscript sources of the *Catecheses* give strong arguments for attributing the work to Cyril's successor John II of Jerusalem (387–417).[65] The *Catecheses* were first attributed to John II in 1574, after the discovery of a manuscript that named him as their author. This led scholars to assign a later date to the work, in an attempt to explain how the lectures could describe certain liturgical rites, such as the Lord's Prayer and the veneration of the eucharistic species, which were considered post-Cyrilline.[66] Currently scholars are divided on the question, some suggesting that Cyril wrote the eighteen *Prebaptismal Catecheses* and John II composed the five *Mystagogical Catecheses* later, without being recognized as their author, or that John II revised Cyril's complete catecheses after he used them himself as teaching notes and subsequently revised them. Piédagnel concludes that the manuscript information is not conclusive enough for us to reject Cyril's authorship.[67] More recently, Juliette Day has questioned Cyril's authorship and dates the text of the *Mystagogical Catecheses* between 380 and 415.[68] Without entering further into the debate on authorship, it is sufficient to say that rejection of Cyril's authorship of the *Mystagogical Catecheses* has not been unanimously accepted or definitively proven.[69] Since the text is known to have originated in Jerusalem no later than 415, this affects neither its importance as a fundamental text for the study of early Hagiopolite liturgy nor its use here for understanding the early elements of the eucharistic liturgy in Jerusalem, which

---

[64] For the decline of the catechumenate, see Robert F. Taft, 'When Did the Catechumenate Die Out in Constantinople?' in Ἀναθήματα ἑορτικά: *Studies in Honor of Thomas F. Mathews*, ed. by Joseph D. Alchermes with Helen C. Evans and Thelma K. Thomas (Mainz am Rhein: Verlag Philipp von Zabern, 2009), 288–95.

[65] AL, 230–3; Johannes Quasten, *Patrology*, vol. 3 (Westminster, MD: Newman Press, 1960), 390–1.

[66] See Piédagnel's introduction in *Mystagogical Catecheses*, p. 18; Cross, *Lectures on the Christian Sacraments*, xxxvii.

[67] See *Mystagogical Catecheses*, pp. 38–40 and 50–9; Cross, *Lectures on the Christian Sacraments*, xxxix; Johannes Quasten, *Patrology*, vol. 3 (Westminster, MD: Newman Press, 1960), 366. See also Auguste Piédagnel, 'Les Catéchèses Mystagogiques de Saint Cyrille de Jérusalem: Inventaire de la tradition manuscrite grecque', in *Studia Patristica*, vol. 10, part 1: *Editiones, critica, philologica, biblica, historica, liturgica et ascetica*, ed. by Frank L. Cross (TU 107, Berlin: Akademie Verlag, 1970), here 141–5.

[68] Juliette Day, *The Baptismal Liturgy of Jerusalem: Fourth- and Fifth-Century Evidence from Palestine, Syria, and Egypt* (Aldershot: Ashgate, 2007), 12.

[69] See Alexis J. Doval, *Cyril of Jerusalem, Mystagogue: The Authorship of the Mystagogic Catecheses* (Washington: Catholic University Press, 2001); Maxwell Johnson, 'Baptismal Liturgy in Fourth-Century Jerusalem in Light of Recent Scholarship', in *Inquiries into Eastern Christian Worship*, ed. by Basilius J. Groen, Steven Hawkes-Teeples, and Stefanos Alexopoulos (Eastern Christian Studies 12, Leuven: Peeters, 2012), 81–98. For the most recent examination of the question, see *Lectures on the Christian Sacraments: The Procatechesis and the Five Mystagogical Catecheses Ascribed to St Cyril of Jerusalem*, trans. and intro. Maxwell E. Johnson (Popular Patristics Series 57, Yonkers, NY: St Vladimir's Seminary Press, 2017).

was attributed in later sources to St James the brother of the Lord and known by the name 'the Liturgy of St James' (JAS).[70]

In his explanation of the rites of the Eucharist to the newly initiated in the fifth mystagogical catechesis, Cyril allows one to distinguish the following structure of the eucharistic liturgy (see Table 1.1):[71]

Table 1.1. Structure of the Eucharist in the fifth mystagogical catechesis

1. Liturgy of the Word	The Liturgy of the Word is not included, presumably because it would have been already known to the newly baptized while they were catechumens.
2. Transfer of Gifts	The transfer of the gifts is assumed to have occurred at this point on the basis of the structure of JAS and of the Georgian *Iadgari* hymnal.[72]
3. Hand Washing (*Mystagogical Catecheses* 5:2)	The deacon washes the bishop's (ἱερεύς)[73] and the presbyters' (πρεσβύτεροι) hands once they are standing around the altar (τὸ θυσιαστήριον).
4. Kiss of Peace (*Mystagogical Catecheses* 5:3)	After hand washing, the deacon exclaims: 'Welcome one another and let us kiss one another' (ἀλλήλους ἀπολάβετε καὶ ἀλλήλους ἀσπαζώμεθα) and people exchange the kiss of peace.
5. Dialogue (*Mystagogical Catecheses* 5:4–5)	The anaphora proper begins with the dialogue initiated by the bishop's exclamation: 'Let our hearts be on high' (Ἄνω τὰς καρδίας). People respond: 'We have them with the Lord' (Ἔχομεν πρὸς τὸν Κύριον). The dialogue continues with the bishop's exclamation: 'Let us give thanks to the Lord' (Εὐχαριστήσωμεν τῷ Κυρίῳ), to which people respond: 'It is right and just' (Ἄξιον καὶ δίκαιον).
6. Sanctus (*Mystagogical Catecheses* 5:6)	The full text of the anaphora is not given, although Cyril does summarize its anamnetic aspects and gives a more complete summary of the Eucharist in the fourth mystagogical catechesis. People recite the Sanctus from Isaiah 6:2–3 (Ἅγιος, ἅγιος, ἅγιος Κύριος Σαβαώθ), directing it to God the Father and without mention of the Benedictus, 'Blessed is he who comes' (Εὐλογημένος ὁ ἐρχόμενος).[74]
7. Epiclesis (*Mystagogical Catechesis* 5:7)	After the faithful are sanctified through the singing of hymns, the Holy Spirit descends to make the bread the body of Christ and the wine the blood of Christ. There is no mention of an institution narrative before the epiclesis.[75]

(continued)

---

[70] See Chapter 3 in this book.

[71] *Mystagogical Catecheses* 5:2–22 (pp. 146–73 Piédagnel); Cross, *Lectures on the Christian Sacraments*, 30–9 and 71–80.

[72] Mercier, *Liturgie de Saint Jacques*, 176–80. See Chapter 3, 'The Hymn for Hand Washing' and 'The Hymn of the Holy Gifts'.

[73] Alongside πρεσβύτεροι, ἱερεύς can mean more than 'priest' and is variously translated as 'bishop' by McCauley and 'pontiff' by Piédagnel. See Liddel, Scott, and Jones, *Greek Lexicon*, s.v. ἱερεύς.

[74] See Chapter 3, 'The Anaphora of the Liturgy of St James'.

[75] The institution narrative is explained in *Mystagogical Catecheses* 4: 1.

Table 1.1. Continued

8. Diptychs/Anaphoral Intercessions (*Mystagogical Catechesis* 5:8–9)	After the eucharistic gifts are 'perfected' (ἀπαρτισθῆναι), they pray for the whole world, its rulers, hierarchs, the sick, the suffering, and all who need God's assistance. It is not mentioned who makes these commemorations, whether the presider or the deacon.
9. The Lord's Prayer (*Mystagogical Catechesis* 5:11–18)	After the 'Our Father' (Matthew 6:9–13), the people say 'Amen'. Although Cyril explains each phrase and petition of the Lord's Prayer, he does not indicate any embolism at the conclusion of the prayer other than the 'Amen' of the people to 'set the seal' (ἐπισφραγίζειν) on the prayer. Although 'Our Father' had been recited three times daily in early Christian prayers, this is the earliest mention of it within the eucharistic liturgy. By Saint Augustine's day in the fifth century, it had become commonplace and expected.[76]
10. 'Holy Things' Exclamation (*Mystagogical Catechesis* 5:19)	After 'Our Father', the bishop exclaims 'Holy things for the holy' (Τὰ ἅγια τοῖς ἁγίοις), to which the people respond: 'One is holy, one is Lord, Jesus Christ' (Εἷς ἅγιος, εἷς Κύριος, Ἰησοῦς Χριστός). This exclamation is accompanied by the presentation of the gifts, which were 'visited' (ἐπιφοίτησιν) by the Holy Spirit—a term peculiar to Cyril's Catechesis, the anaphora of JAS, and the Hagiopolitan baptismal rite.[77]
11. Communion Hymn (*Mystagogical Catechesis* 5:20)	In preparation for Communion, Psalm 33:9 'Taste and see that the Lord is good' (Γεύσασθε καὶ ἴδετε, ὅτι χρησιτὸς ὁ Κύριος) is sung. This is the oldest form of the Communion hymn.[78]
12. Reception of Communion (*Mystagogical Catechesis* 5:21–22)	The body of Christ is received in the hand, with 'Amen'. The blood of Christ is received from the chalice, with 'Amen'.[79] Cyril suggests that those who receive Communion sanctify their other senses by touching their hands, eyes, and brows with the moisture from the blood of Christ, which is still on their lips.
13. Thanksgiving Prayer (*Mystagogical Catechesis* 5:22)	Cyril commands the people to wait for the prayer, which was presumably followed by dismissal at the end of the liturgical service.

This catechesis contains one of the earliest mentions of the Lord's Prayer in the Divine Liturgy and of the Sanctus in the anaphora.[80] Georg Kretschmar shows that the structure and content presented by the fifth mystagogical catechesis are very similar to those of the Syrian version of JAS, which is

---

[76] See *Didache* 8:2–3, in *La doctrine des douze apôtres (Didachè)*, ed. by Willy Rordorf and André Tuilier (SC 248, Paris: Cerf, 1978), 172–5; Taft, *Hours*, 5, 13, and 64; Taft, *Precommunion Rites*, 129 and 135–40.

[77] Taft, *Precommunion Rites*, 231–2.   [78] See Chapter 3, 'The Hymn for Communion'.

[79] The practice of receiving Communion through a spoon is first attested in Palestine in the seventh century. See Robert F. Taft, 'Byzantine Communion Spoons: A Review of the Evidence', DOP 50 (1996), 209–38.

[80] Robert F. Taft, SJ, 'The Interpolation of the Sanctus into the Anaphora: When and Where? A Review of the Dossier. Part II', OCP 58 (1992), 85–8, 114–21.

considered to be an indication of the early presence of JAS in Jerusalem.[81] The introductory dialogue to the anaphora in *Mystagogical Catecheses* 5:4–5 is consistent with the *Urtext* and with the Byzantine *textus receptus*, present also in the earlier *Apostolic Constitutions* 8:12.5.[82] Although the first member of the dialogue is missing, the greeting was already present in late fourth-century Byzantine tradition and in later redactions of JAS.[83] The absence of an institution narrative here has also attracted attention, but Bryan Spinks' advice regarding this text is invaluable: he reminds readers that 'the material is catechetical and does not yield the accuracy demanded by modern liturgical scholarship. Where Cyril agrees with the anaphora of St James we may check his accuracy, but where he disagrees it is difficult to know whether he knew a different text or was simply relying on memory or the licence of a preacher and orator.'[84] It should be kept in mind that the Eucharist and the anaphora are the focus of the whole fourth chapter of the *Mystagogical Catecheses*.[85]

The *Itinerarium* of Egeria

The insatiable curiosity and enthusiastic narration of a fourth-century female pilgrim offers a rare glimpse into the lived liturgical life of Jerusalem and its environs.[86] Her diary, which had last been transcribed in the twelfth century at Monte Cassino by Peter the Deacon (*c*.1107–after 1159) and then lost for several centuries, was rediscovered in 1884 by Gian Francesco Gamurrini (1835–1923) in Arezzo and subsequently published.[87] The identity of the author—known today as the French or Spanish nun Egeria—was corroborated

[81] Georg Kretschmar, 'Die frühe Geschichte der Jerusalemer Liturgie', *Jahrbuch für Liturgie und Hymnologie* 2 (1956), 22–46, here 29–31.

[82] *Mystagogical Catecheses*, pp. 149 n. 1 and 188–9 (Appendix II); *Les Constitutions Apostoliques*, vol. 3: *Livres VII et VIII*, ed. by Marcel Metzger (SC 336, Paris: Cerf, 1987), 178–80; Robert F. Taft, SJ, 'The Dialogue before the Anaphora in the Byzantine Eucharistic Liturgy. III: "Let us give thanks to the Lord – It is fitting and right"', in OCP 55 (1989), here 66.

[83] Robert F. Taft, SJ, 'The Dialogue before the Anaphora of the Byzantine Eucharistic Liturgy. I: The Opening Greeting', in OCP (1986), 299–324.

[84] Bryan D. Spinks, *The Sanctus in the Eucharistic Prayer* (New York: Cambridge University Press, 1991), 62–3.

[85] *Mystagogical Catecheses* 4 (pp. 34–45 Piédagnel); Cross, *Lectures on the Christian Sacraments*, 26–9 and 67–71.

[86] CPL 2325. I rely on Maraval's edition, which is accompanied by a French translation. For an English translation, see Wilkinson, *Egeria's Travels*. The text itself, where the beginning, the end, and several pages in between (at 16: 4 and 25: 6) are missing, gives some information on Egeria's origins: she was a woman (*Antiochia autem cum fuissem regressa*, 22: 1) from Spain or France (Y 10, 18: 2, 19: 5), of sufficient means to be able to go on pilgrimage for three years (17: 1), and she was probably part of the women's religious community to which she addresses her letters (23: 10).

[87] *Arezzo, Biblioteca Città di Arezzo 405* (*c*.11th–12th cent.), fol. 17r–38r. See Maraval's introduction to Egeria, *Itinéraire*, here 40–9.

through a letter from the seventh-century Galician hermit Valerius to his fellow monastics in Bierzo that praised the maiden's voyage to the East.[88]

Egeria's diary can be dated with relative certainty between 381 and 384 thanks to several factors. Her use of the term 'confessor' (Latin *confessor*, equivalent to the Greek term ὁμολογητής) to describe certain bishops suggests a period not too distant from church persecution. The title made reference to hierarchs who suffered persecution but had not been martyred, and have been identified with particular individuals who match Egeria's description, namely the bishops of Batanis, Edessa, and Carrae.[89] The date of Easter between 382 and 386 and the twenty-five days needed to travel between Jerusalem and Edessa suggest that Egeria stayed in Jerusalem from Easter in 381 until Easter in 384.[90] Hence her visit coincided with Cyril's (d. 387) episcopacy there, and he is probably the bishop she was speaking of as leading the liturgical services.

The last third of her account is most valuable for its liturgical information.[91] Here she describes the daily (§ 24: 1–24: 7) and the Sunday (§ 24: 8–25: 6) cycle of services, the celebration of fixed feasts such as Theophany and Hypapante (§ 25: 6–26), the movable paschal cycle (§ 27: 1–44: 3) and baptismal catechesis (§ 45: 1–47: 5), and the feast of the Enkainia of the Anastasis (§ 48: 1–49: 3)—at which point the text breaks off.

From this information it is possible to recover the structure of the daily, fixed, and movable cycles at the cathedral of Jerusalem in the fourth century. Given the importance of Egeria's accounts for Jerusalem's liturgy, her travel diary is useful in examining continuity or rupture between authentic Hagiopolitan practices and later, foreign practices during the period of Byzantinization.

Because of its enigmatic character, Egeria's description of the Sunday Eucharist requires some explanation. In essence, the celebration of the Eucharist proper is summarized through the phrase 'they do all that is usual, as is done here and everywhere on Sunday' (*fiunt omnia secundum consuetudinem, qua et ubique fit die dominica*, § 25: 1; cf. § 27: 3) at daybreak at the Martyrium. This makes it impossible to draw parallels between Egeria's description and the testimony of other witnesses. Egeria's greatest interest in the Sunday Eucharist revolves around preaching: all the priests who wish to preach did so, and the sermon of the bishop concluded the preaching. Since the homilies were meant to be an instruction on the Scriptures, it can be assumed that various scriptural lections were read, although Egeria fails to

---

[88] Valérius du Bierzo, *Lettre sur la bienheureuse Égérie*, ed. by Manuel C. Díaz y Díaz (SC 296, Paris: Cerf, 1982), 336–48. For the account of how scholars arrived at the pilgrim's correct name, see Wilkinson, *Egeria's Travels*, 167–8.

[89] See Egeria, *Itinéraire*, § 19: 1, 19: 5, 20: 2 (pp. 29–31 Maraval).

[90] Egeria, *Itinéraire*, § 17: 2. See P. Devos, 'La date du voyage d'Égérie', AB 85 (1967), 165–94, especially 178. This date has been widely accepted by most scholars. See also Wilkinson, *Egeria's Travels*, 169–71.

[91] Egeria, *Itinéraire*, § 24: 1–49: 3.

mention any readings at all.[92] The reading continued until the fourth or fifth hour of the day (10–11 a.m.) every Sunday and was followed by a dismissal, as usual (*iuxta consuetudinem*, § 25: 1–2).[93] A service of thanksgiving at the Anastasis followed the Sunday Eucharist and included prayers by the bishop (*oratio pro omnibus*, § 25: 3), an individual blessing of all those present, and then a dismissal, so that the whole service ended between the fifth and the sixth hour of the day (11 a.m.–12 p.m.). The phrase 'give thanks to God' (*aguntur gratiae Deo*) is unusual in Egeria's vocabulary and has aroused discussion concerning the nature of the service held in the Anastasis.[94] Although the division of the eucharistic celebration between two different churches was known in later Hagiopolitan and Palestinian sources, such as the Typikon of the Anastasis of the Holy Sepulchre and several Sabaite monastic regulations,[95] such an interpretation of the evidence provided by Egeria here has been rejected by scholars.[96] Later studies of Egeria's *Itinerarium* suggest that her description actually comprised two distinct celebrations of the Eucharist, or a form of morning prayer such as matins (§ 25: 1) followed by the Eucharist (§ 25: 2–4).[97] Wilkinson presents a probable structure for the Eucharist in Jerusalem that is based on the Armenian lectionary, Egeria, and Cyril's fifth mystagogical catechesis but is unclear about accepting a second Eucharist, except for those days when a second Eucharist is explicitly mentioned, namely on Holy Thursday, on the vigil of Pascha, and on Pentecost.[98] Baldovin is clearer about rejecting this as a single

[92] *[U]t semper erudiatur populus in Scripturis et in Dei dilectione* ('so that the people may always be instructed in the Scriptures and in the love of God'). Ibid., §25: 1.

[93] Gamurrini added *non* to the text of Egeria, thus rendering the phrase 'the dismissal, which takes place not before the fourth or fifth hour' (*ante quartam horam aut forte quintam missa <non> fit*; Egeria, *Itinéraire*, § 25: 1). All subsequent editions follow Gamurrini, adding *non*, although this is not found in the manuscript. See apparatus in Maraval's edition, 246.

[94] This is not the usual term Egeria uses for the anaphora, although her reference to the tomb of Christ in the Anastasis as a *martyrium* (§ 25: 3) is also unusual. See Egeria, *Itinéraire*, p. 247 n. 2; Antonius A. R. Bastiaensen, *Observations sur le vocabulaire liturgique dans l'Itinéraire d'Égérie* (Latinitas Christianorum primaeva 17, Nijmegen: Dekker and van de Vegt, 1962), 81–8, and especially 85–8.

[95] See Papadopoulos-Kerameus, *Anastasis Typikon*, 43, 48, 65, 76, 80, for presanctified in Holy Week, where vespers was served in one church and then Communion was received at the Anastasis. Similarly, Sabaitic practice permitted the Liturgy of the Word to be celebrated in various languages in different churches, provided that all monks came together for the Eucharist. See 'Τύπος καὶ παράδοσις καὶ νόμος τῆς σεβασμίας λαύρας τοῦ ἁγίου Σάββα', in Dmitrievskii, *Описание* I, 222–3. This was also the case during the summer, from Ascension to Enkainia, in the usage of the East Syrian Chaldean tradition. See Jammo, *La structure de la messe chaldéenne*, 120; Taft, 'The βηματίκιον', 685 n. 57.

[96] This was the view of Cabrol, *Les églises de Jérusalem*, 54–8.

[97] For more views on the question of one or two eucharistic celebrations on Sunday, see Egeria, *Itinéraire*, p. 247 n. 3; Egeria, *Reisebericht*, ed. and trans. by Georg Röwenkamp, 2nd edn (Fontes Christiani 20, Freiburg: Herder, 2000), 235–7; Juan Mateos, SJ, 'La vigile cathédrale chez Égérie', OCP 27 (1961), 281–312; Zerfass, *Schriftlesung*, 15–20.

[98] See Egeria, *Itinéraire*, § 35: 1–2 (Holy Thursday), 38: 2 (vigil of Pascha), 43: 2–3 (Pentecost); Wilkinson, *Egeria's Travels*, 55, 145 n. 5.

Sunday eucharistic liturgy; he insists that 'we have no evidence for a separation of the word synaxis and eucharist proper at this time'[99] and refers to the fact that, assuming that the procession of the bishop to the Anastasis also included the transfer of the gifts, the Liturgy of the Word and the Liturgy of the Eucharist would take place in two different churches. He thus prefers to understand *aguntur gratiae Deo* as a thanksgiving prayer after Communion, similar to the one given in *Apostolic Constitutions* 7:26—a reading that has become accepted among most liturgiologists.[100]

When attempting to understand difficult passages in Egeria's account, it is important to remember that her descriptions were not exhaustive, especially if one considers her frequent use of the phrase 'one does there that which is also customary for us to do' (*aguntur ibi quae consuetudinis est etiam et aput nos*)[101] to describe central—and often complex—liturgical services.[102] Her primary interest throughout the Sunday Eucharist was in its numerous homilies, which she considered to be unusual.

Apart from the often ambiguous descriptions of liturgical practice in the fourth century, several prescriptive liturgical books have survived that go back as early as the fifth century and are directly connected to the Jerusalem lectionary. These are the Armenian lectionary, the Georgian lectionary, and the *Iadgari*. Although the extant manuscripts preserving these texts do not date from the era before the liturgical Byzantinization of Jerusalem, liturgical scholars have determined that they preserve the ancient liturgical practice of Jerusalem from before later modifications. All three sources were published and made accessible in critical editions during the twentieth century.

The Armenian Lectionary

Although a complete version of the original Greek version of the Jerusalem lectionary no longer exists, the manuscripts of the Armenian clergy, which was serving in Jerusalem already from the fourth century, preserved the Greek Hagiopolite lectionary in Armenian translation.[103] Frederick Cornwallis Conybeare (1856–1924) was the first to edit the sources of the original Hagiopolite lectionary in Armenian translation in 1905.[104] His translations were based on two manuscripts: *Paris BNF Arm. 44* (formerly *Ancien fonds arménien 20*)

[99] Baldovin, *Urban Character*, 59.

[100] *Apostolic Constitutions* 7:26; *Les Constitutions Apostoliques*, vol. 3: *Livres VII et VIII*, ed. by Marcel Metzger (SC 336, Paris: Cerf, 1987), 54–7; Baldovin, *Urban Character*, 59. See also Baldovin, *Liturgy in Ancient Jerusalem*, 21–2, for various theories about the structure of the Eucharist described by Egeria.

[101] Egeria, *Itinéraire*, § 38: 2.   [102] See ibid., p. 290 n. 1.

[103] Renoux, *Introduction*, 21–2; AL, 24; Verhelst, 'Jerusalem in the Byzantine Period', 430.

[104] Conybeare and Maclean, *Rituale armenorum*, 507–27.

(10th cent.)[105] and *Bodleian MS. Arm. d. 2* (before 1359).[106] The most recent edition, by Charles (Athanase) Renoux (b. 1925), refers to these manuscripts, collectively, as the 'Armenian lectionary' (AL).[107] Although the earliest extant manuscripts date to the tenth century, Renoux's critical edition of three manuscripts is believed to reflect the ancient practice of Jerusalem between 415 and 439, a dating based on references to the deposition of the relics of St Stephen and to the development of the protomartyr's cult.[108] The manuscripts that Renoux employed are *Jerusalem St James Monastery Arm. 121* (1192 and 1318), labelled AL (J); *Paris BNF Arm. 44* (10th cent.), labelled AL (P); and *Yerevan Matenadaran Arm. 985* (10th cent.), labelled AL (E).[109] The title of this liturgical lectionary, preserved only in AL (P), is:

Յիշատակարան ժողովոցն որք կատարէն յԷՄ ի սուրբ ի տեղիսն Քի որբցուցանէն զ թանիխնութթիւն ամսանյն եւ զաւուրն ընթերցուատծն. եւ զասղմոսն յանդիման կացցողաան. զտալնիցն առանձին. եւ զյիշատակացն:[110]	Memorial of the synaxes that are held in Jerusalem at the holy place of Christ, in which is indicated the number of the month and the reading of the day, and in which is indicated the psalm proper to the feast and memory.

The liturgical year begins with Theophany (6 January), which commemorates the birth of Christ, and the Octave of Theophany (13 January). The first cycle of saints begins with St Peter Apselamus (11 January)[111] and continues until the commemoration of Sts Cyril and John of Jerusalem (29 March). The movable cycle of Lent and Easter is inserted between 29 March and 1 May and includes scriptural readings for the mystagogical catecheses. The second fixed cycle of saints begins with the commemoration of the Prophet Jeremiah (1 May) and continues until Sts James and John, sons of Zebedee (29 December).[112] In total, there are twenty-five commemorations of saints, of which sixteen are of local Palestinian derivation.[113] Despite the relative scarcity of commemorations in the AL, its bare sanctoral cycle should not necessarily be seen as a sign of

---

[105] AL 157–9; Raymond H. Kévorkian and Armèn Ter-Stéphanian, with Bernard Outtier and Guévord Ter-Vardanian, *Manuscrits arméniens de la Bibliothèque nationale de France: Catalogue* (Paris: Bibliothèque nationale de France, 1998), cols 84–5.

[106] Conybeare and Maclean, *Rituale armenorum*, xv and 507; Sukias Baronian and Frederick C. Conybeare, *Catalogue of the Armenian Manuscripts in the Bodleian Library* (Oxford: Clarendon Press, 1918), 26–7 (manuscript no. 26).

[107] All citations of the AL refer to page numbers from Renoux's edition in PO 36.2. For a bibliography of Renoux's works, see *Sion, mère des Églises: Mélanges liturgiques offerts au Père Charles Athanase Renoux*, ed. by Daniel Findikyan, Daniel Galadza, and André Lossky (Semaines d'études liturgiques Saint-Serge Subsidia 1, Münster: Aschendorff, 2016), 19–34.

[108] Renoux, *Introduction*, 171–81.   [109] Ibid.   [110] AL, 210–11.

[111] For the identity of this rarely mentioned saint, see AL, 225 n. 3; Eusebios of Caesarea, *De martyribus Palestinae*, 10; PG 20:1497; Delehaye, *Synaxarium*, 1151. See also Chapter 4, 'New Martyrs'.

[112] AL, 330–73.   [113] AL, 188.

antiquity, but rather of selectivity. Sermons of the presbyter Hesychius of Jerusalem (d. after 451) exist for several saints or commemorations that are not found in the AL, such as the Conception of St John the Baptist.[114] Likewise, a contemporaneous Syriac list of saints dated to 411 indicates a commemoration for every day of the year.[115] The numerous divergences between the three manuscripts comprising Renoux's critical edition point to both development and variety within the Hagiopolitan tradition at a very early point in the city's liturgical history.[116] Like the *Itinerarium* of Egeria, the AL serves as a witness to Hagiopolitan worship before Byzantinization and the Arab conquest, helping us to trace liturgical evolution in later sources.

The general structure of the eucharistic synaxis in the AL is presented as follows (see Table 1.2):

Table 1.2. The eucharistic synaxis in the Armenian lectionary

1. Psalm with Refrain (կցուրդ, *kcʻurd*)	The refrain is repeated by the faithful. A psalm is chosen to express the theme of the feast or saint being commemorated. A *lectio continua* of psalms existed at certain periods.[117] The most frequent psalms used are 114 and 115.[118]
2. Scriptural Readings	Up to three lections were read, depending on the commemoration. Old Testament figures had readings from the Old Testament, always followed by a reading from Acts or Epistle. New Testament figures did not have an Old Testament reading, unless the commemoration was for more than one New Testament figure.[119]
3. Alleluia with Psalm[120]	Alleluia is not always indicated at this point. The psalm is chosen because of its connection to the stational liturgy site.[121]
4. Gospel Reading	The Gospel is never immediately preceded by an Old Testament reading in the AL, i.e. there was always a reading from Acts or from an Epistle between an Old Testament reading and the Gospel. Out of all four Gospels, the Gospel of Matthew was most frequently read during the liturgical year.[122]

[114] See Aubineau, *Hésychius de Jérusalem*, vol. 2, 668–704.

[115] For more on this source and the development of the calendar, see Chapter 4, 'The Development of the Calendar'.

[116] Renoux, *Introduction*, 188.

[117] From the fourth to the sixth week of Lent, Psalms 132–6 were read continuously at this point. See AL, 110–15.

[118] Renoux notes that *kcʻurd* can be translated as chant, refrain, antiphon, chanted response, and hymn. While he opts for antiphon, I adopt refrain since the text of the *kcʻurd* in the AL is always derived from the Psalms. See AL, 35–6; Findikyan, *Commentary*, 525–31. See also Chapter 3, 'Responsorial Psalmody'.

[119] AL, 36–7. See also Chapter 3, 'Lection(s)', and Chapter 5, 'Epistle Readings in the Jerusalem Lectionary' and 'Old Testament Readings at the Liturgy of St James and Their Disappearance'.

[120] The manuscripts only provide the first verse. Whether or not the whole psalm was read is unclear. See Renoux, *Introduction*, 58.

[121] AL, 38–40. Renoux notes that it is difficult to make a general rule for the presence or absence of the 'Alleluia' solely on the basis of the information in the AL. See also Chapter 3, 'The Gospel Reading'.

[122] AL, 37. See also Chapter 3, 'The Gospel Reading', and Chapter 5, 'The Byzantinization of the Hagiopolite Calendar: Case Studies'.

The Liturgy of the Word concluded after the Gospel reading and the other rites of the Liturgy of the Eucharist began. The central part of the Liturgy of the Eucharist, the anaphora, would be found in an Euchologion or another book other than a lectionary.[123] Deviations from the structure found here include the second eucharistic synaxis on major feasts, which was not preceded by any Liturgy of the Word, namely on Holy Thursday and in the paschal vigil—but these are exceptional.[124]

Within the lectionary of the church of Jerusalem in its Armenian translation there were also other liturgical services, which included readings from Scripture and psalmody. Renoux identifies five types of synaxes in the AL: (1) the eucharistic synaxis, which had an unregulated *lectio continua* pericope system not preserved in the AL;[125] (2) a Lenten synaxis at the tenth hour in the Church of the Anastasis; (3) processions to commemorative stations where a reading took place or a psalm connected to the event or theme of the specific holy site was read;[126] (4) vigils on the eve of Theophany, Holy Thursday, and Pascha; and (5) stations for the catechesis, for which the AL indicates nineteen readings from the Old Testament and the Pauline Epistles for Lent[127] and readings from the General Epistles for the post-baptismal catechesis.[128] These are developed over time, in sources such as the GL and the Typikon of the Anastasis.[129]

The Georgian Lectionary

The expanded Jerusalem lectionary of the fifth through to eighth centuries has been preserved in Georgian translation. Kornelii Kekelidze published the earliest edition of this lectionary in 1912, on the basis of one manuscript from Georgia.[130] A critical edition based on six fragmentary manuscripts, known as 'the Georgian lectionary' (GL), was prepared by Michael Tarchnishvili and

---

[123] The letter of Bishop Macarius regulates liturgical practices concerning baptism and the Eucharist, but offers few details concerning the structure of their celebration or the liturgical year. See Abraham Terian, *Macarius of Jerusalem, Letter to the Armenians, AD 335* (AVANT Series 4, Crestwood, NY: St Vladimir's Seminary Press, 2008), 76–91, who argues for the letter's fourth-century dating.

[124] See AL, 40.

[125] Renoux notes that these are only explicitly identified as 'Eucharist' twice, but it is understood that the psalms and readings for Feasts of the Lord and saints are intended for the Eucharist. Sundays, not indicated in the AL, had a regulated *lectio continua*. See Renoux's introduction in AL, 40.

[126] Theophany (AL, 72–3), Palm Sunday (AL, 120–1), the Passion (AL, 136–57), Christ's Resurrection (AL, 174–5), and his appearance to Thomas (AL, 186–7). For a summary of the stational liturgy of Jerusalem in the AL, see Baldovin, *Urban Character*, 64–72.

[127] AL, 40–3, 95–9.   [128] AL, 188–91.

[129] See the section 'Old Testament Readings at the Liturgy of St James and Their Disappearance' in Chapter 5 here for the Liturgy of the Word structure at matins on certain days of Holy Week.

[130] Kekelidze, Канонарь, which is based on the Lathal (L) manuscript.

appeared in 1959 and 1960, shortly after his death.[131] The six manuscripts Tarchnishvili employed in his edition are: *Paris BNF Geo. 3* (10th–11th cent.), labelled GL (P);[132] *Sinai Geo. O. 37* (formerly *Cagareli 30*) (982), labelled GL (S), copied by the scribe Iovane Zosime on Sinai; *Mestia Historic–Ethnographic Museum 51* (10th cent.), copied by Iovane Zosime in his early period, probably at St Sabas Lavra and labelled GL (L) for Lathal, the place in Georgia where it was discovered;[133] *Tbilisi Erovnuli Library 40* (10th cent.), copied by Michael Č'ikauri and referred to as GL (K), for Kala or Lakurga;[134] *Universitätsbibliothek Graz Pergament 27* (7th cent.), GL (Gr), a fragment of 19 folios copied at Sinai; and *Tbilisi Geo. 1831* (8th cent.), a palimpsest labelled GL (H).[135] Although subsequent scholars have identified additional Georgian manuscript witnesses to the Jerusalem lectionary and have published new editions that incorporate recently discovered manuscripts, Tarchnishvili's edition is still the standard one.[136] The Greek original from the GL was translated but has not survived. Thanks to the discoveries or 'new finds' at Sinai, however, we have at least one fragmentary manuscript, *Sinai Gr. N.E. MΓ 8* (10th cent.), which preserves a Greek version of the Jerusalem lectionary—not only its scriptural lections, but also its hymnography—and whose structure is very similar to the GL.[137]

Like the AL, the GL contains readings and psalms for the eucharistic synaxis that include references to the location of liturgical stations. Two particular developments in the GL are prescriptions for liturgical services, including readings, for every day of the year and the inclusion of hymnography in the eucharistic synaxis; the AL does not provide propers for liturgical services on every day of the year, nor does it include any hymnography. The GL contains a commemoration for almost every day that relies on a general 'canon', according to the type of commemoration: of the Theotokos, the Cross, the Apostles, the prophets, the martyrs, the hierarchs, the confessors, and various other categories. Certain days have their own specific readings and hymns, though there are often similarities in theme and content between the common texts

---

[131] All citations of the GL refer to paragraph numbers (§) from Tarchnischvili's edition in CSCO. For a biography of Tarchnishvili, see G. Garitte, 'Necrologue de Michel Tarchnisvili', Mus 71 (1958), here 398; D. Lang, 'Father Michael Tarchnishvili', BK 4–5 (1958), here 30–1.

[132] Employed by Tarchnishvili for GL § 16–729 and 766–1696.

[133] Employed by Tarchnishvili for GL § 1–53, 65–6, 83, 146–286, 325–589, 612–19, 644–898, 930–1019, 1055–543, and 1668–72.

[134] Employed by Tarchnishvili for GL § 355–882.

[135] See the introduction to the GL by Tarchnishvili (CSCO 188, vi–xii). This edition is now available online at TITUS. Because of the more expansive nature of the GL in comparison with the AL, the great variety of readings in the edition's manuscripts, and the closer connection between the GL and Greek witnesses of the Jerusalem lectionary, the specific manuscripts comprising Tarchnishvili's edition of the GL will occasionally be cited, when necessary.

[136] For example Outtier, 'Sinaï géorgien 54'; Outtier, 'Un nouveau témoin partiel', especially 172–4, where Outtier indicates corrections to the GL; Verhelst, *Lectionnaire de Jérusalem*; Verhelst, 'Liturgy of Jerusalem', 430.

[137] Galadza, 'Sinai Gr. N.E. MΓ 8'. See also Appendix 1.

and the hymns and scriptural readings proper to specific services and commemorations.[138] The general structure for the synaxis presented in the GL can be found in Table 1.3.[139]

Table 1.3. The eucharistic synaxis in the Georgian lectionary

1. *Introit* (ოხითაჲ, *oxitay*)	An entrance hymn for the beginning of the liturgy is sung, with an indication for the tone (ჴმაჲ, *xmay*) in which it is to be sung.[140]
2. Psalm with Verse	Similar to the AL, but a tone is indicated in which the psalm is to be sung.[141]
3. Scriptural Readings	Between two and five readings are prescribed from the Old and New Testaments, depending on the commemoration.[142]
4. Alleluia with Verse	Similar to the AL, with an indication of the tone.[143]
5. Gospel Reading	The Gospels of Matthew and Luke are read most frequently. The prominence of Luke is probably due to the expansion of feasts that celebrate episodes from the early life of Christ and John the Baptist.[144]
6. Hymn for Hand Washing (ჴელთბანისაჲ, *xeltbanisay*)	As many as two or three hymns can be prescribed after the Gospel reading. Their theme is often based on the Gospel pericope. Clergymen wash their hands during the singing of this hymn.[145]
7. Hymn of the Holy Gifts[146] (სიწმიდისაჲ, *sicmidisay*)	This hymn, which varied depending on the commemoration, was sung during the transfer of the gifts to the altar before the anaphora. The GL indicates the tone in which it was to be sung.[147]
8. Communion Hymn (განიცადე, *ganic'ade*)	Only two days in the GL (Holy Thursday and Holy Saturday) prescribe a specific Communion hymn.[148]
9. Dismissal of the People (ერის განტევებაჲ, *eris gantevebay*)	There are four occurrences of this text in the GL, all of them on Lent Sundays. On two occasions there are indications of a musical mode, which suggests that the text is a hymn to be sung.[149]

---

[138] For definitions and explanations of this terminology, see Glossary.

[139] This table is based on the fullest structure of the eucharistic Synaxis, which can be seen in the general services for the Cross (GL § 1446–54) and for Apostles (GL § 1455–68), among other services.

[140] Leeb, *Die Gesänge*, 38–49. ჴმაჲ (*xmay*) is the Georgian equivalent of the Greek ἦχος. See also Chapter 3, 'The *Introit*'.

[141] See Chapter 3, 'Responsorial Psalmody'.

[142] See Chapter 5, 'Epistle Readings in the Jerusalem Lectionary' and 'Old Testament Readings at the Liturgy of St James and Their Disappearance'.

[143] See Chapter 3, 'Alleluia'.

[144] See the scriptural index of the GL (CSCO 205, 132–3). See also See also Chapter 3, 'The Gospel Reading', and Chapter 5, 'Structures of the Jerusalem Lectionary: Gospel Cycles'.

[145] See Chapter 3, 'The Hymn for Hand Washing'.

[146] Tarchnischvili translated the Georgian term as *Sanctificatorum* or *Sanctificationis*, initially believing the text to be a prayer, but Leeb understands it as a hymn, i.e. *Gesang der heiligen Gaben*. I follow Leeb here. See GL § 1468, 1492; Leeb, *Die Gesänge*, 113–15; Taft, *Great Entrance*, 71–3.

[147] See Chapter 3, 'The Hymn of the Holy Gifts'.

[148] GL § 739 and GL Appendix 1 § 50–2; Leeb, *Die Gesänge*, 134. See Chapter 3, 'The Hymn for Communion'.

[149] GL § 329, 364, 402, 527. See Chapter 3, 'Hymns and Prayers for the Dismissal'.

This structure reveals the expansion of hymnography, especially for the 'soft points' of the entrance, washing of hands, and the transfer of the gifts during the liturgy, when the silence of ritual actions would be covered by the singing of hymns.[150] This structure is developed even further in some commemorations, which include hymns for Communion and dismissal.[151]

The expanded calendar found in Tarchnishvili's edition of the GL, which includes a commemoration for every day of the year, begins with Christmas Eve on 24 December and continues until the commemoration of the dedication of Constantinople's Hagia Sophia on 23 December. The movable cycle of Lent and Easter is inserted between 30 March and 1 April.[152] An appendix includes general services for Georgian saints (§1434–6), the Mother of God (§1437–45), the Cross (§1446–54), the Apostles (§1455–68), the prophets (§1469–74), the martyrs (§1475–92), the hierarchs (§1493–1507), the just, the blessed, and the confessors (§1508–22), the kings (§1523–7), and the foundation and dedication of a church, including the subsequent octave (§1528–59). Additional cycles of Old Testament, Epistle, and Gospel readings are also found in the appendix of Tarchnishvili's edition.[153]

The Tropologion (*Iadgari*)

The Tropologion (τροπολόγιον), known in Georgian as *Iadgari* (იადგარი) or even as *Iadgari Tropologion* (იადგარი ტროპოლოჯინ, *iadgari tropolojin*), is an anthology of liturgical hymnody or a 'universal hymnographical source' for the weekly, annual, and fixed cycles that predates the Byzantine hymnals and liturgical books known as the Oktoechos, the Triodion, and the Menaion.[154] The *Iadgari* can be considered their Georgian ancestor.[155] Like

---

[150] For Taft's term 'soft points', see Robert F. Taft, 'How Liturgies Grow: The Evolution of the Byzantine Divine Liturgy', in idem, *Beyond East and West*, here 204. See also Frøyshov, 'Early Development', 171–2.

[151] Leeb, *Die Gesänge*, 38.

[152] The movable cycle (pre-Lent, Lent, Easter, and Pentecost) is found at GL § 283–906 and in GL, Appendix 1. For a presentation of the liturgical year in Jerusalem, see the section 'The Structure and Characteristics of the Hagiopolite Liturgical Year' in Chapter 4 here.

[153] For a detailed summary of the GL's contents, see Leeb, *Die Gesänge*, 23–6; Bertonière, *Easter Vigil*, 10–12; Bertonière, *Sundays of Lent*, 38.

[154] All citations from the *Iadgari* refer to page numbers in the edition of Metreveli, Čankievi, and Xevsuriani. Unless otherwise noted, translations from the Georgian text of the *Iadgari* are my own. For an explanation of these terms, see the Glossary. See also Tinatin Chronz, 'Das griechische Tropologion-Fragment aus dem Kastellion-Kloster und seine georgischen Parallelen', OC 92 (2008), 113–18.

[155] *Iadgari*, 931; Wade, 'The Oldest *Iadgari*', 451; *Biobibliografia di Elene Met'reveli (1917–2003)*, ed. by Gaga Shurgaia (Eurasiatica 80, Rome: Edizioni Studium, 2009), 227–8; Andrew Wade, 'The Oldest Iadgari: The Jerusalem Tropologion: 4th to 8th Centuries, 30 Years after the Publication', in *ΣΥΝΑΞΙΣ ΚΑΘΟΛΙΚΗ*, 2: 717–50.

the Jerusalem lectionary, the complete Greek equivalent of this book, known as the Tropologion, has been lost. Its oldest form, the 'ancient *Iadgari*', survives only in Georgian translation, while the 'new *Iadgari*' has been preserved in Georgian and partially preserved in Greek in several manuscripts of the Sinai 'new finds'. The oldest, most complete Greek manuscript of the Tropologion is *Sinai Gr. N.E. MΓ 5* (8th–9th cent.), which was discovered on Mount Sinai among the new manuscripts in 1975.[156] The reference to two redactions of the *Iadgari* can be found in Iovane Zosime's notes of the content of *Sinai Geo. O. 34* (fol. 123r), where he mentions 'ancient' and 'new' hymns from Lent and the Oktoechos. Stig Frøyshov identifies the new redaction as being 'identical to the ancient Palestinian layer of the present Orthodox hymnography', which began to replace the ancient *Iadgari* in the first half of the seventh century.[157] The new redaction retained about 5 per cent of the hymnography of the ancient *Iadgari*.[158] Metreveli believes that the poetic forms of the Georgian *Iadgari*, written in both prose and meter, represent the earliest forms of Greek poetic prose once found in the original Tropologion. A comparison of the texts preserved in Georgian, which come from the seventh-century Hagiopolite liturgical tradition, with later Byzantine texts that reflect tenth- to fourteenth-century Constantinopolitan usage shows that the monostrophic prose hymns of the Tropologion were used as models for the meter, theme, and structure of later Byzantine hymns.[159]

That the extant version of the Greek original often exists only in Georgian translation should no longer surprise us, as we have witnessed the same phenomenon in the case of Hagiopolite lectionaries. It is only within the last four decades that scholars have begun to study this book, explaining why even the name Tropologion is absent from many authoritative sources on Byzantine music and hymnography.[160] While the Georgian word *iadgari* (იადგარი) is believed to mean 'memorial' or to refer to a collection of memorial hymns for the saints,[161] the meaning of the term *tropologion* is still unexplained. The connection with the derivative verb τροπολογέω, 'to expound allegorically', is

---

[156] Géhin and Frøyshov, 'Nouvelles découvertes sinaïtiques', 178–9; Nikiforova, *Из истории Минеи в Византии*, especially 195–235; Appendix 1.

[157] Frøyshov, 'Early Development', 143–4.

[158] Métrévéli, 'Manuscrits liturgiques géorgiens', 47–8; *Iadgari*, 932.

[159] Métrévéli et al., 'Le plus ancien Tropologion géorgien', 56–8. See *Iadgari*, 643–50, for an index of Georgian hymns and their Greek equivalents.

[160] The term is absent from Egon Wellesz, *A History of Byzantine Music and Hymnography*, 2nd edn (Oxford: Clarendon, 1971) and from ODB but is discussed in Husmann, 'Hymnus und Troparion', 27–9, and in Momina, 'О происхождении греческой триоди', 114–15.

[161] 'Памяти' or 'сборник поминальных песнопений святых'. *Iadgari* (იადგარი) can also be found in the plural (იადგარნი, *iadgarni*). See Xevsuriani, *Tropologion*, 14; Nikolaos Trunte, Ἄσατε τῷ Κυρίῳ ᾆσμα καινόν: Vor- und Frühgeschichte der slavischen Hymnographie', in *Sakrale Grundlagen slavischer Literaturen*, ed. by Hans Rothe (Vorträge und Abhandlungen zur Slavistik 43, Munich: Otto Sagner, 2002), 27–76, here 38–51.

tempting, since the hymnody of this type of book was often an exegetical elaboration on Scripture; but *tropologion* is most likely connected to τρόπος ('way, manner') and λόγος, as is the technical term *troparion* (τροπάριον).[162] The etymology of the proper name Tropologion, then, remains to be explained.

Extant Greek books bearing the name Tropologion include several manuscripts analysed by Heinrich Husmann and Stig Frøyshov.[163] Their contents include elements that later became the liturgical books of the Byzantine rite—books titled Menaion, Triodion, Pentekostarion, and the Great Parakletike or Oktoechos. The dating of the Tropologion manuscripts, however, reveals that they are contemporary with books from a latter period in the development of these books. As the original hymnographical source was expanded through new compositions by monastic hymnographers from the Anastasis in Jerusalem—possibly the monks known as *spoudaioi* in certain liturgical and historical texts—and from Mar Saba Lavra in the Judean desert, its contents were eventually divided among other books, on the basis of the type of hymn.[164] When the liturgical cycles and seasons had more or less taken shape, the hymnody was once more divided and expanded, primarily by Stoudite hymnographers. At this point it was merged with scriptural readings, synaxaria, rubrical indications, and even some of the fixed parts of the ordinary, to create the first versions of the books now known as the Oktoechos, the Triodion, and the Menaion.[165] Without knowledge of the recent discoveries in Sinai and new research in this field, the name Tropologion was often misunderstood by liturgiologists without an understanding of musical manuscripts, and used—not surprisingly—to refer both to the ancient and to more recent Tropologia.[166]

[162] See Liddell, Scott, and Jones, *Greek–English Lexicon*, s.v. τροπάριον; Lampe, *Patristic Greek Lexicon*, 1412. See also Oliver Strunk, 'Tropus and Troparion', in *Speculum Musicae Artis: Festgabe für Heinrich Husmann*, ed. by Heinz Becker and Reinhard Gerlach (Munich: Wilhelm Fink Verlag, 1970), 305–11, reprinted in Oliver Strunk, *Essays on Music in the Byzantine World* (New York: Norton, 1977), 268–76.

[163] Husmann mentions *Sinai Gr. 777* (11th cent.), *Sinai Gr. 784* (12th cent.), and *Sinai Gr. 789* (12th cent.), all of which contain various *stichera*, *kathismata*, and canons from the Oktoechos. *Sinai Gr. 556* (11th cent.), *Sinai Gr. 579* (11th cent.), *Sinai Gr. 607* (9th–10th cent.), and *Sinai Gr. 759* (11th cent.) are more like Menaia, to judge from their contents. *Grottaferrata Δ.γ. XII* (970) is also mentioned. See Husmann, 'Hymnus und Troparion', here 29–31 and Frøyshov, 'Early Development', here 165.

[164] Frøyshov, 'Early Development', 144–5. For more on the *spoudaioi*, see Chapter 2, 'Palestinian Monasticism'.

[165] See Nikiforova, *Из истории Минеи в Византии*; Frøyshov, 'Early Development', 165; Elena Velkova Velkovska, 'Byzantine Liturgical Books', in *Handbook for Liturgical Studies* I, 225–40; Manel Nin, 'Other Liturgical Books in the East', in *Handbook for Liturgical Studies*, vol. 1, 241–4; Momina, 'О происхождении греческой триоди', 113, 117.

[166] Taft, *Byzantine Rite*, 58, uses the term to refer to newer books, while Frøyshov, Wade, and others who deal with early Hagiopolitan liturgy intend the earlier, unified source.

Akaki Shanidze (1887–1987) prepared the first edition of the *Iadgari* from the 'parchment papyrus' manuscript at the National Centre of Manuscripts,[167] *Tbilisi H2123* (9th–10th cent.), which was copied at St Sabas Lavra in Palestine.[168] The manuscript contains 313 folios and is a witness to older orthographic conventions, which suggests that it was copied from an older source than the other witnesses of the *Iadgari*.[169] A team of Georgian scholars that including Elene Metreveli (1917–2003), Caca Čankievi, and Lili Xevsuriani undertook a critical edition of the *Iadgari* in 1980 on the basis of six additional manuscripts: *Sinai Geo. O. 18* (10th cent.), copied by an unknown scribe, but with later notes by Iovane Zosime;[170] *Sinai Geo. O. 40* (10th cent.), copied by Symeon the Hymnographer at the order of Theodore of Palavra at St Sabas Lavra (fol. 253r), but later acquired by Presbyter Gregory of Sinai (fol. 253v–254r) after the exodus of Georgians from Palestine to Sinai in the decade after 960;[171] *Sinai Geo. O. 41* (10th cent.);[172] *Sinai Geo. O. 26* (10th cent.);[173] *Sinai Geo. O. 20* (987);[174] and *Sinai Geo. O. 34* (10th cent.), copied by Iovane Zosime. This highly studied manuscript was considered to be a 'liturgical encyclopaedia of its time' and contains both the ancient and the newer redactions of the *Iadgari*.[175]

Because the *Iadgari* is a hymn book, its content does not present a complete structure of the services. Even with regard to its hymnographic content for the commemorations that took place throughout the year, the calendar of the *Iadgari* records fewer feasts than the Jerusalem lectionary in the GL.

---

[167] Formerly the Korneli Kekelidze Institute of Manuscripts.

[168] ჯილ-ეტრატის იადგარი [*Čil-etratis iadgari*, Papyrus-Parchment Iadgari], ed. by Akaki Shanidze et al. (Tbilisi: Metsniereba, 1977). For a description of the manuscript, see *Description* I, 229–39; B. Outtier, 'Review of *Le Iadgari sur papyrus et parchemin*, A. Chanidzé et al. (Tbilissi 1977)', BK 37 (1979), 336–41; Xevsuriani, *Tropologion*, 23–8; Renoux, *Hymnaire de Saint-Sabas*, 249–50.

[169] Xevsuriani, *Tropologion*, 27–8.

[170] *Description* I, 53–73; Xevsuriani, *Tropologion*, 28–30; Renoux, *Hymnes de la résurrection* I, 7–8. For more on the Georgian scribe Iovane Zosime, see Chapter 2, 'Georgian Monastic Liturgy'.

[171] *Description* I, 143–52; Xevsuriani, *Tropologion*, 30–2; Renoux, *Hymnes de la résurrection* II, 8–10. For more on the Georgian exodus, see Chapter 2, 'Georgian Monastic Liturgy'.

[172] *Description* I, 153–6; Xevsuriani, *Tropologion*, 32; Renoux, *Hymnes de la résurrection* II, 10–11.

[173] *Description* I, 77–93; Renoux, *Hymnes de la résurrection* III, 6–7.

[174] *Description* I, 73–7; Renoux, *Hymnes de la résurrection* III, 7–8.

[175] Xevsuriani, *Tropologion*, 32–6, esp. 33; *Description* I, 94–131; Renoux, *Hymnes de la résurrection* II, 11–17; Frøyshov, *Horologe 'géorgien'*. For more on this manuscript, see Chapter 2, 'Georgian Monastic Liturgy', and Appendix 1. The complete 1980 edition of the *Iadgari* is also available online: *The Most Ancient Hymn-Book*, ed. by Eka Kvirkvelia, Cicino Guledani, and Jost Gippert (Tbilisi-Frankfurt am Main: Thesaurus Indogermanischer Text- und Sprachmaterialien, 2011). At http://titus.uni-frankfurt.de/texte/etcs/cauc/ageo/liturg/udzviad/udzvi.htm (accessed on 1 June 2017).

This can be explained by the fact that the *Iadgari* was a hymnographic companion to the lectionary and therefore included only major feasts, which required hymns and general services whose hymns were repeated on various occasions.[176] Nevertheless, most services contained an entrance hymn (ოხითაჲ, *oxitay*), verses for the responsorial psalm and for the Alleluia, a hymn for hand washing (ჴელთბანისაჲ, *ẋeltbanisay*), and a hymn for the transfer of the gifts (სიჩმიდისაჲ, *sicmidisay*)—apart from the hymns for vespers and matins or other services for each commemoration that preceded the Divine Liturgy.[177] The *Iadgari*'s calendar is virtually identical to that of the GL, except for the repetition and rearrangement of certain feasts; it runs from Annunciation (25 March) to Christmas (25 December), then to Hypapante (2 February), and then to pre-Lent, Lent, Easter, Pentecost, and the summer months, until the feast of archangels (14 November).[178] Michael Schneider's study of the *Iadgari* has helped to understand the book's structure and its theology of the incarnation of Christ in the major feasts of Christmas (25 December) and Theophany (6 January),[179] while recent editions of French translations by Charles Renoux have examined the *Iadgari*'s various sources and origins, as well as the correlations with its Greek originals. Renoux's translations not only make the Georgian text of the Tropologion accessible, but his approach to the text—which was to translate the text of one manuscript at a time, rather than the whole critical edition prepared by Metreveli and her colleagues—makes it easier to understand the diversity of the various manuscripts with regard to their liturgical contents.[180] Unlike in the manuscripts of the Jerusalem lectionary, which often indicate the place or liturgical station where a given commemoration was to be celebrated in the city, in many of the manuscripts of the Tropologion or *Iadgari* holy sites are noticeably absent. This is likely due to the slow decline of stational liturgy in Jerusalem at the time when hymnography was developing, making its way into the structures of the eucharistic Divine Liturgy, and finding a permanent place in liturgical books.

---

[176] Métrévéli, 'Le plus ancien Tropologion géorgien', 55–6. See the section 'General Commemorations' in Chapter 5 here for more on general commemorations.

[177] See, for example, the structure of the eucharistic liturgy on Christmas day (25 December) in the *Iadgari* edition, *Iadgari*, 21–2.

[178] *Iadgari*, 7–327. For an English summary, see Wade, 'The Oldest *Iadgari*', 451–2.

[179] For studies of Christmas and Theophany, see Schneider, *Lobpreis im rechten Glauben*; for the Sunday services, see Peter Jeffery, 'The Sunday Office of Seventh-Century Jerusalem in the Georgian Chantbook (Iadgari): A Preliminary Report', *Studia Liturgica* 21 (1991), 52–75.

[180] Renoux, *Hymnes de la résurrection* I; Renoux, *Hymnaire de Saint-Sabas*; Renoux, *Hymnes de la résurrection* II; Renoux, *Hymnes de la résurrection* III.

MONASTIC LITURGY IN BYZANTINE
JERUSALEM AND PALESTINE

Holy sites, however, were not limited to cities and towns; they included monasteries as well. The majority of monastic holy sites were associated with coenobitic or communal monasticism rather than with lavriote monasticism (which was a mixture of communal and solitary or eremitical monasticism); and the most important coenobia were the monastery next to the Kathisma Church[181] and the monastery at St Peter's Church.[182] Monasteries with holy sites were often located along major roads, showing their connection to Palestinian society and the daily life of the church of Jerusalem.[183] The *Life of Sabas* reveals strong ties between monastic life of the desert and city life, showing St Sabas to be a spokesman for the whole church of Jerusalem during his visit to Emperor Justinian in 531.[184] Desert and city were brought even closer together once baptisms at monasteries became a frequent practice.[185]

Understanding the role of monks in all the aspects of liturgical life in the Jerusalem patriarchate is crucial for an analysis of Hagiopolite liturgy and its Byzantinization. Archaeological and literary sources offer glimpses into the rise of monasticism in Palestine and into daily life as carried out in the numerous monasteries of Jerusalem and of the Judean desert. At its peak, in the fifth and sixth centuries, the region housed at least sixty-four monasteries.[186]

The general practice in lavriote monasticism followed a pattern whereby the monks would pray privately in their cells, then gather for common services in the monastery's main church on Saturday and Sunday.[187] This is the origin of the Sabaite and lavriote 'all-night vigil' ($\dot{\alpha}\gamma\rho\upsilon\pi\nu\dot{\iota}\alpha$), which in turn explains the absence of the latter in coenobitic monasticism, for example in Stoudite

---

[181] GL § 1143, 1395; Verhelst, 'Lieux de station' II, here 262–3. For more on the Kathisma Church, see the section 'Liturgy at the Cathedral of Jerusalem' in this chapter.

[182] GL § 1295; Yizhar Hirschfeld, *The Judean Desert Monasteries in the Byzantine Period* (New Haven, CT: Yale University Press, 1992), 56–8; Verhelst, 'Lieux de station' I, here 40–3.

[183] Leah Di Segni, 'Monk and Society: The Case of Palestine', in Patrich, *Sabaite Heritage*, 35–6.

[184] See *Life of Sabas*, in Schwartz, *Cyril of Scythopolis*, 175.

[185] M. Ben-Pechat, 'Baptism and Monasticim in the Holy Land: Archaeological and Literary Evidence', in *Christian Archaeology in the Holy Land*, 501–22; Perrone, 'Monasticism', 80.

[186] The best surveys are perhaps Derwas J. Chitty, *The Desert a City: An Introduction to the Study of Egyptian and Palestinian Monasticism under the Christian Empire* (Oxford: Basil Blackwell, 1966) and Yizhar Hirschfeld, *The Judean Desert Monasteries in the Byzantine Period* (New Haven, CT: Yale University Press, 1992). For a list of these monasteries, see S. Vailhé, 'Répertoire alphabétique des monastères de Palestine', *Revue de l'Orient Chrétien* 4 (1899), 512–42 and 5 (1900), 19–48 and 272–92. For an updated list, including recent archaeological discoveries, see Y. Hirschfeld, 'List of the Byzantine Monasteries in the Judean Desert', in *Christian Archaeology in the Holy Land*, 1–90.

[187] Allusions are made to this practice in the *Life of Sabas*, chapters 18, 20, and 58, in Schwartz, *Cyril of Scythopolis*, 102, 105, and 159; *Life of John the Hesychast*, chapter 7, in Schwartz, *Cyril of Scythopolis*, 206; Patrich, *Sabas*, 206.

monasteries. Nikolai Uspensky and Miguel Arranz suggested that the absence of the all-night vigil in Stoudite sources indicates that the service arose, or was revived, only in the twelfth century,[188] despite the description of the practice of the Saturday night vigil in Palestine both in the *Life of Sabas* (written in the sixth century by Cyril of Scythopolis) and in the testament of St Sabas.[189]

Because there are no extant Sabaite or other Palestinian monastic liturgical manuscripts from the Byzantine period, hagiographical accounts and edifying texts from Palestinian monasteries prove to be extremely valuable. The numerous hagiographies of Palestinian monks written by Cyril of Scythopolis suggest that, leaving aside the stational character of Jerusalem's liturgy, Palestinian monks shared the main features of Hagiopolite liturgy. For example, one can assume, from hagiographic accounts and later liturgical manuscripts copied at Mar Saba Lavra, that the eucharistic liturgy both in Jerusalem and in Palestinian monasteries would have been the Liturgy of St James (JAS), at least until the beginning of Byzantinization.[190] Apart from such a conclusion, it is difficult to know more details about Palestinian monastic liturgical practices during the Byzantine era with any certainty. The saints' lives composed by Cyril of Scythopolis suggest that the Eucharist was not celebrated every day.[191] Spiritually edifying tales, such as the *Spiritual Meadow* by John Moschus, often use liturgical services as the background for spiritual advice or theological instruction, but give little detail about the liturgical practice itself.[192] By far the most informative text on monks and liturgy in the Jerusalem patriarchate during the Byzantine era is the *Narration of the Abbots John and Sophronius*, which describes a meeting between Hagiopolitan monks and a hermit on Mount Sinai. The monks in question are the Abbots John and Sophronius, believed to be John Moschus (*c.*540–634),[193] author of the *Spiritual Meadow*, and Sophronius (*c.*560–638), future patriarch of Jerusalem,[194] who travelled from Palestine to visit the monk Neilus on Sinai and prayed with him there. During their prayer, the two abbots noted that the monks on Sinai did not sing any hymns

---

[188] See Miguel Arranz, SJ, 'N. D. Uspensky: The Office of the All-Night Vigil in the Greek Church and in the Russian Church', SVTQ 24 (1980), here 174.

[189] ἐθέσπισεν δὲ ὥστε κατὰ δὲ κυριακὴν εἰς τὴν θεοτόκου ἐπιτελεῖσθαι ἐκκλησίαν καὶ ἀπαραλείπτως ἀπὸ ὀψὲ ἕως πρωὶ ἀγρυπνίαν ἐν ἀμφοτέραις γίνεσθαι ταῖς ἐκκλησίαις κατά τε κυριακὴν καὶ δεσποτικὴν ἑορτήν. *Life of Sabas*, chapter 32, in Schwartz, *Cyril of Scythopolis*, 118. For the testament, see *Sinai Gr. 1096* (12th cent.), 148r; Dmitrievskii, *Описание* I, 222–3; Gianfranco Fiaccadori, '42. Sabas: Founder's *Typikon* of the Sabas Monastery near Jerusalem', BMFD IV, here 1316.

[190] See Appendix 1 for the various Georgian 'liturgical collections' copied at Mar Saba Lavra that contain JAS, presumably a sign that this liturgy was celebrated in Palestinian monasteries.

[191] See, for example, *Life of Sabas*, chapter 32, in Schwartz, *Cyril of Scythopolis*, 117–18.

[192] John Moschos, Λειμών (*Pratum*), PG 87.3:2852–3112; *The Spiritual Meadow by John Moschos (also known as John Eviratus)*, trans. by John Wortley (Cistercian Studies Series 19, Kalamazoo, MI: Cistercian Publications, 1992).

[193] Barry Baldwin, 'Moschos, John', ODB II, 1415.

[194] Aristeides Papadakis, 'Sophronios', ODB III, 1928–9.

during their services; they were also informed by Nilus that these monks were not ordained and hence were not permitted to sing hymns or to intone litanies, as these duties would have been reserved for chanters or deacons. Among the pieces of psalmody and hymnody listed for the Divine Liturgy by John and Sophronius are the *trisagion* (τρισάγιον, which opens with the line Ἅγιος ὁ Θεός), responsorial psalmody called *prokeimenon* (προκείμενον) and *propsalmon* (πρόψαλμον), an Alleluia, a hymn sung after the Gospel and called by the rare name *bematikion* (βηματίκιον),[195] the *cheroubikon*, sung during the entrance of the Mysteries or eucharistic gifts,[196] and the Communion hymn (κοινωνικόν).[197] It is worth noting that certain manuscripts mention the hymn 'Let all mortal flesh keep silent' (Σηγησάτω πᾶσα σάρξ), which is known from manuscripts of JAS, as another possible hymn sung during the transfer of the gifts.[198] Although the account dates to the seventh or eighth century according to most scholars, the earliest extant source for this text is the tenth-century *Explanation of the Commandments of the Lord* (Ἑρμηνεῖαι τῶν ἐντολῶν τοῦ Κυρίου), compiled by Nicon of the Black Mountain, north of Antioch (*c.*1025–before 1110).[199] While extremely valuable, the account of John and Sophronius makes it clear that one ought to be cautious about labelling all monastic practice in Palestine as 'Sabaite', since various monastic forms of worship existed side by side, some of them being part of—or even indistinguishable from—liturgical practices such as those performed in the Church of the Anastasis in Jerusalem.[200] Nevertheless, both forms of worship were considered to reflect the 'order of the Catholic and Apostolic Church' (ἡ τάξις τῆς καθολικῆς καὶ ἀποστολικῆς ἐκκλησίας) and

---

[195] See Taft, 'The βηματίκιον', 680–5.

[196] καὶ εἰς τὴν προέλευσιν τῶν Μυστηρίων τὸ Οἱ τὰ Χερουβίμ. Longo, 'Narrazione', 254.

[197] Ibid., 254 and 266.

[198] See ibid., 254 (line 53 and apparatus). We will revisit these descriptions of ordained clergy offices in Jerusalem and the use of Hagiopolitan liturgical terminology when examining the Liturgy of the Word in JAS. See the section 'The Liturgy of the Word' in Chapter 3 here.

[199] Alexander Kazhdan, 'Nikon of the Black Mountain', ODB III, 1484–5. For the Typikon of the Black Mountain, see *Das Taktikon des Nikon vom Schwarzen Berge*, vol. 1, 48–135; BMFD I, 377–424. While Basil Lourié has attempted to push the date of the *Narration* to the ninth or tenth century, most authors accept it as an account of seventh-century pre-Arab liturgical practices in the Jerusalem patriarchate. See Basil M. Lourié, 'Повествование отцов Иоанна и Софрония (BHG 1438w) как литургический источник', *Византийский Временник* 54 (1993), 62–73, here 62–3; Longo, 'Narrazione', 236–8; Uspensky, 'Чин всенощного бдения', 37–42; Taft, 'The βηματίκιον', 676. Although deficiencies in the text used for Longo's edition cause some confusion, this is currently the only edited version of the *Narration* available. See, for example, 'Mesedi – Μεσῴδιον', in Parenti, *A oriente e occidente di Costantinopoli*, 98 n. 43. Taft, 'The βηματίκιον', 676 n. 4 mentions the unpublished dissertation of Stig Ragnvald Frøyshov, *La narration de Jean et Sophrone (BHG 1438w): Édition, traduction et étude contextuelle* (Unpublished master's thesis, Paris: Université de Paris-Sorbonne and Institut Catholique de Paris, 1998).

[200] It is unclear whether the service that John and Sophronius were familiar with was the result of the 'Palestinian synthesis' of 'cathedral' and 'monastic' usage, as Taft claims, or simply the practice of the monks of the Church of the Anastasis. See Taft, 'The βηματίκιον', 677 and 692.

any alternative was considered anathema.[201] By the eighth century, Palestinian monks had set both Jerusalem and Mar Saba Lavra as the standard by which all practices, liturgical and other, should be measured: 'just as Jerusalem is the queen of all cities, so is the Lavra of St Sabas the prince of all deserts, and in so far as Jerusalem is the norm of other cities, so too is Mar Sabas the exemplar for other monasteries'.[202]

EARLY CONSTANTINOPOLITAN LITURGY

Even if the Church of the Anastasis or the Holy Lavra of St Sabas were the models for liturgy in the Jerusalem patriarchate, there were other important liturgical centres elsewhere in the Byzantine East. From the perspective of the Byzantine empire, the most important such centre was certainly Hagia Sophia, the 'Great Church' of Constantinople, imperial capital and see of the ecumenical patriarchate.[203] In order to understand the process of Byzantinization in the Jerusalem patriarchate, it is necessary to compare Hagiopolite liturgical practice with contemporaneous Constantinopolitan practice. However, unlike the liturgy in Jerusalem, the liturgy in Constantinople before Byzantine iconoclasm in the eighth and ninth centuries is relatively little known to us. The fourth-century homilies of St Gregory of Nazianzus (d. *c*.390), known by the epithet 'the Theologian', as well as those of St John Chrysostom (d. 407), Severian of Gabala (d. *c*.430), and Proclus (d. 446/7), all of whom were bishops and lived in Constantinople in the fourth and fifth centuries, remain to be examined for what they can yield about the liturgical year in Constantinople in the fourth and fifth centuries.[204] The sixth century yields the *kontakia* of Romanus the Melodist (d. after 555) and the sermons of

---

[201] Longo, 'Narrazione', 253.

[202] Korneli S. Kekelidze, *Monumenta hagiographica georgica, Pars prima: Keimena* (Tbilisi: Sumptibus Rossicae Academiae scientiarum edidit, 1918), 172–3 ('და 3~ა ი~წმი მეუფე არს ყ~ლისა ქალაქთაა ეგრევე ლავრაა საბაისი მთავარია ყ~თთა უდაბმოთაა. და უკუეთუ ი~წმისაა რაა სწორების არს სხჳსა ქალაქისაა: ეგრევე საბაწმიდისაა რაა მსავსების არს სხჳსა მონასტრისაა'.); Paul Peeters, 'La passion de S. Michel le Sabaïte', *Analecta Bollandiana* 48 (1930), 76, § 14 (*Sicut Hierosolyma regina est omnium urbium, ita etiam laura Sabae omnium solitudinum est princeps, adeoque, si Hierosolyma aliarum urbium norma est, sic etiam (laura) sancti Sabae exemplo est ceteris monasteriis*); English translation from Griffith, 'The Church of Jerusalem and the "Melkites"', 185. See also Monica J. Blanchard, 'The Georgian Version of the Martyrdom of Saint Michael, Monk of Mar Sabas Monastery', *ARAM* 6 (1994), 149–63.

[203] For liturgy at Hagia Sophia, see Rowland J. Mainstone, *Hagia Sophia: Architecture, Structure and Liturgy of Justinian's Great Church* (London: Thames & Hudson, 1988), 226–35.

[204] See Barry Baldwin, Alexander Kazhdan, Robert S. Nelson, Nancy P. Ševčenko, 'Gregory of Nazianzos', ODB II, 880–2; Barry Baldwin, Alexander Kazhdan, Robert S. Nelson, 'John Chrysostom', ODB II, 1057–8; Barry Baldwin, 'Severianos', ODB III, 1883–4; Barry Baldwin, 'Proklos', ODB III, 1729.

Leontius (*c*.5th–6th cent.), presbyter in Constantinople.[205] These texts and other passing references only provide information on general reading cycles, certain pericopes on specific days, and a certain commemoration or the celebration of a saint. As Gary Philippe Raczka has pointed out, the vague references to the lectionary and calendar from fourth- and fifth-century homilies begin to take form in the sixth century, and already by then they show greater similarities with later (and extant) liturgical books, particularly with the Constantinopolitan kanonarion–synaxarion, commonly (albeit speciously) known as the Typikon of the Great Church of Constantinople.[206] The term *typikon* can designate a book of liturgical prescriptions, a monastic rule, or the accepted unwritten tradition of a local church and can be used in references to all three in liturgical studies.

The first liturgiologists to refer to the kanonarion-synaxarion as a Typikon were the Russian pre-revolutionary liturgists Krasnosel'tsev and Dmitrievskii, who made contact with the library of the Monastery of St John the Theologian on Patmos in 1891 and were able to study the manuscript *Patmos Gr. 266* (9th–10th cent.).[207] The manuscript catalogue of the monastery's library, compiled by Ioannis Sakellion (1815–91), referred to *Patmos Gr. 266* as a Typikon.[208] After Dmitrievskii, Juan Mateos (1917–2003) edited the liturgical prescriptions of the Patmos manuscript and several other Constantinopolitan synaxaria in 1962–3 and continued the tradition of naming the text 'the Typicon de la Grande Église'.[209] The manuscript sources of Mateos' edition of this Typikon of the Great Church are in reality hagiographic collections known as synaxaria, which contain the lives of saints along with liturgical prescriptions and topographical notices for the city of Constantinople.[210] The

---

[205] See Barry Baldwin, 'Romanos the Melode', ODB III, 1807–1808; Alice-Mary Talbot, 'Leontios', ODB II, 1212.

[206] Raczka, *The Lectionary*, 8–11 and 139–45. The specific manuscript of Mateos' edition that Raczka refers to is *Hagios Stavros Gr. 40* (10th–11th cent.). See Mateos, *Typicon*, vol. 1, iv.

[207] Nikolai Krasnosel'tsev, 'Типикъ церкви Св. Софіи въ Константинополѣ (IX в.)', *Лѣтопись Историко-филологического общества при Императорском Новороссийском университетѣ* (Одесса) 2 (1892), *Византийское отдѣленіе*, vol. 1, 156–254, especially 159–62, where Krasnoselt'sev describes receiving a copy of the manuscript.

[208] The library's manuscript catalogue lists *Patmos Gr. 266* (9th–10th cent.) in the category 'Typikon', hence the tradition of calling this synaxarion a 'Typikon'. See 'σξς'. Ὁμοίον [Τυπικόν]', in Πατμιακὴ Βιβλιοθήκη ἤτοι ἀναγραφὴ τῶν ἐν τῇ βιβλιοθήκῃ τῆς κατὰ τὴν νῆσον Πάτμον, ed. by Ioannes Sakellion (Athens: Alexandros Papageorgios, 1890), 136.

[209] This is based primarily on codices *Hagios Stavros Gr. 40* (10th–11th cent.) [= H] and *Patmos Gr. 266* (9th cent.) [= P]. See Mateos, *Typicon*, vol. 1 , iv–v and viii–xix. See also Robert F. Taft and Alexander Kazhdan, 'Typikon of the Great Church', ODB III, 2132–3.

[210] See Delehaye, *Synaxarium*, v–l, for an outline of the various manuscript families of Byzantine synaxaria. See also Robert F. Taft and Nancy Patterson Ševčenko, 'Synaxarion', ODB III, 1991; Jacques Noret, 'Le Synaxaire Leningrad gr. 240: Sa place dans l'évolution du Synaxaire byzantin', in *Античная древность и средние века* (Сборник 10, Sverdlovsk: Уральский государственный университет, 1972), 124–30, here 124–5. Noret, 'Ménologes, Synaxaires, Ménées' notes the inadequacy and ambiguity of this and similar terms in Byzantine

Bollandist Hippolyte Delehaye (1859–1941) focused on the hagiographical texts and published them in 1902 under the title *Synaxarium ecclesiae constantinopolitanae*. The primary manuscripts that Mateos employed are *Hagios Stavros Gr. 40* (10th–11th cent.), labelled H, and *Patmos Gr. 266* (9th–10th cent.), labelled P, both of which provide the lives of various saints in abbreviated form (βίοι ἐν συντόμῳ), along with four other manuscripts.[211] Mateos' two-volume edition follows the structure of the liturgical year in Constantinople:[212] the fixed cycle runs from 1 September to 31 August and the movable cycle begins with the Sunday before Meatfare, continues through Lent, Easter, Pentecost, and all the Sundays after Pentecost, until the year arrives again at the period of Meatfare. The text contains the names of the saints to be commemorated, liturgical prescriptions indicating the location of a station within the city of Constantinople, the basic structure of services, and liturgical set pieces such as troparia, *prokeimena*, and the Communion hymn (κοινωνικόν).[213]

Extant eleventh-century manuscripts of the Constantinopolitan Praxapostolos (πραξαπόστολος), a liturgical book containing scriptural readings from Acts (πράξεις), from the Epistles (ἀπόστολος) of St Paul, and from the General Epistles, also provide information on liturgy at the Great Church of Constantinople. Apart from the texts of the scriptural readings themselves, these books contain the full liturgical ordo (ἀκολουθία) of services in the form of troparia, *prokeimena*, verses for the Alleluia, Communion hymns, and other liturgical prescriptions.[214] Two important examples of the Constantinopolitan Praxapostolos are *Dresden Sächsische LB Gr. A.104* (11th cent.) and *Moscow GIM*

studies. While the reading of the lives of saints from synaxaria in monastic environments is better known, it is not clear when they were read in cathedral liturgy. The most probable location of a synaxarion reading at the Cathedral Orthros in Constantinople would have been at the end of the service, between the end of the Orthros and the beginning of the Divine Liturgy. See Delehaye, *Synaxarium*, v–vi; Skaballanovich, *Толковый Типиконъ*, vol. 2, 189; Mateos, *Typicon*, vol. 1, xxiii–xxiv; Miguel Arranz, 'Les prières presbytérales des matines byzantines', OCP 37 (1971), 406–36; Miguel Arranz, 'L'office de l'Asmatikos Orthoros (matines chantées) de l'ancien Euchologe byzantin', OCP 44 (1978), 126–32.

[211] See Mateos, *Typicon*, vol. 1, iv–vi. For more on the individual manuscripts, see Andrea Luzzi, 'Il Patmiacus 266: Un testimone dell'utilizzo liturgico delle epitomi premetafrastiche', RSBN 49 [2012] (2013), 239–61; Andrea Luzzi, 'Synaxaria and the Synaxarion of Constantinople', in *The Ashgate Research Companion to Byzantine Hagiography*, vol. 2: *Periods and Places*, ed. by Stephanos Efthymiadis (Burlington, VT: Ashgate, 2014), 197–210, esp. 200–3.

[212] For further explanations of the structure of the liturgical year, see Chapter 4, 'The Structure and Characteristics of the Hagiopolite Liturgical Year', and Chapter 5, 'Structures of the Jerusalem Lectionary: Gospel Cycles'.

[213] See Mateos, *Typicon*, vol. 1, xxii–xxiv for a reconstruction of the various services indicated in this source.

[214] Andreou, *Praxapostolos*, 46.

Gr. Vladimir 21/Savva 4 (11th cent.), each containing significant rubrics that connect it with the imperial capital.[215] The structure of the liturgical arrangement of the Praxapostolos is similar to that of the Typikon of the Great Church: the arrangement begins with the synaxarion from Pascha through Holy Saturday, then a menologion is inserted from 1 September until 31 August.[216] The codices end with general commemorations.[217]

Apart from the cathedral of Constantinople, there were also monasteries in the imperial capital that played an important role in the development of the liturgy there after iconoclasm. The Typikon of the Stoudios Monastery[218] in Constantinople is a prescriptive liturgical book used to regulate the liturgical life of the monastery.[219] The earliest extant source is the Typikon of Alexis the Stoudite, patriarch of Constantinople (r. 1025–43), which was composed for the Monastery of the Dormition of the Theotokos founded by Alexis in Constantinople, but was preserved exclusively in Slavonic translation.[220] One of the main characteristics of this book is that it begins with Easter or with the Lenten cycle, and not with the Saturday night vigil characteristic of Sabaite Typika.[221] The liturgical year in the Stoudite Typika runs from the

[215] *Dresden Sächsische LB Gr. A.104* (11th cent.) was damaged during the Second World War, but large portions of this manuscript were transcribed in Dmitrievskii, *Древнѣйшіе Патріаршіе Типиконы*, especially 214–347. See also Mateos, *Typicon*, vol. 1, viii; K. K. Akentiev, 'Следы дрезденского списка (А 104) Типика Св. Софии в архиве А. А. Дмитриевского', Конференция к 150-летию со дня рождения А. А. Дмитриевского 12 мая 2006 г, *Βυζαντινορ-ωσσικα*. *Санкт-Петербургское Общество византино-славянских исследований*. At http://byzantinorossica.org.ru/seminar_dresden104.html (accessed on 1 August 2016). A full reconstruction of the Dresden manuscript can be found in Konstantin K. Akentiev, *Типикон Великой Церкви. Cod. Dresde A 104. Реконструкция текста по материалам архива А. А. Дмитриевского* (Subsidia Byzantinorossica 5, St Petersburg: Византинороссика, 2009), especially 42–127. For *Moscow GIM Gr. Vladimir 21/Savva 4* (11th cent.), see Andreou, *Praxapostolos*, 10–11.
[216] 'Sinassario', fol. 1v–211r: see Andreou, *Praxapostolos*, 12, 106–202; 'Menologio', fol. 211r–306v: see Andreou, *Praxapostolos*, 13, 202–402.
[217] See Andreou, *Praxapostolos*, 12–13 and 106–411 for an edition of the complete text.
[218] Alexander Kazhdan, Alice-Mary Talbot, and Anthony Cutler, 'Stoudios Monastery', ODB III, 1960–1.
[219] Robert F. Taft, 'Typikon, liturgical', ODB III, 2121–32; Alice-Mary Talbot, 'Typikon, monastic', ODB III, 2132.
[220] Alexander Kazhdan, 'Alexios Stoudites', ODB I, 67; Pentkovsky, *Типикон*, 42–8. The two editions of the Stoudite liturgical Typikon are Petras, *Typikon*, based on *St Petersburg RNB, Novgorod St Sophia 1136* (13th cent.) of which he has only edited the Lenten cycle and Bright Week; and Pentkovsky, *Типикон*, which has edited the complete movable and fixed cycles, supplementing *Novgorod St Sophia 1136* with *Sinai Slav. 330* (11th cent.) and *Sinai Slav. 333* (11th cent.). See Pentkovsky, *Типикон*, 21–41, for a history of the study of these manuscripts. Clark, *Sinai Checklist*, does not include these manuscripts.
[221] *Sinai Gr. 150* (10th–11th cent.), Dmitrievskii, *Описаніе* I, 173; *Vatopedi Gr. 322 (956)* (13th–14th cent.), Dmitrievskii, *Описаніе* I, 225; Petras, *Typikon*, 41; Pentkovsky, *Типикон*, 233; Robert F. Taft, 'Stoudite Typika', ODB III, 1961.

Sunday of the Publican and the Pharisee, through Easter, to the Sunday of All Saints, and then from 1 September to 31 August for the fixed cycle.

Along with the Typikon of the Great Church, the Praxapostolos, and monastic liturgical Typika, Constantinopolitan psalters also contain a wealth of information. Stichometric distinctions in versification between a Hagiopolitan psalter of twenty *kathismata* and a Constantinopolitan or ecclesiastical (ἐκκλη-σιάστης) psalter of sixty-eight antiphons are significant in that they help to identify the origin of a manuscript.[222] Apart from the 150 psalms in various versifications, psalters may also contain refrains (ὑποψάλματα),[223] biblical odes,[224] or supplemental material such as hymnody or canticles for various services, for example the *cheroubikon* in Constantinopolitan psalters, or calendar indications.[225] Unlike the Constantinopolitan psalter, which gives refrains for every antiphon, the Jerusalem psalter had no refrains.[226] Frøyshov notes that each type of psalter—whether Constantinopolitan or Hagiopolitan—was not associated with monastic or cathedral practice, but was used throughout its respective city.[227] For example, the versification of the psalter was the same across Palestinian manuscripts, regardless of whether they were copied and used at the Monastery of St Catherine on Mount Sinai or at the Church of the Anastasis in Jerusalem.[228] One of the most notable Constantinopolitan sources is *Moscow GIM Gr. 129D* (9th cent.), known as 'the Khludov Psalter'.[229]

The structure of the Divine Liturgy can be discerned from the variable elements—hymns and texts—that are found in the Constantinopolitan liturgical sources discussed in this section (see Table 1.4).[230]

---

[222] Parpulov, *Byzantine Psalters*, 56–7; H. Schneider, 'Die biblischen Oden in Jerusalem und Konstantinopel', *Biblica* 30 (1949), 442–7.

[223] Oliver Strunk, 'The Byzantine Office at Hagia Sophia', DOP 9–10 (1956), 175–202, here 200–1.

[224] H. Schneider, 'Die Biblischen Oden im Christlichen Altertum', *Biblica* 30 (1949), 28–65, here 64.

[225] Parpulov, *Byzantine Psalters*, 52–65.

[226] Juan Mateos, SJ, 'Quelques problèmes de l'orthros byzantin', *Proche-Orient Chrétien* 11 (1961), 17–35, here 18.

[227] Frøyshov, *Horologe 'géorgien'*, vol. 2, 359.

[228] See the examples given by Parpulov, *Byzantine Psalters*, 80–2.

[229] *Salterio Chludov*, facsimile edn (Madrid: Archivo Histórico de la Ciudad de Moscú and AyN Ediciones, 2006); *Salterio griego Jlúdov (ms. gr. 129, Museo Histórico del Estado, Moscú): Libro de Estudios* (Madrid: Museo Histórico del Estado, Moscú, / AyN Ediciones, 2007).

[230] This table is based on the information for the Divine Liturgy on Christmas day (25 December) in the Typikon of the Great Church and in the Praxapostolos. See Mateos, *Typicon*, vol. 1, 156–9; Andreou, *Praxapostolos*, 288–90. Psalters do not give specific information on the Divine Liturgy or on the structure of the Divine Liturgy on December 25, but their appendices sometimes do include information on the fixed hymns sung at the Divine Liturgy. See Parpulov, *Byzantine Psalters*, 176 (Appendix D3).

Table 1.4. The Divine Liturgy in Constantinopolitan sources

1. Antiphons	Three antiphons are sung, each with its own refrain. The hymn 'Only-begotten Son' (ὁ μονογενὴς) is sung between the second and third antiphon.[231]
2. Troparia and *kontakia*	After the small entrance, various hymns are sung, depending on the day and on the commemoration. These are sung according to one of the eight tones.[232]
3. Responsorial Psalmody	A type of responsorial psalmody called *prokeimenon* is sung after the *trisagion* and before the scriptural readings. The psalm verse or, occasionally, a verse from another biblical canticle is sung according to one of the eight tones, as indicated in the liturgical books.[233]
4. Epistle Reading	One New Testament reading is indicated, either from Acts or from an Epistle. The Book of Revelation was not read liturgically in Constantinople.[234]
5. Alleluia with Verse	Similar to the AL and the GL, with the indication of a tone in which to sing the Alleluia.[235]
6. Gospel Reading	One Gospel reading, depending on the commemoration or the time of year (e.g. Lent, Easter, after Pentecost).[236]
7. Communion Hymn	Usually a psalm verse, sung while the clergy and the faithful receive Communion.[237]

On certain commemorations, variable hymns are indicated for the *trisagion*, which comes after the troparia and *kontakia* (Table 1.4, no. 2) and before the *prokeimenon* (Table 1.4, no. 3).[238] Likewise, the hymn of the great entrance—usually the *cheroubikon*, which takes place after the Gospel reading—can be replaced on certain days of the year.[239] Otherwise the structure presented in Table 1.4 is quite stable and does not differ for the Divine Liturgy.[240]

The Constantinopolitan liturgical sources outlined so far are not exhaustive but can be considered representative of the liturgy in Constantinople around the tenth century and give information on the structure of the liturgical year and the lectionary, which are the focus of this study. As Georgios Andreou

[231] For more on the antiphons, see Chapter 3, 'Antiphons'.

[232] For more on the troparia and *kontakia*, see Chapter 3, 'The *Introit*'.

[233] For more on the *prokeimenon*, see Chapter 3, 'Responsorial Psalmody'.

[234] For more on the Epistle reading, see Chapter 3, ' Lection(s)', and Chapter 5, 'Epistle Readings in the Jerusalem Lectionary'.

[235] For more on the Alleluia, see Chapter 3, 'Alleluia'.

[236] See the index of Gospel readings in Mateos, *Typicon*, vol. 2, 223–7. For more on the Gospel reading, see Chapter 3, 'The Gospel Reading', and Chapter 5, 'Structures of the Jerusalem Lectionary: Gospel Cycles'.

[237] For more on the Communion hymn, see Chapter 3, 'The Hymn for Communion'.

[238] For more on the *trisagion*, see Chapter 3, 'The *Trisagion*'.

[239] For more on the hymns sung during the Great Entrance, see Chapter 3, 'The Hymn for Hand Washing' and 'The Hymn of the Holy Gifts'.

[240] After the fourteenth century, the Marian troparion became a fixed element at the end of the diptychs of the anaphora, thereby adding a degree of variability to hymnography in the Liturgy of the Eucharist within the Byzantine rite Divine Liturgy, depending on the commemoration being celebrated. See the section 'The Liturgy of the Eucharist' in Chapter 3 here.

notes, Juan Mateos' edition of the Typikon of the Great Church has been, perhaps inadvertently, accepted as the sole witness of liturgical life in Constantinople. For this reason, a comparison with other liturgical books, particularly the Praxapostolos and its rich rubrics and other information, is of utmost importance.[241] Nevertheless, the uniformity in the ordering of pericopes in lectionaries in Constantinople and in the Byzantine rite is surprising, especially when compared with the diverse and irregular order of the pericopes in Jerusalem's various lectionaries.[242] With regard to the Divine Liturgy itself, Constantinople celebrated the Liturgy of St Basil the Great (BAS) and the Liturgy of St John Chrysostom (CHR), whose texts were found in the Euchologion along with that of other sacraments, liturgical rites, and prayers.[243] Apart from the liturgical texts themselves, Constantinople has an abundance of commentaries on, and mystagogies of, the Divine Liturgy that explained its rites, rituals, and liturgical actions to the faithful in mystical, anamnetic, and mimetic terms—something that did not happen in Jerusalem.[244] Because current knowledge of the assimilation of the Stoudite and Sabaite traditions alongside that of the Great Church, as well as of the development of sacraments in the Byzantine rite, is still in its infancy, this study will steer clear of questions not directly related to the liturgical calendar and to the lectionary within the eucharistic liturgy.

HAGIOPOLITE LITURGICAL MANUSCRIPTS IN THE PERIOD OF BYZANTINIZATION

Any study of a change in liturgical practice must examine the practice in question before, during, and after the purported change. The eucharistic synaxis in the *Mystagogical Catecheses* of Cyril of Jerusalem, the *Itinerarium*

---

[241] [L]'*approccio esplicativo secondo cui l'unico punto di riferimento per la comprensione della tradizione liturgica bizantina sarebbe un solo libro, per esempio, il Typikon della Grande Chiesa, è insufficiente. La ricerca liturgica dovrebbe guardare a questo testo in modo diverso, visto che non può presentare realtà liturgiche del periodo in cui esso è stato redatto* ('The explanatory approach according to which the only point of reference for understanding the Byzantine liturgical tradition would be one book, for example, the Typikon of the Great Church, is inadequate. Liturgical research should look to this text in a different way, since it cannot present the liturgical realities of the period in which it was redacted'). Andreou, *Praxapostolos*, 102.

[242] For more on the various orderings of pericopes, see Chapter 5 here.

[243] See P. Joannou, 'Euchologion', *Lexikon für Theologie und Kirche*, vol. 3, ed. by Josef Höfer and Karl Rahner, 2nd edn (Freiburg: Herder, 1959); Robert F. Taft, 'Euchologion', ODB II, 738; Stefano Parenti, 'Euchologion', in *Lexikon für Theologie und Kirche*, vol. 3, ed. by Walter Kasper, 3rd edn (Freiburg: Herder, 1995), 976; Parenti, 'La "vittoria"'. For more on sacraments, see the conference proceedings on Orthodox sacraments in ПУЦТ; Parenti, 'Towards a Regional History'.

[244] See Chapter 3, 'Mystagogies of the Liturgy of St James', for a discussion of this question.

of Egeria, the Armenian lectionary (AL), the Georgian lectionary (GL), and the Tropologion (*Iadgari*) were presented here side by side with the corresponding sources from Constantinople precisely for this purpose: to make us understand liturgy in Jerusalem before its Byzantinization. The next chapter will consider them within the historical context of Palestine, from the eighth century to the thirteenth, and will use them as a standard against which one could (1) determine whether later liturgical manuscripts without specific topographical or palaeographical information may in fact originate from Jerusalem and (2) assess the level to which they have been Byzantinized. Although not all of these sources will be used to the same degree in the following chapters, they have nevertheless been presented here in order that the reader may understand what sources of the Hagiopolite liturgical tradition still exist; besides, such an inventory could facilitate further study of Jerusalem's liturgy. It must be noted, however, that, although the sources reviewed here are accepted as representative of liturgical practice in Jerusalem before the eighth century, hardly any of their manuscript sources predate the eighth century. Thus the liturgical practices they transmit are dated to the period between the fourth and the eighth century not on the basis of palaeography or codicology, but because liturgical scholars believe that they reflect, and are consistent with, what is known of early Hagiopolitan usage. There are in fact very few manuscripts that predate the eighth century. The earliest Greek liturgical manuscript, *Barberini Gr. 336* (8th cent.), is an Euchologion from southern Italy copied during the period just before iconoclasm. Although it was copied and used in southern Italy, it reflects the liturgical practice of Constantinople, some of its strata also representing Constantinopolitan patriarchal usage, local southern Italian practices, and certain Middle Eastern and Hagiopolitan elements.[245] It is thus possible to find various liturgical traditions even within one manuscript, which means that clear criteria are necessary in order to establish the provenance, date, and reliability of a liturgical manuscript.

How one selects manuscript sources and determines whether they witness a changing liturgical tradition—and one that gets eventually uprooted and reformed—can be a complicated matter. Concerning the liturgical Byzantinization of Jerusalem, there are three main criteria for selecting liturgical manuscripts and sources relevant to the study of this phenomenon. Each source and liturgical manuscript must:

1. present concrete codicological and palaeographic evidence connecting the source to (a) the geographic territory of the Jerusalem patriarchate or to (b) the chronological period between the eighth and thirteenth centuries, within the Arab-occupied region of Palestine under the Ummayads and ʿAbbasids;

---

[245] Parenti and Velkovska, *Барберини гр. 336*, 52–63, 70.

2. reveal direct links to the Jerusalem lectionary or its sanctoral cycle (or both); or

3. reveal a partial connection to the Jerusalem lectionary or its sanctoral cycle (or both), namely a connection not shared with the later, synthesized Byzantine rite.[246]

As noted, the first criterion is assessed on the basis of studies conducted by competent authorities in Greek, Georgian, and Syriac palaeography and codicology. This is extremely important, since not all manuscripts are dated by their copyists or include clear colophons. The study of the corpus of Greek manuscripts has made it possible for palaeographers to identify a type of writing, called 'inclined uncial script', that originated in Palestine.[247] Thus, even when a manuscript is not dated or its place of origin is not indicated by the scribe himself, the scribal hand can often betray the manuscript's origin. Nevertheless, one must remember that, just as manuscripts travelled with their owners, so too scribes trained in one region that had its own distinct script could travel elsewhere.[248] Besides, books were often given as gifts. Colophons and notes from manuscripts currently at the library of the Greek Orthodox patriarchate in Jerusalem reveal that many manuscripts from the tenth through to the fourteenth centuries were received as gifts, often from Constantinople.[249]

The second criterion is assessed on the basis of established sources of the Jerusalem lectionary, such as the Armenian lectionary and the Georgian lectionary.[250] Although the term 'lectionary' has been used for editions of liturgical manuscripts, it is used here—much like the term *typikon*—as shorthand for the distinct order of scriptural readings and celebrations of holy days throughout the complete liturgical year in Jerusalem.[251] Taken as a whole, this order of biblical readings and saints' days was more than a liturgy schedule for the Christians in Jerusalem: it served to facilitate the mediation of Christ's presence in their daily life and united all members of society.[252] That scriptural readings according to their ordering in the Jerusalem pericope are found in

---

[246] These criteria have been employed to select the manuscripts listed in Appendix 1.

[247] Perria, *Repertorio*, 15; Perria, 'Scritture e codici di origine orientale', 22–3.

[248] The example of Georgius Basilicus, a sixteenth-century scribe from Constantinople who also worked in Venice and Messina, is a case in point. See Ernst Gamillscheg and Dieter Harlfinger, *Repertorium der griechischen Kopisten, 800–1600*, vol. 1: *Handschriften aus Bibliotheken Grossbritanniens*, part A: *Verzeichnis der Kopisten* (Vienna: Österreichischen Akademie der Wissenschaften, 1981), 53–4.

[249] For example *Hagios Sabas Gr. 412* (11th cent.). See William Henry Paine Hatch, *The Greek Manuscripts of the New Testament in Jerusalem* (Paris: Librarie Orientaliste Paul Geuthner, 1934).

[250] See 'The Armenian Lectionary' and 'The Georgian Lectionary' in this chapter.

[251] For more details on the specific commemorations of this calendar, see Chapter 4, 'The Byzantinization of the Hagiopolite Calendar: Case Studies'. For the scriptural readings, see Chapter 5, 'Structures of the Jerusalem Lectionary: Gospel Cycles' and 'Epistle Readings in the Jerusalem Lectionary'.

[252] See 'Lent: A Meditation', in Taft, *Beyond East and West*, 73–85, here 84–5.

liturgical manuscripts other than lectionaries reveals the importance of this distinct way of reading Scripture within the Holy City's liturgical tradition. The presence of this established ordering of pericopes and of the liturgical calendar in manuscripts for other liturgical rites, such as eucharistic liturgies, shows the important place held by scripture and hymnography in liturgical celebrations.

The third criterion is extremely important precisely because, as will be seen in subsequent chapters of this book, the process of liturgical Byzantinization was gradual. There are many 'transitional' sources that witness to both Hagiopolitan and Constantinopolitan practice. Naturally, these manuscripts will be examined with due caution.

Of the manuscripts that will be examined in this study, some are better examples of authentic Hagiopolite liturgy, while others show strong signs of Byzantinization and are difficult to classify as Hagiopolitan. Georgian manuscripts copied before the eleventh century are the most faithful witnesses of Jerusalem's stational liturgy; they often include even the name of liturgical stations within the city of Jerusalem. This is apparent even in the transitional calendar of Iovane Zosime in *Sinai Geo. O. 34* (10th cent.).[253] Other Georgian manuscripts, such as *Sinai Geo. O. 54* (10th cent.) and *Sinai Geo. O. 12* (10th–11th cent.), also preserve JAS and elements of the Hagiopolitan Euchologion most faithfully. When Georgian sources depart from the Hagiopolitan rite, they often note this change and explicitly state that they follow the 'Greek' order or rite. The best examples are Iovane Zosime's calendar and the Gospel lectionary *Sinai Geo. N. 12* (1075).[254]

The colophons of Syriac manuscripts also provide similar information, although Syriac liturgical sources show much greater signs of Byzantinization. *Vatican Syr. 20* (1215) notes that its pericopes follow the 'Greek rite', while *Vatican Syr. 19* (1030) points to the transmission of Byzantine liturgical practice from Antioch into northern Palestine.[255]

Greek manuscripts reflect the greatest changes. Ninth- and tenth-century lectionaries, such as *Sinai Gr. 210* (861/2) and *Sinai Gr. N.E. MΓ 8* (10th cent.), still preserve the order of pericopes common to the AL and the GL. First-hand examination of the Greek lectionaries *Sinai Gr. N.E. M 35* (11th–12th cent.), *Sinai Gr. N.E. M 66* (11th–12th cent.), *Sinai Gr. N.E. X 73* (13th cent.), and *Sinai Gr. N.E. X 159* (14th–16th cent.) has shown that Kurt Aland's observation that these manuscripts are witnesses of 'the Jerusalem order of pericopes, but contain the Byzantine readings' is problematic.[256] Until these manuscripts

---

[253] For more on this manuscript, see Chapter 2, 'Palestinian Monasticism', and Appendix 1.
[254] See Aleksidze et al., *Catalogue of Georgian Manuscripts*, 256, as well as Appendix 1.
[255] For more on the historical context of these Syriac manuscripts and the contact between Constantinople, Antioch, and Jerusalem, see Chapter 2, 'Byzantine Contact', and Appendix 1.
[256] Aland, *Kurzgefaßte Liste*, 356. See Appendix 1 for more information on each of these manuscripts.

are edited, it is perhaps better to state that they represent a 'mixed type' of lectionary rather than being witnesses of the Jerusalem order of pericopes. The Typikon of the Anastasis, *Hagios Stavros Gr. 43* (1122), notes the presence of two rites—the local Hagiopolitan and the Constantinopolitan—but the contemporary liturgical Typika, *Sinai Gr. 1096* (12th cent.) from Sabas Lavra and *Sinai Gr. 1097* (1214) from Sinai, are almost completely Byzantinized.[257]

Many manuscripts with connections to Jerusalem or Palestine have not been discussed here for various reasons, which will be explained presently. The provenance of a liturgical manuscript is of the utmost importance for this study, devoted as it is to the liturgical practice of a specific region at a specific time. Provenance can be a difficult matter to establish and, thus, it is best addressed at the outset of this work. Liturgical and codicological evidence can be both a help and a hindrance in understanding the origin of a liturgical source. Several examples of differing opinions between liturgists and codicologists can be provided here.

Liturgists often establish the provenance of a manuscript on the basis of the presence or absence of certain liturgical elements. For example, the Euchologion *Moscow RGB Gr. 27 [Sevastianov 474]* (10th cent.), edited by Stephan Koster, was initially believed to be of Middle Eastern origin because of the presence of certain Hagiopolitan prayers.[258] More recently, however, this thesis has been challenged as a result of closer analysis of the script and of the decoration of the manuscript, both of which connect the codex to a scribe clearly formed in Constantinople.[259] These factors, as well as the manuscript's later history and the additions made by a second scribal hand in 'epsilon' style typical of Palestine and Cyprus, only complicate matters.[260]

Nevertheless, the evidence from codicology is more certain for establishing a manuscript's origin. According to the colophon of the Gospel book *Vatican Barberini Gr. 319* (1039/1168), the first part of the codex (fol. 1r–174v) was copied by presbyter Leon in 1039 in Jerusalem. It makes mention of a pilgrimage to Jerusalem and of the holy fire at the Anastasis in Jerusalem.[261] The second part (fol. 191r–196v) contains tables with readings from the

[257] For more on these manuscripts, see Chapter 2, 'The Development of Stational Liturgy', 'Palestinian Monasticism', and 'Hagiopolite Patriarchs in Exile'; also Appendix 1.

[258] Stephan Josef Koster, *Das Euchologion Sevastianov 474 (X. Jhdt.) der Staatsbibliothek in Moskau* (Rome: Pontifical Oriental Institute, 1996).

[259] Inna P. Mokretsova, M. M. Naumova, Elina N. Dobrynina, Boris L. Fonkitch, *Материалы и техника византийской рукописной книги (по реставрационной документации Государственного научно-исследовательского института реставрации)* (Moscow: Indrik, 2003), 107–9 (Russian) and 262–3 (English).

[260] Koster, *Das Euchologion Sevastianov* (see n. 226), 474, 15–24.

[261] Pahlitzsch, *Graeci und Suriani im Palästina der Kreuzfahrerzeit*, 330–1; *Dated Greek Minuscule Manuscripts to the Year 1200*, edited by Kirsopp Lake and Silva Lake, vol. 7: *Manuscripts in Rome, Part I* (Boston: American Academy of Arts and Sciences, 1937), 15 (no. 285).

Gospels, while the end of the codex (fol. 197v–214v) contains Epistles for various general commemorations written in another hand. The table, however, was copied in southern Italy and reflects local Italo-Greek—and not Hagiopolitan—usage.[262] This illustrates Nigel Wilson's point, that 'a number of books travelled with their owners, and it would be rash to assert that an ex-libris is a reliable indication of the place of origin'.[263] Dealing specifically with liturgical manuscripts, Robert Taft states: 'among manuscript scholars it is axiomatic that books travel with their owners, and the fact that a liturgical manuscript is now found in a monastery library does not mean it was copied in the same monastery or used in its liturgical services'.[264] The Gospel lectionary *Sinai Gr. 213* (967) is a perfect example. Written in uncial script by the priest Eustathius, probably in southern Italy, the codex was given to the Monastery of the Theotokos on Mount Horeb (i.e. Sinai) by Macarius, bishop of Pharan and Sinai (d. 1224).[265] The canon table (fol. 2r) originally belonged to another manuscript—a later one, from the thirteenth or fourteenth century.[266] This might suggest that the clergy and the readers who used the Gospel book salvaged it by replacing the older canon table—if one previously existed—with a newer version, which reflected the lectionary of the region in which it was to be used. Such theories, however, are speculation and show how dangerous it is to assume that a manuscript reflects the liturgical practice of the place where it was found.

These examples only illustrate the problems that arise when one must select sources for analysis in any liturgical study and define the limits of what is to be studied and what can justifiably be omitted.

CONCLUSIONS

As the patronage of Byzantine emperors and the diaries of foreign pilgrims testify, liturgy in Byzantine Jerusalem was intimately connected to the holy sites; and the Holy City's most holy place, the Church of the Anastasis, was

---

[262] Aland classifies the manuscripts as minuscule manuscript 164 with the designation 'e', meaning that it contains Gospel readings for every day of the week (ἑβδομάδες). See Aland, *Kurzgefaßte Liste*, 56; Santo Lucà, 'Su due sinassari della famiglia C*: il Crypt. Δ.α.XIV (ff. 291–292) e il Roman. Vallic. C 34^III (ff. 9–16)', *Archivio storico per la Calabria e la Lucana* 66 (1999), here 56.

[263] Nigel G. Wilson, 'Archimedes: The Palimpsest and the Tradition', BZ 92 (1999), 89–101, here 99.

[264] Taft, 'Worship on Sinai', 167–8.

[265] Fedalto, *Hierarchia ecclesiastica orientalis*, vol. 2, 1044; Adrian Marinescu, 'The Hierarchs' Catalogue of Monastery St Catherine in Mount Sinai', in *Études Byzantines et Post-Byzantines* IV, ed. by Emilian Popescu and Tudor Teoteoi (Iaşi: Editura Trinitas, 2001), here 279.

[266] Harlfinger, Reinsch, and Sonderkamp, *Specimina sinaitica*, 62.

influential in establishing the order of liturgical practices throughout Jerusalem. The structure of the eucharistic synaxis gleaned from the writings of Cyril of Jerusalem and from Egeria's account corresponds to the simple structure given in the AL. This was further expanded in the GL through hymnography sung at the entrance and transfer of the gifts and found in the Tropologion. Despite the fluidity between monastic and cathedral worship in Jerusalem, there were nevertheless practices specific to the city and practices specific to the Judean desert, most notably the absence of stational liturgy and the reduced frequency of the celebration of the Eucharist.

Early liturgy in Constantinople during the same period is not as well known, primarily due to the absence of detailed descriptions or liturgical books. Nevertheless, as individual elements of the liturgical traditions of Jerusalem and Constantinople are compared in subsequent chapters, the contrast between the two cities will become more apparent. This contrast is accentuated by the topographies of two cities: one was the place where Christ lived, and its topography depended on the holy sites that were venerated by local Christians and pilgrims, while the other strove to become a holy place through the accumulation of relics from Jerusalem. Robert Ousterhout summarizes the distinction well:

> In Jerusalem, sacred events *happened*—and were memorialized. In Constantinople, throughout its long history, sanctity was introduced and perpetuated within a complex system that interwove power and status; it was carefully imported, invented, constructed, and celebrated—in image and relic, in streets and buildings, in metaphor and ritual.[267]

With this introduction to the general features of liturgical worship in Jerusalem and to the structure of the eucharistic synaxis during the Byzantine period behind us, it is now possible to move on to the worship traditions of post-Byzantine Jerusalem preserved in liturgical sources that were copied after the Arab conquest of 638. After the seventh century, Hagiopolitan Christians and their liturgical tradition experienced a dramatic change, one that we will examine in the next chapter.

---

[267] Ousterhout, 'Sacred Geographies', 109.

2

The Historical Contexts of Byzantinization

To understand how the liturgical sources from Jerusalem presented in Chapter 1 functioned and underwent change through the process of Byzantinization, one must examine and understand the context in which they were copied and used. As Baumstark writes, 'liturgical forms are so intimately bound up with the external history of the world and of the church and with the development of the religious sentiment, itself conditioned by historical happenings, that they are constantly being subjected to very great modifications'.[1] Before I proceed to the specific topics developed in the following chapters—the eucharistic liturgy, the calendar, and the lectionary—this chapter will address the questions of why, how, and when liturgical Byzantinization occurred. Full descriptions of the manuscripts of the Hagiopolite liturgy in the period of Byzantinization, mentioned in their historical contexts in this chapter, can be found in Appendix 1.

Several theories exist as to *why* liturgical Byzantinization occurred. Some have suggested that the Jerusalem patriarchate lost its liturgical tradition through the depredations that resulted from the Arab occupation and through a desire to be more closely allied to Constantinople, the defender of Chalcedonian Orthodoxy. Faithfulness to the Greek language, especially among the Sabaite monks, is also cited as a factor influencing the desire to imitate Constantinopolitan liturgy.

Questions of precisely *how* and *when* the phenomenon of liturgical Byzantinization occurred are often avoided. The few popular works that describe it suggest that it happened in one fell swoop, either immediately after the destruction of the Holy Sepulchre in 1009[2] or as a result of the return from Constantinople of exiled Hagiopolitan patriarchs who brought with them the Byzantine rite to Jerusalem.[3] While this theory is tempting, it betrays a simplistic understanding of the history, internal functioning, and evolution of the Byzantine rite and of liturgy in general.

---

[1] Baumstark, *Comparative Liturgy*, 1.
[2] See, for example, Pentkovsky, 'Богослужебные уставы'.
[3] See the section 'History of the Question of Byzantinization' in the Introduction here.

In the absence of any synthetic, authoritative study of the Hagiopolite liturgy, I shall endeavour to re-examine the questions of why, how, and when Byzantinization occurred by looking at the historical context.[4] The following 'braided' narrative of analysis and storytelling is by no means complete or free of bias.[5] The liturgical history of Jerusalem for the period between the Arab conquest and the First Crusade presented in this chapter takes into account the fragmentary nature of the sources for this era—especially the so-called 'dark centuries' from the ninth through to the eleventh—where contemporaneous sources often ignore coexisting religious groups or the works of authors who write in other languages. For example, Jewish historical accounts often make no mention of the presence of Christians in Jerusalem. This is the impression one gets from the various histories of the period.[6] Likewise, Latin and Greek liturgical sources from the Holy Sepulchre of the twelfth-century Latin kingdom make no mention of each other's existence, and churches and holy sites described in accounts written in one language are extremely difficult to corroborate with those of another language.[7] According to literary historian Hayden White,

> all original descriptions of any field of phenomena are *already* interpretations of its structure... The plot-structure of a historical narrative (*how* things turned out as they did) and the formal argument or explanation of *why* 'things happened or turned out as they did' are *prefigured* by the original description (of the 'facts' to be explained) in a given dominant modality.[8]

The modality in question here is that of the liturgy and of the dynamic interaction between the various people and powers that influenced it.

[4] Several adequate histories of the Jerusalem patriarchate that consider the variety of linguistic sources do exist. The recent article on the Jerusalem patriarchate from the seventh to the thirteenth centuries by Constantin A. Panchenko, 'Иерусалимская православная церковь', ПЭ 21: 466–76, serves as an excellent introduction to this complex period.

[5] This expression, used to define narrative, comes from David Hackett Fischer, *Albion's Seed: Four British Folkways in America* (New York: Oxford University Press, 1989), xi. See also Anna Green and Kathleen Troup, *The Houses of History: A Critical Reader in Twentieth-Century History and Theory* (Manchester: Manchester University Press, 1999), 211.

[6] See for example Gil, *History of Palestine*, esp. 430–89, whose detailed history of the period between 634 and 1099 gives little information on the relations between Christians and Jews.

[7] See ibid., 436–42; Johannes Pahlitzsch and Daniel Baraz, 'Christian Communities in the Latin Kingdom of Jerusalem (1099–1187 CE)', in *Christians and Christianity in the Holy Land: From the Origins to the Latin Kingdoms*, ed. by Ora Limor and Guy G. Stroumsa (Turnhout: Brepols, 2006), 205–35.

[8] Hayden White, 'The Fictions of Factual Representation', in Anna Green and Kathleen Troup, *The Houses of History: A Critical Reader in Twentieth-Century History and Theory* (Manchester: Manchester University Press, 1999), 214–29, here 221–2. Originally published in *The Literature of Fact*, ed. by Angus Fletcher (New York: Columbia University Press, 1976), 21–44.

THE JERUSALEM PATRIARCHATE

The focus of this study is the liturgical practice of the Orthodox Chalcedonian patriarchate of Jerusalem from the eighth to the thirteenth centuries and within its own territory, which covered the Roman provinces of Palestine. The position of Sinai on the Hagiopolitan periphery raises the question of other 'peripheries'. How far from Jerusalem did its liturgical tradition and influence spread? Certain liturgical documents originating well beyond Palestine—as far as the Khwārezmian empire near the Caspian Sea, as documented by al-Bīrūnī—suggest Hagiopolitan connections and will be examined here briefly.[9] Jerusalem's own position on the Constantinopolitan periphery is what makes it of interest within the study of Byzantine liturgy.[10]

Orthodoxy

In this study, 'Orthodox' refers to those Chalcedonian hierarchs who were in Communion with the ecumenical patriarch of Constantinople; and the designation 'Chalcedonian' means that they accepted the teaching of the Fourth Ecumenical Council held in Chalcedon in 451, which defined Christ as one person in two natures.[11] The majority of Christians in Palestine before and after the Arab conquest of Jerusalem were Chalcedonian Christians. Anastasius of Sinai (7th cent.) believed that all the holy sites of Jerusalem and of the Holy Land were in the hands of the Chalcedonian church because the latter's teaching was the true one.[12] Incidentally, non-Chalcedonian pilgrims were sometimes reluctant to visit Jerusalem on account of Chalcedonian control there.[13] That said, pilgrimage to the Holy Land was still important for non-Chalcedonians after the Arab conquest and Jacobite monastic establishments probably existed in Jerusalem from the end of the eighth century onwards.[14] Boundaries of religious affiliation in Byzantine Palestine were also quite flexible, as Christians from various jurisdictions, Jews, and even pagans often venerated the same holy sites or relics of holy monks.[15] A quick glance

---

[9] See al-Bīrūnī, *Fêtes des Melchites*. This source is connected to 'Melkites' in Khwārazm, near the Aral Sea. See Hugh Kennedy, ed., *An Historical Atlas of Islam*, 2nd rev. edn (Brill: Boston, MA, 2002), 8, 9. For more on 'Melkite' liturgy beyond Palestine and Jerusalem, see Taft, 'Worship on Sinai', 161–2 n. 58; Jean-Maurice Fiey, 'Rūm à l'est de l'Euphrate', Mus 90: 3–4 (1977), 365–420.

[10] Parenti, *L'Eucologio slavo del Sinai*, esp. 21–22; Parenti, 'Towards a Regional History'.

[11] Timothy Ware, *The Orthodox Church*, rev. edn (London: Penguin, 1993), 4; John Meyendorff, *Byzantine Theology: Historical Trends and Doctrinal Themes* (New York: Fordham University Press, 1987), 32–41.

[12] Anastasius of Sinai, *Quaestiones et Responsiones*, PG 89:767–70.

[13] Schick, *Christian Communities of Palestine*, 9–10.   [14] Ibid., 72–82.

[15] Perrone, 'Monasticism', 74.

at a list of bishops of the church of Jerusalem confirms that the Orthodox presence was dominant; but it also reveals the complexity of the ecclesial situation in the Holy City after the fallout of the fourth ecumenical council at Chalcedon. Apart from the bishops common to the whole early Christian church in Jerusalem (whose successors the Greek Orthodox patriarchate of Jerusalem claims for itself until the present day), continuous lists of parallel hierarchies begin to appear after the Arab conquest in 638. Fragmentary lists of individual archbishops of Jerusalem are identified as Arian, semi-Arian, or Miaphysite; but bishops of the non-Chalcedonian West Syrian and Armenian churches that claimed descent from James, the traditional first bishop of Jerusalem, have been present in Jerusalem from the seventh century until today.[16] The Armenian bishops were elevated to patriarchal status in 1311. Testimonies for a continuous Coptic hierarchy in Jerusalem begin to appear in 1236. In lists of the bishops of various Christian jurisdictions in Jerusalem, bishops claiming the title of 'Anglican bishop of Jerusalem' begin in 1841 and bishops claiming the title of 'Latin patriarch of Jerusalem' begin in 1847. The latter were restored by Rome after having been effectively eliminated from the Holy Land in 1291.[17]

Finding an Arian or a Miaphysite bishop among the lists of the church of Jerusalem may be surprising, but one must be aware that certain theological debates, resolved in Byzantium, continued to linger on in Palestine.

In the face of Muslim occupation, Communion between Jerusalem and Constantinople was never disrupted, as it had been in Antioch and Alexandria, where the ecumenical patriarch could not be commemorated after the arrival of the Umayyads (*c*.661) until 937.[18] Nevertheless, the situation did make it difficult for Hagiopolitan patriarchs to participate in church councils within the Byzantine empire.[19] Diminished contact between Jerusalem and Constantinople was exacerbated by Constantinopolitan support for Monotheletism, encouraging closer ties between Jerusalem and Rome. In the years following the Arab conquest, and in the absence of a patriarch of Jerusalem, Pope Martin I (649–53) mediated ecclesiastical appointments within the Jerusalem patriarchate, which Palestinian monks welcomed owing to Rome's opposition to Monotheletism.[20]

---

[16] For greater clarity on this terminology, see Sebastian P. Brock, 'The Syriac Orient: A Third "Lung" for the Church?', OCP 71 (2005), 5–20; *Les liturgies syriaques*, ed. by François Cassingena-Trévedy and Izabela Jurasz (Études syriaques 3, Paris: Geuthner, 2006), 296–7.

[17] For more on the presence of non-Chalcedonians in Jerusalem, see George Every, 'Syrian Christians in Jerusalem, 1183–1283', *Eastern Churches Quarterly* 7 (1947–8), here 50–1; Andrew Palmer, 'The History of the Syrian Orthodox in Jerusalem', *Oriens Christianus* 75 (1991), 16–43, esp. 25–38. For complete lists of all these jurisdictions, see Fedalto, *Hierarchia ecclesiastica orientalis*, vol. 2, 999–1013.

[18] Nasrallah, *Histoire* II.2, 17.   [19] Nasrallah, *Histoire* II.1, 56–7.

[20] Pope Martin I, *Epistola VIII, ad Georgium archimandritam monasterii sancti Theodosii*, PL 87:167–8; id., *Epistola IX, ad Pantaleonem*, PL 87:169–74; Gil, *History of Palestine*, 433–4.

The titles of liturgical texts from Jerusalem reflect the developing doctrinal and ecclesial situation. The title of the AL is 'Memorial of the synaxes that are held in Jerusalem in the holy place of Christ, in which is indicated the number of the month and the reading of the day, and in which is indicated the psalm proper to the feast and memory'.[21] Here there is no question of 'right worship', only an emphasis on the importance of the holy sites for the church of Jerusalem. The title of the kanonarion–synaxarion of Constantinople is similar, mentioning only the place and the content of the liturgical source:

Κανὼν τῆς ἁγίας τοῦ Θεοῦ Μεγάλης Ἐκκλησίας ἀναγνώσεων πράξεων, ἀποστόλων, εὐαγγελίων καὶ προφητικῶν, καὶ ἑκάστης ἀκολουθίας ἀπὸ τῆς κυριακῆς πρὸ τῆς ἀπόκρεω μέχρι τῆς Ν΄ ἐπιδημίας τοῦ Ἁγίου Πνεύματος.[22]	Canon of the holy Great Church of God of the readings of the Acts, Epistles, Gospels, and Prophets, and every service from the Sunday of Meatfare until the Descent of the Holy Spirit on Pentecost.

Back in Palestine, the later, post-Chalcedonian GL emphasizes its own Orthodoxy within the city of Jerusalem with a different title:

ესე განწესებაჲ და განგებაჲ მოძღუართა მიერ მართლმორწმუნეთა-თა რომელსა ჰყოფენ იჱრუსალჱმს.[23]	This is the rite and order from Orthodox teachers (*možġowart'a mier mart'lmorcmowney*), which they do in Jerusalem.

Holy sites are taken for granted, but the need to establish the orthodoxy of the text is made clear. This is echoed in St Theodosius the Cenobiarch's (d. 11 January 529)[24] vehement response to the anti-Chalcedonian Patriarch John III of Jerusalem (r. 516–24): 'If someone does not accept the four councils as the four Gospels, let him be anathema!'[25] Such tensions between Chalcedonian and non-Chalcedonian Christians in Jerusalem are not as readily discernible today, because much of the Greek anti-Chalcedonian hagiography and other

---

[21] AL, 72–3. For more on the AL, see 'The Armenian Lectionary' in Chapter 1 here.

[22] Mateos, *Typicon*, vol. 2, 2.

[23] GL § 1. See Kekelidze, *Kanonarion*, 12 n. 2, for a discussion of this title and its translation. Kekelidze translates the word მოძღუართა as 'hierarchs' (святителей), although its literal meaning is 'teachers'.

[24] Alexander Kazhdan and Nancy Patterson-Ševčenko, 'Theodosios the Koinobiarches', ODB III, 2053.

[25] εἴ τις οὐ δέχεται τὰς τέσσαρας συνόδους ὡς τὰ τέσσαρα εὐαγγέλια, ἔστω ἀνάθεμα. *Life of Sabas*, chapter 56, in Schwartz, *Cyril of Scythopolis*, 152. For an analysis of the parallel between the Scriptures and the ecumenical councils, see also Schwartz, *Cyril of Scythopolis*, 155; Cirillo di Scitopoli, *Storie monastiche del deserto di Gerusalemme*, trans. by Romano Baldelli and Luciana Mortari (Praglia: Edizioni Scritti Monastici, 1990), 272 n. 186.

literature—which clearly opposed the doctrinal statements of the Council of Chalcedon—was destroyed after the Constantinopolitan synodal intervention in 536.[26] The surviving hagiography, such as the work of Cyril of Scythopolis, has been considered a 'propagandist regional history in the service of Chalcedonian orthodoxy and the Jerusalem patriarchate'.[27]

The Christian Population and Its Languages

Egeria's account gives us valuable, though perhaps idealized, information on the life of Christians in Jerusalem, a heterogeneous and multilingual assembly consisting of Greek and Christian Palestinian Aramaic speakers, monastics and lay people—both locals and foreign pilgrims. Apart from their intense liturgical schedule, which required them to rise before cockcrow and to return to services several times during the day, they also fasted extensively during Lent, eating nothing but gruel and water.[28] Egeria's visit to Jerusalem not only made her an eyewitness to liturgical life but also alerted her to the separation and unity among the diverse language groups in Jerusalem. Her account reads as follows:

Et quoniam in ea prouincia pars populi et grece et siriste nouit, pars etiam alia per se grece, aliqua etiam pars tantum siriste, itaque quoniam episcopus, licet siristenouerit, tamen semper grece loquitur et nunquam siriste: itaque ergo stat semper presbyter, qui episcopo grece dicente, siriste interpretatur, ut omnes audient quae exponuntur. Lectiones etiam, quecumque in ecclesia leguntur, quia necesse est grece legi, semper stat, qui siriste interpretatur propter populum, ut semper discant. Sane quicumque hic latini sunt, id est qui nec siriste nec grece nouerunt, ne contristentur, et ipsis exponitur eis, quia sunt alii fratres et sorores grecolatini, qui latine exponent eis.[29]	Now in that province some of the people know both Greek and Syriac, while some know Greek alone and others only Syriac; and because the bishop, although he knows Syriac, always speaks Greek and never Syriac, there is always a priest standing by who, when the bishop speaks Greek, interprets into Syriac, so that all may understand what is being taught. And because all the lessons that are read in the church must be read in Greek, he always stands by and interprets them into Syriac, for the people's sake, that they may always be edified. Moreover, the Latins here, who understand neither Syriac nor Greek, in order that they not be disappointed, have (everything) explained to them, for there are other brothers and sisters, knowledgeable of both Greek and Latin, who translate into Latin for them.

---

[26] *Acta conciliorum oecumenicorum*, vol. 3: *Collectio Sabbaitica contra acephalos et origeniastas destinata: insunt acta synodorum Constantinopolitanae et Hierosolymitanae A. 536*, ed. by Eduard Schwartz (Berlin: W. de Gruyter, 1940), 113, 121; Flusin, 'L'hagiographie palestinienne', 39.

[27] Bitton-Ashkelony and Kofsky, 'Monasticism in the Holy Land', 261.

[28] Egeria, *Itinéraire*, § 28: 1–4 (pp. 264–6 Maraval).

[29] Ibid., § 47: 3–4 (p. 314 Maraval).

It is often unclear what language is intended, since terms such as Syriac, Syro-Palestinian, and Aramaic are often used interchangeably. The term *siriste* here may actually designate 'the Syrian language', which was not exactly Christian Palestinian Aramaic, nor the written language of Edessene Syriac.[30] Egeria seems to imply that the relevance of the prayers, hymns, antiphons, and readings to the feast being commemorated and to the site where participants were celebrating made it easier for her to comprehend what was going on, even if she did not understand Greek.[31]

Although the bishop preached in Greek, he may not have been a native speaker of that language. Pierre Maraval senses Cyril of Jerusalem's frustration with the difficulties of the Greek language despite his classical education and knowledge of Greek philosophy.[32] As an example of Cyril's exasperation, Maraval points to the bishop's comment on students and education: 'they spend so many years learning grammar and other subjects only to speak Greek well; and yet not all of them speak Greek equally well'.[33] This suggests that Cyril's native tongue was probably Christian Palestinian Aramaic.[34]

Apart from the indigenous Aramaic-speaking population, Armenians and Georgians were also a significant presence in the Holy Land from the time of their Christianization. These two groups are of particular importance for the study of the Hagiopolite liturgy, because they have preserved the most comprehensive manuscripts describing liturgical life in early Christian Jerusalem—specifically the AL, GL, and the *Iadgari*—which have been mostly lost in the original Greek or in other possible translations, such as Syriac or Christian Palestinian Aramaic. During the Christological controversies of the fifth century Armenians opposed the Chalcedonian doctrinal formulations, but they did not break Communion with Constantinople until the second council of Dvin in 555.[35] Ecclesiastical union between Armenia and Byzantium had been achieved twice after the Council of Chalcedon, in 572 and 591, but the Armenians in Palestine were no longer in Communion with the Jerusalem and Constantinople patriarchates after the seventh century.[36] Therefore their sources do not represent the liturgical practice of the Chalcedonian Orthodox patriarchate of Jerusalem during the period of Byzantinization and are not examined here.

---

[30] See Nasrallah, *Histoire* II.2, 183; Nasrallah, 'Liturgie des Patriarcats melchites', 160; Scott Fitzgerald Johnson, 'Introduction: The Social Presence of Greek in Eastern Christianity, 200–1200 CE', in *Languages and Cultures of Eastern Christianity: Greek*, ed. by Scott Fitzgerald Johnson (Farnham: Ashgate, 2015), 1–122, here 4–7.

[31] Egeria, *Itinéraire*, § 47: 5 (pp. 314–16 Maraval).

[32] See Jan Willem Drijvers, *Cyril of Jerusalem: Bishop and City* (Leiden: Brill, 2004), 31.

[33] τοσούτοις ἔτεσι διὰ γραμματικῆς καὶ διὰ τεχνῶν μανθάνουσι μόνον Ἑλληνιστὶ καλῶς λαλεῖν. Καὶ οὐδὲ πάντες λαλοῦσιν ὁμοίως. Cyril of Jerusalem, *Catechesis* 17: 16 (= PG 33: 988).

[34] See Maraval's observation in Egeria, *Itinéraire*, 315 n. 3.

[35] See Thomson, *Armenian History Attributed to Sebeos*, 37.

[36] Charles Renoux, *Le lectionnaire de Jérusalem en Arménie: Le Čašocʿ. I: Introduction et liste des manuscrits* (PO 44.4, Turnhout: Brepols, 1989), 18.

Except for a brief period of separation after the time of Peter the Iberian (*c*.409–88), the Georgians maintained Communion with Constantinople and constituted an important minority in the Hagiopolitan church.[37] Georgians were already present in Palestine in the fifth century during the reign of King Vaxtang I Gorgasali (r. 447–522) and are mentioned by the name of Bessoi (*Βέσσοι*) in the *Life* of St Theodosius the Cenobiarch by Theodore of Petra.[38] For them, Jerusalem was the 'mother of all churches' and the cradle of Georgian Christianity, whence they willingly received their liturgical and religious traditions. The importance of Jerusalem for Georgians can also be gleaned from their relations with Byzantium: according to the church-political sense of the Georgians, Constantinople was not 'New Rome' but 'New Jerusalem'.[39]

Melkites: A Subgroup?

Another term that requires closer examination is 'Melkite', today often used to designate the Greek Catholic Church in the Middle East.[40] The first patriarch to restore Communion with Rome (in 1724) was Patriarch Cyril VI Tanas of Antioch (1680–1760), who is considered the first Melkite Greek Catholic patriarch. But in scholarly circles the adjective 'Melkite' could be used inter-changeably with 'Orthodox' when referring to Christians in Jerusalem before 1724, often without further elaboration. The Greek name *μελκῖται* or *μελχῖται* derives from the Syriac *mălkāyā* and the Arabic *malakī*, which means 'royal' or 'imperial' and refers to the imperial church or those who followed the faith of the Byzantine emperor.[41] The term *μάλχος* was already used by the sophist and historian Eunapius of Sardis in the fourth and fifth centuries; it meant

---

[37] Robert W. Thomson and Timothy E. Gregory, 'Peter the Iberian', ODB III, 1642; Horn and Phenix, *Lives*, xxxi–xxxii; Tarchnishvili, 'Ecclesial Autocephaly of Georgia', 98–9.

[38] BHG 1776. The *Βέσσοι* are probably Georgians and not Thracians, as in Strabo, *Geography* 7.5.12. See Kekelidze, *Канонарь*, 33; *Le nouveau manuscrit géorgien sinaïtique N Sin 50: Édition en fac-similé*, introduced by Z. Aleksidzé, trans. by J.-P. Mahé (CSCO 586, Louvain: Peeters, 2001), 1; Stephen Rapp, *Studies in Medieval Georgian Historiography: Early Texts and Eurasian Contexts* (CSCO 601, Leuven: Peeters, 2003), 305–6 and 319.

[39] Tarchnishvili, 'Ecclesial Autocephaly of Georgia', 102.

[40] See Korolevsky, *Christian Antioch*, 153–67 for the history of the separation from the Orthodox patriarchate and 255–64 for a list of the hierarchy. See also Griffith, 'The Church of Jerusalem and the "Melkites"', 190; Panchenko, *Arab Orthodox Christians*, 2, 4–7, 506.

[41] Timothy E. Gregory, 'Melchites', ODB II, 1332; Griffith, 'The Church of Jerusalem and the "Melkites"', 203–4; Sidney H. Griffith, *The Church in the Shadow of the Mosque: Christians and Muslims in the World of Islam* (Princeton, NJ: Princeton University Press, 2008), 139; '*Μελχῖται*', in *ΘΗΕ* 8: 990; Sebastian P. Brock, 'Melkite', in GEDSH, 285. The term is completely absent from Lampe, *Patristic Greek Lexicon*, and from Trapp, *Lexikon zur byzantinischen Gräzität*. There is, to my knowledge, no scholarly study of the origins and use of this Greek term.

'king' or 'royal', which Eunapius noted was a Syriac loan word.[42] There appear to be few examples of Chalcedonian Christians using this term self-referentially before the fifteenth century and, when they did use it themselves, it was to affirm their faithfulness to God—the 'heavenly king', as opposed to the Byzantine (or some other temporal) ruler.[43] In fact the term was used more commonly by members of non-Chalcedonian churches, who meant it pejoratively to describe Chalcedonians. The Coptic Bishop Severus ibn al-Muqaffaʿ (d. 987) applied the term to 'the members of that council [of Chalcedon] and all the followers of their corrupt creed' who, according to him, 'follow the opinion of the prince and his wife, in proclaiming and renewing the doctrine of Nestorius'.[44] Incidentally, this is somewhat ironic if one recalls that the Melkites of Jerusalem remained Orthodox even when the Byzantine emperor had become Monothelite or iconoclast.[45]

Despite the common recourse of all members of the Orthodox patriarchate of Jerusalem to the Byzantine emperor and his faith, the term 'Melkite' could have more than just dogmatic connotations. Sidney Griffith has shown that the crusaders distinguished between 'Syrians', who spoke the 'Saracen' language but used Greek for liturgy, and the 'Greek Orthodox', also known as 'Rūm Orthodox' or 'ar-Rūm'.[46] This distinction is the source of Griffith's proposed Melkite Arab Orthodox Christian identity, characterized by a theology formulated in Greek by St John of Damascus (c.675–753/4), the foremost Melkite theologian who also knew Arabic.[47] Theodore Abū Qurrah (c.740–825), bishop of Ḥarrān and probably a native of the city of Edessa,

---

[42] Charles du Fresne du Cange, *Glossarium ad scriptores mediæ et infimæ Græcitatis* (Lyons: Anissonion, Posuel, and Rigaud, 1688), 859 and 902. See also Henri Estienne, *Thesaurus graecae linguae*, vol. 6 (Geneva: H. Stephani Oliva, 1580; repr. Graz: Akademische Druck, 1954), 558 and 763. Du Cange notes that Theophanes Kerameus, *In pretiosam Jesu Christi Passionem*, PG 132: 550–606, uses the term 'Melkite' and explains it as equivalent to 'royal'. For more on this figure, see Alexander Kazhdan, 'Theophanes of Sicily', ODB 3:2062–3; M. Théarvic [Jules Pargoire], 'A propos de Théophane le Sicilien', *Échos d'Orient* 7 (1904), 31–4, 164–71.

[43] Alexander Treiger, 'Unpublished Text from the Arab Orthodox Tradition (1): On the Origin of the Term "Melkite" and On the Destruction of the Maryamiyya Cathedral in Damascus', *Chronos: Revue d'Histoire de l'Université de Balamand* 29 (2014), 7–37.

[44] Severus ibn al-Muqaffaʿ, *History of the Patriarchs of the Coptic Church of Alexandria*, vol. 2: *Peter I to Benjamin I (661)*, ed. and trans. by B. Evetts (PO 1.4, Paris: Firmin-Didot, 1907), 443–4 (Part 1, Chapter 13).

[45] Mango, 'Greek Culture in Palestine', 159. Auzépy, however, delves further into this question and suggests that Chalcedonian Palestine may not have been as iconophile as we have been led to believe. See Auzépy, 'De la Palestine à Constantinople', 192–3. For more on this question, see 'Byzantine Iconoclasm and Its Impact on Palestine' in this chapter.

[46] Griffith, 'The Church of Jerusalem and the "Melkites"', 175–6.

[47] Alexander Kazhdan, 'John of Damascus', ODB II, 1063–4; Daniel J. Sahas, *John of Damascus on Islam: The 'Heresy of the Ishmaelites'* (Leiden: Brill, 1972); Louth, *St John Damascene*, 3–14; Petrynko, *Weihnachtskanon*, 51–83; Mango, 'Greek Culture in Palestine', 159; Griffith, 'The Church of Jerusalem and the "Melkites"', 186–90. For a list of hymnographic works by St John of Damascus, see Sophronios Leontopoleos, "Ὁ ἅγιος Ἰωάννης ὁ Δαμασκηνὸς καὶ τὰ ποιητικὰ αὐτοῦ ἔργα', ΝΣ 26 (1931), 497–512, 530–8, 610–17, 666–81, 721–36; ΝΣ 27

was one of the first to compose Melkite apologetics in Arabic in order to respond to non-Chalcedonian Christians and to Islam.[48] Thus Griffith views the Melkites as a 'culturally, historically, and socially distinguishable subset' of the Rūm Orthodox or Jerusalem patriarchate.[49]

When examined from the perspective of liturgical texts, such a distinction between Melkites and the other Orthodox of the Jerusalem patriarchate is, however, not as clear as Griffith presents it. Granted, the context of Palestine—which is significantly different from that of Constantinople—helps to explain why Melkites viewed themselves as the 'church of the six councils' long after the seventh ecumenical council in 787. Jerusalem's church had no need for its own ecclesiastical council to combat Christian iconoclasm internally, because it was concerned with external accusations of idolatry from Jews and Muslims.[50] This is reflected in liturgical manuscripts, which often make reference to only six ecumenical councils, even if they were copied after 787.[51] Several references are made to the 'six synods' in liturgical texts after the eighth century that include the calendar of al-Bīrūnī and several manuscripts of JAS.[52] Nevertheless, the omission of the seventh ecumenical council is not limited to liturgical manuscripts used by Arab Orthodox. Despite the apparent urgency to have the fourth ecumenical council included in diptychs within the Sabaite monastic milieu during the sixth-century Christological controversies,[53] the first extant Hagiopolite liturgical manuscript to mention the seventh ecumenical council at Nicaea was copied as late as the fourteenth-century and is found in the Diakonikon for JAS preserved in manuscript *Sinai Gr. 1040*.[54] Only two other known Greek manuscripts of JAS mention seven ecumenical councils in the diptychs, namely *Koutloumoussiou Gr. 194* (14th cent.) and *Paris Suppl. Gr. 476* (15th cent.).[55] Georgian manuscripts of JAS are also resistant to having more than six councils commemorated in the diptychs.[56] Likewise, the Testament of St Theodore the Stoudite, read aloud

(1932), 28–44, 111–23, 165–77, 216–24, 329–53, 415–22, 450–72, 514–34, 570–85, 644–64, 698–719; ΝΣ 28 (1933), 11–25.

[48] Sidney H. Griffith and Alexander Kazhdan, 'Theodore Abu-Qurra', ODB III, 2041; John C. Lamoreaux, 'The Biography of Theodore Abū Qurrah Revisited', DOP 56 (2002), 25–40; John C. Lamoreaux, *Theodore Abū Qurrah* (Library of the Christian East 1, Provo, UT: Brigham Young University, 2005).

[49] Griffith, 'The Church of Jerusalem and the "Melkites"', 204.

[50] Ibid., 191–7.   [51] Ibid., 197.

[52] al-Bīrūnī, *Fêtes des Melchites*, 18–19, 26; Mercier, *Liturgie de Saint Jacques*, 104.

[53] *Life of Sabas*, ch. 60, in Schwartz, *Cyril of Scythopolis*, 162.

[54] Καὶ τῶν ἁγίων μεγάλων ἑπτὰ Συνόδων...('And of the seven holy great councils...'). Brightman, *Eastern Liturgies*, 502. This part of the diptychs for the dead from JAS is not included in Dmitrievskii's transcription. See Dmitrievskii, Описание II, 134. For more on this source, see Appendix 1.

[55] See Mercier, *Liturgie de Saint Jacques*, 218; Kazamias, Θεία Λειτουργία τοῦ Ἁγίου Ἰακώβου, 206.

[56] *Liturgia ibero-graeca*, 96 and 165.

just before his death in 826, only refers to 'six holy and ecumenical councils' and then to the 'Second Council of Nicaea which was recently assembled'.[57] Thus the title 'church of the six councils' cannot be limited to those members of the Jerusalem patriarchate that match other criteria of Arab Christian identity. This may explain why the term 'Melkite' has never been more clearly defined within Byzantine studies and Byzantine liturgiology, and why it is used broadly to define any liturgical practice originating on the territory of the patriarchates of Alexandria, Antioch, and Jerusalem, regardless of language— Greek, Georgian, Arabic, or Syriac.[58]

Even if they could be considered a 'distinguishable subset' of the Rūm Orthodox, Melkites were always an integral part of the Jerusalem patriarchate, alongside Greek- and Georgian-praying Christians, united under a single hierarchy that was not divided along ethnic or linguistic lines. The depiction of Christian Arabs in Byzantine art confirms their integration and assimilation into the ecclesial community. In Byzantine illumination, Christian monks of Arab origin were indistinguishable from their Greek brethren, while nomadic or Muslim Arab aggressors could be depicted as Romans, recalling the time of pre-Constantinian persecution.[59] Arabs could, however, be grouped under their own bishop. For example, the Bedouin sheikh Peter Aspebet, who had his tribe baptized by Euthymius, was later consecrated bishop of Parembolae (ἐν Παλαιστίνῃ Πέτρος τῶν Παρεμβολῶν ἐπίσκοπος) by Juvenal in the fifth century for the Arab tribes in the region.[60]

Jerusalem's liturgical practices were also shared by Melkite Christians in the Khwārezmian empire near the Aral Sea—in the very distant periphery of the Hagiopolite liturgical world.[61] The Muslim scholar and polymath Abū Rayḥān

---

[57] PG 99:1816; 'Theodore Studites', BMFD 1:76.

[58] The origins of this usage may be connected to Cyril Korolevsky, who associated the liturgical practices of the ancient eastern patriarchates with their eastern Catholic successors. See Charon, 'Le rite byzantin', 475. Anton Baumstark also refers to ancient Jerusalem liturgy as 'the Old Palestinian Melkite Rite'; see Baumstark, *Comparative Liturgy*, 223–4. This usage seems to have been followed by other liturgiologists of the Roman school, such as Robert Taft, Stefano Parenti, Elena Velkovska, and others, who refer generally to Greek prayers or practices originating from Middle Eastern liturgical manuscripts as 'Melkite'. See, for example, Taft, *Byzantine Rite*, 57; Parenti and Velkovska, *Барберини гр. 336*, 62; Radle, 'Sinai Gr. NE MΓ 22', 176–7.

[59] Vassilios Christidès, 'Pre-Islamic Arabs in Byzantine Illuminations', *Mus* 83 (1970), 167–81; Samir Arbache, 'Les moines chez les Arabes chrétiens avant l'islam', in *Le monachisme syriaque: Aux premiers siècles de l'Église, IIᵉ–début VIIᵉ siècle*, vol. 1 (Antélias, Lebanon: Editions du CERP, 1998), 299–304.

[60] *Life of Euthymios*, ch. 15, in Schwartz, *Cyril of Scythopolis*, 24–5; Siméon Vailhé, 'Le monastère de Saint Théoctiste (411) et l'évêché de Paremboles (425)', *Revue de l'Orient Chrétien* 3 (1898), 58–76; Irfan Shahîd, *Byzantium and the Arabs in the Fifth Century* (Washington, DC: Dumbarton Oaks, 2006), 40–1 and 181–4; Samir Arbache, 'Bible et liturgie chez les arabes chrétiens (VIᵉ–IXᵉ siècle)', in *The Bible in Arab Christianity*, ed. by David Thomas (Leiden: Brill, 2007), 37–48, here 39.

[61] *The Chronology of Ancient Nations* [al-Āthār al-bāqiya min al-qurūn al-khāliya], in Al-Bīrūnī, *Fêtes des Melchites*, 294–312. See also Anton Baumstark, 'Ausstrahlungen des

Muḥammad Ibn Aḥmad al-Bīrūnī (972/3–1050) recorded the calendar of the Khwārezmian Melkites—not actually a liturgical source but a list of feasts he observed them celebrate—in the fifteenth chapter of his *Chronology of Ancient Nations*.[62] The Melkite calendar is a fusion of the encyclopaedism prevalent in Constantinople, in the works of al-Bīrūnī's contemporary Symeon Metaphrastes,[63] as well as at Sinai, in the calendar of Iovane Zosime;[64] and it also shares similarities with a ninth-century Greek mixed-uncial fragment of a calendar found on Sinai.[65] Al-Bīrūnī presents a laconic inventory of saints and commemorations, along with occasionally enthusiastic first-hand observations that recall certain passages from Egeria's diary.

Al-Bīrūnī's calendar contains 141 entries, distinguishes between seventeen 'feasts' of greater solemnity and 124 'commemorations', and runs from 1 October (*Tishrīn I*) to 29 September (*Elul*), according to the Syrian year. The author's digressions from the list include descriptions of the ecclesiastical and civil hierarchy of the Greeks, the feast of Calends, the rite of baptism, the teachings of the six councils, the burial of John the Baptist, and the story of the Seven Sleepers of Ephesus, to name a few topics. Forty-eight entries are characteristically Hagiopolitan commemorations such as the feast of Sts James and David on 26 December; several commemorations of the Cross on 7 May and 14 September; feasts of the Anastasis Church on 3 and 13 June and 24 September; of John the Baptist on 10 and 26 October, 24 February, 1 and 25 June, and 29 August; and joint commemorations of prophets, Evangelists, and Apostles.[66] Despite the great distance between the Khwārezmian Melkites and Jerusalem, their calendar contained many of the same holidays as the Holy City.

vorbyzantinischen Heiligenkalenders von Jerusalem', OCP 2 (1936), 129–44; Galadza, 'Melkite Calendar'; Jean-Maurice Fiey, 'Rūm à l'est de l'Euphrate', Mus 90 (1977), 365–420; Ken Parry, 'Byzantine-Rite Christians (Melkites) in Central Asia in Late Antiquity and the Middle Ages', *Modern Greek Studies* 16 (2012), 91–108.

[62] Edward S. Kennedy, 'Al-Bīrūnī, Abū Rayḥān Muḥammad Ibn Aḥmad', *Dictionary of Scientific Biography*, vol. 1, ed. by Charles Coulston Gillispie (New York: Charles Scribner's Sons, 1981), 148–51; Lawrence I. Conrad, 'Bīrūnī, Al-', ODB I, 291. For the complete work, see Al-Bīrūnī, *The Chronology of Ancient Nations*, ed. and trans. by E. Sachau (London: William H. Allen, 1879).

[63] Alexander Kazhdan, 'Encyclopedism', ODB I, 696–7; Alexander Kazhdan and Nancy Patterson-Ševčenko, 'Symeon Metaphrastes', ODB III, 1983–4; Christian Høgel, *Symeon Metaphrastes: Rewriting and Canonization* (Copenhagen: Museum Tusulanum Press of the Univeristy of Copenhagen, 2002).

[64] Garitte, *Calendrier palestino-géorgien*. See Appendix 1 here.

[65] Stefano Parenti and Elena Velkovska, 'Two Leaves of a Calendar Written in "Mixed" Uncial of the 9th Century', BBGG (terza serie) 7 (2010), 297–306.

[66] The 15 May feast of the Theotokos is also found in some Syriac Jacobite calendars. See the entries for this date in F. Nau, *Un Martyrologe et douze Ménologes syriaques* (PO 10.1, Paris: Firmin-Didot, 1915), 1–163.

Sacred Topography

The importance of the holy sites of Jerusalem is emphasized in every genre of literature connected to the Holy City, from liturgical texts to travel diaries and even theological writings. Hadrian's destruction of the city in 135 had cleared the way for a new topography, which completely expunged any previous symbolism. But the written accounts of the Scriptures, as well as the oral tradition, filled this void and provided a sacred topography on which churches and shrines were built.[67] In Jerusalem itself, the Romans introduced two main axes, the 950-metre north–south *cardo maximus* and the 600-metre east–west *decumanus maximus*. Incidentally, this created an urban area much smaller than in other major urban centres of the time, such as Antioch or Rome.[68]

In JAS, the first lines of the Diptychs for the Living, echoing Galatians 4:26 and Psalm 86:5, read:

Προσφέρομέν σοι, δέσποτα, καὶ ὑπὲρ τῶν ἁγίων σου τόπων, οὓς ἐδόξασας τῇ θεοφανείᾳ τοῦ Χριστοῦ σου καὶ τῇ ἐπιφοιτήσει τοῦ παναγίου σου πνεύματος, προηγουμένως ὑπὲρ τῆς ἁγίας καὶ ἐνδόξου Σιὼν τῆς μητρὸς πασῶν τῶν ἐκκλησιῶν...[69]	We make this offering to you, O Master, also for your holy places, which you glorified by the divine manifestation of your Christ and by the visitation of your all-holy Spirit, first of all for the holy and glorious Sion, mother of all the churches.

The same passage reads as follows in the Georgian text of JAS:

შევსწირავთ შენდა, უფალო, საშინელსა ამას და უსისხლოსა მსხუერჯლსა წმიდათა შენთა ადგილთათჳს, რომელნი ადიდენ გამოჩინებითა ქრისტე შენისათა; პირველად წმიდისათჳს და დიდებულისა სიონისა, დედისა ყოველთა ეკლესიათათისა...[70]	We offer you, O Lord, this awful and bloodless sacrifice for your holy places which you have glorified by the appearance of your Christ; first of all, for the holy and glorious Sion, the mother of all churches...

The meteoric rise of Jerusalem in late antiquity, from the honour granted its bishop in the seventh canon of the first ecumenical council to its recognition as patriarchate in 451 thanks to the efforts Bishop Juvenal of Jerusalem, gave it a prominent place in the imperial church and made it *the* central pilgrimage

---

[67] Virgilio Canio Corbo, 'Le fonti del Nuovo Testament sul pellegrinaggio ai luoghi santi della Palestina', in *Kongress für Christliche Archäologie*, 167–83.

[68] Baldovin, *Urban Character*, 45.   [69] Mercier, *Liturgie de Saint Jacques*, 206.

[70] *Sinai Geo. N. 58* (9th–10th cent.), fol. 21v; *Liturgia ibero-graeca*, 86–7, along with the English translation.

site in the Roman empire, a position it preserved even among those who rejected Chalcedon.[71]

Pilgrimage

While much has been written about Christian pilgrimage to the Holy Land until the seventh century, the same is not true for the period after the Arab conquest.[72] The earliest Byzantine description of these holy sites comes from the eighth or ninth century and was written by Epiphanius Hagiopolites, of whom little is known.[73] A pilgrimage to Palestine under Emperor Leo III (r. 717–41)[74] around 734 turned into a one-way trip to martyrdom for sixty pilgrims when they were put to death by Muslim authorities. Their *Passio* was originally written in Syriac and soon translated into Greek.[75] Subsequent pilgrims also experienced persecution and were memorialized in Constanti-nopolitan synaxaria.[76]

Despite these difficulties, it is known that Greek pilgrims continued to visit Jerusalem and the holy sites without interruption. Right up until a few years before the destruction of the Anastasis in 1009, the Holy City enjoyed a status far superior to that of any pilgrimage site and beyond its patriarchal status as authorized by any church council.[77] A major difference in the middle and late Byzantine periods is the absence of women pilgrims. During the late antique and early Byzantine periods their presence was common and included many

---

[71] Siméon Vailhé, 'L'Érection du Patriarcat de Jérusalem, 451', *Revue de l'Orient Chrétien* 4 (1899), 44–57; Wilkinson, *Jerusalem Pilgrims*, 7–8; Perrone, 'Christian Holy Places', 15 and 36–37.

[72] Maraval, *Lieux saints*; Josef Engemann, 'Das Jerusalem der Pilger. Kreuzauffindung und Wallfahrt', in *Kongress für Christliche Archäologie*, 24–35.

[73] Alexander Kazhdan, 'Epiphanios Hagiopolites', ODB I, 714; Külzer, *Peregrinatio*, 14–20; H. Donner, 'Palästina-Beschreibung des Epiphanios Hagiopolita', *Zeitschrift des Deutschen Palästina-Vereins* 87 (1971), 42–91; Vasilii G. Vasilevskii, Διήγησις Ἐπιφανίου περὶ τῆς Ἱερουσαλὴμ καὶ τῶν ἐν αὐτῇ τόπων (ППС 11 [4.2], St Petersburg: Православное Палестинское Общество, 1886).

[74] Peter A. Hollingsworth, 'Leo III', ODB II, 1208–9.

[75] BHG 1217; Anastasios Papadopoulos-Kerameus, Μαρτύριον τῶν ἁγίων ἑξήκοντα νέων μαρτύρων τῶν ἐν τῇ ἁγίᾳ Χριστοῦ τοῦ Θεοῦ ἡμῶν πόλει ἐπὶ τῆς τυραννίδος τῶν Ἀράβων μαρτυρησάντων (ППС 34 [12.1], St Petersburg: Православное Палестинское Общество, 1892). The authenticity of the eleventh-century version by Symeon the Hesychast (BHG 1218) has been questioned. See A. Papadopoulos-Kerameus, 'IX. Ὀκτωβρίῳ κα'. Μαρτύριον τῶν ἁγίων ἐνδόξων μαρτύρων τοῦ Χριστοῦ ἑξήκοντα καὶ τρίων', in Συλλογὴ παλαιστινῆς καὶ συριακῆς ἁγιολογίας 1 (ППС 57 [19.3], St Petersburg: Православное Палестинское Общество, 1907), 136–63; George Huxley, 'The Sixty Martyrs of Jerusalem', *Greek, Roman and Byzantine Studies* 18 (1977), 369–74.

[76] See the notice for St Gregory of Acritas (*c*.780) in the synaxarion of Constantinople: Delehaye, *Synaxarium*, 372–3.

[77] Griffith, 'The Church of Jerusalem and the "Melkites"', 185.

noble women.[78] As for non-Chalcedonians, they came to be unwelcome, though this did not stop them from visiting Jerusalem and the Holy Land as pilgrims.[79] In the 650s, Catholicos Ishoʻyahb III of Adiabene (d. 659) was in contact with the church of Jerusalem and even solicited financial aid for the restoration of the Anastasis.[80] Later Byzantine authors from the twelfth century onward have left accounts of their own pilgrimages to Jerusalem. One of the most notable is that of John Phocas (*c*.1177), a well-educated pilgrim who provides unique accounts of the holy sites.[81]

For the liturgical historian, however, the most useful pilgrimage accounts are generally the earlier narrations. Egeria's account is unique in that it clearly describes daily liturgical services at the Anastasis.[82] For monastic liturgy, the *Narration of the Abbots John and Sophronius* also provides copious detail regarding the differences between rural Egyptian and Palestinian monastic traditions.[83] Kekelidze, however, is justified in lamenting that the descriptions of the holy sites left by pilgrims are often unable to satisfy scholarly accuracy and curiosity, due to their own contradictions.[84] In any case, I must note that the use of such sources can never replace the investigation of actual liturgical texts.[85]

The Development of Stational Liturgy

Despite their lacunary and fragmentary information, pilgrimage accounts bring elements of liturgical books to life. This is especially true of Egeria's account, in particular with regard to stational liturgy.[86] The system of stations

---

[78] Alice-Mary Talbot, 'Byzantine Pilgrimage to the Holy Land from the Eighth to the Fifteenth Century', in Patrich, *Sabaite Heritage*, 97–110, here 98–9.

[79] See the *Life of Euthymios*, in Schwartz, *Cyril of Scythopolis*, 47–9; Jean-Maurice Fiey, 'Le pèlerinage des Nestoriens et Jacobites à Jérusalem', *Cahiers de civilisation médiévale* 12 (1969), 113–26.

[80] Sebastian Brock, 'Syriac into Greek at Mar Saba: The Translation of St Isaac the Syrian', in Patrich, *Sabaite Heritage*, 201–8, here 202.

[81] PG 133:923–62; Ivan E. Troitskii, Ἰωάννου τοῦ Φωκᾶ, Ἔκφρασις ἐν συνόψει τῶν ἀπ᾽ Ἀντιοχείας μέχρις Ἱεροσολύμων κάστρων καὶ χωρῶν Συρίας, Φοινίκης καὶ τῶν κατὰ Παλαιστίνην ἁγίων τόπων (ΠΠС 23 [8.2], St Petersburg: Православное Палестинское Общество, 1889); *The Pilgrimage of Joannes Phocas in the Holy Land*, trans. by Aubrey Stewart (London: Adelphi, 1889); Alexander Kazhdan, 'Phokas, John', ODB III, 1667; Külzer, *Peregrinatio*, 20–1. For the later period, see Denys Pringle, *Pilgrimage to Jerusalem and the Holy Land, 1187–1291* (Crusade Texts in Translation 23, Surrey: Ashgate, 2012).

[82] See Chapter 1, 'The *Catecheses* of St Cyril of Jerusalem'.

[83] See Chapter 1, section 'Monastic Liturgy in Byzantine Jerusalem and Palestine'.

[84] Kekelidze, *Канонарь*, 29.

[85] Such a distinction is not made by Verhelst, who refers to the hypothetical 'Euchologia' of St Cyril of Jerusalem and of Egeria. See Verhelst, 'Liturgy of Jerusalem', 446.

[86] For more on stational liturgy, see Chapter 1, 'Stational Liturgy and the Topography of Jerusalem'.

in Jerusalem was further developed in the GL, providing commemorations for every day of the year at various churches and holy sites throughout the Holy City. Stéphane Verhelst notes that the GL uses various terms to describe its seventy-three stations.[87] These can be divided into three groups on the basis of their geography and titles in the GL. The first group of stations are biblical or apocryphal sites, such as Golgotha, the Church of Bethlehem, or the Cathedral of Sion.[88] The second category consists of foundations (შჱნებული, *šēnebuli*), that is, urban monastic communities of foreign monks who did not speak Aramaic, such as the Monastery of the Spoudaioi, the Foundation of Eudokia, or the Foundation of Melania.[89] The third category consists of villages (დაბაჲ, *dabay*) settled by local Aramaic-speaking monks.[90] Verhelst cautions that these categories, however, are not exclusive, serving more as a means of systematizing the numerous stations.[91] Nevertheless, Verhelst has noted that the GL omits stations at Euthymian or Sabaite monasteries, which he speculates may be due to the fallout from Miaphysite controversies around the time of Chalcedon and the ensuing Origenist disputes.[92] All stations listed in the GL date from before the Persian sack of Jerusalem in 614, showing simplification and reduction rather than expansion and development of the network of Hagiopolitan stational liturgy.[93]

In Constantinople, the synaxis of the day indicated in liturgical books was not the only liturgical celebration of the cathedral liturgy for that day.[94] What designated the primary celebration of the day was the presence of the bishop, and not necessarily the location where the synaxis was held. Whether or not this was the case in Jerusalem is unclear. However, it is clear that monks played a part in cathedral services in Jerusalem. This is, perhaps, how the calendar was generalized and the readings and hymns appropriate to the place and time gradually lost their importance and force: the cathedral monastics and the local monasteries that had a daily cycle of services and did not participate in the stational liturgy would hold the same services as the cathedral liturgy, but without moving from place to place within the space of the city. The *Narration of the Abbots John and Sophronius* confirms that monks were familiar with the services and ordo of cathedral liturgy in Jerusalem.[95] The absence of Euthymian and Sabaite monasteries from the GL's stations means these monasteries would have had greater freedom to modify their liturgical calendar and sanctoral cycle. Local monastic saints certainly figure

[87] For a complete list, see Verhelst, 'Lieux de station' I, 16–26. For a map, see 'Map of the City of Jerusalem, 4th–11th cent' in Appendix 2 here.

[88] Verhelst, 'Lieux de station' II, 247–73.

[89] Verhelst, 'Lieux de station' I, 35–58.

[90] Ibid., 28–35.

[91] Ibid., 58–60; Verhelst, 'Lieux de station' II, 273–4.

[92] Verhelst, 'Lieux de station' I, 58–9. For more on these disputes, see Booth, *Crisis of Empire*.

[93] Verhelst, 'Lieux de station' II, 275; Baldovin, *Urban Character*, 100–2.

[94] See '*λειτουργία*', in Mateos, *Typicon*, vol. 2, 302–3; Baldovin, *Urban Character*, 205–6.

[95] Longo, 'Narrazione', 236.

more prominently in the earliest extant Sabaite liturgical calendars, such as *Sinai Gr. 1096* (12th cent.) and *Sinai Gr. 1097* (1214). Whether monastic revisions to the common Hagiopolitan sanctoral cycle began before 614 or only after the Arab conquest is unclear. Nevertheless, a Sabaite calendar distinct from the cathedral rite of Jerusalem must have been well established by the tenth century, since Iovane Zosime is able to distinguish between a 'Jerusalem model' (იერუსალémიsაyta, *ierusalēmisayta*) and a contemporaneous Sabaite model (საბაწმიდისაyta, *sabacmidisayta*) in the calendar he copied in manuscript *Sinai Geo. O. 34* (10th cent.).

Palestinian Monasticism

The common language of these monasteries was Greek, but Syrian and Georgian monks were integral members of these communities. I will examine the liturgy in the general context of Palestinian monasticism before turning to the particularities of Greek, Syrian, and Georgian monasticism in the Jerusalem patriarchate. However, a complete picture of Byzantine monasticism in the Holy Land is still lacking, because most studies of fifth-century theological controversies generalize the situation in Palestine and equate it with that of Syria or Egypt.[96] More recently, Phil Booth has focused on the activity of three Palestinian monks—John Moschus, Sophronius of Jerusalem, and Maximus Confessor—showing the important role of a more 'sacramentalized' and liturgically integrated monasticism at the service of the church in the sixth and seventh centuries.[97]

Liturgical sources reveal two kinds of monastic rites: the communal and/or private services obligatory for monks every day, and the less frequent communal services for the whole community. These existed side by side in Jerusalem, with monastic influence eventually causing the expansion of the cathedral *cursus* from a daily morning and evening service to a multiplicity of daily offices observed even by the laity.[98]

The Horologion of *Sinai Geo. O. 34* (10th cent.) is particular because it contains a daily cursus of twenty-four hours, divided between 'public' (საჲროჲ, *saeroy*) services and simpler services of ascetics. The public services were intended for the whole monastic community and contained elements from cathedral usage, such as prayers from the Jerusalem Euchologion and a programme of reading selected—rather than continuous—psalmody.[99] As the ascetic services were also prayed in common in the church, rather than privately in the monks' cells, the main characteristic of the ascetic services

[96] See Perrone, 'Monasticism', 68.   [97] Booth, *Crisis of Empire.*
[98] Baumstark, *Comparative Liturgy*, 111–13.
[99] Frøyshov, *Horologe 'géorgien'*, vol. 2, 425–546, esp. 542–6.

was in their simple structure, consisting primarily of a fixed psalm, a continuous reading of variable psalmody, and a prayer.[100] Until Frøyshov's work on *Sinai Geo. O. 34* (10th cent.), only Palestinian monastic Horologia, such as the manuscript *Sinai Gr. 863* (9th cent.) edited by Juan Mateos, were known in liturgical studies.[101] The discovery of hitherto unknown manuscripts among the Sinai new finds of 1975 has changed this. Among the most interesting manuscripts is the Horologion in *Sinai Geo. N. 23* (986), copied in Constantinople by Iovane-Meli from a Constantinopolitan model. This, then, appears to be the earliest manuscript of a Constantinopolitan Horologion and its potential implications for our knowledge of the development of the Liturgy of the Hours are significant.[102]

It is believed that the contents of the Horologion of *Sinai Geo. O. 34* (10th cent.) originated at the cathedral of Jerusalem, where a monastic group called *spoudaioi* (οἱ μοναχοὶ Σπουδαῖοι; სპონდიელნი, *spondielni*), the 'zealous ones', served at the Anastasis and at nearby churches, assisting in the liturgical services.[103] In the Typikon of the Anastasis, the *spoudaioi* are identified as a group responsible for the beginning of the vigil on the eves of Palm Sunday[104] and Holy Saturday[105] and are said to have had their own order of services.[106] A similar duty is given to the *hagiosionitai* (Ἁγιοσιωνῖται) in the Typikon of the Anastasis, which indicates that this group was responsible for a vigil (ἀγρυπνία) in the upper room (ἐν τῷ ὑπερῴῳ) on Holy Thursday.[107] The *spoudaioi* lived in the Monastery of the Theotokos of the Spoudaioi (ἡ Θεοτόκος τῶν Σπουδαίων), founded in 494 in Jerusalem near the Anastasis, by Patriarch Elias (r. 494–516).[108] Dmitrievskii believed that they prayed uninterrupted services at the holy sites and filled in the times until the patriarch arrived, just as the *monazontes* and *parthenai* did, according to Egeria's observations of them.[109] Because the Typikon of the Anastasis covers only two weeks of the year, it is impossible to say whether this group of monks performed the same duties during the remainder of the year.

---

[100]　Ibid., vol. 2, 547–666, esp. 665–6.

[101]　Mateos, 'Horologion'; Parenti, 'Fascicolo ritrovato'.

[102]　Aleksidze et al., *Catalogue of Georgian Manuscripts*, 396–7.

[103]　Frøyshov, *Horologe 'géorgien'*, vol. 2, 335–6 and 670–1.

[104]　Papadopoulos-Kerameus, *Anastasis Typikon*, 3.　　　　[105]　Ibid., 161–2.

[106]　οἱ δὲ Σπουδαῖοι...ψάλλουν ἐκεὶ τὸν κανόνα καὶ πᾶσαν τὴν ἀκολουθίαν καὶ ἀπολύ[ονται], καθὼς ἐστιν ὁ τύπος αὐτῶν ('The *spoudaioi*...sing there the canon and the whole service and make the dismissal, as is their custom'). Ibid., 7; Dmitrievskii, Древнѣйшіе Патріаршіе Типиконы, 84; Kekelidze, Канонарь, 265–7.

[107]　Papadopoulos-Kerameus, *Anastasis Typikon*, 83.

[108]　See ch. 31 of the *Life of Sabas*, in Schwartz, *Cyril of Scythopolis*, 116, lines 4–8. See also GL § 1140 for the feast of the dedication of the Church of the Theotokos of the Spoudaioi on 11 August.

[109]　Dmitrievskii, Древнѣйшіе Патріаршіе Типиконы, 111–13; Egeria, *Itinéraire*, § 24: 1 and 25: 6 (= pp. 234–6 and 248–50 Maraval).

According to Sophrone Pétridès, the *spoudaioi* are also attested in Constantinople and in Cyprus.[110] Other similar groups, such as the *philoponoi* (φιλόπονοι), 'lovers of toil', are found in Alexandria, Beirut, and Antioch, the most famous member being the sixth-century Alexandrian philosopher John Philoponus, one the best-known commentators of Aristotle.[111] It is not clear, however, whether these terms are ever used in a liturgical context. The examples provided by Pétridès suggest that they do not in fact refer to a coherent, liturgical group, whether monastic or lay. Nevertheless, the presence of groups designated by such names in Jerusalem as late as the twelfth century—if we are to trust the references in the Typikon of the Anastasis—is significant.

Another influential constituency of the Jerusalem patriarchate that had its own liturgical order was that of the monks of Palestine. The Typikon of the Anastasis describes Palestinian monastics participating in services at the Holy Sepulchre, which indicates that monks from the monasteries of St Sabas, St Chariton, and St Theodosius were present at Golgotha for the Hours of Holy Friday, while the patriarch and the rest of the people simultaneously held another service outside, across from Golgotha.[112] Other testimonials to the daily life of Palestinian monks come from the *Vitae* of the most exemplary ones, composed by Cyril of Scythopolis (*c*.525–59).[113] The *Life of Stephen the Sabaite* also contains such material.[114]

The largest and most famous of all lavras in Palestine was the Great Lavra, known today as the Lavra of St Sabas, 14.5 km south-east of Jerusalem. Initially established in 483 as a lavriote community by St Sabas the Sanctified (439–532),[115] the monastery later adapted to coenobitic life.[116] The architectural corpus of the Lavra was scattered across the Kidron Valley but was subsequently consolidated in an elevated area of approximately 100 by 600 m². This is where St Sabas built the first prayer house (εὐκτήριον). The house was replaced by the Great Church of the Annunciation, consecrated on 1 July 501 by Patriarch Elias,[117] and by the 'God-built' (θεόκτιστος) cave church now dedicated to St Nicholas of Myra.[118] The tomb of St Sabas is presently located in the main courtyard (μεσίαυλον) of the monastery. Other structures included a hostel, a bakery (μαγκιπεῖον), a hospital (νοσοκομεῖον), and numerous

[110] Pétridès, 'Spoudæi'; Sophrone Pétridès, , 'Spoudæi et Philopones', *Échos d'Orient* 7 (1904), 341–8.

[111] Barry Baldwin and Alice-Mary Talbot, 'Philoponos, John', ODB III, 1657.

[112] Papadopoulos-Kerameus, *Anastasis Typikon*, 147.

[113] Barry Baldwin and Alice-Mary Talbot, 'Cyril of Skythopolis', ODB I, 573.

[114] *The Life of Stephen of Mar Sabas*, ed. by John C. Lamoreaux (CSCO 578–579, Louvain: Peeters, 1999).

[115] Alexander Kazhdan and Nancy Patterson-Ševčenko, 'Sabas', ODB III, 1823.

[116] Patrich, *Sabas*, 57–66. See also Siméon Vailhé, 'Le monastère de Saint-Sabas', *Échos d'Orient* 2 (1898-9), 332–41 and *Échos d'Orient* 3 (1899–1900), 18–28 and 168–77.

[117] *Life of* Sabas, Chapter 32, in Schwartz, *Cyril of Scythopolis*, 117–18; Patrich, *Sabas*, 72–5.

[118] *Life of* Sabas, ch. 18, in Schwartz, *Cyril of Scythopolis*, 102; Patrich, *Sabas*, 69–72.

monastic cells.[119] Joseph Patrich admits that little is known of the construction of the original Great Church, as the present structure dates back to a much later period.[120] This helps to explain why certain liturgical documents and pilgrim accounts attest to a different arrangement. According to the liturgical Typikon of St Sabas Lavra preserved in the codex *Sinai Gr. 1096* (12th cent.), in a stational procession during vigils known as *lite* (λιτή) as well as at the end of matins, the monks walked from the cave church to the Church of the Forerunner, where they would chant *stichera* slowly, for as long as it took to anoint the brethren with holy oil.[121] The Slavic pilgrim Abbot Daniel (*c*.1106–8) notes:

Суть же 3 церкви...И ту есть гробъ святаго Савы посредѣ церквий тѣх трій, вдалѣе отъ великія сажень 4; и есть теремець над гробомъ святаго Савы, учинено красно.[122]	There are three churches here...and between the three churches is the tomb of St Sabas, about four fathoms [7.3 m] from the great church, and there is a beautifully executed chapel over the tomb.[123]

However, Denys Pringle notes that the identity and location of the third church mentioned by Abbot Daniel is uncertain.[124]

The close proximity between Jerusalem and the monasteries of the Judean desert had an impact on debates within Palestinian monasticism regarding Christological controversies in the sixth and seventh centuries. The main goal of the *Life of Euthymios* and *Life of Sabas*—to portray the organization of the powerful movement of Chalcedonian monasticism in the Judean wilderness[125]—makes it easy to

---

[119] For plans of the monastery, see Patrich, *Sabas*, 60 fig. 8, 69 fig. 12, and 78 fig. 22.

[120] Ibid., 72.

[121] λιτανεύομεν ἐξερχόμενοι εἰς τὸ θεόκτιστον...Καὶ ἀπεκεῖσε ἀπερχόμεθα εἰς τὸν ναὸν τοῦ Προδρόμου· ψάλλονται στιχηρά, πλ. β΄ Προφῆτα κῆρυξ Χριστοῦ, Δόξα, θεοτοκίον· Ἁγία παρθένε Μαρία, μείζων ἀγγέλων...ψάλλονται δὲ ταῦτα ἀργῶς διὰ τὸ δίδοσθαι ἅγιον ἔλαιον τοῖς ἀδελφοῖς ἀπὸ τῆς ἐπισκέψεως παρὰ τοῦ ἡγουμένου ἢ τοῦ ἱερέως· λαμβάνομεν δὲ τοῦτο ἐν τῇ ἀριστερᾷ παλάμῃ καὶ χριόμεθα διὰ τῆς δεξιᾶς τὸ μέτωπον καὶ τὴν καρδίαν ('We process, going out to the God-built cave...and we depart thence to the shrine of the Forerunner. Stichera, Tone 2 plagal [Tone 6] are sung: "O Prophet, preacher of Christ...", Glory...Theotokion: "Holy virgin Mary, greater than the angels..." These are sung slowly throughout the distribution of the holy oil to the brothers after the visitation by the hegoumenos or the priest. We take it in the palm of the left hand and anoint the forehead and heart with the right'). Dmitrievskii, *Описаніе* III, 21–2.

[122] *Житье и хожденье Данила руськыя земли игумена, 1106–1107 гг.*, ed. by Mikhail A. Venevitinov (ППС 3, St. Petersburg: Типографія В.Ѳ. Киршбаума, 1885), 54–5; 'Хождение игумена Даниила', ed. and trans. by Gelian M. Prokhorov, in *Библиотека литературы Древней Руси*, vol. 4: *XII век*, ed. by Dmitrtii S. Likhachev, Lev A. Dmitriev, Anatolii. A. Alekseev, Natalia V. Ponyrko (St Petersburg: Наука, 1997), 60.

[123] This translation follows Pringle, *Churches of the Crusader Kingdom*, vol. 2, 259. See also Wilson, *Abbot Daniel*, 34.

[124] Pringle, *Churches of the Crusader Kingdom*, vol. 2, 260.

[125] Flusin, 'Palestinian Hagiography', 210.

forget the strong opposition to Chalcedon and certain Origenist leanings among Palestinian monks.[126]

Attempts by Byzantine emperors to reconcile Miaphysite and Chalcedonian Christological positions through compromise led to more disputes in Palestine. Emperor Justinian's attempt to interpret Chalcedon from a perspective acceptable to moderate Miaphysites led to the posthumous condemnation in 553, at the fifth ecumenical council of Constantinople II, of the writings of three church fathers central to Antiochene Christology: Theodore of Mopsuestia (*c.*350–428), Theodoret of Cyrrhus (*c.*393–466), and Ibas of Edessa (d. 28 October 457).[127] Origen was also condemned at this council, in particular for his views on the preexistence of the soul, universal salvation (ἀποκατάστασις πάντων), and restoration of the undifferentiated unity in God and for his belief that each intellect will become identical to Christ at the last judgement, hence the Greek name *isochristoi* ('Christ's equals') given to Origen's followers.[128] Origenism, however, was a broad label in Palestine and also denoted a spiritual tradition of individual monastic contemplation.[129] Further compromise under Emperor Heraclius led to declarations of a 'single activity' (Monoenergism) and a 'single will' (Monotheletism) in Christ, which only complicated matters and resulted in imperial legislation that banned discussion of these questions. Once the majority of non-Chalcedonians found themselves outside the Byzantine empire after the Arab occupation of Antioch and Alexandria, both Monoenergism and Monotheletism were condemned at the sixth ecumenical council of

---

[126] Perrone, *La chiesa di Palestina*, 89–202; Flusin, 'L'hagiographie palestinienne', 26–7. For more on this question, see also Cornelia B. Horn, *Asceticism and Christological Controversy in Fifth-Century Palestine: The Career of Peter the Iberian* (Oxford Early Christian Studies, Oxford: Oxford University Press, 2006); Aryeh Kofsky, 'What Happened to the Monophysite Monasticism of Gaza?', in *Christian Gaza in Late Antiquity*, ed. by Brouria Bitton-Ashkelony and Arieh Kofsky (Jerusalem Studies in Religion and Culture 3, Leiden: Brill, 2004), 183–94. See also n. 26 in this chapter.

[127] Timothy E. Gregory, 'Three Chapters, Affair of the', ODB III, 2080–1; Barry Baldwin, 'Theodore of Mopsuestia', ODB III, 2044; Barry Baldwin, 'Theodoret of Cyrrhus', ODB III, 2049; Timothy E. Gregory, 'Ibas', ODB II, 970–1.

[128] For the anathemas against Origen, see 'Iustiniani edictum contra Origenem', in *Collectio Sabbaitica contra Acephalos et Origeniastas destinata*, ed. by Eduard Schwartz (Acta Conciliorum Oecumenicorum 3, Berlin: Walter de Gruyter, 1940), 213–14; 'Canones XV (contra Origenem sive Origenistas)', in *Concilium Universale Constantinopolitanum sub Iustiniano habitum*, ed. by Johannes Straub (Acta Conciliorum Oecumenicorum 4.1, Berlin: Walter de Gruyter, 1971), 248–9.

[129] For a discussion of the nature of Origenism in Palestine during this period, see Andrew Louth, 'The *Collectio Sabaitica* and Sixth-Century Origenism', in *Origeniana Octava: Origen and the Alexandrian Tradition: Papers of the 8th Internationl Origen Congress, Pisa, 27–31 August 2001*, 2 vols, ed. by Lorenzo Perrone (Bibliotheca Ephemeridum Theologicarum Lovaniensium 164, Leuven: Peeters, 2003), vol. 2, 1167–75; Timothy E. Gregory, 'Origen', ODB III, 1534; Booth, *Crisis of Empire*, 18–22.

Constantinople III in 680–1 and compromise formulae aimed at appeasement were abandoned.[130]

The ensuing 'crisis of empire' in the fallout from Chalcedon and the Arab conquest of vast tracts of Byzantine territory resulted in a new monastic ideological programme promoted by John Moschus, Sophronius of Jerusalem, and Maximus Confessor—the 'Moschan circle', as Phil Booth refers to the three Palestinian monks. The role of the monk at the service of the church and as an active participant in its sacramental life—rather than as an aloof hermit in the Judean wilderness—was accompanied by

> first, an absolute refusal to contemplate compromise or Communion with heretics (against the advocates of oikonomia); second, a recognition of papal preeminence within the church (against the dictatorial stance of the capital); and third, the exclusion of the emperor from religious narratives (against the political culture of the Christian empire).[131]

This view of the imperial capital and of the emperor changed drastically in Palestine after the victory over Constantinopolitan iconoclasm and increased the persecution of Christians by Muslim rulers.[132] Nevertheless, former rifts within the Jerusalem patriarchate were still visible in liturgical sources such as the later manuscripts of the GL, where Euthymian and Sabaite monastic foundations were excluded from the stational liturgy of Jerusalem. Whether this was the result of these monasteries' opposition to the Monotheletism and Origenism endorsed by the patriarchate in Jerusalem is unclear.[133] In any case, exclusion from the Holy City's stational liturgy would have affected the liturgical calendar of the Euthymian and Sabaite monasteries and provided them with an opportunity to distinguish themselves by developing liturgical practices that were different from those of heretics. This may explain why even the earliest extant Sabaite liturgical calendars, such as *Sinai Gr. 1096* (12th cent.), are highly Byzantinized and show few similarities to other Hagiopolitan liturgical calendars of the same period.

Such was the situation in which Greek, Syriac, and Georgian monastic life in the Judean desert developed. After the Arab conquest, however, our knowledge of the ninth through to the eleventh centuries consists of fragmentary

---

[130] Timothy E. Gregory, 'Monoenergism', ODB II, 1396–7; Timothy E. Gregory, 'Monotheletism', ODB II, 1400–1. For a basic bibliography and summary of these disputes, see *The Acts of the Council of Chalcedon*, vol. 1: *General Introduction, Documents before the Council, Session I*, trans. by Richard Price and Michael Gaddis (Translated Texts for Historians 45, Liverpool: Liverpool University Press, 2005), 51–6.

[131] Booth, *Crisis of Empire*, 338.

[132] For these changing views, see 'Islamic Occupation', 'Byzantine Iconoclasm and Its Impact on Palestine', and 'Theodore Balsamon and the Rite of Constantinople' in this chapter.

[133] Verhelst, 'Lieux de station' I, 58–9. For more on this question, see 'The Development of Stational Liturgy' in this chapter.

glimpses rather than seamless narratives.[134] The focus of historical witnesses in the period after the Arab conquest is mainly on the larger monasteries, which suggests that many monasteries did not survive the Persian and Arab attacks of the seventh century.[135]

Greek Monastic Liturgy

The primary liturgical language of most Palestinian monasteries was Greek, so what is said generally of monasticism applies equally to Greek-speaking monasticism. However, the same multilingualism that Egeria witnessed in fourth-century Jerusalem is also reflected in Hagiopolitan and Palestinian monasteries until the crusades.[136] For example, in the *Life of St Sabas* we read that Armenian monks were permitted to serve the canonical hours ($τῆς ψαλμῳδίας κανόνα$)[137] in their own language ($τῇ τῶν Ἀρμενίων διαλέκτῳ$), but were to join the Greeks for the Divine Liturgy,[138] which is indicated here by the term $προσκομιδή$.[139]

Contrary to what one might assume, the Lavra of St Sabas in Palestine became the centre of a Greek intellectual revival after the Arab conquest. This revival not only influenced Jerusalem and Palestine but also had an impact upon Constantinople and the rest of the Byzantine empire, where a decline in literary production had been felt since the time of the Emperor Heraclius (d. 641).[140] The monastery served as the home of great hymnographers and theologians, although some of them spent only a part of their creative careers at the monastery, often leaving on account of ordination to the episcopate, or in order to carry out some other appointments assigned to them by the patriarch.[141] Many Hellenophone monks of Palestine—such as St Sophronius,

---

[134] Nasrallah, *Histoire* II.1, 69; Constantin A. Panchenko, 'Иерусалимская православная церковь', ПЭ 21: 472.

[135] Bitton-Ashkelony and Kofsky, 'Monasticism in the Holy Land', 288.

[136] For more on bilingualism among Palestinian monks, see Nasrallah, *Histoire* II.1, 65–6.

[137] For an explanation of this term, see Alexei A. Dmitrievskii, 'Что такое $κανὼν τῆς ψαλμῳδίας$, так нерѣдко упоминаемый въ жизнеописаніи препод. Саввы Освященнаго?' *Руководство для сельскихъ пастырей* 38 (1889), 69–73. For more on Armenian monasticism in the Holy Land, see Nina G. Garsoïan, 'Introduction to the Problem of Early Armenian Monasticism', *Revue des Études Arméniennes* 30 (2005–7), 177–236, here 185 and 220–6.

[138] $ἐν τῷ καιρῷ τῆς θείας προσκομιδῆς ἔρχεσθαι μετὰ τῶν Ἑλληνισταρίων καὶ τῶν θείων μεταλαμβάνειν μυστηρίων$ ('At the time of the divine offering join the Greek-speakers and partake of the divine mysteries.'). *Life of Sabas*, ch. 32, in Schwartz, *Cyril of Scythopolis*, 117.

[139] For an explanation of the term $προσκομιδή$, see Stefano Parenti, 'Nota sull'impiego del termine $προσκομιδὴ$ nell'eucologio Barberini gr. 336 (VIII sec.)', *Ephemerides Liturgicae* 103 (1989), 406–17; Pavlos Koumarianos, '*Prothesis* and *Proskomide*: A Clarification of Liturgical Terminology', *Greek Orthodox Theological Review* 52: 1–4 (2007), 63–102, esp. 68–72.

[140] Mango, 'Greek Culture in Palestine', 149.

[141] For a general overview of the literary work of the residents of St Sabas Lavra, see Archbishop Aristarchos Peristeris, 'Literary and Scribal Activities at the Monastery of St Sabas', in Patrich, *Sabaite Heritage*, 171–94.

later patriarch of Jerusalem (*c.*560–638);[142] St Andrew, bishop of Crete and composer of the Great Canon (d. 4 July 740);[143] the hymnographer and apologist St John of Damascus;[144] the Damascene's adopted brother, Cosmas, bishop of Maiouma (*c.*675–752) and composer of hymnographic canons for Palm Sunday, the Nativity of Christ, the Dormition, the Exaltation, and Holy Week;[145] the polemicist Theodore Abū Qurrah, bishop of Ḥarrān;[146] Michael Syncellus (*c.*761–846), hieromonk of the Lavra, grammarian, and homilist as well as emissary of Patriarch Thomas to Rome and Constantinople;[147] and Mark, hymnographer and bishop of Otranto (9th–10th cent.)[148]—were considered to have been monks of St Sabas Lavra at some point during their lives. Some aspects of their biographies, however, have been questioned in recent scholarship and connect them rather to a monastery at the Anastasis in Jerusalem or with other unidentified monastic communities in Jerusalem or Palestine.[149]

Incidentally, the reference to a calligrapher (καλλιγράφος), the Galatian monk Eustathius,[150] as well as the numerous biblical and patristic citations in the writings of Cyril of Scythopolis suggest the presence of a significant library at St Sabas already in the fifth century.[151] Two libraries existed at the monastery, one on the south side of the Great Church and the other in the tower of Justinian, and contained all the books of the Lavra's Jerusalemite *metochion* of the archangels. Many of the most valuable manuscripts and church objects were, however, destroyed by fire during the middle of the eighteenth century.[152]

---

[142] Christoph von Schönborn, *Sophrone de Jérusalem: Vie monastique et confession dogmatique* (Paris: Beauchesne, 1972); Aristeides Papadakis, 'Sophronios', ODB III, 1928–9.

[143] Alexander Kazhdan, 'Andrew of Crete', ODB I, 92–3.

[144] See n. 47 here ('Melkites: A Subgroup?').

[145] Alexander Kazhdan and Nancy Patterson-Ševčenko, 'Kosmas the Hymnographer', ODB II, 1152.

[146] See n. 48 here ('Melkites: A Subgroup?').

[147] Robert Browning and Alexander Kazhdan, 'Michael Synkellos', ODB II, 1369–70; Mary B. Cunningham, *The Life of Michael the Synkellos: Text, Translation and Commentary* (Belfast Byzantine Texts and Translations 1, Belfast: Belfast Byzantine Enterprises, 1991); Claudia Sode, *Jerusalem–Konstantinopel—Rom: Die Viten des Michael Synkellos und der Brüder Theodoros und Theophanes Graptoi* (Altertumswissenschaftliches Kolloquium 4, Stuttgart: Franz Steiner Verlag, 2001).

[148] Panagiotes G. Nikolopoulos, 'Μᾶρκος, Ἐπίσκοπος Ὑδροῦντος', ΘΗΕ 8: 759; Paolo Cesaretti, 'Da "Marco d'Otranto" a Demetrio: Alcune note di lettura su poeti bizantini del Salento', RSBN 37 (2000), 183–208.

[149] See, for example, Auzépy, 'De la Palestine à Constantinople'; Louth, *St John Damascene*, 6–7.

[150] *Life of Sabas*, ch. 84, in Schwartz, *Cyril of Scythopolis*, 189.

[151] For an index of Cyril of Scythopolis' sources, see the index in Schwartz, *Cyril of Scythopolis*, 254–6; Bernard Flusin, *Miracle et histoire dans l'œuvre de Cyrille de Skythopolis* (Paris: Études augustiniennes, 1983), 43–73; Cirillo di Scitopoli, *Storie monastiche del deserto di Gerusalemme*, trans. by Romano Baldelli and Luciana Mortari (Abbazia di Praglia: Edizioni Scritti Monastici, 1990), 409–17; Patrich, *Sabas*, 189–92; Cynthia Jean Stallman-Pacitti, *Cyril of Skythopolis: A Study in Hagiography as Apology* (Brookline, MA: Hellenic College Press, 1991).

[152] For a brief survey of the scribal production of Mar Sabas Lavra, see Siméon Vailhé, 'Les écrivains de Mar-Saba', *Échos d'Orient* 2 (1898–9), 1–11 and 33–47; Archbishop Aristarchos

Syriac Monastic Liturgy

A reference to the practice of multiple, multilingual services is repeated in the twelfth-century redaction of the founder's Typikon of St Sabas Lavra, which is considered the will and testament of St Sabas (439–532) himself, although no contemporaneous copies are extant. The description of the liturgical services within the monastery is as follows:

Μὴ ἔχειν δὲ ἐξουσίαν μήτε τοὺς Ἴβηρας, μήτε τοὺς Σύρους, ἢ τοὺς Φράγγους λειτουργίαν τελείαν ποιεῖν ἐν ταῖς ἐκκλησίαις αὐτῶν, ἀλλὰ συναθροιζομένους ἐν αὐταῖς ψάλλειν τὰς ὥρας καὶ τὰ τυπικά, ἀναγινώσκειν δὲ τὸν Ἀπόστολον καὶ τὸ Εὐαγγέλιον τῇ ἰδίᾳ διαλέκτῳ, καὶ μετὰ ταῦτα εἰσέρχεσθαι εἰς τὴν μεγάλην ἐκκλησίαν καὶ μεταλαμβάνειν μετὰ πάσης τῆς ἀδελφότητος τῶν θείων καὶ ἀχράντων καὶ ζωοποιῶν μυστηρίων.[153]	Nor shall it be permitted that the Georgians, or the Syrians, or the Franks celebrate a complete liturgy in their churches. Let them instead gather over there, and sing the canonical hours and Typika in their own language, and read the Epistle and the Gospel as well, and then go to the Great Church and take part in the divine, undefiled, and life-giving sacraments together with the whole brotherhood.[154]

At least for major feasts, the Divine Liturgy that the monastic brotherhood would celebrate in common in the Lavra's Great Church was probably still JAS until the twelfth century.[155] Both the *Life of Stephen the Sabaite*, which mentions that Stephen served BAS frequently on the basis of ancient traditions, and liturgical manuscripts from Palestine and Sinai containing both BAS and CHR, such as *Sinai Geo. N. 54* (10th cent.) and *Sinai Gr. 1040* (14th cent.), suggest that the position of JAS as the primary eucharistic Divine Liturgy of Palestinian monasticism was in decline by the twelfth century.[156] This seems even more likely when one considers that the Typikon in *Sinai Gr. 1096* (12th cent.)—the same manuscript that contains the Testament of St Sabas—makes no reference to JAS. The reference to 'Franks' may be a later interpolation into a much older original text. However, it should be noted that Latin speakers were present in Jerusalem both as pilgrims and as permanent monastics. The priest Gabriel of the Anastasis, as the *Life of Euthymius*, was

---

Peristeris, 'Literary and Scribal Activities at the Monastery of St Sabas', in Patrich, *Sabaite Heritage*, 171–94, here 175–7.

[153] *Sinai Gr. 1096* (12th cent.), 148r; Dmitrievskii, Описание I, 222–3.

[154] English translation from Gianfranco Fiaccadori, '*Sabas*: Founder's *Typikon* of the Sabas Monastery near Jerusalem', BMFD IV, 1316, with my emendations.

[155] See Charon, 'Le rite byzantin', 495.

[156] See Auzépy, 'De la Palestine à Constantinople', 190; Aleksidze et al., *Catalogue of Georgian Manuscripts*, 413–15. See also Chapter 3, 'Eucharistic Liturgies' and 'Sources of the Liturgy of St James'.

fluently trilingual in Latin, Greek, and Syriac, and there were monks from the West, on the Mount of Olives, who prayed in Latin.[157]

'Syrian' served as a unifying designator for speakers of Syriac, Christian Palestinian Aramaic, and Arabic in Palestine until the ninth or tenth century.[158] From the time of Egeria until the twelfth century, Syriac had a prominent place in the daily life of Jerusalem, as witnessed by another directive of St Sabas' testament:

Ἐπεὶ δὲ φθοροποιοὶ δαίμονες ἐν ταῖς προχειρήσεσι τῶν ἡγουμένων εἰώθασι δειχωνίας καὶ στάσεις ἀναρύπτειν τῶν δύο γλωσσῶν, μεταξὺ Ῥωμαίων τε φημὶ καὶ Σύρων, ἐκ μέσου τὸ σκάνδαλον ἐξελαύνοντες, διοριζόμεθα· μηδένα τῶν Σύρων ἀπό γε τοῦ νῦν τῆς τοῦ ἡγουμένου ἐπιβαίνειν ἀρχῆς, οἰκονόμους δὲ καὶ δοχειαρίους καὶ εἰς τὰς λοιπὰς διακονίας προτιμᾶσθαι τοὺς Σύρους καὶ διαταττόμεθα καὶ ἀποδεχόμεθα, ὡς ἀνυστικωτέρους ὄντας καὶ δραστικοὺς ἐν ταῖς πατρά[ι]σιν αὐτῶν.[159]	Since in the act of the nomination of the superiors pernicious demons are accustomed to raise disagreements and divisions between the two languages (I mean between Romans [i.e. Byzantines] and Syrians), in order to get rid of this scandal, we ordain that no Syrian should be appointed to the office of superior; but we both decide and accept that Syrians, being more efficient and practical in their native country, should be preferred for the stewardship and treasurership as well as for other ministries.[160]

But, despite their efficiency and practicality, Syrians were never permitted to be abbots in these monasteries, and thus Syriac never held liturgical primacy in the multilingual monastic communities of Palestine or in the Jerusalem cathedral. One example of a bilingual Melkite liturgical manuscript of uncertain provenance is *Sinai Gr. N.E. X 239* (12th–13th cent.), a peculiar Greek–Syriac manuscript containing CHR that presumes that the clergy would know both Greek and Syriac, since it indicates that most of the prayers were said inaudibly in Syriac and the exclamations were made in Greek.[161] The earliest Syriac liturgical manuscript relevant to my study is *Sinai Syr. M52N* (9th–10th cent.), dated to the late ninth and early tenth century, which contains a complete calendar of fixed commemorations for the whole liturgical year (10 folios); this calendar follows closely the sanctoral cycle of the Jerusalem lectionary, from 1 October (*Teshri I*) until 30 September (*Elul*). André Binggeli's preliminary study of this calendar has stressed its importance

[157] ἔμαθεν ὀρθῶς λαλεῖν τε καὶ γράφειν κατά τε τὴν Ῥωμαίων καὶ Ἑλλήνων καὶ Σύρων φωνήν ('he had learnt to speak and to write accurately in the Latin, Greek, and Syriac languages'). *Life of Euthymius*, ch. 37, in Schwartz, *Cyril of Scythopolis*, 56; McCormick, *Survey of the Holy Land*, 206–7.
[158] Leeming, 'The Adoption of Arabic as a Liturgical Language', 240–1.
[159] *Sinai Gr. 1096* (12th cent.), fol. 149v; Dmitrievskii, Описание I, 224.
[160] English translation from Gianfranco Fiaccadori, '*Sabas*: Founder's *Typikon* of the Sabas Monastery near Jerusalem', BMFD IV, 1317.
[161] Nikolopoulos, *Νέα εὑρήματα*, 224; Brock, 'Manuscrits liturgiques', 278.

for the study of liturgy in Jerusalem between the appearance of new martyrs—namely martyrs of the Arab conquest, who were integrated into the sanctoral cycle—and the final liturgical Byzantinization of the Jerusalem patriarchate.[162]

Nevertheless, very few Syriac liturgical manuscripts show a clear connection with the Orthodox patriarchate of Jerusalem. The lack of Syriac and Arabic liturgical sources is also explained by the fact that not all Syriac- and Arabic-speaking Christians were Chalcedonian Melkites who shared the faith promoted by Constantinople.[163] The majority of sources reflect the East and West Syrian liturgical traditions, which had closer ties to Antioch.[164] Because of the liturgical limitations imposed on the various linguistic communities, Arabic liturgical texts are generally restricted to lectionaries such as *Sinai Ar. 72* (897), *Sinai Ar. 54* (9th cent.), *Sinai Ar. 74* (9th cent.), *Sinai Ar. 70* (9th–10th cent.), or *Sinai Ar. 97* (1123/4).[165] Another, similar source, the New Testament codex *Vatican Ar. 13* (9th cent.), was probably used among Arabic monks in a multilingual environment such as St Sabas or Mount Sinai.[166] The most important Arabic Gospel lectionary for this study is the bilingual Greek–Arabic codex *Sinai Ar. 116* (995/6) in the hand of Presbyter John, son of Victor of Damietta, who copied both the Greek and the Arabic text on Sinai while he was a priest in the monastery. He had previously entered the monastery and became monk on Sinai in 984/5.[167]

Although the provenance of the extant liturgical manuscripts is very difficult to determine, colophons of most extant Syriac Melkite liturgical manuscripts indicate that they were copied in parts of Syria and Cappadocia —within the Antiochene patriarchate, not in Jerusalem.[168] This is particularly the case with *Vatican Syr. 19* (1030) and *Vatican Syr. 20* (1215).[169] Regarding liturgical content, most manuscripts contain CHR or BAS and very few

---

[162] Binggeli, 'Calendrier melkite de Jérusalem', 193. See Appendix 1 for more on this manuscript.

[163] Nadia El Cheikh and Clifford E. Bosworth, 'Rūm', in *Encyclopaedia of Islam*, vol. 8, 601–6; Griffith, 'The Church of Jerusalem and the "Melkites"'; Johannes Pahlitzsch, 'Griechisch, Syrisch, Arabisch: Zum Verhältnis von Liturgie- und Umgangssprache bei den Melkiten Paläs-tinas im 12. und 13. Jahrhundert', in *Language of Religion, Language of the People: Medieval Judaism, Christianity and Islam*, ed. by Ernst Bremer, Jörg Jarnut, Michael Richter, and David J. Wasserstein, with assistance from Susanne Röhl (Mittelalter Studien 11, Munich: Wilhelm Fink Verlag, 2006), 37–47.

[164] Sebastian Brock, 'Liturgy', GEDSH, 248–51.

[165] See 'Melkites: A Subgroup?' and 'Arabization' in this chapter; also Appendix 1.

[166] Francesco D'Aiuto, '*Graeca* in codici orientali della Biblioteca Vaticana', in Perria, *Tra oriente e occidente*, 227–96, here 241–5 and tables 1–3 there. See also Joshua Blau, 'A Melkite Arabic Literary "Lingua Franca" from the Second Half of the First Millennium', *Bulletin of the School of Oriental and African Studies* 57 (1994), 14–16.

[167] Aland, *Kurzgefaßte Liste*, 356; Harlfinger, Reinsch, and Sonderkamp, *Specimina sinaitica*, 17–18 and tables 18–22; Garitte, 'Évangéliaire grec-arabe', 208–9. See Appendix 1 for more on this manuscript.

[168] For more on the problem of colophons, see Ševčenko, 'Manuscript Production'.

[169] See Appendix 1 for more on these manuscripts.

contain JAS.[170] However, they often do make note of distinctions between various liturgical practices, for example by referring to liturgical usages 'according to the Greek order' (*'ik ṭ̣ks' ioni'*) or to differences between liturgical usage in Edessa and in Melitene; and they generally originate from the area around the Black Mountain near Antioch, making it difficult to situate any of them within the environs of the Jerusalem patriarchate.[171]

Georgian Monastic Liturgy

As noted already, Georgians had a significant presence in Palestine from the fifth century, and St Sabas Lavra was one of their primary bases. Between the eighth and the tenth centuries, this monastery was the focal point of Georgian scribal activity outside the Caucasus. It was here that a major redaction of the Georgian bible, known as 'the St Sabas redaction' (საბაწმიდური, *sabacmiduri*), took place between the eighth and the tenth centuries.[172] After 980 Georgian scribes abandoned the Lavra and moved to Sinai, where Georgians were known already since the late sixth century.[173] Contact between Sinai and Palestine was quite common at the time and several routes facilitated travel.[174]

Among the Georgian monks who migrated from Mar Sabas to Sinai was the scribe Iovane Zosime, the most notable Georgian figure in Palestine in the tenth century.[175] Little is known of his early life, and some have speculated

---

[170] Sebastian P. Brock, *Catalogue of Syriac Fragments (New Finds) in the Library of the Monastery of Saint Catherine, Mount Sinai* (Athens: Mount Sinai Foundation, 1995), esp. 57–9; Philothée, *Nouveaux manuscrits syriaques*.

[171] Heinrich Husmann, 'Eine alte orientalische christliche Liturgie: Altsyrisch-melkitisch', OCP 42 (1976), 156–96, esp. 156–64.

[172] Tarchnishvili, *Geschichte*, 62–3.

[173] The earliest mention of Georgians is under the name *bessas* in the *Itinerarium* of Antoninus of Piacenza (*c*.570). See *Antonini Placentini Itinerarium*, ed. by Johann Gildemeister (Berlin: Reuthers, 1889), § 37: 27 (Latin), 56 n. 48 (German). For a more recent edition, see *Antonini Placentini Itinerarium*, ed. by Paul Geyer (CCSL 175, Turnhout: Brepols, 1965), 148 (§ 37, V 184.4). This name corresponds to the word βέσσοι in the *Life of Theodosius the Cenobiarch* (BHG 17766). See n. 38 here ('The Christian Population and its Languages'); Tarchnishvili, *Geschichte*, 62, 69.

[174] For the various routes connecting Jerusalem and Sinai, see Pau Figueras, 'Pilgrims to Sinai in the Byzantine Negev', in *Kongress für Christliche Archäologie*, 756–62. See also Yoram Tsafrir, 'The Maps Used by Theodosius: On the Pilgrim Maps of the Holy Land and Jerusalem in the Sixth Century CE', DOP 40 (1986), 129–45; Israel Roll, 'Roads and Transportation in the Holy Land in the Early Christian and Byzantine Times', in *Kongress für Christliche Archäologie*, 1166–70.

[175] Tarchnishvili, *Geschichte*, 109–14; Garitte, *Calendrier palestino-géorgien*, 16; Bernard Outtier, 'Langue et littérature géorgiennes', in *Christianismes orientaux: Introduction à l'étude des langues et des littératures*, ed. by Micheline Albert, Robert Beylot, René-G. Coquin, Bernard Outtier, Charles Renoux, and Antoine Guillaumont (Initiations au christianisme ancien, Paris: Éditions du Cerf, 1993), 263–96, here 289. The most recent and complete biography of Iovane Zosime is in Frøyshov, *Horologe 'géorgien'*, vol. 2, 217–30. Zosime's name is absent from PmbZ II.

that he was born around 920 and became a novice at the monastery of Šatberdi in Georgia around 940.[176] Various manuscript colophons preserved at Sinai show that he lived at St Sabas Lavra around 962[177] and then moved to the Monastery of St Catherine on Sinai, where he resided between 973[178] and 986,[179] dying shortly thereafter. One of the most important liturgical texts for the study of the liturgical Byzantinization of Jerusalem is the calendar that Zosime copied in codex *Sinai Geo. O. 34* (10th cent.). It bears the title 'Synaxes of the Months of the Year' (კრებაჲ თთუეთაჲ წელიწადისათაჲ), where the term 'synaxis' (კრებაჲ, *krebay*) is equivalent to the Greek σύναξις, a liturgical gathering intended to celebrate a feast or a commemoration.[180] The contents of this calendar reflect a mixed Hagiopolitan transitional liturgy. Gérard Garitte believed that the liturgical calendar was not intended for actual use but rather as a kind of encyclopaedic synaxarion that revealed the compiler's awareness of two sanctoral traditions active in his time—a hybrid and a *compilation artificielle*.[181] Zosime himself identifies four sources for his collection:

ესე კრებანი და დღეთა დამიწერიან, თავად კანონისათა და საბერძნეთი-სათა და იერუსალჶმისათა და საბაწმიდისათა.[182]	I have described these synaxes from four sources: chiefly the canon (*kanoni*), and also of the Greeks, and of Jerusalem, and of St Sabas.

Garitte has made suggestions as to what these sources may have been: the canon (კანონისაჲთა, *kanonisayta*) refers to the Jerusalem lectionary;[183] a Greek model (საბერძნეთისაჲთა, *saberznetisayta*) is perhaps a synaxarion of Palestinian origin;[184] the 'Jerusalem model' (იერუსალჶმისაჲთა, *ierusalēmisayta*) was something other than the Jerusalem lectionary, perhaps something like the hymnals or the Menaia found in *Sinai Geo. O. 1, Sinai Geo. O. 59, Sinai Geo. O. 64,* and *Sinai Geo. O. 65*;[185] and there is a contemporaneous

---

[176] Frøyshov, *Horologe 'géorgien'*, vol. 2, 221. For more on the Monastery of Šatberdi, which was founded by Gregory of Khandzta in the ninth century in Tao-Klardžeti, Georgia, see Valeri Silogava and Kakha Shengelia, *Tao-Klardjeti* (Tbilisi: Caucasus University Press, 2006).

[177] *Sinai Geo. O. 34* (10th cent.); Frøyshov, *Horologe 'géorgien'*, vol. 2, 220.

[178] *Sinai Geo. O. 35* (973); Frøyshov, *Horologe 'géorgien'*, vol. 2, 219.

[179] *Sinai Geo. Tsagareli 92* (986); Frøyshov, *Horologe 'géorgien'*, vol. 2, 219.

[180] Mateos, *Typicon*, vol. 2, 319–20; Garitte, *Calendrier palestino-géorgien*, 20, 43.

[181] [L]e calendrier de Jean Zosime est un document hybride…Il ne semble pas qu'un tel document puisse être considéré comme un ordo destiné à régir réellement la vie liturgique d'une communauté. Garitte, *Calendrier palestino-géorgien*, 37.

[182] Ibid., 114.   [183] Ibid., 23–31.   [184] Ibid., 31–3.

[185] Ibid., 33. For a description of these manuscripts, see Nikolai Marr, *Описание грузинских рукописей синайского монастыря* (Moscow: Академия Наук СССР, 1940), 99–107, 135–41, 141–52; *Description* I, 13–38 (*Sinai Geo. O. 1*), 162–86 (*Sinai Geo. O. 59*), 187–208 (*Sinai Geo. O. 64*), 208–9 (*Sinai Geo. O. 65*).

Sabaitic model (საბაწმიდისათა, *sabacmidisayta*), which Garitte does not identify.[186] Iovane Zosime's familiarity with a variety of liturgical traditions in Palestine and Sinai has inspired Stig Frøyshov to consider him—along with Nicon of the Black Mountain one century later (*c.*1025–*c.*1100/10)[187]—'a precursor to comparative liturgy in our time'.[188]

Unlike the Arabic sources, extant Georgian liturgical manuscripts from the ninth century onward contain more than just lectionaries. A great number also contain JAS and various prayers of Palestinian origin no longer extant in Greek sources. As with the GL, the Georgian manuscripts of JAS and other prayers from the Euchologion are invariably translations from Greek originals that have in many cases been lost. These include *Sinai Geo. N. 58* (9th–10th cent.), *Sinai Geo. O. 54* (10th cent.), and *Sinai Geo. O. 12* (10th–11th cent.), liturgical books that contain Divine Liturgies, sacraments, readings from the Jerusalem lectionary, and an assortment of other prayers and rites.[189] For lack of a better term, they have been dubbed 'liturgical collections' (ლიტურგიკული კრებული, *liturgikuli krebuli*; συλλογὴ λειτουργικῶν κειμένων).[190] Since these types of manuscripts are often acephalous (i.e. they do not bear any title) and are not intended exclusively for the presiding bishop or presbyter but contain hymns and readings for chanters or the laity, Georgian scholars are hesitant to call them Euchologia (εὐχολόγια).[191] Because of the potpourri of its contents within a codex of generally small dimensions,[192] Bernard Outtier refers to this type of book as a *missel de voyage*.[193] The all-encompassing nature of its content recalls the western Latin liturgical books known as *libelli missarum*, where liturgical action was concentrated in the presider's hands.[194] While the Georgian 'liturgical collections' do derive from a monastic environment, either at the St Sabas Lavra in Palestine or at St Catherine's Monastery on Mount Sinai, these books are not intended exclusively for a monastic community, which is obvious from the inclusion of marriage services and prayers for pregnant women.

If Sabaite monks from the various language groups were to come to the Great Church to celebrate together the Divine Liturgy in Greek, as mentioned

---

[186] Garitte, *Calendrier palestino-géorgien*, 35–7.
[187] Alexander Kazhdan, 'Nikon of the Black Mountain', ODB II, 1484–5.
[188] 'Zosime fut ainsi, en compagnie de Nicon de la Montagne-Noire un siècle plus tard, un précurseur à la Liturgie comparée de notre temps'. Frøyshov, *Horologe 'géorgien'*, vol. 2, 230.
[189] For a description of each of these manuscripts, see Appendix 1.
[190] *Liturgia ibero-graeca*, 29–31. This term is also followed by Aleksidze et al., *Catalogue of Georgian Manuscripts*.
[191] Robert F. Taft, 'Euchologion', ODB II, 738; Stefano Parenti, 'Euchologion', in *Lexikon für Theologie und Kirche*, vol. 3, ed. by Walter Kasper, 3rd edn (Freiburg: Herder, 1995), 976.
[192] The codices range from 200 × 150 mm to 50 × 90 mm.
[193] Outtier, 'Sinaï géorgien 54', 88.
[194] Eric Palazzo, *A History of Liturgical Books from the Beginning to the Thirteenth Century*, trans. by Madeleine Beaumont (Collegeville, MN: Liturgical Press, 1998), 107, 109–10.

in the *Life of Sabas* and regulated by the Testament of St Sabas, how would these Georgian liturgical manuscripts have been used in the Greek-dominated monastic liturgical environment? It is most likely that they were used in smaller communities or in monastic dependencies where the majority of monks were Georgians or liturgical services were conducted in Georgian. Regardless of their use, the very existence of these sources is of great importance for the study of the Hagiopolite liturgy during this period.

HAGIOPOLITAN DECLINE

Before the Arab conquest, the Jerusalem church was flourishing, monasticism was thriving, and new hymnography and literature was being composed. Conflicts and theological disputes caused significant disruption to ecclesiastical life, but Chalcedonian Christians were still in the majority and controlled the holy sites. The worst was yet to come.

The turbulence of sixth-century theological disputes in Palestine was replaced by war and bloodshed in seventh-century Jerusalem. The Persian conquest of Jerusalem (614–30) caused considerable loss of life and inflicted significant destruction upon the city. The advancing Persian army pushed towards Palestine nomadic Bedouin raiders, who massacred monks at the Great Lavra a week before the Persians seized Jerusalem.[195] Despite such upheavals, a building programme was immediately initiated under Patriarch Modestus of Jerusalem (d. 634).[196] Rather than being a restoration of the status quo, this was simply the calm before another storm.

Islamic Occupation

The defining event of the period of Byzantinization, which has implications for the history of Jerusalem even until today, is the capture of the Holy City by the Muslim forces of Caliph 'Umar in 638.[197] Jerusalem was thereafter no

---

[195] Antiochus Strategos, *Epistula ad Eustathium*, PG 89:1421–8; Dauphin, *La Palestine byzantine*, vol. 2, 357.

[196] Thomson, *Armenian History Attributed to Sebeos*, 70–2; Constantin A. Panchenko et al., 'Иерусалим', ПЭ 21: 397–441, here 413. For more on this question, see 'Changes in Topography' in this chapter.

[197] The exact date of Jerusalem's conquest is not completely clear. The traditional date is February 638, although the city may have already fallen by December 637. In either case, the conquest occurred before the death of Patriarch Sophronius of Jerusalem on 11 March 638. See André Guillou, 'Prise de Gaza par les Arabes au VIIe siècle', *Bulletin de correspondance hellénique* 81 (1957), 396–404.

longer within the same empire as Constantinople, and Chalcedonian Christians found themselves a powerless majority ruled by a minority from another religion and culture. The Christian perspective on the occupation of Jerusalem varied from one group to another. The monks of St Sabas believed that the preceding fall of Palestine to the Persians in 614 was punishment for the sin of Monotheletism and for the separation from Constantinople.[198] At the other extreme, Michael I Rabo (1126–99),[199] Miaphysite patriarch of Antioch, believed that God had sent the Arabs to deliver Palestine from the tyranny of the Byzantines—a popular topos that was adapted and repeated in Byzantine post-Florentine reactions to the fall of Constantinople in 1453.[200]

Chalcedonian authors also employed literary topoi to describe the events surrounding the arrival of the Muslim invaders.[201] St Maximus Confessor writes of a civilization-destroying 'barbarous nation of wild beasts' that only resemble humans in physical appearance,[202] and St Sophronius of Jerusalem compares the events he witnessed to the apocalyptic abomination of desolation from the prophecy of Daniel.[203] Certainly parallels between the biblical battle of the Israelites and Philistines (1 Samuel 17:1) and that of the Byzantine and Muslim armies, which was taking place before these authors' very eyes, were tempting. But, according to Claudine Dauphin, the invading Arabs did not carry out any systematic massacres. Their invasion was a 'war of usury' and siege more than one of military invasion,[204] and the demographic decline in Palestine under the Arabs had already begun during the Byzantine period, as established by archaeological and demographic studies.[205]

Despite diverging perceptions of the event, it is clear that the Arab occupation of Palestine ushered in a long transitional period of cultural, social, and political—but especially liturgical—change. A key figure at the beginning of this period was Patriarch Sophronius of Jerusalem (c.560–638), who witnessed the Arab conquest of his city. It was Sophronius, and not any military or civil leader, who negotiated with Caliph 'Umar the treaty that led to Jerusalem's

---

[198] Frederick C. Conybeare, 'Antiochus Strategos: The Capture of Jerusalem by the Persians in 614 AD' [*sic*], *English Historical Review* 25 (1910), 502–17.

[199] Sidney H. Griffith, 'Michael I the Syrian', ODB II, 1362–3; D. Weltecke, 'Michael I Rabo'; GEDSH, 287–90.

[200] Michael the Syrian, *Chronicle*, vol. 2, pp. 431–2 (= 11: 8). For more on anti-Byzantine sentiment, see Nasrallah, *Histoire* II.1, 58; Ostrogorsky, *History of the Byzantine State*, 568.

[201] Dauphin, *La Palestine byzantine*, vol. 2, 360.

[202] Maximus Confessor, *Epistulae*, XIV, PG 91:540.

[203] Sophronius of Jerusalem, *Homilia in Theophaniam*, 10: 24–31 (6 January 637); Sophronius of Jerusalem, 'Λόγος εἰς τὸ ἅγιον βάπτισμα', in A. Papadopoulos-Kerameus, Ἀνάλεκτα Ἱεροσολυμητικῆς Σταχυολογίας, vol. 5 (St Petersburg: Kirschbaum, 1898), 151–68, here 166. See also Daniel 9:27, 11:31, 12:11; 1 Maccabees 1:54, 6:7; Matthew 24:15.

[204] Dauphin uses the term *guerre d'usure*. See Dauphin, *La Palestine byzantine*, vol. 2, 363–8.

[205] Ibid., 371–2.

submission.[206] The role of Sophronius as a kind of ethnarch suggests the rise in importance of Jerusalem's hierarchy during the period when Greek-praying Christians in Jerusalem found themselves outside the Byzantine empire; it also bears witness to the progressive development of a top-down model of leadership within the patriarchate of Jerusalem. Sophronius was not only an ecclesiastical leader but also the chief hymnographer in the new phase of hymnographic composition found in the *Iadgari*.[207]

In the first years of Muslim occupation, little changed for the Jerusalem patriarchate in terms of demographics and civil administration; and the relations between Muslims and Christians were good. Cities remained Christian, while Muslims established new towns and villages or occupied houses abandoned by Christians who had fled with the Byzantines. The Umayyad dynasty's founder, Mu'āwiya (r. 661–80), retained the existing civil tax infrastructure administration established under the Byzantines, adding only a new personal (*ğizya*) and territorial (*ḫarāğ*) tax, so that only the ruler who governed and received the taxes changed. Not only did churches and monasteries remain open, but new ones with visible external crosses could be constructed in newly established Muslim towns.[208]

Although the Umayyads preferred not to involve themselves in Christological controversies, they were forced to oversee strained inter-Christian relations.[209] Conflicts between Chalcedonians, Miaphysites, and Monothelites were intensified, because the Chalcedonians, now no longer the established and state-approved church, were occasionally viewed with suspicion by Muslim authorities,[210] while non-Chalcedonians received preferential treatment due to their opposition to Constantinople and support for the occupation.[211] Although this is often repeated as a commonplace and may in fact have been true in Egypt, Samuel Noble and Alexander Treiger have pointed out that there is no evidence for such attitudes in Syria, since 'the earliest Miaphysite literary responses to the conquest in both Syria and Egypt take the form of apocalypses that portray the arrival of the Muslims as a catastrophe presaging the end of times'.[212]

---

[206] *Theophanis Chronographia*, 339; Mango and Scott, *Chronicle of Theophanes*, 472. See also Daniel J. Sahas, 'The Face to Face Encounter between Patriarch Sophronius of Jerusalem and the Caliph 'Umar ibn al-Khaṭṭāb: Friends or Foes?', in *The Encounter of Eastern Christianity with Early Islam*, ed. by Emmanouela Grypeou, Mark N. Swanson, and David Thomas (History of Christian–Muslim Relations 5, Brill: Leiden, 2006), 33–44.

[207] Frøyshov, 'Early Development', 144; Aleksidze et al., *Catalogue of Georgian Manuscripts*, 367. See also Stig Frøyshov, 'Sophronios of Jerusalem', *The Canterbury Dictionary of Hymnology* (Canterbury Press, 2013). At http://www.hymnology.co.uk/s/sophronios-of-jerusalem (accessed 25 April 2016).

[208] Nasrallah, *Histoire* II.1, 40–3.   [209] Ibid., 209–10.

[210] Ibid., 54.   [211] Ibid., 39.

[212] Noble and Treiger, *The Orthodox Church in the Arab World*, 14.

In time, the occupiers' initial tolerance for the adapting Christian majority began to fade. Once the antithesis between Arabs and non-Arabs had disappeared, the divide between Muslims and non-Muslims sharpened.[213] This antagonism coincides with the reign of the ʿAbbasid dynasty (*c*.750–1258) and, particularly from 959, with the rule of Fatimid caliphs from Egypt, who were known for their severity towards Christians.[214] Their hostile attitude turned Jerusalem into a setting for theological debates and martyrdom for many Arab Melkite new martyrs, Anthony Rawḥ and Peter Capitolias among them.[215]

Despite these difficulties, there was still freedom of movement and contact between Jerusalem and the other patriarchates. One of the better known figures of the ʿAbbasid period, Patriarch Thomas of Jerusalem, was initially a doctor and a deacon in Jerusalem who in 797 became a monk at the Lavra of St Sabas. After serving as *hegoumenos* of the Old Lavra, Thomas became patriarch some time before 807.[216] It was this same Patriarch Thomas who sent his secretary Michael Syncellus to Rome via Constantinople in 815. Resources permitted Thomas to restore the Anastasis, which he did after the death of Hārūn al-Rashīd in 809, even without the caliph's permission.[217] Contact between the Judean monasteries and the patriarchate were also maintained at this time. There were many cases of *hegoumenoi* of St Sabas Lavra being promoted to the episcopate, both within the patriarchate of Jerusalem and elsewhere. For example, Theodore Abū Qurrah, previously believed to have been a monk of St Sabas and then its *hegoumenos*, became bishop of Edessa in the Antiochene patriarchate.[218] Thus mobility and fluid exchange of clergy existed between Palestinian monasteries and areas beyond the Jerusalem patriarchate.

Jerusalem's foreign contacts were not limited to the other eastern patriarchates. In 808, after hearing of suffering and poverty in Jerusalem, Charlemagne (*c*.742–814) sent a delegation to the Holy Land to assess

[213] Arthur Stanley Tritton, *The Caliphs and Their Non-Muslim Subjects: A Critical Study of the Covenant of ʿUmar* (London: Frank Cass, 1970), 3.

[214] Vittorio Peri, *La 'Grande Chiesa' Bizantina: L'ambito ecclesiale dell'Ortodossia* (Brescia: Queriniana, 1981), 146.

[215] Griffith, 'The Church of Jerusalem and the "Melkites"', 183–5. See Chapter 4, 'New Martyrs'.

[216] See BHG 1670, *De S. Stephano sabaita thaumaturgo monacho* (in AASS, Julii, tomus III), 588, § 136 (13 July); BHG 1200, *Martyrium SS. XX patrum sabaitarum* (in AASS, Martii, tomus III), *2–*14, here *5, § 24 (20 March). For other supplemental edited folios from the passion of the twenty martyrs, see Robert P. Blake, 'Deux lacunes comblées dans la *Passio XX Monachorum Sabaitarum*', AB 68 (1950), 27–43.

[217] Eutyches Patriarcha Alexandrini, *Annales*, pars 2 (CSCO 51, Beirut: Typographeo Catholico, 1909), 55–6; Constantin A. Panchenko, 'Иерусалимская православная церковь', ПЭ 21: 470. See n. 147 ('Greek Monastic Liturgy') here in this chapter.

[218] John C. Lamoreaux, 'The Biography of Theodore Abū Qurrah Revisited', DOP 56 (2002), 25–40. For more on Theodore Abū Qurrah, see 'Melkites: A Subgroup?' in this chapter.

the financial situation of the church there and to provide support.[219] Its report reveals the existence of 162 members of personnel, including sixty ordained clergy attached to the Holy Sepulchre complex alone:[220] a number comparable, for example, to that of the Church of Blachernai in Constantinople but far smaller than the 600 clergy at Hagia Sophia in 612.[221] The total patriarchal budget that the delegation calculated was comparably small, around 1,660 solidi, or 7.06 kilograms of gold.[222] This amount provided for the salaries of all the clergy, which the patriarch distributed after matins on Holy Thursday[223] and also during the foot washing later in the day, according to the Typikon of the Anastasis;[224] a peculiar choice, considering the condemnation of Judas' love of money sung throughout the hymnography for that day.[225]

Migrations

Despite the turmoil that followed the Arab conquest of the Holy City, Palestine and Jerusalem were considered hospitable and relatively safe regions. According to the *Life of St Stephen the Younger*, Palestine—Muslim rule notwithstanding—was a safer refuge than Constantinople or other regions of the Byzantine empire for persecuted iconophile monks during the eighth century.[226] In the early ninth century, another Byzantine account paints a decidedly different picture of the apparent stability of the church of Jerusalem. The monastic chronicler Theophanes (d. 818) describes the situation:

---

[219] McCormick, *Survey of the Holy Land*, xiii.
[220] Ibid., 31 table 2.3.   [221] Ibid., 24–5.   [222] Ibid., 16.
[223] ἐν ταύτῃ γὰρ τῇ ἁγίᾳ ἡμέρᾳ ῥογεύει ὁ πατριάρχης [εἰς] τὸν κλῆρον τὴν ῥόγαν αὐτῶν οὕτως· μετὰ τὸ ἀπολῦσαι ὁ ὄρθρος, ἀλλάξει καὶ καθήσει εἰς τὸ Σέκρετ[ον] καὶ φορεῖ τὸ ὠμοφόριον αὐτοῦ· καὶ εὐθὺς ἀλλάζουν οἱ ιβ′ ἀρχ[ιερεῖς] καὶ παραστήκουν αὐτῷ, καὶ ἄρξεται ῥογεύειν αὐτῶν πάντων ἐμβάθμως καὶ κατὰ τάξιν ('On this holy day the patriarch distributes the largesse to the clergy thus: after the dismissal of matins, he leaves and sits in the council chamber and wears his *omophorion*. Immediately the twelve bishops leave and stand by him, and he begins to distribute to all of those in ministry and according to order'). Papadopoulos-Kerameus, *Anastasis Typikon*, 99.
[224] καὶ [ὁ πατριάρχης] φιλᾷ τὸν πόδα καί δίδει ἑκάστῳ αὐτῶν ἀπὸ νομίσματος ('And the patriarch kisses their feet and gives each one of them a coin'). Ibid., 113.
[225] See ibid., 96–116.
[226] See BHG 1666, Stephanus Constantinopolitanus Diaconus, *Vita Sancti Stephani junioris, monachi et martyris*, PG 100:1120; and *La Vie d'Etienne le Jeune par Etienne le Diacre*, ed. by Marie-France Auzépy (Birmingham Byzantine and Ottoman Monographs 3, Aldershot: Variorum, 1997), 125–6. See also Marina Detoraki, 'Greek *Passions* of the Martyrs in Byzantium', in *Ashgate Companion to Byzantine Hagiography* II, 85–9.

τῷ δ' αὐτῷ ἔτει πολλοὶ τῶν κατὰ Παλαιστίνην Χριστιανῶν μοναχοὶ καὶ λαϊκοὶ καὶ ἐκ πάσης Συρίας τὴν Κύπρον κατέλαβον φεύγοντες τὴν ἄμετρον κάκωσιν τῶν Ἀράβων. ἀναρχίας γὰρ καθολικῆς κατασχούσης Συρίαν καὶ Αἴγυπτον καὶ Ἀφρικὴν καὶ πᾶσαν τὴν ὑπ' αὐτοὺς ἀρχήν, φόνοι τε καὶ ἁρπαγαί καὶ μοιχεῖαι, ἀσέλγειαί τε καὶ πᾶσαι πράξεις θεοστυγεῖς ἐν κώμαις καὶ πόλεσι ὑπὸ τοῦ θεολέστου ἔθνους αὐτῶν ἐπράττοντο, οἵ τε κατὰ τὴν ἁγίαν Χριστοῦ τοῦ θεοῦ ἡμῶν πόλιν σεβάσμιοι τόποι τῆς ἁγίας ἀναστάσεως, τοῦ κρανίου καὶ τῶν λοιπῶν ἐβεβηλώθησαν. ὁμοίως δὲ καὶ αἱ κατὰ τὴν ἔρημον διαβόητοι λαῦραι τοῦ ἁγίου Χαρίτωνος καὶ τοῦ ἁγίου Σάβα, καὶ τὰ λοιπὰ μοναστήρια καὶ αἱ ἐκκλησίαι ἠρημώθησαν. καὶ οἱ μὲν ἀνῃρέθησαν μαρτυρικῶς, οἱ δὲ τὴν Κύπρον κατέλαβον καὶ ἐκ ταύτης τὸ Βυζάντιον, οὓς Μιχαήλ, ὁ εὐσεβὴς βασιλεύς, καὶ Νικηφόρος, ὁ ἁγιώτατος πατριάρχης, φιλοφρόνως ἐξένισαν. τοῖς μὲν γὰρ ἐλθοῦσιν ἐν τῇ πόλει μοναστήριον ἐπίσημον ἐδωρήσατο, τοῖς δὲ κατὰ τὴν Κύπρον ἐναπομείνασι μοναχοῖς τε καὶ λαϊκοῖς τάλαντον χρυσίου ἀπέστειλεν, καὶ παντοίως τούτους ἐθεράπευσεν.[227]

In the same year [812/13] many of the Christians of Palestine, monks and laymen, and from all of Syria arrived in Cyprus, fleeing the excessive misdeeds of the Arabs. For, as a result of the general anarchy that prevailed in Syria, Egypt, Africa, and their [i.e. the Arabs'] entire dominion, murders, rapes, adulteries, and all manner of licentious acts that are abhorred by God were committed in villages and towns by that accursed nation. In the holy city of Christ our God the venerable places of the holy Resurrection, of Golgotha, and the rest were profaned. Likewise the famous *lavras* in the desert, that of St Chariton and that of St Sabas, and the other monasteries and churches were made desolate. Some Christians were killed like martyrs, while others proceeded to Cyprus and thence to Byzantium and were given kindly hospitality by the pious emperor Michael and the most holy patriarch Nikephoros. The emperor made a gift of an important monastery to those who had come to the City, while to those who had remained in Cyprus, both monks and laymen, he sent a talent of gold and provided for them in every way.[228]

It is generally accepted that the great migrations of 'Christian monks and laity' described by Theophanes were those of an 'intellectual élite' fleeing Monotheletism as well as Persian and Arab invasions in the seventh century, and then iconoclasm in the eighth and ninth centuries. The picture painted by Theophanes was not that simple. Just as the persecution of Christians in the early church did not continue without interruption but went in fits and spurts, in tandem with periods of peace, so too was the situation for Christians in Palestine. The Byzantine recapture of Syrian territories in the late tenth century subjected the region to pillaging and a scorched earth policy, as well as to psychological pressure designed to disrupt the unity of the non-Chalcedonian Christian population.[229] The chronicles of the period, especially those of Michael the Syrian (d. 1199) and Bar Hebraeus (c.1226–86), suggest that the Miaphysites moved north and east, towards Militene and Edessa,

---

[227] *Theophanis Chronographia*, 499. For biographical information on Theophanes, see Mango and Scott, *Chronicle of Theophanes*, xliii–lii; Alexander Kazhdan, 'Theophanes the Confessor', ODB III, 2063.
[228] Translation from Mango and Scott, *Chronicle of Theophanes*, 683. See also Griffith, 'Holy Land in the Ninth Century', 232.
[229] Dagron, 'L'immigration syrienne', 183–5.

rather than towards Constantinople and southern Italy, where numerous new dioceses and monasteries had been established during the late tenth and early eleventh centuries.[230] Byzantine attempts to submit the Syrians to Chalcedonian Orthodoxy failed, most notably after the delegation of Yuḥanon VIII bar ʿAbdun (1004–31) and his bishops to Constantinople in 1029.[231] It should be noted that the exiled Chalcedonian Patriarch Elias of Antioch was consecrated in Constantinople on 1 April 1030 and most probably remained there. However, his signature did not appear on the acts of excommunication against the Miaphysites until 1032,[232] perhaps because he did not approve of the Byzantine tactic of forced reunion, as Dagron suggests.[233]

However, certain members of the Palestinian 'intellectual élite' did arrive in southern Italy and made a significant impact on the church there. Patriarch Orestes of Jerusalem (r. 986–1005), whose sister was the wife of the fifth Fatimid Caliph al-Azīz (r. 976–96) and whose brother Arsenius became patriarch of Alexandria in 1000, spent most of his time as patriarch outside of Jerusalem, accompanying Byzantine ambassadors in voyages to Arab-occupied lands,[234] and died in Constantinople after living there for four years.[235] Orestes was engaged in church life in southern Italy and wrote the *Vitae* of three Sicilian saints: Sabas, Christopher, and Macarius.[236] Southern Italian contact with such figures as Patriarch Orestes, as well as earlier contact between Palestinian and southern Italian monasticism,[237] explains how certain Middle Eastern prayers, such as the prayer for presenting bread and wine found in the Alexandrian BAS, made their way to southern Italy and Constantinople.[238] Since, however, similar Palestinian influence is already found

---

[230] Michael the Syrian, *Chronicle*, vol. 3, 130; Bar Hebraeus, *Chronicon ecclesiasticum*, vol. 1, trans. by Joannes Baptista Abbeloos and Thomas Josephus Lamy (Leuven: Peeters, 1872–7), 412 and 418.

[231] Ibid., 430–2; H. Takahashi, 'Melitene', GEDSH, 283.

[232] 'Confirmation du tome précédent contre les Jacobites', in Grumel, *Regestes* I.2–3, 346 (n. 840, April 1032).

[233] Dagron, 'L'immigration syrienne', 203.

[234] Yaḥyā al-Anṭakī, *Cronache*, 190; Marius Canard, 'al-ʿAzīz Bi'llāh', in *Encyclopaedia of Islam*, vol. 1, 823–5.

[235] Yaḥyā al-Anṭakī, *Cronache*, 227.

[236] St Sabas: BHG 1611 and 1611b; Sts Christopher and Macarius: BHG 312. André Jacob and Jean-Marie Martin, 'L'Église grecque en Italie (v. 650–v. 1050)', in *Histoire des Christianisme des origines à nos jours*, vol. 4: *Évêques, moines et empereurs (610–1054)*, ed. by Gilbert Dagron, Pierre Riché, and André Vauchez (Paris: Desclée, 1993), 347–71; Lidia Perria, Vera von Falkenhausen, and Franceso D'Aiuto, 'Introduzione', in Perria, *Tra oriente e occidente*, ix.

[237] Antonino Gallico, 'Su una citazione di Teodoreto nel bios di San Nilo: Trace del cristianesimo siro-palestinese in Calabria', in *Chiesa e Società nel Mezzogiorno. Studi in onore di Maria Mariotti*, vol. 2 (Soveria Mannelli: Rubbettino, 1998), 35–45.

[238] Heinzgerd Brakmann, 'Zu den Fragmenten einer griechischen Basileios-Liturgie aus dem koptischen Makarios-Kloster', *Oriens Christianus* 66 (1982), 118–43, here 127–30; 'Vino e olio nelle liturgie bizantine', in Parenti, *A oriente e occidente di Costantinopoli*, 54; Radle, 'Liturgical Ties between Egypt and Southern Italy'.

in the oldest surviving Byzantine Euchologion, *Barberini Gr. 336* from the eighth century, for example in the rite of foot washing on Holy Thursday and in the prayer of the cathedra, this process must have begun long before Patriarch Orestes.[239]

Byzantine Contact

In response to the persecution of the church of Jerusalem, the Byzantines attempted to reconquer Jerusalem several times. The military campaign of John I Tzimisces (r. 969–76) liberated Nazareth, Mount Tabor, and Caesarea in 975, while the campaign of Emperor Basil II (r. 976–1025) only reached Baalbek in present-day Lebanon, according to the letter from Tzimisces to Ashot III of Armenia, preserved by Matthew of Edessa.[240]

The recapture of Antioch in 969 provided a second pole for the Byzantine empire, which had been the virtual capital of the Roman East.[241] The rise of Antioch, however, did not go unchecked by Constantinople, at least not in ecclesiastical matters. Subsequent candidates for the position of patriarch of Antioch, such as the monk Theodore in the tenth century, were subjected to an examination by the synod prior to their enthronement.[242] According to Yaḥyā al-Anṭakī, Patriarch Agapius of Antioch (r. 978–96) was urged by Emperor Basil II to resign as patriarch of Antioch in exchange for a monastery in Constantinople and a salary.[243] Agapius was replaced on 4 October 996 by John, who had been *chartophylax* at Hagia Sophia in Constantinople. Patriarch John was ordered to 'bring order [*rattaba*] to the church of Cassian in Antioch, on the basis of the model [*mithāl*] of St Sophia in Constantinople'.[244] The church of Cassian (al-Qusyān in Arabic) was not the

---

[239] See Parenti and Velkovska, *Barberini 336*, 205–8 (§ 222–5); 60 and 73 (§ 7 and 26), respectively. See also Parenti, 'Preghiera della cattedra'.

[240] Alexander Kazhdan and Anthony Cutler, 'John I Tzimiskes', ODB II, 1045; Charles M. Brand and Anthony Cutler, 'Basil II', ODB I, 261–2; Canard, 'La destruction de l'église de la Résurrection', 43. For a recent review of some aspects of Tzimiskes' campaigns, see Anthony Kaldellis, 'Did Ioannes I Tzimiskes Campaign in the East in 974?', *Byzantion* 84 (2014), 235–40.

[241] Dagron, 'L'immigration syrienne', 205. See also Todt, 'Region und griechisch-orthodoxes Patriarcht von Antiocheia', 239–67; Todt, 'Zwischen Kaiser und ökumenischem Patriarchen', 137–76.

[242] 'Examen synodal de l'aptitude du moine Théodore, désigné par l'empereur pour être patriarche d'Antioche', in Grumel, *Regestes* I.2–3, 305 (n. 795, January 970). See also V. Grumel, 'Le patriarcat et les patriarches d'Antioche sous la seconde domination byzantine, 969–1084', *Échos d'Orient* 33 (1934), 129–47.

[243] The name of the monastery is unclear, but Kratchkovsky and Vasiliev suggest it may have been Πικριδίου. See Janin, *Les églises et les monastères*, 403–4.

[244] Yaḥyā al-Anṭakī, *History* II, 445–6.

same as the Great Church of Antioch, but had assumed the status of the city's cathedral perhaps as early as the sixth century.[245] In the eleventh century, Abbot Elias of the monastery 'of the star' brought back books from Antioch to 'Abūd in Samaria, present-day Palestine,[246] for use there. This community was a Chalcedonian stronghold and the region was a source of many other liturgical manuscripts.[247]

One such liturgical book is *Vatican Syr. 19* (1030), a Gospel book showing the strong influence of Byzantine liturgical practice on the Antiochene patriarchate. A very detailed colophon of the manuscript, written in Arabic Garshuni—that is, Arabic text in Syriac script—reads as follows:[248]

> I, Abbot Elias, presbyter, disciple of Abbot Moses, confirm to have written this Gospel and the books of the feasts, of the Resurrection, and the six Menaia, to the service of the holy church, and the rest of the books that I brought with me from Antioch in Arabia as a gift [*waqf*] for the monastery of St Elias, known as the monastery of the star [*kawkab*], which I built. May this Gospel and these books be for those who live in this monastery.[249]

Another note (fol. 194v) indicates that the manuscript was completed on Wednesday 7 August 1030, that the aforementioned Elias was from the town of 'Abūd, and that Antioch is described as part of the region of 'Adqūs.[250] This wealth of geographic information has attracted attention since the manuscript's initial description by Joseph Simonius Assemani (1687–1768) and by his nephew, Stephanus Evodius Assemani (1711–82) in 1758.[251] They believed that 'Adqūs was a corruption of *Al-quds*, meaning 'Jerusalem'.[252]

---

[245] For more on the Antiochene church of Cassian, see Wendy Mayer and Pauline Allen, *The Churches of Syrian Antioch (300–638 CE)* (Leuven: Peeters, 2012), 52–5, 174–82. See also Todt, 'Zwischen Kaiser und ökumenischem Patriarchen', 154–7.

[246] Giovanni Lenzi, 'Lezionario dei Vangeli: Aramaico palestinese', in *Vangeli dei popoli*, 230.

[247] Bellarmino Bagatti, *Antichi villaggi cristiani di Samaria* (Jerusalem: Tipografia dei Padri Francescani, 1979), 117–18; Schick, *Christian Communities of Palestine*, 240–1.

[248] Nasrallah, 'Liturgie des Patriarcats melchites', 160; Alessandro Mengozzi, 'Garshuni', GEDSH, 172–3.

[249] *Io, abba Elia, presbitero, discepolo di abba Mosè, affermo di aver scritto questo Vangelo e i libri delle solennità, della resurrezione e i sei menei a servizio della santa Chiesa, e il resto dei libri che ho portato con me da Antiochia in Arabia come dono [waqf] per il monastero di S. Elia, conosciuto come il monastero della stella [kawkab], che è stato costruito da me. Che questo Vangelo e i libri siano per chi abita in questo monastero.* The original text of the manuscript, transcribed in Assemani, *Catalogus*, vol. 2, 102, is no longer legible. This Italian translation is from Giovanni Lenzi, 'Lezionario dei Vangeli: Aramaico palestinese', in *Vangeli dei popoli*, 228–30, here 229, with his corrections to the Assemani transcription.

[250] 'Seventh day of Ab in the year of the Greeks 1341', ibid.

[251] Assemani, *Catalogus*, vol. 2, 70–103. For more on the scholars of the Assemani family, see Sebastian P. Brock, 'Assemani, Joseph Aloysius', GEDSH, 43; Sebastian P. Brock, 'Assemanus, Joseph Simonius', GEDSH, 43–44; Sebastian P. Brock, 'Assemani, Stephanus Evodius', GEDSH, 44. See also Franciscus M. Erizzo, *Evangeliarium Hierosolymitanum ex codice vaticano palæstino* (Verona: Vicentini et Franchini, 1864).

[252] Assemani, *Catalogus*, vol. 2, 101.

Francis Crawford Burkitt (1864–1935) identified ʾAdqūs and Kawkab as Dux (τὸ Δούξ) and Cavcas (Καύκα), two regions in Celesyria (Κοίλη Συρία) near Antioch, mentioned by Anna Comnene (1083–53) in the *Alexiad*.[253] Burkitt also proposed that the monastery of St Elias was the famous Lavra of St Elias on the Black Mountain.[254] Sebastian Brock follows Burkitt on the origin of the manuscript but disagrees that the monastery of St Elias refers to the Black Mountain.[255] However, more recent studies have identified the monastery 'of the star' (Kawkab) to be 1.5 km from Abbot Elias' home town of ʿAbūd in Samaria, present-day Palestine.[256]

Although John Tzimisces and Basil II were unable able to recapture Jerusalem militarily, the reconquest of Antioch facilitated the transmission of Byzantinized liturgical books from Constantinople and Antioch to northern Palestine and Jerusalem, which eventually led to the adoption of the Byzantine rite in Jerusalem. By the time of the crusader conquest of the Holy City in 1099, the liturgical Byzantinization of Jerusalem was in its final stages.

Arabization

One of the most complex aspects of the history of liturgical Byzantinization in Jerusalem is the shift from a Greek-speaking to an Arabic-speaking Orthodox Church, which is surprising at first if one considers that the Holy Land was under increasing Constantinopolitan liturgical influence during the ninth and tenth centuries and that many Arabic speakers continued to pray in Greek. This problem is compounded by certain scholars' selective attempts to favour the presence of one language over another among Chalcedonian Christians in Jerusalem. For example, Korolevsky divides liturgical developments between a 'Syro-Byzantine' and 'Arab-Byzantine' period and claims that Arabic became a liturgical language only in the seventeenth century.[257] Nasrallah refined Korolevsky's work and suggested that, with the revived use of Greek in the tenth century, Arabic became increasingly common as a liturgical language,

---

[253] *Alexiad* XIII, 12: 18, in *Annae Comnenae Alexias*, ed. by Diether R. Reinsch and Athanasios Kambylis (Berlin and New York: W. de Gruyter, 2001), 419.

[254] Francis C. Burkitt, 'Christian Palestinian Literature', JTS 2 (1901), 174–86, esp. 176–9.

[255] Sebastian Brock, 'Syriac Manuscripts Copied on the Black Mountain, near Antioch', in *Lingua Restituta Orientalis. Festgabe für Julius Assfalg*, ed. by Regine Schulz and Manfred Görg (Wiesbaden: Harrassowitz, 1990), 59–67, here 62 n. 19.

[256] Giovanni Lenzi, 'Lezionario dei Vangeli: Aramaico palestinese', in *Vangeli dei popoli*, 230. It is also worth noting that the manuscript is a palimpsest with the underwriting in Greek minuscule, formerly a Triodion. See Francesco D'Aiuto, '*Graeca* in codici orientali della Biblioteca Vaticana', in Perria, *Tra oriente e occidente*, 283–90, esp. 288–9 for the Greek text of the Triodion; Francesco D'Aiuto, 'Per la storia dei libri liturgico-innografici bizantini: Un progetto di catalogazione dei manoscritti più antichi', BBGG (terza serie) 3 (2006), 53–66, here 61–3.

[257] Charon, 'Le rite byzantin', 27.

surpassing Syriac in most regions by the thirteenth century.[258] More recently, Sidney Griffith, followed by Noble and Treiger, have pushed the date even earlier, pointing to Arabic translations of lectionaries and theological works as early as the second half of the eighth century and continuing into the ninth.[259] The influx of Muslims into urban areas such as Homs in Syria—rather than the exodus of Greek speakers to Constantinople and the West—is what accelerated the process of Arabization.[260]

Ninth-century *Vatican Gr. 2282* has numerous marginal notes in Arabic to explain the Greek rubrics. This shows that, while the liturgy may still have been celebrated in Greek, the vernacular was already becoming Arabic.[261] Arabic marginal notes in the Gospel lectionaries *Sinai Gr. 212* (9th cent.) and *Sinai Gr. N.E. MΓ 11* (9th cent.) are so frequent that they are sometimes present when no Greek rubric was copied, which means that the reader who was using the manuscripts had to know Arabic in order to navigate and read the Greek text during liturgical services.[262] Other manuscripts, such as *St Petersburg RNB Gr. 44* (9th cent.) and *Sinai Gr. N.E. MΓ 8* (10th cent.), contain Arabic rubrics and notes within the text block of folios, which indicates that knowledge of Arabic was assumed by the reader—and certainly not marginal. In some cases the Arabic rubrics and notes provide supplemental information that helps to interpret the Greek text of a rubric properly.[263] Caliph 'Abd al-Malik (r. 685–705) and his son, al-Walīd I (r. 705–15), precipitated the process of Arabization by forbidding scribes to copy certain legal documents in Greek.[264] Similarly, the 'Abbasid translation movement was marked by stark 'anti-Byzantinism', which portrayed Byzantines as holding illogical beliefs and as having no philosophers of their own, and favoured 'philhellenism' instead—though expressed in Arabic.[265]

Because of the multilingual environment in Jerusalem and its monasteries, it is often difficult to determine the extent to which Arabic was used liturgically.

---

[258] Nasrallah, 'Liturgie des patriarchats melchites', 158.

[259] Griffith, 'From Aramaic to Arabic', 24–30; Noble and Treiger, *The Orthodox Church in the Arab World*, 21–2.

[260] Nasrallah, *Histoire* II.1, 43; Nasrallah, *Histoire* II.2, 183.

[261] See 'Ad liturgiam antiochenam: Notulae', in *Novae patrum bibliothecae*, compiled by Angelo Mai, vol. 10.2: *Liturgica*, ed. by J. Cozza-Luzi (Rome: Bibliotheca Vaticana, 1905), 113–16; Charon, 'Le rite byzantin', 19; Nasrallah, *Histoire* II.1, 70.

[262] Galadza, 'Two Sources of the Jerusalem Lectionary', 79–111. See Appendix 1 for more on this manuscript.

[263] Thibaut, *Monuments*, 3*–11*; Galadza, 'Sinai Gr. N.E. MΓ 8'. See Appendix 1 for more on this manuscript.

[264] Michael the Syrian, *Chronicle*, 2: 481; Juan Pedro Monferrer-Sala, 'Between Hellenism and Arabization: On the Formation of an Ethnolinguistic Identity of the Melkite Communities in the Heart of Muslim Rule', *Al-Qanṭara* 33: 2 (2012), 445–71, here 447.

[265] Dmitri Gutas, *Greek Thought, Arabic Culture: The Graeco-Arabic Translation Movement in Baghdad and Early 'Abbāsid Society (2nd–4th/8th–10th centuies)* (London: Routledge, 1998), 83–95.

As already noted, the majority of Arabic liturgical texts that do survive are lectionaries. This may reflect the prescription that only the Liturgy of the Word and the Liturgy of the Hours be celebrated in the vernacular, while on the other hand the eucharistic liturgy was to be celebrated in Greek alone. A passage from the Typikon of the Anastasis witnesses to the increased importance of Arabic in the liturgy. During matins on Easter morning, we find a rubric reminiscent of passages from Egeria concerning the place of Syriac (*siriste*) and the founder's Typikon of the Lavra of St Sabas mentioned above:

Καὶ εὐθὺς ὁ πατριάρχης ἵσταται εἰς τὸ σύνθρονον, καὶ ὁ ἀρχιδιάκονος λέγει ʻΠρόσχωμενʼ, καὶ εὐθὺς ἄρξεται ἀναγινώσκειν τοῦτο μεγάλη φωνῇ· «Τοῦ ἐν ἁγίοις πατρὸς ἡμῶν Ἰωάννου τοῦ Χρυσοστόμου, λόγος εἰς τὸ ἅγιον πάσχα», (οὗ ἡ ἀρχή)· «Εἴ τις εὐσεβὴς καὶ φιλόθεος» κτλ. Εἶθ' οὕτως μεταφράσει αὐτὸν τὸν λόγον ὁ β' τῶν διακόνων εἰς ἀραβικὴν γλῶσσαν, ὥστε παρακληθήσονται οἱ μὴ εἰδότες ἀναγινώσ(κειν) ῥωμαϊκὰ [sic], καὶ γίνεται χαρὰ καὶ ἡ ἀγαλλίασις καὶ ἡ εὐφροσύνη παντὶ τῷ λαῷ, μικροῦ τε καὶ μεγάλου [sic].[266]	And immediately the patriarch stands on the synthronon and the archdeacon says 'Let us attend!' and immediately begins to read this in a loud voice: 'Of our father among the saints, John Chrysostom, Homily for Holy Pascha', (which begins) 'If anyone is pious and God-loving' etc. Then the second of the deacons translates the homily into the Arabic language so that those who do not read Greek may be comforted and that all the people may have joy, exultation, and merriment—both the small and the great.

This suggests that, by the twelfth century, Arabic had taken the place that Syriac once held as the liturgical vernacular among the local Palestinian population of the church of Jerusalem.

Despite Arabic's function as a kind of liturgical vernacular, there are few if any solely Arabic liturgical manuscripts of the Hagiopolite liturgy. Syriac may have continued to be used alongside Greek for certain parts of the liturgical services, such as hymns or litanies, as can be seen in *Sinai Gr. N.E. X 239* (12th–13th cent.). Nasrallah believes that Arabic was used less in Jerusalem than in Antioch, because of the loyalty to Constantinople of monasteries like the Lavra of St Sabas.[267] As already noted, despite the presence of Greek, Syriac, Aramaic, Georgian, and even Armenian and Frankish monks resident at Mar Sabas Lavra, Greek was the common official liturgical language and Arabic-speaking monks attended Syriac services, since there was a lack of complete liturgical texts in Arabic.[268] Although Arabic liturgical Typika were

---

[266] Papadopoulos-Kerameus, *Anastasis Typikon*, 200. The homily referred to in the manuscript is in John Chrysostom, *Sermo catecheticus in pascha*, CPG 4605; PG 59:721–4; Arabic version in *Sinai Ar. 455* (12th cent.), fol. 90–92 and *Paris B.N. Ar. 262* (15th cent.), fol. 189v (no. 17). See Gérard Troupeau, *Catalogue des manuscrits arabes: Première partie: Manuscrits chrétiens*, vol. 1 (Paris: Bibliothèque Nationale, 1972), 228.
[267] Nasrallah, 'Liturgie des patriarchats melchites', 159–60.
[268] Leeming, 'The Adoption of Arabic as a Liturgical Language', 240–1; Nicolas Egender, 'La formation et l'influence du *Typikon* liturgique', in Patrich, *Sabaite Heritage*, here 210.

copied in Syria and Egypt, no such manuscripts are extant from Palestine or from the Jerusalem patriarchate, which lends support to the view that Arabic really did play a significantly secondary role as a liturgical language in Hagiopolite liturgy.[269] On the basis of the results obtained from Georgian and Syriac discoveries, Kate Leeming has suggested that the 'new finds' at Sinai may contain Arabic hymnographic and liturgical texts as the underwriting of palimpsests; these Arabic texts would have been written over because the liturgy they contained was Hagiopolitan and eventually rejected during the period of liturgical Byzantinization.[270] This claim, however, remains to be verified.

Changes in Topography

Owing to archaeological surveys and historical analysis of the seventh and eighth centuries in Palestine, it can now be stated with greater certainty that much of the destruction of churches and holy sites attributed to the Persians in 614 and to the Arabs in the years immediately after 638 actually occurred in the ninth century.[271] Despite pillaging and burning the Anastasis and numerous other churches in Palestine, as described by Antiochus Strategus, the Persians subsequently funded the complete restoration of the Anastasis, which was initiated by Patriarch Modestus (r. 630–34).[272] Robert Schick believes that more churches were restored during the early years of the Muslim conquest than during the brief period of Byzantine recovery under Emperor Heraclius (r. 610–41), a conclusion based on the lack of evidence of building activity in Jerusalem during the reign of Heraclius.[273] Klaus Bieberstein suggests that descriptions of the destruction of other churches, such as the Nea Church of the Theotokos, were actually projections by historians of more recent, ninth-century events onto the murky past.[274]

---

[269] Martin Lüstraeten, *Die handschriftlichen arabischen Übersetzungen des byzantinischen Typikons* (Jerusalemer Theologisches Forum 31, Münster: Aschendorff Verlag, 2017).

[270] Leeming, 'The Adoption of Arabic as a Liturgical Language', 245.

[271] Bieberstein, 'Gesandtenaustausch'. For new seventh-century sources, see Laurent Blancs, 'Autour de quelques textes chrétiens concernant les premiers temps de la conquête musulmane', in *Byzance et ses périphéries: Hommage à Alain Ducellier*, ed. by Bernard Doumerc and Christophe Picard (Toulouse: CNRS/Université de Toulouse-Le Mirail, 2004), 41–55.

[272] Frederick C. Conybeare, 'Antiochus Strategos, the Capture of Jerusalem by the Persians in 614 AD' [sic], *English Historical Review* 25 (1910), 502–17; Alexander Kazhdan, 'Antiochus Strategos', ODB I, 119–20. See 'Islamic Occupation' in this chapter.

[273] Schick, *Christian Communities of Palestine*, 65–6.

[274] Bieberstein, 'Gesandtenaustausch', 159. See also Sidney Griffith, 'What Has Constantinople to Do with Jerusalem? Palestine in the Ninth Century: Byzantine Orthodoxy in the World of Islam', in *Byzantium in the Ninth Century: Dead or Alive? Papers from the Thirtieth Spring Symposium of Byzantine Studies, Birmingham, March 1996*, ed. by Leslie Brubaker (Aldershot:

From the perspective of the liturgical historian, the use of 'threshold dates' such as 614 or 1009 by liturgical scholars such as Arranz raises the question of the connection of a liturgical rite to a liturgical space precisely because these dates often do not correspond to the variety found in the actual liturgical sources. How quickly would changes to topography affect liturgical practices or be reflected in liturgical rites copied down in manuscripts? For example, according to the account of Arculf, the Imbomon was already without a roof around 670; Willibald of Eichstätt (*c.*700–7/8) confirms there was no roof there around 724 or 725, and the church remained so until the arrival of the crusaders. Nevertheless, liturgical services continued to be held at the Imbomon.[275] Would such a state of disrepair affect liturgical practice? The state of affairs might discourage any processions to this church in the stational liturgy of Jerusalem, but would it immediately alter more than just the location of the service? Would it alter its internal structure, prayers, hymns, and scriptural readings? If the liturgical changes witnessed in liturgical books during the period of Byzantinization resulted not from internal ecclesiastical and canonical regulation but as a local response to external circumstances in the local environment, it is not surprising that diversity and variation are present in the liturgical sources. A principle of comparative liturgical studies attributed to Baumstark, that 'the development of liturgy is but a series of individual developments' and the 'history of the liturgy consists not in one progressive unilinear growth of entire rituals as single units, but via distinct developments of their individual components',[276] certainly supports such a conclusion. Let us look more closely at some of these changes to the sacred topography of Jerusalem to understand what impact they had on liturgy.

Ashgate, 1998), 181–94; Nahman Avigad, 'The Nea: Justinian's Church of St Mary, Mother of God, Discovered in the Old City of Jerusalem', in *Ancient Churches Revealed*, ed. by Yoram Tsafrir (Jerusalem: Israel Exploration Society, 1993), 128–35; Renata Salvarani, 'Il modello gerosolimitano: continuità e trasformazione nella liturgia di Gerusalemme', in *Liturgie e culture tra l'èta di Gregorio Magno e il pontificato di Leone III: Aspetti rituali, ecclesiologici e istituzionali*, ed. by Renata Salvarani (Monumenta Studia Instrumenta Liturgica 64, Vatican City: Libreria Editrice Vaticana, 2011), 37–55.

[275] Dmitrievskii, *Древнѣйшіе Патріаршіе Типиконы*, 33; Pringle, *Churches of the Crusader Kingdom*, vol. 3, 72–88, esp. 72–3. This station is indicated six times in the GL: § 645, 752, 856, 890, 1126, 1279; Verhelst, 'Lieux de station' I, 22; id., 'Lieux de station' II, 261. See Chapter 1, 'Stational Liturgy and the Topography of Jerusalem'.

[276] Although Taft attributes this 'law' to Baumstark, neither he nor Fritz West is able to trace this reference to Baumstark's publications. See Robert F. Taft, SJ, 'Comparative Liturgy Fifty Years after Anton Baumstark (d. 1948): A Reply to Recent Critics', *Worship* 73 (1999), 521–40, here 525; Robert F. Taft, SJ, 'Anton Baumstark's Comparative Liturgy Revisited', in *Liturgy Fifty Years after Baumstark*, 198. My thanks to Robert Taft and Fritz West for their assistance with this question.

The Destruction of the Anastasis

Many authors consider the destruction of the Anastasis church in 1009 to be the most significant date in the process of Byzantinization, a date that marked the Holy City forever, leaving it a completely changed landscape. Arranz and Pentkovsky are just a few liturgists who flag the year 1009 as a crucial date in their general studies of Byzantine liturgy.[277] Yet a closer examination of the events surrounding the destruction and rebuilding of the Anastasis reveals that this date, too, may be not so much a watershed as an unnuanced landmark date in the process of Byzantinization in Jerusalem.

Before discussing the destruction of the Anastasis, it should be noted that the church we are familiar with today is not the original Holy Sepulchre. The present structure dates to the reconstruction after the fire of 1808 and was preceded by three other structures, the first being that of Constantine the Great in the fourth century.[278] Following numerous sacks and sieges, the Anastasis complex underwent several repairs throughout the seventh century and down to the tenth. The church complex suffered extensive damage on 28 May 966, when it was burned and Patriarch John VII (r. 964–6) was brutally murdered and his body immolated in the atrium of the Martyrium.[279] Patriarch Christodulus II (r. 966–9) began restoration. Work continued under Patriarchs Thomas II (r. 969–79), Joseph II (r. 980–4), Agapius (r. 984–5), and Orestes (r. 986–1006) of Jerusalem and Patriarch Arsenius of Alexandria (r. 1000–10).[280] The reconstruction was funded by Ibn al-Ḥammār, a Miaphysite Christian, and later supervised by *synkellos* Ṣadaqah Ibn Bišr, so that the Anastasis was 'restored to its pristine splendour'.[281]

The rule of Caliph al-Ḥākim bi-Amri'llāh from 996 to 1021 ushered in an era of particular animosity towards Christians, despite the fact that his mother

---

[277] See Arranz, 'Grandes étapes'; Pentkovsky, 'Богослужебные уставы'. See also *Konflikt und Bewältigung: Die Zerstörung der Grabeskirche zu Jerusalem im Jahre 1009*, ed. by Thomas Pratsch (Berlin: De Gruyter, 2011).

[278] Ousterhout, 'Rebuilding the Temple', 66–8. For a diagram of the various reconstructions, see Appendix 2, 'Plan of the Church of the Anastasis (4th, 11th, and 12th cent.)' in this volume.

[279] Yaḥyā al-Anṭakī, *History* I, 708; Yaḥyā al-Anṭakī, *Cronache*, 114–15; Fedalto, 'Liste vescovili', 17.

[280] See 'Patriarchae Hierosolymitani. 98.1.2 Hierosolyma, Aelia Capitolina, Urusalîm, al-Quds, Yarušalaym, Jerusalem, Gerusalemme', in Fedalto, *Hierarchia ecclesiastica orientalis*, vol. 2, 999–1005 for varying names and dates of the patriarchs in this period.

[281] *[I]l tetto della chiesa di san Costantino fu portato a termine ed essa venne restituita al suo pristino splendore: fu allora che la chiesa fu completata in ogni sua parte, poco tempo prime dell'ultima distruzione abbattutasi su di essa nel mese di ṣafar dell'anno 400 dell'egira* ('The roof of the church of St Constantine was completed and it was restored to its pristine splendour. It was at this time that all the parts of the church were completed, shortly before the last destruction struck it down in the month of Ṣafar in the year 400 of the Hegira'). Yaḥyā al-Anṭakī, *Cronache*, 116; Yaḥyā al-Anṭakī, *History* I, 708; Ousterhout, 'Rebuilding the Temple', 69; Gil, *History of Palestine*, 463–4.

was a Melkite. His persecutions ranged from indiscriminate arrests and executions in 1001 to banning the celebration of Pascha and Theophany in 1004.[282] He also forbade the use of wine during the celebration of the Eucharist, forcing the clergy to use the residue from raisins soaked in water.[283] According to the account of Ibn-al-Qalānisī, al-Ḥākim ordered the destruction of the Holy Sepulchre complex in AH 399 (17 September 1007 to 4 September 1008).[284] The account of the destruction of the Anastasis is also found in the history of Yaḥyā-ibn-Saʿīd of Antioch, who dates it to the following year, 5 Ṣafar AH 400 (27 September 1009).[285] The account describes the destruction of churches in Egypt and Syria ordered by al-Ḥākim, and then presents the scene in Jerusalem:

> He [al-Ḥākim] also wrote to Yārūḫ in Syria, governor of Ramla, that he must demolish the church of the Holy Resurrection, to make its [Christian] symbols disappear, and to rip out its traces and memory. Then Yārūḫ sent his sons Yūsuf and al-Ḥusayn b. Ẓāhir al-Wazzān, in the company of Abū'l-Fawāris al-Ḍayf, who seized all the moveable property found there, after which [the church itself] was destroyed down to the foundations, except for that which was impossible to destroy and too difficult to seize and carry away. Afterwards the ʿCranion, Calvary', the church of St Constantine, and all the other buildings in their vicinity were destroyed, and the sacred remains [holy relics] were completely annihilated. Ibn Abū al-Ẓāhir attempted to remove the Holy Sepulchre and to make any trace of it disappear by breaking it and demolishing the greatest part. There was a monastery of nuns in the neighbourhood [of the Holy Sepulchre], known by the name of the monastery of as-Sari, which was also demolished. The destruction [of the Church of the Resurrection] began on Tuesday, the fifth day of Ṣafar in the year 400. All its possessions and property [*waqf*] were seized, including the vessels, sacred objects, and jewellery.[286]

---

[282] Al-Ḥākim's life and his numerous campaigns against Christians are recorded in Yaḥyā al-Anṭakī, *History* II, 450–520.

[283] Yaḥyā al-Anṭakī, *History* II, 503; Yaḥyā al-Anṭakī, *Cronache*, 257. See also Marius Canard, 'al-Ḥākim Bi-amr Allāh', in *Encyclopaedia of Islam*, vol. 3, 77–8 for more on al-Ḥākim's policies towards Christians.

[284] *History of Damascus, 363–555 a.h. by Ibn al-Qalânisi from the Bodleian Ms. Hunt. 125 Being a Continuation of the History of Hilâl al-Sâbi*, ed. by Henry F. Amedroz (Leyden: Brill, 1908), 67–8 and 15 (English summary); Canard, 'La destruction de l'église de la Résurrection', 26, 28, 30–4, 42. Canard's comparison of the various historical sources shows that the role of the miracle of the Holy Fire as al-Ḥākim's motivation to destroy the Holy Sepulchre is unclear.

[285] Yaḥyā al-Anṭakī, *History* II, 490–3; Yaḥyā al-Anṭakī, *Cronache*, 246–53; Gil, *History of Palestine*, 373–4.

[286] *Il [al-Ḥākim] fit également écrire en Syrie à Yaroukh, gouverneur de Ramlah, qu'il ait à démolir l'église de la Sainte-Résurrection, de faire disparaître ses emblèmes [chrétiens], d'en arracher les traces et souvenirs. Alors Yaroukh envoya son fils Yousout et al-Houséïn-ibn-Thahir-al-Wazzan en compagnie d'Abou-l-Fawaris-ad-Dhaïf, qui se saisirent de tout le mobilier qui s'y trouvait; et après quoi [l'église elle-même] fut abattue jusqu'aux fondements à l'exception de ce qu'il était impossible à détruire et difficile à arracher à enlever. Puis le «Cranion, Calvaire» l'église de Saint-Constantin et tous les autres édifices renfermés dans leur enceinte furent détruits, et les vestiges sacrés [saintes reliques] furent complètement anéantis. Ibn-Abou-Zhahir, s'efforça*

Only that which was too difficult to destroy was spared. This action was accompanied by other anti-Christian decrees, including the confiscation and destruction of all other churches in Palestine and the banning of processions. Fortunately the patriarch was warned, which gave him time to hide all the precious relics, gold, silver, and vestments before al-Ḥākim's order could be carried out.[287] Lazarus of Mount Galesion (d. 7 November 1053) personally witnessed the destruction of the Anastasis and decided that it was safer to return to Anatolia, in view of the persecution of Christians that accompanied this event.[288]

That such destruction had a devastating impact on worship in Jerusalem is without question. Yet within two years Christians were permitted to rebuild the Anastasis. Reconstruction began during the reign of the more tolerant local Bedouin emir, al-Mufarriǧ Ibn al-Ǧarrāḥ, and was overseen by a new patriarch, Theophilus I (r. 1012–20), previously bishop of Ḥibāl near al-Karak.[289] The emir al-Mufarriǧ issued an edict of protection for the complex in 1020, referring to it as the Church of Resurrection (al-Qiyāma), and Yahyā-ibn-Saʿīd notes that parts of the church were once again restored to their 'ancient splendour' according to the means and resources of al-Mufarriǧ.[290] The death of al-Ḥākim in 1021 in mysterious circumstances pacified the situation even further, allowing a treaty to be signed in 1030 between the Byzantine Emperor Romanus III Argyrus (r. 1028–34) and al-Ḥākim's heir, Ẓāhir.[291] This permitted a more complete reconstruction of the Anastasis at Byzantine expense, although the reconstruction was delayed until 1042, after an earthquake in 1033 or 1034 that had already destroyed virtually all the remaining churches in Jerusalem.[292]

---

d'enlever le Saint-Sépulchre et d'en faire disparaître la trace, en brisa et démolit la plus grande partie. Il y avait dans le voisinage [du saint-Sépulchre] un monastère de religieuses, connu sous le nom de monastère d'as-Sari, qui fut également démoli. La ruine de [l'église de la Résurrection] fut commencée le mardi cinquième jour de çafar de l'an 400. Tous ses domaines et legs pieux [waqf] furent saisis, ainsi que tous les vases et objets sacrés et les pièces d'orfèvrerie. Yaḥyā al-Anṭakī, *History* II, 491–2; Yaḥyā al-Anṭakī, *Cronache*, 249–50.

[287] Canard, 'La destruction de l'église de la Résurrection', 20–4.

[288] BHG 979, *De Sancto Lazaro Monacho in Monte Galesio* (in AASS, Novembris, tomus III), 515 (7 November, § 19, D–F); Alice-Mary Talbot, 'Byzantine Pilgrimage to the Holy Land from the Eighth to the Fifteenth Century', in Patrich, *Sabaite Heritage*, 97–110, here 101; *The Life of Lazaros of Mt Galesion: An Eleventh-Century Pillar Saint*, trans. by Richard P. H. Greenfield (Washington, DC: Dumbarton Oaks, 2000), 102–3.

[289] Yaḥyā al-Anṭakī, *Cronache*, 258; M. Canard, 'Djarrāḥids or Banu 'l-Djarrāḥ', in *Encyclopaedia of Islam*, vol. 2, 482–5, esp. 483.

[290] Yaḥyā al-Anṭakī, *History* II, 505; Yaḥyā al-Anṭakī, *Cronache*, 259; Ousterhout, 'Rebuilding the Temple', 69–70.

[291] Charles M. Brand and Anthony Cutler, 'Romanos III Argyros', ODB III, 1807.

[292] Yaḥyā al-Anṭakī, *History* III, 444–5; Yaḥyā al-Anṭakī, *Cronache*, 373–4; Ousterhout, 'Rebuilding the Temple', 70. According to some accounts, the Muslim party agreed to the rebuilding on condition that a mosque be restored in Constantinople. See Gil, *History of Palestine*, 373–4.

The Byzantine emperor who initiated construction of the second Holy Sepulchre around 1042 was Constantine IX Monomachus (1042–55).[293] A close reading of Michael Psellus had led Robin Cormack to point out that Constantine IX was conscious of the importance and potential that artistic patronage had in Constantinople, in the Byzantine empire, and throughout the eastern Mediterranean. Constantine also desired to overshadow the previous donations of Romanus Argyrus, who was noted by Psellus to have aspired to greatness, imagining himself as a second Solomon, Constantine the Great, and Justinian, both as a defender of the faith and as patron of monumental architectural projects.[294] According to William of Tyre, the only source that gives any details on the eleventh-century rebuilding process, the on-site supervisor was Johannes Carianitis, a Byzantine nobleman who had retired to Jerusalem as a monk and who monitored the work of the two teams of Byzantine and local Palestinian craftsmen directed by a chief architect from Constantinople.[295] Surprisingly, however, no Byzantine historians of the period, such as Michael Psellus, mention any imperial patronage from Constantinople for the rebuilding of the Anastasis, and it is only through historians writing in Arabic or Latin that we learn anything of the rebuilding process. How should the silence of Byzantine sources be interpreted? Is it of greater importance that Arabic chronicles were eager to attribute Byzantine imperial patronage to the rebuilding of Jerusalem's greatest shrine? Even though the faithful of Jerusalem's Chalcedonian church were gradually becoming more Arab in terms of culture and language, they still looked to Constantinople for spiritual guidance—and for financial support.

Regardless of patronage, the resulting building was impressive by the standards of the time. It was constructed from Roman and Byzantine *spolia* and the structure of the rotunda of the Anastasis followed the original fourth-century

---

[293] Charles M. Brand and Anthony Cutler, 'Constantine IX Monomachos', ODB I, 504.

[294] Michel Psellos, *Chronographie ou histoire d'un siècle de Byzance (976–1077)*, vol. 1, ed. and trans. by Émile Renauld (Paris: Les Belles Lettres, 1926), 41–4; Robin Cormack, *Writing in Gold: Byzantine Society and Its Icons* (London: Philip, 1985), 182–94.

[295] *Quomodo pari nequam Daher filius egregius moderator regni successit et precibus domini Romani Constantinopolitani imperatoris reedificatur ecclesia cooperante Iohanne Carianite, Constantino Monomacho sumptus ministrante…Procurabat autem eorum legationem quidam Iohannes cognomento Carianitis, Constantinopolitanus natione, bobilis quidem secundum carnem sed moribus multo nobilior. Hic postposita seculi dignitate Christum sequutus, religionis assumpto habitu Ierosolimis pauper pro Christo habitabat.* Willelmi Tyrensis Archiepiscopi, *Chronicon*, ed. by Robert B. C. Huygens, Hans E. Mayer, and Gerhard Rösch (CCCM 63, Turnhout: Brepols, 1986), vol. 1, 112–13 (1.6.rub and 1.6.17–19); Ousterhout, 'Rebuilding the Temple', 70–1, 76. For other examples of Byzantine craftsmen working in the East, see Ernst Kitzinger, 'Byzantine Art in the Period between Justinian and Iconoclasm', in *Berichte zum XI. Internationalen Byzantinisten-Kongress* (Munich: C. H. Beck, 1958), 1–50, esp. 11 and fig. 10; reprinted in Ernst Kitzinger, *The Art of Byzantium and the Medieval West: Selected Studies*, ed. by W. Eugene Kleinbauer (Bloomington, IN: Indiana University Press, 1976), 157–232; Henri Stern, 'Notes sur les mosaïques du Dôme du Rocher et de la Mosquée de Damas à propos d'un livre de Mme. M.G. van Berchem', *Cahiers Archéologiques* 22 (1972), 201–32.

plan. Its twenty-one-metre span, colossal for that time, may have caused concern for the builders, who covered it with a wooden roof. The courtyard was retained and lined with chapels related to events from Christ's Passion, as well as to St James and Old Testament saints. It should be noted that no pastophorium was included in the design, an omission common in Byzantine plans until the sixth century.[296] One major aspect of the Golgotha complex that was not rebuilt was the five-aisled basilica of the Martyrium.[297] However, the abandonment of the basilica plan and the spatial reduction of churches were both quite common in this period, which suggests an approach to the rebuilding programme consistent with Byzantine architectural practices of the time.[298]

Although Byzantines played an important role in the reconstruction process, the final result was an amalgam of Byzantine and local Palestinian styles and methods, something found in other artistic disciplines of the same period.[299] Certain masonry sections were built according to the hallmark Byzantine recessed-brick technique, while others used the Muslim-influenced flat-brick method. The execution of the vaults, usually groin vaults in series, also reveals local workmanship in the thoroughly Byzantine plan. It is unclear whether the Byzantines began the project and left it to the Palestinians to finish, or whether the two teams worked side by side.[300] In any case, Richard Krautheimer has suggested that the collaboration of Byzantine and Islamic architectural schools on the Holy Sepulchre project may have influenced subsequent Byzantine church plans with an octagonal dome in the eleventh century.[301] Likewise, the twin dome plan of the Anastasis is reflected in the Comnenian dynasty's (1081–1185) mausoleum at the Pantocrator Monastery Church of St Michael, suggesting a direct example of Hagiopolitan influence on Byzantine architecture.[302]

At the same time, other churches were rebuilt and new foundations established during the period between the destruction of the Anastasis and the arrival of the crusaders. One of the most notable is the Holy Cross Monastery, built by the Sabaite Georgian monk Giorgi P'roxore around the year 1030.[303] King Bagrat IV of Georgia (1027–72) funded the monastery, which eventually became the focus of Georgian monastic activity in Palestine and a centre for the

---

[296] Patrich, 'Transfer of Gifts', 342–3.
[297] Ousterhout, 'Rebuilding the Temple', 70–2.
[298] An example of this is Hagia Sophia in Thessalonike, a basilica converted into a centrally planned, smaller church. See Cyril Mango, *Byzantine Architecture* (Milan: Electa Editrice, 1978), 89–90; Kalliopi Theoharidou, *The Architecture of Hagia Sophia, Thessaloniki: From Its Erection up to the Turkish Conquest* (Oxford: British Archaeological Reports, 1988).
[299] Vera N. Zalesskaia, 'Некоторые Мелькитские памятники X–XI вв.', ПС 29 [92] (1987), 137–42.
[300] Ousterhout, 'Rebuilding the Temple', 73–6.
[301] Richard Krautheimer, *Early Christian and Byzantine Architecture* (Harmondsworth: Penguin Books, 1965), 244; Ousterhout, 'Rebuilding the Temple', 78.
[302] Ousterhout, 'Sacred Geographies', 108–9.   [303] Tarchnishvili, *Geschichte*, 75.

whole Jerusalem patriarchate.[304] From the Holy Cross Monastery, Giorgi Pʻroxore promoted a liturgical rule similar to that of St Sabas Lavra, where he had
previously been a monk.[305] Information gathered from colophons reveals that
this monastery became an important scribal centre and is the place of origin of
the heavily Byzantinized Dumbarton Oaks Georgian Menaion, *Dumbarton
Oaks MS 2* (11th cent.).[306] Despite the absence of any specific date, the mention
of the Abbot Giorgi Pʻroxore (d. 12 February 1066), the monk Iovane Dvali, and
the 'blessed brother' Nistʻereoni in the detailed colophon of this and other
manuscripts copied during the same period in Jerusalem helps to date the
Dumbarton Oaks Menaion to the middle of the eleventh century. The commemorations for the months of December, January, and February closely follow
the Constantinopolitan Typikon of the Great Church, although commemorations of Georgian saints are also included.[307]

The new Holy Sepulchre was rededicated in 1048, only thirty-nine years
after its destruction in 1009 by al-Ḥākim, and adorned with opulent gifts
from Emperors Michael VI Stratioticus (r. 1055–7) and Michael VII Doucas
(r. 1071–8).[308] Despite the complete destruction of the Martyrium and the
reorganization of the basilica to occupy the former forecourt and to face in the
opposite direction, the rebuilt Anastasis church was faithful to the original
Constantinian church—at least for the purposes of the liturgical services. The
restorers were motivated to create many new, smaller places of worship that
amassed the various traditions previously spread throughout the city in one
building complex.[309] The rearrangement of the reliquary chapels around the
Anastasis, which occurred during the fifty-one years from rededication to the
capture of Jerusalem by the crusaders in 1099, is reflected in certain liturgical
actions in the Typikon of the Anastasis. Robert Ousterhout believes that this is
particularly evident in the events of Good Friday and in the procession with
the Holy Cross.[310] Once the crusaders replaced the courtyard and chapels of

[304] Nino Khutsishvili, იერუსალიმის ჯვრის მონასტრის მიწათმფლობელობა საქართველოში (*Holy Cross Monastery of Jerusalem: Georgian Land Ownership*) (Tbilisi: Artanuji Publishers, 2006), 141.

[305] Michael van Esbroeck, 'Le couvent de Sainte-Croix de Jérusalem selon les sources géor-giennes', *Studi sull'Oriente Cristiano* 4: 2 (2000), 139–70, here 142.

[306] Garitte, 'Menée'; Tarchnishvili, *Geschichte*, 75; Sakvarelidze, 'Byzantinization of Georgian Liturgy', 284–90.

[307] For more on the Dumbarton Oaks Menaion, see Appendix 1.

[308] Willelmi Tyrensis Archiepiscopi, *Chronicon* I.6 (CCCM 63, Turnhout: Brepols, 1986), 112–14; translated into English as William, Archbishop of Tyre, *A History of Deeds Done Beyond the Sea*, vol. 1, ed. and trans. by Emily Atwater Babcock and August Charles Krey (New York: Columbia University Press, 1943), 69–71; Charles M. Brand, 'Michael VI Stratiotikos', ODB II, 1366; Charles M. Brand and Anthony Cutler, 'Michael VII Doukas', ODB II, 1366–7; Ousterh-out, 'Rebuilding the Temple', 77 n. 40. Yaḥyā al-Anṭakī's history ends in 1033; thus he does not describe the completed restoration of the Anastasis.

[309] Corbo, *Santo Sepolcro*, vol. 1, 145–6.

[310] Papadopoulos-Kerameus, *Anastasis Typikon*, 144–7; Ousterhout, 'Rebuilding the Temple', 78.

the Anastasis with a single, domed transept and a pilgrims' choir dedicated in 1149, the authentic stational character of the Golgotha complex was lost, the church turning into a kind of concentrated Byzantine microcosm of the life of Christ.[311] Only in 1099 did the Orthodox patriarchate lose control of the Anastasis to the Latin hierarchy that accompanied the First Crusade; then the Greek language was reduced to a secondary role in services at the Holy Sepulchre for the first time ever since the latter's construction by Constantine in the fourth century.[312]

This closer look at the events surrounding 1009 explains why liturgical books from this period do not always fall neatly into the historical periods delineated by modern liturgical historiography and do not themselves reveal a drastically different rite immediately after the year 1009. Liturgical changes were already being introduced during the tenth century, as evidenced by many 'transitional' liturgical sources. This is especially clear in the liturgical calendar of *Sinai Geo. O. 34* (10th cent.), which confirms the presence of Constantino-politan liturgical books in Palestine before the eleventh century.

Ecclesiastical Reorganization

The fact that Christianity was no longer the official state-sponsored religion of the Holy City after the Arab conquest in 638 had a great impact on church structures and administration in the Orthodox patriarchate of Jerusalem. This is reflected in several organizational changes made after the Arab conquest. Previously, diocesan boundaries paralleled those of Byzantine civil adminis-trative divisions, and Muslim authorities generally preserved such existing administrative structures. But the Muslim occupation saw significant demo-graphic changes to the religious composition of the population, particularly in the eighth and ninth centuries. Urban centres such as Damascus, Antioch, Emessa, and Jerusalem retained their Christian identity and population in the first century of the Hegira, but regions that saw heavy fighting, such as Caesarea and the coast north of Arsūf, witnessed the displacement of the indigenous Christian population by Muslim inhabitants.[313] All these factors, along with a devastating earthquake in 747/8, showed the need for a reorgan-ization of the hierarchy in the patriarchate of Jerusalem.[314]

---

[311] Ibid.; Taft, 'Liturgy of the Great Church', 66.
[312] For accounts of liturgical services at the Anastasis shortly after the arrival of the crusaders, see Wilson, *Abbot Daniel*, 77–8. See also ППС 106 (2008), dedicated to the millennium commemorations of Abbot Daniel's pilgrimage.
[313] Nasrallah, *Histoire* II.1, 43; Levy-Rubin, 'The Reorganisation of the Patriarchate of Jerusalem', 218–20.
[314] For the natural disasters of the period, see Gil, *History of Palestine*, 89–90 n. 15.

In the absence of any register of the patriarchate of Jerusalem for the period after the Arab conquest (which does not parallel the situation one finds in the patriarchate of Constantinople), the primary source for this reorganization is the ninth-century work by Basil of Ialimbana entitled *Order of the Episcopal Placement of the Venerable Patriarchs* (*Τάξις προκαθεδρίας τῶν ὁσιωτάτων πατριαρχῶν*), a list of bishoprics in the Holy Land.[315] Basil's list is a copy of previous works that he updated, showing great knowledge of the ecclesial situation in Palestine, as well as of the Arabic and Syriac languages. The work provides a list of twenty-five archbishoprics within the patriarchate of Jerusalem, some of them raised from the status of suffragan bishoprics (*synkelloi*).[316] This was presumably done in order to facilitate church administration at a time when contact and activity had become more difficult.

Analysis of the list shows a change in focus from pastoral care for the flock of the local church to an interest in preserving holy sites. Of the four major archbishoprics attached to the patriarchal court in Jerusalem and considered patriarchal *synkelloi*, three were connected to holy sites without communities: Diospoleos (*ὁ Διοσπόλεως*), Neapolis (*ἡ Νεάπολις*), and the Jordan River (*ὁ τοῦ ἁγίου Ἰορδάνου ποταμοῦ*); and only Ioppe/Jaffa (*ὁ Ἰόππης*) was exclusively responsible for pastoral care.[317] As in the Byzantine period, the importance of holy sites was again stressed in the Jerusalem patriarchate under Arab control. For this reason Theodore the Stoudite wrote to Patriarch Thomas of Jerusalem that, although only the fifth in the order of the Orthodox patriarchates, his see should be counted first (*Σὺ πρῶτος πατριαρχῶν, κἂν πεντάζοις τῷ ἀριθμῷ*), because it was on its holy sites that Christ lived, died, and was buried.[318] Thus it could be understood that, given the demographic changes, the preservation of the holy sites became a priority in the Jerusalem patriarchate, since it was a means to justify its existence and to emphasize its prestige.

With a decreasing number of faithful in Palestine, the responsibility of caring for these holy sites passed almost exclusively to monks. The archbishopric of the Holy River Jordan, second only to the patriarch and entrusted with the duties of patriarchal advisor, *protosynkellos* (*πρωτοσύγκελλος*), and deputy, *antiprosopos* (*ἀντιπρόσωπος*), became responsible for both the Jordan holy sites and the Judean monastic communities.[319] Likewise, the centre of

---

[315] Ernst Honigmann, 'Die Notitia des Basileios von Ialimbana', *Byzantion* 9 (1934), 208–11; Vitalien Laurent, 'La *Notitia* de Basile l'Arménien', *Échos d'Orient* 34 (1935), 459–71; Levy-Rubin, 'The Reorganisation of the Patriarchate of Jerusalem', 199–202.

[316] A full list is presented in Levy-Rubin, 'The Reorganisation of the Patriarchate of Jerusalem', 203.

[317] Ibid., 221.

[318] St Theodore of Stoudios, *Epistolarum liber secundus*, PG 99:1160–1.

[319] Patriarch Timothy (Themelis) of Jerusalem, '*Τὰ Τακτικὰ τῶν Πατριαρχείων*', *ΝΣ* 34 (1939), 65–85, here 82. For more on these titles, see Alexander Kazhdan, 'Antiprosopon', ODB I, 120; Aristeides Papadakis, 'Synkellos', ODB III, 1993–4.

the Jericho diocese was moved to the Monastery of St John the Evangelist on the banks of the river Jordan after the earthquake of 747/8. This showed that monasteries were favoured at a time when the Orthodox Christian population was struggling.[320] Where the earthquake of 747/8 had destroyed whole dioceses, as happened at Scythopolis and Petra, the bishop moved to Jerusalem, becoming a titular bishop in residence at the patriarchal court.[321] Once the administration of Bethlehem, Emmaus, Thekoa, Hebron, and ʿAbūd—all within the diocese of Jerusalem—was left to senior priests of the patriarchate, the Hagiopolitan patriarchal court became the centralized locus of power and influence in Orthodox Palestine and a point of contact with other Orthodox patriarchates, including Constantinople.[322] From the perspective of liturgy, this centralization of power facilitated greater control over, and oversight of, liturgical practices. Any changes or developments made at the patriarchal court could more easily spread to the rest of its territory.

The First and Second Crusades

The persecution of Christians continued after the destruction of the Holy Sepulchre in 1009. Theodore Prodromos' *Life of Meletios of Myoupolis* (c.1070–3) describes Christians being persecuted and tortured at the hands of Arabs in Jerusalem.[323] Such news, along with the desire to ward off Muslim advances into Anatolia, motivated Emperor Alexius I Comnenus (r. 1081–1118) to appeal for help to Pope Urban II (r. 1088–99) at the Council of Piacenza in March 1095.[324] Alexius was a shrewd diplomat and knew how to exploit the western church's interests in relics and in the Holy Land. By highlighting the presence of exiled patriarchs of Jerusalem, such as Patriarch Euthymius (c.1083), at the Constantinopolitan imperial court, Alexius made it clear that Constantinople and Jerusalem were to be considered as one: any attack on the Byzantine empire would also be an affront to the Holy City.[325]

---

[320] Levy-Rubin, 'The Reorganisation of the Patriarchate of Jerusalem', 217.

[321] Ibid., 220. For a map of the territory of the Jerusalem patriarchate, see Appendix 2, 'Map of the Patriarchate of Jerusalem (4th–11th cent.').

[322] Themelis, '*Τὰ Τακτικά*' (n. 319 here), 84.

[323] Vasilii G. Vasilevskii, Νικολάου ἐπισκόπου Μεθώνης καὶ Θεοδώρου τοῦ Προδρόμου συγγραφέων τῆς ΙΒ´ ἑκατονταετηρίδος βίοι Μελετίου τοῦ νέου (ΠΠC 17 [6.2], St Petersburg: Православное Палестинское Общество, 1886), 46 (Greek) and 127–8 (Russian). For more accounts of the period of the First Crusade, see John Wilkinson, *Jerusalem Pilgrimage, 1099–1185* (London: Hakluyt Society, 1988).

[324] Robert Sommerville, *Pope Urban II's Council of Piacenza* (Oxford: Oxford University Press, 2011); 15–16; Charles M. Brand, Philip Grierson, and Anthony Cutler, 'Alexios I Komnenos', ODB I, 63; Alexander Kazhdan, 'Urban II (Odo of Châtillon)', ODB III, 2143–4.

[325] P. Gautier, 'Le Typikon de sébaste Grégoire Pakourianos', REB 42 (1984), 6–145, here 131; Peter Frankopan, *The First Crusade: The Call from the East* (Cambridge, MA: Harvard University Press, 2012), 92, 95.

The arrival of the First Crusade in 1099 initially did little to alleviate the situation for the church of Jerusalem. The first years of the Latin kingdom were marked by massacres of non-Latins—both Christians and Muslims—because the earliest crusaders were often unable to distinguish between the two groups. From the perspective of crusader chronicles, 'being Christian was synonymous with being Latin', and those chroniclers who knew the situation better nevertheless elided the various Christians and their churches in Palestine and Syria, or ignored them altogether.[326] After the First Crusade, Byzantine pilgrimage accounts such as those of twelfth-century Constantine Manasses and John Phocas do not focus on the difficulties caused by Muslims, which suggests that in this respect the situation had improved for the local Christian population.[327] But, while the holy sites were now preserved from destruction and desecration, this did not mean that local Orthodox Christians had regained access to or control of them.[328]

In fact the Orthodox Church was subject to the hierarchy of the Latin patriarchate of Jerusalem after the arrival of the crusaders.[329] This also carried liturgical implications. The services witnessed by the Slav *hegoumenos* Daniel between 1106 and 1108 were presided over by Latin clergy.[330] Surprisingly, liturgical manuscripts from the Jerusalem patriarchate copied during the twelfth century rarely mention Latin clergy. The twelfth-century copy of St Sabas' testament in *Sinai Gr. 1096* mentions Franks in passing among the various groups that lived in the monastery.[331] Similarly, the Typikon of the Anastasis makes absolutely no mention of any Latin presence during Holy Week services at the Holy Sepulchre, despite *hegumenos* Daniel's eyewitness testimony to the contrary. The silence of liturgical manuscripts is, however, reciprocal: Latin liturgical books of the Canons Regular of the Holy Sepulchre of Jerusalem make no mention of Greek clergy at the Anastasis.[332]

But the silence of liturgical manuscripts and chronicles is not representative of the reality on the ground. Local Palestinian and Byzantine Christians had contact with the crusaders after their arrival in Jerusalem, and the crusaders

[326] MacEvitt, *Crusades and the Christian World of the East*, 45–7, here 47.
[327] Alice-Mary Talbot, 'Byzantine Pilgrimage to the Holy Land from the Eighth to the Fifteenth Century', in Patrich, *Sabaite Heritage*, 97–110, here 101; Andreas Külzer, *Peregrinatio graeca in Terram Sanctam*, 17–21; Alexander Kazhdan, 'Phokas, John', ODB III, 1667.
[328] See Wilson, *Abbot Daniel*, 77–8; Jonathan Phillips, 'The Latin East, 1098–1291', in *The Oxford History of the Crusades*, ed. by Jonathan Riley-Smith (New York: Oxford University Press, 1999), here 113–15.
[329] Bernard Hamilton, *The Latin Church in the Crusader States: The Secular Church* (London: Variorum Publications, 1980), 159–71 and 179–87.
[330] Dmitrievskii, *Древнѣйшіе Патріаршіе Типиконы*, 98–9; Bertonière, *Easter Vigil*, 13.
[331] See fol. 148r–149v; also Appendix 1 here.
[332] See Cristina Dondi, *The Liturgy of the Canons Regular of the Holy Sepulchre of Jerusalem: A Study and a Catalogue of the Manuscript Sources* (Bibliotheca Victorina 16, Turnhout: Brepols, 2004).

used the local Christians to their strategic advantage. The marriage of King Baldwin III of Jerusalem (1143–63) to Theodora, niece of Emperor Manuel I Comnenus, in 1158 was only one of the many strategic marriages between rulers of Constantinople and the crusaders of the Levant.[333] Strategic marriages were accompanied by Manuel's imperial patronage of the holy sites. The most notable examples are the mosaics of the Church of the Nativity in Bethlehem, which used imagery of the seven ecumenical councils and other local church councils, as well as portraits of Emperor Manuel Comnenus himself, to promote the idea of the Byzantine emperor as custodian of the Orthodox faith as much as patron of the holy places.[334] The unstable situation of bishops within the Jerusalem patriarchate before the crusades improved significantly under the crusaders and there are frequent, albeit brief, mentions of Greek-praying bishops—often referred to as Melkites—in Palestine.[335] However, by the time of Latin King Guy de Lusignan's (d. 1194) loss to Saladin (1138–93) at the Battle of Ḥaṭṭīn near Tiberias on 4 July 1187, which ultimately led to the fall of Jerusalem to Saladin's forces,[336] Christians had already adapted to their Arab environment and their liturgical practices, which had been in flux during this period of transition, began to consolidate and take form.

Once Muslim rule was restored in Jerusalem after 1187, the Orthodox returned to the Anastasis. Nevertheless, the provisions of the Treaty of Jaffa of 2 September 1192 also allowed Latin clergy back to the Holy Sepulchre, and it was only through the intervention of Emperor Isaac II Angelus (r. 1185–95, 1203–4) that Greek clergy were permitted to return to the Anastasis, although they had to share the church with as many as seven other denominations, all of them vying for the same place of worship.[337] The monopoly of the Orthodox patriarchate on other shrines in the Holy Land had also come to an end after the arrival of the crusaders. The twelfth-century divisions of the Holy Sepulchre and the divided state of affairs under Saladin laid the foundation for the division of the Anastasis complex between various Christian

---

[333] Charles M. Brand, 'Baldwin III', ODB I, 247. For the policy of Emperor Manuel, see Paul Magdalino, *The Empire of Manuel I Komnenos, 1143–1180* (New York: Cambridge University Press, 1993).

[334] Lucy-Anne Hunt, 'Art and Colonialism: The Mosaics of the Church of the Nativity in Bethlehem (1169) and the Problem of "Crusader" Art', DOP 45 (1991), 69–85; MacEvitt, *Crusades and the Christian World of the East*, 157–9.

[335] MacEvitt, *Crusades and the Christian World of the East*, 110–12.

[336] *De expugatione terrae sanctae per Saladinum* (*The Capture of the Holy Land by Saladin*), ed. by Joseph Stevenson (Rolls Series, London: Longmans, 1875); James Brundage, *The Crusades: A Documentary History* (Milwaukee, WI: Marquette University Press, 1962), 153–9; Charles M. Brand, 'Saladin', ODB III, 1830.

[337] al-Maqrīzī, *A History of the Ayyūbid Sultans of Egypt*, trans. by Ronald J. C. Broadhurst (Boston, MA: Twayne, 1980), 85; Denys Pringle, *Pilgrimage to Jerusalem and the Holy Land, 1187–1291* (Crusade Texts in Translation 23, Surrey: Ashgate, 2012), 2 and 193; Charles M. Brand and Athony Cutler, 'Isaac II Angelos', ODB II, 1012.

denominations until the present day.[338] Efforts by Orthodox clergy from abroad, such as by St Sava of Serbia (1175–1235), to promote pilgrimage to the Holy Land from other Orthodox regions and to 'enhance the Orthodox presence in the Latin Kingdom' helped to strengthen the ties between Jerusalem, Constantinople, and Mount Athos.[339] The need to share the holy sites with other Christians and the influx of Orthodox clergy and pilgrims from the Balkans and Eastern Europe meant that liturgy in the Jerusalem patriarchate would never be the same.

CRISIS AND CONTACT

Now that we have a sense of the chronology of the period of crisis for the church of Jerusalem between the Arab conquest of Palestine and the ousting of the crusaders by Saladin, let us return to examine a few aspects of this history that are of particular importance for liturgical Byzantinization. Within a century of the Arab conquest of Jerusalem, crisis also struck the church of Constantinople in the form of iconoclasm. According to the narrative of the development of the Byzantine rite, this turmoil brought together like-minded monks, such as Theodore Stoudite and the monks of St Sabas Lavra, setting in motion what is now known among Byzantine liturgiologists as the Stoudite and Sabaite synthesis.[340]

Byzantine Iconoclasm and Its Impact on Palestine

It is widely held that Palestinian monks were united in their opposition to iconoclasm and focused much of their energy on combating this Byzantine phenomenon. The synaxarion of Constantinople not only attributes to Sts John of Damascus and Cosmas of Maiouma the composition of hymnography but also highlights their defence of icons against the iconoclasts, which suggests that this was perhaps the main subject of their writings.[341]

---

[338] See Narcyz S. Klimas, OFM, 'L'inserimento delle diverse communità cristiane nel complesso del santo sepolcro e lo *status quo* ottomano', in *Una città tra terra e cielo: Gerusalemme: Le religioni, le chiese*, ed. by Cesare Alzati and Luciano Vaccaro (Storia Religiosa Euro-Mediterranea 3, Vatican City: Libreria Editrice Vaticana, 2014), 361–91.

[339] David Jacoby, 'Three Notes on Crusader Acre', *Zeitschrift des Deutschen Palästina-Vereins* 109 (1993), 83–96, here 87; Robert Browning, 'Sava of Serbia', ODB III, 1847.

[340] Taft, *Byzantine Rite*, 58.

[341] ὁ μὲν ὅσιος Ἰωάννης τῇ τῶν λόγων αὐτοῦ δυνάμει καὶ ταῖς τῶν γραφῶν σοφαῖς ἀποδείξεσι πλεῖστα στηλιτεύσας τὴν δυσσεβῆ τῶν εἰκονομάχων αἵρεσιν καὶ πολλὰ συγγράμματα καταλελοιπώς ('The venerable John, by the power of his words and by the skilled making of writings, held up to scorn the impious heresy of the iconoclasts and left behind many treatises'). Delehaye, *Synaxarium*, 279.

Certainly the opposition of the eastern patriarchs to Constantinopolitan iconoclasm was unanimous. In the year 764, Theophanes recounts that, 'by common consent, Theodore, patriarch of Antioch, Theodore of Jerusalem, and Kosmas of Alexandria, together with their suffragan bishops, unanimously anathematized him [*sc.* Emperor Constantine V Copronymus (718–75)] on the day of holy Pentecost after the reading of the holy Gospel, each in his own city'.[342] They also sent letters to the pope of Rome, which were read at the Lateran Council in 769.[343] Yet the involvement of Palestinian monks in the debate over icon veneration in Constantinople may be somewhat exaggerated. Marie-France Auzépy suggests that a 'Palestinian lobby' promoted John of Damascus and exonerated certain Palestinian monks who were indifferent to icon veneration, such as Stephen the Sabaite, after the second wave of iconoclasm in Constantinople.[344] After a painstaking analysis of literary and archaeological evidence, Robert Schick concludes that

> iconoclasm as it manifested itself in the Byzantine empire is fundamentally different from what appears in Palestine, where images of ordinary people and animals, and not just icons, were destroyed. This makes it difficult to accept any claim that the damage [to Palestinian mosaic floors] was inspired by the iconoclastic practices of the Christians in the Byzantine empire.[345]

The motivation for this destruction—and then near-immediate repair—is unclear. Archaeological evidence suggests that Christians carried out the destruction under duress, perhaps in response to the iconoclastic edict of the Umayyad Caliph Yazīd II (r. 720–4) from 721 to 723.[346] Accusations of idolatry from Muslims and Jews certainly motivated the destruction of icons. Later on, however, the Chalcedonians repaired these icons, perhaps in order to distinguish themselves from Miaphysites and Nestorians, who were indifferent to icon veneration. Theodore Abū Qurrah's treatises on icon veneration clearly show an attempt to dispel Chalcedonian deference to unorthodox views on icon veneration, whether of Muslim, Jewish, or of other intra-Christian origin.[347]

---

[342] ὃν κοινῇ γνώμῃ Θεόδωρος, ὁ πατριάρχης Ἀντιοχείας, καὶ Θεόδωρος Ἱεροσολύμων, καὶ Κοσμᾶς Ἀλεξανδρείας σὺν τοῖς ὑπ᾽ αὐτοὺς ἐπισκόποις τῇ ἡμέρᾳ τῆς ἁγίας πεντηκοστῆς μετὰ τὴν ἀνάγνωσιν τοῦ ἁγίου εὐαγγελίου ὁμοφρόνως ἀνεθεμάτισαν ἕκαστος κατὰ τὴν ἑαυτοῦ πόλιν. *Theophanis Chronographia*, 434; Mango and Scott, *Chronicle of Theophanes*, 600. The letter of their anathemas is preserved in the acts of the Seventh Ecumenical Council. See Norman J. Tanner, SJ, *Decrees of the Ecumenical Councils*, vol. 1 (London: Sheed & Ward, 1990), 137–8; 'Concilium Jerosolymitanum in causa sacrarum imaginum', Mansi XII, 679–80 and 1135.

[343] Mansi XII, 720B–D; Mansi XIII, 720B–2C; Pope Hadrian, *Epistola ad beatum Carolum regem de imaginibus*, PL 98:1256B–7A.

[344] Auzépy, 'De la Palestine à Constantinople', 191–2.

[345] Schick, *Christian Communities of Palestine*, 213.

[346] Henry Lammens and Khalid Y. Blankinship, 'Yazīd (II) b. 'Abd al-Malik', in *Encyclopaedia of Islam*, vol. 11, 311; Schick, *Christian Communities of Palestine*, 219.

[347] *Théodore Abuqurra: Traité du culte des icônes*, ed. by Ignace Dick (Patrimoine arabe chrétien 10, Jounieh/Rome: Librarie Saint-Paul/Pontifical Oriental Institute, 1986), 88. For more

Stoudite Monastic and Liturgical Reforms

Although Stoudite monasticism never reached Palestine, the monastic reform attributed to St Theodore Stoudite (759–826) had an immeasurable impact on the whole Byzantine liturgical tradition.[348] What monastic and liturgical practice was like among the Stoudites before Theodore is difficult to know because of the absence of any sources.[349] As Thomas Pott acknowledges, 'the Studite reform, prior to being a reorganization of Byzantine monastic life, sought to be a spiritual reform of monasticism itself'.[350] Theodore was interested in preserving monastic tradition, 'renewing the life that brings salvation' by a 'return to the ancient way of life',[351] which he believed was represented by eastern monasticism, particularly by the Palestinian monks of Mar Sabas Lavra. But the claim is that the monks of Mar Saba, reacting to Theodore's call for help in response to the synod of 809 around the second marriage of Emperor Constantine VI (771–805), did not immediately bring a Palestinian monastic liturgy with them.[352] There is no evidence that anything changed in the liturgy among the Stoudites when the Palestinian monks arrived in Constantinople, between 809 and 818.[353] Neither does any liturgical practice seem to have changed in 799, when some of the Stoudite monastic brotherhood moved from the Sakkoudion Monastery in Bithynia to the Stoudios Monastery in Constantinople.[354] Thus it is believed that Theodore was already familiar with some form of the Palestinian monastic Horologion

on Theodore Abū Qurrah, see 'Melkites: A Subgroup?' in this chapter. See also Schick, *Christian Communities of Palestine*, 219.

[348] Alexander Kazhdan, 'Theodore of Stoudios', ODB III, 2044–2045; Pott, *Byzantine Liturgical Reform*, 115–51.

[349] Julien Leroy, 'La réforme studite', in *Il monachesimo orientale: Atti del Convegno di studi orientali, 9, 10, 11 e 12 aprile 1958* (OCA 153, Rome: Pontifical Oriental Institute, 1958), 181–214. See also Pott, *Byzantine Liturgical Reform*, 116.

[350] Ibid., 142.

[351] ζητῶν εἰς τὴν ἐμαυτοῦ σωτηρίαν τινὰ βοήθειαν, ἵνα μὴ ἀπόλωμαι, ἢ θείαν ἢ ἀνθρωπίνην, τὴν δυναμένην ἀνανεώσασθαι τὴν σωτήριον πολιτείαν καὶ ὁδοποιῆσαι καὶ εὐτακτῆσαι ἕκαστα ἡμῶν εἰς τὸ ἀρχαῖον σχῆμα καὶ πολίτευμα, τοῦ κανονικῶς καὶ ἐννόμως, ὡς ὑποφαίνουσιν αἱ τῶν θείων πατέρων βίβλοι ('I seek the divine or human assistance that will allow me to save myself and that will be capable of renewing the life that brings salvation, of marking the path, of restoring order to our affairs, and of return to the ancient way of life, of the canons and ordained by law, as the books of the holy fathers bring to light'). Theodore of Stoudios, *Great Catecheses* 25, in A. Papadopoulos-Kerameus, *Τοῦ ὁσίου Θεοδώρου τοῦ Στουδίτου μεγάλη κατήχησις* (St Petersburg: Kirschbaum, 1904), 173; Pott, *Byzantine Liturgical Reform*, 120.

[352] Paul A. Hollingsworth, 'Moechian Controversy', ODB II, 1388–9.

[353] Theodore of Stoudios, Letter 555 (809–811), Letter 277 (818), Letter 278 (818). See *Theodori Studitæ epistulæ*, vol. 2, ed. by Georgios Fatouros (Berlin: Walter de Gruyter, 1991–2), 849–52, 412–15, 415–18.

[354] B. Menthon, *Une terre de légendes: L'Olympe de Bithynie: Ses saints, ses couvents, ses sites* (Paris: Bonne Presse, 1935), 21; Alexander Kazhdan, Alice-Mary Talbot, Anthony Cutler, 'Stoudios Monastery', ODB III, 1960–1; Delouis, *Saint-Jean-Baptiste de Stoudios à Constantinople*, 166–7.

before any conscious effort was made to implement Palestinian monastic liturgical practices. These Hagiopolitan practices may have arrived in Bithynia via Palestinian monks who migrated from Palestine to Syria and then continued north towards Constantinople.[355] Nevertheless, this remains speculation.

Upon his arrival in Constantinople, Theodore is credited with initiating certain liturgical reforms that would set in motion what liturgiologists have called the 'Middle-Byzantine synthesis'.[356] Taft has described the resulting 'hybrid Stoudite office' as 'a Palestinian Horologion with its psalmody and hymnody grafted onto a skeleton of litanies and prayers from the Euchologion of the Great Church'.[357] The Constantinopolitan Euchologion, or prayer book of the presider, contains the texts of prayers necessary for celebrating the Divine Liturgy and other sacraments and blessings. The most notable change to this book during the Stoudite reforms was the reordering of the Divine Liturgies: BAS was moved from the beginning of the Euchologion to second place, after CHR. Because of Theodore Stoudite's promotion of a frequent reception of Communion, CHR was celebrated daily by the Stoudites and came to be performed more frequently than BAS. By the tenth century it replaced BAS as the primary Divine Liturgy of the Byzantine rite and began to appear at the beginning of Euchologion manuscripts.[358] Hagia Sophia, which served the Liturgy of the Hours daily, initially performed the Divine Liturgy exclusively on Saturdays, Sundays, and feast days; but it expanded this practice in 1044, after Emperor Constantine IX Monomachus—the same emperor credited with the restoration of the Church of the Anastasis in Jerusalem—assigned funds to pay the cathedral clergy to celebrate the Divine Liturgy daily.[359] JAS, the primary eucharistic liturgy of Jerusalem, was never transmitted to the Stoudites and did not figure in their reforms, ultimately disappearing from liturgical practice even in Jerusalem around the thirteenth century. The impact of the Stoudite reforms on the Horologion is much more complex and cannot be dealt with here. The impact of the Stoudite synthesis on other elements of Hagiopolitan and Constantinopolitan liturgical usages imposed by Theodore Stoudite—particularly those related to the calendar and

---

[355] Julien Leroy, 'Le cursus canonique chez saint Théodore Studite', *Ephemerides Liturgicæ* 68 (1954), 5–19, here 13; Pott, *Byzantine Liturgical Reform*, 128.

[356] Taft, *Byzantine Rite*, 61.   [357] Ibid., 58.

[358] Parenti, *L'eucologio slavo del Sinai*, 5–9; Parenti, 'La "vittoria"'.

[359] *Georgius Cedrenus Ioannis Scylitzae ope*, ed. by Immanuel Bekker (Corpus Scriptorum Historiae Byzantinae 14, Bonn: Weber, 1839), vol. 2, 609; Robert F. Taft, SJ, 'The Frequency of the Celebration of the Eucharist throughout History', in *Between Memory and Hope: Readings in the Liturgical Year*, ed. by Maxwell E. Johnson (Collegeville, MN: Liturgical Press 2001), 77–96, here 83–4. See also Robert F. Taft, SJ, 'Changing Rhythms of Eucharistic Frequency in Byzantine Monasticism', in *Il monachesimo tra eredità e aperture: Atti del Simposio 'Testi e temi nella tradizione del monachesimo cristiano' per il 50° Anniversario dell'Istituto Monastico di Sant'Anselmo, Roma, 28 maggio–1 giugno 2002*, ed. by Maciej Bielawski and Daniel Hombergen (Studia Anselmiana 140, Rome: Pontificio Ateneo S. Anselmo, 2004), 419–58.

the lectionary—is still unclear, perhaps because liturgiological studies of the 'Middle-Byzantine synthesis' never adequately explain the place of the sanctoral or lectionary within this reform, despite the important role that Stoudite hymnographers played in shaping the liturgical year, its feasts, and scriptural readings. The impact of the Stoudites is seen particularly in their codification of disparate collections of liturgical hymnography, originally found in books based on the hymn genre, into books of liturgical seasons. The results of this codification were the Oktoechos (ὀκτώηχος) in the eighth century, the Menaion (μηναῖον) in the ninth century, and the Triodion (τριῴδιον) in the tenth century. The earliest extant manuscripts of the Menaion are *Sinai Gr. 607*, *Sinai Gr. 596*, *Sinai Gr. 608*, and *Sinai Gr. N.E. MΓ 28* from the end of the ninth and beginning of the tenth century.[360] Older Hagiopolitan liturgical books, such as the *Iadgari* or the Tropologion, contained all the liturgical seasons of the year in one volume, as demonstrated by the oldest extant Greek Hagiopolitan Tropologion, *Sinai Gr. N.E. MΓ 56* and *Sinai Gr. N.E. MΓ 5* (8th–9th cent.).[361] By the end of the eleventh century, the oldest dated Greek liturgical manuscripts from Mar Sabas Lavra, *Sinai Gr. 741* and *Sinai Gr. 742* (25 January 1099), were completely Byzantinized Lenten Triodia.[362]

Already by the end of the tenth century, the centre of influence shifted from the Jerusalem patriarchate to Mount Athos. This was especially felt within Georgian monasticism and visible in Georgian scribal activity at the Iveron Monastery on Mount Athos.[363] Despite this decisive move and the use of the Stoudite Hypotyposis (Ὑποτύπωσις) by Athanasius of Athos (925–1001), Georgian liturgical sources still evidenced their Hagiopolitan origin and identified the Typikon of St Sabas as the order and Typikon of the 'Greek' Church.[364] Kekelidze points to a note in a Georgian Gospel manuscript copied at Gethsemane in 1048, once held in the private collection of priest Besarion

---

[360] Robert F. Taft and Nancy Patterson-Ševčenko, 'Oktoechos', ODB II, 1520; Frøyshov, 'Early Development'; Momina, 'О происхождении греческой триоди'; Robert F. Taft, 'Triodion', ODB III, 2118–19; Nikiforova, *Из истории Минеи в Византии*, 94. Nikiforova's research dates the Menaion at least one century earlier than was previously held. See Robert F. Taft, 'Menaion', ODB II, 1338. For additional information on the development of liturgical books, see the discussion of the *Iadgari* here in Chapter 1, 'The Georgian Lectionary'.

[361] Nikiforova, *Из истории Минеи в Византии*, 195–235. See Appendix 1 for more on this manuscript.

[362] See Appendix 1 for more on these manuscripts.

[363] Kekelidze, *Литургические грузинские памятники*, 478; Grégoire Peradse, 'L'activité littéraire des moines géorgiens au monastère d'Iviron, au Mont Athos', RHE 23 (1927), 530–9; Taft, 'Mount Athos', esp. 184–6; Alice-Mary Talbot and Anthony Cutler, 'Iveron Monastery', ODB II, 1025–1026; Tamara Grdzelidze, *Georgian Monks on Mount Athos: Two Eleventh-Century Lives of the Hegoumenoi of Iviron* (London: Bennett and Bloom, 2009).

[364] George T. Dennis, 'Ath. Rule: Rule of Athanasios the Athonite for the Lavra Monastery', BMFD I, 205–31; Taft, 'Mount Athos', 183; Alexander Kazhdan and Nancy Patterson-Ševčenko, 'Athanasios of Athos', ODB I, 219.

Nizharadze but now under the shelf mark *Tbilisi Centre of Georgian Manuscripts H1741* (1048):

ესე წესი და განგებაჲ საბა წმიდისაჲ არს ბერძული, ვის ქართულ უნდეს კანონსა მიუდგეს და მისგან ისწავე რომელ დედასა ეწვსა და იგი დამიწვსია წმიდაჲ და ჭეშმარიტი წესი საბა წმიდისაჲ.[365]	This is the rite and order of the Greek Church, of St Sabas the Sanctified. If someone wants the Georgian version, let them turn to the canon (*kanoni*) and learn it from there. I wrote that which was in the original, the holy and true order of St Sabas the Sanctified.

The shift from Jerusalem to Athos also resulted in two redactions of the text of the Bible, the pre-Athonite Georgian text[366] and the new Georgian translation, which help to date the contents of liturgical manuscripts.[367] The Epistle book *Sinai Geo. O. 10* (11th cent.) not only reflects this new textual redaction but also follows the order of the Greek Church (საკჳთხელთა ბერძულსა წესსა, fol. 1r), including its liturgical calendar.[368] Although the reforms and the liturgical synthesis attributed to St Theodore Stoudite may have looked to Palestinian monasticism for their models, the Stoudite rite and its calendar and lectionary ultimately replaced the Hagiopolitan rite.

CONSTANTINOPOLITAN HEGEMONY

Following the iconoclastic controversy and the ascendancy of Byzantine monasticism, the balance of influence began to shift from Palestine and its Sabaite monks to Constantinople as the centre of imperial and religious power. It was in Constantinople that the Orthodox patriarchs of Jerusalem sought refuge from depredations in an increasingly hostile, Muslim-controlled Palestine.

---

[365] Kekelidze, *Канонарь*, 36–7; Peradse, 'Liturgiegeschichte Georgiens', 74–5.

[366] See 'Georgian Monastic Liturgy' in this chapter. The text of the pre-Athonite version is available online; see *Novum Testamentum georgice e codibus praeathoniensibus. The Old Georgian Four Gospels: Pre-Athonian Redaction*, ed. by Elguja Giunashvili, Manana Machkahneli, Sophio Sarjveladze, Zurab Sarjveladze, Darejan Tvaltvadze, and Jost Gippert (Tbilisi and Frankfurt-am-Main: Fundamentals of an Electronic Documentation of Caucasian Languages and Cultures Alternative Resources, Materials, Applications and Zipped Information [ARMAZI] Project, 1999–2007). At http://titus.uni-frankfurt.de/texte/etca/cauc/ageo/nt/cinant/cinan.htm (accessed 30 May 2016).

[367] Mzekala Šaniʒe, 'Remarques au sujet de la bible géorgienne', BK 41 (1983), 105–22; Daredshan Twaltwadse (Darejan Tvaltvadze), 'Aus der Geschichte der Übersetzung der Tetraevangelien ins Georgische', *Georgica* 31 (2008), 107–19.

[368] *Description* III, 8–33, here 8. See Appendix 1 for more on this manuscript.

Byzantine Political Ideology and Motivation

While Chalcedonian Orthodoxy had already come to be identified with allegiance to the Byzantine empire in Palestine since the diffusion of the label 'Melkite', Orthodoxy and imperial allegiance were not necessarily inter-dependent within the Byzantine empire. According to Dagron, it was the immigration of Syrian refugees on the frontier of the Byzantine empire in Asia Minor during the eleventh and twelfth centuries that reinforced Byzantine self-identification with Orthodoxy, so that 'Orthodox' received a political designation—the Roman (that is, Byzantine) religion (οἱ τὰ 'Ρωμαίων θρησκεύοντες)—that became the definition of *romanitas*.[369] An example of external ecclesiastical intrusion into the affairs of Christians in the East came in the year 937, during the rule of Patriarch Theophylactus of Constantinople (r. 933–56).[370] Patriarch Theophylactus sent a decree to the patriarchs of Antioch, Alexandria, and Jerusalem asking them to commemorate the patriarch of Constantinople by name in their prayers and liturgies, something that had not been done since the time of Umayyad rule (*c.*661–750). Patriarch Eutychius of Alexandria (877–940) recounts that the reaction to this request was positive and that the eastern patriarchs complied with Constantinople's request.[371] Another example of Byzantine intrusion is the treatment of Miaphysites within Byzantine territory by Emperor Romanus III Argyrus. Upon hearing that the Syrian non-Chalcedonian bishop Yūḥannā bore the title of 'patriarch of Antioch', Romanus summoned him and his metropolitans before Patriarch Alexius the Stoudite of Constantinople (r. 1025–43) and insisted that Yūḥannā renounce his errors and join the church of Constantinople. When Yūḥannā refused, he was banished and died in exile.[372]

Numerous such examples exist, but there has been very little analysis of the implications of these policies for liturgical practice. Christian Hannick's pro-vocatively titled article, 'Annexions et reconquêtes byzantines: Peut-on parler

---

[369] [L]*es orthodoxes, impuissants à contenir cette invasion de l'intérieur, reçoivent une désig-nation purement politique:* οἱ τὰ 'Ρωμαίων θρησκεύοντες. *L'Orthodoxie demeure, en dernier ressort, la définition de la romanité* ('The Orthodox, powerless to contain this invasion from within, receive a purely political designation: the Byzantine religion. Orthodoxy remains, as a last resort, the definition of Romanitas'). Dagron, 'L'immigration syrienne', 214.

[370] Alexander Kazhdan, 'Theophylaktos', ODB III, 2068.

[371] Eutichio, Patriarca di Alessandria, *Gli Annali*, trans. by Bartolomeo Pirone (Studia Orientalia Christiana Monographiae 1, Cairo: Franciscan Centre of Christian Oriental Studies, 1987), 436. See Constantin A. Panchenko, 'Иерусалимская православная церковь', ПЭ 21: 472; Sidney H. Griffith, 'Eutychius of Alexandria', in *Encyclopædia Iranica*, vol. 9 (New York: Columbia University Press, 1999), 77–8.

[372] Yaḥyā al-Anṭakī, *History* III, 488–91; Yaḥyā al-Anṭakī, *Cronache*, 341–2. For more information on Romanus III Argyrus, see 'The Destruction of the Anastasis' in this chapter.

d'"uniatisme" byzantin?', has been the only study to address the question of Byzantine religious hegemony in areas beyond the Byzantine empire or its direct control.[373] Focusing on the period between the seventh and the eleventh centuries, Hannick traces several historical events that demonstrate the extension of ecclesiastical jurisdiction and liturgical practices beyond their natural borders and points out tendencies towards unification that erased local particularities. He provides examples of Constantinopolitan interventions in the life of the diocese of Otranto in southern Italy,[374] attempts of Greek hierarchs to influence church life in Kievan-Rus',[375] and the passive albeit unsuccessful assimilation of Armenians in the Caucasus.[376] In spite of the provocative title of his study, Hannick concludes that there was no consistent implementation or imposition of Constantinople's Orthodox Christianity as a policy of the Byzantine empire. Constantinople was only interested in regulating Greek liturgical texts, if at all, and had no interest in Slavonic or Armenian liturgical books, at least not conscientiously. Likewise, jurisdictional disputes were never settled systematically and their resolution depended heavily on *oikonomia*.[377]

Without clear evidence of a Byzantine policy designed to impose the rite abroad, it is worth shifting focus to Jerusalem to see how the dynamic of Byzantinization worked locally. From this vantage point, the liturgical influence of Constantinople on Jerusalem may also be explained by the desire of the Hagiopolitan church to adopt Byzantine liturgical practices, rather than simply by Constantinople's desire to impose them upon others. Observing the liturgy of Constantinople could have been seen as a sign of Orthodoxy, as it certainly was in the Caucasus. Georgian anti-Armenian religious polemics arose in response to tense political Georgian–Armenian relations during the ninth and the tenth centuries.[378] Liturgical rites for the reintegration of heretics in Georgian liturgical books were often extremely harsh on Armenians, while Greek sources were more lenient.[379] This rise in Georgian emphasis on Orthodoxy and severity towards heresy also corresponds to the period in which the Georgian liturgy was Byzantinized, which suggests that adopting another, more 'Orthodox' liturgy or changing one's own liturgical tradition was entirely acceptable if it served as a sign of unity in the face of interconfessional enmity and as a means to bolster one's own Orthodoxy.

[373] Hannick, 'Annexions et reconquêtes byzantines'.   [374] Ibid., 452–5.
[375] Ibid., 456–64.   [376] Ibid., 464–74.   [377] Ibid., 474.
[378] Bernadette Martin-Hisard, 'Le discours des Géorgiens sur leur orthodoxie', RSBN 47 (2010), 195–264.
[379] Ibid., 260–4.

Theodore Balsamon and the Rite of Constantinople

Extant correspondence between clergy and monks shows that the Orthodoxy of different liturgical rites was a significant concern in the eleventh and twelfth centuries. Athonite *hegoumenos* Euthymius Mt'acmideli (d. 1028) had to reassure the monk Theodore from the Lavra of St Sabas in Palestine that JAS was both acceptable and authentic, even if it was not being celebrated as frequently as BAS and CHR.[380] Theodore IV Balsamon (1186–1203), absentee patriarch of Antioch residing in exile in Constantinople, replied to similar questions about JAS from Patriarch Mark of Alexandria.[381] But, while Euthymius emphasizes the continuity of JAS with BAS and CHR, thereby legitimizing and acknowledging the Byzantinization of the Georgian liturgy, Balsamon takes a different position.[382]

What exactly this position is, however, depends upon which version of Balsamon's responses one follows.[383] The most commonly cited version is the Ἐρωτήσεις κανονικαί in *Patrologia Graeca*, which is based on Leunclavius and Rhalles and chosen for its completeness and greater number of questions and responses.[384] The first question posed by Patriarch Mark to Balsamon deals specifically with the legitimacy of JAS:

Αἱ περὶ τὰ μέρη τῆς Ἀλεξανδρείας καὶ τῶν Ἱεροσολύμων ἀναγινωσκόμεναι λειτουργίαι, καὶ λεγόμεναι συγγραφῆναι παρὰ τῶν ἁγίων ἀποστόλων, Ἰακώβου τοῦ ἀδελφοθέου, καὶ Μάρκου, δεκταί εἰσι τῇ ἁγίᾳ καθολικῇ Ἐκκλησίᾳ, ἢ οὔ;[385]	Concerning the liturgies read in the regions of Alexandria and Jerusalem, and said to have been written by the holy Apostles, James the Brother of the Lord and Mark, are they received by the holy Catholic Church, or not?

Balsamon replies that, while canon 32 of the Council in Trullo (692) does admit the Apostle James as the author of JAS, the Liturgy of St Mark is questionable. Despite this acknowledgement, however, Balsamon says that neither liturgy is acceptable because the holy ecumenical throne of Constantinople has not accepted them.[386] 'For this reason all churches of God should

---

[380] Peradse, 'Liturgiegeschichte Georgiens', 77. See also Verhelst, 'Liturgie melkite de saint Jacques', 230–2; Parenti, 'La "vittoria"', 31. For more on this correspondence and the origins of JAS, see Chapter 3, 'The Origins and History of the Liturgy of St James'.

[381] Alexander Kazhdan, 'Balsamon, Theodore', ODB I, 249; Charon, *History of the Melkite Patriarchates*. vol. 1, 16; Viscuso, *Guide for a Church under Islām*, 3–9.

[382] Verhelst, 'Liturgie melkite de saint Jacques', 237.

[383] Viscuso, *Guide for a Church under Islām*, 43–6.

[384] PG 138:952–1012; Grumel, 'Les Réponses canoniques', 324; Nasrallah, 'Liturgie des patriarchats melchites', 163.

[385] PG 138:953A.

[386] Ψηφιζόμεθα οὖν μὴ εἶναι δεκτὰς αὐτάς ('Therefore, we declare that they are not acceptable'). PG 138:953C; Viscuso, *Guide for a Church under Islām*, 68. See also *The Council in Trullo Revisited*, ed. by George Nedungatt and Michael Featherstone (Kanonika 6, Rome: Pontifical Oriental Institute, 1995), 106–10.

follow the practice of New Rome or Constantinople' and celebrate according to the tradition of St John Chrysostom and St Basil the Great.[387] The other redaction of Balsamon's correspondence is found in the oldest manuscripts of the library of the ecumenical patriarchate in Constantinople and was edited by Manuel Gedeon.[388] This version is shorter both because it has fewer questions and because its responses are more succinct. The same first question appears in Gedeon's version thus: 'Ought one to serve liturgy with the scrolls [of the liturgies] of St James and St Mark?' (Χρὴ μετὰ τῶν κοντακίων ἱερουργεῖν τοῦ ἁγίου Ἰακώβου καὶ τοῦ ἁγίου Μάρκου;).[389] The word κοντακίων here refers to a scroll containing liturgical texts rather than to the hymnographic composition by the same name. Balsamon's response repeats much of what was stated above but, rather than dismissing the celebration of JAS, he suggests an examination and study of its texts by the Holy Synod.[390] The honour accorded to Jerusalem here is more in keeping with Balsamon's comments elsewhere on the ecumenical councils, acknowledging the possibility of celebrating JAS for certain feasts, in a way similar to that in which BAS was celebrated in Constantinople and is still celebrated in the Byzantine rite today:[391]

... πρῶτος ὁ ἅγιος Ἰάκωβος ὁ ἀδελφόθεος ὡς πρῶτος ἀρχιερατεύσας τῆς Ἱεροσολυμιτῶν Ἐκκλησίας παρέδωκε τὴν θείαν ἱεροτελεστίαν, ἥτις παρ' ἡμῖν ἀγνοεῖται, παρὰ δὲ τοῖς Ἱεροσολυμίταις καὶ τοῖς Παλαιστιναίοις ἐνεργεῖται ἐν ταῖς μεγάλαις ἑορταῖς.[392]	First St James the Brother of the Lord, as first high priest of the church of Jerusalem, taught the divine sacred rites, which are unknown to us, but which the Jerusalemites and Palestinians practice on great feasts.

Thus the ideological dominance of Constantinople over the liturgy of other churches and patriarchates, elevating its rite to the status of a *ritus praestantior*, as it were, began at Trullo, but came to impact the Orthodox patriarchate of Jerusalem only when its chief eucharistic liturgy, JAS, began to be questioned. A few decades prior to Balsamon, the Metropolitan Elias of Crete (r. *c*.1120) expressed similar preference for a liturgical centralization that was based on the model of the Hagia Sophia in Constantinople. In response to a

---

[387] Διά τοι τοῦτο καὶ ὀφείλουσι πᾶσαι αἱ Ἐκκλησίαι τοῦ Θεοῦ ἀκολουθεῖν τῷ ἔθει τῆς νέας Ῥώμης, ἤτοι τῆς Κωνσταντινουπόλεως. PG 138:953D; Viscuso, *Guide for a Church under Islām*, 66–70.

[388] Balsamon, 'Λύσεις ἐπὶ ταῖς ἀπορίαις'; Grumel, 'Les Réponses canoniques', 324.

[389] Balsamon, 'Λύσεις ἐπὶ ταῖς ἀπορίαις', 135.

[390] Ibid., 137; Grumel, 'Les Réponses canoniques', 325; Parenti, *L'eucologio slavo del Sinai*, 6–9.

[391] Theodore Balsamon, *Canones Nicænæ Primæ Sanctæ et Œcumenicæ Synodi*, PG 137:261; Parenti, 'La "vittoria"', 47.

[392] Theodore Balsamon, *Canones Sanctorum Patrum qui in Trullo Imperialis Palatii Constantinopoli Convenerunt*, PG 137:621B. Charon provides an erroneous reference for this citation. See Charon, 'Le rite byzantin', 495.

question from one of his priests about the developing and varied prothesis rite at the beginning of the Divine Liturgy, he expressed to his interlocutor that 'what is not done in the Great Church of God should not be sought in other churches'.[393] This attitude reaches its height with Symeon of Thessalonike (d. 1429), who often critically compares allegedly questionable Hagiopolitan monastic or Armenian liturgical practices with those of the Great Church of Constantinople. For Symeon, 'especially this Church of the city of Constantinople, more than the others, holds what is perfect, pure, correct, and unadulterated of the faith in Christ, and what is indestructible of the divine traditions from the very beginning'.[394] The views of Elias of Crete or Symeon of Thessalonike would probably not have had a direct impact on Jerusalem, but they show the sentiments of Byzantine clergy towards foreign Hagiopolite liturgical practices—and it is likely the Jerusalem church was aware of these views. By the time of Symeon, however, Jerusalem had already lost its authentic traditions and JAS was no longer celebrated.

Such views of Constantinople as the paragon of right faith and liturgical practice spread south and east relatively quickly—and even beyond the domain of the Chalcedonians. A twelfth-century treatise by the Syrian Orthodox Metropolitan of Amid in northern Mesopotamia, Dionysius bar Ṣalibi (d. 1171), which takes the form of a discussion with a West Syrian monk named Rabban ʾIshōʿ, reveals that even non-Chalcedonians were enticed by the splendour of Constantinople.[395] Dionysios bar Ṣalibi scolds Rabban ʾIshōʿ for his views and for putting words into the mouth of the Prophet Jeremiah. Rabban alleges that

> the beautiful Metropolis which Jeremiah has foreseen when lamenting over Jerusalem is our Metropolis [Constantinople]. God showed him her towers, her beauty, her ramparts, and her buildings and said to him: 'Do not weep over Jerusalem, lo I have found a house better than Jerusalem, and I will bring all people and all tongues to its glory'; and it happened as he said.[396]

---

[393] ὃ δὲ ἐν τῇ Μεγάλῃ τοῦ θεοῦ Ἐκκλησίᾳ μὴ τελεῖται οὐδὲ ἐν ταῖς λοιπαῖς οἶμαι τῶν Ἐκκλησιῶν ζητεῖσθαι ὀφείλει. Vitalien Laurent, 'Le rituel de la proscomidie et le métropolite de Crète Élie', REB 16 (1958), 116–42, here 134 (lines 261–3).

[394] 'Καὶ ἡ ἐκκλησία ἐξαιρέτως αὕτη τῆς Κωνσταντίνου παρὰ τὰς ἄλλας τὸ ἠκριβωμένον ἔχει καὶ καθαρὸν καὶ ὀρθὸν τῆς πίστεως Χριστοῦ καὶ ἀκίβδηλον, καὶ τὸ τῶν θείων ἀπαρχῆς παραδόσεων ἀπαράθραυστον'. St Symeon of Thessalonika, *The Liturgical Commentaries*, ed. and trans. by Steven Hawkes-Teeples (Studies and Texts 168, Toronto: Pontifical Institute of Mediaeval Studies, 2011), 210–11 (L 74). See also PG 155:277D–280C, 701, 908; Alice-Mary Talbot, 'Symeon', ODB III, 1981–2.

[395] Sebastian P. Brock, 'Dionysios bar Ṣalibi', GEDSH, 126–7. See also Rifaat Ebied, 'Dionysius bar Ṣalībī's Syriac *Polemitcal Treatises*: Prejudice and Polarization towards Christians, Jews and Muslims', *The Harp* 20 (2006), 73–86, esp. 83. My thanks to Jack Tannous for bringing this text to my attention.

[396] Alphonse Mingana, 'A Treatise of Barṣalībi against the Melchites', in *Woodbrooke Studies: Christian Documents in Syriac, Arabic, and Garshūni*, vol. 1 (Cambridge: W. Heffer & Sons, 1927), 17–63, here 40.

Dionysios bar Ṣalibi then explains to Rabban 'Ishoʿ that there is no such passage in Jeremiah's *Lamentations* and, even if there were, Rabban's interpretation of the passage is completely wrong. Jeremiah was taken to Egypt, not to Constantinople. Nevertheless, the beauty of the city's buildings and the liturgical songs of the Byzantines had made an impression on non-Chalcedonians.[397] In the absence of similar statements from actual Chalcedonians in Palestine, one can only assume that the clergy and the faithful of the Jerusalem patriarchate would have seen allegiance to Constantinople as prestigious and been proud to be associated with the church of such a magnificent city.

Hagiopolitan Patriarchs in Exile

Before continuing the discussion of exiled eastern patriarchs, it is necessary to mention the problems of the lists that outline their succession. The absence of a trustworthy list of the successors to the patriarchal see of Jerusalem is another obstacle in studying the relationship between Constantinople and Jerusalem from the eleventh through to fourteenth centuries. Even a cursory examination of some primary sources from this period shows that the standard lists compiled by Venance Grumel and Giorgio Fedalto must be consulted with caution.[398] The exact dates when the patriarchs of Jerusalem went into exile and returned are unclear. As part of the agreement between the Byzantine Emperor Romanus Argyrus and Caliph al-Ẓāhir to rebuild the Anastasis, the church of Jerusalem received the right to appoint its own candidates to the patriarchal throne.[399] The previous arrangement required approval from the caliph and meant that the see of Jerusalem was often vacant or that appointments were arbitrary. For example, the vacancy after the death of Patriarch Theophilus I (r. 1012–20) was filled by Patriarch Nicephorus I (r. 1020–48), who had been a married priest working in the palace of al-Ḥākim in Jerusalem as a carpenter. His appointment was confirmed in Constantinople only after he visited the imperial capital and proved his Orthodoxy by reading a profession of faith before Patriarch Eustathius of Constantinople.[400] Some of the dates and accounts during this period do not correspond either across the

---

[397] Ibid., 40–5 (Chapter 6: 'Against the Pride of the Chalcedonians, and on the Building of Their Capital').

[398] Grumel, *Chronologie*, 451–2; V. Grumel, 'La Chronologie des patriarches grecs de Jérusalem au XIIIᵉ siècle', REB 20 (1962), 197–201; Fedalto, *Hierarchia ecclesiastica orientalis*, vol. 2. See the review by Jean Darrouzès in REB 48 (1990), 297–9 for more information on episcopal lists in the Christian East.

[399] For more on the rebuilding of the Anastasis, see 'The Destruction of the Anastasis' in this chapter.

[400] Yaḥyā al-Anṭakī, *History* III, 432–3, 436–7, 468–71, 532–3.

different sources in Greek and Arabic or between the Arabic sources themselves, as was seen in the case of the dates of the destruction of the Anastasis by al-Ḥākim.[401]

An important and well-known document of this period, the eleventh-century Typikon of Gregory Pacourianus for the Monastery of the Mother of God Petritzonitissa in Bachkovo, present-day Bulgaria, dated December 1083, reveals that the monastery's patron, Gregory Pacourianus (d. 1086), signed the Typikon along with Patriarch Euthymius of Jerusalem,

> to guarantee and confirm that all that has been written is the same, since [Patriarch Euthymius] happened to be here [in Bulgaria] by order of our mighty and Holy Emperor requiring him to be in Thessalonike for peace with the hateful Frank and on his return again arrived here with us at my estates at Philippoupolis.[402]

The text under the patriarch's signature is as follows: 'I, Euthymius, through God's mercy patriarch of Jerusalem, the city of the Holy Resurrection of Christ our God, have signed with my own hand the present *typikon*.'[403] This signature is the only information we have for dating the reign of Patriarch Euthymius.[404]

The situation is the same in the case of Patriarch Nicholas, mentioned in the manuscript *Hagios Stavros Gr. 43* (1122). Known popularly as the 'Typikon of the Anastasis', this important document transmits the liturgy of Holy Week, Pascha, and Bright Week as it was celebrated at the Church of the Anastasis in Jerusalem. Originally it began with the now missing services of Lazarus Saturday and ended with the service for the Saturday after Easter.[405] But the manuscript is now acephalous, in other words without a beginning, hence it bears no title either. However, it contains a lengthy colophon:

---

[401] See Wolfgang Felix, *Byzanz und die islamische Welt im früheren 11. Jahrhundert: Geschichte der politischen Beziehungen von 1001 bis 1055* (Vienna: Verlag der Österreichischen Akademie der Wissenschaften, 1981), 39–44.

[402] *Typikon de Grégoire Pacourianos pour le monastère de Pétritzos (Bačkovo) en Bulgarie*, ed. by Louis Petit (Византийскій Временник, Приложеніе къ XI тому, no. 1, St Petersburg: Типографія Императорской Академіи Наукъ, 1904), 557; Paul Gautier, 'Le typikon du sébaste Grégoire Pakourianos', REB 42 (1984), 5–145; Robert Jordan, '*Pakourianos: Typikon* of Gregory Pakourianos', BMFD II, 507–63; Nina G. Garsoïan, 'Pakourianos', ODB III, 1553.

[403] *Typikon de Grégoire Pacourianos* (n. 402), 557. See also Chrisostomos A. Papadopoulos, Ἱστόρια τῆς ἐκκλησίας Ἱεροσολύμων (Jerusalem and Alexandria: ἐκ τοῦ Πατριαρχικοῦ Τυπογραφείου Ἀλεξανδρείας, 1910), 368–9.

[404] See *Typikon de Grégoire Pacourianos* (n. 42), 560 n. 70; Grumel, *Chronologie*, 452.

[405] The full title given to the manuscript by Athanasios Papadopoulos-Kerameus is Διάταξις τῶν ἱερῶν ἀκολουθιῶν τῆς μεγάλης τῶν παθῶν ἑβδομάδος τοῦ κυρίου ἡμῶν Ἰησοῦ Χριστοῦ, κατὰ τὸ ἀρχαῖον τῆς ἐν Ἱεροσολύμοις ἐκκλησίας ἔθος, ἤτοι τὸ ἐν τῷ ναῷ τῆς Ἀναστάσεως ('Arrangement of the sacred services of the great week of the passion of our Lord Jesus Christ, according to the ancient customs of the church in Jerusalem, in the Church of the Resurrection'). Papadopoulos-Kerameus, *Anastasis Typikon*, 1. See Appendix 1.

Ἐκτίσθη ἡ δέλτος αὕτη κατὰ πρόσταξιν τοῦ εὐλαβοὺς Γεωργίου, ἄρχων καὶ κριτὴς τῆς ἁγίας πόλεως καὶ σακελλίου [supra] χαρτοφύλακος] τὲ καὶ μεγάλου σκευοφύλακος τῆς ἁγίας Χριστοῦ τοῦ Θεοῦ ἡμῶν Ἀναστάσεως· καὶ ἐδόθη παρ'αὐτοῦ εἰς τὴν ἐκκλησίαν τῆς ἁγίας Χριστοῦ τοῦ Θεοῦ ἡμῶν Ἀναστάσεως ὑπὲρ ἀφέσεως ἁμαρτιῶν αὐτοῦ.

This book was published at the command of the pious George, archon and judge of the Holy City and *sakellios* [*chartophylax*] as well as great *skeuophylax* [of the Church] of the Holy Resurrection of Christ our God. And it was given by him to the Church of the Holy Resurrection of Christ our God for the remission of his sins.

Ἐγράφη δὲ καὶ εἱρμώσθη διὰ χειρὸς Βασιλείου τοῦ Ἁγιοπολίτου, γραφεῦς τὲ καὶ ἐλαχίστου ἀναγνώστης τῆς ἁγίας Χριστοῦ τοῦ Θεοῦ ἡμῶν Ἀναστάσεως ἐν τῇ ἁγίᾳ πόλει Ἰερουσαλήμ. εἴληφεν δὲ τέλος ἡ αὕτη δέλτος ἡμέρα β' ὥρα γ'τῆς ἡμέρας εἰς τὴν κζ' τοῦ φευρουαρίου μηνός· ἔτους κόσμου ἑξακισχιλιοστῶι ἑξακοσίω τριάκοντα· ἰνδικτιῶνος ιε': παρακαλῶι οὖν καὶ λιπαρῶ τοὺς ἐντυγχάνοντας καὶ ἀναγινώσκοντας ἐν τῆι ταύτηι δέλτω εὔχεσθε ὑπὲρ ἀμφοτέρων τῶ γράψαντι ἅμα καὶ τῶ κτισαμένω· ἵνα ῥυσθῶμεν ἀμφότεροι τῆς αἰωνίου κολάσεως ἀμήν.

Written and bound by the hand of Basil the Hagiopolite, copyist and humble reader [of the Church] of the Resurrection of Christ our God in the Holy City of Jerusalem. This book was completed at the third hour of the day [9 a. m.], on Monday 27 February, in the year of the world 6063 [= AD 1122], the fifteenth indiction. Therefore I earnestly beseech those who come across this book and read it: pray for both the writer as well as for the patron, so that both of us may be delivered from eternal punishment. Amen.

Ἐτυπώθη δὲ τὸ παρὸν τεῦχος κατὰ τὴν τάξιν τῆς ἁγίας Χριστοῦ τοῦ Θεοῦ ἡμῶν Ἀναστάσεως καὶ οὐ δεῖ τίς προσθήσει ἢ ἐκλήψει ἀπαυτόν τι.[406]

It was modelled after the present roll according to the order [of the Church] of the Holy Resurrection of Church our God and no one should add to it or omit from it anything at all.

The editor of the manuscript, Athanasios Papadopoulos-Kerameus (1856–1912), gave it the title 'Τυπικὸν τῆς ἐν Ἰεροσολύμοις ἐκκλησίας', perhaps following the example of other pre-Revolutionary Russian liturgiologists such as Nikolai Krasnosel'tsev, who applied the title 'Typikon' to the kanonarion-synaxarion of the Great Church of Constantinople.[407] Although it does not actually bear this anachronistic title, the 'Typikon of the Anastasis' bears a Typikon's characteristic traits of regulating the divine services of the church and has become accepted shorthand for the church's order and practice, whether in the form of a book or as an unwritten living tradition.[408] However, because the 'Typikon of the Anastasis' provides complete texts of hymnography, scriptural readings, and rubrics for the services, it is clear that it was a liturgical book possibly used during services. Thus certain authors have suggested that it should be considered a Tropologion or a hymnal rather than a Typikon.[409]

---

[406] Papadopoulos-Kerameus, *Anastasis Typikon*, 252–3.

[407] For the Constantinopolitan kanonarion-synaxarion, see Chapter 1, 'Early Constantinopolitan Liturgy'.

[408] Dmitrievskii, *Описаніе* I, iv; Mateos, *Typicon*.

[409] See Gaga Shurgaia, 'Formazione della struttura dell'ufficio del Sabato di Lazzaro nella tradizione cattedrale di Gerusalemme', *Annali di Ca' Foscari* 36.3 (1997), 147–68, here 148 n. 4. For further discussion of the term *typikon*, see Chapter 1, 'Early Constantinopolitan Liturgy'.

Numerous scholars have studied this text, among them its editor, of course, Papadopoulos-Kerameus, and then Dmitrievskii, Krasnosel'tsev, Bertonière, Janeras, and Baldovin, all of whom have pointed out the difficulty of accurately dating it.[410] Dmitrievskii shows that many of the basic elements of the Typikon of the Anastasis resemble those of Egeria's accounts.[411] For example, the *spoudaioi* are central to the continuity of the services, some of which, such as the Hours of Good Friday attributed to Patriarch Sophronius, are completely dependent on the participation of monks from the monasteries of Sts Sabas, Chariton, Theodosius, and others.[412] Furthermore, JAS is still the main Hagiopolitan eucharistic liturgy;[413] the stational character of the services has been retained, and there are processions to and from the Cross at Golgotha during Vigil[414] and synaxeis (gatherings) at the Mount of Olives, Gethsemane, the Martyrium (ὁ ναὸς τοῦ ἁγίου Κωνσταντίνου), Sion, Golgotha, and the Anastasis, among other places.[415]

Moreover, the hymnography and the structure of the services are similar to those of the current Byzantine rite. For example, the structure of vespers and matins is virtually identical to the one they have in the current Byzantine rite: they retain the same structure as in the *Narration of the Abbots John and Sophronius*, but they fill it in with hymnody, according to the custom of the abbots themselves.[416] Much of the hymnody found in the Typikon of the Anastasis is also identical to that of the current Byzantine rite, especially the main hymns of each day of Holy Week and of Pascha. These include troparia,[417] *exaposteilaria*,[418] *stichera*,[419] liturgical canons,[420] and the antiphons of the Divine Liturgy,[421] as well as several of the fixed hymns of services such as the 'resurrectional festal troparia for "the undefiled" [Psalm 118 LXX]' (τροπάρια τοῦ ἀμώμου τῆς ἑορτῆς ἀναστάσιμα), although there are also additional troparia with specific Palm Sunday themes.[422] Such similarities

---

[410] Papadopoulos-Kerameus, *Anastasis Typikon*; Dmitrievskii, *Богослуженіе страсной и пасхальной седмицъ*; Dmitrievskii, *Древнѣйшіе Патріаршіе Типиконы*; Krasnosel'tsev, 'Review'; Bertonière, *Easter Vigil*, 12–18; Janeras, *Vendredi-Saint*, 40; Baldovin, *Urban Character*, 80–82.

[411] Dmitrievskii, *Древнѣйшіе Патріаршіе Типиконы*, 66–70.

[412] Papadopoulos-Kerameus, *Anastasis Typikon*, 7 and 147; GL § 115–157; Pétridès, 'Spoudæi'; Janeras, *Vendredi-Saint*, 250–9.

[413] Papadopoulos-Kerameus, *Anastasis Typikon*, 23.

[414] Ibid., 12.   [415] Ibid., 17, 18, 23, 99, 147, 190.

[416] This can be seen in vespers and matins for the first days of Holy Week. See ibid., 28–31, 32–41.

[417] See 'Ἰδοὺ ὁ νυμφίος ἔρχεται' (Troparion for Holy Monday, Tuesday, and Wednesday), ibid., 32, 52, 66; "Ὅτε οἱ ἔνδοξοι μαθηταῖ' (Troparion for Holy Thursday), ibid., 83.

[418] See 'Τὸν νυμφῶνά σου βλέπω, Σωτῆρ μου' (First Exaposteilarion for Holy Monday and Tuesday), ibid., 38, 56; 'Σαρκὶ ὑπνώσας ὡς θνητός' (Exaposteilarion of Pascha), ibid., 196.

[419] See for example the numerous identical stichera of Palm Sunday, although their order is not always the same as the current Byzantine rite, ibid., 1–31.

[420] For example the canons of Palm Sunday and Pascha, ibid., 7–15, 191–6.

[421] Ibid., 24, 201.   [422] Ibid., 6–7.

explain why the Typikon of the Anastasis is considered a source for the ancient Hagiopolitan rite as well as one of the earliest testimonials for the 'Byzantine' Holy Week,[423] showing the Anastasis Typikon's truly transitional character. This is evidenced even further by the Anastasis Typikon's familiarity with the practice in Constantinople (τῆς Ῥωμανίας τάξις), which provides certain alternative rubrics for Constantinopolitan pericopes.[424] It should be noted, however, that the manuscript also includes characteristic Hagiopolitan cathedral liturgical practices, such as numerous processions, that are not part of the current Byzantine rite. Thus, while the structure and content of the services may be similar, the liturgical action often is not.

Alexei Dmitrievskii was the most vocal scholar to question this source's authenticity. He spends almost thirty pages refuting Papadopoulos-Karameus' claim that the manuscript reflects the liturgical practice of 1122, suggesting that the destruction of various holy sites, especially the destruction of the Anastasis in 1009, made it impossible for many of the services to take place as they were described.[425] Dmitrievskii used the commemoration of Patriarch Nicholas of Jerusalem, mentioned in the prayer for those who bring offerings on Palm Sunday, to date the manuscript.[426] According to Dmitrievskii, Patriarch Nicholas reigned from 932 to 945 or 947, and his name was simply recopied in the manuscript.[427] For Dmitrievskii, all these factors pointed to a *terminus ante quem* of 1009, the latest accepted date of the destruction of the Anastasis by al-Ḥākim, and a *terminus post quem* of 886, which is based on the names of the hymnographers mentioned in the text. Thus Dmitrievskii believed that the monk Basil copied the text for posterity's sake and intended it as a historical artefact.[428]

However, as was already noted, the destruction of 1009 did not have as great an impact on Jerusalem's liturgy as liturgists have assumed.[429] In the same vein, more recent studies of Byzantine prosopography revise some of Dmitrievskii's conclusions surrounding the identity of Patriarch Nicholas. The *Prosopographie der mittelbyzantinischen Zeit* identifies 267 Nicholases known to have lived between 867 and 1025, and none of them matches Dmitrievskii's proposed patriarch of Jerusalem.[430] Giorgio Fedalto places Patriarch Nicholas'

[423] See Janeras, 'La Settimana Santa'; Taft, 'Holy Week'.

[424] Papadopoulos-Karameus, *Anastasis Typikon*, 106.

[425] Dmitrievskii, Древнѣйшіе Патріаршіе Типиконы, 74–83; Papadopoulos-Karameus, *Anastasis Typikon*, αʹ–θʹ.

[426] Ibid., 26. See Brakmann, 'Zur Εὐχὴ τῆς καρποφορίας'.

[427] Dmitrievskii, Древнѣйшіе Патріаршіе Типиконы, 101, 109. Bertonière, *Easter Vigil*, 13–14 follows Dmitrievskii.

[428] Bertonière, *Easter Vigil*, 13–14; Janeras, *Vendredi-Saint*, 40.

[429] See 'The Destruction of the Anastasis' in this chapter.

[430] The only figures that bear some resemblance with that portrait are Patriarch Nicolaus I Mysticus of Constantinople (d. 925, #25885), who ruled twice in Constantinople, Patriarch Nicolaus II Chrysoberges of Constantinople (d. 992, #26019), who is commemorated in diptychs in *Messina Gr. 177*, and Patriarch Nicolaus II of Antioch (d. 1030, #26124). See PmbZ, #25885–#26152. Copyists

reign in an interval between shortly before February 1122, when *Hagios Stavros Gr. 43* was copied, and after January 1156, when he is mentioned at a synod in Constantinople.[431] All this recent evidence should persuade liturgical scholars to reconsider the Typikon of the Anastasis as a twelfth-century witness to the late stages of liturgical Byzantinization in Jerusalem. The manuscript's transitional character is evidenced by its scribe's familiarity with the practice and ordo of both Jerusalem (ὁ τύπος τῆς Ἁγίας Ἀναστάσεως) and Constantinople (ἡ δὲ τῆς Ῥωμανίας τάξις).[432] Such notices are often the sign of a redactor who reports a change taking effect or a conflict in liturgical practice, as we have seen with the calendar copied by Iovane Zosime in *Sinai Geo. O. 34* (10th cent.), with the Melkite calendar copied by al-Bīrūnī, and with the liturgical Typikon *Sinai Gr. 1096* (12th cent.).[433] Krasnosel'tsev pointed out the neglected role of the copyist Basil the Hagiopolite as a redactor.[434] The patronage of the pious archon George, who was *sakellios, chartophylax,* and great *skeuophylax* of the Church of the Anastasis, should not be overlooked either when considering the role of the manuscript in the church of Jerusalem during the twelfth century.[435] Basil himself was a reader at the Anastasis who attempted to reconcile conflicting elements of the Hagiopolitan rite as he saw it being Byzantinized before his very eyes. This all suggests that the manuscript should be regarded as a twelfth-century witness of how the important figures mentioned in the colophon *would* have celebrated Holy Week and Pascha at the Anastasis in 1122, if this had been possible.

Thus, were it not for the commemoration of Patriarch Nicholas in this manuscript, it would be impossible to date his reign as patriarch of Jerusalem, let alone to know his name.

Perhaps one of the more complete sources for the hierarchy of the patriarchate of Jerusalem is contained at folios 77–103 in *Hagios Sabas Gr. 153* (1275), edited by Papadopoulos-Kerameus.[436] Although the editor calls this

---

named Basil are known from the period between 867 and 1025, but none of them matches the description of the copyist of the Typikon of the Anastasis. See the index in *Prosopographie der mittelbyzantinischen Zeit. 2. Abteilung (867–1025)*, vol. 8, 391.

[431] Fedalto shows some uncertainty about the period from 932 to 945. See Fedalto, 'Liste vescovili', 17; Fedalto, *Hierarchia ecclesiastica orientalis*, vol. 2, 1003. See also Papadopoulos-Kerameus, *Anastasis Typikon, η'*; Angelo Mai, *Spicilegium Romanum*, vol. 10: *Synodus Constantinopolitana* (Rome: Typis Collegii Urbani, 1844), 16.

[432] Papadopoulos-Kerameus, *Anastasis Typikon*, 106.

[433] For *Sinai Geo. O. 34* (10th cent.), see 'Georgian Monastic Liturgy' in this chapter, as well as Appendix 1. For *Sinai Gr. 1096* (12th cent.) see Appendix 1.

[434] Cited in Bertonière, *Easter Vigil*, 16, and followed by Brakmann, 'Zur Εὐχὴ τῆς καρποφορίας', 78.

[435] Alexander Kazhdan and Paul Magdalino 'Sakellarios', ODB III, 1828–9; id., 'Sakellion', ODB III, 1829–30; R. J. Macrides, 'Chartophylax', ODB I, 414–15; Paul Magdalino and Alice-Mary Talbot, 'Skeuophylax', ODB III, 1909–10.

[436] Athanasios Papadopoulos-Kerameus, 'Δίπτυχα τῆς ἐν Ἱεροσολύμοις ἐκκλησίας', in Ἀνάλεκτα Ἱεροσολυμητικῆς Σταχυολογίας 1 (St Petersburg: Kirschbaum, 1891), 124–43; Kenneth

text 'Diptychs of the church in Jerusalem' (*'Δίπτυχα τῆς ἐν Ἱεροσολύμοις ἐκκλησίας'*), in view of its nature, the text appears to be more of a service (*ἀκολουθία*) for the joint commemoration of the patriarchs of Jerusalem. The names of the patriarchs are listed within hymnography preceded by rubrics that indicate the tone in which the hymns are to be sung. No date is given for the celebration of this feast in the edited text itself, but we know from significantly earlier Hagiopolitan sources that a joint commemoration of the patriarchs or bishops of Jerusalem fell on 17 or 18 May.[437] Despite the numerous names provided, this source is problematic because it does not give dates for any of the hierarchs, and there is no certainty that it includes the names of all the patriarchs or that it lists them in chronological order. Byzantine histories, such as that of Theophanes the Confessor, are of little help here because they lose track of the hierarchy of the church of Jerusalem after the Arab conquest.[438]

Several sources provide more reliable information on the life of the patriarchs of Alexandria, Antioch, and Jerusalem in Constantinopolitan exile, although they are certainly not as abundant as those for the patriarchs of the imperial capital. No register has survived for any of the eastern patriarchates, and most of what is known comes from Byzantine sources. From these we generally know that the exiled patriarchs were held in high esteem and were involved in the liturgical life of Constantinople. Given the paucity of sources, I will examine the activity of Patriarch Leontius of Jerusalem and Patriarch Athanasius II of Alexandria as examples of how exiled eastern patriarchs functioned in Constantinople and what relations they had to their episcopal sees.

Leontius of Jerusalem

A significant figure of the Comnenian dynasty (1081–5) is Leontius of Jerusalem (*c*.1110–85). His *Life*, written by Theodosius Goudeles probably after 1204, is one of the few *vitae* that survive from the period. As patriarch of Jerusalem, he is perhaps the only one to have visited his see while in Constantinopolitan exile.[439] Although Michel Kaplan doubts the veracity of the

W. Clark, *Checklist of Manuscripts in the Libraries of the Greek and Armenian Patriarchates in Jerusalem Microfilmed for the Library of Congress, 1949–1950* (Washington, DC: Library of Congress, 1953), 11.

[437] GL § 982; Garitte, *Calendrier palestino-géorgien*, 232, 227–8, 400; Verhelst, 'Lieux de station' I, 56–7.

[438] *Theophanis Chronographia*, 339; Mango and Scott, *Chronicle of Theophanes*, 472. See also the general remarks about the patriarchs of Jerusalem listed by Theophanes in Mango and Scott, *Chronicle of Theophanes*, lxxii–lxxiii.

[439] For other contemporary saints and their *vitae*, see Tsougarakis, *Life of Leontios*, 2 n. 5. Tsougarakis believes that Leontius' voyage to Jerusalem, described below, lasted between ten and twelve months and took place around 1178. See Tsougarakis, *Life of Leontios*, 205.

account of Leontius' trip to Jerusalem and even questions whether it actually occurred, he acknowledges that it provides a unique source for knowledge of Byzantine views of Jerusalem and of Constantinople's political and religious policy towards Palestine and its occupying forces.[440]

Born in Strumvitza (*Στρούμβιτζα*), Macedonia, between 1110 and 1115, Leontius became a monk (*c*.1130–2) and subsequently *hegoumenos* (*c*.1157–8) on Patmos, where—according to his biographer—he was renowned for his ascetical life and humility.[441] During several visits to Constantinople he behaved as a holy fool.[442] In an unusual change of affairs, he became the oeconomus of Patmos, which required him to make a trip to Constantinople in order to restore property taken from his monastery.[443] There he met Emperor Manuel I Comnenus (1143–80) who, after restoring the monastery's property, was so impressed with Leontius' knowledge of Scripture and his piety that he decided to ordain him bishop.[444] Leontius declined the sees of Kiev (*Ρῶς*) and Cyprus (*Κύπρος*), both recently vacated, declaring that God had destined him to be patriarch.[445] With the death of Patriarch Nicephorus II sometime between July 1173 and 1177,[446] Leontius was named patriarch of Jerusalem (*ἀρχιερέα τῆς Σιών... τῆς Ἱερουσαλήμ... τοῦ θρόνου τῆς μητρὸς πασῶν τῶν ἐκκλησιῶν*) by the emperor, who urged him to go to Jerusalem.[447] Whether the emperor's exhortation was motivated by devotion, as Leontius' response suggests, or had political reasons, as some modern scholars suggest, is uncertain.[448] Episcopal consecration during this period often included the stipulation that the newly consecrated bishop should visit his see, as witnessed in several cases.[449]

---

[440] Kaplan, 'Leontios', 479, 487–8.   [441] Tsougarakis, *Life of Leontios*, 34.

[442] For more on this phenomenon, see Alexander Kazhdan, 'Fools, Holy', ODB II, 795.

[443] The amount of 700 *modioi* of wheat was exchanged for two pounds of gold by imperial decree. See Tsougarakis, *Life of Leontios*, 193 n. 5.

[444] *Life of Leontios*, 106, § 63: 30–3; Charles M. Brand, Alexander Kazhdan, and Anthony Cutler, 'Manuel I Komnenos', ODB II, 1289–90.

[445] *Ὅτι με τοῦ ἐπουρανίου βασιλέως πατριάρχην ἔχοντος, οὔκουν ὁ ἐπίγειος ἐπίσκοπον ποιῆσαι δεδύνται* ('When the celestial king destines me for patriarch, the earthly one cannot make me bishop'). Tsougarakis, *Life of Leontios*, 108, § 65: 26–8. For more on the metropolia of *Ρῶς* with its seat in Kiev, see Tsougarakis, *Life of Leontios*, 194; Simon Franklin and Anthony Cutler, 'Kiev', ODB II, 1128.

[446] Tsougarakis, *Life of Leontios*, 108, § 66; 195–6. For the reference to patriarch Nicephorus II, see Grumel, *Regestes* I.2–3, n. 1126. Other lists include patriarchs between the reigns of Nicephorus II and Leontius.

[447] *Ἐπεὶ δὲ καὶ προχειρισθείη ἀρχιερεὺς τῆς Σιών, ὡς εἴρηται, καὶ εἰς αὐτὴν ἀπιέναι παρὰ τοῦ κρατοῦντος ὑπεμιμνήσκετο* ('Since he was appointed archpriest of Sion, as has been said, he was being reminded by the ruler to go there'). Tsougarakis, *Life of Leontios*, 110, § 67: 12–14.

[448] Rose, 'Saint Leontios', 254–6. Kaplan emphasizes that Leontius departed for Jerusalem and then returned to Constantinople at the emperor's express command. See Kaplan, 'Leontios', 480.

[449] See Luca Pieralli, 'Benedetto, metropolita di Seleucia negli anni della Guerra di Candia', OCP 66 (2000), 395–418.

Comnenian claims to Antioch were revived after the city's capture by the Byzantine forces of Emperors Nicephorus II Phocas (r. 963–9) in 969,[450] John II Comnenus (r. 1118–43) in 1138,[451] and Manuel I Comnenus in 1159. Because Jerusalem had not been in Byzantine hands since 638, the Constantinopolitan political understanding of Palestine was different: a Byzantine advance into Palestine would not be a restoration of its own territories, but rather a conquest of new lands.[452] That Manuel's delicate diplomacy employing 'military alliances, dynastic marriages, and religious or ecclesiastical arrangements' sought to bring Jerusalem into the Byzantine sphere of influence is quite clear, especially through the marriage of Maria Comnena to King Amalric, whom Leontius may have visited during his stay in Jerusalem, as Richard Rose suggests.[453]

Leontius dealt with both ecclesial and political matters during his voyage. On his way to Palestine, he stopped in Cyprus at a monastery believed to have served as a *metochion* of the patriarchate of Jerusalem. The identity of this monastery—or of any other *metochia* that belonged directly to the Jerusalem patriarchate—is unfortunately unknown before the sixteenth century, and the patriarchate's archive has no relevant records predating the eighteenth century.[454] Upon arrival in Palestine, Leontius passed through Akka (Acre) and Nazareth, where he performed many healings.[455] In Leontius' *Vita*, his secret miracles are compared with the works of Christ, while the termination of a drought through his intercession elicits a parallel with the life of Prophet Elias.[456] In order to avoid Latin authorities, Leontius entered Jerusalem by night and prayed privately at the Anastasis.[457] The absence of any account of public worship is unfortunate for liturgical historians, as any information would certainly provide some insight into Hagiopolite liturgical practices during the period of Byzantinization.

The *Life* states that Leontius' fame spread throughout Syria and Phoenicia, among Isaurians and Cilicians, and even reached Constantinople, where Manuel I Comnenus began to fear for the patriarch's safety and called him back to Byzantine territory. On Leontius' return voyage to Constantinople, Saladin received him in Damascus and offered him a church and a salary to

---

[450] Alexander Kazhdan, 'Nikephoros II Phokas', ODB II, 1478–9.
[451] Charles M. Brand, Alexander Kazhdan, and Anthony Cutler, 'John II Komnenos', ODB I, 1046–7.
[452] Kaplan, 'Leontios', 480–1.   [453] Rose, 'Saint Leontios', 253.
[454] Καὶ ἀπάρας πρὸς τὴν μονήν, τὴν εἰς μικρὰν ἀνάπαυλαν τοῦ πατριαρχοῦντος τῆς Ἰερουσαλὴμ χρηματίζουσαν ... ('And when he left for the monastery, which served as a place for a little rest for the patriarchs of Jerusalem ...'). Tsougarakis, *Life of Leontios*, 112, § 70: 4–6; 198. For the relevant documents, see s.v. 'Κύπρος' in the index of Agamemnon Tselikas, Καταγραφή τοῦ Ἀρχείου τοῦ Πατριαρχείου Ἱεροσολύμων (Δελτίο τοῦ Ἱστορικοῦ καὶ Παλαιογραφικοῦ Ἀρχείου 5, Athens: Μορφωτικό Ἵδρυμα Ἐθνικῆς Τραπέζης, 1992).
[455] Tsougarakis, *Life of Leontios*, 126–32, § 80–83.
[456] Ibid., 132–4, § 84–85.   [457] Ibid., 132, § 84.

make him stay in Syria. Leontius declined the offer, requesting instead letters of safe passage to Constantinople.

From the account of Leontius' visit to Palestine we gain some insight into interecclesial and political relations between Constantinople and the other parties present in the Holy Land. First, the patriarch's mission was not to all Christians of the heterogeneous 'crowd' (ὄχλος ἀμφιμιγής) of the territory of the Jerusalem patriarchate, but to those who needed 'greater attention',[458] and 'especially the pious ones and those who depended on his arrival'.[459] This was presumably the Hagiopolitan Orthodox population, among them Palestinian monks.[460]

Second, tense relations with the Latins prevented Leontius from publicly celebrating the liturgy,[461] an act that the Latin Patriarch Amalric of Nestle (1158–80) previously permitted to Armenian hierarchs.[462] Thus Leontius was forced to venerate the holy sites as a simple pilgrim, and his visit is not even recorded in any Latin sources from the period.[463] Such an account is consistent with tense relations between Constantinople, Rome, and the crusader states. A direct example of the Latins' open opposition to the re-establishment of the Orthodox patriarchate of Antioch is found in a letter from Pope Alexander III to the Latin clergy of Antioch in 1178.[464]

On the other hand, the generous offer of a church in Damascus from Saladin—who is described as 'a believer in Muhammad's hallucinations', yet only 'half-wicked and in many things virtuous and honourable'[465]—reflects the Ayyubid emir's willingness to use the Orthodox as pawns in political relations between the Latins and the Byzantines, as well as a certain sympathy for the Muslim rulers of Palestine from the Byzantine author of Leontnius' life. Whether or not Saladin's confirmation of Orthodox supremacy over all other Christians in his territory—as found in a decree after his capture of Jerusalem—is true or not is unclear.[466]

---

[458] Ἔδει γὰρ χρείας καλούσης μᾶλλον ἐπιγνωσθῆναι αὐτὸν ἐν τοῖς καὶ πλείονος δεομένοις τῆς ἐπισκέψεως. Ibid., 126–8, § 80: 8–9.

[459] ταῦτα τοὺς εὐσεβοῦντας καὶ τῆς αὐτοῦ ἐξηρτημένους ἀφίξεως. Ibid., 132, § 84: 7–8.

[460] See ibid., 202.   [461] Ibid., 138, § 88: 1–6.

[462] Ibid., 205; Michael le Quien, *Oriens Christianus in quatuor patriarchatus digestus*, vol. 3 (Paris: Typographia Regia, 1740), 1250–1.

[463] Tsougarakis, *Life of Leontios*, 205.

[464] Ostrogorsky, *History of the Byzantine State*, 289–90. See *Epistulae pontificorum romanorum ineditae*, ed. by Samuel Löwenfeld (Leipzig: Veit et comp., 1885), n. 287.

[465] τὸ μὲν σέβας ἀσεβὴς καὶ τὰς τοῦ Μωάμεθ πρεσβεύων ὀνειρώξεις ἢ ἐξ ὑπογύου μυθεύματα, ἡμιμόχθηρος δέ τις ὢν καὶ τὰ πολλὰ χρηστευόμενος καὶ τιμῶν. Tsougarakis, *Life of Leontios*, 136, § 87: 12–14.

[466] See ibid., 204; Nikephoros Moschopoulos, *La Terre Sainte: Essai sur l'histoire politique et diplomatique des Lieux Saints de la chrétienté* (Athens: N. Moschopoulos, 1956), 365; Girolamo Golubovich, *Biblioteca bio-bibliografica della Terra Santa e dell'Oriente francescano*, vol. 4 (Florence: Collegio Internazionale di San Bonaventura, 1923), 200.

Athanasius II of Alexandria

The identity of Patriarch Athanasius II of Alexandria (*c*.1275–1315) is a complicated matter, due to the multiplicity of hierarchs with the name Athanasius in thirteenth-century Constantinople. Among them are Patriarch Athanasius of Constantinople (*c*.1235–1315)[467] and Bishop Andronicus of Sardes, who took the name Athanasius when he donned the monastic habit.[468] The historian George Pachymeres (1242–1310?),[469] who was *protekdikos* (the sixth highest office in the hierarchy of archons of Hagia Sophia) and *dikaiophylax* within the imperial offices,[470] knew Athanasius of Alexandria personally and corresponded with him. According to Pachymeres, Athanasius was a monk of Sinai who had fled to a *metochion* of Sinai on Crete.[471] In Constantinopolitan sources Athanasius II comes across as the best known and most respected of the eastern Chalcedonian patriarchs in Constantinopolitan exile.[472]

Athanasius was greatly revered in important circles in Constantinople. He was regarded as a man of culture, open and appreciative of literature, and was a confidant of Emperor Michael VIII.[473] At synods Athanasius normally received a seat to the right of the patriarch of Constantinople, and even presided occasionally when the latter was absent. For example, Athanasius presided at the first synod of Blachernai (8–12 January 1283), representing both Alexandria as its patriarch and Constantinople in the absence of its patriarch, because John XI Beccus (r. 1275–83) had been deposed.[474] Despite Athanasius' chairmanship of the synod, it was the blinded Galaction the Galesiote[475] who led the services of the great blessing of waters for Theophany, held at Saint Sophia three days before the commencement of the synod.[476] According to Pseudo-Codinus, in the absence of the patriarch of Constantinople,

[467] PLP, n. 415; Pachymérès, *Relations historiques*, vol. 3, 122 n. 86, 157–69; Alice-Mary Talbot, 'Athanasios I', ODB I, 218–19.

[468] Pachymérès, *Relations historiques*, vol. 1, 171: 3; vol. 2, 357: 4

[469] Alice-Mary Talbot, 'Pachymérès, George', ODB III, 1550. Pachymérès' primary historical work is the Συγγραγικῶν ἱστοριῶν, which records the events of the reigns of Michael VIII Palaeologus and ends abruptly in the summer of 1307, perhaps due to illness or the death of Pachymérès himself. I rely upon Failler and Laurent's edition and translation (Pachymérès, *Relations historiques*).

[470] For more on these positions, see J. Darrouzès, *Recherches sur les ὀφφίκια de l'Église byzantine* (Archives de l'Orient Chrétien 11, Paris: Institut Français d'Études Byzantines, 1970), 596 and 609; Pachymérès, *Relations historiques*, vol. 1, xix–xx.

[471] Pachymérès, *Relations historiques*, vol. 4, 633: 1–16 (Book XII, 8).

[472] PLP, n. 413; Alice-Mary Talbot, 'Athanasios II', ODB I, 219; Pachymérès, *Relations historiques*, vol. 2, 407: 17; 547.

[473] Failler, 'Le séjour d'Athanase à Constantinople', 55.

[474] 'Περὶ τῶν τελουμένων συνόδων'. Pachymérès, *Relations historiques*, vol. 2, 25: 6f.; vol. 3, 35 (Book VII, 7–8); Vitalien Laurent, AA, *Les regestes des actes du patriarcat de Constantinople*, vol. 1, fasc. 4: *Les regestes de 1208 à 1309* (Paris: Institut Français d'Études Byzantines, 1971), 245–6 (no. 1456); Alice-Mary Talbot, 'John XI Bekkos', ODB II, 1055.

[475] Pachymérès, *Relations historiques*, vol. 2, 617: 20; vol. 3, 25–7; PLP, n. 3473 (Γαλακτίων).

[476] Pachymérès, *Relations historiques*, vol. 3, 31.

one of the eastern patriarchs was to preside over the services of Theophany and over the water blessing, which pointed to the established role that such celebrations had received in the liturgy of Constantinople.[477]

The exiled patriarchs also found themselves involved in the disputes of the imperial capital. In May 1283, during the fallout of the Arsenite schism[478] and anti-unionist activity, the synod requested that Athanasius and Empress Theodora give a profession of faith in order to be commemorated in the diptychs along with the other patriarchs in Constantinople, namely Gregory of Cyprus, patriarch of Jerusalem (d. 1291),[479] and Theodosius IV Villehardouin, patriarch of Antioch (r. 1278–83).[480] It is worth noting that both Athanasius II and Theodosius Princips had been monks on Sinai, which suggests a close connection between Constantinople and Sinai during this phase of the Palaiologan period.[481] Because of his refusal to take sides in ecclesiastical conflicts, Athanasius was eventually exiled to Rhodes, and then to a *metochion* of the patriarchate of Alexandria on Crete.[482] Before his banishment from Constantinople, Athanasius had been dragged into a quarrel over the ownership of the Lavra of the Archangel (ἡ Λαύρας τοῦ Ἀρχιστρατήγου μονή) located in the region of Leosthenion (Λεωσθένιον) or Sosthenion (Σωσθένιον) near the Bosphorus. The Church of Alexandria had this monastery in its possessions already from the sixth century, along with the Monastery of the Great Field (ἡ τοῦ Μεγάλου Ἀγροῦ μονή), founded by the monk Theophanes around 787 and granted to Alexandria by Emperor Michael VIII.[483] Patriarch Athanasius of Constantinople annexed the Monastery

---

[477] ὁ δὲ μετὰ τὴν λειτουργίαν ἁγιασμός, εἰ πατριάρχης εὑρίσκεται οἰκουμενικός, γίνεται παρ' αὐτοῦ, εἰ δὲ μή, παρά τινος τῶν ἑτέρων πατριαρχῶν, ἢ τοῦ Ἀλεξανδρείας ἢ τοῦ Ἀντιοχείας ἢ τοῦ Ἱεροσολύμων, ἐὰν ἐνδημῶν τύχῃ ('The blessing of water after the liturgy is done by the ecumenical patriarch, if he is present, otherwise by one of the other patriarchs, either of Alexandria, or of Antioch, or of Jerusalem, if they are present'). Pseudo-Kodinos, *Traité des offices*, ed. by Jean Verpeaux (Le Monde byzantin 1, Paris: Centre national de la recherche scientifique, 1966), 220 lines 11–17.

[478] Alice-Mary Talbot, 'Arsenites', ODB I, 188. For more information on other figures involved in this conflict, see Alice-Mary Talbot, 'Arsenios Autoreianos', ODB I, 187; Alice-Mary Talbot, 'Joseph I', ODB II, 1073; Michael J. Angold, 'John IV Laskaris', ODB II, 1048–9.

[479] PLP, n. 4589.

[480] Pachymérès, *Relations historiques*, vol. 3, 67–9. For more on Patriarch Theodosius of Antioch, also known as Θεοδόσιος IV, see PLP, n. 7181; Laurent, *Les regestes des actes du patriarcat de Constantinople*, I 4: *Les regestes de 1208 à 1309* (Paris: Institut Français d'Études Byzantines, 1971), n. 1438; Vitalien Laurent and Jean Darrouzès, *Dossier grec de l'union de Lyon (1273–1277)* (Archives de l'Orient Chrétien 16, Paris: Institut Français d'Études Byzantines, 1976), 45; Paul Gautier, 'Le Typikon du Christ Sauveur Pantocrator', REB 32 (1974), 23.

[481] Failler, 'Le séjour d'Athanase à Constantinople', 54.

[482] Pachymérès, *Relations historiques*, vol. 3, 137; Failler, 'Le séjour d'Athanase à Constantinople', 47 and 54.

[483] Pachymérès, *Relations historiques*, vol. 3, 229. For the Lavra of the Archangel Michael, see Janin, *Les églises et les monastères*, 346–50; Janin, *Églises des grands centres byzantins*, 195–9.

of the Great Field, and the patriarchate of Alexandria received the Monastery of Christ Evergetis in exchange.[484]

Despite such ill treatment in Constantinople, Athanasius II still viewed it as the unifying centre of Christendom, whence all evangelization was to flow. This view is most clearly expressed in his letter to the Church of Rus', where he acts as a proponent of Byzantine ecclesiastical policy.[485] Like Leontius, Athanasius had been sent abroad as an ambassador of Constantinople. His voyage to Armenia was intended to arrange a potential marriage between Andronicus II and the Armenian royal family, but pirates at Phocaea interrupted the trip and he was forced to turn back.[486]

A Hagiopolitan Metochion in Constantinople?

The stories of Palestinian monks and hierarchs in the imperial capital raises the question: was there a Hagiopolitan *metochion* ($\mu\epsilon\tau\acute{o}\chi\iota o\nu$)[487] in Constantinople? A permanent church in Constantinople with direct ties to Jerusalem would certainly be the place to look for possible Byzantine liturgical influence on the Holy Land. Numerous examples mentioned above show that monks and hierarchs were given churches for their use in New Rome. As already noted, Theophanes wrote in his ninth-century account of monks fleeing Palestine that 'Emperor Michael and the holy patriarch Nikephoros kindly entertained them. Michael helped them in every way. He gave the men who entered the city a famous monastery, and sent a talent of gold to the monks and laymen still on Cyprus.' This 'famous monastery' is believed to have been the Monastery of Chora, today Kariye Camii.[488] The life of St Anthony the Younger (d. 11 November 865), a native of Palestine, indicates yet another monastery in the vicinity: the *metochion* of All Saints, which was home to several monks from Palestine.[489] However, the Monastery of All Saints was a dependency of monasteries in Bithynia, not Palestine, and the

[484] Pachymérès, *Relations historiques*, vol. 4, 633. The Monastery of the Great Field is known to be the source of two manuscripts: *Paris Gr. 216* (10th cent.), a Praxapostolos; and *Paris Gr. 1538* (12th cent.). See Janin, *Les églises et les monastères*, 198–9.
[485] The whole letter is edited in Failler, 'Le séjour d'Athanase à Constantinople', 59–63.
[486] Pachymérès, *Relations historiques*, vol. 2, 203: 18–205: 6.
[487] 'Dependance eines Klosters', in Trapp, *Lexikon zur byzantinischen Gräzität*, here 1017.
[488] Mary B. Cunningham, *The Life of Michael the Synkellos: Text, Translation and Commentary* (Belfast Byzantine Texts and Translations 1, Belfast: Belfast Byzantine Enterprises, 1991), 62–3; Griffith, 'Holy Land in the Ninth Century', 233. For more on the Monastery of Chora, see Janin, *Les églises et les monastères*, 531–9 ($X\rho\iota\sigma\tauo\hat{\upsilon}$ $\tau\hat{\eta}\varsigma$ $X\acute{\omega}\rho\alpha\varsigma$, $Mo\nu\grave{\eta}$ $\tauo\hat{\upsilon}$); Anthony Cutler and Alice-Mary Talbot, 'Chora Monastery', ODB I, 428–30.
[489] $\check{\epsilon}\sigma\tau\iota\nu$ $\dot{\eta}\mu\hat{\iota}\nu$ $\dot{\epsilon}\nu$ $\tau\hat{\eta}$ $\pi\acute{o}\lambda\epsilon\iota$ $\mu\epsilon\tau\acute{o}\chi\iota o\nu$ $\tau\grave{\eta}\nu$ $\dot{\epsilon}\pi\omega\nu\upsilon\mu\acute{\iota}\alpha\nu$ $\tau\hat{\omega}\nu$ $\dot{A}\gamma\acute{\iota}\omega\nu$ $\Pi\acute{\alpha}\nu\tau\omega\nu$ $\varphi\acute{\epsilon}\rho o\nu$ ('There is in the city a *metochion* for us bearing the name of All Saints'). BHG 142; François Halkin, 'Saint Antoine le Jeune et Pétronas le vainqueur des arabes en 863 (d'après un texte inédit)', AB 62 (1944), 187–225, here 213. For another version of the saint's life, see Athanasios Papadopoulos-Kerameus, 'XII. $B\acute{\iota}o\varsigma$ $\kappa\alpha\grave{\iota}$ $\pi o\lambda\iota\tau\epsilon\acute{\iota}\alpha$ $\tauo\hat{\upsilon}$ $\dot{o}\sigma\acute{\iota}o\upsilon$ $\dot{A}\nu\tau\omega\nu\acute{\iota}o\upsilon$ $\tauo\hat{\upsilon}$ $N\acute{\epsilon}o\upsilon$', $\Sigma\upsilon\lambda\lambda o\gamma\grave{\eta}$ $\pi\alpha\lambda\alpha\iota\sigma\tau\iota\nu\hat{\eta}\varsigma$ $\kappa\alpha\grave{\iota}$

presence of Palestinian monks was too sporadic and coincidental to suggest a whole 'Palestinian quarter', as Jean Gouillard provocatively proposes—and then definitively refutes.[490] Even so, no churches or monasteries remained continuously in the hands of the Jerusalem patriarchate.

All of this makes it difficult to speak of a specific location that served as the continuous seat of the Jerusalem patriarchate in Constantinople or as a point of liturgical contact between Jerusalem and Constantinople. To summarize, then, what has been said above about the exiled eastern patriarchs, their position in Constantinople was purely honorific, although in some cases they played the role of a replacement for the patriarch of Constantinople, both in his administrative and in his liturgical functions. Their identities and backgrounds were diverse, but they were usually foreigners, with occasional connections to Sinai, although they were not themselves necessarily from Palestine or from the East. The residence in Constantinople of these eastern patriarchs was unstable and depended on monasteries they received from the emperor. They also relied heavily on their *metochia* in other parts of the empire for their survival and upkeep. The patriarchs were caught in power struggles between Constantinople and Latins and Arabs, or in tensions between the emperor and the patriarch of Constantinople. As hierarchs with little if any accountability to their own episcopal sees between the eleventh and fourteenth centuries, the eastern patriarchs were free to serve as spokesmen for Byzantine ecclesiastical and political foreign policy and to travel on missions assigned to them by the Byzantine emperor.

CONCLUSIONS

Racing through the contextual history of Hagiopolite liturgy over the course of more than six centuries and considering this mass of information alongside the Hagiopolite liturgical manuscripts copied after the eighth century, I arrive at the following conclusions:

1. The occupation of Jerusalem and Palestine by non-Christian rulers and the destruction of holy sites weakened the stability of the Jerusalem patriarchate and negatively affected authentic, Hagiopolite liturgical practice. This crisis caused a decline in the Christian population, led to neglect of the destroyed holy sites, and necessitated the reorganization of

---

συριακῆς ἁγιολογίας 1 (ΠΠC 57 [19.3], St Petersburg: Православное Палестинское Общество, 1907), 186–216.

[490] Jean Gouillard, 'Un "quartier" d'émigrés palestiniens à Constantinople au IXᵉ siècle?' *Revue des Études Sud-Est Européennes* 7 (1969), 73–6; Griffith, 'Holy Land in the Ninth Century', 233.

the hierarchy around the cathedral of Jerusalem, as well as that of its major outlying monasteries and some of the remaining holy sites. The relocation of episcopal sees from centres of local Christian population to holy sites of pilgrimage exposed Hagiopolite liturgy to even greater contact with foreign liturgical practices.

2. Despite the diffusion of Arabic as the official language of the Muslim state, Greek thrived in the multilingual Palestinian monasteries and remained the common official liturgical language of the Jerusalem patriarchate without interruption. Nevertheless, Georgian, Syriac, and Arabic were also used as liturgical languages among Chalcedonians, and Georgian scribes copied and transmitted the contents of many Greek Hagiopolite liturgical manuscripts, which are crucial witnesses of Byzantinization today.

3. Despite both the Constantinopolitan and the Jerusalem patriarchates' concern to maintain Orthodoxy, there is no evidence of a concerted effort or systematic programme on the part of the Byzantine empire to impose the Byzantine rite in the Jerusalem patriarchate.

4. The chronological limits used in liturgical historiography to explain changes in Hagiopolitan worship are not reflected in the corresponding liturgical sources themselves. Liturgical sources show great variety and suggest that liturgical Byzantinization was a gradual phenomenon, with a transitional phase that was carried out locally within the patriarchate of Jerusalem.

This chapter has addressed questions of when, how, and why liturgical Byzantinization occurred by mapping out a timeline of significant events in Jerusalem and Constantinople. To explain a liturgical change, one must know its context; but ultimately one has to search for the answer within the liturgical sources themselves. This will be my goal in the next three chapters.

Part II

Byzantinization of the Liturgy of St James, the Calendar, and the Lectionary

3

The Liturgy of St James

The Liturgy of St James (JAS) was the local eucharistic liturgy of the Jerusalem patriarchate during the late antique, Byzantine, and early Islamic periods, until it fell into disuse as a result of Byzantinization. The purpose of this chapter on JAS is twofold. On the one hand it aims to present all the known Hagiopolitan manuscripts that contain JAS in order to help readers to understand this liturgy's continued presence and disappearance within the Jerusalem patriarchate. On the other hand it aims to examine the structure of that liturgy's initial part, the Liturgy of the Word (or 'liturgy of the catechumens'), during which hymns were sung and scriptural lections were read, in order to help readers to understand the liturgical context of the calendar and lectionary, which will be examined in the following chapters.

EUCHARISTIC LITURGIES

It goes without saying that the celebration of the Eucharist was central to the church, but it is perhaps not as obvious that particular eucharistic liturgies were inherent—and strictly connected—to specific local churches. For example, the anaphora of CHR had its origins in Antioch,[1] while the local eucharistic liturgy of Alexandria was once the Liturgy of St Mark.[2] Similarly, the local eucharistic liturgy of the patriarchate of Jerusalem was JAS. The JAS is noteworthy for its lengthy and detailed intercessions, made by repeating the imperative 'remember' (μνήσθητι; ძოგჷ§ხჲ6ჲნ, moixsenen).[3] The anaphoras of BAS, CHR, and JAS are all classified as Antiochene or West Syrian according

---

[1] Hänggi and Pahl, *Prex eucharistica*, 223–9; Robert F. Taft, SJ, 'St John Chrysostom and the Byzantine Anaphora That Bears His Name', in *Essays on Early Eastern Eucharistic Prayers*, 195–226 (and the bibliography there).

[2] Hänggi and Pahl, *Prex Eucharistica*, 101–23; Cuming, *Liturgy of St Mark*. On new manuscript sources for this liturgy, see Michael Zheltov, 'The Byzantine Manuscripts of the Liturgy of Mark in the Sinai New Finds', *ΣΥΝΑΞΙΣ ΚΑΘΟΛΙΚΗ*, 2: 801–8.

[3] Mercier, *Liturgie de Saint Jacques*, 206–20; *Liturgia ibero-graeca*, 86–102.

to their structure, as distinct from East Syrian and Alexandrian anaphoras, which have a different structure.[4] By comparison with anaphoras in BAS,[5] CHR,[6] and other liturgies, the anaphora in JAS is marked by (1) connection to the local geography of Jerusalem through the mention of holy sites and (2) concern for doctrinal precision, especially for Trinitarian theology. It also shows signs of careful textual elaboration, for example two epicleses, and has a penitential character.[7] In spite of the frequent accusations of historicism in Hagiopolite liturgy, JAS 'reflects a remarkable awareness of the entire sweep of salvation history and a strong sense of the forward movement of salvation history toward eschatological fulfilment'.[8]

Over the course of two millennia many have sought to understand the origin of these liturgies and the diversity of their forms. Study of eucharistic liturgies led to what can be called the 'progressive development theory', according to which all eucharistic liturgies allegedly stemmed from one original liturgy and were subsequently edited and revised. According to this theory, the original liturgy was JAS. It was then revised and abbreviated to become BAS, which was in turn revised and became CHR. While accepted in the past,[9] this theory has since been rejected.[10] Today it is believed that the evolution goes in the opposite direction—from shorter to longer prayers. Originally smaller prayers were added together through connecting links between the various 'discrete prayer units', moving from diversity to uniformity, at least until the medieval period.[11]

It is also worth noting that there were local redactions of certain liturgies. For example, differences existed between the text of JAS in various languages, so that one can speak of a Syrian JAS[12] as distinct from a Greek JAS or Georgian JAS, each with its own structure, depending on its regional

[4] See Bradshaw and Johnson, *Eucharistic Liturgies*, 77.
[5] Hänggi and Pahl, *Prex eucharistica*, 230–43.
[6] Ibid., 224–5; Brightman, *Eastern Liturgies*, 321–37.
[7] Hänggi and Pahl, *Prex eucharistica*, 244–61; Witvliet, 'The Anaphora of St James', here 160–2.
[8] Ibid., 167. For a summary of the criticism of historicism in Jerusalem's liturgy, see Taft, *Beyond East and West*, 44–5.
[9] 'James the Apostle is the original author of the divine liturgy...To save time St Basil the Great shortened the liturgy of St James; and St Chrysostom shortened that of St Basil.' Hieromonk Agapios and Nikodemos the Hagiorite, *The Rudder (Pedalion)*, ed. by Denver Cummings (Chicago, IL: Orthodox Christian Educational Society, 1957), xxvii; *Литургія св. Іакова* (Ladomirova), 105–6.
[10] Swainson, *Greek Liturgies*, xxx–xxxi; Brightman, *Eastern Liturgies*, liv; Dmitri E. Conomos, *Byzantine Trisagia and Cheroubika of the Fourteenth and Fifteenth Centuries: A Study of Late Byzantine Liturgical Chant* (Thessaloniki: Patriarchal Institute for Patristic Studies, 1974), 13–18.
[11] Paul F. Bradshaw, 'The Evolution of Early Anaphoras', in *Essays on Early Eastern Eucharistic Prayers*, 1–17, esp. 3 and 16; Robert F. Taft, SJ, 'How Liturgies Grow: The Evolution of the Byzantine Divine Liturgy', in idem, *Beyond East and West*, 203–5.
[12] Hänggi and Pahl, *Prex eucharistica*, 269–75.

provenance.[13] PRES also had various local redactions, including a version from Jerusalem—which is referred to as the Hagiopolitan presanctified liturgy (HagPRES)—and a version from Rome.[14] The exchange and cross-fertilization between various regions, including those of Jerusalem and Constantinople, add to the complexity of the question and explain the fluidity of eucharistic liturgical rites. Nevertheless, in Jerusalem, JAS was usually referred to as simply the 'Divine Liturgy', without any specific reference to its author. This can be seen in the GL, where the eucharistic liturgy is called 'the canon of the sacrifice of the Hours' (კანონი ჟამის წირვისაჲ, *kanoni žamis cirvisay*), 'the sacrifice of the Hours' (ჟამის წირვაჲ, *žamis cirvay*), or 'the noonday [office]' (სამხრად, *samxrad*), which is equivalent to the office of Typika.[15]

The Origins and History of the Liturgy of St James

Despite the fact that JAS has always been regarded as an ancient prayer, the current text is considered by John Fenwick to be 'too long, too carefully structured, too theologically and biblically precise' to be a 'primitive composition'.[16] Fenwick believes the anaphora of JAS is a 'conflation of that of Ur-Basil with a Cyrilline/Eusebian form' from the fifth mystagogical catechesis.[17] This would suggest that the eucharistic liturgy witnessed by Egeria and celebrated by St Cyril of Jerusalem in the fourth century was a kind of ancestor to our earliest known manuscript sources of the anaphora of JAS from the eighth and ninth centuries. Nevertheless, the insufficient understanding of the relationship between the various manuscripts and languages of JAS makes it impossible to draw any definitive conclusions about the origins of JAS.[18] Thus, I will limit my speculation on this question to what can be ascertained on the basis of the historical sources.

The first mention of a liturgy attributed to St James is believed to come in Canon 32 of the Council of Trullo (692),[19] although fragments of JAS are cited

[13] See Witvliet, 'The Anaphora of St James', 155; Fenwick, *Anaphoras of St Basil and St James*, 48.

[14] Michael Tarchnišvili, 'Die *Missa praesanctificatorum* und ihre Feier am Karfreitag nach georgischen Quellen', *Archiv für Liturgiewissenschaft* 2 (1952), 75–80; Alexopoulos, *Presanctified Liturgy*, 95–127.

[15] 'Opfergottesdienst, Offizium des Meßopfers, Meßopfer'; 'der Süden, der Mittag, die Mittagzeit und das Mittagessen'. Leeb, *Die Gesänge*, 37–8. For the last term, which is related to the office of Typika, see Mateos, *Parole*, 68–71; Evgenii [full name, plse?] Diakovskii, Послѣдованіе часовъ и изобразительныхъ. Историческое изслѣдованіе (Kiev: Типографія Мейдлера, 1913), 269–300.

[16] Fenwick, *Anaphoras of St Basil and St James*, 33.

[17] Ibid., 303. See *Mystagogical Catecheses*, 146–74; Hänggi and Pahl, *Prex eucharistica*, 206–9; Kent J. Burreson, 'The Anaphora of the Mystagogical Catecheses of Cyril of Jerusalem', in *Essays on Early Eastern Eucharistic Prayers*, 131–51, here 150–1.

[18] Witvliet, 'The Anaphora of St James', 156; Bradshaw and Johnson, *Eucharistic Liturgies*, 76.

[19] For the literature on this question, see Fenwick, *Anaphoras of St Basil and St James*, 32.

in the life of St Anastasius the Persian (d. 628).[20] It is also believed that St Jerome (d. 420) was familiar with a version of JAS; this view is based on his use of the phrase 'the only sinless one' (ὁ μόνος ἀναμάρτητος),[21] which is found in JAS and in the second *Catechesis* of St Cyril of Jerusalem.[22] An account by St Anastasius of Sinai (d. after 700) describing how Communion was administered with a spoon to a stylite near Damascus includes phrases that suggest that the liturgy celebrated was JAS.[23] In the ninth century, in the letter of the Holy Roman Emperor Charles the Bald (823–77) to the clergy of Ravenna, JAS is *the* quintessence of the Jerusalem rite, while Constantinople is connected to BAS.[24]

Two centuries later JAS is already noted to be in decline. In the response to Theodore of St Sabas Lavra near Jerusalem, Euthymius, abbot of Iveron monastery of Athos, the Holy Mountain (ⴇⴍⴀⴌⴈⴇⴍⴚⴑⴈ, *mt'acmideli*),[25] writes that all Greeks once used JAS but, because of its length, it fell into disuse and now people prefer CHR and BAS.[26] The discourse over the length of JAS that Euthymius cites was attributed to Proclus of Constantinople, formerly identified as the fifth-century bishop of the imperial capital,[27] but now known as Pseudo-Proclus, an author of the sixteenth century who was familiar with the works of Mark of Ephesus (1394–1445).[28] Pseudo-Proclus' text asserted that St James, the brother of the Lord and first bishop of Jerusalem, established the liturgy, which was then adopted by St Basil the Great. However,

---

[20] See Heinzgerd Brakmann, 'Ein jerusalemer Anaphora-Zitat in den *Acta Anastasii Persae* (BHG 84)', AB 113 (1995), 115–16.

[21] St Jerome, *Dialogus adversus pelagianos* II.23, PL 23:561.

[22] *Catechesis* II, 10, PG 33:396; McCauley and Stephenson, *Works of Saint Cyril of Jerusalem*, vol. 1, 101–2.

[23] CPG 7758 (B. Narrationes 9 (9): Ἡ Ἀμαθοῦς πόλις ἐστὶ καὶ αὐτὴ μία τῆς Κυπρίων νήσου); *Narrationes utiles animae* 43, ed. by F. Nau, 'Le texte grec des récits utiles à l'âme d'Anastase (le Sinaïte)', in OC 3 (1903), here 62; Robert F. Taft, 'Byzantine Communion Spoons: A Review of the Evidence', DOP 50 (1996), 209–38, here 220–1.

[24] *Celebrata sunt etiam coram nobis Missarum officia more Hierosolymitano auctore Iacobo Apostolo, et more Constantinopolitano auctore Basilio* ('In our presence were also celebrated the liturgies in the manner of Jerusalem, by James the Apostle, and in the manner of Constantinople, by Basil'), quoted in the preface of *De liturgia gallicana*, PL 72:103; André Jacob, 'Une lettre de Charles le Chauve au clergé de Ravenne?' RHE 67 (1972), 409–22; Parenti, 'La "vittoria"', 28–9.

[25] For the *Vita* of St Euthymius, see Paul Peeters, 'Histoires monastiques géorgiennes', AB 36/7 (1922) [1917–19], 8–68. For St Euthymios' work on Mount Athos, see Grégoire Peradse, 'L'activité littéraire des moines géorgiens au monastère d'Iviron, au Mont Athos', RHE 23 (1927), 530–9.

[26] For the German translation, see Gregor Peradse, 'Ein Dokument aus der mittelalterlichen Liturgiegeschichte Georgiens', *Kyrios: Vierteljahresschrift für Kirchen- und Geistesgeschichte Osteuropas* 1 (1936), 74–9, here 77.

[27] Λόγος περὶ παραδόσεως τῆς θείας λειτουργίας, PG 65:849–52; CPG 5893.

[28] F. J. Leroy, 'Proclus, "de traditione divinae missae": Un faux de C. Palaeocappa', OCP 28 (1962), 288–99. For more on Proclus, bishop of Constantinople (d. 446/7), see Barry Baldwin, 'Proklos', ODB III, 1729.

Ὁ δὲ μέγας Βασίλειος μετὰ ταῦτα τὸ ῥάθυμον καὶ κατωφερὲς τῶν ἀνθρώπων θεωρῶν, καὶ διὰ τοῦτο τὸ τῆς λειτουργίας μῆκος ὀκνούντων, ταύτην οὐ περιττὴν καὶ μακρὰν εἶναι νομίζων, ἀλλὰ τὸ τῶν συνευχομένων τε καὶ ἀκροωμένων ῥάθυμον διὰ πολὺ τοῦ χρόνου παρανάλωμα ἐκκόπτων, ἐπιτομώτερον παρέδωκε λέγεσθαι.[29]	After these things, Basil the Great saw the people's indolence and moral decline on account of the languorous length of the liturgy, although he did not think it to be useless and long. But while praying it and hearing apathy because of the length of time it took, he shortened it and handed it down to be said in abbreviated form.

As already noted, this view of the origins of eucharistic liturgies has since been rejected in favour of a more nuanced one.[30]

By the twelfth century, Hagiopolite liturgical sources rarely mention JAS. The Typikon of the Anastasis still prescribes JAS on Palm Sunday, Holy Thursday, Holy Saturday, and Pascha,[31] but the near-contemporary liturgical Typikon *Sinai Gr. 1096* (12th cent.) does not mention JAS at all. The chapter of the Typikon on the Divine Liturgy in *Sinai Gr. 1096* describes the way BAS, CHR, and PRES were officiated at the Lavra of St Sabas—a description that agrees with the practice of the Byzantine rite today. The only possible divergence from current Byzantine rite usage in *Sinai Gr. 1096* is the Typikon's prescription for the celebration of BAS during the 'fasts of the feasts of the Lord' (καὶ ἐν ταῖς νηστείαις τῶν δεσποτικῶν ἑορτῶν).[32] Whether this implies more than just the celebration of BAS during Great Lent and on the eves of Christmas, Theophany, and Pascha, as is the current practice, is unclear. Since the manuscript contains many more fasting days ('of Alleluia') than the current Byzantine practice, it is possible—although unlikely—that in this source the celebration of BAS was prescribed more frequently.[33]

A similar liturgical Typikon, *Sinai Gr. 1097* (1214), does mention that 'the liturgy of the Apostle' (ἡ λειτουργία δὲ τοῦ ἀποστόλου) was celebrated during a period of fasting. In the liturgical calendar of this Typikon, the commemoration on 30 April is for an earthquake that occurred on 30 April 1201 and indicates that this was a strict day of fasting on Sinai.[34] The relevant text reads as follows:

[29] *Λόγος περὶ παραδόσεως τῆς θείας λειτουργίας*, PG 65:849.

[30] See nn. 9, 10, and 11 in this chapter ('Eucharistic Liturgies').

[31] Papadopoulos-Kerameus, *Anastasis Typikon*, 23–8, 105–8, 186–9, and 200–3.

[32] See the Typikon's section *Περὶ τῶν ἁγίων λειτουργιῶν*. *Sinai Gr. 1096* (12th cent.), fol. 12; Dmitrievskii, *Описание* III, 25.

[33] See Hieronymus Engberding, 'Die Angleichung der byzantinischen Chrysostomusliturgie an die Basiliusliturgie', *Ostkirchliche Studien* 13 (1964), 105–22.

[34] Alexei A. Dmitrievskii, 'Землетрясеніе на Синаѣ и его послѣдствія для Синайской обители', *Церковныя вѣдомости* 3: 25 (1890), 836–41, here 838.

Καὶ ὀφείλομεν κατὰ τὴν λ' τοῦ Ἀπριλίου μηνὸς νηστείαν ποιεῖν, ἡ λειτουργία δὲ τοῦ ἀποστόλου τελεῖται εἰς τὸν καιρὸν αὐτῆς καὶ λαμβάνουσιν οἱ ἀδελφοὶ τὰ ἀντίδωρα αὐτῶν καὶ ἀπέρχονται εἰς τὰ κελλία αὐτῶν, τηροῦντες αὐτὰ μέχρις ἑσπέρας, ἑσπέρας δὲ μεταλαμβάνουσιν αὐτὸ καὶ ἐσθίουσι ξηροφαγίαν.[35]	And we are to keep a fast from the thirtieth of the month of April, but the liturgy of the apostle is celebrated at its time, and the brothers take their Antidoron and go into their cells, keeping it until evening. In the evening they partake of it and eat dry food.[36]

Although it would be tempting to see this as the conservative celebration of JAS on a solemn fasting day, the context suggests instead a reference to the service (ἀκολουθία) of St James, son of Zebedee and brother of St John the Theologian, whose commemoration falls on 30 April in the Byzantine liturgical calendar.[37]

Once the Orthodox patriarchate of Jerusalem abandoned JAS completely, it came to be considered the liturgy par excellence of the Syriac-praying non-Chalcedonian churches.[38] This presumably helped to seal its fate as a liturgy of questionable orthodoxy among Chalcedonian Christians after the reconquest of Antioch, once the schism between Chalcedonians and Miaphysites was thoroughly entrenched.

The Byzantinization of the Liturgy of St James

Those who have written on JAS often mention in passing that the formularies recorded in the extant manuscripts are highly Byzantinized. However, they rarely explain what this means.[39] Placide de Meester's entry in the *Dictionnaire d'archéologie chrétienne et de liturgie* on the eucharistic liturgies of the patriarchates of Alexandria, Antioch, and Jerusalem is perhaps one of the rare cases where any scholar treats the concrete details of this liturgical Byzantinization.[40] He notes eight points at which Byzantine influence is felt in Hagiopolite liturgy through the introduction or insertion of 'Byzantine importations'. These points are:

1. the prothesis, specifically the verse 'Like a lamb led to the slaughter' (Ὡς πρόβατον ἐπὶ σφαγὴν ἤχθη, Isaiah 53:7) during the cutting of the prosphora, and in general the rite of prothesis as a whole, especially the prayer 'God, our God, who sent forth the heavenly bread' (Ὁ Θεὸς, ὁ Θεὸς ἡμῶν, ὁ τὸν οὐράνιον ἄρτον);[41]

---

[35] *Sinai Gr. 1097* (1214), fol. 122–3; Dmitrievskii, *Описаніе* III, 415.
[36] See Ševčenko, 'Typikon', 282.
[37] Ševčenko mistakenly identifies this as the feast of St James, the brother of the Lord (ibid., n. 51). For more on the earthquake, see Sauget, *Synaxaires Melkites*, 372–7.
[38] Edmund Bishop, 'Liturgical Comments and Memoranda', JTS 11 (1910), 67–73, here 70.
[39] For more on this question, see Introduction, 'Byzantinization'.
[40] Placide De Meester, OSB, 'Grecques (Liturgies)', DACL 6.2:1591–662, especially 1605–10.
[41] Parenti and Velkovska, *Барберини гр. 336*, 267 (§ 1).

2. the prayers of enarxis, that is, the prayer for the initial entrance into the church and for the *trisagion*;

3. the prayers before the Great Entrance, that is, the prayer before the Gospel, 'Make the pure light of your divine knowledge shine in our hearts' (Ἔλλαμψον ἐν ταῖς καρδίαις), the prayer before the Great Entrance, 'No one who is bound to carnal desires' (Οὐδεὶς ἄξιος),[42] and the proskomide prayer of BAS, 'O Lord, our God, who created us and led us to this life' (Κύριε, ὁ Θεὸς ἡμῶν, ὁ κτίσας ἡμᾶς καὶ ἀγαγών εἰς τὴν ζωὴν ταύτην)—which de Meester states are borrowed from the Byzantine rite;[43]

4. the hymnography, specifically 'Only-begotten Son' (Ὁ μονογενὴς Υἱός),[44] the *cheroubikon* (Οἱ τὰ Χερουβίμ),[45] and the troparion after Communion 'May our mouths be filled' (Πλήρωσον τὸ στόμα μου, variant of Πληροθήτω), which come from the Byzantine rite;[46]

5. the kiss of peace, that is, the transfer of the kiss of peace from after the Creed to immediately before the Creed;

6. the anaphora, particularly through the insertion of several phrases into it: 'The grace of our Lord Jesus Christ' (Ἡ χάρις τοῦ Κυρίου ἡμῶν) before the anaphora, 'And may the mercies' (Καὶ ἔσται τὰ ἐλέη) at its conclusion, and 'And make us worthy' (Καὶ καταξίωσον ἡμᾶς) before the Lord's Prayer;

7. the diptychs, that is, the singing of 'Rejoice, full of grace' (Χαῖρε κεχαριτωμένη) at the commemoration of the Theotokos at the diptychs and the commemoration of the first hierarch with the words 'First of all, remember, Lord' (Ἐν πρώτοις μνήσθητι Κύριε); and

8. the litanies, that is, the diaconal litanies and the various exclamations from the Byzantine rite that were inserted at various points, for example the great litany and the litany after Communion (Ὀρθοὶ μεταλαβόντες).[47]

While such a clear scheme of Byzantine influence on JAS is extremely attractive, it is in many cases overly simplistic for a study of the historical progression of liturgical Byzantinization. De Meester's eight points may have been based on a contemporary celebration of JAS with which he was familiar, rather than on Hagiopolite liturgical manuscripts copied before the thirteenth century. Unfortunately he does not provide a source for the text upon which he based his conclusions. Let us analyse some of his observations more closely.

---

[42] Ibid., 272 (§ 12).   [43] Ibid., 272–3 (§ 13); Taft, *Great Entrance*, 364–9.
[44] Follieri, *Initia hymnorum*, vol. 3, 111. For more on the *introit* and the eisodikon, see 'Antiphons' in this chapter.
[45] Follieri, *Initia hymnorum*, vol. 3, 64. For more on the hymn of the holy gifts, see section 'The Hymn of the Holy Gifts' in this chapter.
[46] Ibid., 327. For more on the rites of Communion and on the dismissal, see 'The Hymn for Communion' and 'Hymns and Prayers for the Dismissal' in this chapter.
[47] De Meester, 'Grecques (Liturgies)' (see n. 40 here), 1606.

First, the prothesis rite itself develops quite late throughout the Byzantine rite.[48] Nevertheless, de Meester is correct in asserting that a prothesis rite at the beginning of JAS is foreign to this liturgy. The prayer 'God, our God, who sent for the heavenly bread' (Ὁ Θεὸς, ὁ Θεὸς ἡμῶν, ὁ τὸν οὐράνιον ἄρτον) appears for the first time in *Barberini Gr. 336* (8th cent.) as the prayer the priest says while placing the bread on the paten or *diskos* (δίσκος) during the preparatory rites in the skeuophylakion, before the beginning of BAS.[49] The same prayer is found in the near-contemporary earliest manuscripts of JAS, but is located at the transfer of the gifts before the anaphora, and the manuscript evidence confirms that this prayer is always recited as part of the transfer of the gifts in JAS.[50] Taft dismisses theories according to which the prayer's placement at the transfer of the gifts rather than at the prothesis indicated that a prothesis rite was part of the transfer of the gifts in JAS. While he suggests that the prayer most likely passed from BAS to JAS, he is cautious about making any definitive claims.[51] Were the prayer of the prothesis to be found at the beginning of JAS, as it is found in BAS, it would be considered a clear sign of Byzantine influence.

The various prayers at the beginning of JAS prove equally complicated. Hagiopolitan JAS does not have the same structure of the enarxis as the Constantinopolitan BAS or CHR, and most manuscripts of JAS do not reveal a clear structure as to what ensued between the *introit* at the beginning of the Divine Liturgy and the *trisagion*. However, André Jacob and Stefano Parenti have shown that, for example, the prayer before the Gospel, 'Make the pure light of your Divine knowledge shine in our hearts' (Ἔλλαμψον ἐν ταῖς καρδίαις ἡμῶν), actually comes from JAS and only later enters the Byzantine formularies of CHR and BAS.[52] Taft has shown that the prayer 'No one who is bound to carnal desires' (Οὐδεὶς ἄξιος) has its origins in BAS, while Verhelst

---

[48] For the history and development of the prothesis rite, see Pott, *Byzantine Liturgical Reform*, 197–228; Steven Hawkes-Teeples, 'The Prothesis of the Byzantine Divine Liturgy: What Has Been Done and What Remains', in *Rites and Rituals of the Christian East: Proceedings of the Fourth International Congress of the Society of Oriental Liturgy, Lebanon, 10–15 July, 2012*, ed. by Bert Groen, Daniel Galadza, Nina Glibetic, and Gabriel Radle (Eastern Christian Studies 22, Leuven: Peeters, 2014), 317–28.

[49] Parenti and Velkovska, *Барберини гр. 336*, 267 (§ 1).

[50] Mercier, *Liturgie de Saint Jacques*, 180; Kazamias, Θεία Λειτουργία τοῦ Ἁγίου Ἰακώβου, 170.

[51] Taft, *Great Entrance*, 260–2.

[52] The prayer before the Gospel in the Georgian JAS is different: ᲛᲔᲜ ᲒᲛᲐᲠᲗᲝᲑᲗ, ᲣᲤᲐᲚᲝ, ᲠᲝᲛᲔᲚᲛᲐᲜ ᲒᲐᲛᲝᲐᲑᲠᲬᲧᲘᲜᲔᲕ ᲘᲜᲒᲔᲚᲘᲡᲐᲒᲐᲜ ᲜᲐᲗᲔᲚᲘ ('We thank you, O Lord, who made light shine out of darkness'). See *Liturgia ibero-graeca*, 50–2. For the Greek prayer, see André Jacob, 'L'evoluzione dei libri liturgici bizantini in Calabria e in Sicilia dall'VIII al XVI secolo, con particolare riguardo ai riti eucaristici', in *Calabria bizantina: Vita religiosa e strutture amminis-trative* (Atti del primo e secondo incontro di Studi Bizantini, Reggio Calabria: Parallelo 38, 1974), 47–69, here 64–5. Parenti notes that Jacob's conclusions must be read together with those of S. Lucà, 'I Normanni e la "rinascita" del sec. XII', *Archivio Storico per la Calabria e la Lucania* 60 (1993), here 62. See Stefano Parenti, 'La frazione in tre parti del pane eucaristico nella liturgia Italo-Bizantina', in idem, *A oriente e occidente di Costantinopoli*, 175–95, here 184.

believes that it is of Hagiopolitan origin. On this question I follow Taft.[53] Similarly, the prayer before elevation and Fraction in JAS (Ἀκατάληπτε Θεὲ λόγε; გამოუთქუმელ ღმერთო, საჩუყვან, *gamout'k'umelo ġmerto, sit-quao*), originally found in the Hagiopolitan JAS and in the Alexandrian Liturgy of St Mark,[54] makes its way from those anaphoras into other formularies, such as CHR and BAS.[55] These details point to the influence of JAS upon BAS and upon CHR, which is particularly evident in southern Italian formularies,[56] and at the same time upon the direct influence of BAS on JAS by the ninth century, as witnessed by the presence of several prayers explicitly attributed to St Basil the Great within the formulary of JAS.[57]

With regard to hymnography, some fixed elements in the current Byzantine rite, such as 'Only-begotten Son' (Ὁ μονογενής) and the *cheroubikon* (Οἱ τὰ Χερουβίμ), were found in the old Jerusalem rite, but as variable elements within the lectionary. For example, the GL prescribes 'Only-begotten Son' as the *introit* (*oxitay*) of JAS for Pascha, while the *cheroubikon* is the hymn of the holy gifts for all Sundays of Lent.[58] Otherwise the *introit* and the hymn of the holy gifts varied according to the day and commemoration in the GL. In manuscripts of JAS, however, 'Only-begotten Son' and the *cheroubikon* become fixed in all liturgies as the *introit* and the hymn of the holy gifts respectively.[59] Even in Hagiopolite lectionaries such as *St Petersburg RNB Gr. 44* (9th cent.), 'Only-begotten Son' eventually becomes the *introit* for every Sunday.[60] Although the introduction of 'Only-begotten Son' into the Divine Liturgy in Constantinople is attributed to Emperor Justinian I in AD 535/6, this introduction does not imply that the emperor was also the author of the text.[61]

---

[53] See Taft, *Great Entrance*, 130–4; Verhelst, *Traditions judéo-chrétiennes*, 26–7.

[54] Mercier, *Liturgie de Saint Jacques*, 226–8; *Liturgia ibero-graeca*, 110.

[55] See Stefano Parenti, 'La preghiera di elevazione "Verbo incomprensibile" della liturgia di S. Giacomo ed il suo impiego nell'eucologio Italo-Bizantino', in idem, *A oriente e occidente di Costantinopoli*, 115–28.

[56] See Verhelst, 'Liturgie melkite de saint Jacques', 240–1; Stefano Parenti, 'La frazione in tre parti del pane eucaristico nella liturgia Italo-Bizantina', in idem, *A oriente e occidente di Costantinopoli*, 175–95, here 183; Parenti, 'Preghiera della cattedra'; Radle, 'Liturgical Ties', 618–21.

[57] Mercier, *Liturgie de Saint Jacques*, 178 and 192; *Liturgia ibero-graeca*, 58 and 68; Verhelst, 'Liturgie melkite de saint Jacques', 239 n. 26; Stéphane Verhelst, 'Une prière de Saint-Jacques et deux prières de Saint-Basile: (Ὁ ἐπισκεψάμενος ἡμᾶς; Ὁ κτίσας ἡμᾶς; Οὐδεὶς ἄξιος)', in *Θυσία αἰνέσεως: Mélanges liturgiques offerts à la mémoire de l'Archevêque Georges Wagner (1930–1993)*, ed. by Job Getcha and André Lossky (Paris: Presses S. Serge, Institut de théologie orthodoxe, 2005), 411–29.

[58] GL § 328, 363, 401, 437, 476, 526.

[59] See, for example, *Vatican Gr. 1970* (13th cent.), fol. 64r.

[60] See fol. 19r, 24v, 37r, 41v, 48r, 52r, 56v, 60r; Helmut Leeb, *Die Gesänge im Gemeindegottesdienst von Jerusalem (vom 5. bis 8. Jahrhundert)* (Wiener Beiträge zur Theologie 28, Vienna: Herder, 1970), 49.

[61] *Theophanis Chronographia*, 216; Mango and Scott, *Chronicle of Theophanes*, 314. For the authorship of the hymn, see Venance Grumel, 'L'auteur et la date de composition du tropaire *Ho monogenes*', *Echos d'Orient* 22 (1923), 398–418, esp. 417–18; Robert F. Taft, 'Monogenes, Ho', *ODB* II, 1397.

Since the hymn summarizes the Christological teachings of the early church councils, many non-Chalcedonian churches use the same hymn to this day. Some phrases in the text—particularly the mention that 'one of the holy Trinity' (εἷς ὢν τῆς ἁγίας Τριάδος) suffered crucifixion, death, and rose from the dead—recall the Theopaschite *trisagion*. This, as well as the hymn's adoption by non-Chalcedonian churches, suggests to Sebastià Janeras that 'Only-begotten Son' was strongly promoted—but not necessarily written—by Justinian as an attempt at compromise in the wake of the controversies after Chalcedon.[62] Its fixed place within the Divine Liturgy of Constantinople can only be confirmed from the ninth century on.[63]

The history of the *cheroubikon* is more complicated than that of the hymn 'Only-begotten Son'. According to the twelfth-century historian George Cedrenus, the hymn was, like the hymn 'Only-begotten Son', also introduced into Constantinople's liturgy in the sixth century, but by Emperor Justin II (r. 565–78), who ordered it to be sung in 573/4.[64] Because the *cheroubikon* is the principal hymn of the Great Entrance in the Byzantine rite, Robert Taft has dedicated much attention to that hymn's origins. The earliest Constantinopolitan liturgical manuscript to mention the *cheroubikon* is the ninth-century Chludov Psalter, *Moscow GIM Gr. 129D* (9th cent.), where this hymn is listed among various others in the manuscript's appendix.[65] It is worth noting that contemporaneous Hagiopolitan psalters, most of them preserved today either in St Petersburg or on Mount Sinai, do not include the *cheroubikon* in their appendices, although they almost always contained prayers associated with the Divine Liturgy, such as prayers for preparation before receiving Communion, the Creed, and the Lord's Prayer.[66] Nevertheless, the *cheroubikon* is commonly found in many of the earliest Hagiopolite liturgical sources and during one of the most liturgically conservative periods of the year—on Sundays of Great Lent—just like 'Only-begotten Son'. Taft dismisses its use on Sundays of Lent in Jerusalem as an argument for its Hagiopolitan origin and points instead to the evolution of the place of the *cheroubikon* within the rites surrounding the transfer of the gifts.[67] As we shall see, the *cheroubikon* eventually displaces the hymn of hand washing

---

[62] Sebastià Janeras, 'Le tropaire Ὀ Μονογενής dans les liturgies orientales et sa signification oecuménique', in *Liturgies in East and West: Ecumenical Relevance of Early Liturgical Development*, ed. by Hans-Jürgen Feulner (Österreichische Studien zur Liturgiewissenschaft und Sakramententheologie 6, Vienna: Lit Verlag, 2013), 209–23, esp. 214–20.

[63] Mateos, *Parole*, 50–3.

[64] *Georgius Cedrenus Ioannis Scylitzae ope*, ed. by Immanuel Bekker (Corpus Scriptorum Historiae Byzantinae 13, Bonn: Weber, 1838), vol. 1, 684–5; Alexander Kazhdan, 'Kedrenos, George', ODB II, 1118.

[65] See fol. 166v. For more on Constantinopolitan psalters, see Chapter 1.

[66] Parpulov, *Byzantine Psalters*, 56–64.

[67] Taft, *Great Entrance*, 70–6. For a more recent analysis of this question, see the revised Italian of Taft and Parenti, *Storia della liturgia di S. Giovanni Crisostomo*, 181–90.

and the hymn of the holy gifts in JAS.[68] Although the *cheroubikon* was found in many other liturgical traditions, including Armenian and southern Italian, Taft dismisses Antiochene or Hagiopolitan origins precisely because of the testimony of Emperor Justin's introduction of the hymn in the sixth century—the earliest mention of the *cheroubikon*.[69]

Despite what has been stated here concerning 'Only-begotten Son' and the *cheroubikon*, the introduction of hymnography in Constantinople does not definitively prove its Constantinopolitan authorship or actual provenance. Nor should it—in these two cases—be used as a criterion for identifying liturgical Byzantinization in Jerusalem, especially since both hymns are present in Georgian Hagiopolite liturgical manuscripts from at least the tenth century during solemn points of the liturgical year. More important from the perspective of liturgical Byzantinization is how these hymns eventually displaced other, variable hymns—namely the *introit*, the hymn for hand washing, and the hymn of the holy gifts—which formed an integral part of Jerusalem's authentic liturgical tradition directly connected to its lectionary. For this reason, the degree of a liturgical source's Byzantinization should not be determined by the simple presence or absence of a particular hymn, but by how it is used or reused, whether it has displaced other hymns, and whether it has found a permanent place within the liturgical formulary of JAS.

Consequently, the question of Byzantine influence upon JAS is even more complex than de Meester may have been aware, and still remains unresolved. Here I will not be able to examine the presence or absence of elements of JAS in the formularies of BAS and CHR until more is known of the internal workings and origins of BAS, CHR, and JAS. Until then, it is impossible to accurately label one or another element as a clear sign of Byzantinization. Such information would certainly illuminate our knowledge of the transmission and exchange of euchological material between Jerusalem and other liturgical centres of influence. Regardless, the only way this can be verified is by an examination of the sources.

SOURCES OF THE LITURGY OF ST JAMES

Although numerous witnesses to the euchological prayers and the structure of services in Jerusalem before the Arab conquest do exist, no Euchologion manuscript per se has been preserved from that period. Despite the paucity

---

[68] See 'The Hymn for Hand Washing', 'The Hymn for the Holy Gifts', and 'Conclusions' in this chapter.

[69] Taft, *Great Entrance*, 75–6 and 97–8.

of euchological material, it is still possible to reconstruct some its contents, as proposed by Heinzgerd Brakmann and Tinatin Chronz.[70] The texts of eucharistic liturgies from Jerusalem have received the most attention and will be examined here. Studies of Euchologia have made possible a taxonomy of prayers, which localize many of them in the general 'eastern' region, often labelled as 'Melkite' but without greater specification.[71] Studies of baptism and chrismation,[72] marriage,[73] ordination,[74] unction,[75] consecration of churches and altars[76] have shed more light on the still elusive Jerusalem Euchologion. Nevertheless, there is no liturgical manuscript from the Jerusalem patriarchate that bears the title 'Euchologion', nor is there any complete manuscript containing all the liturgical rites required for the full cycle of services during the life of a Christian in Jerusalem. Editions bearing the name 'Euchologion', such as the *British Museum MS Or. 4951*, edited by Matthew Black under the title *Rituale Melchitarum*, can often be misleading. In this case the incomplete manuscript only contains prayers for ordination, blessing of water, and consecration of churches and altars.[77] Likewise Verhelst's dubbing of the catechesis of St Cyril of Jerusalem or of Egeria's pilgrim accounts as 'Euchologia' cannot be accepted:[78] these may be eyewitness narrations of liturgical services where prayers from the Euchologion were read, but they are nevertheless 'second-hand' sources, and not liturgical books someone would use to perform a liturgical service. The earliest extant Hagiopolitan Euchologia are *Sinai Gr. N.E. MΓ 53* (8th–9th cent.), an acephalous manuscript containing prayers

[70] Brakmann and Chronz, 'Jerusalemer Euchologion'.

[71] See the extremely helpful table of prayers divided according to their hypothetical origin in Parenti and Velkovska, *Евхологий Барберини gr. 336*, 70. For a discussion of the term 'Melkite' and its use in Byzantine liturgiology, see Chapter 2, 'Melkites: A Subgroup?'.

[72] Ekvtime Kochlamazashvili, 'კათაკმეველობისა და ნათლისღების წეს-განგებანი "ეუქითბეგათა" უძველეს ქართულ კრებულებში' ['The catechumenate and baptismal rites and services in "Euchologies" of the old Georgian collections'], ქრისტიანულ-არქეოლოგიური ძიებანი [Studies in Christian archeology (Tbilisi)] 3 (2010), 578–646; Michael Zheltov, 'Сирийский (или палестинский?) чин Крещения в греческой рукописи Sinait. NE MΓ 93', *Вестник Церковной Истории* 33–4 (2014), 116–26.

[73] Gabriel Radle, *The History of Nuptial Rites in the Byzantine Periphery* (Unpublished doctoral thesis, Rome: Pontifical Oriental Institute, 2012).

[74] Heinzgerd Brakmann, 'Die altkirchlichen Ordinationsgebete Jerusalems: Mit liturgiegeschichtlichen Beobachtungen zur christlichen Euchologie in Palaestina, Syria, Iberia und im Sasanidenreich', *Jahrbuch für Antike und Christentum* 47 (2004), 108–27.

[75] Tinatin Chronz, *Die Feier des Heiligen Öles nach Jerusalemer Ordnung mit dem Text des slavischen Codex Hilferding 21, der Russischen Nationalbibliothek in Sankt Petersburg sowie georgischen Übersetzungen palästinischer und konstantopolitanischer Quellen* (Jerusalemer Theologisches Forum 18, Münster: Aschendorff, 2012).

[76] Permiakov, *'Make This the Place Where Your Glory Dwells'*.

[77] See Matthew Black, *Rituale Melchitarum: A Christian Palestinian Euchologion* (Bonner Orientalische Studien 22, Stuttgart: Verlag W. Kohlhammer, 1938).

[78] Verhelst, 'Liturgy of Jerusalem', 446.

for the Liturgy of the Hours and for various blessings,[79] and *Sinai Geo. N. 58* (9th–10th cent.), a 'liturgical collection' with JAS, scriptural readings from the Jerusalem lectionary, and prayers for various blessings.[80] Consequently, although Hagiopolitan JAS is believed to be the eucharistic liturgy of Jerusalem from before the time of St Cyril of Jerusalem (349–87), there is no manuscript that presents a text anterior to the Arab conquest.

Editions of the Liturgy of St James

Because of the presumed antiquity of JAS, its Greek manuscript sources have received significant attention and were often published, despite the fact that this liturgy ceased to be celebrated. The edition of JAS by Joseph Aloysius Assemani (1710–82) as the fifth volume of his series *Codex Liturgicus Ecclesiæ Universæ* includes parts from *Messina Gr. 177* (11th cent.) that have since been lost.[81] Archbishop Dionysius Latas of Zakynthos used Assemani's copy for his 1886 edition of JAS, which he intended for actual liturgical use.[82] Since then, various editions of Greek JAS have been published. The most significant were by Charles Anthony Swainson (1820–87), Frank Edward Brightman (1856–1932), Basile-Charles Mercier (1904–78), Ioannis Phountoulis (1927–2007), whose edition included a twenty-page preface but which was intended for use in liturgical services, and, most recently, Alkiviades Kazamias.[83] For Georgian JAS, Michael Tarchnishvili prepared the first edition, while a Georgian team of scholars comprised of Lili Xevsuriani, Mzekala Shanidze, Michael Kavtaria, and Tinatin Tseradze published a new and updated edition, which contains a commentary by Stéphane Verhelst.[84]

---

[79] *Νέα εὑρήματα τοῦ Σινᾶ*, 150 and table 75; Géhin and Frøyshov, 'Nouvelles découvertes sinaïtiques', 77; Christos Kanavas, *L'eucologio MG 53 (sec. IX) del monastero di S. Caterina del Sinai* (Unpublished doctoral thesis, Rome: Pontifical Oriental Institute, 2013).

[80] Aleksidze at al., *Catalogue of Georgian Manuscripts*, 417–18.

[81] Assemani, *Missale Hierosolymitanum*, 68–99. See Appendix 1, 'Messina Gr. 177 (11th cent.)' for more on this source.

[82] See Brightman, *Eastern Liturgies*, xlix; Tarby, *Prière eucharistique*, 29 n. 12. Brakmann and Chronz, 'Eine Blume der Levante', 106–7.

[83] Swainson, *Greek Liturgies*; Brightman, *Eastern Liturgies*; Mercier, *Liturgie de Saint Jacques*; Ioannis M. Phountoulis, *Θεία Λειτουργία Ἰακώβου τοῦ Ἀδελφοθέου* (Thessalonike: Ἐκδόσεις Πουρνάρα, 1970); Kazamias, *Θεία Λειτουργία τοῦ Ἁγίου Ἰακώβου*, 157–226.

[84] Michael Tarchnišvili, 'Eine neue georgische Jakobosliturgie', *Ephemerides Liturgicae* 62 (1948), 49–82; Tarchnishvili, *Liturgiae ibericae antiquiores*; and *Liturgia ibero-graeca*, 185–452. For reviews of *Liturgia ibero-graeca*, see those of Gabriele Winkler in OCP 77 (2011), 549–53 and of Daniel Galadza in *Logos: A Journal of Eastern Christian Studies* 53: 1–2 (2012), 142–6. For Verhelst's response to Winkler's review, see Stéphane Verhelst, 'Notes sur la recension du livre *Liturgia Ibero-Graeca Sancti Iacobi*', OCP 79 (2013), 227–31.

Scholarly editions have also been accompanied by editions intended for actual use in a variety of languages: Greek,[85] Church Slavonic,[86] English,[87] and many others.[88] Although the revived celebration and spread of JAS in Orthodox and Catholic churches of the Byzantine rite is a recent, twentieth-century phenomenon, the continued use of JAS within the Syrian Orthodox Church in India has more ancient roots.[89]

The Long and Short Versions of the Liturgy of St James

Georgian scholars examining manuscripts of JAS identified two versions of the liturgy, one long and one short, the difference between the two depending on the addition of prayers for Communion and of a longer conclusion of the liturgy. The fact that manuscripts of the long version contain the entire text of the short version has led to the conclusion that the short version is closest to the original translation and the long version is the result of further development and supplementation of the earlier, shorter text.[90] While the text of the short version is more or less stable, there are still significant variants within the

[85] For example, Ἀκολουθία πλήρης τοῦ ἁγίου ἐνδόξου καὶ πανευφήμου ἀποστόλου Ἰακώβου τοῦ ἀδελφοθέου καὶ πρώτου ἱεράρχου τῶν Ἱεροσολύμων, ed. by Archimandrite Euthymios T. Delales (Athens: Τύποις Μπλαζουδάκη, 1922–3); Aristeides Panotes, Λειτουργικὸν Ἱεροσόλυμον: Ἤτοι ἡ Θεία Λειτουργία τοῦ ἁγίου Ἰακόβου τοῦ Ἀδέλφου τοῦ Κυρίου (n.p.: n.p., 1997); Ἡ Θεία Λειτουργία τοῦ ἁγίου Ἰακώβου τοῦ Ἀδελφοθέου, ed. by Archbishop Christodoulos of Athens, 14th edn (Athens: Apostoliki Diakonia, 2007). For further bibliography on Greek editions of JAS, see Kazamias, Θεία Λειτουργία τοῦ Ἁγίου Ἰακώβου, 21–4.
[86] See Литургія св. Іакова (Ladomirova), 104–8, which explains that this edition was translated and edited by Johann von Gardner, formerly Archbishop Philip of Berlin. See also Miloš Velimirović and Svetlana G. Zvereva, 'Гарднер, Иван Алексеевич', ПЭ 10:416–18.
[87] *The Divine Liturgy of Our Father Among the Saints, James of Jerusalem* (Cambridge, NY: Monks of New Skete, 1996); *Liturgy of St James*, trans. by Archimandrite Ephrem Lash. At http://www.anastasis.org.uk/lit-james.htm (accessed 8 June 2016; this website has ceased to exist after Ephrem Lash's death in 2016).
[88] For example, Bulgarian: Божественната литургия на св. апостол Иакова, брат Божий, превел от оригинала левлийский епископ Партений (Sofia: n.p., 1948), noted in Aleksandr G. Kravetskii, 'Проблема богослужебного языка на Соборе 1917–1918 годов и в последующие десятилетия', Журнал Московской Патриархии (1994, February), 83 and 87 n. 98; German: *Griechische Liturgien*, ed. and trans. by Remigius Storf, introduced by Theodor Schermann (Munich: Kösel & Pustet, 1912); Romuald Müller, *Jakobus-Liturgie und Liturgie der vorgeweihten Gaben* (Zurich: Ostreferat des Instituts für Weltanschauliche Fragen, 1986); Russian: Православное Богослужение, vol. 3: Последования Таинства Евхаристии, Литургия св. Василия Великого, Литургия Преждеосвящённых Даров, Литургия св. апостола Иакова (Moscow: Свято-Филаретовский Православно-Християнский Институт, 2010), 117–66; Ukrainian: Божественна Літургія Святого Апостола Якова Брата Божого та першого Ієрарха Єрусалимського (Rome: n.p., 2012).
[89] For more on the contemporary celebration of JAS, see Phillip Tovey, *The Liturgy of St James as Presently Used* (Alcuin/GROW Liturgical Studies 40, Cambridge: Grove Books, 1998).
[90] *Liturgia ibero-graeca*, 32.

short version. The most notable is the absence of two well-known prayers from BAS and CHR attributed to St Basil the Great, 'No one who is bound to carnal desires' (Οὐδεὶς ἄξιος) and the prayer of the proskomide 'O Lord, our God, who created us and led us to this life' (Κύριε, ὁ Θεὸς ἡμῶν, ὁ κτίσας ἡμᾶς καὶ ἀγαγὼν εἰς τὴν ζωὴν ταύτην),[91] which suggests that the short version of JAS may in fact be an earlier, pre-Byzantinized text predating significant influence from BAS and CHR.[92]

How the two versions of the Georgian JAS relate to the original Greek version of JAS is still unclear.[93] Unlike the Georgian text, critical editions of the Greek JAS have not been able to identify a clear distinction between long or short versions of the Greek text of the liturgy. Basile-Charles Mercier, following Brightman, divided his study of twenty-nine manuscripts of JAS along geographic lines and into three groups: 'eastern' manuscripts from Jerusalem and Damascus, 'intermediate' ones from Thessalonike, and 'western' ones from Zakynthos. Among the five eastern manuscripts, only two predate the thirteenth century and one of them is actually not from Jerusalem, but from Damascus.[94] Within this group, Mercier also distinguishes two independent families. This distinction is, however, based not on the criterion of varying liturgical structures, but on seemingly minor textual variants.[95] An initial examination of the concluding rites of each of these Greek sources reveals two manuscripts that correspond to the ending of the Georgian long version, namely *Sinai Gr. N.E. Σ 3* (11th cent.) and *Sinai Gr. 1039* (13th cent.).[96]

Returning to the Georgian sources, there is no clear geographic distinction between the two recensions. However, all four Georgian manuscripts that can be definitively situated at St Sabas Lavra in Palestine by means of codicological and palaeographical methods, namely *Sinai Geo. N. 26* (9th–10th cent.), *Sinai Geo. O. 53* (9th–10th cent.), *Sinai Geo. O. 54* (10th cent.), and *Sinai Geo. N. 63* (10th cent.), are sources of the long version.[97] Nevertheless, both versions—the long and the short—were used side by side during the tenth and eleventh centuries. This adds more weight to the argument that the Hagiopolite liturgy was developing within the territory of the patriarchate of Jerusalem—and not elsewhere, such as Constantinople—and then imported in a ready form by Hagiopolitan patriarchs who returned from Constantinopolitan exile.

---

[91] Mercier, *Liturgie de Saint Jacques*, 178 and 192; *Liturgia ibero-graeca*, 58 and 68. See 'The Byzantinization of the Liturgy of St James' in this chapter.

[92] *Liturgia ibero-graeca*, 31.   [93] Ibid., 32.

[94] Mercier, *Liturgie de Saint Jacques*, 133–4; Brightman, *Eastern Liturgies*, xlix.

[95] Mercier, *Liturgie de Saint Jacques*, 153.

[96] It should be noted that neither Mercier nor Kazamias pay attention to the two diverse endings of JAS.

[97] See *Liturgia ibero-graeca*, 31.

Manuscripts of the Liturgy of St James

The preceding examples from de Meester regarding the internal Byzantinization of JAS and the contradictions from more recent scholarship show the need for an independent study of JAS. Such a study must consider other eucharistic liturgies, such as BAS and CHR. Although this is not the place for such an investigation, it is, however, still possible to investigate Byzantinization in Jerusalem by tracing the presence or absence of JAS in liturgical manuscripts. Here I will follow the observations and method of André Jacob and the conclusions of Stefano Parenti for the Constantinopolitan decline of the celebration of BAS; and I will apply them to the phenomenon of liturgical Byzantinization in Jerusalem.[98] Jacob enumerated seventeen Greek manuscripts and two Georgian manuscripts, namely *Sinai Geo. O. 89* (11th cent.) and *Graz Geo. 5* (12th cent.), of the older Constantinopolitan recension dated before the fourteenth century, to which Taft added even more sources.[99] Since then, more examples of CHR have been discovered, such as *Sinai Gr. N.E. МΓ 22* (9th–10th cent.) and *Sinai Geo. N. 66* (10th cent.).[100] As Jacob notes, however, the geographic origin of most of these manuscripts is completely unknown and they are often fragmentary; thus it is difficult to say much about regional connections between the textual redaction of CHR that they represent or about their use among Chalcedonian Christians in the eastern patriarchates.[101]

Manuscripts of JAS exist in six different languages: Greek, Syriac, Georgian, Armenian, Ethiopic, and Old Church Slavonic.[102] The analysis of the Greek and Georgian manuscripts is based on the most recent studies of JAS by

---

[98] Jacob, *Formulaire*, 19–61; Jacob, 'La tradition manuscrite', 113; Parenti, 'La "vittoria"', 46–7.

[99] Jacob, *Formulaire*, 63–252; Tarchnishvili, *Liturgiae ibericae antiquiores*, vol. 1, 64–83; Taft, *Concluding Rites*, 798–811, esp. 798–803; Taft and Parenti, *Storia della liturgia di S. Giovanni Crisostomo*, 700–30. See Jacob, 'Une version géorgienne', esp. 69–70, where Jacob lists twenty-seven other Georgian manuscript sources of CHR. These, however, are all from after the fourteenth century.

[100] See Radle, 'Sinai Gr. N.E. МΓ 22'; Aleksidze et al., *Catalogue of Georgian Manuscripts*, 422.

[101] Jacob, 'La tradition manuscrite', 136.

[102] Mercier, *Liturgie de Saint Jacques*, 126–30. For editions of languages other than Greek or Georgian, see the bibliography in Tarby, *Prière eucharistique*, 28–44; Witvliet, 'The Anaphora of St James', 155; Gabriele Winkler, *Die Jakobus-Liturgie in ihren Überlieferungssträngen: Edition des Cod. arm. 17 von Lyon, Übersetzung und Liturgievergleich* (Anaphores Orientales 4, Anaphoras Armeniacae 4, Rome: Pontifical Oriental Institute, 2013). For more information on the Syriac text, see Joseph-Marie Sauget, 'Vestiges d'une célébration gréco-syriaque de l'anaphore de Saint Jacques', in *After Chalcedon: Studies in Theology and Church History Offered to Professor Albert Van Roey for His Seventieth Birthday*, ed. by Carl Laga, Joseph A. Munitiz, and Lucas van Rompay (OLA 18, Leuven: Peeters, 1985), 309–45. For the Old Church Slavonic manuscript of JAS written in Glagolitic script, *Sinai Slav. 5/N* (10th–11th cent.), see Ioannis C. Tarnanidis, *The Slavonic Manuscripts Discovered in 1975 at St Catherine's Monastery on Mount Sinai* (Thessaloniki: St Catherine's Monastery, 1988), 103–8; Stefano Parenti, 'Листы Крылова-Успенского: вопросы методики изучения славянского текста византийских литургий', *Palaeobulgarica* 33: 3 (2009), 3–26, here 22–3. The text of this last source is severely damaged and is being examined with the help of ultraviolet quartz lenses by a team of scholars (headed by Heinz Miklas of the University of Vienna) who attempt to decipher the text.

Alkiviades Kazamias and the already mentioned Georgian team of scholars, all of whom had access to the Sinai 'new finds' manuscripts of JAS, as well as to manuscripts from libraries throughout the world.[103] Because of the limited information that fragments provide about the content and internal structure of the original liturgical manuscripts they come from, these are not considered here.[104] Likewise, although there are many later sources of JAS, no manuscripts of JAS later than the fourteenth century are considered here, since these are beyond the scope of my study.

The following list is of known manuscripts of JAS in Greek and Georgian from the earliest known sources until the fourteenth century, not exclusively from the Jerusalem patriarchate, but roughly from the region of Syria and the eastern Mediterranean.

Eighth–Ninth Centuries
Sinai Gr. N.E. MΓ 118: fragmentary manuscript that contains only JAS.[105]

Ninth Century
Vatican Gr. 2282: roll (εἰλητάριον) that contains JAS and bears the title Κύριε εὐλόγησον καὶ συνέτησον τάξις σὺν Θεῷ καὶ ἀκολουθία τῆς κατὰ τὴν σύναξιν ἱερομύστου τελετῆς ('Lord bless and instruct, the order with God and sequence of the rites according to the synaxis of the initiated'). Arabic marginal notes are present and the diptychs commemorate six ecumenical councils. JAS is preceded by a profession of faith. The manuscript is believed to have been copied in Damascus.[106]

Ninth–Tenth Centuries
Sinai Geo. O. 53: acephalous manuscript copied at St Sabas Lavra (fol. 35r) that contains the long version of JAS, as well as New Testament readings according to the Jerusalem lectionary.[107]

Sinai Geo. N. 31: acephalous manuscript containing the long version of JAS and readings of the Jerusalem lectionary.[108]

Sinai Geo. N. 26: defective manuscript that begins with the long version of JAS, followed by HagPRES, litanies, dismissals, and readings according to the Jerusalem lectionary.[109]

---

[103] Kazamias, Θεία Λειτουργία τοῦ Ἁγίου Ἰακώβου; *Liturgia ibero-graeca*.

[104] For a description of some of these fragments, see Kazamias, Θεία Λειτουργία τοῦ Ἁγίου Ἰακώβου, 67–70 (Σιναϊτικὰ σπαράγματα).

[105] Kazamias, Θεία Λειτουργία τοῦ Ἁγίου Ἰακώβου, 58–9 (= H in the apparatus of Kazamias). This manuscript was not included in the Sinai Greek new finds catalogue by P. G. Nikolopoulos. See Nikolopoulos, Νέα εὑρήματα.

[106] Cardinal Angelo Mai, *Novae partum bibliothecae*, vol. 10, part 2, ed. by Joseph Cozza-Luzi (Rome: Bibliotheca Vaticana, 1905), 30–116; Mercier, *Liturgie de Saint Jacques*, 134 (= H in the apparatus of Mercier); Kazamias, Θεία Λειτουργία τοῦ Ἁγίου Ἰακώβου, 77–9 (= R in the apparatus of Kazamias).

[107] *Description* III, 55–8; *Liturgia ibero-graeca*, 20–1 (= D in the apparatus of Khevsuriani et al.).

[108] Ibid., 26 (= M in the apparatus of Khevsuriani et al.).

[109] Ibid., 19 (= B in the apparatus of Khevsuriani et al.).

Sinai Geo. N. 58: acephalous manuscript that begins with the short version of JAS and contains readings according to the Jerusalem lectionary for various commemorations, along with prayers from the Euchologion.[110]

Tenth Century

Graz University Library Cod. No. 2058/4 (985): acephalous Georgian manuscript copied by Iovane Zosime on Mount Sinai that contains the long version of JAS and HagPRES.[111]

Sinai Gr. N.E. M 151: acephalous and defective manuscript that contains the Hieratikon (ἱερατικόν) and the Diakonikon (διακονικόν) of JAS.[112]

Sinai Geo. O. 12: acephalous manuscript that contains the short version of JAS, HagPRES, prayers from the Euchologion—including baptism and marriage—and from the Horologion, and readings from the Jerusalem lectionary.[113]

Sinai Geo. O. 54: acephalous manuscript that contains the long version of JAS, HagPRES, litanies, dismissals, prayers for blessing objects at various feasts of the year, readings following the Jerusalem lectionary, and the rite of monastic tonsure. The manuscript originates in Palestine. Quire marks and the fragment *Sinai Geo. N. 33*, which forms part of *Sinai Geo. O. 54*, all suggest that JAS was the first liturgy in this manuscript.[114]

Sinai Geo. N. 22 + *Sinai Geo. N. 83*: acephalous manuscript that contains the long version of JAS and fragments of readings from the New Testament according to the Jerusalem lectionary.[115]

Sinai Geo. N. 53: acephalous manuscript that contains the short version of JAS, HagPRES, litanies for major feasts, the 'Memorial for the liturgy performed in Jerusalem',[116] and prayers from the Euchologion.[117]

---

[110] Ibid., 18–19 (= A in the apparatus of Khevsuriani et al.).

[111] Ibid., 13–14, 22–4 (= G+Gp in the apparatus of Khevsuriani et al.). Fragments of this manuscript are found in *Prague, Strahov Library Cod. D J VI 1*. See J. Jedlička, 'Das Prager Fragment der altgeorgischen Jakobusliturgie', *Archiv Orientální* 29 (1961), 183–96.

[112] Kazamias, Θεία Λειτουργία τοῦ Ἁγίου Ἰακώβου, 50–2 (= C in the apparatus of Kazamias) and 52–3 (= D in the apparatus of Kazamias); Nikolopoulos, *Νέα εὑρήματα*, 151 and table 139.

[113] *Liturgia ibero-graeca*, 31–2 (= K in the apparatus of Khevsuriani et al.). For more on this manuscript, see Appendix 1.

[114] *Description* III, 58–67; Outtier, 'Sinaï géorgien 54'; *Liturgia ibero-graeca*, 21 (= E+e in the apparatus of Khevsuriani et al.). For more on this manuscript, see Appendix 1.

[115] Ibid., 24–5 (= H+h in the apparatus of Khevsuriani et al.).

[116] 'ამისაჴსენებელი ქადაგწირვისა, რომელი ეჲრუსალემს შინა წართქუმის', fol. 86r–93r, or, in Greek, 'Μνημόνευσις ὀνομάτων (Δίπτυχα ζώντων καὶ τεθνεώτων), τῆς Θείας Λειτουργίας, ἡ ὁποία λέγεται εἰς τὰ Ἱεροσόλυμα' ('Remembrance of names [Diptychs of the living and the dead], of the Divine Liturgy, in the way they are said in Jerusalem'). Aleksidze et al., *Catalogue of Georgian Manuscripts*, 117, 286, 413.

[117] *Liturgia ibero-graeca*, 26–7 (= N in the apparatus of Khevsuriani et al.).

Sinai Geo. N. 54: acephalous manuscript that contains the long version of JAS as well as BAS, CHR, and lections following the Jerusalem lectionary.[118]

Sinai Geo. N. 63: acephalous manuscript that contains the long version of JAS and fragments of readings from the New Testament according to the Jerusalem lectionary.[119]

Sinai Geo. N. 65: acephalous and defective manuscript that contains only the long version of JAS. Georgian scholars who examined the manuscript concluded that, in all probability, it was a 'liturgical collection'.[120]

Sinai Geo. N. 70: acephalous manuscript that contains only the short version of JAS. It is likely that the manuscript was a 'liturgical collection' with more prayers and readings at the end.[121]

Sinai Geo. N. 79: manuscript fragment that contains the short version of JAS.[122]

Sinai Geo. N. 81: manuscript fragment that contains JAS, but it is unclear whether it is the long or short version. It contains additional prayers for incense not found in the other manuscripts.[123]

Eleventh Century

Sinai Gr. N.E. E 59 (1070): bilingual Greek–Arabic manuscript containing the exclamations (ἐκφώνησις) of the presider. It is acephalous and defective and contains only JAS.[124]

Sinai Gr. N.E. E 24: acephalous and defective fragment that contains only JAS.[125]

Sinai Gr. N.E. E 80: contains fragments of JAS.[126]

Sinai Gr. N.E. Σ 3: acephalous manuscript that contains fragments of JAS.[127]

Sinai Gr. N.E. X 156: contains only JAS and is defective. The manuscript begins with JAS and bears the title 'Θεία [Λει]τουργ[ία] τοῦ ἀγίου Ἰακώβου

---

[118] Ibid., 27 (= O in the apparatus of Khevsuriani et al.).
[119] Ibid., 22 (= F in the apparatus of Khevsuriani et al.).
[120] Ibid., 28 (= P in the apparatus of Khevsuriani et al.).
[121] Ibid., 25–6 (= L in the apparatus of Khevsuriani et al.).
[122] Ibid., 28–9 (= Q in the apparatus of Khevsuriani et al.).
[123] Ibid., 29 and 34–5 (= R in the apparatus of Khevsuriani et al.).
[124] Kazamias, Θεία Λειτουργία τοῦ Ἁγίου Ἰακώβου, 65–7 (= Q in the apparatus of Kazamias). The information provided by Kazamias corrects the minimal and erroneous information in Nikolopoulos, Νέα εὑρήματα, 261.
[125] Kazamias, Θεία Λειτουργία τοῦ Ἁγίου Ἰακώβου, 47–50 (= B in the apparatus of Kazamias); Nikolopoulos, Νέα εὑρήματα, 256 and table 226.
[126] Kazamias, Θεία Λειτουργία τοῦ Ἁγίου Ἰακώβου, 60 (= L in the apparatus of Kazamias); Nikolopoulos, Νέα εὑρήματα, 264.
[127] Kazamias, Θεία Λειτουργία τοῦ Ἁγίου Ἰακώβου, 61–5 (= O in the apparatus of Kazamias). This manuscript was not included in the Sinai Greek new finds catalogue by Panagiotes Nikolopoulos. See Nikolopoulos, Νέα εὑρήματα.

τοῦ ἀποστόλου καὶ [ἀ]δελφοῦ τοῦ Κυρίου' ('Divine Liturgy of St James the Apostle and brother of the Lord').[128] The extant eight quires do not reveal whether the manuscript originally contained any other liturgies.

Messina Gr. 177: parchment scroll that contains JAS (recto) and the Liturgy of St Mark (verso).[129]

Tbilisi Centre of Manuscripts A-86: complete short version of JAS, followed by prayers from the Euchologion.[130]

Thirteenth Century

Sinai Gr. 1039: acephalous manuscript that contains JAS.[131]

Vatican Gr. 1970: contains BAS, CHR, PRES, the Liturgy of St Peter, the Liturgy of St Mark, and finally JAS, copied from a manuscript of the eleventh century. Such a dating is based on the commemoration of hierarchs among the dead in the anaphora.[132] Other prayers from the Euchologion, such as for the consecration of Chrism (*myron*),[133] are interspersed among the eucharistic liturgies, in the order listed above. The manuscript originates from the Monastery of Patir in Calabria.[134]

Thirteenth–Fourteenth Centuries

Vatican Borgia Geo. 7: contains JAS and the Liturgy of St Peter. Tarchnishvili refers to it as an Euchologion (ქურთხევანი, *kurtxevani*), but the title appears to be missing and the manuscript's fragmentary state makes it difficult to understand the order in which it originally existed.[135]

---

[128] Kazamias, Θεία Λειτουργία τοῦ Ἁγίου Ἰακώβου, 44–7 (= A in the apparatus of Kazamias); Nikolopoulos, Νέα εὑρήματα, 213 and tab. 189.

[129] Assemani, *Missale Hierosolymitanum*, 68–99; Mercier, *Liturgie de Saint Jacques*, 135–6 (= M in the apparatus of Mercier); Jacob, 'Messanensis gr. 177'. The scroll has been lost. For more on this manuscript, see Appendix 1.

[130] *Liturgia ibero-graeca*, 13–14 and 19–20 (= C in the apparatus of Khevsuriani et al.). For the edition of the text, see Древне-Грузинскій Архіератиконъ. Грузинскій текстъ, ed. by Kornelii S. Kekelidze (Tbilisi: Электро-печатня С.М. Лосаберыдзе, 1912). For the English translation, see Frederick C. Coneybeare and Oliver Wardrop, 'The Georgian Version of the Liturgy of St James', ROC 18 (1913), 396–410 and 19 (1914), 155–73. See also Heinzgerd Brakmann, 'Die altkirchlichen Ordinationsgebete Jerusalems: Mit liturgiegeschichtlichen Beobachtungen zur christlichen Euchologie in Palaestina, Syria, Iberia und im Sasanidenreich', *Jahrbuch für Antike und Christentum* 47 (2004), 108–27, here 110–11 and 118–21.

[131] Dmitrievskii, Описаніе II, 245–6; Kazamias, Θεία Λειτουργία τοῦ Ἁγίου Ἰακώβου, 53–4 (= F in the apparatus of Kazamias).

[132] *Vatican Gr. 1970* (13th cent.), fol. 90v–91v; Mercier, *Liturgie de Saint Jacques*, 137 and 216 (= I in the apparatus of Mercier); Kazamias, Θεία Λειτουργία τοῦ Ἁγίου Ἰακώβου, 79–80 (= U in the apparatus of Kazamias).

[133] Folios with this service are now found at Grottaferrata, under the shelf mark *Grottaferrata Z.δ. CXIX*. See André Jacob, 'Cinq feuillets du Codex Rossanensis (Vat. gr. 1970) retrouvés à Grottaferrata', Mus 87 (1974), 45–57; André Jacob, 'L'euchologe de Sainte-Marie du Patir et ses sources', in *Atti del Congresso Internazionale su S. Nilo di Rossano, 28 settembre–1° ottobre 1986* (Rossano-Grottaferrata: Scuola Tipografica Italo-Orientale S. Nilo, 1989), 75–118.

[134] See Jacob, *Formulaire*, 239–43.

[135] For a minimal description of this manuscript's contents, see Tarchnishvili, *Liturgiae ibericae antiquiores*, vol. 2, ii–iii; *Liturgia ibero-graeca*, 17 (= Z in the apparatus of Khevsuriani

Fourteenth Century

Sinai Gr. 1040: Diakonikon (διακονικόν) that contains diaconal litanies for JAS, HagPRES, BAS, CHR, and PRES of St Basil.[136]

Table 3.1 is intended to illustrate the presence of JAS in liturgical manuscripts, along with the other elements that accompany this eucharistic liturgy.[137]

Table 3.1. Manuscripts of the Liturgy of St James

	JAS	Lectionary	Euchologion	HagPRES	BAS	CHR	St Mark	St Peter
8th–9th cent.								
Sinai Gr. N.E. MΓ 118	✓							
9th cent.								
Vatican Gr. 2282	✓							
9th–10th cent.								
Sinai Geo. O. 53	✓	✓						
Sinai Geo. N. 26	✓	✓			✓			
Sinai Geo. N. 31	✓	✓						
Sinai Geo. N. 58	✓	✓	✓					
10th cent.								
Graz University Library Cod. No. 2058/4	✓				✓			
Sinai Gr. N.E. M 151	✓							
Sinai Geo. O. 12	✓	✓	✓		✓			
Sinai Geo. O. 54	✓	✓	✓		✓			
Sinai Geo. N. 22 + Sinai Geo. N. 83	✓	✓						
Sinai Geo. N. 53	✓		✓		✓			
Sinai Geo. N. 54	✓	✓				✓	✓	
Sinai Geo. N. 63	✓	✓						
Sinai Geo. N. 65	✓							
Sinai Geo. N. 70	✓							
Sinai Geo. N. 79	✓							
Sinai Geo. N. 81	✓							
11th cent.								
Sinai Gr. N.E. E 59	✓							
Sinai Gr. N.E. E 24	✓							
Sinai Gr. N.E. E 80	✓							
Sinai Gr. N.E. Σ 3	✓							

(continued)

et al.); Michael Tarchnishvili, 'Les manuscrits géorgiens du Vatican', BK 13–14 (1962), 61–71, here 67. For an edition of the text, see Tarchnishvili, *Liturgiae ibericae antiquiores*, vol. 1, 35–63.

[136] Kazamias, Θεία Λειτουργία τοῦ Ἁγίου Ἰακώβου, 54–6 (= I in the apparatus of Kazamias). See also Appendix 1.

[137] This table is inspired by a similar table, which Stefanos Alexopoulos used in order to trace the evolution of the title of PRES in liturgical manuscripts. See 'Table 2.2: Titles of the Presanctified in the Manuscript Tradition', in Alexopoulos, *Presanctified Liturgy*, 56.

Table 3.1. Continued

	JAS	Lectionary	Euchologion	HagPRES	BAS	CHR	St Mark	St Peter
Sinai Gr. N.E. X 156	✓							
Messina Gr. 177	✓						✓	
Tbilisi Centre of Manuscripts A-86	✓		✓					
12th cent.								
–								
13th cent.								
Sinai Gr. 1039	✓							
Vatican Gr. 1970	✓		✓		✓	✓	✓	✓
13th–14th cent.								
Vatican Borgia Geo. 7	✓							✓
14th cent.								
Sinai Gr. 1040	✓			✓	✓	✓		

On the basis of Table 3.1 we can make several observations concerning the manuscript contents of these twenty-nine sources and the continued presence of JAS:

1. The greatest number of extant manuscripts containing JAS, both in Greek and Georgian, are from the tenth and eleventh centuries. However, manuscripts of JAS continued to be copied into the twelfth century and beyond, which shows that the disappearance of JAS did not occur immediately after 1009 or with the end of patriarchal exile from Jerusalem, but was gradual.

2. Only Georgian manuscripts of JAS also include readings from the Jerusalem lectionary. The presence of readings from the Jerusalem lectionary in Georgian sources of JAS shows a continued connection between the local Hagiopolitan eucharistic liturgy and the lectionary, while its absence from Greek sources suggests the possible use of another lectionary. The fragmentary nature of some Greek manuscripts of JAS makes it plausible to suggest that once they also contained appendices with lectionaries; *Sinai Gr. N.E. МГ 8* (10th cent.) could be such an appendix. However, if such manuscripts existed, none has survived.

3. Although most sources of JAS contain only this eucharistic liturgy, two manuscripts—one Greek, *Sinai Gr. 1040* (14th cent.), and one Georgian, *Sinai Geo. N. 54* (10th cent.)—contain JAS, BAS, and CHR, in that order. This suggests that BAS or CHR did not immediately replace JAS during the process of Byzantinization and that all three liturgies were used concurrently within the patriarchate of Jerusalem as early as the tenth century.

4. Except for later manuscripts, such as the eclectic *Vatican Gr. 1970* (12th cent.), JAS is never found after BAS or CHR in the manuscripts examined.

In *Sinai Geo. N. 54* (10th cent.) and in *Sinai Gr. 1040* (14th cent.), JAS and BAS come before CHR, which suggests that JAS was still considered the primary eucharistic liturgy of Jerusalem until the arrival of the new Constantinopolitan redaction of the Euchologion, wherein CHR preceded BAS.

THE LITURGY OF THE WORD

It is through the Liturgy of the Word that the liturgical calendar and the lectionary are directly connected to, and most apparent in, the eucharistic liturgy. This is because the contents of this part of the Divine Liturgy—the hymnody, psalmody, and scriptural readings—changed according to the day and the season and hence are not usually found in manuscripts of the formulary of JAS. These propers are found in the specific liturgical books designated for readers or chanters. The major exception is the category of Georgian manuscripts of JAS known as 'liturgical collections', which include readings from the Jerusalem lectionary. While the propers change, the structure of the liturgy remains the same. I shall examine this structure here, especially looking for changes to it in order to observe signs of liturgical Byzantinization.[138]

Because of the process of liturgical Byzantinization of Jerusalem, one needs to be aware of liturgical developments in both Constantinople and Jerusalem in order to verify the influence of the former upon the latter. In Constantinople, between the sixth and the eighth centuries, the beginning of the liturgy consisted of two elements: the new *introit*, consisting of a psalm and troparion or *eisodikon*, and the old *introit* of the *trisagion*.[139] By the eighth century this was expanded to include three antiphons fixed to the beginning of the service, as testified by corresponding prayers for each antiphon in the oldest Euchologion, *Barberini Gr. 336* (8th cent.).[140] Patriarch Germanus' silence on antiphons in his mystagogy makes these prayers the earliest testimonies to the presence of the three antiphons in the Divine Liturgy.[141] The familiar

---

[138] For a description of the contemporary structure of the Liturgy of the Word in the Byzantine rite, see Mateos, *Parole*, 127–9. For a comparison with Armenian practice, which bears certain similarities to the Hagiopolitan rite, see Findikyan, *Commentary*, 442. See also Thibaut, *Monuments*, 20–1.

[139] Mateos, *Parole*, 126.

[140] See Parenti and Velkovska, Евхологий Барберини гр. 336, 267–8 (§ 2–4).

[141] See Taft, 'Liturgy of the Great Church', 50. For bibliography on the enarxis in the Byzantine rite, see Nina Glibetić, 'The Byzantine Enarxis Psalmody on the Balkans (Thirteenth-Fourteenth Century)', in *Rites and Rituals of the Christian East: Proceedings of the Fourth International Congress of the Society of Oriental Liturgy, Lebanon, 10–15 July 2012*, ed. by Bert Groen, Daniel Galadza, Nina Glibetić, and Gabriel Radle (Eastern Christian Studies 22, Leuven: Peeters, 2014), 329–38.

Table 3.2. Structure of the Liturgy of the Word of St James

---

1. Initial rites
2. Entrance, with prayer of entrance and prayer of incense
3. **Introit** and synapte
4. *trisagion*, followed by the
3. Pax given by the presider
4. **Responsorial psalmody**
5. Lection(s) from the Old and/or New Testament
6. Alleluia, with **verse**
7. Ektene
8. **Gospel**
9. Dismissal of catechumens

---

structure of three antiphons was also found at the end of other Constantinopolitan services of the cathedral office, such as vespers or pannychis.[142]
The structure of the Liturgy of the Word of JAS in Jerusalem, however, is less
certain.[143] Despite the lack of clarity, several main elements stand out in the
Liturgy of the Word of JAS, namely the *introit*, the antiphons, the *trisagion*, the
responsorial psalmody with a preceding sign of peace, and scriptural lections
followed by Alleluia, an *ektene*, and the Gospel. Table 3.2 gives a simplified
outline of the Liturgy of the Word of JAS, indicating in bold variable elements
that depended on the commemoration in the liturgical calendar.[144]

The *Introit*

The first variable element of the Liturgy of the Word in Hagiopolitan sources
is a short hymnographic composition to which I will refer as the *introit*. Most
manuscripts of JAS omit any exclamation at the start of the liturgy, beginning
rather with preparatory prayers in the skeuophylakion before the *introit*.[145]
The *Narration of the Abbots John and Sophronius* does not mention any
specific hymn at the start of the liturgy, although it does mention the need
for chanters to know how to chant with 'melody and tone and singing'—all
requirements for the execution of an *introit*.[146] Since these were hymnographic compositions and were always sung, the texts are accompanied by

---

[142] Mateos, *Typicon*, vol. 2, 284 and 311.

[143] Cuming, 'Missa Catechumenorum', 62–71.

[144] For a more detailed outline, including prayer incipts, see Kazamias, Θεία Λειτουργία τοῦ
Ἁγίου Ἰακώβου, 242–3; *Liturgia ibero-graeca*, 188–9.

[145] For more on this question, see Vassa Larin, 'The Opening Formula of the Byzantine
Divine Liturgy, "Blessed is the Kingdom", among Other Liturgical Beginnings', *Studia Liturgica*
43 (2013), 229–55.

[146] ψάλτας μὲν διὰ τὸ ψάλλειν καὶ ᾄδειν μετὰ μέλους καὶ ἤχου καὶ ᾄσματος ('chanters, on the
other hand, to chant and sing with melody and tone and singing'). Longo, 'Narrazione', 254; Taft,
'The βηματίκιον', 677–8; Taft, 'Worship on Sinai', 152–3.

rubrics indicating how they were to be executed according to one of the tones of the eight-tone system.[147] The earliest Hagiopolite lectionary, the AL, has no element comparable to the *introit*, but liturgical sources from the GL and onwards usually include a proper hymn and call it by many different names. Such names are for example, in Greek, troparion (τροπάριον), *sticheron* at the entrance (στιχηρὸν εἰς τὸν εἴσοδον), stichos of the synaxis (στίχος τῆς συνάξεως), and *eisodikon* (εἰσοδικόν) and, in Georgian, *oxitay* (ოხითაჲ). Despite the various names, the function of these hymns was identical: they were opening hymns for JAS. For this reason, it seems appropriate to use the Latin technical term *introit* here as an 'umbrella' name fit to cover all the various forms of this first structural unit of JAS.

Troparia belong to the oldest stratum of Byzantine hymnody. In older literature troparia are often referred to as 'hymns', and hence include old monostrophic, non-scriptural chants such as 'Only-begotten Son' (ὁ μονογενής), the *trisagion*, and the *cheroubikon*. They are often classified according to their contents (e.g. ἀναστάσιμα, for the Resurrection), location in the service (e.g. ἀπολυτίκιον, for the dismissal), or melody (e.g. ἰδιόμελον or προσόμοιον).[148]

The *eisodikon* (εἰσοδικόν, 'hymn of entry') is understood in today's Byzantine rite to designate the introductory verse for the Small Entrance, 'Come, let us worship' (Psalm 94:6a), and the accompanying brief refrain.[149] *Vatican Gr. 1970* (13th cent.) uses the expression 'for the entrance' (εἰς εἴσοδον) to describe the fixed hymn 'Only-begotten Son' (fol. 64r), while *St Petersburg RNB Gr. 44* (9th cent.) offers the same hymn as the *introit* for every Sunday.[150] This hymn is also indicated as the *oxitay* for Pascha in the GL,[151] while the hymn 'Christ is risen from the dead' (Χριστὸς ἀνέστη ἐκ νεκρῶν, θανάτῳ; ქრისტჱ აღსდგა მკოჳდრეთით, *k'riste aġsdga mkowdret'it'*) is given as the *oxitay* of the paschal vigil.[152] In the Typikon of the Anastasis, the *eisodikon* for Palm Sunday is 'Today the grace of the Holy Spirit had gathered us together' (Στιχηρὸν εἰς τὴν ἁγίαν εἴσοδον· ἦχος πλάγιος βʹ· Σήμερον ἡ χάρις τοῦ ἁγίου πνεύματος ἡμᾶς συνήγαγεν), currently a *sticheron* in the Byzantine rite; and the *eisodikon* for Pascha is 'Your angel, O Lord' (Στιχηρὸν εἰς τὴν εἴσοδον· ἦχος πλάγιος δʹ· Ὁ ἄγγελός σου Κύριε, ὁ τὴν ἀνάστασιν).[153] The latter was an

---

[147] For more on the development of the eight-tone system in Jerusalem, see Frøyshov, 'Early Development'.

[148] Elizabeth M. Jeffreys, 'Troparion', ODB III, 2124; Christian Troelsgård, 'Troparion', NGDMM 25:776–7.

[149] Christian Troelsgård, 'Eisodikon', NGDMM 8:42. See also Mateos, *Typicon*, vol. 2, 291–2; Mateos, *Parole*, 85–6.

[150] Leeb, *Die Gesänge*, 49.

[151] 'მხოლოდ შობილი ზჱ და სიტყოჳაჲ' (*mxolod šobili zē da sitqoway*). GL § 745; *Iadgari*, 216. See also Mateos, *Typicon*, vol. 2, 308.

[152] GL § 737; *Iadgari*, 216; Follieri, *Initia hymnorum*, vol. 5.1, 104.

[153] Ibid., vol. 3, 1 and 488.

obscure hymn in the Byzantine rite, until the Hagiopolitan Tropologion *Sinai Gr. N.E. ΜΓ 5* (8th–9th cent.) revealed the same entry hymn for the paschal vigil in the Tropologion.[154] The Typikon of the Anastasis clearly states that this hymn was to be sung while the clergy, including the patriarch, entered the church (Ψάλλοντες τοῦτο [i.e. the στιχηρὸν εἰς τὴν εἴσοδον] εἰσοδεύουν ὁ πατριάρχης καὶ ὁ κλῆρος, καὶ οἱ ψάλται ἐπὶ τὸν ἄμβωνα λέγουν τὰ ἀντίφωνα; 'While singing this, the patriarch and the clergy enter, and the chanters on the ambo say the antiphons').[155] Robert Taft identifies another Hagiopolite liturgical term for the *introit* in JAS: προέλευσις, 'the issuing forth [hymn]'.[156] This same term is used in *Vatican Gr. 2282* (9th cent.) as well as in the *Narration of the Abbots John and Sophronius*,[157] testifying to the use of JAS by the monks of Palestine and Sinai.[158]

Georgian sources refer to this hymn as the *oxitay* (ოხითაჲ) before the entrance and the *trisagion*.[159] The Georgian name comes from the word *oxay* (ოხაჲ), which means 'prayer' or 'intercession'.[160] Helmut Leeb insists that this noun should not be translated as troparion, *pace* Tarchnishvili in the GL, since troparia are, by definition, monostrophic poetic hymns. The Georgian *oxitay* were not necessarily monostrophic and, by definition, always concluded with an invocation, that is, a 'prayer'.[161] Leeb also notes the function of the *oxitay* as the first chant of the changeable part, or propers, of the liturgy.[162]

Nevertheless, the different Greek and Georgian terms for the *introit* are sometimes used for the same hymn in liturgical manuscripts. For example, the *introit* in the first tone, 'Your Nativity, O Theotokos' (Ἡ γέννησίς σου, Θεοτόκε;[163] შენ შობაჲ, ღმრთისმშობელო, šeni šobay, ġmrt'ismšovelo), for the Nativity of the Theotokos on 8 September is called troparion in the

[154] Nikiforova, *Из истории Минеи в Византии*, 220. Here it is the *sticheron* of the synaxis (στιχηρὰ τῆς συνάξεως) on Holy Saturday.
[155] See fol. 12v; Papadopoulos-Kerameus, *Anastasis Typikon*, 24.
[156] Mercier, *Liturgie de Saint Jacques*, 165 (apparatus line 21).
[157] Longo, 'Narrazione', 254. It should be noted that the Hagiopolitan term προέλευσις, which Taft identifies correctly with the eisodikon, is used here for the transfer of the gifts and not for the entrance at the beginning of the liturgy.
[158] Taft, 'Worship on Sinai', 152–3.   [159] *Liturgia ibero-graeca*, 46 (§17).
[160] *Gebet* (prayer), *Bitte* (request), *Bittgebet* (invocation), *inständige Bitte* (supplicatory request), *Fürbitte* (intercession) *und Fürsprache* (intercession) (Leeb, *Die Gesänge*, 38–9); *Vermittlung* (mediation, intercession), *Fürbitte* (intercession) (Sardshweladse and Fähnrich, *Altgeorgisch-Deutsches Wörterbuch*, 935).
[161] Leeb, *Die Gesänge*, 39. Any potential similarities between the Byzantine Akroteleution (ἀκροτελεύτιον), or repeated final verse, and the final phrase of the *oxitay* remain to be investigated. See Mateos, *Typicon*, vol. 2, 325.
[162] *Es wurde von allen Gesängen der Messe als erster, und zwar zu Beginn der Messe gesungen. Es hatte also rein formal eine einleitende, eröffnende Funktion zu erfüllen* ('Of all the chants of the Mass, it was the first, namely it was sung at the beginning of the Mass. It therefore had to perform simply an introductory and opening function'). Leeb, *Die Gesänge*, 43.
[163] Follieri, *Initia hymnorum*, vol. 2, 10.

Constantinopolitan Typikon of the Great Church[164] and *oxitay* in the GL and the *Iadgari*.[165] The same is true for the *introit* in Palm Sunday, already mentioned.

As we shall see in the following chapter, however, many of the opening hymns of the Divine Liturgy in the GL or *Iadgari* are not the same in the Greek sources. For example, the *oxitay* for Pentecost found in the GL and *Iadgari* is:

იშვე ვითარცა ჯერ გიჩმდე, გამოსცენდი, ვითარცა ინებე, იჩნე ჯორგითა, უფალო ცუენო, აღ-რაა-სდეგ მკუდრეთით, სძლე სიკუდილსა, ამაღლდი დიდებითა, რომელმან ყოველივე აღავსე და მოგუევლინნ სული წმიდაი. გალობაი და დიდებაი შენსა ღრთოებასა.[166]	By your nativity, you revealed yourself as you willed. You manifested yourself, as you chose. You suffered in the flesh, O our God. You arose from the dead, trampling down death. You ascended in glory, filling all things. You sent us your divine Spirit, that we may praise and glorify your divinity.

This text summarizes the whole mystery of salvation in Christ, from his birth to his suffering, death, resurrection, and ascension and ultimately to the sending of the Holy Spirit on Pentecost, which this hymn commemorates. The Greek Hagiopolitan Tropologion *Sinai Gr. N.E. ΜΓ 5* (8th–9th cent.) contains a different *introit*, which is called 'the *sticheron* of the synaxis' in that manuscript:

Ὅταν τὸ Πνεῦμά σου κατέπεμψας Κύριε, συνηγμένων τῶν Ἀποστόλων, τότε οἱ τῶν Ἑβραίων παῖδες θεωροῦντες, ἐξίσταντο φόβῳ· ἤκουον γὰρ αὐτῶν φθεγγομένων, ἑτέραις γλώσσαις, καθὼς τὸ Πνεῦμα ἐχορήγει αὐτοῖς· ἰδιῶται γὰρ ὄντες, ἐσοφίσθησαν, καὶ τὰ ἔθνη πρὸς πίστιν ζωγρήσαντες, τὰ θεῖα ἐρρητόρευον· διὸ καὶ ἡμεῖς βοῶμέν σοι· ὁ κατελθὼν ἐπὶ γῆς, καὶ ἐκ τῆς πλάνης σώσας ἡμᾶς, Κύριε, δόξα σοι.[167]	When you sent down your Spirit, Lord, to the Apostles as they were gathered, then the children of the Hebrews saw it and were beside themselves with fear; for they were hearing them speaking in other tongues, as the Spirit gave them; for though simple men, they had been made wise; and having caught the nations for the faith, were preaching things divine; and we also cry out to you: You came down to the earth and saved us; Lord, glory to you.

[164] Mateos, *Typicon*, vol. 1, 18.
[165] GL § 1221; *Iadgari*, 286.
[166] GL § 881; *Iadgari*, 249. The critical edition of the *Iadgari* also indicates Εἴδομεν τὸ φῶς τὸ ἀληθινόν (ვიხილეთ ნათელი ჭეშმარიტი, vixilet' nat'eli češmariti) as the *oxitay* in some manuscripts. See Follieri, *Initia hymnorum*, vol. 1, 359.
[167] Στιχηρὰ τῆς συνάξεως. Ἦχος πλάγιος δ΄. Πρός· Ὅτε τῷ ξύλῳ σε ('Stichera of the synaxis. Tone 4 plagal [Tone 8]. To "When by the tree you..."'). *Sinai Gr. NE ΜΓ 5*, fol. 71r. See Nikiforova, *Из истории Минеи в Византии*, 232. Today in the Byzantine rite this is a *sticheron*

In the earliest sources from Constantinople, however, the troparion of Pentecost is different:

Εὐλογητὸς εἶ Χριστὲ ὁ Θεὸς ἡμῶν· ὁ πανσόφους τοὺς ἁλιεῖς ἀναδείξας καταπέμψας αὐτοῖς τὸ πνεῦμα τὸ ἅγιον· καὶ δι' αὐτῶν τὴν οἰκουμένην σαγηνεύσας, φιλάνθρωπε δόξα σοι.[168]	Blessed are you, Christ our God, who have shown the fishermen to be all-wise, having sent to them the Holy Spirit, and through them you caught the universe. Lover of mankind, glory to you.

This difference could simply be understood as the replacement of the Hagiopolitan hymn by that of Constantinople: a product of Byzantinization. However, the Hagiopolitan hymn cited above is not actually replaced, but rather transferred to another part of the propers for the feast of Ascension, finding itself today as the *doxastikon* for the *stichera* 'at the Praises' (εἰς τοὺς Αἴνους), at matins.[169] Similar examples exist, indicating that this is not an isolated incident.[170] Thus we are dealing with a development that is much more complex than a replacement of one hymn by another.

In the current Byzantine rite, it is not uncommon for variable hymns from the Oktoechos to find their way into other, more prominent fixed positions in the Byzantine rite, for example in BAS or in funeral services. The examples that come to mind in the current Byzantine rite are the sessional hymn for Tone 8 on Sunday at matins (Ἐπὶ σοὶ χαίρει, Κεχαριτωμένη), which is used as a troparion in the diptychs in BAS, and the Tone 4 *sticheron* on Friday evening (Μετὰ πνευμάτων Δικαίων τετελειωμένων), which is used as a troparion for the commemoration of the departed.[171] But how and why this is so is hardly clear. Could the use of one hymn as opposed to another, or the

sung during *lite* at the vespers of Pentecost: Εἰς τὴν Λιτήν, Στιχηρὰ Ἰδιόμελα, Δόξα...Καὶ νῦν... Ἦχος πλ. δ' (For the *lite*, idiolmela stichera, Glory...both now...Tone 4 plagal [Tone 8]). See *Πεντηκοστάριον χαρμόσυνον* (Rome: n.p., 1883), 393.

[168] Mateos, *Typicon*, vol. 2, 136; Andreou, *Praxapostolos*, 130.

[169] Ἐτέχθης, ὡς αὐτὸς ἠθέλησας· ἐφάνης, ὡς αὐτὸς ἠβουλήθης· ἔπαθες σαρκί, ὁ Θεὸς ἡμῶν· ἐκ νεκρῶν ἀνέστης, πατήσας τὸν θάνατον· ἀνέστειλας ἡμῖν Πνεῦμα θεῖον, τοῦ ἀνυμνεῖν καὶ δοξάζειν σου τὴν Θεότητα ('You were born, as you yourself willed. You appeared, as you yourself wished. You suffered in the flesh, O our God. You rose from the dead, having trampled on death. You were taken up in glory, who fill the universe. You sent us the divine Spirit, that we might hymn and glorify your divinity'). Tone 2 *doxastikon* at the praises of matins for Ascension. Follieri, *Initia hymnorum*, vol. 1, 544; Leeb, *Die Gesänge*, 45 n. 29.

[170] The hymn for hand washing for transfiguration at liturgy on August 6 (Πρὸ τοῦ Σταυροῦ σου, Κύριε, ὄρος; პირველ ჯუარცუმისა შენისა, *pirvel juarc'umisa šenisa*) becomes the first *sticheron* at vespers for the same feast. See GL § 1133; *Iadgari*, 265; Follieri, *Initia hymnorum*, vol. 3, 370.

[171] Ibid., vol. 1, 515 and vol. 2, 408. 'Ἐπὶ σοὶ χαίρει, Κεχαριτωμένη' is also found as a fixed element of compline in the Horologion *Sinai Gr. 863* (9th cent.). See Parenti, 'Fascicolo ritrovato', 349.

'competition' between two hymns, be explained by the perceived importance of one point of the liturgical services over another? Among the Stoudites, the sixth ode of the canon at matins had the character of an *introit*, similar to that of the Divine Liturgy.[172] Thus, could the transposition of a troparion for a certain feast or commemoration from the Hagiopolitan *Iadgari* to the contemporary Byzantinized Typikon be connected to the development of the Liturgy of the Hours and to the inner workings of the Stoudite and Sabaite synthesis? The question remains unanswered so long as the detailed development of the liturgical services in Constantinople and Jerusalem around the ninth and tenth centuries is unknown. Nevertheless, indexes of Greek and Georgian hymnographic equivalents do exist and may be deployed if we wish to answer this question.[173] Further examples in the next chapter will also bring us back to it. What becomes clear from these examples of the transfer of hymns to different parts of the liturgical services is that the Orthodoxy of their dogmatic content is not a factor: none of the Hagiopolitan hymns mentioned here that are moved or abandoned expresses dubious Christological formulations; they are all solidly Chalcedonian.

Antiphons

In Constantinople three antiphons were sung at the beginning of the Divine Liturgy. In Hagiopolite liturgical texts, however, no such antiphons were part of JAS; and they are not included in the AL, the GL, the *Iadgari*, or any other Hagiopolite lectionaries. The first witness to antiphons at JAS in Jerusalem is for Palm Sunday and Easter, in the Typikon of the Anastasis. Immediately after the *introit*, the manuscript's scribe Basil placed the Constantinopolitan antiphons, inserted as a unit into JAS, between the Hagiopolitan *eisodikon* and the *trisagion*.[174] The provenance of this borrowing, that is, the Constantinopolitan origin of the antiphons, is revealed by the fact that (1) antiphons are not present in early Hagiopolitan sources of JAS and that (2) the troparion refrain of the third antiphon on both Palm Sunday and Pascha is the same as contemporaneous, or earlier, sources from Constantinople but different from the Hagiopolitan *eisodikon* sung at the beginning of JAS. Although the text of the paschal antiphons of the Typikon of the Anastasis matches those of the Constantinopolitan Typikon of the Great Church and of the Praxapostolos,[175]

---

[172] Miguel Arranz, SJ, 'N. D. Uspensky: The Office of the All-Night Vigil in the Greek Church and in the Russian Church', SVTQ 24 (1980), 190.

[173] Leeb, *Die Gesänge*, 44–8.

[174] Papadopoulos-Kerameus, *Anastasis Typikon*, 24 and 200–1.

[175] Mateos, *Typicon*, vol. 2, 92–6; Andreou, *Praxapostolos*, 106.

neither Constantinopolitan source prescribes antiphons at the liturgy on Palm Sunday. This is certainly no scribal omission, as the Constantinopolitan Typikon of the Great Church specifically indicates that the Divine Liturgy immediately begins with the *trisagion*; the three small antiphons were to be sung on the preceding evening, during pannychis.[176] This same proscription of antiphons at the Palm Sunday liturgy is included in the eleventh-century Constantinopolitan Praxapostolos and two contemporaneous kanonaria-synaxaria of elusive origin found today at Sinai: *Sinai Gr. 150* (10th–11th cent.) and *Sinai Gr. 2095* (9th–10th cent.).[177] The Evergetis Typikon and the Typikon of Patriarch Alexius the Stoudite both prescribe a *lite* (λιτή) procession at the end of matins, but without any antiphons, and the Typika psalms and Beatitudes at the Divine Liturgy.[178] The twelfth-century Typikon of the Monastery of the Holy Saviour in Messina in southern Italy is the first to include Palm Sunday antiphons in the Divine Liturgy.[179] Another southern Italian Typikon, *Grottaferrata Γ.α. I* (1300), prescribes the service of *trithekte* and Beatitudes as part of a *lite* procession before the Palm Sunday Divine Liturgy.[180] Thus, to my knowledge, there is no evidence for Palm Sunday antiphons in the Divine Liturgy before the Typikon of the Anastasis. Rather than suggest that the Constantinopolitan Palm Sunday antiphons first found their place in JAS in Jerusalem, it is more likely that the presence of these antiphons at the Divine Liturgy in a Hagiopolitan source reveals the date of the redaction of this source, namely the early twelfth century. In other words, it seems more likely that the Palm Sunday antiphons would have been introduced first into the Divine Liturgy, where the practice of antiphons at the normal Divine Liturgy already existed, for example in Constantinople, southern Italy, or Antioch, and only later adopted at the Holy Sepulchre.

After the first testimony of antiphons at JAS in the Typikon of the Anastasis, other twelfth-century Hagiopolitan manuscripts also begin to prescribe antiphons. These include the liturgical Typika *Sinai Gr. 1096* (12th cent.) and *Sinai Gr. 1097* (12th cent.), although the Divine Liturgy they prescribe is no longer JAS, but CHR. In general, the presence of antiphons at the Divine Liturgy in Hagiopolite liturgical manuscripts is a sign of the end stages—or completion—of liturgical Byzantinization in Jerusalem.

---

[176] Mateos, *Typicon*, vol. 2, 64–6.

[177] Andreou, *Praxapostolos*, 196–7; *Sinai Gr. 150* (10th–11th cent.): 'Τῷ πρωῒ εἰς τὴν λειτουργίαν ἀντίφωνα οὐ λέγονται [*Sinai Gr. 2095* (9th–10th cent.): γίνοται]. Εἰσοδικόν· Συνταφέντες'. Dmitrievskii, *Описание* I, 190.

[178] Dmitrievskii, *Описание* I, 542; Pentkovsky, *Типикон*, 247.

[179] Miguel Arranz, *Le typicon du monastère du Saint-Sauveur à Messine: Codex Messinensis Gr. 115 AD 1131* (OCA 185, Rome: Pontifical Oriental Institute, 1969), 228–99.

[180] See Dmitrievskii, *Описание* I, 909.

The *Trisagion*

The *trisagion* hymn, whose name means 'thrice-holy', is found among the initial rites of every eastern eucharistic liturgy.[181] Most manuscripts of JAS include a prayer to be said by the presider in conjunction with the *trisagion*, 'Compassionate and merciful, long-suffering and abounding in mercy, and true Lord' (Οἰκτίρμον καὶ ἐλεῆμον, μακρόθυμε καὶ πολυέλεε καὶ ἀληθινὲ Κύριε; მოწყალეო, მრწყალომბერო, სუელგრძელო, მრავალმოწყალეო და ჭეშმარიტო უფალო).[182] Some Georgian sources also have a long introduction to the prayer's ekphonesis, labelling it another prayer.[183] *Vatican Gr. 1970* (13th cent.) gives the full text of the *trisagion*, which concludes with the phrase 'Holy Trinity have mercy on us' (ἁγία τριὰς ἐλέησον ἡμᾶς) after the doxology, once the *trisagion* has been sung three times by the reader (ἀναγνώστης). Most manuscripts of JAS, however, do not contain the actual text of the *trisagion*; but those that include the propers for the Liturgy of the Word often do.[184] For example, *St Petersburg RNB Gr. 44* (9th cent.) has rubrics that prescribe the *trisagion*.[185] Variants of the *trisagion* in the Byzantine rite today, namely 'As many as have been baptized into Christ' (Ὅσοι εἰς Χριστὸν ἐβαπτίσθητε, Galatians 3:27)[186] and 'To your Cross' (Τὸν Σταυρόν σου),[187] exist for certain feast days, and their focus is noticeably Christological. Still other manuscripts prescribe even more variant hymns in place of the *trisagion*. For example, *Sinai Gr. N.E. ΜΓ 8* (10th cent.) indicates a variant hymn for the *trisagion*, 'Christ is born upon the earth' (Χριστὸς ἐτέχθη ἐπὶ γῆς), on the fourth day following Christmas.[188] The full text of the hymn, found in *Sinai Gr. 150*

---

[181] Ἅγιος ὁ Θεός, Ἅγιος ἰσχυρός, Ἅγιος ἀθάνατος, ἐλέησον ἡμᾶς; წმიდაო ღმერთო, წმიდაო ძლიერო, წმიდაო უკვდავო, შეგვეწყალენ ჩუენ, *cmidao ġmert'o, cmidao zliero, cmidao ukvdavo, šegwcqalen č'uen* (Holy God, holy mighty, holy immortal, have mercy on us). For more on the *trisagion*, see John of Damascus, Περὶ τοῦ τρισαγίου ὕμνου, PG 95:21–61, CPG 8049; Mateos, *Parole*, 91–126; Robert F. Taft, 'Trisagion', ODB III, 2121; Sebastià Janeras, 'Le Trisagion: une formule brève en Liturgie comparée', in *Liturgy Fifty Years after Baumstark*, 495–562; 'How Liturgies Grow. The Evolution of the Byzantine Divine Liturgy', in Taft, *Beyond East and West*, 215–16; Kenneth Levy and James W. McKinnon, 'Trisagion', NGDMM 25:745–6. For the non-Chalcedonian defence of the 'Theopaschite' form, see Mingana, 'Treatise of Barṣalībī against the Melchites', 57–63.

[182] Kazamias, Θεία Λειτουργία τοῦ Ἁγίου Ἰακώβου, 161–2; *Liturgia ibero-graeca*, 48–9 (§ 23).

[183] *Liturgia ibero-graeca*, 46–7 (§ 21).

[184] *Vatican Gr. 1970* (13th cent.), fol. 66r–66v.

[185] See fol. 60r; Thibaut, *Monuments*, 10*.

[186] Mateos, *Parole*, 110–11. This is also found in the GL § 736.

[187] Ibid., 118–19.

[188] For more on this manuscript, see Galadza, 'Sinai Gr. N.E. ΜΓ 8' and Appendix 1.

(10th–11th cent.), a manuscript of unknown provenance and liturgical content, is as follows:

Χριστὸς ἐτέχθη ἐπὶ γῆς ἐν φάτνῃ, σπάργανα φορέσας, τὰ δεσμὰ διαρρύξας τῶν ἀνομιῶν ἡμῶν.[189]	Christ is born upon the earth in a manger; wearing swaddling clothes he broke the bonds of our transgression.

The hymn follows a meter almost identical to that of the paschal troparion 'Christ is risen from the dead' (Χριστὸς ἀνέστη ἐκ νεκρῶν)[190] and is preceded here by the rubric 'Instead of the *trisagion*, plagal (tone) four' (Ἀντὶ δὲ τοῦ Τρισαγίου (ἦχος) πλ. δ'). The lections after this replacement for the *trisagion* are Hebrews 2:11–18 and Matthew 2:13–23, thematically related to the Nativity of Christ and the massacre of the innocents.[191] Whether this variable hymn was introduced in an attempt to avoid using the *trisagion* through an additional Christological phrase related to Christ's birth or incarnation cannot be verified. The Armenian tradition preserves to this day a variable *trisagion* for more solemn holy days, which is similar to the Theopaschite *trisagion*. A concluding phrase that refers to the feast being celebrated is added to the hymn, pointing to a Christological understanding of the *trisagion*.[192]

Apart from the possible Theopaschite hints in the *trisagion*, the liturgical function of this hymn is worth examining. Although the earliest evidence for the *trisagion* is from Constantinople around 438/9, this hymn was already present in Palestine from at least the time of St Sabas (*c*.439–532), whose life mentions the polemic over the Theopaschite *trisagion* formula.[193] Polemics surrounding the phrase 'who was crucified for us' (ὁ σταυρωθεὶς δι' ἡμᾶς) continued into the eighth century, despite attempts to settle the question at the Council of Trullo. Syrian Chalcedonians continued to use the Theopaschite *trisagion* and the issue remained a point of contention at the Lavra of

---

[189] See Dmitrievskii, *Описаніе* I, 207. My thanks to Dimitrios K. Balageorgos for this reference. For more on the origins of the manuscript *Sinai Gr. 150*, see Stefano Parenti, 'Per l'identificazione di un anonimo calendario italo-greco del Sinai', AB 115 (1997), 281–7, updated in idem, *A oriente e occidente di Costantinopoli*, 155–9. For more on the connections between the birth of Christ at Christmas and his death and resurrection at Pascha, see Galadza, 'Various Orthodoxies', 191–3; Ioannis M. Phountoulis, 'Τό «Πάσχα» τῶν χριστουγένων', Τελετουργικά Θέματα, vol. 2 (Σειρά «Λογική λατρεία» 12, Athens: Apostoliki Diakonia, 2006), 101–21.

[190] See 'Eucharistic Liturgies' in this chapter.

[191] GL § 815–17. The same reading is also found in *Sinai Ar. 116* (10th cent.), fol. 98r–100r.

[192] *The Armenian Church Choirmaster's Manual*, ed. by Arra Avakian (New York: Diocese of the Armenian Church of North America, 1965).

[193] *Life of Sabas*, in Schwartz, *Cyril of Scythopolis*, 117–18. For more on this question, see Mateos, *Parole*, 101–2; Timothy E. Gregory, 'Theopaschitism', ODB III, 2061.

Eutychius in the eighth century.[194] Nevertheless, most scholars find it likely that the *trisagion* came to Jerusalem from Constantinople.

Despite the *trisagion*'s suggested Constantinopolitan origin, its function varied depending on the liturgical tradition. In Constantinople, the *trisagion* was an entrance chant at the beginning of the liturgy. In other traditions, however, this hymn was associated with a solemnized rite that preceded the Gospel, and not with the initial entrance into the church. Sarhad Y. Hermiz Jammo noted that the *trisagion* entered the Chaldean East Syrian tradition by the time of Catholicos Isho'yahb I (r. *c*.581/2–95), once the structure of the Liturgy of the Word with its own *introit* had been established. The location of the inserted *trisagion*—immediately before the scriptural readings— emphasizes its function as an introduction to the readings rather than to the clergy's initial entrance into the church.[195] Gabriele Winkler took issue with this view, pointing to the development of the *trisagion* in the Byzantine tradition as an additional entrance hymn.[196] For the Armenian tradition, Daniel Findikyan's study of the commentaries of Bishop Step'anos Siwne'ci of Siwnek' (*c*.685–735) has revealed the *trisagion*'s function as an introduction to the lections of the Liturgy of the Word sung during the Gospel procession, rather than as an *introit* hymn. The proximity of this variable hymn to the reading of the Gospel, both of which depended upon the liturgical commemoration being celebrated, further strengthened the Armenian Christological understanding of the *trisagion*.[197]

The function of the *trisagion* in Jerusalem may have been in fact more akin to its function in the Armenian and East Syrian traditions. This view is further strengthened by the presence and—more importantly—by the placement of Constantinopolitan antiphons on Palm Sunday and Pascha in the Typikon of the Anastasis. In both cases, the antiphons are not inserted before the *eisodikon* and the *trisagion*, as in Constantinople, but between the *eisodikon* and *trisagion*. As the function of the *trisagion* in Jerusalem is connected to the scriptural readings and not to the entry rites of the liturgy, foreign—namely Constantinopolitan—liturgical elements could be inserted between the *eisodikon* and *trisagion*, as one can see in the Typikon of the Anastasis. This example illustrates that the history of the development of a liturgical unit in one

---

[194] Auzépy, 'De la Palestine à Constantinople', 197–9.

[195] Jammo, *La structure de la messe chaldéenne*, 97–9. For more on Isho'yahb I, see Sebastian P. Brock, 'Isho'yahb I', GEDSH, 218.

[196] See Gabriele Winkler's review of Jammo in *Oriens Christianus* 66 (1982), 240–1.

[197] Findikyan, *Commentary*, 456–8, and 43–55 for details of Step'anos' life. Gabriele Winkler's review of Findikyan's book does not address this theory, which leads one to assume that she accepts Findikyan's corrective. Instead Winkler herself stresses the connection between the Armenian *introit* (Psalm 92) and the Georgian *oxitay*. Gabriele Winkler, 'M. D. Findikyan's New and Comprehensive Study of the Armenian Office', OCP 72 (2006), 383–415, especially 399–400.

liturgical rite or tradition is not necessarily the same as that of its development in another tradition.

The *Pax*

The greeting of the faithful by the presider with the words 'Peace be with all!' (*Εἰρήνη πᾶσι*; მშჳდობაჲ ყოველთა, *mšwdobay qovelt'a*), known by its Latin name *pax* ('peace'), followed the *trisagion* and the *introit* and was the beginning of the liturgy in the most ancient sources.[198] In JAS the greeting came before the responsorial psalmody,[199] although Greek sources give the pax twice: once at the beginning of the liturgy[200] and again before the responsorial psalmody.[201]

Responsorial Psalmody

Various terms are used in liturgical sources to describe responsorial psalmody. This variety has led some to hypothesize that specific terms have proper geographical connections.[202] I shall briefly examine this matter here in order to determine whether it is possible to find signs of Constantinopolitan influence upon the Hagiopolitan sources on the basis of the use of specific terms for responsorial psalmody.

Before proceeding, however, I need to make a few points. This type of psalmody was variable and directly connected to the liturgical year. For example, in the AL, the eucharistic liturgy began with a psalm and a refrain (*kc'urd*). The psalm was chosen to express the theme of the feast or saint commemorated. A *lectio continua* of psalms also existed in certain periods,[203] and generally the most frequent sources for responsorial psalmody were Psalms 114 and 115.[204]

The term *prokeimenon* is first documented in the ninth century.[205] Although many liturgiologists and musicologists have drawn parallels between

---

[198] Mateos, *Parole*, 129–30.   [199] *Liturgia ibero-graeca*, 50–1 (§ 24).
[200] Mercier, *Liturgie de Saint Jacques*, 162; Kazamias, Θεία Λειτουργία τοῦ Ἁγίου Ἰακώβου, 158.
[201] Mercier, *Liturgie de Saint Jacques*, 168; Kazamias, Θεία Λειτουργία τοῦ Ἁγίου Ἰακώβου, 162.
[202] For example, Stefano Parenti, 'Mesedi – μεσῴδιον', in idem, *A oriente e occidente di Costantinopoli*, 91–102.
[203] From the fourth to the sixth week of Lent, Psalms 132 to 136 were read continuously at this point. See AL, 110–15.
[204] Ibid., 35–6.
[205] Mateos, *Parole*, 7–13, 133–4; Gisa Hintze, *Das byzantinische Prokeimena-Repertoire. Untersuchungen und kritische Edition* (Hamburger Beiträge zur Musikwissenschaft 9, Hamburg: Verlag der Musikalienhandlung Karl Dieter Wagner, 1973); Elena Velkovska, 'I "dodici

the *prokeimenon* and other forms of responsorial psalmody, such as the Roman *responsorium* or gradual, Simon Harris points out that there is little justification for such a comparison.[206] Further disagreements exist regarding the meaning of the name of this responsorial chant. Mateos argues that the term *prokeimenon* was coined in order to capture the fact that the responsorial verse was chosen and 'placed before' the rest of the psalm, in order to serve as a refrain. Geoffrey W. H. Lampe, however, explains the term as referring to a text that 'preced[es the] reading of the Epistle'.[207] The disagreement lies therefore in the fact that the indirect object of this participle is unknown. What is it that the responsorial verse precedes: the readings or the remainder of the psalm? Since Mateos believes that the *prokeimenon* came between the Old Testament reading and the Epistle in Constantinople, the prefix *pro-* must refer to the psalm. This would make the *prokeimenon* a responsorial psalm set between two readings. There are, however, numerous examples where a *prokeimenon* is found before only one lection, or even without any lection, as happens during the service of lucernary (λυχνικόν) at Constantinopolitan cathedral vespers.[208] However, if we turn to Jerusalem, where the presence of Old Testament readings at the eucharistic liturgy is documented in Greek and Georgian sources,[209] there is only one occasion where the responsorial psalmody is a *Zwischengesang*—a hymn between two readings. This occasion is the commemoration of St Cyriacus on 15 July in the GL.[210] Otherwise the responsorial psalmody is always placed before all readings, both from the Old and from the New Testament.

Before the term *prokeimenon* was used, the chant was probably referred to simply as a 'psalm' (ψαλμός), judging by the testimony of *St Petersburg RNB Gr. 44* (9th cent.) and by the fact that the lector gave a chanted announcement

---

prokeimena" del mattutino cattedrale bizantino', in *Crossroad of Cultures: Studies in Liturgy and Patristics in Honor of Gabriele Winkler*, ed. by Hans-Jürgen Feulner, Elena Velkovska, and Robert F. Taft, SJ (OCA 260, Rome: Pontifical Oriental Institute, 2000), 705–16; Simon Harris, 'The Byzantine Prokeimenon', *Plainsong and Medieval Music* 3 (1994), 133–47.

[206] Ibid., 133. See Hintze, *Das byzantinische Prokeimena-Repertoire* (see n. 205 here), 17–19.
[207] Lampe, *Patristic Greek Lexicon*, 1153.
[208] Mateos, *Typikon*, vol. 2, 316–17.
[209] For more on the question of Old Testament readings in the eucharistic liturgy, see 'Lection(s)' in this chapter and 'Old Testament Readings at the Liturgy of St James and Their Disappearance' in Chapter 5.
[210] GL § 1089. *Im Georgischen Lektionar ist nur ein einziger Fall bezeugt, an dem das 'p'salmuni' ein Zwischengesang sein kann... An allen anderen Eucharistiefeiern des Georgischen Lektionars werden aber die beiden Begriffe für den Psalmengesang 'p'salmuni' und 'dasdebeli' immer vor den Lesungen des Alten Testamentes notiert* ('In the Georgian lectionary there is only one attested case in which the "p'salmuni" can be a hymn between two readings [Zwischenge-sang]...At all the other eucharistic celebrations of the Georgian lectionary, however, the two terms for the psalmody "p'salmuni" and "dasdebeli" are always before the readings from the Old Testament'). Leeb, *Die Gesänge*, 52.

of the form 'a psalm of David' (ψαλμὸς τῷ Δαυΐδ).[211] This same term—'psalm' (ფსალმუნი, *p'salmuni*)—is found throughout Georgian sources such as the GL and in manuscripts of JAS.[212] Mercier's edition gives the following structure for the introduction of responsorial psalmody in JAS:

Καὶ μετὰ ταῦτα ὁ ἱερεὺς σφραγίζει λέγων· Εἰρήνη πᾶσιν. Ὁ ψάλτης τὸ προκείμενον, ὁ ἀπόστολος, τὸ ἀλληλούϊα.[213]	And after [the prayer and the *trisagion*], the priest signs [them] saying: 'Peace be to all'. The chanter [intones] the *prokeimenon*, the Epistle, and the Alleluia.

After this the priest continues with 'the prayer for the incense before the Gospel reading' (εὐχὴ θυμιάματος πρὸ τοῦ εὐαγγελίου): 'To you, Lord our God, who are filled with all fragrance and joy' (Σοὶ τῷ πεπληρωμένῳ πάσης εὐωδίας καὶ εὐφροσύνης, Κύριε ὁ Θεὸς ἡμῶν).[214] This rubric, however, is only indicated in one manuscript, *Messina Gr. 177* (11th cent.).

Georgian sources show some variation in terminology. In manuscripts of JAS, the term *prokeimenon* is not used at all:

მღდემან: მშჳდობაჲ ყოველთა. ერმან: სულისა შენისა თანა. დიაკონმან: ფსალმუნი დავითისი. მოხედეთ. ფსალმუნი თქუან და საკითხავნი წაჲკითხნენ.[215]	*Priest*: Peace to all. *People*: With your spirit. *Deacon*: Psalm of David. Be attentive! *Let them say the Psalm and read the Lections.*

Elsewhere, Georgian sources use the term *dasdebeli* (დასდებელი), or the more complete form *dasadebeli* (დასადებელი), to designate the refrain for responsorial psalmody.[216] This technical term derives from the word *dadebay* (დადებაჲ),[217] which is literally equivalent to the Greek verb κατατίθημι,[218] although Leeb suggests the meaning to be *Beifügung*—'enclosed, attached,

[211] Christian Troelsgård, 'Prokeimenon', NGDMM 20:403–4; Hintze, *Das byzantinische Prokeimena-Repertoire* (see n. 205 here), 8–10.
[212] For example, GL § 6, 14, 16, 19, etc.; *Liturgia ibero-graeca*, 50–1 (§ 25).
[213] Mercier, *Liturgie de Saint Jacques*, 168; Kazamias, Θεία Λειτουργία τοῦ Ἁγίου Ἰακώβου, 162.
[214] Mercier, *Liturgie de Saint Jacques*, 168.
[215] *Liturgia ibero-graeca*, 50–1 (§ 24–6). The English translation has been adapted and corrected here.
[216] 'Gesang', in Sardshweladse and Fähnrich, *Altgeorgisch-Deutsches Wörterbuch*, 354.
[217] 'Legen, Hinlegen', ibid., 310.
[218] 'Put down, ordain, record'. Lampe, *Patristic Greek Lexicon*, 723.

addition, inclusion'.[219] However, the text designated by *dasdebeli* is closer to an antiphon than to a *prokeimenon*.[220] Gisa Hintze notes that Middle Byzantine music manuscripts from the eighth and tenth centuries also use the term *doche* (δοχή), literally 'reception' or 'receptacle', but probably meaning 'respond' when applied to responsorial psalmody similar to a *prokeimenon*.[221]

The repertoire of forty-eight *prokeimena* in the Byzantine rite was already fully developed by the thirteenth century and can be divided into three groups, following Hintze and Harris. The first group, *prokeimena* of the liturgy (προκεί-μενα τῆς λειτουργίας) or *prokeimena* of the Epistle (προκείμενα τοῦ ἀποστόλου), consists of thirty possible chants to be sung at the Divine Liturgy in one of the eight tones. The second group, made up of eight *prokeimena*, was reserved for daily vespers (προκείμενα τοῦ λυχνικοῦ or προκείμενα τοῦ ἑσπερινοῦ), although it also included the *prokeimenon* 'Arise, O Lord our God' (Ἀνάστηθι Κύριε ὁ Θεός) for Sunday matins, while the third group, that of 'great *prokeimena*' (μεγάλα προκείμενα), consisted of ten possible chants.[222] One should also mention the *prokeimena* for weekdays during Great Lent, which consisted of psalms sung sequentially, from first to last, throughout Lent, and the *prokeimena* for sacraments such as marriage, which do not fall into these three neat categories.[223] As has been noted, the texts for this responsorial psalmody are psalms, although verses from two biblical canticles, namely Daniel 3 and Luke 1, also feature among the repertoire of Byzantine *prokeimena*. In most of the forty-eight *prokeimena*, the refrains are not from the first verse of the psalm but are selected from some other verse. However, the majority of *prokeimena* verses from psalms—thirty-one to be precise—do begin with the first verse of their source—whether a psalm or a biblical canticle.[224]

The Propsalmon

The *propsalmon* (πρόψαλμον) is a technical term derived from the verb προψάλλειν, 'to sing in anticipation', or perhaps 'to sing in the presence of', 'to sing before someone'.[225] Although this specific term is rarely found in Greek sources, it does appear in two texts that are significant for liturgical history. One

---

[219] Leeb, *Die Gesänge*, 50–1.   [220] Renoux, *Hymnes de la résurrection* I, 14–17.

[221] Hintze, *Das byzantinische Prokeimena-Repertoire*, 11–12 and Harris, 'The Byzantine Prokeimenon', 135 (for both, see n. 205 here).

[222] Hintze, *Das byzantinische Prokeimena-Repertoire*, 12–16 and Harris, 'The Byzantine Prokeimenon', 134 (for both, see n. 205 here).

[223] Alexopoulos, *Presanctified Liturgy*, 167 and 329–34.

[224] Harris, 'The Byzantine Prokeimenon' (see n. 205 here), 134.

[225] ὁ Δαβίδ, τὸν ἐπιτάφιον προψάλλει ψαλμόν ('David sings the funeral psalm in anticipation'). St Asterios, bishop of Amasea, Εἰς τὸν αὐτὸν ε΄ ψαλμὸν, ἄλλως. Λόγος γ΄, PG 40:424A; Lampe, *Patristic Greek Lexicon*, s.v. προψάλλω (p. 1198). The Latin term used to translate προψάλλει is *praecinere*, which could also mean 'to introduce or lead the singing'. See P. G. W. Glare, *Oxford Latin Dictionary* (Oxford: Clarendon, 1983), s.v. *praecino* (p. 1423).

is the *Narration of the Abbots John and Sophronius*, where the *propsalmon* is listed as one of the hymns sung according to tone and requiring chanters to execute it properly.[226] The second occurrence is in a sixth-century Syriac document from western Syria that details the ceremony of a bishop's visit (*adventus*)—a document recopied and preserved in a much later manuscript, *Charfet Fonds patriarcal 87* (19th cent.), then published by the Syrian Catholic Patriarch Ignatius Ephrem Rahmani (1848–1929). In this source, during the Liturgy of the Word, the chanter ascends the bema and announces 'a psalm of David' (*Ψαλμὸς τοῦ Δαυΐδ*). The archdeacon orders the chanter to sing (*Πρόψαλλε*), who then sings the *propsalmon*. The archdeacon then directs the congregation to sing along (*ὑποψάλλωμεν*). The same instructions are repeated by the archdeacon for the Alleluia, except that the last formula is longer: 'Let us all sing together in harmony' (*Συμφώνως πάντες ὑποψάλλωμεν*).[227]

Although the use of a verbal form (here in the subjunctive, *ὑποψάλλωμεν*) may make it seem that these are invitations and not actual technical terms, certain manuscripts confirm that the noun *propsalmon* can be used as a technical liturgical term. Marginal notes around the readings in *Sinai Gr. 212* (9th cent.) include rubrics for the *propsalmon* (see Table 3.3).

It is worth noting that the psalms associated here with certain commemorations of saints are completely different from those in the standard Byzantine repertoire identified by Hintze.[228] The responsorial psalmody for Prophets (fol. 104v) is the only one in the manuscript that is clearly called 'psalm' and not *propsalmon*. Thus it should be noted that, in this source, the responsorial psalm is called *propsalmon* before Gospels, but, before an Epistle, it is called simply a psalm. A later manuscript of JAS, *Vatican Gr. 1970* (13th cent.), refers to the responsorial psalmody as a *propsalmon*, not as a *prokeimenon*.[229]

The Hypopsalma

The *hypopsalma* (*τὸ ὑπόψαλμα*), plural *hypopsalmata* (*τὰ ὑποψάλματα*), 'chanted response', is also used to indicate responsorial psalmody.[230] Leeb

[226] Longo, 'Narrazione', 254; Taft, 'Worship on Sinai', 152.

[227] Patriarch Ignatius Ephraem Rahmani, *Vetusta documenta liturgica* (Studia Syriaca 3, Scharfe, Lebanon: Typis Patriarchalibus, 1908), 16–22; Gabriel Khouri-Sarkis, 'Réception d'un évêque syrien au VIᵉ siècle', *L'Orient Syrien* 2 (1957), 137–84, here 161; Mateos, *Parole*, 9. The text has been re-examined and translated by Sebastian Brock as 'an episcopal *adventus* in Syriac' and is to appear under this title in a forthcoming Festschrift edited by Elena Draghici-Vasilescu. My thanks to Sebastian Brock for sending me a copy of his article in advance of publication.

[228] See Hintze, *Das byzantinische Prokeimena-Repertoire* (in n. 205 here), 13–16 for a table and index of the Byzantine *prokeimena*.

[229] λέγουσιν οἱ ἀναγινώσκοντες πρόψαλμα· καὶ ἀπόστολον· καὶ στιχολογίαν ('The readers say the propsalma and the Epistle and the verses'), fol. 66v. See also Leeb, *Die Gesänge*, 54.

[230] Lampe, *Patristic Greek Lexicon*, 1465; Mateos, *Parole*, 8; Parpulov, *Byzantine Psalters*, 69 and 100; Irina V. Starikova, 'Ипопсалмы', ПЭ 26:175–6.

Table 3.3. *Propsalmon in Sinai Gr. 212* (9th cent.)

	Commemoration	Propsalmon (Marginal Note)	Accompanying Scriptural Reading
fol. 69r	Martyrs	Φοβήθ[ητε τὸν Κύριον πάντες οἱ ἅγιοι] ('Fear the Lord, all you his saints', Ps 33:10)	Mt 10:16–22
fol. 73r	Martyrs (other)	1. Φοβ[ήθητε...] ('Fear the Lord...' Ps 33:10) 2. Θαυμαστὸς [ὁ Θεὸς ἐν τοῖς ἁγίοις αὐτοῦ] ('God is wonderful in his saints', Ps 67:36)	Mt 10:24–33
fol. 78r	St Stephen	Ἔθηκας ἐπὶ τὴν κεφαλὴν [αὐτοῦ στέφανον...] ('You have placed upon his head a crown', Ps 20:4b)	Jn 12:24–6
fol. 82v	Women Virgins and Martyrs	Ἀπενεχθήσον[ται τῷ βασιλεῖ παρθένοι...] ('The virgins behind her shall be brought to the king', Ps 44:15)	Mt 25:1–13
fol. 87r	Venerable Monks	Οἱ ἀγαπῶν[τες τὸν Κύριον, μισεῖτε πονηρά...] ('You who love the Lord, hate evil', Ps 96:10)	Mt 5:1–12a
fol. 90r	Hierarchs	[Illegible]	Jn 10:11–16
fol. 92v	Archangels	Ὁ ποιῶν τοὺς ἀγγέλους [αὐτοῦ πνεύματα...] ('He makes angels his spirits', Ps 103:4)	Mt 16:24–27
fol. 104v	Prophets	Μὴ ἅπτεσθε τῶν χριστῶν μου καὶ ἐν τοῖς προφήταις μου μὴ πονηρεύεσθε ('Do not touch my anointed ones, and do not act wickedly towards my prophets', Ps 104:15)	1 Cor 12:27–13:3

Note: An earlier version of this table has appeared in Galadza, 'Two Sources of the Jerusalem Lectionary', 105–6.

suggests that in the GL the term *hypopsalma* should be used instead of *hypakoe*, to indicate refrains for biblical odes.[231] As we shall see, the term is most often used outside the context of the Liturgy of the Word.

An account from the fifth-century life of St Melanie (383–439) at a women's monastery on the Mount of Olives also uses the *hypopsalma* in the context of matins:

Ἦν γὰρ αὐτῶν ὁ μὲν νυκτερινὸς κανὼν τρία ὑποψάλματα καὶ τρεῖς ἀναγνώσεις καὶ πρὸς τοῖς ὀρθρινοῖς ἀντίφωνα δεκαπέντε.[232]	Their night office included three *hypopsalmata*, three readings, and fifteen antiphons for the morning office.

[231] Leeb, *Die Gesänge*, 222.
[232] Gerontius, *Vie de Sainte Mélanie*, ed. and trans. by Denys Gorce (SC 90, Paris: Éditions du Cerf, 1962), 216. A similar practice is confirmed by St John Cassian as part of vigil from Friday to Saturday. See Cassianus, *De institutis coenobiorum*, ed. by Michael Petschenig, rev. and suppl. Gottfriend Kreuz (Corpus Scriptorum Ecclesiasticorum Latinorum 17, Vienna: Österreichische Akademie der Wissenschaften, 2004), 43 (III, 8–9); Mateos, *Parole*, 8.

This account goes on to give explanations for praying at the third, sixth, and ninth hours of the day. These explanations are based on events from Acts and Genesis rather than on the Marcan account of the Passion of Christ, which suggests a knowledge of Scripture broader than the Gospels, as well as an alternative tradition about the meaning of the times of the Liturgy of the Hours—a tradition that differs from that of *Apostolic Tradition* and St Cyprian of Carthage (d. 258).[233]

The life of St Hypatius of Rouphinianai (d. 466), abbot of a monastery in the suburbs of Constantinople, mentions that the saint intoned the *hypopsalmon*, which in this case was 'Come let us sing to the Lord' (Psalm 94:1). The saint did so while distributing Communion to the brothers of the monastery, who in turn responded with the Communion verse.[234]

Because the descriptor *hypopsalma* is used in Jerusalem and Constantinople for psalm verses in services that range from matins to the eucharistic Divine Liturgy, its occurrnce cannot serve either as a distinguishing factor between Hagiopolitan and Constantinopolitan liturgical practice or a measure of liturgical Byzantinization.

The Epakouston

Etymologically, the noun *epakouston* (τὸ ἐπακουστόν, often used in the plural, τὰ ἐπακουστά) is related to the noun *hypakoe* (ὑπακοή), since both derive from compounds of the same verb ἀκούειν, 'to hear' (ἐπακούειν and ὑπακούειν, both meaning 'give ear to', 'pay attention'), and both came to mean, as nouns, 'that which is to be responded'.[235] In this sense the word can either refer to a simple response or have a technical usage.[236] Mateos concedes that the *hypakoe* is closer to a troparion and the Syriac *'enyana* than to a *prokeimenon*.[237] It is

---

[233] Paul F. Bradshaw, Maxwell E. Johnson, and L. Edward Phillips, *The Apostolic Tradition: A Commentary*, ed. by Harold W. Attridge (Minneapolis, MN: Augsburg Fortress, 2002), 194–215 (§ 41: 1–18); Taft, *Hours*, 13–29, 77. For more on the life of Melanie, see Alexander Kazhdan and Nancy Patterson-Ševčenko, 'Melania the Younger', ODB II, 1331–2.

[234] Καὶ ἐν ἐκστάσει ἤδη γενόμενος, ἐν τῷ διδόναι τὴν εὐλογίαν ἄλλου παρακρατοῦντος τὴν χεῖρα αὐτοῦ, ὑποβάλλει ὑπόψαλμα· «Δεῦτε ἀγαλλιασώμεθα τῷ Κυρίῳ.» Ψάλλοντες δὲ οἱ ἀδελφοὶ καὶ τὴν κοινωνίαν δεχόμενοι ἐκ τῆς χειρὸς αὐτοῦ ἔκλαιον πάντες γινώσκοντες, ὅτι ἀληθῶς ἀγαλλιῶνται οἱ ἄγγελοι οἱ παραλαμβάνοντες αὐτὸν καὶ διὰ τοῦτο ἔψαλλον· «Δεῦτε ἀγαλλιασώμεθα τῷ Κυρίῳ». Callinicos, *Vie d'Hypatios*, ed. and trans. by Gerhardus J. M. Bartelink (SC 177, Paris: Éditions du Cerf, 1971), 286–8. See also Alexander Kazhdan, 'Hypatios of Rouphinianai', ODB II, 963; Alice-Mary Talbot, 'Rouphinianai', ODB III, 1814.

[235] In the neuter, the term is equated with προκείμενον. See Trapp, *Lexikon zur byzantinischen Gräzität*, 549. For discussion of the term, see Dmitrievskii, Древнѣйшіе Патріаршіе Типиконы, 81; Bertonière, *Easter Vigil*, 80–7. The term is absent from Mateos, *Parole*; see Mateos, *Typikon*, vol. 2, 66–76, and 294, 306–7 (index).

[236] For example: Χαίροις, νικοποιὲ σταυρέ, δεομένων δοτὴρ, καί βοώντων ἐπακουστά. St John Chrysostom, Εἰς τὴν προσκύνησιν τοῦ τιμίου ξύλου, PG 62:753; CPG 4672; BHG 415.

[237] Mateos, *Parole*, 20–1.

worth noting that the term *hypakoe* (ი̇ბაკ̇ო, *ibakoy*) is used in the GL to designate the verse sung instead of the *trisagion* on Holy Saturday.[238] *Hypakoe* is also used in the GL for the four hymns sung during the procession preceding the water blessing on Theophany that are part of the current Byzantine rite.[239]

The *epakouston*, on the other hand, is a brief psalm verse that corresponds to the *prokeimenon*. Bertonière identifies three possible *epakousta*: (1) a simple psalm verse; (2) a psalm verse with Christian adaptation through the addition of the word 'Christ'; or (3) a psalm verse with additional hymnographic modification.[240] There are also parallels between the *epakouston* and Egeria's description of three psalms at the Sunday vigil,[241] as well as the '*prokeimena evangelica*' [*sic*] in the GL.[242] The Typikon of the Anastasis includes the *epakouston* (τὸ ἐπακουστόν) and a psalm verse before Gospel readings for matins of Easter Week, but it never appears at the eucharistic liturgy.[243] In fact the term *prokeimenon* is used for the responsorial psalmody at the Divine Liturgy that immediately follows the same matins where the *epakouston* was sung.[244]

The Mesodion

Etymologically, the *mesodion* (μεσῴδιον) is a biblical hymn (ᾠδή) placed in the middle (μέσον) between two readings. It functions in the same way as a responsorial psalm. The monks John and Sophronius were surprised not to find the *mesodion* at the third and sixth odes of matins when they visited Nilus on Sinai. This, however, should not prompt us to equate the *mesodion* with a troparion or another type of hymn found at that point of matins. During their exchange, all three monks agree that the former is equivalent in execution to 'The Lord is God' (Θεὸς Κύριος), which is performed in the manner of a responsorial psalm.[245]

The *mesodion* is also equivalent to the Constantinopolitan *prokeimenon*, but it is of Palestinian origin.[246] Certain sources, such as the Gospel lectionary in

---

[238] Ὅσοι εἰς Χριστὸν ἐβαπτίσθητε ('As many as have been baptized into Christ'); (რომელთა ეკა ხართა გილებისა...). GL § 736.
[239] GL appendix § 27.
[240] Bertonière, *Easter Vigil*, 80–6, esp. 86. See also Dmitrievskii, *Древнѣйшіе Патріаршіе Типиконы*, 81.
[241] Egeria, *Itinéraire*, § 24: 9 (= p. 242 Maraval).
[242] GL § 741; Bertonière, *Easter Vigil*, 81.
[243] Papadopoulos-Kerameus, *Anastasis Typikon*, 211, 220, 227, 235, 244, 252.
[244] See Papadopoulos-Kerameus, *Anastasis Typikon*, 211.
[245] Following Stefano Parenti, 'Mesedi – μεσῴδιον', in idem, *A oriente e occidente di Costantinopoli*, here 100. See also Longo, 'Narrazione', 253; Skaballanovich, *Толковый Типиконъ*, vol. 2, 209–15.
[246] See Brightman, *Eastern Liturgies*, 582; 'Mesedi' in Peter D. Day, *The Liturgical Dictionary of Eastern Christianity* (Collegeville, MN.: The Liturgical Press, 1992), 191; Stefano Parenti,

Besançon Bibliothèque Municipale Gr. 42 (13th cent.), use the terms inter-changeably: '*prokeimena* and *mesodia* of the liturgy according to the tone' ('*προκείμενα καὶ μεσῴδια τῆς λειτουργίας κατὰ ἦχον*').[247] The eighth-century Euchologion *Barberini Gr. 336* uses both terms, but reserves *prokeimenon* for those offices that have a connection to the Constantinopolitan cathedral, such as vespers, matins, and PRES, while *mesodion* is retained for services of Palestinian origin, such as the series of eight psalms and lections for each day of the octave after monastic tonsure and profession.[248] Unlike the Con-stantinopolitan *prokeimenon*, which during the tenth century could still in-clude multiple psalm verses in its refrain, the *mesodion* in *Barberini Gr. 336* consistently has only one verse.[249] Other southern Italian Euchologia use the term *mesodion* for the order of marriage rites, funerals, kneeling vespers (*γονυκλισία*) of Pentecost, and the Hours of Good Friday.[250] The terms *prokeimenon* and *mesodion* are also found side by side in some Triodia and Pentekostaria copied at Grottaferrata.[251]

However, apart from the account of John and Sophronius, our Hagiopolite liturgical manuscripts do not mention the *mesodion*.

Lection(s)

The variable scriptural lections read during JAS were directly connected to the movable and fixed cycles of the liturgical year.[252] The AL contained up to three readings and the GL could have up to five readings at the eucharistic liturgy, including both Old Testament and New Testament readings.

Manuscripts of JAS are unclear about the number and type of readings.[253] Although Greek versions of the Liturgy of St Mark have only one Epistle reading at this point, Coptic and Ethiopian versions of the Liturgy of St Mark

---

'Mesedi – *μεσῴδιον*', in idem, *A oriente e occidente di Costantinopoli*, 91–102, especially 94–7; Findikyan, *Commentary*, 463–4.

[247] fol. 140r. Aland, *Kurzgefaßte Liste*, 255 (*ℓ* 583); Stefano Parenti, 'Mesedi – *μεσῴδιον*', in idem, *A oriente e occidente di Costantinopoli*, 94.

[248] Parenti and Velkovska, *Barberini 336*, 227–9 (§ 256.1–8).

[249] Unfortunately no text of any *prokeimenon* is given in *Barberini Gr. 336* (8th cent.) in order to confirm this within the same manuscript. For examples of *prokeimena* at the Divine Liturgy in Constantinople with more than one verse, see Mateos, *Typicon*, vol. 1, 20, 158, etc., and vol. 2, 316–17 (index). See also Stefano Parenti, 'Mesedi – *μεσῴδιον*', in idem, *A oriente e occidente di Costantinopoli*, 95.

[250] Ibid., 94–6.

[251] *Vatican Gr. 771* (11th–12th cent.) and *Grottaferrata Δ.β. XVII* (11th–12th cent.). Ibid., 97.

[252] For more on the Jerusalem calendar and lectionary system, see Chapters 4 and 5 in this book.

[253] For the question of Old Testament readings, see Chapter 5, 'Epistle Readings in the Jerusalem Lectionary'.

have up to four readings.[254] This agrees with Georgian manuscripts of JAS such as *Sinai Geo. N. 63* (10th cent.), *Sinai Geo. N. 22* (10th cent.), and *Tbilisi Centre of Manuscripts A-86* (11th cent.), which indicate more than one lection, either from the Old Testament or from the New Testament, to be read at this point during the Liturgy of the Word.[255] Greek sources explicitly refer to the Epistle but are silent about Old Testament readings.[256] Phountoulis notes that *Paris Supplement Gr. 303* (16th cent.) is the only Greek manuscript of JAS to prescribe an Old Testament reading in JAS, although Mercier omits this information in his edition.[257] As Mercier himself notes, the manuscript is an unreliable copy made by an unreliable copyist, Constantine Palaeocappa (*c.*1560), who is known to have added and supplemented information in manuscripts where it was absent.[258] Thus, while Old Testament readings in Greek at JAS have been preserved in lectionaries such as *Sinai Gr. N.E. МГ 8* (10th cent.) and many Georgian manuscripts of JAS call for an Old Testament reading, there is no reliable explicit witness to Old Testament readings in Greek manuscripts of JAS.

The Alleluia

Although manuscripts of JAS do not mention the singing of Alleluia before the Gospel, we know from the AL, the GL, and other lectionaries that it was present at this point, both in Greek and in Georgian sources. Generally the manuscripts only provide the first verse of the psalm, as do *St Petersburg RNB Gr. 44* (9th cent.) and *Sinai Gr. 212* (9th cent.). Whether or not the whole

---

[254] Cuming, *Liturgy of St Mark*, 97–8.

[255] *Liturgia ibero-graeca*, 50 (§26). The English translation in *Liturgia ibero-graeca*, 51, mistakenly takes the word for 'lections' (სკითხავნი, *sakitxavni*) to be in the singular, i.e. 'reading' instead of 'readings'.

[256] Mercier, *Liturgie de Saint Jacques*, 168–9; Kazamias, Θεία Λειτουργία τοῦ Ἁγίου Ἰακώβου, 162.

[257] Ἐκ τῶν χειρογράφων τῆς λειτουργίας τοῦ Ἰακώβου μόνον ὁ κῶδιξ Παρισίων S. 303 μαρτυρεῖ ὅτι ἀναγινώσκονται «διεξοδικώτατα τὰ ἱερὰ λόγια τῆς Παλαιᾶς Διαθήκης καὶ τῶν Προφητῶν» ('From among the manuscripts of the liturgy of James, only the codex Paris S. 303 testifies that they read "in particular the holy words of the Old Testament and the Prophets"'). Ioannis M. Phountoulis, Θεία Λειτουργία Ἰακώβου τοῦ Ἀδελφοθέου (Thessalonike: Ἐκδόσεις Πουρνάρα, 1970), 14.

[258] See the entries for Κωνσταντῖνος Παλαιόκαππας in *Repertorium der Griechischen Kopisten 800–1600*, 3 vols, ed. by Ernst Gamillscheg and Dieter Harlfinger (Veröffentlichungen der Kommission für Byzantinistik 3, Vienna: Verlag der Österreichischen Akademie der Wissenschaften, 1981–1997), vol. 1: 126 (§ 225), vol. 2: 124–5 (§ 316), vol. 3: 139 (§ 364); François Joseph Leroy, 'Les énigmes Palaeocappa: Notes sur un copiste grec du XVIᵉ siècle', in *Recueil commémoratif du Xᵉ anniversaire de la Faculté de philosophie et lettres* (Publications de l'Université Lovanium de Kinshasa 22, Louvain: Éditions Nauwelaerts, 1968), 191–206. See also 'The Origins and History of the Liturgy of St James' in this chapter. For a description of this manuscript, see Mercier, *Liturgie de Saint Jacques*, 141 (= G in Mercier's apparatus).

psalm was recited is unclear.[259] In the AL, the psalm was chosen because of its connection to the stational liturgy site or because of the theme of the commemoration.[260]

The *Ektene*

Certain manuscripts of JAS, both Greek and Georgian, include an *ektene* (ἐκτενής; კურექსი, *kuerek'si*) at this point, between the Alleluia and the Gospel.[261] These are *Messina Gr. 177* (11th cent.), *Vatican Gr. 1970* (13th cent.),[262] and *Sinai Geo. N. 22* (10th cent.).[263] The *ektene*, or litany, makes no specific reference to the Gospel but includes petitions for the church, the hierarchy, the ruler, the city, and the faithful who are present and awaiting God's mercy. This list concludes with a petition similar to that found today at the *lite* (λιτή) in the Byzantine rite: 'O God, save your people and bless your inheritance' (Σῶσον, ὁ Θεός, τὸν λαόν σου καὶ εὐλόγησον τὴν κληρονομίαν σου). After the general commemoration of the Theotokos (Τῆς παναγίας, ἀχράντου), the petition adds the names of specific saints. The list of saints often varies from one litany to the next, even in the same manuscript; but each litany usually includes a great number of Old Testament figures and local Hagiopolitan saints.[264]

The Gospel Reading

The specific rites surrounding the reading the Gospel in JAS are not found in all manuscripts, since the liturgical books containing JAS are often intended

---

[259] Renoux, *Introduction*, 58.

[260] AL, 38–40. Renoux notes that it is difficult to make a general rule for the presence or absence of the Alleluia only on the basis of the information in the AL. For more on the Alleluia, see Mateos, *Parole*, 134–5; Leeb, *Die Gesänge*, 81–99.

[261] Geoffrey J. Cuming, 'The Litanies in the Liturgy of St James', *Ecclesia Orans* 3 (1986), 175–80, here 176. The Greek term derives from an adjective, ἐκτενής, which meant 'stretched out'. For the etymology of the Georgian term კურექსი (*kuerek'si*), see Gabriele Winkler, 'Einige Randemerkungen zum österlichen Gottesdienst in Jerusalem vom 4. bis 8. Jahrhundert', OCP 39 (1973):481–90, here 481–2.

[262] Mercier, *Liturgie de Saint Jacques*, 170–2.

[263] *Liturgia ibero-graeca*, 50–1, 146, 238–9, 311–13.

[264] For other similar litanies, see *Sinai Gr. 1040* (14th cent.), fol. 7v–8r; Dmitrievskii, *Богослуженіе страсной и пасхальной седмицъ*, 272–80; Mercier, *Liturgie de Saint Jacques*, 166–8, 174, 188. For the Georgian version, see Bernard Outtier and Stéphane Verhelst, 'La *kéryxie catholique* de la liturgie de Jérusalem en Géorgien (*Sin. 12 et 54*)', *Archiv für Liturgiewissenschaft* 42 (2000), 41–64, especially 55 and 57–9. The complete text of the litanies is not present in *Liturgia ibero-graeca*. See also Skaballanovich, *Толковый Типиконъ*, vol. 2, 91–4. See also Chapter 4, 'Joint Commemorations of Old Testament Figures', for more on these litanies.

for the presider, not for the deacon or chanters. Thus these manuscripts contain prayers before and after the Gospel.[265] Certain Greek sources, such as *Messina Gr. 177* (11th cent.), do, however, contain the rubrics for the priest and the deacon in the dialogue that introduces the Gospel reading:

Ὁ Ἀρχιδιάκονος· Ὀρθοί. Ἀκούσωμεν τοῦ ἁγίου εὐαγγελίου.	*Archdeacon*: Stand aright. Let us listen to the holy Gospel.
Ὁ Ἱερεύς· Εἰρήνη πᾶσιν.	*Priest*: Peace be with all.
Ὁ Διάκονος· Ἐκ τοῦ κατὰ Ματθαῖον.	*Deacon*: [Gospel] according to Matthew.
Ὁ Ἀρχιδιάκονος· Πρόσχωμεν.	*Archdeacon*: Let us be attentive.
Καὶ ὅτε πληρωθῇ τὸν Εὐαγγέλιον λέγει ὁ Διάκονος· Σχολάσωμεν...[266]	*And when the Gospel is complete, the Deacon says*: Be at ease...

Both a deacon and an archdeacon are also mentioned in the Typikon of the Anastasis, where the division of their duties surrounding the readings is clear and distinct.[267] The indication of the Gospel according to Matthew here in *Messina Gr. 177* (11th cent.) certainly points to it just as a model; it does not mean that only the Gospel of Matthew was read. Nevertheless, in the AL Matthew was the most frequently read Gospel.[268] In the GL, Matthew and Luke were read most frequently, probably due to the expansion of liturgical feasts that commemorated the early life of Christ and John the Baptist.[269]

THE LITURGY OF THE EUCHARIST

The Liturgy of the Eucharist had fewer variable elements than the Liturgy of the Word, since its primary focus was not the reading of Scripture in the lectionary but rather the eucharistic gifts, their transfer to the altar, their consecration during the anaphora, and their distribution to the faithful during Communion. Until the fourteenth century, the only variable element of the liturgy in Constantinople after the Gospel was the Communion verse. The Marian troparion 'It is truly right' (Ἄξιον ἐστίν), *heirmos* of the ninth biblical ode (Luke 1:46–55) sung towards the end of the anaphora during the diptychs for the departed, only became a fixed element of CHR in the fourteenth century, when it replaced the more common hymn found in earlier manuscripts of CHR, 'Rejoice, full of grace' (Χαῖρε κεχαριτωμένη), which was also found in

---

[265] *Liturgia ibero-graeca*, 50–4.
[266] Assemani, *Missale Hierosolymitanum*, 71–2. See also Mateos, *Parole*, 141–6.
[267] Papadopoulos-Kerameus, *Anastasis Typikon*, 25, 200, 201.   [268] AL, 37.
[269] See the scriptural index of the GL.

Table 3.4. Structure of the Liturgy of the Eucharist of St James

---

1. **Hymn for hand washing**, followed by the
2. **Hymn of the holy gifts** during the transfer of the gifts
3. Anaphora
4. Ektene and Lord's Prayer
5. 'Holy things for the holy' exclamation and Fraction
6. **Prayer for those bringing offerings**
7. Communion accompanied by
8. **Hymn for Communion**
9. **Prayer/hymn for dismissal**
10. Return of the clergy to the diakonikon/skeuophylakion with additional prayers

---

JAS.[270] Once one of these hymns found a permanent place within the structure of the Divine Liturgy of CHR or BAS, festive or thematic variants connected to particular commemorations of the liturgical year could be introduced, but not before.

In Jerusalem, however, the variety of hymnody in JAS continued from the Liturgy of the Word into the Liturgy of the Eucharist, with particular and changing hymnody for the ritual hand washing, for the transfer of the gifts, and for Communion. Table 3.4 gives a simplified outline of the Liturgy of the Eucharist of JAS, indicating through bold the variable elements that depended on particular commemorations.[271]

The Hymn for Hand Washing

The hymn for hand washing (ჴელთაბანისაჲ, *ḫelt'abanisay*), as the name suggests, was sung while the clergy washed their hands before the transfer of the gifts.[272] St Cyril of Jerusalem mentions the washing of hands—the *lavabo* rite—in his *Mystagogical Catecheses* but, surprisingly, not the transfer of the gifts.[273] Tarchnishvili thought that the text related to this ritual was a prayer, but then, when he published the GL, he retracted this view and presented the text in question as a hymn.[274] This goes to show how important it is to look at lectionaries alongside Euchologia in order to understand liturgical rites and

---

[270] Winkler, 'Die Interzessionen I', 320–36; Winkler, 'Die Interzessionen II', 351–4; Taft, *Diptychs*, 118–19; Follieri, *Initia hymnorum*, vol. 5.1, 57.

[271] For a more detailed outline, including prayer incipits, see Kazamias, Θεία Λειτουργία τοῦ Ἁγίου Ἰακώβου, 243–52; *Liturgia ibero-graeca*, 189–92.

[272] Leeb, *Die Gesänge*, 99–113.

[273] *Mystagogical Catecheses*, 146–8 (Catechesis 5:2). See Taft, *Great Entrance*, 163–4.

[274] *Liturgia ibero-graeca*, 315–16.

practices described in liturgical manuscripts. That we are dealing with a hymn and not with a prayer becomes evident once we look at the diaconal command in JAS:

Οἱ ψάλται· στιχηρόν. [Διάκονος·] Ἐν εἰρήνῃ Χριστοῦ ψάλλατε.[275]	*Chanters*: Sticheron. [*Deacon*:] Sing in the peace of Christ.

In the Georgian version, the order between injunction and hymn is clearer, although Tarchnishvili's confusion regarding the term *xelt'abanisay* is understandable:

დიაკონმან: მშჳდობით გალობდით. და ჴელთაბანისაჲ.[276]	*Deacon*: Chant in peace. *And the [hymn of] hand washing [is sung].*

The *sticheron* mentioned in the Greek version is the same hymn for hand washing mentioned in Georgian. Although there are at least sixty-two different Georgian hymns for hand washing,[277] there are to my knowledge no extant Greek hymns bearing this or a similar title. Their Greek counterparts are called simply a 'verse' (στίχος) or a *sticheron* (στιχηρόν), as seen in *St Petersburg RNB Gr. 44* (9th cent.) for the Sunday services.[278]

The reason for the disappearance of this hymn is presumably its thematic content, which Leeb associates with the preceding Gospel reading from the Liturgy of the Word.[279] Taking Cheesefare Sunday as an example, Leeb identifies three themes in the Gospel reading from Matthew 6:1–33 prescribed in the GL—fasting, prayer, and service to the Lord—and finds these same themes in the hymn for hand washing. The text is as follows:

ვიწყოთ, ერნო, უბიწოსა მარხვისა, რომელ არს სულთა ცხორებაა. ვჰმონებდეთ უფალსა შიშით, ზედა სიხარულისაა ვიცხოთ თავთა ჩუენთა და წყლითა სიწმიდისაათა პირნი	Let us begin, O people, the pure fast, which is the salvation of our souls. Let us serve the Lord with fear, let us anoint our heads with the oil of good deeds and let us was our faces with the waters of purity. Let us not use empty phrases

---

[275] *Sinai Gr. 1040* (14th cent.), fol. 2v–3r; Dmitrievskii, Богослуженіе страсной и пасхальной седмицъ, 271.

[276] *Liturgia ibero-graeca*, 56–7.

[277] For an index of these hymns in the GL, see Leeb, *Die Gesänge*, 106–10.

[278] *St Petersburg RNB Gr. 44* (9th cent.), fol. 21v, 34v; Thibaut, *Monuments*, 7*.

[279] Leeb, *Die Gesänge*, 106.

ჩუენნი განვბანნეთ. ნუემცა
მრავლისმეტყუელ ვართ ლოცვასა შინა,
არამედ, ვითარცა გუისწავიებს, ესრეთ
ვღაღადებდეთ: მამაო ჩუენო, რომელი
ხარ ცათა შინა, მოგუიტევენ შეცოდებანი
ჩუენნი, ვითარცა კაცთმოყუარე ხარ.²⁸⁰

in prayer, but as we have been taught, let us
cry out: Our Father, who are in heaven, forgive
us our trespasses, for you are the lover of
mankind.

The parallels between the themes of Matthew 6 and the text of the hymn,
including the direct quotations from the Lord's Prayer, are unmistakeable.
Like many other Hagiopolitan hymns, this Georgian hymn was not lost in the
process of Byzantinization but migrated to the end of matins on another day
of Lent, so that it has been preserved in Greek within the Byzantine rite today
as a *sticheron* in the *aposticha* of matins for Tuesday of the First Week of
Great Lent.²⁸¹ The same connection between the themes of the Gospel
reading and the hymn for hand washing is apparent in other cases as well,
for instance in the hymn for hand washing on Pascha, which comments on
Mark 16:1–8, or on various feasts of saints. In all these cases, the hymn is
either a hymnographic response—an *Antwortsgesang*—to the Gospel reading
or a chant that connects the themes of the Gospel to the saint or commemoration being celebrated.²⁸²

Ultimately, the disappearance of the Jerusalem lectionary led to the
decline of the hymn for hand washing. The absence of readings from this
lectionary made the hymns inspired by it lose their relevance; hence
such hymns were abandoned from the transfer of the gifts in the Liturgy
of the Eucharist. However, the conservative structure of JAS preserved
the position of the hymn for hand washing, putting in its place the hymn
of the holy gifts. And, as we shall see in the next section, this hymn was
in turn replaced by the *cheroubikon* or other related hymns sung in
Constantinople.

After hand washing, the deacon dismisses those who are unable to pray due
to weakness, unworthiness, or lack of initiation and summons all to 'recognize
one another' (ἀλλήλους ἐπίγνωτε· [ἀλλήλους γνωρίσατε])—that is, to spot
anyone in the gathering who was not a member, perhaps a remnant of the
disciplina arcani, or 'discipline of the secret', whereby the uninitiated were
not permitted to participate in the sacraments in order to preserve the secret of

²⁸⁰ GL § 327; *Iadgari*, 100; Leeb, *Die Gesänge*, 110–11.
²⁸¹ Ἀρξώμεθα, λαοί, τῆς ἀμώμου νηστείας, ἥτις ἐστὶ τῶν ψυχῶν σωτηρία· δουλεύσωμεν τῷ
Κυρίῳ ἐν φόβῳ· ἐλαίῳ ἐγκρατείας τὰς κεφαλὰς ἀλείψωμεν, καὶ ὕδατι ἀωνείας τὰ πρόσωπα
νιψώμεθα· μὴ βαττολογήσωμεν ἐν ταῖς προσευχαῖς, ἀλλ' ὡς ἐδιδάχθημεν, οὕτω βοήσωμεν·
Πάτερ ἡμῶν, ὁ ἐν τοῖς οὐρανοῖς, ἄφες ἡμῖν τὰ παραπτώματα ἡμῶν, ὡς φιλάνθρωπος. Τριῴδιον
κατανυκτικόν (Rome: n.p., 1879), 151; Follieri, *Initia hymnorum*, vol. 1, 176. See the Georgian
and English translations in this section at n. 280.
²⁸² Leeb, *Die Gesänge*, 111–13.

the mysteries—and to stand up.[283] Although several prayers are said by the presider at this point, none of them dwells on the action of washing one's hands. Instead they focus on the offering of incense and on the rites associated with the imminent transfer of gifts and anaphora.[284] This is in keeping with St Cyril's comments on hand washing: its purpose is not to clean one's hands from the external dirt but to purify oneself from sin.[285]

The Hymn of the Holy Gifts

The hymn of the holy gifts accompanied the procession of the holy gifts to the altar for the anaphora, a rite that later became known as 'the Great Entrance'.[286] The rite in Constantinople once involved the transfer of the gifts from the skeuophylakion to the altar of the church. For Jerusalem, Tarchnishvili originally translated the Georgian term *sicmidisay* (სიწმიდისაჲ) as 'hymn of sanctification',[287] but Leeb correctly understood it to mean 'hymn of the holy gifts',[288] with reference to the holy gifts being transferred at the time when the hymn was sung. As Taft notes, hymns were often introduced at the 'soft points' of the liturgy in order to cover periods of silence. Three examples of such points are (1) the beginning of the liturgy, when the entrance of the clergy is accompanied by the *introit*; (2) the transfer of the gifts; and (3) the end of the liturgical service.[289] In JAS, the transfer of the gifts was related to two separate hymns: the hymn for hand washing and the hymn of the holy gifts, which were designed to accompany the two distinct parts of the rite of the transfer of the gifts.

[283] Mercier, *Liturgie de Saint Jacques*, 176; Kazamias, Θεία Λειτουργία τοῦ Ἁγίου Ἰακώβου, 169; Taft, *Great Entrance*, 374. For the *disciplina arcani*, see Adolf Hampel, 'Arkandisziplin', in *Lexikon für Theologie und Kirche*, 3rd edn, ed. by Walter Kasper (Freiburg im Breisgau: Herder, 1993), 990–1; Alexander A. Tkachenko, 'Disciplina arcani', ПЭ 15:413–14.

[284] [πρόσδεξαι] ἐκ χειρὸς ἡμῶν τῶν ἁμαρτωλῶν τὸ θυμίαμα τοῦτο εἰς ὀσμὴν εὐωδίας, ὡς προσεδέξω τὴν προσφορὰν Ἄβελ καὶ Νῶε καὶ Ἀαρὼν καὶ Σαμουὴλ καὶ πάντων τῶν Ἁγίων σου' ('Receive from the hands of us sinners this incense as a sweet smelling fragrance, as you received the offering of Abel and Noah and Aaron and Samuel and of all your holy ones'). Kazamias, Θεία Λειτουργία τοῦ Ἁγίου Ἰακώβου, 171. For more on the *lavabo*, see Taft, *Great Entrance*, 163–77.

[285] Οὐ πάντως δὲ διὰ τοῦτο ἐδίδου διὰ τὸν σωματικὸν ῥύπον...Ἀλλὰ σύμβολον τοῦ δεῖν ἡμᾶς πάντων καθαρεύειν τῶν ἁμαρτημάτων τε καὶ ἀνομημάτων, τὸ νίψασθαι ('[The deacon] gave [the water to the priest] not at all because of bodily uncleanness...but the washing is a symbol that we all should be clean of sinfulness and unlawfulness'). *Mystagogical Catecheses*, 148 (Catechesis 5:2).

[286] For specific reference to the hymn during the Great Entrance, see Taft, *Great Entrance*, 70–6, 99–102, 112–16.

[287] *Sanctificatorum* or *sanctificationis*; for example, see GL § 1468 and 1492.

[288] 'Gesang der heiligen Gaben'. Leeb, *Die Gesänge*, 113–15.

[289] Robert F. Taft, SJ, 'How Liturgies Grow: The Evolution of the Byzantine Divine Liturgy', in idem, *Beyond East and West*, 204–5.

The Byzantine rite today knows three possible hymns for the Great Entrance at the Divine Liturgy.[290] The most frequently used one—the *cheroubikon*—is replaced only twice during the year: on Holy Thursday, when its place is taken by the hymn 'Your mystical supper' (Τοῦ δείπνου σου μυστικοῦ); and on Holy Saturday, when its place is taken by the hymn 'Let all mortal flesh keep silent' (Σιγησάτω πᾶσα σὰρξ βροτεία).[291] The hymn 'Your mystical supper' is already established in the Constantinopolitan Typikon of the Great Church, where there was very little variation for the fixed parts of the Divine Liturgy.[292] However, the hymn 'Let all mortal flesh keep silent' is not mentioned on Holy Saturday either in the Typikon of the Great Church or in the tenth-century Constantinopolitan Praxapostolos. In the former, the rubric explicitly calls for the *cheroubikon*, while the latter is silent concerning the Great Entrance hymn, not providing any instructions.[293] That the *cheroubikon* is replaced only during Holy Week calls to mind Baumstark's observation about the conservative nature of liturgy in solemn seasons, whereby 'primitive conditions are maintained with greater tenacity in the more sacred seasons of the Liturgical Year'.[294]

While Constantinople and the Byzantine rite prescribed variable Great Entrance hymns only during Holy Week, the variability of the hymns during the transfer of the gifts in Jerusalem was a constant feature. Hagiopolitan Georgian sources provide over twenty-six possible variants in the GL and twenty-three more in various manuscripts of the Oktoechos.[295] Two Greek sources also offer examples of the hymn of the holy gifts, which was known as 'the *sticheron* sung for the holy [gifts]' (Στιχηρὸν ψαλλόμενον εἰς τὰ ἅγια).[296] For Pascha, the Typikon of the Anastasis prescribes such a hymn to be sung in the first tone—'Today a holy Pascha has been revealed to us' (Πάσχα ἱερὸν ἡμῖν σήμερον)—along with the hymn that takes the *cheroubikon*'s place (ἀντὶ τοῦ χερουβικοῦ)—'You were raised from the tomb, O Christ' (Ἐξηγέρθης, Χριστέ, ἐκ τοῦ μνήματος). The copyist deliberately repeated both hymns from the preceding service of matins in the same manuscript and directed the reader to find the full text of the *stichera* for the holy gifts among

---

[290] Taft, *Great Entrance*, 54–5; Renoux, 'Hymne des saints dons', 295–7.

[291] Dmitri Conomos, 'Cheroubikon', NGDMM 5:571; Follieri, *Initia hymnorum*, vol. 3, 64.

[292] Mateos, *Typicon*, vol. 2, 76. For the history of the hymn, see Taft, *Great Entrance*, 54, 68–70, and 487–8; Taft and Parenti, *Storia della liturgia di S. Giovanni Crisostomo*, 174–180.

[293] Ibid., 90; Andreou, *Praxapostolos*, 201.

[294] Baumstark, *Comparative Liturgy*, 27. See also Robert Taft, SJ, 'Comparative Liturgy Fifty Years after Anton Baumstark', in *Liturgy Fifty Years after Baumstark*, 527, 535–8 and Robert Taft, SJ, 'Anton Baumstark's Comparative Liturgy Revisited', in *Liturgy Fifty Years after Baumstark*, 191–232, here 200, 206–8 ('Law 9').

[295] Leeb, *Die Gesänge*, 120–4; Renoux, 'Hymne des saints dons', 297–307.

[296] Papadopoulos-Kerameus, *Anastasis Typikon*, 201. See also Gerda Wolfram, 'Stichēron', NGDMM 24:386.

the hymns for matins.[297] *Stichera* for the holy gifts and hymns sung instead of the *cheroubikon* are also found on Palm Sunday and Holy Thursday in this manuscript.[298] The other source, St Petersburg RNB Gr. 44 (9th cent.), refers to this hymn as the '*sticheron* of the synaxis' (στιχηρὸν εἰς σύναξιν) on sixteen different days: eight Sundays and eight other commemorations.[299] Other Greek names for the hymn at the transfer of the gifts are 'verse' (singular στίχος), as found in St Petersburg RNB Gr. 44 (9th cent.), *stichera* or 'verses of the day' (στιχηρά or στίχοι κατὰ τὴν ἡμέραν) in Sinai Gr. 1040 (14th cent.), and '*kathisma* of the day' (τὸ κάθισμα τῆς ἡμέρας) in a very late manuscript used in Kazamias' edition of JAS, Alexandria Gr. 288 (911) (16th–17th cent.).[300]

In Greek manuscripts of JAS, the only chant other than the *cheroubikon* hymn is the hymn 'Let all mortal flesh' (Σιγησάτω πᾶσα σάρξ). Its text is as follows:[301]

Σιγησάτω πᾶσα σὰρξ βροτεία καὶ στήτω μετὰ φόβου καὶ τρόμου καὶ μηδὲν γήϊνον ἐν ἑαυτῇ λογιζέσθω· ὁ γὰρ βασιλεὺς τῶν βασιλευόντων, Χριστὸς ὁ Θεὸς ἡμῶν, προέρχεται σφαγιασθῆναι καὶ δοθῆναι εἰς βρῶσιν τοῖς πιστοῖς, προηγοῦνται δὲ τούτου οἱ χοροὶ τῶν ἀγγέλων μετὰ πάσης ἀρχῆς καὶ ἐξουσίας, τὰ πολυόμματα χερουβὶμ καὶ τὰ ἑξαπτέρυγα σεραφίμ, τὰς ὄψεις καλύπτοντα καὶ βοῶντα τὸν ὕμνον, ἀλληλούϊα.[302]	Let all mortal flesh keep silent and stand with fear and trembling, and let it take no thought of any earthly thing, for the King of Kings, Christ our God, comes forth to be slaughtered and to be given as food to the faithful. Before him go the choirs of angels with all principalities and powers, the many-eyed cherubim and the six-winged seraphim, covering their faces and crying the hymn: Alleluia.

However, not all sources of JAS include this hymn. Some, for example *Vatican Gr. 1970* (13th cent.), have 'Let all mortal flesh' (Σιγησάτω πᾶσα σάρξ) and provide the *cheroubikon* as an alternate hymn, while others, such as *Messina Gr. 177* (11th cent.), provide only the *cheroubikon*.[303] Although the hymn 'Let all mortal flesh' (Σιγησάτω πᾶσα σάρξ) has been associated with Hagiopolitan JAS and has become synonymous with modern editions and the revived celebration of JAS, 'Let all mortal flesh' is completely absent from the GL. In fact the hymn's earliest testimonies are all in the twelfth century: in the

[297] *Hagios Stavros Gr. 43* (1122), fol. 134r; Papadopoulos-Kerameus, *Anastasis Typikon*, 201–2.
[298] Papadopoulos-Kerameus, *Anastasis Typikon*, 25 and 106–7.
[299] Thibaut, *Monuments*, 1*–11*.
[300] Kazamias, Θεία Λειτουργία τοῦ Ἁγίου Ἰακώβου, 75–7, 169.
[301] Follieri, *Initia hymnorum*, vol. 3, 498; Taft, *Great Entrance*, 76–7; Parenti, 'Σιγησάτω πᾶσα σάρξ', 191–9.
[302] Mercier, *Liturgie de Saint Jacques*, 176.
[303] *Vatican Gr. 1970* (13th cent.), fol. 70r–70v; Assemani, *Missale Hierosolymitanum*, 75.

twelfth-century Constantinopolitan Psalter *Harvard University Houghton Library Gr. 3* it is called 'the *cheroubikon* of the Great Church' (Χερουβικὸν τῆς μεγάλης ἐκκλησίας) and prescribed to be sung in Tone 2;[304] and it is mentioned as the hymn of the Great Entrance of BAS on Holy Saturday in the Prophetologion *Sinai Gr. 14* (12th cent.)[305] and as the hymn of the transfer of the gifts at JAS in *Vatican Gr. 1970* (13th cent.), an Euchologion from southern Italy discussed several times in this chapter.[306] But, as Bertonière admits, it is impossible to find the origins of the introduction of this hymn either into JAS or into BAS.[307] What can be said is simply that the first sources to mention this hymn are from the twelfth century and are not Hagiopolitan.

Turning now to the content of the hymns, many observers have connected the texts sung during the liturgy with the action of transfering the gifts, which was taking place at the same time. Theological commentaries, such as that of Theodore of Mopsuestia (d. c.428), describe the gifts before the anaphora as already being Christ and compare the procession with his passion and burial procession.[308] Renoux's study of the content of the Georgian version of the hymn for the holy gifts has led him to a different conclusion. Rather than expressing in words the liturgical action of the procession, Renoux believes that the themes of the hymns in the GL and *Iadgari* focus on the union between celestial and terrestrial praise. This, in turn, has led Charles Renoux and Stéphane Verhelst after him to imagine a more sombre rite surrounding the transfer of the gifts in Jerusalem—or that there was no transfer of gifts at all—by contrast with to the solemnity of the Constantinopolitan rite.[309]

Such a conclusion seems, however, to assume too much from the very concise ideas and images expressed and presented by these hymns. The text of the *cheroubikon* itself makes more references to other parts of the liturgy—such as the *trisagion*, the pre-anaphoral dialogue, and Communion—than to the Great Entrance and to the transfer of the gifts.[310] Accordingly, attempting to extract the precise organization of the Great Entrance rite from its hymnography may be inferring too much from the limited descriptions they provide. The architectural and archaeological evidence has led Joseph Patrich

---

[304] *Harvard University Houghton Library Gr. 3* (1105), fol. 281v; Parenti, 'Σιγησάτω πᾶσα σάρξ', 193; Parpulov, *Byzantine Psalters*, 103; Jeffrey C. Anderson and Stefano Parenti, *A Byzantine Monastic Office, 1105 AD* [sic]: *Houghton Library, MS gr. 3* (Washington, DC: The Catholic University of America Press, 2016), 252–3 n. 187.

[305] Bertonière, *Easter Vigil*, 116–17.

[306] See Parenti, 'Σιγησάτω πᾶσα σάρξ', 194.   [307] Bertonière, *Easter Vigil*, 286–7.

[308] Leeb, *Die Gesänge*, 120; Taft, *Great Entrance*, 35–9; Barry Baldwin, 'Theodore of Mopsuestia', ODB III, 2044.

[309] Renoux, 'Hymne des saints dons', 308–11; Stéphane Verhelst, 'La liturgie de Saint Jacques: Rétroversion grecque et commentaires', in *Liturgia ibero-graeca*, 305, 390–2.

[310] The specific reference is in the phrase ταῖς ἀγγελικαῖς ἀοράτως δορυφορούμενον τάξεσιν ('escorted invisibly by ranks of angels'). The themes of the *cheroubikon* are clearly and succinctly summarized in Robert F. Taft, 'Cheroubikon', ODB I, 418. See also Taft, *Great Entrance*, 62–8.

to conclude that there was a solemn Great Entrance procession in Palestine already in the sixth century. The transformation of church architecture so as to include a lateral prothesis chapel, whence the gifts were taken to the altar, continued until the eighth century and was not the result of a developed cult of martyrs' relics, as some have suggested.[311] While this reveals a change in Hagiopolite liturgical practice, the transformation begins in the sixth century and ends in the eighth, which means that it predates Byzantinization. At the same time there is no evidence to show that this modification of procession routes and of church architecture was the result of Constantinopolitan influence; it was more likely a local, independent development.

The change of hymns, however, can indeed be seen as a sign of Byzantinization. Taft observed that in the Typikon of the Anastasis the variable hymn of the holy gifts had been pushed back into the place of the hymn of hand washing. The hymn of hand washing was eventually lost and forced out of the eucharistic liturgy, most likely because of its dependence on the themes of the lectionary. Thus, the Great Entrance hymn in Jerusalem was no longer the variable hymn of hand washing but the Constantinopolitan *cheroubikon*, or another hymn known from several Hagiopolite manuscripts as the hymn 'in place of the *cheroubikon*' (ἀντὶ τοῦ χερουβικοῦ).[312]

Once the transfer of the gifts has been completed and the hymn of the holy gifts has been sung, the liturgy continues with several pre-anaphoral rites. Unlike in CHR and in BAS, here in JAS the Creed is recited (Πιστεύω εἰς ἕνα Θεόν; მრწამსისა, *mrcamsisa*, 'I believe') before the kiss of peace, which has its own prayer, 'God and Lord of all' (Ὁ πάντων Θεὸς καὶ Δεσπότης; ღმერთი ყოველთა უფალი ხარ და უფალი).[313] The presider recites this prayer before the kiss of peace. Next comes the main part of the liturgy: the eucharistic prayer of the anaphora.

The Anaphora of the Liturgy of St James

The anaphora of JAS—the eucharistic prayer at the core of the Divine Liturgy of Jerusalem—has the following structure, typical of what liturgiologists have classified as West Syrian anaphoras (see Table 3.5):[314]

---

[311] Patrich, 'Transfer of Gifts', 358–9.   [312] Taft, *Great Entrance*, 75.

[313] Assemani, *Missale Hierosolymitanum*, 75; Mercier, *Liturgie de Saint Jacques*, 182; *Liturgia ibero-graeca*, 60–2. Some Georgian sources of JAS prescribe the 'Prayer of St Basil: None of us, who are bound by carnal desires' to be recited at this point, during the Creed. See *Liturgia ibero-graeca*, 58–60.

[314] An English translation of the anaphora of JAS can be found in Ronald C. D. Jasper and Geoffrey J. Cuming, *Prayers of the Eucharist: Early and Reformed* (Collegeville, MN: Liturgical Press, 1990), 89–99.

Table 3.5. Structure of the anaphora of St James

Opening Dialogue and Pre-Sanctus Prayer	Opening dialogue between the priest and the people, 'The love of God the Father' (ʿΗ ἀγάπη τοῦ Θεοῦ καὶ πατρός) and preface, 'It is truly fitting and right' (Ὡς ἀληθῶς ἄξιόν ἐστι καὶ δίκαιον)[315]
Sanctus/Benedictus	'Holy, holy, holy, Lord of Sabaoth...Blessed is he who came and who comes in the name of the Lord' (Ἅγιος, ἅγιος, ἅγιος, κύριος σαβαώθ...εὐλογημένος ὁ ἐλθὼν καὶ ἐρχόμενος ἐν ὀνόματι κυρίου)[316]
Post-Sanctus	'Holy are you, King of the ages and Lord and Giver of all holiness...' (Ἅγιος εἶ, βασιλεῦ τῶν αἰώνων καὶ πάσης ἁγιωσύνης...)[317]
Institution Narrative	'And when he was about to endure his voluntary and life-giving death on the Cross' (Μέλλων δὲ τὸν ἑκούσιον καὶ ζωοποιὸν διὰ σταυροῦ θάνατον)[318]
Anamnesis	'Do this for my remembrance' (Τοῦτο ποιεῖτε εἰς τὴν ἐμὴν ἀνάμνησιν)[319]
(For...)	'For as often as you eat this bread and drink this cup, you proclaim the death of the Son of Man and confess his Resurrection, until he comes' (ὁσάκις γὰρ ἂν ἐσθίητε τὸν ἄρτον τοῦον καὶ τὸ ποτήριον τοῦτο πίνητε, τὸν θάνατον τοῦ υἱοῦ τοῦ ἀνθρώπου καταγγέλλετε καὶ τὴν ἀνάστασιν αὐτοῦ ὁμολογεῖτε, ἄχρις οὗ ἂν ἔλθῃ)[320]
Epiclesis	'and send out upon us and upon these holy gifts set before you your all-Holy Spirit' (καὶ ἐξαπόστειλον ἐφ᾽ ὑμᾶς καὶ ἐπὶ τὰ προκείμενα ἅγια δῶρα ταῦτα τὸ πνεῦμα σου τὸ πανάγιον)[321]
Intercessions/Diptychs	'We offer to you, Master, for your holy places also, which you glorified by the theophany of your Christ and the visitation of your all-Holy Spirit; principally for holy and glorious Sion, the mother of all the churches' (Προσφέρομεν σοι, δέσποτα, καὶ ὑπὲρ τῶν ἁγίων σου τόπων, οὓς ἐδόξασας τῇ θεοφανείᾳ τοῦ Χριστοῦ σου καὶ τῇ ἐπιφοιτήσει τοῦ παναγίου σου πνεύματος, προηγουμένως ὑπὲρ τῆς ἁγίας καὶ ἐνδόξου Σιὼν τῆς μητρὸς πασῶν τῶν ἐκκλησιῶν). The Intercessions include lengthy commemorations beginning with the repeated 'Remember' (Μνήσθητι)[322]
Doxology	'By the grace and compassion and love for mankind of your Christ...' (Χάριτι καὶ οἰκτιρμοῖς καὶ φιλανθρωπίᾳ τοῦ Χριστοῦ σου...)[323]

The phrase from the Benedictus, 'who came and who comes' (ὁ ἐλθὼν καὶ ἐρχόμενος), is particular to liturgical texts from Jerusalem, which explains its appellation as the 'Hagiopolite Benedictus'.[324] Even more characteristic of

---

[315] Mercier, *Liturgie de Saint Jacques*, beginning at 198, line 12.
[316] Ibid., 200, lines 4–6.   [317] Ibid., beginning at 200, line 8.
[318] Ibid., beginning at 200, line 29.   [319] Ibid., beginning at 202, line 22.
[320] Ibid., beginning at 202, line 22.   [321] Ibid., beginning at 204, line 22.
[322] Ibid., beginning at 206, line 25.   [323] Ibid., beginning at 222, line 5.
[324] *Vatican Gr. 1970* (13th cent.), fol. 81r; Mercier, *Liturgie de Saint Jacques*, 200, lines 5–6; Jasper and Cuming, *Prayers of the Eucharist* (see n. 314), 91; Brightman, *Eastern Liturgies*, 86.

Jerusalem are the lengthy intercessions and diptychs of JAS, which recall numerous saints and commemorate various categories of people and events. Kazamias' survey of the Greek manuscripts of JAS has revealed more than 250 individuals commemorated by name, as many as twenty-two apostles and disciples, forty prophets, thirty-two male martyrs, thirteen confessors, thirty-five female martyrs, sixty church fathers and teachers, and forty-one ascetics and monks, as well as thirteen categories of clergy commemorated as groups.[325] The number of the saints commemorated is so overwhelming that Taft refers to other diptychs with a large infusion of saints as 'Jerusalemized'.[326]

Prayer for Those Bringing Offerings

Immediately after the anaphora, the Lord's Prayer (Matthew 6:9–13), and the elevation of the eucharistic bread, known as the Lamb, with the exclamation of the presider 'Holy things for the holy' (*Τὰ ἅγια τοῖς ἁγίοις*; ⲅ̄ⲇⲟⲥⲟⲥⲁ ⲅ̄ⲇⲟⲥⲟⲥⲟⲥⲁ, *cmiday cmidat'ay*),[327] comes the 'Prayer for those bringing offerings' (*εὐχὴ τῆς καρποφορίας*).[328] On the basis of a similar text found in a manuscript of the Liturgy of St Mark, *Vatican Gr. 2281* (1209), Geoffrey Cuming originally believed that this was a prayer for those who brought first fruits or tithes to the church immediately before Communion, so that the offerings could be shared between the clergy and the poor when the latter approached to receive Communion.[329] Heinzgerd Brakmann noticed that some manuscripts of JAS, such as *Sinai Gr. 1040* (14th cent.) and *Hagios Stavros Gr. 43* (1122), contained a similar prayer. The witness of these manuscripts, as well as references to prayers for the living and dead before

While this phrase is found in Syriac and Armenian versions of JAS, it is not found in Greek manuscripts from the Sinai 'new finds' or in Georgian translations of JAS. See Kazamias, *Θεία Λειτουργία τοῦ Ἁγίου Ἰακώβου*, 190; *Liturgia ibero-graeca*, 76 and 210. The 'Hagiopolite Benedictus' is also found in the Greek and Coptic versions of the anaphora of St Gregory Nazianzus and in the prayer for blessing palms on Palm Sunday in *Barberini Gr. 336*. See Bryan D. Spinks, *The Sanctus in the Eucharistic Prayer* (Cambridge: Cambridge University Press, 1991), 116–21, esp. 121; Parenti and Velkovska, *Барберини гр. 336*, 59. See also Gabriele Winkler, *Das Sanctus: Über den Ursprung und die Anfänge des Sanctus und sein Fortwirken* (OCA 267, Rome: Pontifical Oriental Institute, 2002).

[325] Kazamias, *Θεία Λειτουργία τοῦ Ἁγίου Ἰακώβου*, 273–82.

[326] See Taft, *Diptychs*, 61–6, 190; *Liturgia ibero-graeca*, 261–77, 352–5. For an examination of the liturgical commemoration of some of these saints, see the case studies in next chapter on the liturgical calendar, Chapter 4, 'The Byzantinization of the Hagiopolite Calendar: Case Studies'.

[327] Mercier, *Liturgie de Saint Jacques*, 228; Kazamias, *Θεία Λειτουργία τοῦ Ἁγίου Ἰακώβου*, 214; *Liturgia ibero-graeca*, 110–11. Note that the Georgian phrase presents the subject in the singular and the indirect object in the plural. See also Taft, *Precommunion Rites*, 199–211.

[328] Kazamias, *Θεία Λειτουργία τοῦ Ἁγίου Ἰακώβου*, 214–15. The prayer is missing from Mercier's edition.

[329] Geoffrey J. Cuming, "*Η καρποφορία*', *Ephemerides Liturgicae* 95 (1981), 556–8; Cuming, *Liturgy of St Mark*, xxx.

the Fraction in JAS, allowed Brakmann to conclude that this was not a prayer for those who brought offerings of first fruits at that specific moment of the Divine Liturgy, but rather for those who had brought offerings—and for the living and the dead in general.[330] Thus, the 'Prayer for those bringing offerings' was similar to the anaphoral diptychs but with possible festal variants, as in the case of the diaconal prayer on Palm Sunday before Communion in the Typikon of the Anastasis.[331] Unfortunately, few examples of this prayer exist and the one from the Typikon of the Anastasis is the only known variable example specifically connected to the liturgical calendar.

The Hymn for Communion

After the 'Prayer for those bringing offerings' came the Fraction and Communion, during which the hymn for Communion was sung. The oldest texts for Communion chants were Psalm 33:9, 'Taste and see that the Lord is good' (Γεύσασθε καὶ ἴδετε ὅτι χρηστὸς ὁ κύριος), and Psalm 148:1, 'Praise the Lord from the heavens' (Αἰνεῖτε τὸν κύριον ἐκ τῶν οὐρανῶν). In the Byzantine rite, Psalm 33:9 has been preserved for PRES, reinforcing Baumstark's observation of the conservatism of more solemn seasons of the liturgical year.[332] Today, however, the repertory consists of twenty-six different possible Communion verses for the Divine Liturgy.[333]

Curiously, the Hagiopolitan sources of JAS rarely mention the Communion chant. Most sources only indicate the exclamation of the presider, 'Holy things for the holy' (τὰ ἅγια τοῖς ἁγίοις). However, the long version of JAS does include many psalm verses in the prayers of the clergy before they receive Communion.[334] These may have also been sung or read by the chanters or by people other than the clergy.

Specific chants after Communion in the GL include: the *ganic'ade* (განიცადე), a word that means 'taste' (see Psalm 33:9) and is equivalent to γεύσασθε in the Byzantine *koinonikon* (κοινωνικόν);[335] and the *agavse* (აღავსე), a word that means 'fulfilled' (see Psalm 70:8) and is equivalent to

[330] Brakmann, 'Zur Εὐχὴ τῆς καρποφορίας', 80.
[331] *Hagios Stavros Gr. 43* (1122), fol. 13v–14r; Papadopoulos-Kerameus, *Anastasis Typikon*, 25–6.
[332] Thomas H. Schattauer, 'The Koinonicon of the Byzantine Liturgy', OCP 49 (1983), 91–129, here 123–4. For more on Baumstark's rule of conservative solemn liturgical seasons, see section 'The Hymn of the Holy Gifts' in this chapter.
[333] Dmitri E. Conomos and Robert F. Taft, 'Koinonikon', ODB II, 1136; Christian Troelsgård, 'Koinōnikon', NGDMM 13: 744–5; Dmitri E. Conomos, *The Late Byzantine and Slavonic Communion Cycle: Liturgy and Music* (Washington, DC: Dumbarton Oaks Research Library and Collection, 1985), 19–51.
[334] *Liturgia ibero-graeca*, 114–27.   [335] Leeb, *Die Gesänge*, 124–7.

πληρωθήτω in the Byzantine hymn 'May our mouths be filled'.[336] Because Greek manuscripts of JAS and Greek lectionaries, such as *St Petersburg RNB Gr. 44* (9th cent.), omit these Hagiopolitan hymns, the primary source for all of them is the GL.

Hymns and Prayers for the Dismissal

JAS concluded with variable hymns and prayers specific to the commemoration that looked much like the *introit*, the hymn for hand washing, and the hymn of the holy gifts. Apart from the hymn for 'the dismissal of the people' (ერის განტევებაჲ, *eris gantevebay*), which was equivalent to the Byzantine *apolytikion* (ἀπολυτίκιον),[337] similar prayers, called *opisthambonoi* or ambo prayers (in the singular, εὐχὴ ὀπισθάμβωνος) in Constantinopolitan or Byzantine sources and *apolyseis* (in the singular, ἀπόλυσις) or dismissal prayers in Hagiopolitan sources, are found in the Byzantine rite. It is believed that these prayers were a 'foreign import' into the Byzantine BAS and CHR and that many of them were of Hagiopolitan origin.[338] Italo-Greek Euchologia *St Petersburg Gr. 226* (10th cent.), *Grottaferrata Γ.β. IV* (10th cent.), *Grottaferrata Γ.β. VII* (10th cent.), and *Grottaferrata Γ.β. X* (11th cent.) even include special *opisthambonoi* for the Sundays of Great Lent, prayers whose themes are inspired by readings from the Jerusalem lectionary.[339] Despite this connection to JAS and to Jerusalem, Mercier omitted the anthology of ambo prayers contained in *Vatican Gr. 2282* (9th cent.) from his edition of that manuscript, making it more difficult to access these prayers and giving the impression that the formulary of JAS that he edited was disconnected from the liturgical calendar and lectionary of Jerusalem. However, Mercier's choice to omit these prayers from his edition may have been pragmatic, since it is often difficult to understand where JAS actually ends. The 'last prayer' (εὐχὴ τελευταία), 'May God be blessed, he who blesses and sanctifies' (Ηὐλόγηται ὁ Θεός, ὁ εὐλογῶν καὶ ἁγιάζων), can be followed by several more prayers, such as the one said in the Diakonikon (εὐχὴ λεγομένη ἐν τῷ διακονικῷ μετὰ τὴν ἀπόλυσιν), the one for the dismissal after the synaxis (εὐχὴ ἀπολυτικὴ τῆς συνάξεως), or

---

[336] Ibid., 127–8 and 136–44.   [337] See Mateos, *Typikon*, vol. 2, 285.

[338] Taft, *Concluding Rites*, 611 and 639–40; Stefano Parenti, 'Testimoni sconosciuti di preghiere dell'ambone', OCP 62 (1996), 197–205.

[339] Taft, *Concluding Rites*, 615; Gaetano Passarelli, *L'Eucologio Cryptense Γ.β. VII (sec. X)* (Ἀνάλεκτα Βλατάδων 36, Thessalonike: Patriarchal Institute for Patristic Studies, 1982), 80–1 (fol. 16v–18r); Pavlos Koumarianos, *Il Codice 226 della Biblioteca di San Pietroburgo: L'Eucologio Bizantino di Porfyrio Uspensky* (Unpublished doctoral thesis, Rome: Pontifical Oriental Institute, 1996), 14–18 (fol. 7v–11r). See Chapter 5, 'Gospel Readings for Great Lent' for the cycle of readings for Lent according to the Jerusalem lectionary.

the one delivered from the ambo (εὐχὴ ὀπισθάμβωνος).[340] Many of these prayers contained expressions of thanksgiving for the reception of Communion and mentioned the return to daily life in the world with the help of the intercession of various saints. The variable prayers added aspects of the commemoration or of the saint being celebrated to the standard prayer requests. Giuseppe Cozza-Luzi edited three prayers from *Vatican Gr. 2282* (9th cent.), while Taft, continuing the work of Teodoro Minisci on the *opisthambonoi* prayers in Grottaferrata manuscripts, has identified 118 different variable Greek ones for BAS, CHR, and PRES.[341] Stéphane Verhelst has compared Greek *opisthambonoi* prayers (what is known of them) with prayers from Georgian manuscripts, particularly from the 'liturgical collection' *Sinai Geo. O 12* (10th–11th cent.), which contains fifty-five prayers for dismissal (განტევება, *ganteveba*, fol. 35r–90r) arranged according to the Hagiopolite liturgical year. Verhelst notes that many of the prayers allude to readings from the Jerusalem lectionary and that the Georgian texts are virtually identical to the Greek in those cases where the Greek texts have been preserved (i.e. mainly in southern Italian manuscripts).[342] Nevertheless, most of these prayers are either omitted from the formulary of JAS or ignored in studies of the Hagiopolitan eucharistic liturgy.

MYSTAGOGIES OF THE LITURGY OF ST JAMES

Before concluding this chapter on JAS, it is worth asking the question: How did Hagiopolitan theologians explain the Divine Liturgy of JAS and its sacred rites to their fellow Christians? In Constantinople, Patriarch Germanus is well known for explaining the Divine Liturgy through the genre of mystagogy and thus for literally leading the faithful into the mysteries celebrated in the liturgical services.[343] Despite the revival of Greek literature in Palestine in the ninth century, theological literature from the Jerusalem patriarchate after

---

[340] Mercier, *Liturgie de Saint Jacques*, 240–9; Kazamias, Θεία Λειτουργία τοῦ Ἁγίου Ἰακώβου, 222–6; *Liturgia ibero-graeca*, 134–41.

[341] *Novae patrum bibliothecae*, vol. 10, part 2, ed. by Giuseppe Cozza-Luzi (Rome: Typis Sacri Consilii Propagando Christiano Nomini, 1905), 105–10; Taft, *Concluding Rites*, 623–30, 645–98; Teodoro Minisci, 'Le preghiere opistamvoni dei codici criptensi', BBGG n.s. 2 (1948), 65–75, 117–26; 3 (1949), 3–10, 61–6, 121–32, 185–94; 4 (1950), 3–14.

[342] Stéphane Verhelst, 'Prières géorgiennes de renvoi et prières grecques de l'ambon: Premières comparaisons', BBGG (terza serie) 6 (2009), 287–305. See also André Jacob, 'Une prière du skeuophylakion de la Liturgie de saint Jacques et ses parallèles byzantins', *Bulletin de l'Institut historique belge de Rome* 37 (1966), 53–80; Taft, *Concluding Rites*, 623–30.

[343] Bornert, *Commentaires*; Taft, 'Liturgy of the Great Church'; Robert F. Taft, SJ, 'Commentaries', ODB I, 488–9.

the eighth century is not especially prominent.[344] Maximus Confessor (*c.*580–662), John of Damascus (*c.*675–753/4), Anastasius of Sinai (7th–8th cent.), and Theodore Abū Qurrah (*c.*740–825) are among the best-known authors of the period immediately after the Arab conquest. However, many of their extant works, such as the *Liber asceticus* of Maximus Confessor and the *Sermon on the Divine Liturgy* by Anastasius of Sinai, remain to be examined for their liturgical content.[345] For many other authors of the period, however, even basic biographical details are completely unknown. For example, Hesychius of Sinai (8th–9th cent.?) was the *hegoumenos* of the Monastery of the Burning Bush on Mount Sinai and wrote *On Watchfulness and Holiness*, but it is not certain when he actually lived. His apparent familiarity with John Climacus and Maximus Confessor suggest that he lived in the eighth or the ninth century.[346] A certain Philotheus of Mount Sinai (9th–10th cent.?) is also known only through a few works.[347]

The only known exception is the classic *Mystagogia* of St Maximus Confessor.[348] Although it is known that Maximus was a Palestinian monk who also spent time in Constantinople, his origins have been fiercely debated since the publication of the Syriac version of the *Vita* by Sebastian Brock. In the Syriac life, Maximus is not born to a noble family in Constantinople but rather out of wedlock, in Palestine, and is the disciple of a heretic.[349] Because Maximus' Palestinian origins are now seen as credible, recent studies have attempted to settle the question of which liturgy—that of Constantinople or Jerusalem—was the subject of his mystagogy.[350] The general consensus is that Maximus was describing the liturgy of Constantinople, despite his intimate knowledge of Jerusalem's liturgy as a Palestinian monk.

Apart from Maximus, Palestinian hierarchs and theologians seem to have rarely written *about* the liturgy, preferring instead to write hymnography or homilies *for use in* the liturgy itself. The rare exceptions are spiritually edifying

---

[344] Hans-Georg Beck, *Kirche und theologische Literatur im byzantinischen Reich* (Byzantinisches Handbuch 2.1, Munich: C. H. Beck'sche Verlagsbuchhandlung, 1977), 97–8.

[345] See CPG 7692; St Maximus Confessor, Λόγος ἀσκητικός, PG 90:912–56; St Maximus Confessor, *The Ascetic Life: The Four Centuries on Charity*, ed. and trans. by Polycarp Sherwood, OSB (Ancient Christian Writers 21, Westminster, MD: Newman Press, 1955), 103–35. The text has quotations from JAS. CPG 7750; Anastasius of Sinai, *Homilia de sacra synaxi*, PG 89:825–49.

[346] CPG 7862.

[347] Ibid., 7864–6. For the few patristic writers from the Jerusalem patriarchate after the Arab conquest, see *Patrology: The Eastern Fathers from the Council of Chalcedon (451) to John of Damascus (†750)*, ed. by Angelo di Berardino, trans. by Adrian Walford (Cambridge: James Clarke, 2008), 307–34.

[348] CPG 7704; Boudignon, *Maximi Confessoris Mystagogia*.

[349] BHG 1231–6d; Sebastian P. Brock, 'An Early Syriac Life of Maximus the Confessor', AB 91 (1973), 299–346; Alexander Kazhdan, 'Maximos the Confessor', ODB II, 1323–4. The most recent analysis of the two contradictory accounts of Maximus' life is found in Booth, *Crisis of Empire*, 143–9.

[350] Patrich, 'Transfer of Gifts', 347–50; Taft, 'Maximus'.

tales, such as the *Spiritual Meadow* by John Moschus, or hagiographies by Cyril of Scythopolis, although in all these cases liturgy is mainly the background for the message the author is trying to express. Thus, unlike Constantinople, Jerusalem offers us no theological treatises or mystagogies on the liturgy after the Arab conquest. The closest example of a Hagiopolitan text that explains the liturgy is the *Treatise Containing the Complete Interpretation of the Church and the Detailed Exposition of All the Ceremonies of the Divine Liturgy*, attributed to a Patriarch Sophronius of Jerusalem.[351] Patriarch Sophronius I (d. 638) has been ruled out as the author, and thus the most likely candidate is Patriarch Sophronius II (11th cent.).[352] René Bornert has shown that this text is a derivation of the *Protheoria*, written by Nicholas of Andida in Pamphylia between 1054 and 1067,[353] and of the *Historia ecclesiastica* attributed to Patriarch Germanus I of Constantinople (r. 715–30),[354] which the author of the *Treatise* attempted to synthesize. Both Patriarch Germanus and Nicholas of Andida focus on the liturgy of the Great Church of Constantinople. Although five known manuscripts contain the text of Sophronius' *Treatise*, this text still remains to be edited.[355]

In view of all this, the *Catecheses* of Cyril are the only known examples of mystagogy in Jerusalem. Since '[m]ystagogy is to liturgy what exegesis is to scripture', it is difficult to know what liturgy meant to Christians in Jerusalem after Cyril and to understand its symbolic form.[356] The absence of subsequent mystagogies might be explained in several ways. It may be that Cyrilline mystagogy continued to be read in Jerusalem and maintained its relevance for the church there. Nevertheless, the absence of any mystagogical texts connected with the liturgy of Jerusalem after the fourth century is enigmatic, particularly considering the multiplicity of such texts written in Constantinople and its environs in order to explain the liturgy of the imperial capital. Whether this genre foundered in Jerusalem because of the dangerous political environment after the Arab conquest is unclear. It is certainly possible to think of the need to protect the secrecy of the mysteries from the heterodox in a multireligious ambience constantly plagued by Christian divisions and to

---

[351] Σωφρονίου πατριάρχου Ἱεροσολύμων λόγος περιέχων τὴν ἐκκλησιαστκὴν ἅπασαν ἱστοριαν καὶ λεπτομερῆ ἀφήγησιν πάντων τῶν ἐν τῇ θείᾳ ἱερουργίᾳ τελουμένων. PG 87: 3981–4001; CPG 7677.

[352] Bornert, *Commentaires*, 210–11; Panagiotes G. Nikolopoulos, 'Σωφρόνιος ὁ Β', ΘΗΕ 11: 645.

[353] PG 140:417–68; Alexander Kazhdan, 'Nicholas of Andida', ODB II, 1468.

[354] St Germanus of Constantinople, *On the Divine Liturgy*, ed. by Paul Meyendorff (Crestwood, NY: St Vladimir's Seminary Press, 1984); Alexander Kazhdan, 'Germanos I', ODB II, 846–7.

[355] *Vatican Ottoboni Gr. 459* (15th cent.); *Vatican Palatine Gr. 367* (13th cent.), fol. 18v–33v; *Laurentian Gr. LIX, 13* (15th–16th cent.), fol. 326r–346v; *Paris Coislin Gr. 114* (14th–15th cent.), fol. 330r–340r; *Vatican Gr. 112* (14th cent.), fol. 66r–73v. See Bornert, *Commentaires*, 210–11.

[356] Taft, 'Liturgy of the Great Church', 46–7, 59.

suppose that this may have inspired a return to some kind of *disciplina arcani*. But this is not very likely and would not explain the dearth of mystagogical texts from the fifth or sixth centuries, when Jerusalem was still in Byzantine hands. Likewise, non-Chalcedonian authors in similarly unfavourable contexts wrote liturgical commentaries.[357]

The real reason for the absence of liturgical mystagogies in Jerusalem after the fourth century may lie in the development of hymnography. Hymnography, by its very nature, is a kind of liturgical exegesis and catechesis, and it continued to be intrinsic to the structure of Jerusalem's JAS.[358] As long as Jerusalem's lectionary survived, the variable hymns of JAS—such as the *introit*, the hymn for hand washing, and the hymn of the holy gifts— expounded the rites and actions of the liturgy and connected them to the particular feast or saint being celebrated. The continued use of these hymns and the eruption of hymnography as a literary genre around the eighth century may have attracted authors who might have otherwise expressed their theology in mystagogies. Once foreign Byzantine liturgical practices were adopted in Jerusalem and the variable hymnography of JAS no longer had a place within the Divine Liturgy, liturgical rites and actions would have been explained by corresponding Byzantine mystagogies. The Constantino-politan contents of the *Treatise* attributed to Sophronius—the only Hagiopo-litan mystagogy, and one that qualifies only remotely, for that matter—seem to confirm such a hypothesis.

CONCLUSIONS

This investigation of the liturgical manuscripts and structures of JAS here is intended to facilitate the examination of Jerusalem's calendar and lectionary in the next chapters. Since the calendar and lectionary are directly connected to JAS through hymnody, psalmody, and scriptural readings, it is necessary to keep these structures in mind when analysing the calendar and lectionary. The following conclusions can be drawn with regard to the continued presence of JAS and its subsequent disappearance in the Jerusalem patriarchate:

1. The similarities between all versions of JAS—Greek and Syriac as well as non-Chalcedonian versions—meant that Constantinople had doubts

---

[357] See, for example, *Two Commentaries on the Jacobite Liturgy by George Bishop of the Arab Tribes and Moses Bar Kepha: Together with the Syriac Anaphora of St James and a Document Entitled* The Book of Life, ed. and trans. by Richard H. Connolly and Humphrey W. Codrington (London: Williams and Norgate, 1913).

[358] José Grosdidier de Matons, 'Liturgie et Hymnographie: Kontakion et Canon', DOP 34 (1980–1981), 31–43, here 36–7.

about a usage of the anaphora in Jerusalem that was similar to non-Chalcedonian usage. This is apparent from Patriarch Theodore Balsamon's writings that deal with liturgical practices in the twelfth century. Nevertheless, the internal Byzantinization of JAS and the bidirectional influence of Hagiopolitan and Constantinopolitan elements on the Byzantine Euchologion suggest that the disappearance of JAS was a gradual phenomenon, which occurred not as a result of external historical events but through internal development and evolution of the liturgy within the Jerusalem patriarchate. The final decision to abandon JAS, which had already undergone gradual Byzantinization, was due to canonical considerations.

2. The various terms for, and changes to, responsorial psalmody do not provide a clear criterion for evaluating liturgical Byzantinization. The only term with a greater Constantinopolitan connection is *prokeimenon*, which appears in Hagiopolitan sources side by side with older terms, such as *mesodion* or *epakouston*.

3. The celebration of JAS was directly linked to the Jerusalem lectionary. This is most clear in Georgian manuscripts of JAS that also contain readings from the Jerusalem lectionary in an appendix and whose Liturgy of the Word structure still includes multiple readings, Old Testament ones among them. With the loss of the Jerusalem lectionary, the connection between the scriptural readings and the hymnography inspired by the themes of these readings was lost.

4. The celebration of JAS was dependent upon the structure provided by its particular hymnography in the Liturgy of the Eucharist. Its gradual disappearance, summarized in Table 3.6, is first manifested in the discarding of the hymn for hand washing, then in the introduction of the *cheroubikon* or *cheroubikon* replacement as a fixed hymn, and ultimately in the loss of the hymn for the holy gifts.

5. What Stefano Parenti has dubbed 'orational atrophy', in which creativity and the composition of new prayers wanes and a generic prayer

Table 3.6. Hymnography at the transfer of the gifts in the Liturgy of St James

Constantinople	Jerusalem		
Typikon of the Great Church	GL	*Hagios Stavros Gr. 43*	*Messina Gr. 177*
	Hymn for hand washing →	X	X
	Hymn of the holy gifts →	Hymn of the holy gifts →	X
cheroubikon		[Anti-]*cheroubikon* →	*cheroubikon*

becomes fixed,[359] can be compared to a phenomenon that I would call 'hymnographic petrification', whereby formerly variable hymns, hymns related to the themes of the feast being celebrated and its scriptural readings, are replaced by more generic hymns, often once variable themselves. These hymns become entrenched and fixed for diverse rites and actions. The best examples are Ὁ μονογενής and the Χερουβικόν, which are variable hymns in the GL but become fixed in later manuscripts of JAS.

---

[359] Stefano Parenti, 'Towards a Regional History of the Byzantine Euchology of the Sacraments', *Ecclesia Orans* 27 (2010), 109–21, here 114–16.

4

The Liturgical Calendar of Jerusalem

We now turn our attention to the liturgical calendar of Jerusalem. Previous studies of the Hagiopolite liturgical year focused primarily on the celebrations of Pascha, Christmas, and Theophany but rarely delved into the details of the sanctoral cycle. This was due to the latter's complexity and to the fact that scholars' interest was focused on the calendars considered to be the earliest, which contained a less developed or more sparse sanctoral.[1] Anton Baumstark believed that studying the development of the commemoration of saints and the relationship between the 'native country of certain feasts' and their subsequent extension to different churches raises anew questions of reciprocal

[1] See for example, Talley, *Liturgical Year*. Those studies that did include details of the sanctoral cycle were often guided by the necessity of resolving questions connected to the reforms of the Second Vatican Council and targeted current Roman Catholic practices. See, for example, Adolf Adam, *The Liturgical Year: Its History and Its Meaning after the Reform of the Liturgy*, trans. by Matthew J. O'Connell (New York: Pueblo, 1981). Exceptions are found in the work of the Bollandists: Hippolyte Delehaye, *Cinq leçons sur la méthode hagiographique* (SH 21, Bruxelles: Société des Bollandistes, 1934), 9. See also an appraisal and summary of Delehaye's work: Flor Van Ommeslaeghe, 'The *Acta Sanctorum* and Bollandist Methodology', in *The Byzantine Saint: 14th Spring Symposium of Byzantine Studies*, ed. by Sergei Hackel (Crestwood, NY: St Vladimir's Seminary Press, 1981), 155–63; Bernard Joassart, 'Hippolyte Delehaye (1859–1941): Un bollandiste au temps de la crise moderniste', in *Sanctity and Secularity during the Modernist Period: Six perspectives on hagiography around 1900*, ed. by Lawrence Barmann and Charles J. T. Talar (SH 79, Bruxelles: Société des Bollandistes, 1999), 1–45. See also Hippolyte Delehaye, *L'ancienne hagiographie byzantine: Les sources, les premiers modèles, la formation des genres: Conférences prononcées au Collège de France en 1935*, ed. by Bernard Joassart and Xavier Lequeux (SH 73, Bruxelles: Société des Bollandistes, 1991); Bernard Joassart, *Hippolyte Delehaye: Hagiographie critique et modernisme*, 2 vols (SH 81, Bruxelles: Société des Bollandistes, 2000). Other attempts to systematize hagiographic material include Archbishop Sergei, Полный мѣсяцесловъ востока, 3 vols (Vladimir: Типо-Литографія В.А. Паркова, 1901); François Halkin, *Recherches et documents d'hagiographie byzantine* (SH 51, Bruxelles: Société des Bollandistes, 1971). Also useful are the detailed calendar entries in Nancy Patterson Ševčenko, *Illustrated Manuscripts of the Metaphrastian Menologion* (Chicago, IL: University of Chicago Press, 1990); Christian Høgel, *Symeon Metaphrastes: Rewriting and Canonization* (Copenhagen: Museum Tusulanum Press of the University of Copenhagen, 2002), 172–204; Sofia Kotzabassi and Nancy Patterson Ševčenko, *Greek Manuscripts at Princeton, Sixth to Nineteenth Century: A Descriptive Catalogue* (Princeton, NJ: Princeton University Department of Art and Archaeology, 2010). For a thorough survey of the most recent bibliography from liturgical studies, see Buchinger, 'Origin and Development', 14–18.

dependence between one territory and another, opening the path to recon-sidering and resolving issues of origins and diffusion of saints' cults.[2] Con-tinuing in this vein, Robert Taft has repeatedly pointed to hagiography as a tool in the study of what he calls 'liturgy from the bottom up'. This approach seeks to enliven and supplement the 'too often stodgy' textual and archaeo-logical studies of the history of liturgy, from late antiquity through to the Byzantine and medieval periods.[3] Hagiographies provide reliable evidence for actual liturgical services and for what people thought of those services.[4] But, apart from these uses of hagiography, there is a very practical and more basic reason for turning to hagiography in this study: to understand why a given feast is celebrated on a given day. The presence of a commemoration with a specific geographic connection in a given liturgical book does not mean beyond doubt that this liturgical book was copied in that same place or region.[5] Harald Buchinger has recently proposed new directions for heorto-logical research, noting that, 'if the standard works of liturgical studies are to be a mirror of the discipline, they will in the future have to examine more clearly than they have how the feasts in the rhythm of time have actually expressed and influenced the life and faith of the church'.[6] Thus the investi-gation of heortology is conducted both externally, in relation to the influence of feasts upon the praxis of society, and internally, with respect to how celebrations were expressed in words through liturgical texts.[7] Hippolyte Delehaye considered local sources to be most reliable for confirming the veneration of a saint—the whole object of the historical science of hagiography—because such sources presented the 'living and authentic trad-ition of the community'.[8] It is the living and authentic tradition that is the ultimate focus of any investigation of a liturgical change such as the Byzanti-nization of the Jerusalem patriarchate—my primary focus here. How did the shift from a local Hagiopolite calendar to a universal Byzantine calendar affect the church of Jerusalem? And is this change reflected in the liturgical texts? As Buchinger admits, however, 'a lot of detailed investigation will have to take place before responsible attempts at a synthesis can be undertaken'.[9] This chapter proposes an investigation into the details of the Hagiopolite liturgical year and its Byzantinization in order to provide a foundation on which both analysis and synthesis can be built in response to these challenges.

---

[2] Baumstark, *Comparative Liturgy*, 152.

[3] For a bibliography of studies in other disciplines that support such a study of liturgy, see Taft, *Through Their Own Eyes*, 4–10; Taft, *Concluding Rites*, 67–71.

[4] For an example of the application of such a method, see Robert F. Taft, SJ, 'Byzantine Liturgical Evidence in the Life of St Marcian the Œconomos: Concelebration and the Preana-phoral Rites', OCP 48 (1982), 159–70; Taft, *Through Their Own Eyes*, 12–14.

[5] See Sauget, *Synaxaires Melkites*, 432.   [6] Buchinger, 'Das Jerusalemer Sanctorale', 120.

[7] Buchinger, 'Origin and Development', 29.

[8] Delehaye, *Cinq leçons* (see n. 1 here), 46–7.

[9] Buchinger, 'Origin and Development', 29.

THE STRUCTURE AND CHARACTERISTICS OF
THE HAGIOPOLITE LITURGICAL YEAR

Before I turn to the problem of the Byzantinization of the liturgical year, let me first examine the basic aspects of Jerusalem's calendar, namely its structure, its development, and the categories of feasts.[10]

Kornelii Kekelidze's study of the Georgian manuscript GL (L) from Mestia, one of the manuscripts used by Tarchnishvili for his edition of the GL, allowed Kekelidze to note several characteristics of the liturgical year in Jerusalem. Most important were the beginning of the year in December, the presence of octaves after Theophany (6 January) and the feast of Enkainia (13 September), and the insertion of the movable Lenten content between March and April.[11] Lent in the AL, with readings exclusively from the Old Testament on weekdays, lasted for six weeks plus the week of the 'paschal fast' before Easter (i.e. Holy Week), although there are traces of an older, shorter structure of Lent within the lectionary.[12] This movable Lenten and paschal cycle was inserted between 29 March and 1 May in the AL, the same period of the year in which part of Lent and the fifty days of Pentecost would fall.

The Beginning of the Liturgical Year

The way in which calendars or liturgical books begin is noteworthy. The liturgical year in the Jerusalem patriarchate began with feasts of the Incarnation.[13] Thus Jerusalem did not highlight Pascha as the first feast of the liturgical year, as we see in liturgical books from Constantinople. Certain Syriac and Arabic sources, such as *Sinai Syr. M52N* (9th–10th cent.) and al-Bīrūnī's eleventh-century Melkite calendar, celebrate the indiction on 1 September,[14] but this is not considered to be the beginning of the liturgical year; nor is 1 September the physical beginning of these liturgical books or calendars, since they all begin with celebrations on 1 October (*Teshri I/Tishrīn I*). The Hagiopolite liturgical station of the feast of Indiction specified in *Sinai Syr. M52N* (9th–10th cent.) is the Probaitic Pool.[15] Georgian sources such as the GL and *Sinai Geo. O. 34*

---

[10] For a similar introduction to the Byzantine liturgical year, see Albert Ehrhard, 'Das griechische Kirchenjahr und der byzantinische Festkalender', in idem, *Überlieferung*, vol. 1, 25–53. See also Alexander A. Tkachenko, 'Год церковный', ПЭ 11, 672–83; Alexander A. Lukashevich, 'Годовой неподвижный богослужебный круг', ПЭ 11, 668–9.

[11] Kekelidze, *Канонарь*, 27.

[12] For a discussion of this question, see AL 24–6 and 45–9; Bradshaw and Johnson, *Origins of Feasts*, 92–113.

[13] See Talley, *Liturgical Year*, 129–34.

[14] Mateos, *Typicon*, vol. 1, 54; Grumel, *Chronologie*, 193–203; Nicolas Oikonomides, 'Indiction', ODB II, 993.

[15] See Philothée, *Nouveaux manuscrits syriaques*, 515; al-Bīrūnī, *Fêtes des Melchites*, 312.

(10th cent.) also commemorate the Indiction, but these liturgical books begin either with the Nativity of Christ or with 1 January. The station in these two sources is also the Probaitic Pool.[16]

The way the liturgical year began could be theologized—for example, according to the meaning that certain church fathers have attributed to the beginning of each of the four Gospels.[17] It appears, however, that the date for the beginning of the liturgical year was chosen rather for practical or polemical reasons. In Constantinople, beginning the year on 1 September had the practical purpose of connecting the fiscal and the ecclesiastical years. Note, however, that until 1 September 462 the beginning of the liturgical year (τὸ νέον ἔτος) in Constantinople was celebrated on 23 September, the date of St John the Baptist's conception, which was, chronologically speaking, the first New Testament event recorded in the Gospels.[18] In Jerusalem the shift to the Nativity of Christ as the beginning of the liturgical year comes amid post-Chalcedonian tensions between various denominations and factions as well as from the need to observe the imperially ordered feast of Nativity (which will be examine in greater detail here).

Octaves

An important element in the liturgical year of the AL was the celebration of an octave after Easter and Theophany. Each day of the octave included a eucharistic synaxis in a different Hagiopolitan church. As the 6 January feast of Theophany was originally a celebration of the manifestation of Christ, its octave had readings that narrated events from the early life of Christ and ended with the feast of Jesus' Presentation in the Temple on 14 January.[19]

While Egeria describes octaves after certain major feasts and these are found in the GL, their Hagiopolitan origin is confirmed through a comparative examination of Constantinopolitan sources.[20] Juan Mateos indicates that, except for the eve of certain feasts and the octave of Easter, pre-feasts (προεόρτια), post-feasts, and octaves are completely unknown in *Hagios Stavros Gr. 40* (10th cent.), the principal manuscript used in his edition of

---

[16] See GL § 1198; Garitte, *Calendrier palestino-géorgien*, 88.

[17] For example, St Gregory the Great, *Homilies on Ezekiel* 1.4.1, in *Ezekiel, Daniel*, ed. by Kenneth Stevenson and Michael Glerup (Ancient Christian Commentary on Scripture, Old Testament XIII, Downers Grove, IL: InterVarsity Press, 2008), 5 (Ezekiel 1:4–24).

[18] Mateos, *Typicon*, vol. 1, 54–5; Stefano Parenti, 'Il tempo della Liturgia', in *Tempus mundi umbra aevi: Tempo e cultura tra Medioevo e Età moderna: Atti dell'incontro nazionale di studio (Brescia, 29–30 marzo 2007)*, ed. by Gabriele Archetti and Angelo Baronio (Brescia: Fondazione Civiltà Bresciana, 2008), 123–36, here 134.

[19] AL, 210–25.

[20] Egeria, *Itinéraire*, § 25: 10–11 and § 49: 3 (= pp. 252–5 and 318–19 Maraval); GL § 1535–59.

the Typikon of the Great Church.[21] Later, non-Constantinopolitan sources used in Mateos' edition do mention more pre-feasts and vigils on the eve of feasts (παραμονή), giving suport to the hypothesis of a Hagiopolitan origin of octaves.[22] It is noteworthy that the tenth-century Sinaitic monk Iovane Zosime, who was conversant with both Hagiopolite and Constantinopolitan liturgical practices, mentions the observance of post-feasts and octaves only within the Jerusalem patriarchate:

ხოლო არს დღესასწაული რომელსა ბ-სა და გ დღესა ზედაასხზედა პატივსცემენ იერუსალჱმს და საბა წმიდას და მსგებსითაცა. ხოლო თქუენ ვითა გინებ ყავთ. ლოცვა ყავთ ჩუენ თჳს. ამენ.[23]	There are many feasts that are celebrated for two and three days in Jerusalem and at Saint Sabas, and some even for an octave. But you do as you wish. Pray for us. Amen.

The phrase 'But you do as you wish' suggests that there was some disagreement over octaves and that another practice, possibly Constantinopolitan, regarding octaves and post-feasts was observed among Zosime's brotherhood on Sinai. Nearly two centuries after Iovane Zosime, the Typikon of *Sinai Gr. 1096* (12th cent.) testifies to the continued practice of octaves around special feasts—in this case the feast of the Lavra's founder, St Sabas the Sanctified, on 5 December.[24] The same source also indicates that the Dormition of the Theotokos on 15 August was celebrated for nine days (ἑορτάζομεν δὲ ἡμέρας θ').[25]

Some calendars provided general commemorations for every day of the week. These were presumably held when there was no major celebration of a saint and no other holiday. Iovane Zosime's note on the weekly cycle of commemorations describes the Sabaite practice of his time:

დღჱ კჳრიაკჱ დღესასწაულ არს წმიდისა აღდგომისაა, და ბ-შაბათი და გ-შაბათი სინანულისაა, და დ-შაბათი და პარასკევი ჯუარისაა, და ე-შაბათი ღმრთისმშობელისაა, და შაბათი წმიდათაა და სულისაა.[26]	Sunday is the day of the holy Resurrection, Monday and Tuesday are of repentance, Wednesday and Friday are of the Cross, Thursday is for the Theotokos, and Saturday is for the saints and departed.

---

[21] Mateos, *Typicon*, vol. 2, 294.   [22] Ibid., 311.
[23] Garitte, *Calendrier palestino-géorgien*, 114.
[24] *Sinai Gr. 1096* (12th cent.), fol. 55r–57v; Dmitrievskii, *Описание* III, 34–5.
[25] *Sinai Gr. 1096* (12th cent.), fol. 126r; Dmitrievskii, *Описание* III, 54.
[26] Garitte, *Calendrier palestino-géorgien*, 119.

This order of weekday commemorations, particularly the dedication of Mondays and Tuesdays to repentance, reflects the more primitive system recorded in the *stichera* and sessional hymns (καθίσματα) of some Stoudite Oktoechoi and Triodia.[27] However, the fact that Zosime's calendar dedicates Thursday to the Theotokos instead of the Apostles—who were commemorated on Thursdays in Stoudite sources—shows his adherence to Sabaite practice of the time, which can be confirmed by the commemoration of the Theotokos in the hymnography for Thursdays in the Sabaite Horologion *Sinai Gr. 863* (9th cent.).[28]

The Fixed and Movable Cycles

The complicated harmonization of the fixed and movable cycles led to the development of the Byzantine rite's liturgical Typikon, a type of book intended to resolve problems when certain feasts from one cycle or the other coincided or collided. This occurs most commonly in late winter and in spring, when the movable paschal cycle has its major holidays. In early Hagiopolite liturgical books, the problem was obviated by the presence of both cycles in the same book. Thus, in the GL, the movable cycle of Great Lent, Pascha, and Pentecost was inserted between 30 March and 1 April,[29] while in the *Iadgari* it was inserted between the feast of Hypapante on 2 February and the commemoration of St George on 23 April.[30] The GL reveals its compiler's awareness of the possible overlap of the two cycles, since there are places where the manuscripts of the GL provide alternative readings in case a fixed feast should fall within the paschal season. An example of this is the commemoration of St Peter, Archbishop of Jerusalem, on 19 April.[31]

Many of the liturgical calendars that will be examined here, such as *Sinai Syr. M52N* (9th–10th cent.) and *Sinai Geo. O. 34* (10th cent.), only include the fixed cycle. This presupposes that these calendars were used in conjunction with other liturgical books, which regulated the movable cycle according to the date of Easter. However, the intricate connection between the fixed and the movable cycles is more clearly visible in Gospel books—especially *Sinai Ar. 116* (995/6)—many of which connect the movable cycle of Gospel readings in the lectionary to fixed commemorations such as the Exaltation of the Cross,

---

[27] Olga Aleksandrovna Krasheninnikova, 'К истории формирования седмичных памятей октоиха', *Богословские труды* 32 (1996), 260–8, here 263. For more on the weekly cycle, see also Irénée-Henri Dalmais, 'Les commémorations des saints dans l'office quotidien et hebdomadaire des liturgies orientales', *La Maison-Dieu* 52 (1957), 98–108; Elena Velkova Velkovska, 'The Liturgical Year in the East', in *Handbook for Liturgical Studies*, vol. 5, 157–76, here 169–70.

[28] Mateos, 'Horologion', 62; Parenti, 'Fascicolo ritrovato', 355–6.

[29] Between GL § 281 and GL § 907.

[30] The movable cycle is found in *Iadgari*, 99–233.   [31] See GL § 924.

Nativity, and Theophany.[32] François Halkin has noticed this connection between the movable cycle of Gospel readings and fixed commemorations in several Greek menaia. For example, the July Menaion in the *Berlin Staatsbibliothek (Preußischer Kulturbesitz) Gr. 277 (Fol. 41)* (12th cent.) provides homilies by St John Chrysostom on Matthew for each day, supposing that Pascha would fall on 16 April and Pentecost on 4 June that year. The Constantinopolitan Praxapostolos *Moscow GIM Gr. Vladimir 21/ Savva 4* (11th cent.) also connects the fixed and movable cycles by prescribing the reading of Lazarus and the Rich Man (Luke 16:19–31), from the Gospel cycle of Luke depending on Pentecost, which was expected to fall on the Sunday after 6 November.[33]

The Development of the Calendar

While the fifth-century AL is the earliest Hagiopolite liturgical calendar, earlier examples of church calendars from elsewhere in Christendom do exist. The most noteworthy are the Roman *Depositio episcoporum et martyrum*, dated to 354,[34] and the ancient Syrian martyrology from *British Museum Add. 12150*, a document in Syriac from Nicomedia in Bithynia dated to 411.[35] These, however, are simply lists of commemorations of feasts and saints' days without any liturgical indications of lections, psalms, hymns, or rubrics for stations or the location of the liturgical synaxis. The Syrian martyrology and the extant homily of Hesychius of Jerusalem (d. after 451) on the feast of the Conception of St John—a commemoration not found in the AL—both suggest that the sanctoral cycle of the AL may have been selective rather than exhaustive.[36] For example, Egeria mentions that feasts of martyrs were celebrated during Lent, but few such commemorations are found in the AL.[37] Does this suggests that the feasts of martyrs interrupted the fast if they were

---

[32] Andreou, *Praxapostolos*, 253.

[33] See Ehrhard, *Überlieferung*, vol 3.1, 85–90, especially 89; F. Halkin, 'Fêtes fixes et fêtes mobiles: Leur fusion dans des calendriers byzantins', AB 86 (1968), 372.

[34] For an introduction to this source, see Michele Renee Salzman, *On Roman Time: The Codex-Calendar of 354 and the Rhythms of Urban Life in Late Antiquity* (Berkeley, CA: University of California Press, 1990).

[35] William Wright, 'An Ancient Syrian Martyrology', *Journal of Sacred Literature and Biblical Record* 8.15 (1865), 45–56 and 8.16 (1866), 423–32; François Nau, *Martyrologes et Ménologes orientaux*, I–XIII: *Un martyrologue et douze Ménologes syriaques* (PO 10.1, Paris: Firmin-Didot, 1915), 7–26; *Breviarium syriacum, seu Martyrologium syriacum saec. IV iuxta Cod. SM. Musaei Britannici Add. 12150*, ed. by Bonaventura Mariani, OFM (Rerum Ecclesiasticarum Documenta Subsidia Studiorum 3, Rome: Herder, 1956).

[36] See Homiliae XVI, *In conceptionem venerabilis Praecursoris*; BHG 860c; CPG 6587; Aubineau, *Hésychius de Jérusalem*, vol. 2, 668–704; Barry Baldwin, 'Hesychios of Jerusalem', ODB II, 924–5.

[37] Egeria, *Itinéraire*, § 27: 5 (= p. 246 Maraval); Buchinger, 'Das jerusalemer Sanctorale', 117.

celebrated on Wednesday or Friday, or does it simply point to further discrepancies between texts from the early history of Jerusalem that describe liturgical celebrations and liturgical texts that were used to regulate the services themselves?

In Constantinople, the dating of the formation of the synaxarion has been the topic of significant debate.[38] While Deacon Euaristus' (10th cent.) dedicatory Epistle in the synaxarion can be dated to the sole rule of Constantine VII Porphyrogenitus (27 January 945–15 November 959), knowledge of the earlier text and structure of the synaxarion is less clear.[39] Cyril Mango brought into attention a type of book of the second half of the seventh century called a *synaxographi(o)n* (συναξογράφι[ο]ν) mentioned in the *Miraculi s. Artemii*.[40] Andrea Luzzi suggests this book to be a kind of brief list of synaxes with no more than the name of the commemoration and no descriptions or narrations, unlike the later synaxarion, which contains longer texts.[41] Joseph-Marie Sauget's study of Arabic Melkite synaxaria has revealed their similarity to Byzantine synaxaria, in particular the Constantinopolitan Greek Synaxarion G, whose primary manuscript is *Milan Bibliotheca Ambrosiana Gr. C. 101 Sup.* (12th cent.), and Synaxarion D*, which is based on *Paris BNF Gr. 1587* (12th cent.).[42] However, the divergences between Arabic synaxaria from Syria and Greek synaxaria from Constantinople reveal the retention of local layers among Arabic-praying Rūm in the Jerusalem patriarchate, which Sauget has identified as a 'Melkite proper', as well as elements from Mount Sinai and from Coptic calendars.[43]

Categories of Feasts

The bare sanctoral cycle of the AL included about twenty-five celebrations, which Charles Renoux was able to divide into three categories.[44] Similarities can

---

[38] For a summary of the bibliography on this question, see Luzzi, 'Epoca di formazione del sinassario di Costantinopoli', 75.

[39] Delehaye, *Synaxarium*, xiii–xiv; Luzzi, 'Epoca di formazione del sinassario di Costantinopoli', 86–7 and 90–1; Alexander Kazhdan, 'Evaristos', ODB II, 762.

[40] BHG 173. See Cyril Mango, 'The Relics of St Euphemia and the Synaxarion of Constantinople', BBGG n. s. 53 (1999), 79–87, here 81–2. For the relevant passage from the martyrdom of St Artemios, see *Varia Græca Sacra: Сборникъ греческихъ неизданныхъ богословскихъ текстовъ IV–XV вѣковъ*, ed. by Athanasios Papadopoulos-Kerameus (St Petersburg: Kirschbaum, 1909), 76; *The Miracles of St Artemios: A Collection of Miracle Stories by an Anonymous Author of Seventh-Century Byzantium*, ed. by Virgil S. Crisafulli and John W. Nesbitt (Leiden: Brill, 1997), 208.

[41] Luzzi, 'Epoca di formazione del sinassario di Costantinopoli', 77–9.

[42] For a basic comparison of the Melkite synaxarion with these synaxaria, see Sauget, *Synaxaires Melkites*, 115–60.

[43] Ibid., 162–96.   [44] AL, 50.

be found when this cycle is compared with commemorations in the GL. The three categories are as follows:

1. Dedications of churches (նաւակատիք, *nawakatik*ʿ; სატფური, *satpuri*), for example the feast of Dedication (*enkainia*) of the Anastasis on 13 September, with the commemoration and display of the precious Cross on the following day;[45]

2. Depositions of relics (դիր, *dir*; დადგმაჲ, *dadgmay*) the only two in the AL being for the Prophets Zachariah on 10 June and Isaiah on 6 July,[46] while in the GL there are about twenty-seven depositions; and

3. Commemorations (յիշատակ, *yishatak*; ჴსენებაჲ, *ksenebay*) on anniversaries of the death of saints or days of remembrance, such as for Sts James and David on 25 December in the AL.[47]

Feasts in Greek liturgical calendars cannot be classified so easily, since many calendars do not indicate the reason why a saint is celebrated on a certain day. In fact most calendars simply give the name of the saint, usually in the genitive case, without further elaboration.[48] Most feast days of saints in Greek calendars are simply mentioned as their 'memory', 'remembrance', or 'commemoration' (μνήμη) without specifying the reason for the specific date.[49] St Andrew of Crete (d. 4 July 740) uses the phrase 'annual memory' (ἐτήσιος μνήμη) in a *sticheron* for the feast of St Dionysius the Areopagite, without elaborating on the nature of this commemoration.[50] For lack of any other explanation of why the saint is celebrated on this date, 'memory' (μνήμη) is here understood to refer to a saint's *dies natalis*.[51]

The type of saints' commemorations in the Typikon *Sinai Gr. 1096* (12th cent.) is generally unspecified, although in some cases this Typikon still distinguishes a pre-feast (προεόρτιον) from a deposition of relics.[52] A distinction also exists between 'transfer' (ἀνακομιδή), for example the

---

[45] Ibid., 222–5.   [46] Ibid., 206 and 212.   [47] Ibid., 228–31, 54–4.

[48] For example, 'the memory of our venerable father Symeon Stylite' (ἡ μνήμη τοῦ ὁσίου πατρὸς ἡμῶν Συμεὼν τοῦ Στυλίτου) on 1 September. *Sinai Gr. 1096* (12th cent.), fol. 25r; Dmitrievskii, *Описаніе* III, 28.

[49] The word μνήμη can mean memory, remembrance, commemoration (of the departed, of Christ's sacrifice, of the Resurrection, of creation); the faculty of memory; act of memory, recollection, and record. See Lampe, *Patristic Greek Lexicon*, s.v. μνήμη.

[50] Δόξα. Ἦχος βʹ. Ἀνδρέου Ἱεροσολυμίτου· οἱ δὲ Βυζαντίου. 'Δεῦτε συμφώνως, οἱ πιστοί, τὴν ἐτήσιον μνήμην των Ἱεραρχῶν εὐφημήσωμεν' ('Glory. Tone 2 [doxastikon at vespers for Hieromartyr Dionysius the Areopagite on 3 October] by Andrew the Jerusalemite, now the Byzantine: 'Come, O faithful, let us praise the annual memory of the hierarchs with one accord'). Follieri, *Initia hymnorum*, vol. 1, 295.

[51] See Garitte, *Calendrier palestino-géorgien*, 349; Francesco Spadafora, 'Dionigi l'Areopagita', BS 4, 634–6; D. V. Zaitsev, 'Дионисий Ареопагит', ПЭ 15, 309–24.

[52] For example, the pre-feast of the Nativity of the Theotokos on 7 September, *Sinai Gr. 1096* (12th cent.), fol. 29r; Dmitrievskii, *Описаніе* III, 29.

transfer of the relics of St Stephen on 2 August,[53] and 'deposition' (κατάθεσις), such as the deposition of the relics of St Bartholomew on 24 August,[54] although the two terms are often used interchangeably. The textual examples cited by Geoffrey H. Lampe and Erich Trapp for the two terms both come from Greek authors with a connection to Antioch or Syria; and the terms in question are also used in Constantinople and Jerusalem. Thus, it is not possible to distinguish them as being either Constantinopolitan or Hagiopolitan.[55]

Apart from the octaves discussed above, some feasts are celebrated for more than one day through the inclusion of 'concomitant feasts'. These are commemorations of New Testament figures that follow the major feasts in which those figures are involved. Baumstark has hypothesized that concomitant feasts are of Antiochene origin.[56] Although the extension of a feast through supplemental celebrations related to the primary theme of the feast agrees with the idea of a Hagiopolitan octave, concomitant feasts are not explicitly present in the GL. As one might expect, however, the most common concomitant feasts of the Byzantine rite—such as those of St John the Baptist on 7 January after Theophany, of Sts Symeon and Anna on 3 February after Hypapante, and of Sts Joachim and Anna on 9 September after the Nativity of the Theotokos—are already present in Iovane Zosime's calendar *Sinai Geo. O. 34* (10th cent.).[57] In *Sinai Gr. 1096* (12th cent.), there are rubrics for what to do 'on the second day of the feast' (εἰς τὴν δευτέραν ἡμέραν ἀπὸ τῆς ἑορτῆς) for feasts of the Lord (δεσποτικαῖς ἑορταῖς).[58] Thus, the classification of saints' days and commemorations changes significantly over the course of the roughly eight hundred years between the AL and the Sabaite Typikon in *Sinai Gr. 1096*.

HAGIOGRAPHY, HOMILIES, AND HYMNOGRAPHY

In order to approach the study of the liturgical calendar, we must rely on the associated literary genres of hagiography, homily, and hymnography—the

---

[53] *Sinai Gr. 1096* (12th cent.), fol. 121v; Dmitrievskii, *Описание* III, 53; Lampe, *Patristic Greek Lexicon*, 107; Trapp, *Lexikon zur byzantinischen Gräzität*, 81 (ἡ ἀνακομιδή [λειψάνων]: *Überführung* ['transfer']).

[54] *Sinai Gr. 1096* (12th cent.), fol. 127r; Dmitrievskii, *Описание* III, 55; Lampe, *Patristic Greek Lexicon*, 708; Trapp, *Lexikon zur byzantinischen Gräzität*, 778 (τὸ καταθέσιον: *Bestattung* ['interment, burial'], *Beisetzung von Reliquien* ['sepulture, burial']).

[55] For ἀνακομιδή, the example is from John of Damascus, *Passio Artemii* 9, PG 96: 1260B. For κατάθεσις, see John Malalas, *Chronographia* XVIII, PG 97: 701B. For more on this author, see Barry Baldwin, 'Malalas, John', ODB II, 1275.

[56] Baumstark, *Comparative Liturgy*, 157, 163, 182–3.

[57] Garitte, *Calendrier palestino-géorgien*, 44, 48, 89.

[58] *Sinai Gr. 1096* (12th cent.), fol. 123v; Dmitrievskii, *Описание* III, 53.

'three Hs', as Alexander Kazhdan (1922–97) called them.[59] These 'interpretative genres' (to use Frances Young's formula) all revolve around worship, liturgy, and prayer, which are at the heart of scriptural interpretation and cultural identity.[60] Their methods and how they relate to the liturgical calendar will be briefly described here.

Early twentieth-century Bollandists, especially Hippolyte Delehaye (1859–1941),[61] compiled, edited, and systematized numerous hagiographic materials, grouping them as either literary monuments or liturgical documents.[62] Liturgical documents, mainly martyrologia, were further classified as local or general. Delehaye considered the local sources to be the most reliable ones when it came to confirming the veneration of a saint—the whole object and primary focus of the historical science of hagiography— because they presented the 'living and authentic tradition of the community'.[63]

Because of the prestige of the Holy Land and the numerous pilgrims and monks that visited and settled in Palestine, 'the dimension of Palestinian hagiography is not merely local. Produced in part by Christians who came from elsewhere, with their own literary culture, it spread swiftly throughout Christendom, in turn exerting its own influence and becoming integrated in the traditions of other Churches.'[64] For this reason it is possible to trace changes in the reception of Palestinian hagiography not only within the

---

[59] Alice-Mary Talbot, 'Alexander Kazhdan: In Memoriam', in Patrich, *Sabaite Heritage*, xii–xvii, here xvi.

[60] Young, *Biblical Exegesis*, 217–20. It is worth noting that Young does not explicitly mention hymnography, which grows as a genre after the early Christian period on which she focuses. Thus it is unclear whether hymnography would be included in the category 'Liturgy, Spirituality, Prayer' or in another category, such as 'Commentaries'.

[61] For an appraisal and summary of Delehaye's work, see Flor Van Ommeslaeghe, 'The *Acta Sanctorum* and Bollandist Methodology', in *The Byzantine Saint: 14th Spring Symposium of Byzantine Studies*, ed. by Sergei Hackel (Crestwood, NY: St Vladimir's Seminary Press, 1981), 155–63; Bernard Joassart, 'Hippolyte Delehaye (1859–1941): Un bollandiste au temps de la crise moderniste', in *Sanctity and Secularity during the Modernist Period: Six perspectives on hagiography around 1900*, ed. by Lawrence Barmann and Charles J. T. Talar (SH 79, Bruxelles: Société des Bollandistes, 1999), 1–45. See also Hippolyte Delehaye, *L'ancienne hagiographie byzantine: Les sources, les premiers modèles, la formation des genres: Conférences prononcées au Collège de France en 1935*, ed. by Bernard Joassart and Xavier Lequeux (SH 73, Bruxelles: Société des Bollandistes, 1991); Bernard Joassart, *Hippolyte Delehaye: Hagiographie critique et modernisme*, 2 vols (SH 81, Bruxelles: Société des Bollandistes, 2000).

[62] Delehaye, *Cinq leçons* (see n. 1 here), 9. See also François Halkin, *Recherches et documents d'hagiographie byzantine* (SH 51, Bruxelles: Société des Bollandistes, 1971). Other attempts to systematize hagiographic material include Archbishop Sergei, Полный мѣсяцесловъ востока, 3 vols (Vladimir: Типо-Литографія В.А. Паркова, 1901). Also useful are the detailed calendrical entries in Nancy Patterson Ševčenko, *Illustrated Manuscripts of the Metaphrastian Menologion* (Chicago, IL: University of Chicago Press, 1990); Sofia Kotzabassi and Nancy Patterson Ševčenko, *Greek Manuscripts at Princeton, Sixth to Nineteenth Century: A Descriptive Catalogue* (Princeton, NJ: Princeton University Department of Art and Archaeology, 2010).

[63] *On y reconnaît la tradition vivante et authentique de la communauté, et aucun témoignage ne l'emporte sur celui-là en valeur et en précision.* Delehaye, *Cinq leçons* (see n. 1 here), 46–7.

[64] Flusin, 'Palestinian Hagiography', 200.

patriarchate of Jerusalem, but also elsewhere, such as in Constantinople. Bernard Flusin divides Palestinian hagiography into three periods: (1) from Constantine (*c*.325) to the Council of Chalcedon (451); (2) from 451 until the Arab conquest; and (3) from the 630s onward, without any clear terminus.[65] Although Flusin is aware of the complexity and variety of the hagiographical texts, he does not pay the attention that is due to Old Testament figures and their persistent cults in the Hagiopolite sanctoral.

Delehaye's contemporary, Anton Baumstark, put hagiographical material to use in the study of liturgy and transformed it by extracting laws of liturgical evolution from mere data, by means of systematic comparative analysis. The development of the commemoration of saints, particularly the relationship between the 'native country' of certain saints and feasts and their subsequent diffusion to different churches and regions, points to a mutual dependence between one territory and another; in other words it points to the existence of a centre and a periphery of a saint's cult. To understand this development, one must look at the primitive meaning and historical background of these feasts.[66]

One way to understand this meaning is by entering into the mental world of those who celebrated the feast or venerated the saint. Robert Taft, one of the strongest advocates of Baumstark's comparative method, balances top-down perspectives from official ecclesiastical texts that hand down the 'approved line' against popular literature and hagiography.[67] Hagiographies provide reliable testimonies of 'liturgy from the bottom up', since they describe actual liturgical services and what people thought of them. The reliability of such accounts can be better established today due to advances in the contextual history of hagiographical texts.[68] Taft points out that the 'ingenuousness' of the hagiographer renders the account 'reliable beyond suspicion' for the liturgical historian: 'If a legend recounts how an unworthy monk's hand withered when he extended it to receive Communion, the point the liturgical historian gleans from the narrative is that at that time one still received Communion in the hand.'[69] The diary of Egeria is the best example of what such an approach can furnish for liturgical research, particularly for the early liturgy of Jerusalem. The lives of Palestinian monks written by Cyril of Scythopolis, as well as the life of Peter the Iberian, are also useful under this aspect.[70] Another example, this time from Constantinople, is that of a *Life* of St Marcian of Constantinople (d. *c*.474), dated to the fifth or sixth century,

---

[65] Ibid., 200. [66] Baumstark, *Comparative Liturgy*, 152.

[67] See Taft, *Through Their Own Eyes*, 12–14.

[68] For various criteria in evaluating hagiographic texts, see Thomas Pratsch, 'Exploring the Jungle: Hagiographical Literature between Fact and Fiction', in *Fifty Years of Prosopography: The Later Roman Empire, Byzantium and Beyond*, ed. by Averil Cameron (Proceedings of the British Academy 118, Oxford: Oxford University Press, 2003), 59–72.

[69] Taft, *Through Their Own Eyes*, 14. [70] For more on these texts, see Chapter 1.

which provides clear evidence of a pre-anaphoral lavabo rite four or five hundred years before any liturgical manuscript confirms its existence.[71] But, quite apart from these uses of hagiography, there is a very practical and basic reason to turn to hagiography in the study of liturgical calendars: the desire to understand why a certain feast is celebrated on a given day. The connection between a saint and a date is not always clear in the liturgical books. Besides, although commemorations often make geographic specifications, the books themselves may have been copied in a different region from the one in which they were used, and hence may reflect completely different traditions.[72]

The variety of subjects covered by homilies give them great value in throwing light upon what was going on in church during the liturgical year.[73] For this reason Harald Buchinger classifies homilaries into the category of 'Liturgie-interpretative Quellen'.[74] The multivolume work of Albert Ehrhard (1862–1940) serves as an important resource in the study of homilies in the context of liturgy.[75]

In the case of Jerusalem, the genre of liturgical mystagogy seems to have disappeared after Sts Cyril and John of Jerusalem in the fourth and fifth centuries, but liturgical homilaries endure.[76] The ones most significant for their information on the liturgical year are those of Hesychius, a presbyter from Jerusalem (d. after 451),[77] and of St Sophronius (c.560–638), patriarch of Jerusalem.[78] Some of these homilies are preserved in the *Mravaltavi* (მრავალთავი), a Georgian calque of the Greek adjective *polykephalos* (πολυκέφαλος), which means 'with many headings/chapters'.[79] The *Mravaltavi*

---

[71] BHG 1032–1033d. For an example of the application of such a method, see Robert F. Taft, SJ, 'Byzantine Liturgical Evidence in the Life of St Marcian the Œconomos: Concelebration and the Preanaphoral Rites', OCP 48 (1982), 159–70. For a recent study of the life of St Marcian, see John Wortley, 'Vita Sancti Marciani Oeconomi', BZ 103: 2 (2010), 715–72.

[72] Sauget, *Synaxaires Melkites*, 432.

[73] For a clear introduction of the topic, see Robert F. Taft, 'Sermon', ODB III, 1880–1, and the bibliography presented there.

[74] Buchinger, 'Das Jerusalemer Sanctorale', 114.

[75] Ehrhard, *Überlieferung*. For indexes of this work, see Lidia Perria, *I manoscritti citati da Albert Ehrhard* (Testi e Studi Bizantino-Neoellenici IV, Rome: Istituto di Studi Bizantini e Neoellenici, 1979); Ernst Risch, *Handschriften-Register zu Albert Ehrhard* (Berlin: Griechischen Christlichen Schriftsteller, n.d.). At http://gcs.bbaw.de/bilder/handschriften-register-zu-albert-ehrhard (accessed on 31 March 2017).

[76] For more on this question, see Chapter 3, 'Mystagogies of the Liturgy of St James'.

[77] Aubineau, *Hésychius de Jérusalem*. For a complete list of the works of Hesychius, see J. Kirchmeyer, 'Hésychius de Jérusalem', in *Dictionnaire de spiritualité ascétique et mystique, doctrine et histoire*, vol. 7, ed. by Marcel Viller, SJ, Charles Baumgartner, and André Rayez (Paris: G. Beauchesne et ses fils, 1968), 399–408.

[78] Sophrone de Jérusalem, *Fêtes Chrétiennes à Jérusalem*, ed. and trans. by Jeanne de la Ferrière and Marie Hélène-Congourdeau (Les Pères dans la foi 75, Paris: Migne/Brepols, 1999). For more on St Sophronius, see Chapter 2, 'Greek Monastic Liturgy' and 'Islamic Ocupation'.

[79] See Trapp, *Lexikon zur byzantinischen Gräzität*, 1338. The Greek noun *polykephalon*, formed on the neuter forms of this adjective, is not used frequently. For more on the Georgian version of this book, see Tarchnishvili, *Geschichte*, 427–9.

is a collection of texts designed to be read during the liturgical year at various church services. Initially the texts were exclusively homilies for feasts of the Lord or of the Theotokos and were predominantly connected to the movable cycle. Eventually the collections grew to include hagiography and the lives of saints.[80] By the eleventh century, the term *Mravaltavi* had the same use as the Greek term *synaxarion* (συναξάριον) and designated a synaxarion—a book from which lives of saints were read at matins.[81] Like other Hagiopolite liturgical books, the *Mravaltavi* followed the order of the liturgical year: it began with the Annunciation on 25 March, went on to Christmas on 25 December and Theophany on 6 January, then to the Lenten and Easter cycles, and then to the summer months, which included the commemorations of Sts Peter and Paul and St Athenogenes.[82] Thus its order was similar to that of the *Iadgari*. Michel van Esbroeck has edited and analysed six manuscripts with the most ancient versions of *Mravaltavi* that survived.[83] However, Sauget laments that the study of specifically Melkite homiliaries is still in its preliminary stages, just like that of the synaxarion.[84] Stéphane Verhelst has continued van Esbroeck's study of the *Mravaltavi* and edited several homilies attributed to John of Bolnisi, a Georgian bishop about whom virtually nothing is known—except that his homilies were probably written around the eighth or ninth century. Many of these homilies refer to the pericopes of the Jerusalem lectionary that were read on the days and in the commemorations connected with the homilies.[85]

Hymnography is the 'privileged bearer of scriptural exegesis'. Using the formats of troparia and *stichera*, hymnography provides a 'commentary on individual books of Scripture and between the Old and New Testaments, in order to reconstruct the entirety of salvation history in relation to the *telos*, the *teleiosis*'.[86] Because this form of exegesis is used within the liturgy and is composed in various styles and forms, hymnography is one of the most complex aspects of liturgical studies. The extensive work of cataloguing Greek hymnography done by Enrica Follieri (1929–99) and Giuseppe Schirò

[80] Esbroeck, *Homéliaires géorgiens*, 2–5.

[81] Ibid., 6–7; Kekelidze, *Литургическіе грузинскіе памятники*, 301. For more on the history of the reading of the synaxarion at matins, see Skaballanovich, *Толковый Типиконъ*, vol. 2, 285–7.

[82] Esbroeck, *Homéliaires géorgiens*, 326–46.

[83] Ibid., 63–229. See also Hélène Métreveli, 'Un nouvel ouvrage sur le "Mravaltavi" géorgien', BK 35 (1977), 73–96; Tamila Mgaloblishvili, 'The Georgian Sabaite (Sabatsminduri) Literary School and the Sabatsmindian Version of the Georgian *Mravaltavi* (Polykephalon)', in Patrich, *Sabaite Heritage*, 229–33.

[84] Joseph-Marie Sauget, *Deux Panegyrika Melkites pour la seconde partie de l'année liturgique: Jérusalem S. Anne 38 et Ḥarīṣā 37* (ST 320, Città del Vaticano: Biblioteca Apostolica Vaticana, 1986), 7.

[85] Jean de Bolnisi, *Homélies*, ed. by S. Sardjveladze, T. Mgaloblišvili, and E. Koçlamazašvili, trans. by Stéphane Verhelst (SC 580, Paris: Cerf, 2015).

[86] Hannick, 'The Theotokos in Byzantine Hymnography', 76 (for both quotations).

(1905–84) still only skims the surface of what is needed in order to gain a fuller picture of the breadth and scope of Greek hymnography, since their catalogues index a limited number of sources. Follieri restricted her index of incipits to published texts, while Schirò edited only hymnographic canons in manuscripts connected to southern Italy.[87] Despite the enormous quantity and variety of Greek hymnography that has been studied, most hymnographic manuscripts remain unedited, let alone examined. Without a complete picture of the manuscript sources, our understanding of the development of hymnographic genres, of their liturgical books, and of their place in the liturgical tradition is still incomplete.[88] Translations of Greek hymns into Georgian,[89] Syriac,[90] or Church Slavonic[91] also complicate matters, since it is unclear whether hymns that are extant only in these languages come from lost liturgical traditions, such as the ancient liturgy of Jerusalem, or are simply alternative hymns that never found their way into the later Byzantine hymnographic repertoire and became part of the *textus receptus* of the current Byzantine rite.[92]

Hymnography is extremely important to the study of Hagiopolite liturgy because it was in Jerusalem and Palestine that the explosion of new hymns occurred after the Arab conquest.[93] As has been mentioned already in Chapter 3, Egeria's observation that readings and hymns were always appropriate to the time and place where they were used in the liturgy is reflected in

---

[87] Follieri, *Initia hymnorum*; Giuseppe Schirò, *Analecta hymnica graeca e codicibus eruta Italiae inferioris*, 13 vols (Rome: Istituto di studi bizantini e neoellenici, 1983). For an introduction to Follieri's work, see Enrica Follieri, 'The "Initia Hymnorum Ecclesiae Graecae" Bibliographical Supplement', in *Studies in Eastern Chant*, ed. by Egon Wellesz and Miloš Velimirović, vol. 2, ed. by Miloš Velimirović (New York: Oxford University Press, 1971), 35–50.

[88] For an index of hymnographers, see Casimir Émereau, 'Hymnographi byzantini quorum nomina in litteras digessit notulisque adornavit', *Échos d'Orient* 21 (1922), 258–79; *Échos d'Orient* 22 (1923), 11–25, 419–39; *Échos d'Orient* 23 (1924), 195–200, 275–85, 407–14; *Échos d'Orient* 24 (1925), 163–79; *Échos d'Orient* 25 (1926), 177–84. For more recent scholarship on the origin of hymnographic liturgical books, see Momina, 'О происхождении греческой триоди'; Irina E. Lozovaia, '"Новый октоих" св. Иосифа Гимнографа (Grottaferrata, Δ.γ. XIV) и его отражение в древнерусских параклитах студийской традиции', *Хризограф* 3 (2009), 190–203.

[89] See Frøyshov, 'Early Development', 140.

[90] Heinrich Husmann, *Ein syro-melkitisches Tropologion mit altbyzantinischer Notation Sinai syr. 261*, 2 vols (Wiesbaden: Otto Harrassowitz, 1975); Natalia Smelova, 'Melkite Syriac Hymns to the Mother of God (9th–11th centuries): Manuscripts, Language and Imagery', in *The Cult of the Mother of God in Byzantium: Texts and Images*, ed. by Leslie Brubaker and Mary B. Cunningham (Burlington VT: Ashgate, 2011), 117–31.

[91] Krivko, 'Гимнографические параллели'.

[92] For references to the standard printed Greek hymnographic liturgical books, in particular the Roman editions of the second half of the nineteenth century, see Follieri, *Initia hymnorum*, vol. 1, xi–xxvii.

[93] Frøyshov, 'Early Development', 144; Peter Jeffery, 'The Lost Chant Tradition of Early Christian Jerusalem: Some Possible Melodic Survivals in the Byzantine and Latin Chant Repertories', *Early Music History* 11 (1992), 151–90. For a new study of Jerusalem hymnography before the Arab conquest, see Petrynko, *Weihnachtskanon*, 21–39.

the great variability of the hymns used in liturgical services—especially in the structure of JAS, which retained variable hymns as an integral element until at least the twelfth century in Jerusalem.[94] This variability nevertheless depended upon the forms of other hymns used as models, which revealed connections in meaning, through mimesis, between the original and the hymn that imitated it, as well as intertextuality through intra- and extratextual cross-references.[95] For example, on Palm Sunday at matins the Typikon of the Anastasis includes troparia during Psalm 118 (*Εὐλογητάρια* or *Ἄμωμος*)[96] that paraphrase the usual troparia with a resurrectional theme; but here they are proper to Palm Sunday.[97] This should not be so astonishing if one considers that such variants exist in musical manuscripts even today for the Theotokos, St John the Baptist, various other saints, and the deceased. [98] Some of these variant hymns, for example the '*amomos* for the Theotokos' from the fourteenth century, have been retained in current Byzantine liturgical usage in some regions, while others are no longer part of liturgical practice and are preserved only in manuscripts.[99] Ioannis Phountoulis has published the hymns for a 'Holy Week' of St Demetrius—celebrated in Thessalonike from 19 October, which is dubbed 'Palm Sunday' (*Κυριακὴ τῶν Βαΐων*), until the actual feast of Demetrius' martyrdom on 26 October, called 'Pascha' (*Πάσχα*)—where the hymnography for every day of Holy Week and Pascha is slavishly imitated and adapted to focus on St Demetrius.[100] Thus, the *sticheron* for St Demetrius

[94] Egeria, *Itinéraire*, § 47: 5 (= p. 314 Maraval). For a study of the variable hymnody as it fits within the structure of JAS, see Charles Renoux, 'Песнопения Божественной литургии в савваитском Тропологии V–VIII веков', ПУЦТ 2, 96–110. See also the discussion of Egeria's comments in Chapter 2, 'The Christian Population and Its Languages'.

[95] See Young, *Biblical Exegesis*, 119–39 (Chapter 6, 'Reference and Cross-Reference'); Olkinuora, *Feast of the Entrance of the Theotokos*, 17–18.

[96] *Τῶν Ἀγγέλων ὁ δῆμος κατεπλάγη ὁρῶν σε ἐν νεκροῖς λογισθέντα, τοῦ θανάτου* ('The company of the Angels was amazed, seeing you numbered among the dead, [yet destroying the power] of death'). See Taft, *Hours*, 280, 288–9; Follieri, *Initia hymnorum*, vol. 4, 334; Sophronios Leontopoleos, *'Η Ἀκολουθία τοῦ Μεγάλου Σαββάτου καὶ τὰ Μεγαλυνάρια τοῦ Ἐπιταφίου* [part I]', *ΝΣ* 32 (1937), 273–88, especially 279; Sophronios Leontopoleos, *'Η Ἀκολουθία τοῦ Μεγάλου Σαββάτου καὶ τὰ Μεγαλυνάρια τοῦ Ἐπιταφίου* [part II]', *ΝΣ* 33 (1938), 370–7.

[97] Papadopoulos-Kerameus, *Anastasis Typikon*, 6.

[98] The troparia for the deceased found in tenth-century sources were originally sung on Saturdays in the regular weekly cycle and, as such, also mentioned martyrs and other saints who are commemorated on Saturdays throughout the year. These became part of funeral rites in the twelfth century. See Stefano Parenti, 'Тропарите-евлогитарии за покойници', in *Death and Funeral in Jewish–Christian Tradition*, ed. by Regina Koycheva and Anisava Miltenova (Studia Mediaevalia Slavica et Byzantina 1, Sofia: Българска академия на науките институт за литература, 2011), 155–70.

[99] See Diane H. Touliatos-Banker, *The Byzantine Amomos Chant of the Fourteenth and Fifteenth Centuries* (Ἀνάλεκτα Βλατάδων 46, Thessalonike: Πατριαρχικὸν Ἴδρυμα Πατερικῶν Μελετῶν, 1984), 201–2.

[100] Ioannis M. Phountoulis, *Μεγάλη Ἐβδομάς' τοῦ ἁγίου Δημητρίου* (*Κείμενα Λειτουργηκῆς* 17, Thessaloniki: n.p., 1979). My thanks to Alexander Lingas for bringing this source to my attention.

'Today the glory of the martyr has gathered us together'[101] parrots the *sticheron* from Palm Sunday 'Today the grace of the Holy Spirit has gathered us together';[102] and the canon of Pascha 'O day of Resurrection'[103] morphs into a hymn in praise of St Demetrius.[104] However, as we have seen in the previous chapter and shall see in several more cases here, although the hymns found in the GL are often retained in the Byzantine rite, their position within the ordo changes. Thus, for example, what was once a troparion in JAS becomes a *sticheron* during vespers or matins.[105] This exchangeability also existed at the level of texts themselves. It was not uncommon for the content and ideas expressed in hymnography to depend on 'systematic borrowing' from patristic homilies. From the seventh to ninth century, numerous hymnographers in Palestine adapted the works of early Christian writers and transformed them into hymns. One particular source of inspiration for hymnography was St Gregory of Nazianzos (*c.*329/30–90), whose discourses—not his poetry—often served verbatim as texts of newly composed hymnographic canons and *stichera*.[106]

THE BYZANTINIZATION OF THE HAGIOPOLITE CALENDAR: CASE STUDIES

The vast number of saints—a veritable 'great cloud of witnesses' (Hebrews 12: 1)—commemorated in the liturgical calendar might appear as a nebulous fog to the liturgical scholar who is trying to find a way forward through the various holidays and to make sense of the history, development, and theology of the sanctoral cycle. The pre-Sanctus prayer in the anaphora of JAS indicates four categories of saints—the righteous, the prophets, the Apostles, and the martyrs—but no specific names are given at this point.[107] As already mentioned, the diptychs of JAS contain such an overwhelming number of saints that a large infusion of saints in the diptychs of other anaphoras is labelled

[101] 'Σήμερον ἡ δόξα τοῦ ἐνθένου μάρτυρος ἡμᾶς συνήθροισε'. Phountoulis, 'Μεγάλη Ἑβδομὰς' τοῦ ἁγίου Δημητρίου, 19. This *sticheron* is not found in Follieri, *Initia hymnorum*.

[102] 'Σήμερον ἡ χάρις τοῦ ἁγίου Πνεύματος ἡμᾶς συνήγαγε'. Follieri, *Initia hymnorum*, vol. 3, 488.

[103] 'Ἀναστάσεως ἡμέρα, λαμπρυνθῶμεν λαοί'. Follieri, *Initia hymnorum*, vol. 1, 103. For the canon of Pascha, see Hugues Gaïsser, OSB, 'Les Heirmoi de Pâques dans l'Office grec: Etude rythmique et musicale', OC 3 (1903), 416–510.

[104] 'Ἀναστάσεως ἡμέρα, Δημητρίου σφαγή'. Phountoulis, 'Μεγάλη Ἑβδομὰ' τοῦ ἁγίου Δημητρίου, 118; Follieri, *Initia hymnorum*, vol. 1, 102.

[105] Kekelidze, *Канонарь*, 26; Leeb, *Die Gesänge*, 44–8. See Chapter 3, 'The *Introit*' for examples of this phenomenon.

[106] Peter Karavites, 'Gregory Nazianzinos and Byzantine Hymnography', *Journal of Hellenic Studies* 113 (1993), 81–98.

[107] Mercier, *Liturgie de Saint Jacques*, 198; *Liturgia ibero-graeca*, 77 (§79).

Table 4.1. Comparison table of liturgical calendars

Feast	AL	GL	*Sinai Geo. O.38 (979)*	*Sinai Syr.M52N* (9th–10th cent.)	*Sinai Geo. O.34* (10th cent.)	*Vatican Syr. 19 (1030)*	*Al-Bīrūnī* (11th cent.)	*Sinai Gr. 1096* (12th cent.)	*Typikon of the Great Church*	*Constantinople Praxapostolos* (11th cent.)

'Jerusalemized'.[108] The evidence from the sanctoral cycle is even more elaborate and 'requires an almost Talmudic casuistry to navigate through the morass' of often conflicting liturgical detail.[109] Hence this chapter cannot pretend to be definitive or exhaustive, but simply descriptive and representative of the complex interaction between liturgical calendars and commemorations. Rather than examine every single day of each calendar, my investigation of the Jerusalem calendar will be based on several case studies of individual saints who had a specific importance for the church of Jerusalem but also enjoyed universal church veneration, especially in Constantinople. Tracing the development of the liturgical commemoration of one saint or event at a time helps to break down the question of liturgical Byzantinization by infusing more concrete examples into this elaborate puzzle. The conclusions of each case study are summarized in a table that traces each commemoration diachronically, through eight calendar sources from within the Jerusalem patriarchate, and then compares it synchronically with two Constantinopolitan sources.[110] Table 4.1 serves as a general example.

The ten sources included in Table 4.1 offer the most complete information for the whole liturgical year. Nevertheless, examples from other, more fragmentary calendars, described in detail in Chapter 1 for the earliest sources and in Appendix 1 for Hagiopolite manuscripts after the eighth century, will also be discussed in each case study at the points where these manuscripts offer relevant information. Because of the complexity of the material presented here in an admittedly cursory manner, the function of the tables is to give the

---

[108] See Taft, *Diptychs*, 61–6, 190. For preliminary studies of the saints in the diptychs of JAS, see Kazamias, Θεία Λειτουργία τοῦ Ἁγίου Ἰακώβου, 273–82; *Liturgia ibero-graeca*, 261–77, 352–5.

[109] Robert F. Taft, SJ, 'The Veneration of the Saints in the Byzantine Liturgical Tradition', in Θυσία αἰνέσεως: *Mélanges liturgiques offerts à la mémoire de l'Archevêque Georges Wagner (1930–1993)*, ed. by Job Getcha and André Lossky (Paris: Presses S. Serge, Institut de théologie orthodoxe, 2005), 353–68, here 356.

[110] For a description of these sources, see Chapter 1 and Appendix 1.

reader an immediate visualization of the process of Byzantinization of the Hagiopolite calendar, to see the oldest strata of Hagiopolite feasts on the left side of the table in comparison with the Constantinopolitan calendars on the right, and to see where certain commemorations continue or are changed in the 'transitional' liturgical calendars.

Major Feasts of Christ

There is relatively little variation in the dates on which feasts of Jesus Christ were celebrated in Hagiopolite liturgical sources. In Constantinople certain feasts of Christ—such as Easter, Ascension, Pentecost, the eves and days of Nativity and Theophany, Transfiguration—were indicated as having a universal character. The Typikon of the Great Church refers to these feasts by the following phrase:

| ἑορτάζεται ἐν τῇ Μεγάλῃ Ἐκκλησίᾳ καὶ ἐν ταῖς κατὰ τόπον παντὸς τοῦ κόσμου ἁγίαις ἐκκλησίαις.[111] | [This feast] is celebrated in the Great Church and in the holy churches of the world, in all places. |

The similarity and continuity between Hagiopolitan and Constantinopolitan sources can be appreciated from Table 4.2.

Table 4.2. Major feasts of Christ

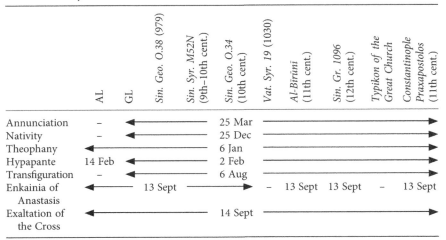

[111] Mateos, *Typicon*, vol. 2, 294.

Despite their universal nature, the chronology or significance of some of these events varied between Jerusalem and Constantinople. This is particularly the case with feasts that celebrated Christ's manifestation and incarnation from birth to baptism, or with the feast of the Exaltation of the Cross. The general cause of this variation is that some extant Hagiopolite calendars predated the introduction of these feasts into the liturgical year. Let us examine the variations among them in greater detail.

The Nativity of Christ and Theophany

The celebration of the Nativity of Christ could be considered one of the first examples of Byzantine liturgical influence upon the Hagiopolite calendar, already in the sixth century.[112] After learning that Jerusalem celebrated Hypapante on 14 February, forty days after the Nativity of Christ was celebrated on 6 January, Emperor Justinian (r. 527–65) issued a decree on 25 March 560 directed at the errors of the church of Jerusalem.[113] Justinian's letter was a reaction to Miaphysitism, which considered the separation of Christ's Nativity from Theophany as an admission of Nestorianism—the doctrine of a division in the person of Christ. The Orthodox position presented in the letter, which was based on Scripture and on the church fathers—specifically Gregory of Nazianzus, Gregory of Nyssa, Augustine of Hippo, and John Chrysostom—understood the Nativity to be the manifestation of Christ's earthly birth in time as a man, while Theophany was his revelation as the eternally-begotten son of God. For a time, under Patriarch Juvenal, Jerusalem celebrated the Orthodox dates of Christmas and Theophany after Chalcedon, as did Byzantinized Armenians in the sixth century.[114] Nevertheless, the fact that Justinian needed to reintroduce these celebrations through a letter shows that the non-Chalcedonian Miaphysites took control in the fifth or sixth centuries. Justinian's letter ordered Jerusalem to adopt the practices of

---

[112] For a study of the theology of the hymns in the *Iadgari* for these feasts, see Schneider, *Lobpreis im rechten Glauben*. For a history of the development of Christmas and Theophany in Palestine, see Botte, *Les origines de la Noël et de l'Épiphanie*, 13–21; Talley, *Liturgical Year*, 134–41; Mimouni, *Dormition et assomption de Marie*, 433–8; Galadza, 'Various Orthodoxies'.

[113] *Ego autem nunc, non coactione quidem nec potestate, sed e divinis sanctis scripturis et per sanctorum magistrorum inquisitionem et doctrinam, festinavi hoc vobis notificare et illis qui subvertunt festa, ad manifestationem ignorantiae eorum, ut convertantur ad scientiam* ('However, I now, not by pressure nor by power, but from the divine and sacred Scriptures and by the questioning and instruction of the holy teachers, hasten to notify you and those who subvert the feasts, so that their ignorance be manifest, in order that they be turned to knowledge'). Esbroeck, 'La lettre de l'empereur Justinien', 358, § 9.

[114] Ibid., 369–71; Charles Renoux, *Le lectionnaire de Jérusalem en Arménie: Le Čašocʻ.* I: *Introduction et liste des manuscrits* (PO 44.4, Turnhout: Brepols, 1989), 18.

Constantinople,[115] namely to transfer Christmas, Theophany, and the Encounter to their Constantinopolitan dates and to add the celebrations of St John the Baptist's Conception on 25 September and Nativity on 25 June, as well as that of the Annunciation to the Theotokos (that is, of Gabriel's announcement to Mary 'the God bearer') on 25 March.[116] This explains why the AL, which reflects the liturgical practices of the beginning of the fifth century, does not contain these commemorations. While these feasts were not instituted for polemical reasons, they were often used as a means to defend dogmas established at the councils of Nicaea, Ephesus, and Chalcedon.[117]

Although such imperial interference in Hagiopolitan practice could be considered an example of Byzantinization, the Jerusalem lectionary still influenced the practices of Constantinople for some time. Likewise, the new feast of the Nativity of Christ was adapted to the Hagiopolitan context, being celebrated at the holy sites with new readings and hymns directly connected to the birth of Christ and distinct from those of the Theophany feast.[118] After the vigil at the sheepfold and in the cave at Bethlehem, the eucharistic liturgy for Christmas day in the GL observed the standard structure of JAS, beginning with the *oxitay*. The text of this hymn for Christmas is as follows:

---

[115] *Nunc non quidem novum quid perquisivimus nos, sed e sanctis libris et patres magistri perquisiverunt et orthodoxi ab initio faciebant et nos etiam facimus et vobis quoque convenit perficere, ut simul magnificemus Patrem et Filium et Spiritum Sanctum* ('Now it is not something new, that which we have acquired, but obtained from holy books, and from the fathers and teachers, and what the Orthodox have been doing from the beginning, so likewise it is fitting for us and for you to do as well, in order that we together may magnify the Father, and the Son, and the Holy Spirit'). Esbroeck, 'La lettre de l'empereur Justinien', 362, § 20.

[116] Ibid., 358, 362. For more on the feast of Hypapante, see Robert F. Taft and Annemarie Weyl Carr, 'Hypapante', ODB II, 961–2; Heinzgerd Brakmann, *'Ἡ ὑπαπαντὴ τοῦ Κυρίου*. Christi Lichtmess in frühchristlichen Jerusalem', in *Crossroad of Cultures: Studies in Liturgy and Patristics in Honor of Gabriele Winkler*, ed. by Hans-Jürgen Feulner, Elena Velkovska, and Robert F. Taft, SJ (OCA 260, Rome: Pontifical Oriental Institute, 2000), 151–72.

[117] Botte, *Les origines de la Noël et de l'Épiphanie*, 86.

[118] For more on the feast of Christmas and its connection to Theophany, see Merja Merras, *The Origins of the Celebration of the Christian Feast of Epiphany*, 2nd edn (Joensuu, Finland: Joensuu University Press, 1995), 157–64; Gabriele Winkler, 'Neue Überlegungen zur Entstehung des Epiphaniefests', *ARAM* 5 (1993), 603–33; Gabriele Winkler, 'Die Licht-Erscheinung bie der Taufe Jesu und der Ursprung des Epiphaniefestes', *OC* 78 (1994), 177–229; Gabriele Winkler, 'The Appearance of the Light at the Baptistm of Jesus and the Origins of the Feast of Epiphany', in *Between Memory and Hope: Readings on the Liturgical Year*, ed. by Maxwell E. Johnson (Collegeville, MN: Liturgical Press, 2000), 291–348; Harald Buchinger, 'Die vielleicht älteste erhaltene Predigt auf das Epiphaniefest: Vier syrische Fragmente des Titus von Bostra (CPG 3578)', in *ΣΥΝΑΞΙΣ ΚΑΘΟΛΙΚΗ*, 1: 65–86.

ოხითაჲ ჴ~ ჲ ა: ყოვე…თა დაბადებუ…თა
შემოქმედი დმერთი, მამისა თანა მჯდომარეი,
შენ, დმრთისმშობელო მარიამ, ჴორციითა შვ.
რომელი მწყემსთა ანგელოზა მიერ ბეთლემს
დმერთი გამოუბრწყინდა და ვარსკულავისა
მიერ მოგუთა ეუწყა და თაყუანის-სცეს მას,
ჩუენცა უღირსნი ესე, დმრთისმშობელო, შენგან
მოზიდულსა ქრისტესა თაყუანის-ვსცემთ და
გადიდებთ შენ, კურთხეულო დედათა
მორის.[119]

Oxitay, Tone 1: The creator of all creation, who is seated with the Father, did you, O Theotokos Mary, bear in the flesh. The one whom the angels announced to the shepherds as God and made known to the Magi through the star who worshipped him, O Theotokos, we the unworthy also worship him—Christ—born of you, and glorify you, O blessed among mothers.

Next come the responsorial psalmody and the scriptural readings:

Psalm, Tone 2: 'The Lord said to me: You are my Son' (Ps 2:7)
Verse: 'Ask of me' (Ps 2:8)
Reading 1: Proverbs 8:22–31, 'Ages ago I was set up, before the beginning of the earth'
Reading 2: Daniel 2:34–35, 'The stone uncut by human hands'
Reading 3: Hebrews 1:1–12, 'You are my Son; today I have begotten you'
Alleluia, Tone 5: 'The Lord said to my Lord' (Ps 109:1)
Gospel: Matthew 2:1–23—Visitation of the Magi, flight to Egypt, and return to Nazareth[120]

After the Gospel comes the hymn of hand washing, which is based on the themes of the preceding Gospel reading:

ჴელთაბანისაჲ: უფალი იშვა ბეთლემს
ურიასტანისასა. ადმოსავალით მოვიდეს
მოგუნი თაყუანის-ცემად დმრთისა
განკაცებასა, საფასეთა მათთა გულსმოდგინედ
აადეს, ძდუენი პატიოსანი მიუპყრნს:
გამოცდილი ოქრო—დეუფესა საუკუნესა,
გუნდრუკი—დმრთისა ყოვე…სა, ვითარცა
[სამისა] დდისა მკუდარსა, მერი—უკუდავსა
მას. ყოველი თესლები მოვედით, თაყუანის-
ვსცეთ, რამეთუ ესე არს მაცხოვარი ჩუენ
ყოველთაჲ.[121]

Hymn of hand washing: The Lord is born in Bethlehem of Judea. From the East came Magi to worship the incarnation of God. They gladly opened their treasures, earnestly bringing gifts there: purified gold for the king of eternity, incense for the God of all, as well as for the one who was three days dead, myrrh for the immortal one. Come all you people and let us worship, for this one is the Saviour of us all.

---

[119] GL § 26; *Iadgari*, 21; Schneider, *Lobpreis im rechten Glauben*, 90.
[120] GL § 26–30.
[121] *Iadgari*, 21; Schneider, *Lobpreis im rechten Glauben*, 91. GL § 31 directs the reader to the hymns of the previous vigil.

This hymn's themes match the content of the preceding Gospel readings from Matthew 1:18–25 and Matthew 2:1–23 perfectly, in that they mention Magi bearing gifts but make no reference to angels and shepherds from the Lucan narrative, which was read at the 'place of the shepherds' during vigil on Christmas Eve. Reference to Christ's death and three-day burial both in this hymn and in the hymn 'Christ is born upon the earth' ($X\rho\iota\sigma\tau\grave{o}s\ \grave{\epsilon}\tau\acute{\epsilon}\chi\theta\eta$ $\grave{\epsilon}\pi\grave{\iota}\ \gamma\hat{\eta}s$)—which was sung instead of the *trisagion* in *Sinai Gr. N.E. MΓ 8* (10th cent.)—shows close intertextual connections between the Nativity of Christ and Pascha. Egon Wellesz has noted further similarities between the Greek hymnography attributed to Sophronius of Jerusalem for the Hours of Christmas Eve and that for Good Friday—similarities that draw out additional parallels between the mystery of Christ's birth and his passion, death, and resurrection.[122]

The last hymn provided for the Christmas Divine Liturgy of JAS in the GL and *Iadgari* is the hymn of the holy gifts sung during the transfer of the gifts:

სიწმიდის შემოყვანებისაჲ: რაჲ-მე შევწიროთ შენდა, ქრისტე? რამეთუ გამოჰჩნდი ჯორციითა, ვითარცა ცაცი, ჩუენ შორის. თითოეულნი, შენგან ქმნულნი, დაბადებულნი, მადლობით დიდებასა შემდგა შესწირვენ: ანგელოზნი—ქებასა, ცანი—მასკულავსა, მოგუნი—ძღუენსა, მწყემსნი—საკჳრველებასა, ხოლო ჩუენ—დედასა და ქალწულსა. რომელი საუკუნითგან ღმერთ ხარ, შეგვწყალენ ჩუენ.[123]

Hymn of the holy gifts: What can we offer you, O Christ, since you appeared through the flesh as a man among us? Each creature that you made brings you thanksgiving of praise: angels—praise, heaven—the star, the Magi—gifts, shepherds—marvel, and we—the mother and virgin. O you, who are God from eternity, have mercy on us!

This last hymn has been preserved in Greek and is sung as a *sticheron* at vespers on Christmas Eve.[124] In general, the themes of these hymns are Christologically sound, emphasizing Christ as the Word of God, seated with the Father, and born in the flesh, as man, from Mary the Theotokos.

---

[122] Egon Wellesz, 'The Nativity Drama of the Byzantine Church', *Journal of Roman Studies* 37: 1–2 (1947), 145–51.

[123] *Iadgari*, 22; Schneider, *Lobpreis im rechten Glauben*, 91. GL § 31 directs the reader to the hymns of the previous vigil.

[124] '$T\acute{\iota}\ \sigma o\iota\ \pi\rho o\sigma\epsilon\nu\acute{\epsilon}\gamma\kappa\omega\mu\epsilon\nu\ X\rho\iota\sigma\tau\acute{\epsilon}\dots$' ('What shall we offer you, O Christ…'). Follieri, *Initia hymnorum*, vol. 4, 155.

The hymns also reveal the important connection between the Jerusalem lectionary's scriptural readings and the hymnography sung during the ritual actions of the liturgy.

The 6 January feast in the GL, here called 'theophany' or 'manifestation' (განცხადებაჲ, *gancxadebay*), retained from the AL structure those readings that had to do generally with the manifestation of Christ and not specifically with Christ's birth, for example Titus 2:11–15, which speaks of the grace of God as appearing and bringing salvation to all people.[125] Otherwise the GL developed new themes for the 6 January feast that were related to washing and purification; it introduced new readings, such as Isaiah 12:1–6, which calls on the faithful 'wash yourselves and make yourselves clean', and 2 Kings 5:9–15, where Eliseus instructs Naaman to wash in the Jordan River seven times, afterwhich his flesh is restored like that of a little child.

Despite the imposition of Christmas on Jerusalem by imperial decree, the liturgical practice of Jerusalem preserved in the GL still maintained influence over Constantinople in other areas, serving as the thematic source for corresponding *stichera*, canons, and patristic readings during liturgical services. Theodore Stoudite (d. 11 November 826) and Joseph the Hymnographer (d. *c*.886) are believed to be the first editors of the Triodion, but its final redaction took place in Palestine.[126] Although the details and chronologies of the interaction between Jerusalem and Constantinople—especially in the realm of hymnography—are still vague, the continued importance of Jerusalem as both liturgical source and redactor until the end of the first millennium is recognized.[127] It is unfortunate that the Greek hymnographic manuscripts from the Sinai 'new finds', in particular the Tropologion *Sinai Gr. N.E. MΓ 56* and *Sinai Gr. N.E. MΓ 5* (8th–9th cent.) and the lectionary *Sinai Gr. N.E. MΓ 8* (10th cent.), are defective precisely at the point where the liturgical services of Christmas would be found.

The order for Christmas in the earliest Sabaite Typikon, *Sinai Gr. 1096* (12th cent.), is the first extant witness in Palestine of a 'purely' Constantinopolitan rite for Christmas. The manuscript makes no mention of JAS and prescribes the Christmas troparion of the Great Church of Constantinople, which was ultimately adopted without any trace of the former hymnography of the GL or *Iadgari*. The Typikon of the Great Church of Constantinople prescribes the following hymn for the Divine Liturgy at Christmas:

---

[125] GL § 83–116.   [126] Bertonière, *Sundays of Lent*, 141.
[127] Taft, *Byzantine Rite*, 56–7; Krivko, 'гимнографические параллели', 74–8.

καὶ τὴν εἴσοδον τῆς λειτουργίας ψάλλονται τροπάρια β΄. Τὸ α΄, ἦχος δ· Ἡ Γέννησίς σου, Χριστὲ ὁ Θεὸς ἡμῶν, ἀνέτειλε τῷ κόσμῳ, τὸ φῶς τὸ τῆς γνώσεως· ἐν αὐτῇ γὰρ οἱ τοῖς ἄστροις λατρεύοντες, ὑπὸ ἀστέρος ἐδιδάσκοντο· σὲ προσκυνεῖν, τὸν Ἥλιον τῆς δικαιοσύνης, καὶ σὲ γινώσκειν ἐξ ὕψους ἀνατολήν. Κύριε δόξα σοι.[128]	And at the entrance of the liturgy two troparia are sung. The first, tone 4: Your Nativity, O Christ our God, has made the light of knowledge dawn on the world, for by it those who adored the stars were taught by a star to worship you, the Sun of justice, and to know you the dayspring from on high. O Lord, glory to you!

Thematically, the Constantinopolitan troparion does not appear any more Chalcedonian or orthodox in its Christology and makes no mention of the Theotokos. Rather the hymn speaks of the replacement of the religion of the Magi with the worship of Christ, the 'Sun of justice'.

Enkainia and the Exaltation of the Cross

In the earliest sources of the Hagiopolitan calendar, such as the AL and the GL, the celebration of the Dedication of the Church of the Anastasis, also known by its Greek name Enkainia (ἐγκαίνια), was one of the most prominent commemorations of the Hagiopolitan liturgical year.[129] This feast is already found in the AL on 13 September and is followed on 14 September by a celebration in the Martyrium dedicated to venerating the Cross. This feast— the Exaltation of the Cross—is called 'the second day' and its liturgical services use the same texts as the ones used on the preceding day. This acknowledges the ascendancy of the 13 September Enkainia over the 14 September Exaltation: the latter is treated as a 'concomitant feast'.[130] The GL celebrates the Enkainia in the Anastasis on 13 September and then an octave follows, just as Egeria had observed in the fourth century.[131] The structure of a homily attributed to St John of Damascus, with the two specific themes of the foundation of the church and of the Cross, also points to the understanding

[128] Mateos, *Typicon*, vol. 1, 156. The second troparion is the *kontakion* 'Today, the virgin' (Ἡ Παρθένος σήμερον). See Follieri, *Initia hymnorum*, vol. 2, 10 and 58–60. For the preparatory period before Christmas in Constantinople, see Winkler, 'Die Interzessionen I', 316–20.

[129] Michael Alexander Fraser, *The Feast of the Encaenia in the Fourth Century and in the Ancient Liturgical Sources of Jerusalem* (Unpublished doctoral thesis, Durham: University of Durham, 1995, rev. 1996), 184–217. At http://encaenia.org/Fraser-MA_encaenia_1996.pdf (accessed on 1 June 2017). For more on the rite of dedication and consecration of churches, see Vincenzo Ruggieri, SJ, 'Consacrazione e dedicazione di chiesa, secondo il *Barberinus graecus 336*', OCP 54 (1988), 79–118; Vitaly Permiakov, 'Чин освящения храма в восточных традициях', ПУЦТ 3, 346–67; Permiakov, *'Make This the Place Where Your Glory Dwells'*.

[130] AL, 222–5. See the section 'Categories of Feasts' in this chapter.   [131] GL § 1234–54.

of the equal status of both the feasts of Enkainia and the Exaltation during the first half of the eighth century.[132]

The majority of the manuscripts employed by Juan Mateos for his edition of the Typikon of the Great Church do not include the Enkainia of the Anastasis in Jerusalem on 13 September or on any other day. Only the chief representative of synaxarion 'Family Fa', manuscript *Paris Gr. 1590* (1063), includes this feast as the first commemoration on 13 September.[133] Although it follows the rite of 'New Rome' (fol. 1r), the manuscript originates from one of the dependencies of the Jerusalem patriarchate, most likely the Monastery of Panagia Asinou (τῶν Φορβίων) on Cyprus, according to Jean Darrouzès, and probably not from a monastery in Palestine proper, as Hippolyte Delehaye had originally suggested.[134]

The Constantinopolitan Praxapostolos *Moscow GIM Gr. Vladimir21/Savva 4* (11th cent.) provides a significant testimony for the development of the celebration of Enkainia. The feast here is already of a secondary importance in relation to the Exaltation of the Cross celebrated on the following day. This is shown by the reference to the veneration of the Cross already in the rubrics for 13 September.[135] The Praxapostolos also reveals the secondary ranking of this Hagiopolite feast in relation to the Constantinopolitan dedication of Hagia Sophia on 23 December. The rubrics for the 13 September feast direct the reader to the commemoration on 23 December, still the principal feast of Enkainia in Constantinople in the eleventh century.[136]

While the Typikon *Sinai Gr. 1096* (12th cent.) does not commemorate the dedication of Hagia Sophia, the decline in prominence of the Enkainia of the Anastasis is clear. Here 13 September is still the Enkainia of the Anastasis, but it is also the pre-feast of the Exaltation, which is treated with greater solemnity and is celebrated with a vigil.[137]

---

[132] See Michel van Esbroeck, 'Le discours de Jean Damascène pour la Dédicace de l'Anastasis', OCP 63 (1997), 53–98, here 70. Van Esbroeck's dating of the homily to around 690–2 is based on information from the Greek *Vita* that is no longer accepted by scholars. A date after 706 is more likely. See Louth, *St John Damascene*, 6.

[133] Mateos, *Typicon*, vol. 1, 26–7.

[134] Jean Darrouzès, 'Manuscrits originaires de Chypre à la Bibliothèque Nationale de Paris', REB 8 (1950), 162–96, here 191; Jean Darrouzès, 'Autres manuscrits originaires de Chypre', REB 15 (1957), 131–68, here 144; Delehaye, *Synaxarium*, xxi; Mateos, *Typicon*, vol. 1, v.

[135] τὰ ἐγκαίνια τῆς ἁγίας Ἀναστάσεως Χριστοῦ τοῦ Θεοῦ ἡμῶν ('The *enkainia* of the Holy Resurrection of Christ our God'). Andreou, *Praxapostolos*, 216.

[136] τὰ ἐγκαίνια τῆς ἁγίας τοῦ Θεοῦ μεγάλης ἐκκλησίας ('The *enkainia* of the Holy Great Church of God'). Ibid., 284.

[137] Εἰ τύχοι ἐν Κυριακῇ ἀναστάσιμα οὐ ψάλλεται, ἡ δὲ στιχολογία γίνεται κατὰ τὸν τύπον τῆς ἀγρυπνίας ('If it should happen on a Sunday, the resurrectional [hymns] are not sung. The verses [of the psalms] follow the order of the vigil'). *Sinai Gr. 1096* (12th cent.), fol. 32v; Dmitrievskii, *Описание* III, 29.

To summarize, the feasts commemorating events in the life of Christ are celebrated universally on the same days both in Jerusalem and Constantinople and throughout Christendom. The development of the calendar in the sixth century introduced changes to the Christmas cycle and new feasts that were not found in the AL, such as the Annunciation and the Nativity of Christ. The Enkainia of the Anastasis was initially a local Hagiopolitan celebration and was not commemorated in Constantinople until the tenth century.

Feasts of the Theotokos

Of all the celebrations of the sanctoral cycle, the most recent feasts are those of the Theotokos.[138] This is surprising, considering that many events from the life of the Theotokos, for example the Annunciation, are found in the canon of Scripture. Most Marian feasts, however, originate in deuterocanonical or apocryphal literature, such as the *Protoevangelium of James*,[139] while biblical events, for example the visitation of Elizabeth by Mary (Luke 1:39–56), receive far less attention.[140] Regardless, the earliest liturgical calendars have few, if any, commemorations of the Theotokos. Some calendars, such as the sixth-century Syriac lectionary *British Museum Add. 14528* edited by Francis Burkitt and the Tropologion *Sinai Gr. N.E. MΓ 5* and *MΓ 56* (8th–9th cent.), contain no commemoration of the Theotokos at all.[141]

Recent studies of the Dormition of the Theotokos have investigated the origins of this feast and have argued that it was initially not a Marian celebration but had ancient Jewish roots or was actually a feast of the

---

[138] Baumstark, *Comparative Liturgy*, 186.

[139] Harm Reinder Smid, *Protoevangelium Jacobi: A Commentary*, trans. by Gertrude E. van Baaren-Pape (Assen: Van Gorcum, 1965); Ronald F. Hock, *The Infancy Gospels of James and Thomas*, with introduction, notes, and original text (The Scholars Bible 2, Santa Rosa, CA: Polebridge Press, 1995), 2–77. See also Henri Leclercq, 'Marie, mère de Dieu', DACL 10.2, 1982–2043; Irénée-Henri Dalmais, 'Les apocryphes de la dormition et l'ancienne liturgie de Jérusalem', *Bible et Terre Sainte* 179 (1976), 11–14; *Mary in the New Testament*, ed. by Raymond E. Brown, Karl P. Donfried, Joseph A. Fitzmyer, and John Reumann (Philadelphia, PA: Fortress Press, 1978); Olkinuora, *Feast of the Entrance of the Theotokos*, 24–38.

[140] Although there is traditionally no feast to commemorate this event in the Byzantine rite, Archimandrite Antonin (Kapustin) established this feast on 30 March at the Gornensky Monastery in Ein Karem, receiving permission from the Holy Synod of the Russian Orthodox Church on 5 August 1883. See N. N. Lisovoy, 'Горненский монастырь', ПЭ 12, 122–5. See also *Диякон Сергей Трубачев. Полное собрание богослужебных песнопений*, vol. 2, ed. by Hegumen Andronik (Trubachev) et al. (Moscow: «Живоносный Источник», 2011), 259–66 ('Въ дѣнь л҃: на срѣтенїе престҍ҇ыꙗ бц҃ы праведною є́лїсавѣтою').

[141] Francis C. Burkitt, *The Early Syriac Lectionary System* (London: British Academy/Oxford University Press, 1923); Nikiforova, *Из истории Минеи в Византии*, 195–235.

Incarnation of Christ.[142] The AL indicates that the 15 August celebration took place a few miles away from Bethlehem, at the Kathisma, the place where the Theotokos rested, showing a connection between her journey to Bethlehem and 15 August, while the GL indicates that the celebration took place at Gethsemane, later associated with the death of the Theotokos.[143] Despite uncertainty about the origins of the celebration of the Dormition of the Theotokos on 15 August, a question that is nevertheless beyond the scope of this study, what is important here is that in both the AL and the GL 15 August is a commemoration of the Theotokos. The earliest patristic Marian homilies by Hesychius of Jerusalem do not specify the day on which they were delivered,[144] but the *Mravaltavi* does provide homilies specifically for the Dormition. Michel van Esbroeck believes that these can be dated to as early as 500 on the basis of the topographical indications described in the journey between Jerusalem and Bethlehem.[145] In Hagiopolite liturgical texts, the earliest evidence of the name 'Dormition of the Theotokos' for this feast appears in *Sinai Syr. M52N* (9th–10th cent.). Unfortunately this name cannot be confirmed in earlier Hagiopolite lectionaries, such as *Sinai Gr. 210* and *Sinai Gr. N.E. Σπ. ΜΓ 12* (861/2), because the title of the pericope from Luke 1:39–56—the presumed Gospel reading for 15 August—has been lost.

The Syrian tradition and, to a certain degree, the liturgical tradition of Constantinople had a different primary Marian feast: the feast of the Synaxis of the Theotokos after the celebration of the Nativity of Christ, a type of 'concomitant feast'.[146] Martin Jugie believed that the first Marian feast in the

---

[142] See Walter Ray, *August 15 and the Development of the Jerusalem Calendar* (Unpublished doctoral thesis, Notre Dame, IN: University of Notre Dame, 2000); Stéphane Verhelst, 'Le 15 août, le 9 av et le Kathisme', *Questions Liturgiques* 82 (2001), 161–91. In evaluating recent scholarship on Mariology, one needs to be cautious of contemporary projections of 'low' or 'high' Mariology onto patristic sources. See A. Edward Siecienski, 'Mariology in Antioch: Mary in the Writings of Chrysostom, Theodoret of Cyrus, and Nestorius', SVTQ 56: 2 (2012), 133–69; Michel van Esbroeck, *Aux origines de la Dormition de la Vierge: Études historiques sur les traditions orientales* (Aldershot: Variorum, 1995). For the commemoration of Mary in the Anaphora of CHR, see Winkler, 'Die Interzessionen I', 320–34.

[143] AL, 354–7; GL § 1148–54; Fassler, 'The First Marian Feast in Constantinople and Jerusalem', 46–7; Mimouni, *Dormition et assomption de Marie*, 378–471. See Chapter 1, 'Stational Liturgy and the Topography of Jerusalem'.

[144] Ἡσυχίου, πρεσβυτέρου Ἱεροσολύμων, εἰς τὴν ἁγίαν Μαρίαν τὴν Θεοτόκον (Hesychius, presbyter of Jerusalem, for St Mary the Theotokos, BHG 1132); PG 93: 1460–68; Aubineau, *Hésychius de Jérusalem*, vol. 1, 158–68. See also Robert S. Pittman, *The Marian Homilies of Hesychius of Jerusalem* (Unpublished doctoral thesis, Washington, DC: Catholic University of America, 1974).

[145] Esbroeck, *Homéliaires géorgiens*, 342–6.

[146] Baumstark, *Comparative Liturgy*, 182–3, 186–9. See also Raes, 'La fête de l'Assomption en Orient', 268–9. For more on concomitant feasts, see the section 'Categories of Feasts' in this chapter.

East was celebrated on the Sunday before the Nativity of Christ and was part of a 'primitive Advent'.[147] However, the sixth-century Syriac translation of the apocryphal *Transitus Mariae* indicates 15 August as the date of the feast of the 'Theotokos of the Vine', along with two other major Marian feasts in the Syrian tradition: 'Theotokos of the Seed' on 15 January and 'Theotokos of the Grain' on 15 May.[148] The calendar in *Sinai Syr. M52N* (9th–10th cent.) also contains a feast of 'Joseph, spouse of Mary' on 14 March and another one, entitled 'Crown of the mother and glory of the child', on 2 August. However, it is not clear whether this second feast refers to the Theotokos or to the preceding feast of the Maccabees on 1 August.[149]

Marian feasts with similar agricultural connections are known from many Hagiopolitan sources. The Melkite calendar of al-Bīrūnī indicates a 'feast of the Roses' on two days in May that commemorated the meeting between St Elizabeth and the Theotokos. The reason for two dates in al-Bīrūnī's calendar is that 4 May was the ancient commemoration, while 15 May was introduced as the modern date because 'roses are very rare on the fourth [of May]'.[150] When and where the modification of this Melkite calendar occurred, and whether it reflected a difference between the climates of the eastern Mediterranean coast and the desert and mountainous region of the Khwār-ezmian kingdom, is unclear. An anonymous Arabic homily traces the origins of this feast back to St Paul the Apostle and explains its pagan origins.[151] In Constantinople, the Typikon of the Great Church mentions two unspecified commemorations of the Theotokos on 13 and 15 May, most likely remnants of the Marian feast of the Roses.[152] A few centuries later, Theodore Balsamon condemns the celebration of this feast as an 'abhorrent custom' from the periphery, an accusation that conforms with his view that all Chalcedonian Christians should follow the example of the Great Church of the imperial capital.[153] This explains the complete absence of the Marian feast of the Roses

[147] Martin Jugie, 'La première fête mariale en Orient et en Occident, l'Avent primitif', *Échos d'Orient* 22 (1923), 129–52, especially 143.

[148] Agnes Lewis Smith, *Apocrypha syriaca: The Protoevangelium Jacobi and Transitus Mariae* (Studia Sinaitica 11, London: C. J. Clay and Sons, 1902), 59–61; Raes, 'La fête de l'Assomption en Orient', 270.

[149] See Philothée, *Nouveaux Manuscrits Syriaques*, 510 and 514.

[150] See al-Bīrūnī, *Fêtes des Melchites*, 306–7.

[151] Michael van Esbroeck, 'Une homélie Mariale étiologique pour la fête des roses au 15 mai', *Studi sull'Oriente Cristiano* 8: 1 (2004), 17–49.

[152] Mateos, *Typicon*, vol. 1, 292–3.

[153] καὶ τὰ λεγόμενα Ῥουσάλια, τὰ μετὰ τὸ ἅγιον Πάσχα ἀπὸ κακῆς συνηθείας ἐν ταῖς ἔξω χώραις γινόμενα ('and the so-called Rousalia [feasts], which are celebrated after holy Pascha because of bad custom in the outer provinces'). *In Can. LXII Conc. in Trullo*, PG 137: 728–9; *The Council in Trullo Revisited*, ed. George Nedungatt and Michael Featherstone (Kanonika 6, Rome: Pontificio Istituto Orientale, 1995), 142–3. See Chapter 2, 'Theodore Balsamon and the Rite of Constantinople'.

from both the Constantinopolitan and the Hagiopolitan calendars after the thirteenth century.

While in Jerusalem the feast of the Dormition was a celebration of a place, in Constantinople it was ideologized to correspond to doctrinal developments. Margot Fassler's comparison of the earliest sources, both homilaries and liturgical texts, explains how this Marian feast developed in order to strengthen Constantinople's ideology and its aura of a holy city, especially through the importation of relics from Jerusalem.[154] Two Constantinopolitan shrines of the Theotokos housed relics of the garments of the Virgin brought from Jerusalem: Mary's vesture, originally from the Church of Sion, was transferred to the Church of Blachernai, and her cincture, originally from Gethsemane, was moved to the Church of Chalkoprateia.[155] Since the time of Patriarch Timothy I of Constantinople (r. 511–18), a procession from Blachernai to Chalkoprateia was held every Friday.[156] Michel van Esbroeck sees the order of this procession as an imitation of the Dormition procession in Jerusalem, from Sion to Gethsemane.[157] It should be noted that the Gospel pericope from Luke 10:38–42 was not read on Dormition in the GL in Jerusalem, but on the commemoration of Martha and Mary on 4 June.[158] Table 4.3 summarizes the development of feasts of the Theotokos, from the single feast of 15 August in the AL to a multiplicity of feasts by the tenth century. Being a compilation of various sources, it is to be expected that Iovane Zosime's calendar *Sinai Geo. O. 34* (10th cent.) describes some obscure commemoration, such as the Meeting of Elizabeth (1 April) and the joint commemoration of the Theotokos and the Myrrhbearing Women (25 April). However, the absence of the Presentation (21 November) and of the Synaxis (26 December) is surprising. Overall, one sees biblical and apocryphal origins as the basis of Marian feasts, which then pass into agricultural feasts dedicated to the Theotokos, before the rise in importance of Marian relics, particularly in Constantinople.

---

[154] Fassler, 'The First Marian Feast in Constantinople and Jerusalem', 46–7 and 61–7 (homilaries), 68–87 (liturgical texts). See also Ousterhout, 'Sacred Geographies', 104; *Neue Quellen zur Geschichte des lateinischen Kaisertums und der Kirchenunion*, vol. 1: *Der Epitaphios des Nikolaos Mesarites auf seinen Bruder Johannes*, ed. by August Heisenberg (Munich: Bayerische Akademie der Wissenschaften, 1922), 27.

[155] Janin, *Les églises et les monastères*, 177 and 249.

[156] Panagiotes G. Nikolopoulos, 'Τιμόθεος', ΘΗΕ 11, 773.

[157] Michel van Esbroeck, 'Le culte de la Vierge de Jérusalem à Constantinople aux 6e–7e siècles', REB 46 (1988), 181–90, here 182.

[158] GL § 1010–12.

Table 4.3. Feasts of the Theotokos

	AL	GL	Sin. Geo. O.38 (979)	Sin. Syr. M52N (9th–10th cent.)	Sin. Geo. O.34 (10th cent.)	Vat. Syr. 19 (1030)	Al-Bīrūnī (11th cent.)	Sin. Gr. 1096 (12th cent.)	Typikon of the Great Church	Constantinople Praxapostolos (11th cent.)
Nativity	–	8 Sept	8 Sept	8 Sept	8 Sept	8 Sept	–[159]	8 Sept	8 Sept	8 Sept
Presentation	–	–	–	–	–	–[160]	–	21 Nov	21 Nov	21 Nov
Annunciation	–	25 Mar	25 Mar	25 Mar	25 Mar	25 Mar	25 Mar	25 Mar	25 Mar	–
Meeting Elizabeth/Feast of Roses	–	–	–	–	1 Apr	–	4/5 May	–	–	–
Synaxis	–	–	–	–	–	26 Dec	–	26 Dec	26 Dec	26 Dec[161]
Fast of Theotokos	–	–	–	13 Aug	–	–	1 Aug	–	1 Sept	1 Sept
Dormition	15 Aug	15 Aug	15 Aug	15 Aug	15 Aug	15 Aug	15 Aug	15 Aug	15 Aug	15 Aug
Theotokos of the Grain	–	–	–	15 May	–	–	–	–	–	–
Theotokos and Myrrhbearing Women	–	–	–	–	25 Apr	–	–	–	–	–
Vesture in Blachernai	–	–	–	–	2 July	2 July	–	2 July	2 July	2 July
Cincture in Chalkoprateia	–	–	–	–	31 Aug	31 Aug	–	31 Aug	31 Aug	–
Weekly	–	–	–	–	Thurs	–	–	–	–	–

[159] In al-Bīrūnī's calendar, 8 September is the date of the commemoration of Sts Joachim and Anna. See al-Bīrūnī, Fêtes des Melchites, 312.

[160] The transcription of Assemanus skips 19, 20, 21, and 24 November without any note. See Assemani, Catalogus, vol. 2, 92.

[161] Also referred to as 'lying in' (τὰ ἐπιλόχια). Andreou, Praxapostolos, 290.

St John the Baptist

One of the most appropriate figures for a case study of the Hagiopolite liturgical calendar is St John the Forerunner and Baptist of the Lord.[162] His conception, birth, life, and death are known through the Gospel narratives, which provide more details about his life in the Judean wilderness than about any other New Testament figure. The Forerunner's cult is of local Palestinian origin, but his veneration quickly extended universally.

The AL presents only one feast of the Forerunner on 29 August, simply 'for John the Baptizer'. No hymnography is provided, but the Gospel reading from Matthew 14:1–12, which narrates John's beheading, points to this event as the focus of the feast. The GL contains eighteen commemorations of St John the Baptist, among them his birth on 24 June, his beheading on 29 August, the finding of his head on 26 October, as well as six depositions (დასდგმაი, *dadgmay*; κατάθεσις in the singular), one dedication (ენკენიაი, *enk'eniay*; ἐγκαίνια), and two commemorations.[163] The finding of John's head, celebrated on 26 October, was the subject of the local Hagiopolitan feast of the deposition of the head of the Forerunner in Jerusalem after the head had been found in Emessa on 24 February 452. In al-Bīrūnī's calendar, this commemoration is referred to as the 'burial of the head of John, son of Zachariah'.[164]

The *Iadgari* contains the two main feasts of St John the Baptist in the Georgian Hagiopolitan sources: these celebrate his nativity on 25 June 'in the Greek manner' (ბერძულად, *berzulad*)[165] and his beheading on 29 August.[166] The hymnography for both feasts corresponds to the *oxitay*

---

[162] For an initial bibliography on St John the Baptist, see BHG 831–867m, BHGna 831–867n; Tarcisio Stamare and Antonietta Cardinali, 'Giovanni Battista, santo', BS 6, 599–624; Amédée Brunot, 'Sur les pas de Jean-Baptiste', *Bible et Terre Sainte* 180 (1976), 10–18; Johannes Irmscher, Alexander Kazhdan, Robert F. Taft, and Annemarie Weyl Carr, 'John the Baptist', ODB II, 1068–1069; Ioli Kalavrezou, 'Helping Hands for the Empire: Imperial Ceremonies and the Cult of Relics at the Byzantine Court', in *Byzantine Court Culture from 829 to 1204*, ed. by Henry Maguire (Washington, DC: Dumbarton Oaks Research Library and Collection, 1998), 53–79, esp. 70–9; Sergei Bulgakov, *The Friend of the Bridegroom: On the Orthodox Veneration of the Forerunner*, trans. by Boris Jakim (Grand Rapids, MI: Eerdmans, 2003); Jean-Claude Cheynet, 'Le culte de saint Jean-Baptiste en Cilicie et en Syrie', in *Byzance et ses périphéries: Hommage à Alain Ducellier*, ed. by Bernard Doumerc and Christophe Picard (Toulouse: CNRS / Université de Toulouse Le Mirail, 2004), 57–66; Alexander A. Tkachenko et al., 'Иоанн Предтеча', ПЭ 24, 528–77.

[163] Kekelidze, Канонарь, 184–6; Baumstark, *Comparative Liturgy*, 181–2.

[164] BHG 840; 'Εἰς τὴν δευτέραν εὕρεσιν τῆς τιμίας κεφαλῆς τοῦ ἁγίου καὶ ἐνδόξου Προφήτου, Προδρόμου, καὶ Βαπτίστου Ἰωάννου' ('For the Second Finding of the Precious Head of the Holy and Glorious Prophet, Forerunner, and Baptist John'), in Charles Ducange, *Traité historique du chef de S. Jean Baptiste* (Paris: Cramoisy & Marbre-Cramoisy, 1645), 215–29; Garitte, *Calendrier palestino-géorgien*, 368. See al-Bīrūnī, *Fêtes des Melchites*, 297.

[165] თთუესა ივნისსა ოთხნ... ჳე, ბერძულად ('Month of June, nativity of John, [June] 25, according to the Greeks'), *Iadgari*, 251–5, here 254–5.

[166] 'თთუესა კე აგჳსტოსსა ოთანნ თავის კუეთაი' ('Month of 29 August, beheading of John'), *Iadgari*, 275–82, here 282.

and hand washing hymns found in the Georgian lectionary. Since neither the Georgian lectionary[167] nor other Georgian liturgical collections[168] have a general liturgical service (ἀκολουθία) for St John the Baptist, the eucharistic synaxis of 29 August provides the hymnography for the other feasts of the Forerunner listed above, especially for the finding of his head on 26 October. For these commemorations of John the Baptist, the rubrics of the GL direct the reader to 29 August ('see all of 29 August', ყოვ̇ელი ჰ̇ჰომ: აგ̇სტოსა: კთ). The service for 29 August is given below:

თთუისა აგ̇სტოსა კთ. იოვანე პიტ̇რეაკისა შ̇წ̇ნე-ბ̇ულსა. ქ̇ალაქისა კიდესა. იოვანე ნათლისმცემელისა თავის მოკ̇უეთაა და ელისე წინასწარმეტ̇ყ̇უელისა.[169] ოხ̇ითაა ჴ̇მაა დ̇ გ̇უერდი. წინამორბედო, ქ̇ადაგო ქ̇რისტ̇ესო, შ̇ენ მეფ̇ესა ამხილებდ უ̇რჩ̇ულ̇ოებისა არა საქ̇მედ, რომლისათუისცა სიმ̇დერამ̇ან უ̇რჩ̇ულ̇ოთა დ̇ედათამან არ̇წ̇მ̇უნა ერ̇ოდ̇ეს მოკ̇უეთაად თავი შ̇ენი და შ̇ემ̇დგომ̇ად სიკ̇უდილისა აღ̇მოსავალითგან მ̇დისაით და დასავალამ̇დ ქ̇ებ̇ულ არს სახ̇ელი შ̇ენი. რომელსა გააჴ̇უს კადნიერებად ქ̇რისტ̇ესა მიმართ, მას ევ̇ედ̇რე შ̇ეწ̇ყ̇ნარებად სულთა ჩ̇უენთა.	29 August. In the building of John the Patriarch, on the edge of the city. The Beheading of John the Baptist, and the Prophet Eliseus.[169] *Oxitay, Tone 8*: Forerunner, herald of Christ, you persuaded the king not to commit iniquity, on account of which the mocking of the lawless women convinced Herod to cut off your head, but after death your name is readily praised from the East unto the West. Since you have boldness before Christ, pray to him to receive our souls.[170]

Psalm, Tone 6: Do not touch, Ps 104:15

Verse: The powerful did not, Ps 104:14 [GL § 1186]

First Reading: Proverbs 20:6–15 [GL § 1187]

Second Reading: Malachi 4:5–6 [GL § 1188]

Third Reading: 2 Kings 2:1–15a, [GL § 1189]

Fourth Reading: Acts 13:17–38(?) [GL § 1190]

Fifth Reading: Hebrews 11:32–40 (*with interpolations*) [GL § 1191]

---

[167] See GL § 1437–527.

[168] *Sinai Geo. N. 58* (9th–10th cent.), fol. 47r–58v; *Sinai Geo. N. 26* (9th–10th cent.) fol. 57v–70v; *Sinai Geo. O. 54* (10th cent.) fol. 66r–175v; *Sinai Geo. N. 22* (10th cent.), fol. 21r–79v; *Sinai Geo. N. 54* (10th cent.) fol. 109r–129v; *Sinai Geo. O. 12* (10th–11th cent.) fol. 284r–286r. See Aleksidze et al., *Catalogue of Georgian Manuscripts*.

[169] The commemoration of the Prophet Eliseus, as well as the second and third readings, are absent from manuscripts GL (P) and GL (L). See the apparatus in GL § 1186. The full Georgian hymnographic texts come from *Iadgari*, 282, as the GL only provides the incipit.

[170] For the French translation of this hymn, see Renoux, *Hymnaire de Saint-Sabas* II, 575. The Greek equivalent of this hymn is Πρόδρομε τοῦ Σωτῆρου, σὺ βασιλεῖς ἤλεγξας ('O forerunner of the Saviour, you reproved the king'), currently the *doxastikon* of the Aposticha at vespers for 29 August in the Byzantine rite. See Follieri, *Initia hymnorum*, vol. 3, 353.

Alleluia, Tone 8: The mouths of the just speak...kill them, Ps 36:30–2 [GL § 1191]

Gospel: Matthew 14:1–12 [GL § 1192]

ჯელთააბანისაჲ: წინამორბედო, ქარაგო ქრისტესო, დაღაცათუ მოკლვასა ბრძანებდა ეროდე შენ ჭეშმარიტისა ქადაგისათჳს, არამედ სულითა შენითა მრწყინვალედ გამოსჩნდი და სიმართლისა იგი მზეჲ ჯოჯოხეთისა მყოფთა პირველ უქადაგე. რომელსა გაქუს კადნიერებაჲ ქირსტეს მიმართ, მას ევედრე შეწყნარებაჲ სულთა ჩუენთა.¹⁷¹	*Hymn for hand washing*: Forerunner, preacher of Christ, although Herod commanded to kill you for preaching the truth, by your soul you shone brilliantly and were the first preacher of the Sun of Truth to those in Hades. Since you have boldness before Christ, pray to him to receive our souls.¹⁷²
სიწმიდისაჲ: შენ გაქენ მჳდრობანი ანგელოზთაანი, შენ გადიდებენ ქერაბინთა ძალნი, შენ უფროისად აგამაღლებენ სერაბინნი მრავალთუალნი, სამებისა წმიდისა გალობასა დაუცხრომელად შესხირვებ: წმიდა ხარ, წმიდა ხარ, წმიდა ხარ შენ, ღერთო ჩუენო.¹⁷³	*Hymn for the holy gifts*: The choirs of angels praise you, the armies of cherubim glorify you, the seraphim with many eyes all exalt you from above. Without ceasing, they offer you the hymn of the Holy Trinity: 'Holy are you, holy are you, holy are you our God'.

Although the hymnography, psalmody, and lections for 29 August are used for all feasts of John, different Gospel pericopes more suitable to the specific commemoration are chosen for St John's other commemorations. In the reading from the Epistle to the Hebrews, those who 'walked around in skins' (Hebrews 11:37) are explicitly named as John, Elias, and Eliseus in the GL.¹⁷⁴ The location of the feasts of St John the Baptist in Jerusalem was 'the building of John the Patriarch, on the edge of the city' (იოვანე პატრეაქისა მშჱნებულსა. ქალაქისა ვიდეჲსა).¹⁷⁵ This foundation is most likely connected to Patriarch John III (r. 516–24), son of Bishop Marcian of Sebaste in Samaria,¹⁷⁶ where St John the Baptist and Prophet

---

¹⁷¹ GL § 1193.
¹⁷² For the French translation of this hymn, see Renoux, *Hymnaire de Saint-Sabas* II, 575. The Greek equivalent of this hymn is Πρόδρομε τοῦ Σωτῆρος, εἰ καὶ φόνῳ ('O forerunner of the Saviour, though the voice'), now the *doxastikon* of the Aposticha at matins for 30 August in the Byzantine rite. See Follieri, *Initia hymnorum*, vol. 3, 353.
¹⁷³ The hymn for the holy gifts is incomplete in the *Iadgari* for 29 August but is found among hymns in Tone 4. See *Iadgari*, 282 and 440; Renoux, *Hymnaire de Saint-Sabas* II, 576.
¹⁷⁴ GL § 149. For more on the variants in this text, see Chapter 5, 'Biblical Textual Criticism and Lectionary Studies'.
¹⁷⁵ GL § 1055, 1186, 1261, 1326, 1412.
¹⁷⁶ *Life of Sabas*, Chapter 56, in Schwartz, *Cyril of Scythopolis*, 146–52; Verhelst, 'Lieux de station' I, 55–6; Pringle, *Churches of the Crusader Kingdom*, vol. 3, 192–207. Kelekidze believes that the reference is to Patriarch John 'the Merciful' of Alexandria (c.606–16) who, along with Patriarch Modestus of Jerusalem (d. 630–7), was responsible for restoring many churches after the Persian occupation of Jerusalem in 614. See Kekelidze, *Канонарь*, 193–4.

Eliseus—not Prophet Elias, as Baumstark mistakenly claims—were both burried and where their cult is believed to have originated.[177]

Constantinople also celebrated a profusion of feasts of St John the Baptist and several churches bore his name, most notably the church of the Stoudios Monastery.[178] The synaxarion of Constantinople indicates ten days on which events related to the Forerunner were commemorated, most notably his conception (σύλληψις) on 23 September; his synaxis (σύναξις) on 7 January after Theophany; the first and third finding of his head, on 24 February and 25 May respectively; his birth on 24 June; and his beheading (ἀποτομή) on 29 August (see Table 4.4).[179] As in Jerusalem, the feast of greatest liturgical solemnity was that of the beheading, and its service was as follows:

Μηνὶ τῷ αὐτῷ κθ΄, μνήμη τῆς ἀποτομῆς τῆς τιμίας κεφαλῆς τοῦ ἁγίου προφήτου καὶ βαπτιστοῦ Ἰωάννου. Τελεῖται δὲ ἡ αὐτοῦ σύναξις ἐν τῷ ἁγιωτάτῳ αὐτοῦ προφητείῳ τῷ ὄντι ἐν τοῖς Σπαρακίου.[180]	29 August. Commemoration of the Beheading of the Holy Prophet and Baptist John. His synaxis takes place in his holy church in the quarter of Sphorakion.
Εἰς τὸν ν΄ καὶ εἰς τὴν εἴσοδον τροπάριον, ἦχος πλ. α΄· Ἡ τοῦ Προδρόμου ἔνδοξος ἀποτομή, οἰκονομία γέγονέ τις θεϊκή, ἵνα τοῖς ἐν Ἄδῃ τοῦ Σωτῆρος κηρύξῃ τὴν ἔλευσιν· θρηνείτω οὖν Ἡρῳδιάς, ἄνομον φόνον αἰτήσασα· οὐ νόμον γὰρ τὸν τοῦ Θεοῦ, οὐ ζῶντα αἰῶνα ἠγάπησεν, ἀλλ' ἐπίπλαστον πρόσκαιρον.[181]	Troparion for Ps 50 in the Orthros and at the entrance during Liturgy, Tone 5: The glorious beheading of the Forerunner became a divine dispensation, so that he might proclaim to those in Hell the coming of the Saviour. So let Herodias, who asked for lawless murder, grieve, for she loved neither the law of God nor the age that lives, but one artificial and temporary.

Prokeimenon, Tone 7: The just man shall rejoice in the Lord, Ps 63:11
Verse: Hear, O God, my voice, Ps 63:1
Second verse: Man shall come to a deep heart, Ps 63:6–7
Reading: Acts 13:25–39
Alleluia, Tone 1: Light is risen to the just, Ps 96:11
Gospel: Mark 6:14–30
Koinonikon: Rejoice in the Lord, Ps 32:1[182]

A glance at other Constantinopolitan liturgical books reveals problems with our information from the synaxarion. According to the Constantinopolitan

[177] See Baumstark, *Comparative Liturgy*, 182.
[178] See Delouis, *Saint-Jean-Baptiste de Stoudios à Constantinople*. For the commemoration of St John the Baptist in the anaphora of CHR, see Winkler, 'Die Interzessionen II', 333–41.
[179] See the relevant dates in Delehaye, *Synaxarium* and in Mateos, *Typicon*.
[180] A *propheteion* (προφητεῖον) is a church specifically dedicated to a prophet. See Lampe, *Patristic Greek Lexicon*, 1193.
[181] Follieri, *Initia hymnorum*, vol. 2, 83. This is currently the *kontakion* of 29 August in the Byzantine rite.
[182] Mateos, *Typicon*, vol. 1, 386.

Praxapostolos, only six feasts of John are celebrated: the synaxis on 7 January; conception on 23 September; his birth (Nativity) on 24 June; beheading on 29 August; and the finding of his head, as well as its deposition, on 24 February and 25 May (see Table 4.4). While the scriptural lections remain the same, the troparion from the synaxarion—actually a *kontakion* of Romanus the Melodist[183]— is replaced by a generic troparion for the Baptist, 'The memory of a just man is with praises' (*Μνήμη δικαίου μετ' ἐγκωμίων*).[184] The synaxarion states that the Church of St John the Baptist in the neighbourhood of Sphorakion (*τὰ Σφορακίου*) was the location for all the feasts of the Forerunner.[185] However, Raymond Janin doubts this. The *προφητεῖον* of the Forerunner in the Sphorakion was no more than a small chapel within the Church of St Theodore. The Church of St John of Hebdomon (*ἐν τῷ Ἑβδόμῳ*) was the real heart of the Forerunner's cult in Constantinople, where the relic of his head was deposited.[186] From the tenth century, John's head and the center of his cult moved to the Stoudios Monastery, where his veneration was added on Tuesdays in the weekly cycle of the Oktoechos.[187]

Returning to the Forerunner's place of origin in Palestine, we find confusion among Hagiopolitan liturgical sources from the tenth to the thirteenth centuries: local commemorations of John the Baptist are now mixed with those of Constantinople (see Table 4.4). The actual Nativity of St John the Baptist is absent from *Sinai Geo. O. 38* (979), but there is a reading for the Sunday before this commemoration, which Garitte presumes must have taken place on 24 June.[188] In *Sinai Geo. O. 34* (10th cent.) the Nativity of St John the Baptist is indicated on both days, as the first commemoration on 25 June and as the second commemoration on 24 June.[189] Some Syriac and Arabic sources commemorate both the Jerusalemite and the Constantinopolitan dates for the finding of the Forerunner's head, as do *Sinai Syr. M52N* (9th–10th cent.)[190] and al-Bīrūnī's eleventh-century Melkite calendar.[191] Similar sources, such as *Vatican Syr. 19* (1030) and *Vatican Syr. 20* (1215), also introduce the previously foreign concomitant feast of John's synaxis on 7 January.[192] Some Hagiopolite

[183] Sophronios Eustratiades, "*Ρωμανός ὁ Μελῳδὸς καὶ τὰ ποιητηκὰ αὐτοῦ ἔργα. Β'*, *Ἐπετηρὶς Ἑταιρείας Βυζαντινῶν Σπουδῶν* 25 (1955), 211–83, here 233; *Ρωμάνου τοῦ Μελῳδοῦ Ὕμνοι*, vol. 3, ed. by Nikolaos A. Libadaras (Athens: *Τυπογραφεῖον Μηνᾶ Μυρτίδη*, 1957), *ϟα', ρλή', σπζ'*; Andreou, *Praxapostolos*, 401–2 (fol. 305v).

[184] Ibid., 401; Follieri, *Initia hymnorum*, vol. 2, 434.

[185] Raymond Janin, AA, 'Les églises byzantines du Précurseur à Constantinople', *Échos d'Orient* 37 (1938), 312–51, here 328–30; Janin, *Les églises et les monastères*, 455–6.

[186] Ibid., 426–9.

[187] Janin, 'Églises byzantines du Précurseur' (see n. 182 here), 319–28; Delouis, *Saint-Jean-Baptiste de Stoudios à Constantinople*, vol. 2, 388–406; Krasheninnikova, 'Седмичные памяти октоиха', 264–5.

[188] See Garitte, 'Index des lectures évangéliques', 386.

[189] See Garitte, *Calendrier palestino-géorgien*, 74.

[190] Philothée, *Nouveaux Manuscrits Syriaques*, 503 and 508.

[191] Al-Bīrūnī, *Fêtes des Melchites*, 297 and 303.

[192] Assemani, *Catalogus*, vol. 2, 94 and 122.

Table 4.4. Commemorations of St John the Baptist

	AL	GL	Sin. Geo. O.38 (979)	Sin. Syr. M52N (9th–10th cent.)	Sin. Geo. O.34 (10th cent.)	Vat. Syr. 19 (1030)	Al-Bīrūnī (11th cent.)	Sin. Gr. 1096 (12th cent.)	Typikon of the GreatChurch	Praxapostolos (11th cent.) Constantinople
Conception	–	27 Sept	27 Sept	–	16 Jan	23 Sept	10 Oct	23 Sept	23 Sept	23 Sept
Nativity	–	24 June	(Sunday before) 24 June	25 June	24/5 June	24 June	25 June	24 June	24 June	24 June
Beheading	29 Aug	29 Aug	29 Aug	29 Aug	29 Aug	29 Aug	29 Aug	29 Aug	29 Aug	29 Aug
Finding of Head	–	26 Oct	–	26 Oct / 24 Feb	24 Feb	24 Feb	26 Oct / 24 Feb	24 Feb / 25 May	24 Feb / 25 May	24 Feb / 25 May
Synaxis	–	–	–	–	7 Jan	7 Jan	–	7 Jan	7 Jan / 23 July	7 Jan
Weekly	–	–	–	–	–	–	1 June	–	–	–
Other	–	29 Sept, 15 Oct, 20 Oct, 14 Nov, 15 Dec, 3 June, 18 July, 25 July, 9 May	–	9 May, 15 Dec	3 June, 18 July	–	–	–	29 Oct, 24 Jan	–

sources, such as the Typikon in *Sinai Gr. 1096* (12th cent.), are completely Byzantinized.[193] Not only is the calendar affected, but the Jerusalem lectionary is also influenced by Constantinople: the typically-Hagiopolite Matthaean Gospel pericope for John's beheading (Matthew 14:1–12) is replaced by the Marcan reading (Mark 6:14–30) most common in Constantinopolitan liturgical sources.

St James the Brother of the Lord

The Byzantine sanctoral cycle today commemorates at least five Jameses, some of them easily confused with one another.[194] The focus of this case study is St James, Brother of the Lord (ἀδελφόθεος) in the flesh, first bishop of Jerusalem, and traditionally the author of the eponymous JAS, who died as a martyr around AD 61.[195] His feast was initially celebrated in Jerusalem on 25 December, replacing a Jewish celebration of the Old Testament Patriarch Jacob in Hebron on that day that was possibly connected to the rededication of the Temple in the time of the Maccabees (1 Maccabees 1:59) on the twenty-fifth day of the Jewish month of Kislev. Thus we have our first confusion of the Brother of the Lord with the Old Testament figure. Various sources of Roman and Spanish rites adopted this celebration and confused the Brother of the Lord with the brother of John, son of Zebedee.[196]

The only commemoration of James in the AL falls on 25 December, along with that of David the Prophet. The James referred to in the readings is the Brother of the Lord and first bishop of Jerusalem. The 'canon' for the feast is as follows:[197]

25 December. James and David.[198] *Synaxis at Holy Sion.*
Psalm: Remember, Lord, David and all his meekness, Ps 131:1
Old Testament Reading: 2 Kingdoms [2 Samuel] 5:1–10, Then all the tribes of Israel came to David at Hebron... for the Lord Almighty was with him.
New Testament Reading: Acts 15:1–29, But some men came down from Judea and were teaching the brethren... If you keep yourselves from these, you will do well. Farewell.
Alleluia: The Lord said to my Lord, Ps 109:1 [This verse is in the Gospel]
Gospel: Matthew 22:41–6, When the Pharisees were assembled... no one dared question him.

[193] Dmitrievskii, *Описание* III, 38, 40, 50.
[194] This section relies upon Galadza, 'Melkite Calendar', 75–83.
[195] Roberto Plotino, 'Giacomo il Minore', BS 6, 401–10; John Painter, *Just James: The Brother of Jesus in History and Tradition* (Columbia, SC: University of South Carolina Press, 1997); Hesychius of Jerusalem, 'Hom. X, *In SS. Iacobum et David*', in Aubineau, *Hésychius de Jérusalem*, vol. 1, 351–68; BHG 763y–766i; BHGna 763z–766p; Galadza, 'Melkite Calendar', 75–83.
[196] Baumstark, *Comparative Liturgy*, 184–5. [197] AL, 368–9.
[198] AL (J) has 'James and David', in keeping with the encomion of Hesychius of Jerusalem in PG 93:1480, while AL (P) and AL (E) have 'David and James'. See AL, 155–60, 368–9.

The AL prescribes a reading from the Epistle of James (1:1–12) for the feast of James and John, sons of Zebedee, on 29 December.[199] This is later added to the canon for the Brother of the Lord, which shows once more the confusion between saints named James.

The main celebration of St James on 25 December in the GL was moved to the next day in order to make room for the Nativity of Christ, in accordance with the imperial decree of Emperor Justinian.[200] In addition to the 26 December commemoration (ჴსენებაჲ, *qsenebay*) celebrated at Holy Sion, the deposition (დადგმაჲ, *dadgmay*) of St James' relics is commemorated on 25 May at the 'building of Paul' (პავლჱს შჱნებული, *p'avlēs šēnebuli*) in the Kidron Valley.[201] At the same church there are also two other feasts of James, together with Symeon and Zachariah: the feast of the finding (პოვნაჲ, *p'ovnay*) on 1 December, and the common commemoration of the three saints on 18 May, both employing the canon prescribed for 25 May. The structure of the two main celebrations is as follows:

თთუეს დეკემბერსა : კვ : სიონს : დავითისი : და იაკობისი : ძმისა ოჳფლისაჲ.[202]	*26 December. Synaxis in Holy Sion. David and James the Brother of the Lord.*
ოხიტაჲ ჴმა ა: ეჰა დიდებული, საკჳრველი საღმრთოჲსა სიმდაბლისაჲ, ოჳფლისა და მონისაჲ, რამეთუ პირველ ეწამების ერთგულებით მონად და კუალად გამოაჩინებს მამად პირველ საოჳკოჳნეთა ძისა ღმრთისა, რომლისაგან გამოგოჳბრწყინდა, ჯორცნი შეიმოსნა ნათესავისაგან ყოლად წმიდისა ქალწოჳლისა, რომლისაგან ჩოჳენნი ცხორებითა საოჳკოჳნოთა სოჳლნი განანათლნა. ეგრეთ შენცა, სანატრელო, მეგობრებაჲ მიგემადლა თოჳისისა ოჳფლისაჲ და მისგან დაცვად მართალი სარწმოჳნოებაჲ მოლოჳაწებითა ეკლესიათა. ითხოე მეოხებით ქრისტეს ღმრთისაგან სოჳლთა ჩოჳენთათოჳის ლხინებაჲ და დიდი წყალობაჲ.[203]	*Oxitay, Tone 1:* Behold, glorious one, the wonder of divine humility, of the master and servant, for as the first witness, you were faithfully hired and guided as a father to the first appearance of the eternal Son of God, in whom we are illuminated, taking flesh from the root of the all-holy Virgin, through whom our souls are enlightened with eternal life. Therefore, O blessed one, unto you is given friendship with Christ and for him to guard the welfare of the churches of the true faith. Pray to Christ God for relief for our souls and great mercy.

---

[199] AL, 372–3.
[200] Esbroeck, 'La lettre de l'empereur Justinien'; Esbroeck, 'Encore la lettre de Justinien'.
[201] Abel, 'La sépulture de saint Jacques', 487–8.
[202] GL § 32–41.   [203] *Iadgari*, 23.

Vespers Psalm: Remember, Lord, David and all his meekness, Ps 131:1
Verse: How he swore to the Lord, Ps 131:2
Psalm, Tone 1: He who magnifies the salvation of the king, Ps 17:51
Verse: My God, his way is blameless, Ps 17:31
Old Testament Reading: 2 Kingdoms [2 Samuel] 5:1–10
New Testament Readings:
Acts 15:13–29
James 1:1–12
Galatians 1:11–20
Alleluia, Tone 2: The Lord swore to David, Ps 131:11
Gospel: Matthew 22:41–6

ჭელთაბანისაჲ ჴმა ა გუერდი:
მდღელნი განწმედილნი, მეფენი და
მსაჯულნი ერთა თანა თაყუანის-
სცემენ ძალსა ჯუარისა შენისასა,
უფალო, და ჩუენ, შენ მიერ
განათლებულნი, ვღაღადებთ და
ვიტყჳით: მამაო ჩუენო, რომელი ხარ
ცათა შინა, მწიდა არს სახელი შენი,
კაცთმოყუარე.[204]

Hymn for hand washing, Tone 5: Purified
priests, kings and judges of the people worship
the might of your Cross, O Lord, and we,
enlightened by you, cry out and say: Our
Father, who are in heaven, hallowed be your
name, O lover of mankind.

სხუაჲ: დავითის მიერ
წინაწარმეტყუელისა, მეფისა და
მამადმთავრისა სიტყუათა, რომლისა
მიერ თქმულთა აღასრულებელ
იქმენ ქალწულისაგან შობილი
ქრისტე, ღმერთი ჩუენ, წინაჲთვე
წოდებულ იყავ უფალი უფლებათაი,
მარჯუენით მამისა თანა მჯდომარეა,
ხოლო მერმედ განეცხადე ძედ,
შობილი დედისაგან.
განმათავისუფლებელ მექმენ ჩუენ,
ყოველთა გამბადებელო უფალო,
ძრიელებითა შენითა მოგუმადლე
ჩუენ აღგომაჲ და ცხორებაჲ
საუკუნოჲ.[205]

Other: By the words of David, of prophets, of
kings, and of patriarchs—through whose
words you were fulfilled, O Christ our God,
born of the Virgin—you were first called Lord
of might, sitting at the right hand of the
Father, but then you revealed yourself as Son,
born from a mother. You were made our
Saviour, O Creator, Lord of all, through your
might granting us resurrection and eternal life.

სიწმიდის შემოყვანებისაჲ ჴმა ა:
ჴორცი უფლისაჲ, სისხლი
მაცხოვრისაჲ წინა-დგეს. ზეცისა
ძალნი უხილავად გმსახურებენ,
ღარადებენ და იტყჳან ჴმითა
დიდებულითა: წმიდა ხარ, წმიდა
ხარ, წმიდა ხარ შენ, უფალო.

Hymn for the holy gifts: The body of the Lord,
the blood of the Saviour are present before us.
The powers of heaven serve invisibly,
proclaiming with one glorious voice and they
sing the hymn of heaven: holy are you, holy
are you, holy are you, Lord.[206]

---

[204] Ibid., 24.   [205] Ibid., 24. This hymn is not found in the GL.
[206] Ibid., 24.

The service for St James on 25 May is as follows:

ოთუესა მაისსა კე. პავლეჲს მჰნებუელსა. დაჲდგმაჲ იაკობისი ძმისა ოჳფლისაჲ.[207]	*25 May. In the building of Paul. Depostion of James the Brother of the Lord.*

Psalm (for Venerables): Many are the afflictions of the righteous, Ps 33:20.
  Verse: The Lord knows the ways of the blameless, Ps 36:18
New Testament Readings:
Acts 15:13–29
James 1:1–12
[Galatians 1:11–20][208]
Alleluia (for Venerables): The righteous shall inherit the earth, Ps 36:29
Gospel: Matthew 23:34–24:1
Hymn for Hand Washing: from the common service for Venerables (?)[209]

The readings from James and Galatians prescribed in the GL on both 26 December and 25 May are the same for this commemoration in Caucasian Albanian lectionaries dated between the fifth and tenth centuries and discovered among the Sinai 'new finds'.[210] The joint celebration of James, Symeon, and Zachariah stems from the discovery of their relics in the fourth or fifth century, certainly before 518, by the Hagiopolitan monks Epiphanius and Peter. The Georgian account of the discovery of these relics in the 'Apocalypse of Zachariah, Simon, and James' states that the two monks received, along with the monk John, an apparition of three saints who identified themselves as Zachariah, priest and father of John the Baptist; Symeon the Elder, successor of Zachariah as priest of the Temple; and James, Brother of the Lord and first bishop of Jerusalem.[211] Thus the connection between the three 'high priests' of Jerusalem—as the Georgian version calls them—derives from the Hagiopolitan tradition.[212] The Arabic version, however, identifies Symeon and Zachariah simply as priests who were contemporaries of James and martyred along with him,[213] while the Latin version does not elaborate on their identities.[214] The discovery of their relics on 1 December may not have happened by chance. This was the day of the

[207] GL § 989–91.   [208] The rubric is unclear. See GL § 990.   [209] GL § 1522.
[210] See Jost Gippert, Wolfgang Schulze, Zaza Aleksidze, and Jean-Pierre Mahé, *The Caucasian Albanian Palimpsests of Mt Sinai* (Turnhout: Brepols, 2008), vol. 2, VII, 4–5, 12–15, 34–7.
[211] Stéphane Verhelst, 'L'Apocalypse de Zacharie, Siméon et Jacques', *Revue Biblique* 105: 1 (1998), 81–104.
[212] Ibid., 91–2, 100–1; Abel, 'La sépulture de saint Jacques', 490.
[213] Sauget, *Synaxaires Melkites*, 323–6.
[214] *Apparitio sanctorum Jacobi apostoli et primi archiepiscoporum, atque sacerdotum Symonis et Zachariae* ('Apparition of saints James the Apostle and first archbishop, as well as of priests Symeon and Zachariah'), in 'Catalogus Carnotensis', AB 8 (1889), 123–4.

death of Peter the Iberian in 491.[215] The appearance of a new feast of the first bishop of Jerusalem on the same day as that of the death of an extremely popular anti-Chalcedonian hierarch in the same region would certainly have an ideological basis and help to displace any potential cult of a non-Chalcedonian saint or hierarch.

In *Sinai Geo. O. 34* (10th cent.) we find the same commemorations of James, Symeon the Elder, and John the Baptist's father Zachariah, along with a commemoration of the patriarchs of Jerusalem from James to Modestus on 17 May. Despite the absence of any liturgical texts or readings, Zosime's calendar connects the feasts to the celebration on 25 May and indicates that the synaxis occurs 'in the building of Paul', already in partial decline by the tenth century.[216] Despite the calendar's multiple sources and numerous commemorations for each day, the indication of James as the first commemoration on each of these days is significant, especially since not all feasts of Hagiopolitan origin occupy first place in Zosime's extensive daily list of saints.

Al-Bīrūnī's Melkite calendar has two feasts of James, one on 1 December, as 'James, the first bishop of Elia', and another on 26 December, as 'Prophet David, and James, first bishop of Elia'.[217] Here the feast of James has been separated from Zachariah and Symeon, who are found elsewhere in the calendar. Neither of these dates receives a note or elaboration from al-Bīrūnī and the very nature of his calendar makes it impossible to learn more about the liturgical celebration. On the basis of this calendar, however, it is certain that St James the Brother of the Lord and first bishop of Jerusalem was celebrated by the Khwārezmian Melkites on 1 December and on the day after the Nativity of Christ as late as the middle of the eleventh century.

In *Vatican Syr. 20* (1215), the day after Christmas is no longer reserved for David and James, but now includes the concomitant feast of the Synaxis of the Theotokos. The Gospel reading for that day, beginning with Matthew 2:13, adopts the theme of the Nativity of Christ and is performed on the following Sunday, by now dedicated to the holy and just David, James, and Joseph.[218] Similarly, the commemoration of St James, previously celebrated on 1 December, now finds itself on 23 October, the Gospel reading beginning with Luke 6:6 recounting the call of the twelve apostles.[219] This same shift from 1 December to 23 October is found in earlier Byzantinized sources, such as the monk Nicon's calendar

---

[215] For a description of the funeral of Peter the Iberian, see *Petrus der Iberer: Ein Charakterbild zur Kirchen- und Sittengeschichte des fünften Jahrhunderts*, ed. by Richard Raabe (Leipzig: J. C. Hinrichs, 1895), 142–3; Cornelia Horn, 'Peter the Iberian and Palestinian Anti-Chalcedonian Monasticism in Fifth- and Early Sixth-Century Gaza', *ARAM Periodical* 15 (2003), 109–28, here 109–10.

[216] Garitte, *Calendrier palestino-géorgien*, 232, 227–8, 400; Verhelst, 'Lieux de station' I, 56–7; Abel, 'La sépulture de saint Jacques', 493.

[217] Al-Bīrūnī, *Fêtes des Melchites*, 298–9.   [218] Assemani, *Catalogus*, vol. 2, 121.

[219] Ibid., 118.

in *Vatican Ar. 76* (1068) and in *Vatican Syr. 69* (1547), which Korolevsky believed reflected tenth-century practices.[220] To fathom the reason for the relocation
of this Hagiopolite feast, we must turn to Constantinople (see Table 4.5).

Contemporary Constantinopolitan sources show celebrations of St James
on the Sunday after Nativity, on 23 October, and on 30 April. The first two
dates are common to the Constantinopolitan synaxarion and the Praxapostolos.
The Praxapostolos contains hymns and readings virtually identical with those in
sources of the present-day Byzantine rite:[221]

Τοῦ ἁγίου ἀποστόλου Ἰακώβου τοῦ ἀδελφοθέου	23 October. Holy Apostle James, the Brother of the Lord
Τροπάριον, ἦχος β'. Ὡς τοῦ κυρίου μαθητὴς ἀνεδέξω δίκαιε τὸ εὐαγγέλιον, ὡς μάρτυς ἔχεις τὸ ἀπαράτρεπτον τὴν παρρησίαν ὡς ἀδελφόθεος τὸ πρεσβεύειν ὡς ἱερεύς, ἱκέτευε Χριστῷ τῷ Θεῷ σωθῆναι τὰς ψυχὰς ἡμῶν.[222]	Troparion, Tone 2: As a disciple of the Lord you received the Gospel, O righteous one; as a martyr, you have unfailing confidence; as the brother of God, prayer; as a hierarch, intercede before Christ God that he may save our souls.

Prokeimenon, Tone 8: Their utterance has gone forth into all the earth, Ps 18:5
Verse: The heavens tell the glory of God, Ps 18:2
Epistle: Brethren, I would have you know that the gospel ... except James the
   Lord's brother, Galatians 1:11–19
Alleluia, Tone 7: Your priests, O Lord, shall clothe themselves in righteous-
   ness, Ps 131:9
[*Gospel*: At that time, Jesus came to his own country, Mark 6: 1ff][223]
Koinonikon: Their utterance has gone forth into all the earth, Ps 18:5

However, several of Delehaye's synaxaria 'families', especially P, specify that
the 23 October commemoration is the Dedication (ἐγκαίνια) of the Church of
St James, along with commemorations of the priest Zachariah and the righteous Symeon[224]—a clear sign of the continuation of the Hagiopolite feasts of
1 December and 25 May. In fact the relics of all three saints were brought to
Constantinople in 415 and placed in the Great Church by Archbishop Atticus

[220] Ibid., 403–17, especially 409–16. See Charon, *History of the Melkite Patriarchates*, vol. 3.1,
19–22, for a brief comparison of these sources.
[221] Andreou, *Praxapostolos*, 243. See also Mateos, *Typicon*, vol. 1, 74–6; Ἀκολουθία τοῦ
ἁγίου ἐνδόξου καὶ πανευφήμου ἀποστόλου Ἰακώβου τοῦ ἀδελφοθέου καὶ πρώτου ἱεράρχου τῶν
Ἱεροσολύμων (Jerusalem: Τυπογραφείου τοῦ Π. Τάφου, 1861), 3–40.
[222] Follieri, *Initia hymnorum*, vol. 5, part 1, 218.
[223] This pericope is in Praxapostoloi *Athens, Byzantine Museum Gr. 131* (12th cent.), which
originates from the Constantinopolitan periphery (to judge from its script) and was used in the
Greek Peloponnesus, and *Athos, Panteleimonos Gr. 86* (11th–12th cent.), which is also of
Constantinopolitan origin and shares certain similarities with Euchologion *Paris Coislin Gr.
213* (1027), copied in Constantinople. See Andreou, *Praxapostolos*, 25–6, 35–6. The current
pericope in the Byzantine rite is Matthew 13:54–8.
[224] Delehaye, *Synaxarium*, 155.

Table 4.5. Commemorations of St James the Brother of the Lord

	AL	GL	Sin. Geo. O.38 (979)	Sin. Syr. M52N (9th–10th cent.)	Sin. Geo. O.34 (10th cent.)	Vat. Syr. 19 (1030)	Al-Birūn (11th cent.)	Sin. Gr. 1096 (12th cent.)	Typikon of the Great Church	Constantinople Praxapostolos (11th cent.)
St James	–	1 Dec	–	1 Dec	23 Oct 1 Dec	23 Oct	1 Dec	23 Oct	23 Oct	23 Oct
David and James	25 Dec	26 Dec	26 Dec	26 Dec	26 Dec	28 Dec	26 Dec	–	Sunday after Nativity	Sunday after Nativity
James and Jerusalem Hierarchs	–	18 May	–	–	17 May	–	–	–	–	–
Deposition	–	25 May	25 May	–	25 May 22 Oct	–	–	–	–	–

of Constantinople (r. 406–25).[225] The Praxapostolos' silence concerning the dedication or Zachariah and Symeon is consistent with other Middle Eastern Praxapostoloi that contain identical rubrics, namely twelfth-century *Sinai Gr. 286* (12th cent.) and *Sinai Gr. 287* (13th cent.). Georgios Andreou suggests that this may be due to the later 'neo-Constantinopolitan' tradition of the Great Church, but he does not elaborate further.[226]

Although archaeologists have not definitively identified the Constantinopolitan church of St James, synaxaria indicate that it was within the confines of the Church of the Theotokos in the neighbourhood of Chalkoprateia (τῷ ὄντι ἔνδον τοῦ σεβασμίου οἴκου τῆς ὑπεραγίας Θεοτόκου τῶν Χαλκοπρατείων), adjacently to Hagia Sophia.[227] Despite the church's uncertain location, a pilgrim account from the eleventh century notes that James' relics were kept

---

[225] μηνὶ Γορπιαίῳ πρὸ ϛ′ Νωνῶν Σεπτεμβρίων, ἡμέρᾳ Σαββάτῳ (ex a[nte].d[iem]. VI Nonas Septembres, die Sabati) ('in the month of Gorpiaios, on the sixth day before the Nones of September, on Saturday'), *Chronicon Paschale*, PG 92: 788. It is unclear when the relics were removed from the Great Church. See also Alexander Kazhdan, 'Attikos', ODB I, 230.

[226] See Andreou, *Praxapostolos*, 10–17 and 37–40.

[227] Delehaye, *Synaxarium*, 155; Thomas F. Mathews, *The Early Churches of Constantinople: Architecture and Liturgy* (University Park, PA: Pennsylvania State University Press, 1971), 28 and 31; Janin, *Les églises et les monastères*, 237; Cyril Mango, 'Chalkoprateia', ODB I, 407–408; Cyril Mango, 'The Chalkoprateia Annunciation and the Pre-Eternal Logos', Δελτίον τῆς Χριστιανικῆς Ἀρχαιολογικῆς Ἑταιρείας per. 4, 17 (1993–1994), 165–70; Cecily Hennessy, 'The Chapel of Saint Jacob at the Church of the Theotokos Chalkoprateia in Istanbul', in *Proceedings of the 7th International Congress on the Archaeology of the Ancient Near East*, vol. 2, ed. by Roger Matthews and John Curtis, with the collaboration of Michael Seymour, Alexandra Fletcher, Alison Gascoigne, Claudia Glatz, St John Simpson, Helen Taylor, Jonathan Tubb, and Rupert Chapman (Wiesbaden: Harrassowitz, 2012), 351–65.

in the crypt of Chalkoprateia, alongside a chest of relics (σορός) associated with the Theotokos.[228] As one of the city's most important Marian shrines, the church was the station for major feasts of the Theotokos originating from the apocryphal *Protoevangelium of James*, as well as of feasts of St James, Symeon the Elder, and the martyrs of Scythopolis.[229] The liturgical practices at Chalkoprateia are of interest especially since the church was served by the clergy of nearby Hagia Sophia but had a connection to Jerusalem and St James, one of the most important Hagiopolitan saints.[230] It is worth repeating here that the hymn 'Let all mortal flesh be silent' (Σιγησάτω πᾶσα σὰρξ βροτεία), prescribed as the Great Entrance hymn in some manuscripts of JAS, was also known as the *cheroubikon* hymn of the Great Church (Χερουβικὸν τῆς μεγάλης ἐκκλησίας) in certain sources.[231] Whether this had anything to do with the cult of St James in Constantinople, which had its centre very close to the Great Church, remains unclear.

St Stephen the Protomartyr

St Stephen, archdeacon of the church of Jerusalem and first martyr, is already mentioned in the Acts of the Apostles (Acts 6:5 and 6:8–7:60).[232] His commemoration is found in the AL, and the development of the cult of St Stephen is the main criterion Charles Renoux employed to date the liturgical content of the AL. In AL (J), Stephen is commemorated on 27 December, while in AL (E) his feast falls on 26 December.[233] This variation between 26 and 27 December is recounted in various patristic homilies and could be explained by the newly established feast of the Nativity of Christ, whose celebration on 25 December shifted the other liturgical commemorations surrounding that date.[234] Gian Domenico Gordini hypothesizes that the date of 26 December was a manifestation of the desire to solemnize the celebration of great saints who were the first witnesses—in Greek literally

---

[228] Janin, *Les églises et les monastères*, 253.

[229] Delehaye, *Synaxarium*, entries under the dates of 1, 8, and 9 September; 23 October; 21 November; 9, 18, 26, and 29 December; 2 and 3 February; 25 March; 12 April; 4 May; and 31 August.

[230] Henri Leclerq, 'Jacques le Mineur', DACL 7.1, 2109–2116, especially 2114; Mathews, *The Early Churches of Constantinople* (see n. 224 here), 28.

[231] For more on this hymn, see Chapter 3, 'The Hymn of the Holy Gifts'.

[232] For more on the life of St Stephen, see *Le Synaxaire Géorgien: Rédaction ancienne de l'union arméno-géorgienne*, ed. by N. Marr (PO 19.5, Paris: Firmin-Didot, 1926), 657–714; Gian Domenico Gordini, 'Stefano, protomartire', BS 11, 1376–87; François Bovon, 'The Dossier on Stephen, the First Martyr', *Harvard Theological Review* 96.3 (2003), 279–315.

[233] AL, 368–9. For questions concerning St Stephen in the AL, see Chapter 1, 'The Armenian Lectionary'.

[234] Sophronius of Jerusalem, *Laudes BB: Apostolorum Petri et Pauli dictae die quarta festi SS. Natalis*, PG 87: 3356–64, especially 3361 (BHG 1495). See also Gregory of Nyssa, *Encomium in Sanctum Stephanum Protomartyrem*, PG 46: 701–21 (BHG 1654); Gregory of Nyssa, *Laudatio altera S. Stephani Protomartyris*, PG 46: 721–36 (BHG 1655); Basil of Seleucia, *Sermo XLI: Laudatio S. Christi protomartyris Stephani deque ejus pretiosi corporis inventione*, PG 85: 461–473 (BHG 1652-3).

'martyrs'—of the incarnation of Christ, rather than the actual date of Stephen's martyrdom.[235] This theory can be corroborated by a sermon of St Gregory of Nyssa (*c.*335–94), who counts the commemorations of Peter, Paul, John, and James as part of the Nativity cycle.[236] All of these saints are found within the octave of the Nativity of Christ in the GL, and it is not surprising to find St Stephen among them, especially considering his importance for the church of Jerusalem and his presence in the Book of Acts.

The GL already reflects the celebration of Christmas on 25 December, and thus displaces the feast of St Stephen from 26 December to 27 December. This primary celebration of St Stephen provides readings and hymns specifically dedicated to the protomartyr, which are also found in the *Iadgari*.

თთუესა: დეკემბერსა: კზ: კრებაჲ სიონს: სადიაკონოს ჴსენებაჲ: წმიდისა: სტეფანჱსი.[237]	*27 December. Synaxis in Sion, in the Diakonikon. Commemoration of Saint Stephen.*
ოხითაჲ ერთი მშუხრი, ერთი სამხრად: ჴ~ჲ [გ]: დიდებულო პირველმოწამეო სტეფანე, მიმსგავსებულ იქმენ მაცხოვრისა. იგი ჯუარცმული იტყოდა: მამაო, შეუნდვენ ამათ ცოდვანი ესე. და შენ ქვადაკრებული ღაღადებდ: უფალო, ნუ შეურაცხავ ამათ ცოდვასა ამას, რომლისა მიერ მიჴსნენ ჩუენ, ქრისტე რმერთო, და შეგუიწყალენ ჩუენ.[238]	*Oxitay for the evening office, Tone 3*: Glorious protomartyr Stephen, you are like the Saviour. The crucified-one said: Father, forgive them these sins. And you, O stoned one, cry out: Lord, do not regard these their sins, from which you have saved us, Christ God, and have mercy upon us.
სხუაჲ დ გ~ი. მჴედარო ზეცისა მეუფისაო, წმიდაო სტეფანე, ერისმთავარ იქმენ მშუდობისაჲ და ღმრთეებაჲ კერპთაჲ დაჰჴსენ და მათი იგი მძლავრებაჲ . . . შეურაცხ-ყავ და აწცა, ერსა შორის დიდებულო, ვითარცა გაქუს კადნიერებაჲ, ქრისტესა ევედრე სულთა ჩუენთათუის.[239]	*For Liturgy, Tone 8*: Soldier of the heavenly king, holy Stephen, you were made commander of peace, you destroyed the divinity of idols, and brought its power to naught. And now, O exalted one among the peoples who has boldness, pray Christ on behalf of our souls.

Psalm, Tone 8: We will glorify you . . . you have crowned us, Ps 5:12b–13
Verse: Let them rejoice in you, Ps 5:12a
New Testament Reading: Acts 6: 8–8:2
Epistle: 2 Corinthians 4:7–15
Alleluia, Tone 8: You put on his head . . . of days forever, Ps 20:4–5
Gospel: John 12:24–41

[235] Gian Domenico Gordini, 'Stefano, protomartire', BS 11, 1383.
[236] Gregory of Nyssa, *Oratio funebris Basilii Magni*, PG 46: 789.
[237] GL § 42–6. [238] *Iadgari*, 26. [239] Ibid., 26.

ჯელთააბანისაძ ჭ~ა და გ~ი: გიხაროდენ
უფლისა მიერ, სტეფანე, გჳირგჳინ-
შემოსილო, მიმსგავსებულო
ანგელოზთაა, ამისთჳის, რამეთუ შენ
პირველაძ სწამე ქრისტეას მეუფისა
ჩუენისა ჩუენთჳის და საცთური
ურჩულოთა ჰურიათაძ დაჰჴსენ. მეოხ
გუეყავ სულთა ჩუენთათჳის.[240]

სიწმიდის შემოყვანებისაწა, ჭ~ა ბ გ~ი:
ვითარმეძ გხადოდით შენ, წმიდაო
სტეფანე, ქეროჲბინაძ, რამეთუ შენ ზეძა
განისუჱნა ქისტემან სერაბინაძ, რამეთუ
სულითა ადიდებდი მას ანგელოზაძ,
რამეთუ ჯორცნი შეურაცხ-უყავ ძლიაძ,
რამეთუ შენ მიერ იქმნებიან კურნებანი
და უფროჲსაძ მადლნი. მეოხ გუეყავ
ცხორებისა ჩუენისათჳის.[241]

Hymn for hand washing, Tone 8: Rejoice in the
Lord, Stephen, adorned with a crown, you
were made like an angel since you were the
first to witness for the sake of Christ our king,
and you ended the folly of the ungodly Jews.
Be the intercessor for our souls.

Hymn for the holy gifts, Tone 6: We call you
cherubim, Saint Stephen, for upon you Christ
reposes; seraphim, for you glorify him in
spirit; angel, for you truly courageously do not
worry for your body; for through you have
come the gifts of healing and grace. Intercede
for our salvation.

Of the eight commemorations of Stephen in the GL, four are of Stephen alone
(on 27 December, 14 January, 15 June, 5 July) and four are joint commemorations with John the Baptist or other martyrs (22 January, 30 June, 18 July,
25 July). The commemorations of Stephen on 15 June, 5 July, 18 July, and
25 July are depositions of the Protomartyr's relics in various shrines (see Table 4.6).

Table 4.6. Commemorations of St Stephen the Protomartyr

	AL	GL	*Sin. Geo. O.38* (979)	*Sin. Syr. M52N* (9th–10th cent.)	*Sin. Geo. O.34* (10th cent.)	*Vat. Syr. 19* (1030)	*Al-Bīrūnī* (11th cent.)	*Sin. Gr. 1096* (12th cent.)	*Typikon of the Great Church*	*Constantinople Praxapostolos* (11th cent.)
Stephen	26/7 Dec	27 Dec 14 Jan 18 July	27 Dec	27 Dec	27 Dec 14 Jan 18 July	27 Dec	27 Dec	27 Dec	27 Dec	27 Dec
Discovery of Relics	–		–	–	15 June 2 Aug	2 Aug	–	–	15 Sept	–
Transfer	–		–	–	–	–	–	–	2 Aug	2 Aug
Deposition	–	15 June 5 July 25 July	–	15 June	–	–	–	2 Aug	–	–

---

[240] The full text of this hymn is found in *Iadgari*, 27.
[241] This text is not found in the GL. For the full text, see *Iadgari*, 27.

None of these depositions indicates the Church of Sion as the location for the station, although this is the church indicated by the synaxarion of Constantinople as the place where the archdeacon's relics were transferred after they were found by the presbyter Lucian of Kĕfar-Gamlā in December 415.[242]

Constantinopolitan sources also share the primary feast of St Stephen on 27 December, although the hymnography of the service varies from source to source. Below is the order found in the Praxapostolos:

Μηνὶ τῷ αὐτῷ κζ΄, ἄθλησις τοῦ ἁγίου ἀποστόλου καὶ πρωτομάρτυρος Στεφάνου.[243] Τροπάριον, ἦχος δ΄· Βασίλειον διάδημα ἐστέφη σῇ κορυφῇ ἐξ ἄθλων ὧν ὑπέμεινας ὑπὲρ Χριστοῦ τοῦ Θεοῦ μαρτύρων πρωτόκλητε· σὺ γὰρ τὴν Ἰουδαίων, ἀπελέγξας μανίαν, εἶδές σου τὸν σωτῆρα τοῦ πατρὸς δεξιόθεν· αὐτὸν οὖν ἐκδυσώπει ἀεὶ ὑπὲρ τῶν ἀνυμνούντων σε.[244] Κονδάκιον, ἦχος γ΄· Ὁ δεσπότης χθὲς διὰ σαρκὸς ἐπεδήμει, καὶ ὁ δοῦλος σήμερον ἐκ τῆς σαρκὸς ἐξεδήμει· χθὲς ὁ βασιλεὺς σαρκὶ ἐτέχθη· σήμερον ὁ οἰκέτης λιθοβολεῖται [δι' αὐτὸν καὶ τελειοῦται,][245] ὁ πρωτομάρτυς καὶ θεῖος Στέφανος.[246]	27 December. *Martyrdom of the holy Apostle, Martyr, and Archdeacon Stephen.* *Troparion, Tone 4*: Your head was crowned by a royal diadem for the struggles you endured, O first-called martyr of Christ God. Confounding the Jews, you saw your Saviour at the right hand of the Father. Pray him, therefore, for those who ever praise you. *Kontakion, Tone 3*: Yesterday the master came to us incarnate, but his servant departs today in the flesh. Yesterday the one who now reigns in the flesh was born, but today his servant is killed by stoning. [For his sake] the first martyr, the divine Stephen [gives up his life].

Prokeimenon, Tone 7: The just man shall rejoice in the Lord, Ps 63:11
Verse: Hear my voice, O God, Ps 63:2
Epistle: Acts 6:8–7:5, 7:47–60
Alleluia, Tone 4: The just man shall flourish like the palm tree, Ps 91:13
Koinonikon: Ps 110:9

It is worth noting that the *kontakion* here makes reference to the Nativity of Christ, in whose octave the commemoration of St Stephen fell. These Constantinopolitan sources also have at least two feasts, namely the discovery of his relics (εὕρησις τοῦ λειψάνου), celebrated on 15 September,[247] and the local feast of the transfer of Stephen's relics (ἀνακομιδὴ τοῦ τιμίου λειψάνου) to

---

[242] Delehaye, *Synaxarium*, 863; S. Vanderlinden, 'Revelatio Sancti Stephani (B.H.L. 7850–6)', REB 4 (1946), 178–217.

[243] Andreou, *Praxapostolos*, 292. For the kanonarion–synaxarion, see Mateos, *Typicon*, vol. 1, 162–4.

[244] See Follieri, *Initia hymnorum*, vol. 1, 222.

[245] This phrase is absent from Andreou's edition.

[246] Not listed in Follieri, *Initia hymnorum*.

[247] Delehaye, *Synaxarium*, 349–50; Mateos, *Typicon*, vol. 1, 34.

Constantinople on 2 August.[248] The year of the transfer to Constantinople is unclear. One source states that a church was built by a certain Juliana for the relics, under the reign of Constantine the Great (324–37), when Metrophanes was bishop of Constantinople (r. *c.*315–27?) and Cyril was bishop of Jerusalem (r. *c.*349–87).[249] This is impossible, since St Stephen's relics were not discovered in Jerusalem until 415 and Constantine's reign in the imperial capital did not coincide with the episcopates of Metrophanes or Cyril. Another source states that Emperor Anastasius I (r. 491–518) and his wife Ariadne constructed a church to house the relics of St Stephen after their arrival in Constantinople.[250] Raymond Janin casts doubt upon both sources, preferring the patronage of Juliana (Ἰουλιανή)—whom he identifies as Emperor Justinian's nemesis, Juliana Anicia—and the dating in the mid-fifth century.[251] The church in question, 'St Stephen in the quarter of Constantine' (Ἅγιος Στέφανος ἐν ταῖς Κωνσταντινιαναῖς), is the station for the 2 August feast.[252]

Joint Commemorations of New Testament Figures

The Jerusalem calendar contains various commemorations of groups of saints. Many of these are connected to depositions of relics and vary from one calendar to another. For example, the GL contains feasts of Sts Peter and Paul along with those of other saints: a commemoration on 2 October in the Church of Procopius (პროკოპის ეკლესიასა, *prokopie eklesiasa*)[253] and a deposition on 9 May in the Church of the Ascension, also known as the Matheteion or Apostoleion (მოწაფეთასა, *mocapetas*).[254] Denys Pringle notes that both churches were damaged after the Arab conquest, which perhaps explains the subsequent abandonment of these commemorations in later Hagiopolite sources. The fact that the Church of St Procopius is

[248] Delehaye, *Synaxarium*, 861–4; Mateos, *Typicon*, vol. 1, 358.

[249] βασιλεύοντος Ῥωμαίων τοῦ μεγάλου καὶ ἁγίου Κωνσταντίνου καὶ ἱεραρχοῦντος Κωνσταντινουπόλεως Μητροφάνους ... Κυρίλλου δὲ τότε τοῦ ἐν ἁγίοις τὸν θρόνον Ἱεροσολύμων διέποντος ('when the great and holy Constantine ruled the Romans and Metrophanes presided in Constantinople ... then Cyril presided over the throne in holy Jerusalem'). Delehaye, *Synaxarium*, 863.

[250] Pseudo George Kodinos, Πάτρια Κωνσταντινουπόλεως III, Περὶ κτισμάτων, in Theodore Preger, *Scriptores originum Constantinopolitanarum*, vol. 2 (Leipzig: Teubner, 1907), 236–7. See also PG 157: 569B.

[251] Janin, *Les églises et les monastères*, 475.

[252] Mateos, *Typicon*, vol. 1, 358; *Les églises et les monastères*, 474–6.

[253] GL §1267–72; Garitte, *Calendrier palestino-géorgien*, 94; Verhelst, 'Lieux de station' I, 40.

[254] GL § 968–71; Garitte, *Calendrier palestino-géorgien*, 65; Verhelst, 'Lieux de station' II, 247–8. See Chapter 1, 'Stational Liturgy and the Topography of Jerusalem'.

mentioned in crusader sources only to identify the location of Mount Gihon also suggests a significant decline in its importance.[255] The Typikon of the Great Church of Constantinople includes a similar commemoration of Sts Peter and Paul together with other saints on 29 October, celebrated at the Orphanage (Ὀρφανοτροφεῖον).[256]

Nevertheless, the principal feast of Sts Peter and Paul in Jerusalem was 28 December, already present in the AL on that date.[257] In the GL, Peter and Paul are celebrated along with a string of martyr feasts after Christmas on 25 December and the commemoration of the Protomartyr Stephen on 27 December. Sever Voicu proposes that the subsequent 28 December feast of Peter and Paul is a commemoration of martyrdom in the West and that the 29 December feast of James the Lesser and of John the Theologian is a commemoration of martyrs from the East. The inclusion of John the Theologian among martyrs is in keeping with an alternative tradition passed on by Papias of Hierapolis (around the second century), whereby John the Theologian was martyred in Jerusalem rather than dying peacefully in old age.[258] The 29 June commemoration is the anniversary of the Roman deposition of the relics of Sts Peter and Paul, which, in true Constantinopolitan fashion, received the concomitant feast of the Synaxis of the Twelve Apostles on the following day.[259] The 29 June commemoration was later introduced to Jerusalem by Emperors Anastasius and Justin.[260] The *Iadgari* presents both traditions, with commemorations of Sts Peter and Paul on both 28 December and 29 June.[261] Eventually the Hagiopolite 28 December celebration was lost, being replaced by the 29 June commemoration, which was universally celebrated in Rome and Constantinople (see Table 4.7).

Another feast of several New Testament figures present in various Hagiopolite calendars is the commemoration of the four Evangelists on 12 June. The feast was certainly of significant importance, considering that it was celebrated in the Anastasis.[262] However, no such commemoration existed in Constantinople.

[255] Pringle, *Churches of the Crusader Kingdom*, vol. 3, 72–88, 353–5.
[256] Mateos, *Typicon*, vol. 1, 82; Janin, *Les églises et les monastères*, 567–8 (not 413–14 as noted in Mateos, *Typicon*, vol. 1, 83 n. 1). For the commemoration of Apostles in the anaphora of CHR, see 'Die Interzessionen II', 341–2.
[257] AL, 370–3.
[258] Sever J. Voicu, 'Feste di Apostoli alla fine di dicembre', *Studi sull'Oriente Cristiano* 8: 2 (2004), 47–77.
[259] Baumstark, *Comparative Liturgy*, 185–6; Dante Balboni, 'Pietro, apostolo. IV. Culto', BS 10, 612–39.
[260] Wade, 'The Oldest *Iadgari*', 454.   [261] *Iadgari*, 27–8, 275.
[262] GL §1023–5; Garitte, *Calendrier palestino-géorgien*, 72.

Table 4.7. Joint commemorations of New Testament figures

	AL	GL	*Sin. Geo. O.38 (979)*	*Sin. Syr. M52N* (9th–10th cent.)	*Sin. Geo. O.34* (10th cent.)	*Vat. Syr. 19 (1030)*	*Al-Bīrūn* (11th cent.)	*Sin. Gr. 1096* (12th cent.)	*Typikon of the Great Church*	*Constantinople Praxapostolos* (11th cent.)
Peter and Paul	28 Dec	28 Dec 29 June	28 Dec	28 Dec	28/29 June[263]	29 June	29/30 June[264]	29 June	29 June	29 June
James and John	29 Dec	29 Dec	29 Dec	29 Dec	29 Dec	–	–	–	–	–
Twelve Apostles	–	–	–	–	30 June	June 30	1 July	30 June	30 June	30 June
Four Evangelists	–	12 June	12 June	12 June	12 June	–	12 June	–	–	–

Joint Commemorations of Old Testament Figures

Figures from the Old Testament could just as well be considered local Palestinian saints. The familiarity of the Hagiopolite liturgical tradition with these figures, and their frequent commemoration in liturgical manuscripts of JAS, are quite clear.[265] After the Theotokos, St John the Baptist, and St Stephen the Protomartyr, the Great Litany of JAS includes seven Old Testament patriarchs and prophets:

Τῆς παναγίας, ἀχράντου, ὑπερενδόξου, εὐλογημένης δεσποίνης ἡμῶν, θεοτόκου καὶ ἀειπαρθένου Μαρίας, τοῦ ἁγίου Ἰωάννου τοῦ ἐνδόξου προφήτου, προδρόμου καὶ βαπτιστοῦ, τῶν ἁγίων ἀποστόλων, Στεφάνου τοῦ πρωτοδιακόνου καὶ πρωτομάρτυρος, Μωϋσέως, Ἀαρών, Ἠλίου, Ἐλισαίου, Σαμουήλ, Δαβίδ, Δανιήλ, τῶν προφητῶν καὶ πάντων τῶν ἁγίων καὶ δικαίων μνημονεύσωμεν...[266]	Having remembered the most holy, pure, glorious, and blessed Lady, Mother of God and ever virgin Mary, the glorious holy Prophet, Forerunner, and Baptist John, of the holy apostles, Stephen the Protodeacon and Protomartyr, the Prophets Moses, Aaron, Elias, Eliseus, Samuel, David, Daniel, and all the saints...

[263] Sts Peter and Paul are indicated on both days, in first place on 29 June and in second place on 28 June. See Garitte, *Calendrier palestino-géorgien*, 75.

[264] St Peter is commemorated on 30 June and St Paul is commemorated on 29 June. See al-Bīrūnī, *Fêtes des Melchites*, 308.

[265] For a comparison of commemorations of prophets in the AL and GL, see Stéphane Verhelst, 'La place des prophètes dans le sanctoral de Jérusalem', *Questions Liturgiques* 84 (2003), 182–204.

[266] Mercier, *Liturgie de Saint Jacques*, 188, also 166–8, 174. See also *Sinai Gr. 1040* (14th cent.), fol. 7v–8r. For the Georgian version, see Bernard Outtier and Stéphane Verhelst, 'La *kéryxie*

Elias and Eliseus, as well as Moses and Aaron, are also found as pairs in the litany of saints at compline in a twelfth-century Syriac Horologion from Palestine, *Berlin Or. Oct. 1019*.[267] Similar litanies with variable saints and petitions are found in other Greek, Coptic, and Syriac liturgical texts, as Baumstark has noted.[268]

The commemoration of Old Testament figures in church calendars is also quite extensive (see Table 4.8). A peculiar series of saints' commemorations surrounds the feast of the Transfiguration in al-Bīrūnī's Melkite calendar. Here we find Moses on 5 August before Transfiguration on 6 August, which is followed by Elias on 7 August and Eliseus on 8 August.[269] Elias' position the day after Transfiguration suggests a kind of 'Synaxis' or concomitant feast. The Synaxis of John the Baptist celebrated seven months prior on the day after Theophany is a possible example of *Gegendatierung*, or 'paired-dating', of two saints or events several months apart proposed by Georg Kretschmar.[270] According to Kretschmar, calendars could highlight the importance of certain holidays or commemorations by this method. A connection between the cult of Elias and that of John the Baptist certainly existed in Palestine, since the two saints were venerated together in Samaria.[271] Whether or not the placement of their feasts exactly seven months apart is a consciously intended connection in the Melkite calendar, a coincidence, or the remaining vestiges of some other pre-Christian calendar is unknown.[272]

Some liturgical Typika from Palestine also treat Old Testament figures with greater solemnity. In *Sinai Gr. 1096* (12th cent.) and *Sinai Gr. 1097* (1214), three readings from Exodus follow the *prokeimenon* at vespers for the feast of the Prophet Moses on 4 September.[273] By comparison with Hagiopolite

---

catholique de la liturgie de Jérusalem en Géorgien (*Sin.* 12 et 54)', *Archiv fürz Liturgiewissenschaft* 42 (2000), 41–64, especially 55 and 57–9. The complete text of the litanies is not present in *Liturgia ibero-graeca*. See Skaballanovich, *Толковый Типиконъ*, vol. 2, 91–4. See also 'The *Ektene*' in Chapter 3 here for more on this litany.

[267] See Matthew Black, *A Christian Palestinian Syriac Horologion (Berlin or. Oct. 1019)* (Cambridge: Cambridge University Press, 1954), 89.

[268] Anton Baumstark, 'Eine syrisch-melchitische Allerheiligenlitanei', *Oriens Christianus* 4: 1 (1904), 98–120, esp. 100–2.

[269] Al-Bīrūnī, *Fêtes des Melchites*, 310.

[270] Georg Kretschmar, 'Die frühe Geschichte der Jerusalemer Liturgie', *Jahrbuch für Liturgie und Hymnologie* 2 (1956), 22–46, esp. 41.

[271] John W. Crowfoot, *Churches at Bosra and Samaria-Sebaste* (British School of Archaeology in Jerusalem, Supplementary Paper 4, London: William Clowes and Sons, 1937), 24–6; Baumstark, *Comparative Liturgy*, 182. See also Anna Lampadaridi, 'Une acolouthie inédite en l'honneur des prophètes Élie et Élisée', BBGG (terza serie) 6 (2009), 167–97. For the cult of Elias in Constantinople and its connection to court ritual, see Paul Magdalino, 'Basil I, Leo VI, and the Feast of the Prophet Elijah', *Jahrbuch der Österreichischen Byzantinistik* 38 (1988), 193–6.

[272] See Hippolyte Delehaye, SJ, *The Legends of the Saints*, trans. by Virginia Marie Crawford (Notre Dame, IN: University of Notre Dame Press, 1961), 180–5.

[273] See *Sinai Gr. 1096* (12th cent.), fol. 27r; Dmitrievskii, *Описаніе* III, 29 and 409; Ševčenko, 'Typikon', 278.

Table 4.8. Joint commemorations of Old Testament figures

	AL	GL	Sin. Geo. O.38 (979)	Sin. Syr. M52N (9th–10th cent.)	Sin. Geo. O.34 (10th cent.)	Vat. Syr. 19 (1030)	Al-Bīrūnī (11th cent.)	Sin. Gr. 1096 (12th cent.)	Typikon of the Great Church	Constantinople Praxapostolos (11th cent.)
Moses	–	4 Sept	–	5 Aug	5/7 Aug	8 Aug	5 Aug	4 Sept	4 Sept	4 Sept
Aaron	–	12 Aug	–	4 Sept / 9 Aug	4 Sept / 12 Aug / 3/4 Sept	–	–	–	1st Sun. Lent / 1st Sun. of Lent	–
Elias	–	2 Aug	–	4 Aug / 4 Sept	4/8 Aug	20 July	7 Aug	20 July	20 July	20 July
Eliseus	14 June	22 June / 14 June	–	–	22 June / 22 June	14 June	8 Aug	14 June	14 June	14 June
Daniel	–	15 Oct	–	21 July / 4 Oct	Aug 3 / 1 May	17 Dec	3 June	17 Dec	17 Dec	17 Dec
Jonah	–	10 Dec	–	4 Jan	25 Aug	–	9 July	–	22 Sept	22 Sept
Isaiah	6 July	5 May / 6 July	5 May	1 Apr / 16 June / 25 Aug	21 Sept / 5 May / 16 June	9 May	9 May	9 May	9 May	9 May
Isaiah, Jeremiah, Zachariah, Ezekiel	–	–	–	1 May	–	–	16 Aug	–	–	–
Zachariah	10 June	10 June	10 June	–	10 June / 16 May	16 May	16 May	8 Feb	8 Feb / 15/16 May	8 Feb / 16 May

sources, the decline in status of Old Testament figures in Constantinopolitan sources is immediately felt. Bernard Botte suggests that the problem of the decline of Old Testament figures lies in an 'evolution of the notion of sanctity' focused more on confessors of the faith and ascetics.[274] Nevertheless, the Constantinopolitan kanonarion–synaxarion included commemorations of the forefathers Abraham, Isaac, and Jacob two Sundays before the Nativity of Christ (κυριακὴ τῶν ἁγίων πατέρων), and of the same Old Testament patriarchs along with Ananias, Azarias, Misael, and Daniel one Sunday before Christmas.[275] The Dumbarton Oaks Menaion also includes this commemoration of Old Testament patriarchs on 21 December, in the days leading up to Christmas, but repeats the same commemoration on 3 January before Theophany, assimilating the pre-festive periods of Christmas and Theophany.[276]

Monastic Saints

The decline of Old Testament figures often came as a result of the increasing cults of monastic saints, in particular Palestinian monks. Certain monastic saints are celebrated on the same day in all calendars because of the antiquity of their commemorations and because of the popularity of their *Vitae*. A perfect example is St Anthony the Great of Egypt (d. 356), who was commemorated on 17 January already in the fifth century, as indicated in the life of St Euthymius (d. 473) by Cyril of Scythopolis.[277]

During the octave of Theophany, the GL indicates the location of each station along with the basic readings for each day, but does not give the subject of the commemoration. The themes of each reading, however, are in keeping with the themes of the feast of Theophany. However, in Iovane Zosime's calendar, the days of the octave of Theophany each bear a unique commemoration and many of these are of Sabaite monastic saints (see Table 4.9).[278] This culminates in the commemoration of the martyrdom of the fathers of Sinai and Raitho on 13 January, the leave-taking (ἀπόδοσις) of Theophany and the end of the octave.[279] As mentioned above, Zosime's calendar attributes the practice of post-feasts and octaves to the liturgical tradition of Jerusalem and

[274] Bernard Botte, OSB, 'Les saints de l'Ancien Testament', *La Maison-Dieu* 52 (1957), 109–20, here 110. Unfortunately I did not have access to Bernard Botte, OSB, 'Le Culte des Saints de l'Ancien Testament dans l'Église chrétienne', *Cahiers Sioniens* 3 (1950), 38–47 and to Bernard Botte, OSB, 'Une Fête du Prophète Élie en Gaule au VIᵉ Siècle', *Cahiers Sioniens* 3 (1950), 170–7.
[275] Mateos, *Typicon*, vol. 1, 134–5; Winkler, 'Die Interzessionen I', 316–18.
[276] Hieronymus Engberding, 'Das Fest aller alttestamentlichen Patriarchen am 3. Januar im georgischen Menäum von Dumbarton Oaks', *Mus* 77 (1962), 297–300.
[277] BHG 140–141h, BHGna 140–141k; Filippo Caraffa, 'Antonio Abate', BS 2, 106–14.
[278] Garitte, *Calendrier palestino-géorgien*, 44.   [279] Ibid.

Table 4.9. Monastic saints

	AL	GL	*Sin. Geo. O.38* (979)	*Sin. Syr. M52N* (9th–10th cent.)	*Sin. Geo. O.34* (10th cent.)	*Vat. Syr. 19* (1030)	*Al-Bīrūnī* (11th cent.)	*Sin. Gr. 1096* (12th cent.)	*Typikon of the Great Church*	*Constantinople Praxapostolos* (11th cent.)
Anthony	17 Jan	17 Jan	17 Jan	17 Jan	17 Jan	17 Jan	16 Jan	17 Jan	17 Jan	17 Jan
Sabas	–	5/9 Dec	–	5 Dec	5/6/9 Dec	5 Dec	5 Dec	5 Dec + octave	5 Dec	5 Dec
John Climacus	–	–	–	–	30 Mar	30 Mar	–	30 Mar	30 Mar	30 Mar
John Damascene	–	–	–	–	4/9 Dec	–	3 Dec	4 Dec	4 Dec 29 Nov	4 Dec
Theodore Stoudite	–	–	–	–	–	–	–	10 Nov	11 Nov	11 Nov
Stephen Sabaite	–	–	–	–	1/2 Apr 23 Dec	–	–	2 Apr	28 Oct	–

St Sabas. Thus it may be that, where the stations of the cathedral liturgy were not observed, as in monasteries, the commemorations of the day included local monastic saints.

In his brief examination of Sinaitic saints, Ioannis Phountoulis notes that several local Sinaitic commemorations absent in Constantinopolitan sources from before the twelfth century, such as those of St John Climacus and the martyrdom of monks on Sinai, found their way into the current Byzantine rite calendar with the diffusion of the Sabaite Typikon in Constantinople.[280] The increased presence of monastic saints is clear in the Sabaite Typikon *Sinai Gr. 1096* (12th cent.), which includes many local Palestinian monks, especially several deceased monks who were founders or patrons of the 'Monastery of Sergius' (τῆς μονῆς τοῦ Σεργίου),[281] as well as foreign monastic saints,

---

[280] Ioannis M. Phountoulis, 'L'eortologhio del Sinai', in *Giovanni Climaco e il Sinai: Atti del IX Convegno ecumenico internazionale di spiritualità ortodossa sezione bizantina, Bose 16–18 settembre 2001*, ed. by Sabino Chialà and Lisa Cremaschi (Bose, Italy: Edizioni Qiqajon, Comunità di Bose, 2002), 301–12; Demetrios G. Tsames, Μαρτυρολόγιον τοῦ Σινᾶ (Thessalonike: Ἐκδόσεις Π. Πουρνάρα, 2003); Σύναξις πάντων τῶν Σιναϊτῶν Ἁγίων (Athens: St Catherine Monastery and Mount Sinai Foundation, 1998), especially 123–96 for the lives and biographical information of the various Sinaitic saints.

[281] ἐκοιμήθη ὁ ὅσιος πατὴρ ἡμῶν Νεόφυτος καὶ κτήτωρ τῆς μονῆς τοῦ Σεργίου ... ἐκοιμήθη ὁ ὅσιος πατὴρ ἡμῶν κὺρ Τίτος καὶ κτήτωρ τῆς μονῆς τοῦ Σεργίου ... ἐκοιμήθη ὁ ὅσιος πατὴρ ἡμῶν Ἰωάννης καὶ κτήτωρ τῆς ἁγίας μονῆς ἡμῶν τοῦ Σεργίου ('our venerable father Neophytus, patron of the monastery of Sergius, reposed ... our venerable father, Lord Titus, patron of the monastery of Sergius, reposed ... our venerable father John, patron of the monastery of Sergius, reposed'). *Sinai Gr. 1096* (12th cent.), fol. 45r (bottom margin); Dmitrievskii, *Описание* III, 32, 51–2, on 25 October, 5 July, and 7 July.

including St Theodore Stoudite. Although St Theodore is considered one of the most famous Constantinopolitan monastics, his commemoration in the Typikon of the Great Church is of minor importance. His commemoration in the Sabaite Typikon *Sinai Gr. 1096* (12th cent.) was added in the margins of the manuscript's folio, which suggests that in the twelfth century St Theodore's memory was not yet widely celebrated in Palestine.[282]

St Athenogenes

A lesser known saint who nevertheless has a significant place in liturgical calendars and lectionaries from Jerusalem is St Athenogenes, bishop of Sebaste (3rd cent.), martyred under Diocletian.[283] Although his date of martyrdom, given as 24 June in the *Breviarium Syriacum* and as 24 July in the *Martyrologium Hieronymianum*,[284] and his geographic connections, variously identified as bishop of Sebaste in Armenia or Bedochton (ἐν Φυλαχθόη, ἐν Πηδαχθόη),[285] are disputed, he is already mentioned by St Basil the Great (d. 379) as a defender of the divinity of the Holy Spirit.[286] St Gregory the Illuminator is said to have found Athenogenes' relics and, uniting them with those of St John the Baptist, to have promoted their common cult in Armenia, which was to replace the pagan agricultural feast of Deorum Hospitalium (ξενοδεκτῶν θεῶν).[287] Despite the early appearance of his cult in Armenia, Athenogenes is not mentioned at all in the AL.

Georgian sources, however, accord him more prominence in the liturgical calendar. The GL indicates his commemoration on the seventh Sunday after Pentecost and provides four readings and a special Gospel reading.[288] Although the seventh Sunday after Pentecost falls within the cycle of Matthew in the Jerusalem lectionary, the Gospel reading for St Athenogenes is from Luke.[289] *Sinai Geo. O. 38* (979) and *Sinai Geo. O. 34* (10th cent.) have

---

[282] *Sinai Gr. 1096* (12th cent.), fol. 48v (left margin); Dmitrievskii, *Описаніе* III, 33.

[283] BHG 197, BHGna 197–197e; Maria Vittoria Brandi, 'Atenogene di Sebaste', BS 2, 562–3.

[284] See *Breviarium syriacum, seu Martyrologium syriacum saec. IV iuxta Cod. SM. Musaei Britannici Add. 12150*, ed. by Bonaventura Mariani, OFM (Rerum Ecclesiasticarum Documenta Subsidia Studiorum 3, Rome: Herder, 1956), 41; *Martyrologium Hieronymianum*, in AASS 72 (Novembri, tomus II, pars I), 95.

[285] See Delehaye, *Synaxarium*, 825; BHG 197.

[286] St Basil the Great, Περὶ τοῦ Ἁγίου Πνεύματος, 29: 73; PG 32: 205; Basile de Césarée, *Sur le Saint-Esprit*, ed. by Benoît Pruche, OP (SC 17bis, Paris: Éditions du Cerf, 1968), 510–11; Barry Baldwin, Alexander Kazhdan, and Nancy Patterson-Ševčenko, 'Basil the Great', ODB I, 269–70.

[287] Agathangelus, *De S. Gregorio episcopo Armeniæ Confessore*, in AASS Septembris, tomus VIII, 320–402, here 384, § 142, and 389–90, § 150 (30 September); BHG 712–712b.

[288] GL § 899–906.

[289] The actual pericope varies among the sources. See Kekelidze, *Канонарь*, 150; GL §905; Garitte, 'Index des lectures évangéliques', 387. See Chapter 5 for more information on Athenogenes in the lectionary.

St Athenogenes and the Holy Apostles on the seventh Sunday after Pentecost, with a special Gospel from Luke,[290] and his fixed commemoration falls on 13 and 17 July.[291] Athenogenes is also mentioned in the *Mravaltavi*, which shows the importance of this day.[292]

Kekelidze points out that in Jerusalem the seventh Sunday after Pentecost was the dividing point for two cycles of readings between Pentecost and Enkainia: seven 'Sundays of the Apostles' and seven 'Sundays of Summer'.[293] Iovane Zosime indicates how this day was calculated:

> If you are searching for the feast of Athenogenes, take the Sunday of Thomas and, depending on the month in which it falls, Athenogenes will be in June or July. If New Sunday is in March, then Athenogenes will be in June. If [New Sunday] is in April, then it will be in July.[294]

In Constantinople sources differ as to the date of Athenogenes' celebration. The Typikon of the Great Church indicates that his feast was celebrated on 17 July in the Church of St George 'in the Cypresses' (ἐν τῷ Κυπαρισσίῳ) without any particular liturgical instructions,[295] while the Constantinopolitan Praxapostolos commemorates Athenogenes on 16 July with readings from the fifth Sunday of Lent (see Table 4.10).[296]

The commemoration of St Athenogenes points to the important connection between the fixed and the movable cycles of the calendar and the lectionary, and how they interacted in the church of Jerusalem before Byzantinization. Athenogenes was originally commemorated on the seventh Sunday after Pentecost but, once the Jerusalem lectionary went into decline, that commemoration was lost. Nevertheless, the fixed commemoration on 16 or 17 July remained in calendars from both Jerusalem and Constantinople, although Athenogenes' feast became less important within the liturgical year.

---

[290] შემდგომად მარტჳლობისა მე-ზ კჳრიაკესა ჴსენებაჲ წმიდისა ათენაგენ მღდელთმთავრისაჲ და წმიდათა მოციქულთაჲ ('Seventh Sunday after Pentecost, memory of St Athenogenes, archpriest, and of the holy Apostles'). Garitte, *Calendrier palestino-géorgien*, 118.

[291] Ibid., 79, 118, 277–8, 432.   [292] Esbroeck, *Homéliaires géorgiens*, 331–4.

[293] Kekelidze, Канонарь, 288–9.

[294] *Si tu cherches la fête d'Athénogène, prends le Dimanche de Thomas et d'après le mois où il se trouvera, l'Athénogène aura lieu en juin ou en juillet; si le nouveau dimanche a lieu en mars, alors l'Athénogène sera en juin; s'il a lieu en avril, alors elle sera en juillet.* M. Brosset, *Études de Chronologie technique* (St Petersburg: Commissionnaires de l'Académie impériale des sciences, 1868), 3, cited in Esbroeck, *Homéliaires géorgiens*, 332.

[295] Mateos, *Typicon*, vol. 1, 344–5; Janin, *Les églises et les monastères*, 70 (not 75, as indicated in Mateos, *Typicon*, vol. 1, 345 n. 1).

[296] Τῇ αὐτῇ ἡμέρᾳ, τοῦ ἁγίου ἱερομάρτυρος Ἀθηνογένους. Ζήτει κυριακῇ ἐ τῶν νηστειῶν ('The same day, [commemoration] of the holy hieromartyr Athenogenes. See the fifth Sunday of Lent'), fol. 298r. Andreou, *Praxapostolos*, 383.

Table 4.10. St Athenogenes

	AL	GL	*Sin. Geo. O.38 (979)*	*Sin. Syr. M52N (9th–10th cent.)*	*Sin. Geo. O.34 (10th cent.)*	*Vat. Syr. 19 (1030)*	*Al-Bīrūnī (11th cent.)*	*Sin. Gr. 1096 (12th cent.)*	*Typikon of the Great Church*	*Constantinople Praxapostolos (11th cent.)*
Athenogenes	–	7th Sun. after Pent.	13, 17 July; 7th Sun. after Pent.	–	13, 17 July; 7th Sun. after Pent.	–	–	–	17 July	16 July

Local Palestinian Saints

Because of the numerous pilgrims and monks who visited and settled in the Holy Land, Palestinian hagiography is not merely local: tales of Hagiopolitan saints and Palestinian ascetic heroes spread quickly and their cults were integrated in the traditions of other local churches.[297] For this reason it is possible to trace changes in the reception of Palestinian hagiography not only within the patriarchate of Jerusalem, but also elsewhere, such as in Constantinople (see Table 4.11).

Hagiopolite calendars are marked by local commemorations of events, for example earthquakes and the commemoration on 17 May of the burning of the city by the Persians in 614.[298] The AL already commemorates Hagiopolitan bishops Cyril and John, authors and editors of the *Mystagogical Catecheses*. Hagiopolitan bishops also receive significant attention in the GL, where a total of fifteen bishops and archbishops of Jerusalem are mentioned: Zachariah (31 January), Sophronius (11 March), Cyril (18 March), John and Modestus (29 March and the Friday before Palm Sunday), Peter (18 April), Euthymius (12 May), Juvenal and Anastasius (1 July), Sallust (24 July), Macarius (16 August), Maximus (26 August), Praulius (27 August), Martyrius (27 October), John (27 November), Modestus and Zachariah (16 December)—along with common commemorations of the martyr-bishops of Jerusalem (13 April and 25 June) and the Memorial of the Bishops of Jerusalem (fourth Saturday of Lent).[299] Most

---

[297] Flusin, 'Palestinian Hagiography', 200.

[298] GL § 219 and § 979. The commemoration of the earthquake in the GL on 13 February, along with St Demetrius, is unclear. Garitte did not find any earthquakes on 13 February. Moshe Gil notes numerous earthquakes in the years 700–48, 856–60, and 1015–33. Gil also notes that 13 February 1021 is the date on which al-Ḥākim was murdered. See Gil, *History of Palestine*, 89–90, 297 and 929.

[299] See the relevant dates in the GL.

Table 4.11. Local Palestinian saints

	AL	GL	Sin. Geo. O.38 (979)	Sin. Syr. M52N (9th–10th cent.)	Sin. Geo. O.34 (10th cent.)	Vat. Syr. 19 (1030)	Al-Bīrūnī (11th cent.)	Sin. Gr. 1096 (12th cent.)	Typikon of the Great Church	Constantinople Praxapostolos (11th cent.)
Cyril of Jerusalem	18 Mar	18 Mar	–	17 Mar	17/18 Mar	–	–	18 Mar	18 Mar	18 Mar
John of Jerusalem	29 Mar	29 Mar	–	–	29 Mar	–	–	–	29 Mar	–
Modestus	–	29 Mar; 16 Dec	–	16 Dec	29 Mar; 16/17 Dec	–	17 Dec	–	19 Oct; 16 Dec	19 Oct
Sophronius	–	11 Mar; 13 July	–	11 Mar	10/11 Mar	10 Mar	11 Mar	11 Mar	10 Mar	10 Mar
Bishops of Jerusalem	–	4th Sat. Lent; 13 April; 25 June	5th Sat. Lent	–	13 April; 25 June	–	–	–	–	–
Cosmas and Damian	–	17 Oct; 3 Mar	17 Oct	17 Oct	17 Oct; 1 Nov	1 Nov; 1 July	17 Oct; 1 July	1 Nov; 1 July	17 Oct; 1 Nov	17 Oct; 1 Nov; 1 July
Abraham the Byzantine	–	–	–	23 Dec	–	–	–	29 Oct	29 Oct	29 Oct

of these dates, however, are not commemorated beyond Jerusalem. *Sinai Syr. M52N* (9th–10th cent.) also contains a similarly expansive list of bishops of Jerusalem, including the only known commemoration of Patriarch Basil of Jerusalem (d. 839), unknown in Greek hagiography.[300]

There are several figures mentioned in Hagiopolite liturgical calendars who could be considered to reside in two different cities or regions. Abraham the Byzantine (6th cent.) is mentioned in the *Spiritual Meadow* as the founder of the monasteries 'of the Abrahamites' (τῶν Ἀβραμιτῶν μονή) in Constantinople and 'of the Byzantines' or 'Constantinopolitans' (μοναστήριον, τὸ ἐπιλεγόμενον τῶν Βυζαντίων) in Jerusalem. He is mentioned in a Hagiopolite calendar on 23 December, but in Constantinopolitan calendars his commemoration is consistently on 29 October.[301] Little is known of his monastery in Jerusalem and its potential role as a centre of diffusion of Constantinopolitan liturgical practices in Palestine within the process of Byzantinization is tempting to consider. However, there is no evidence to suggest that it would have had such a role, especially since virtually nothing is known of this monastery. Similarly, great confusion has arisen regarding the fourth-century martyrs Cosmas and Damian. They are believed to have been from Arabia when commemorated on 17 October,[302] but their commemoration on 1 July—more common in Byzantinized sources—lists them as being from Rome.[303]

In the process of Byzantinization, notable hierarchs of the church of Jerusalem were preserved on their respective days of commemoration in the Byzantine calendar, presumably owing to their importance for Greek-praying Christianity. Commemorations of a strictly local character, such as the joint commemoration of Hagiopolitan bishops, were not adopted in Constantinople. The lack of a clear list of the patriarchs of Jerusalem has made it difficult to confirm the identity of Hagiopolitan hierarchs, let alone to establish the years of their reigns.

---

[300] Philothée, *Nouveaux Manuscrits Syriaques*, 513. See Binggeli, 'Calendrier melkite de Jérusalem', 187–8, for corrections to Philothée's transcription. This saint is not found in BHG or BHGna.

[301] John Moschus, Λειμών 97, PG 87.3: 2956; Binggeli, 'Calendrier melkite de Jérusalem', 189; BHG 5–8e, BHGna 5–8f; Sylvain Destephen, *Prosopographie chrétienne du Bas-Empire*, vol. 3: *Prosopographie du Diocèse d'Asie (325–641)* (Paris: Association des amis du Centre d'histoire et civilisation de Byzance, 2008), 71–2; Giuseppe Morelli, 'Abramo, vescovo di Efeso', BS 1, 117–18. For more on the monastery, see McCormick, *Survey of the Holy Land*, 77 n. 6.

[302] BHG 372–92, BHGna 372–390h; Filippo Caraffa, 'Cosma e Damiano', BS 4, 223–5; Andreou, *Praxapostolos*, 239.

[303] Mateos, *Typicon*, vol. 1, 328; Dmitrievskii, *Описание* III, 51; Phil Booth, 'Orthodox and Heretic in the Early Byzantine Cult(s) of Saints Cosmas and Damian', in *An Age of Saints? Power, Conflict and Dissent in Early Medieval Christianity*, ed. by Peter Sarris, Matthew Dal Santo, and Phil Booth (Leiden: Brill, 2011), 114–28.

Saints from beyond Palestine

Just as the cults of Palestinian martyrs and saints spread to other regions of Christendom, so too great saints from other regions entered the Hagiopolite calendar. While there are many saints foreign to Palestine in the earliest Hagiopolite calendars, I will focus briefly on two groups: bishops from Constantinople and Georgian saints (see Table 4.12).

The sanctity of St John Chrysostom (d. 14 September 407), whose veneration was a point of contention between the patriarchates of the pentarchy, became universally recognized in 438.[304] Although his death on 14 September coincides with the feast of the Exaltation of the Cross, many calendars still mention his name on that day, also celebrating other events from his life on other days, such as his episcopal consecration on 15 December, his return from exile on 13 November, the deposition of his relics on 5 May, and the triumphal return of his relics to Constantinople on 27 January.[305] Another Constantinopolitan bishop, St Gregory of Nazianzus

Table 4.12. Saints from beyond Palestine

	AL	GL	*Sin. Geo. O.38* (979)	*Sin. Syr. M52N* (9th–10th cent.)	*Sin. Geo. O.34* (10th cent.)	*Vat. Syr. 19* (1030)	*Al-Birūni* (11th cent.)	*Sin. Gr. 1096* (12th cent.)	*Typikon of the Great Church*	*Constantinople Praxapostolos* (11th cent.)
John Chrysostom	–	27 Jan 23 Aug	–	27 Jan	27 Jan 15 Sept 13 Nov 23 Aug	27 Jan	27 Jan	27 Jan 14 Sept 13 Nov	27 Jan 14 Sept 13 Nov	27 Jan 13 Nov
Gregory of Nazianzus	–	25 Jan 15 Nov 23 Aug	25 Jan	25 Jan	25 Jan 15 Nov 23 Aug	25 Jan	–	25 Jan	25 Jan	25 Jan
Nino	–	3rd Sat. after Pascha	–	–	14 Jan	–	–	–	–	–
Abo	–	–	–	–	7 Jan	–	–	–	–	–

---

[304] BHG 870–881z, BHGna 870–881z; Daniele Stiernon, 'Giovanni Crisostomo', BS 6, 669–700; Barry Baldwin, Alexander Kazhdan, and Robert S. Nelson, 'John Chrysostom', ODB II, 1057–8.

[305] Daniele Stiernon, 'Giovanni Crisostomo', BS 6, 685.

(*c*.329/30–90), is also commemorated frequently in the GL.[306] The calendar of the Greek Tropologion *Sinai Gr. N.E. МГ 56* and *Sinai Gr. N.E. МГ 5* (8th–9th cent.) includes both St John Chrysostom and St Gregory of Nazianzus on their January dates, providing proper hymnography for the full commemoration of both saints.[307] The commemoration of both saints, as well as of several other hierarchs, on 23 August in the GL and in Iovane Zosime's calendar did not survive Byzantinization in liturgical calendars and was ultimately lost.[308]

Many Georgian Hagiopolite sources reveal a stratum of local Georgian material, including saints foreign to Jerusalem but native to Georgia. There are nine Georgian saints in the GL: Nino (third Saturday of Pascha), Arč'il (8 January), Razden (26 June), Bishop Abibos (6 July), Mebkambi (16 August), Sarmeani (21 August), Šušanik (17 October), John, Stephen, and Isaiah (4 November), and Estati (Eustathius) of Mc'xeta (20 December).[309] Although some of these names are quite obscure even in Georgian hagiography, the most notable of these Georgian saints is St Nino, known in some sources by a Greek name, St Theognosta (Θεογνώστα), and commemorated on 14 January.[310] St Abo, who was martyred on 6 January 786, had his commemoration transferred to the following day because of the celebration of Theophany.[311] His commemoration is not found in the GL, but hymnography is found in the *Iadgari*.[312] Although the presence of these Georgian saints in the GL often raises questions about the faithfulness of Georgian liturgical books to Hagiopolite practices, it should be noted that Syriac and Arabic liturgical books from the Jerusalem patriarchate often include their own 'local' saints among the standard Hagiopolite hagiographic commemorations, and this is particularly noticeable with the category of New Martyrs.[313]

---

[306] BHG 723–730v, BHGna 723–730y; Joseph-Marie Sauget, 'Gregorio di Nazianzio', BS 7, 194–204; Barry Baldwin, Alexander Kazhdan, Robert S. Nelson, and Nancy Patterson-Ševčenko, 'Gregory of Nazianzos', ODB II, 880–2.

[307] Nikiforova, *Из истории Минеи в Византии*, 204–205.

[308] Garitte, *Calendrier palestino-géorgien*, 309–10.

[309] GL §1434. For the lives of many of these saints, see David Marshall Lang, *Lives and Legends of the Georgian Saints* (London: George Allen & Unwin, 1956).

[310] BHG 2175 (*Hiberorum gentis conversio*); Joseph-Marie Sauget, 'Nino', BS 9, 1018–20.

[311] For a translation of the life of St Abo, see Gaga Shurgaia, *La spiritualità Georgiana: Martirio di Abo, santo e beato martire di Cristo di Ioane Sabanisʒe*, introduced by Levan Menabde (Rome: Edizioni Studium, 2003), 185–255.

[312] *Iadgari*, 57–61; Garitte, *Calendrier palestino-géorgien*, 126–7.

[313] See Frøyshov, 'The Georgian Witness', 229 and 266–7.

New Martyrs

The New Martyrs form a unique category of saints for the study of the development of the liturgical calendar.[314] The adjective 'new' denotes that they were killed after the first period of persecution and martyrdom during the first three centuries after Christ, before Christianity became the official state religion of the Roman empire. Because the New Martyrs were generally killed outside the Byzantine empire and their local church found itself in less than favourable conditions, it was difficult for their veneration to acquire a universal character. Despite these difficulties, saints with the title 'New Martyr' are found in Georgian (ახალი მოწამეა, *axali mocamey*) and Syriac (*shd̲ ht̲'*) sources, where these designations are obviously neologisms coined after the corresponding Greek term (*νεομάρτυς* or *νέος μάρτυς*).[315] Greek sources often indicate who killed them, thereby giving an approximate date of their martyrdom. For example, *Sinai Gr. 1096* (12th cent.) lists the fathers of the monastery who were killed by the Persians and the Muslims (*Μαύρων/Ἰσμαηλιτῶν*).[316] In some cases, martyrdom accounts are now believed to be literary creations intended to 'publicize the virtues of a regional church'.[317] The problem of discerning between fact and fiction may explain why it is often difficult to identify some of the New Martyrs in liturgical calendars.

According to the presumably fictional martyrdom account, Michael the Sabaite (7th cent.?), the nephew of a certain Theodore, bishop of Edessa, was a monk of St Sabas Lavra martyred in Jerusalem during the reign of the Umayyad caliph ʿAbd al-Malik (685–705).[318] His commemoration is completely absent from Georgian sources and from Constantinopolitan Greek sources. However, seven Melkite Arabic synaxaria and the Typikon *Sinai Gr.*

---

[314] Demetrios G. Tsames, *Ἁγιολογία τῆς Ὀρθόδοξης Ἐκκλησίας* (Thessalonike: Ἐκδόσεις Π. Πουρναράς, 1999), 108–24. For additional New Martyrs not discussed here, see Griffith, 'Neo-Martyrs'. See also the monograph dedicated to this subject by Christian C. Sahner, *Christian Martyrs under Islam: Religious Violence and the Making of the Muslim World* (forthcoming), especially Chapter 5 ('Creating Saints and Communities'). I thank the author for sharing drafts of his work with me and for offering significant corrections to this section.

[315] Binggeli, 'Calendrier melkite de Jérusalem', 190–2.

[316] *Sinai Gr. 1096* (12th cent.), fol. 93r and 110r; Dmitrievskii, *Описание* III, 42 and 49 (20 March and 15 May).

[317] John C. Lamoreaux, 'Hagiography', in Noble and Treiger, *The Orthodox Church in the Arab World*, 113.

[318] For the life of Michael the Sabaite, see Paul Peeters, 'La Passion de S. Michel le Sabaïte', AB 48 (1930), 65–98, esp. 66–7. For the debate over the authorship of the *Vita*, see Aleksandr A. Vasiliev, 'The Life of Theodore of Edessa', *Byzantion* 16 (1942–1943), 165–225, here 215; Hans-Georg Beck, *Kirche und theologische Literatur im Byzantinischen Reich* (Munich: C. H. Beck'sche Verlagsbuchhandlung, 1959), 558–9. Peeters believes that it is a work of fiction and that Theodore of Edessa is none other than Theodore Abū Qurrah. See also Alexander Kazhdan, 'Theodore of Edessa,' ODB III, 2042–3; Griffith, 'Neo-Martyrs', 170–83.

1096 (12th cent.) indicate his commemoration on 19 July.[319] The veneration of Michael the Sabaite at the Lavra of St Sabas is witnessed by Abbot Daniel, who writes that Michael's relics were found alongside those of St John the Silentiary, St John of Damascus, and St Theodore of Edessa.[320]

Anthony Rawḥ (d. 799/805), also known as Anthony al-Qurashī, was martyred in Raqqa on 25 December 799, during the reign of Harūn al-Rashīd (786–809).[321] Originally from an Arab noble family and hostile to Christians, he converted to Christianity, was baptized at the Jordan River, and was immediately tonsured a monk, receiving the name 'Anthony'. After his pilgrimage to the Jordan River and various monasteries in the Jordan wilderness, Anthony returned to Damascus, where he was denounced for his conversion to Christianity and arrested. After several months in prison, he was released and given the opportunity to renounce his conversion, but instead continued to confess Christ, for which he was decapitated in the city of Raqqa.[322] Anthony's death on 25 December would certainly cause problems for his martyrdom to be commemorated liturgically, since it coincided with Christmas, which explains why those calendars that do commemorate Anthony mention his name on days following 25 December. Ignace Dick notes that, despite the varying dates for the celebration of St Anthony, his cult never left the Arab empire and his memory was lost when the Byzantine calendar supplanted the local calendar, which he calls the 'ancient Syro-Palestinian calendar'.[323]

The veneration of Peter of Capitolias (d. 715), known in Arabic as Bayt Rās in the Transjordan, another cleric martyred at the hands of Muslims, is a more complicated matter.[324] Peter was a father of three children who later became bishop in Bostra, southern Syria, before being martyred in Damascus. Because it appears that the biographies of several Peters—among them a metropolitan of Damascus and a *chartophylax* from Maiouma—have been conflated in hagiographical texts, it is difficult to say anything definitive about Peter of Capitolias. In the *Chronicle* of Theophanes, however, two separate figures

---

[319] Καὶ τῶν ὁσίων πατέρων ἡμῶν Θεοδώρου τοῦ Ἐδεσσηνοῦ καὶ Μιχαὴλ ἀνεψιοῦ αὐτοῦ, τῶν ἀπὸ τῆς λαύρας τοῦ ἁγίου Σάββα ('And of our venerable fathers Theodore of Edessa and Michael, his nephew, of the Lavra of St Sabas'). Dmitrievskii, *Описание* III, 52; Sauget, *Synaxaires Melkites*, 411–14.

[320] Wilson, *Abbot Daniel*, 34.

[321] See Paul Peeters, 'S. Antoine le néo-martyr', AB 31 (1912), 410–50; Paul Peeters, 'L'autobiographie de S. Antoine le néo-martyr', AB 33 (1914), 52–63; Ignace Dick, 'La Passion arabe de S. Antoine Ruwaḥ, néo-martyr de Damas († 25 déc. 799)', Mus 74 (1961), 109–33; Sauget, *Synaxaires Melkites*, 332–4; Griffith, 'Neo-Martyrs', 198–200.

[322] For the Arabic life of St Anthony, see Dick, 'La Passion arabe de S. Antoine Ruwaḥ' (in n. 321 here); Noble and Treiger, *The Orthodox Church in the Arab World*, 117–23.

[323] *L'ancien calendrier syro-palestinien*. Dick, 'La Passion arabe de S. Antoine Ruwaḥ' (see n. 321 here), 110.

[324] Paul Peeters, 'La passion de S. Pierre de Capitolias († 13 janvier 715)', AB 57 (1939), 299–333; Joseph-Marie Sauget, 'Pietro di Capitolias', BS 10, 676–80; Griffith, 'Neo-Martyrs', 184–7; Noble and Treiger, *The Orthodox Church in the Arab World*, 23.

bearing the name Peter are mentioned as martyrs, one the metropolitan of
Damascus and the other a priest martyred near Damascus, both of whom died
for their defence of Christianity in the face of Islam in the year 741/2.[325] His
commemoration is present in several Hagiopolite and Constantinopolitan
calendars, but it is uncertain whether the 'hieromartyr Peter of Damascus'
(ὁ ἅγιος ἱερομάρτυς Πέτρος ὁ Δαμασκηνός) is the same as Peter of Capitolias
(Πέτρος Καπετωλέων) mentioned in the synaxarion of Constantinople.[326] The
various dates on which liturgical calendars commemorate a Peter of ambiguous identity, namely 15 January, 4 October, and 23 November, suggest that the
name of the saint had been passed down from older calendars but his precise
identity and cult of veneration had either died out or become a formality
devoid of further knowledge of the life and deeds of the saint. The AL
commemorates St Peter Apselamus on 11 January, an obscure saint mentioned by Eusebius of Caesarea and commemorated in Constantinopolitan
synaxaria on dates similar to those of St Peter of Capitolias.[327] Whether these
similar dates reveal a direct connection between Peter of Capitolias and Peter
Apselamus is unclear and remains unresolved.

In general, the commemoration of New Martyrs did not find a stable place
within the Hagiopolite calendar, nor did most of them pass into the Byzantinized calendar. This is most likely because of the difficulties of spreading the
cult of martyrs killed during the Muslim occupation. Well-established monasteries, such as Mar Sabas Lavra or the Monastery of Mount Sinai, were,
however, able to promote the cults of their own saints and martyrs. In both
cases, the commemorations of their martyred monks—specifically the twenty
Sabaite monks killed by the Arabs in 797 and commemorated on 19/20 March,
and the forty monks killed at Sinai and Raithou in the fourth century and
commemorated on 13/14 January—were widely celebrated and even adopted
in the Byzantine rite calendar.[328] The Sinai commemoration even has its own
hymnography in the Hagiopolite Tropologion *Sinai Gr. N.E. ΜΓ 56* and *Sinai
Gr. N.E. ΜΓ 5* (8th–9th cent.) on 13 January, sung together with hymns for

[325] Mango and Scott, *Chronicle of Theophanes*, 577–9. Note the many questions that Mango
and Scott raise about the identities of Peter, including the one concerning his other name, 'Peter
of Maiouma'. For further discussion, see Robert G. Hoyland, *Seeing Islam as Others Saw It:
A Survey and Evaluation of Christian, Jewish and Zoroastrian Writings on Early Islam* (Studies in
Late Antiquity and Early Islam 13, Princeton, NJ: Darwin Press, 1997), especially 354–60.

[326] Delehaye, *Synaxarium*, 105–6 and 453–4. See also Joseph-Marie Sauget, 'Pietro di Capitolias', BS 10, 680. Delehaye notes Καπετολέων and Καπιτωλέων as alternative forms of
his name.

[327] AL, 225 n. 3; Eusebius of Caesarea, *De Martyribus Palestinae*, 10; PG 20: 1497; Delehaye,
Synaxarium, 1151.

[328] BHG 1300–7; Garitte, *Calendrier palestino-géorgien*, 129–30 and 420; Marina Detoraki,
'Greek Passions of the Martyrs in Byzantium', in *Ashgate Companion to Byzantine Hagiography*
II, 78–80; Charis Messis, 'Fiction and/or Novelisation in Byzantine Hagiography', in *Ashgate
Companion to Byzantine Hagiography* II, 335.

Table 4.13. New Martyrs

	AL	GL	Sin. Geo. O.38 (979)	Sin. Syr. M52N (9th–10th cent.)	Sin. Geo. O.34 (10th cent.)	Vat. Syr. 19 (1030)	Al-Bīrūnī (11th cent.)	Sin. Gr. 1096 (12th cent.)	Typikon of the Great Church	Constantinople Praxapostolos (11th cent.)
Anthony Rawḥ	–	–	–	30 Dec	18/19 Jan	–	29 Dec	–	–	–
Michael Sabaite	–	–	–	–	–	–	–	19 July	–	–
Peter of Capitolias	–	–	–	–	23 Nov	23 Nov?	15 Jan?	–	4 Oct	4 Oct
Sinai Fathers	–	–	–	13 Jan	13 Jan 28 Dec	14 Jan	13 Jan	14 Jan	14 Jan 27 Dec	14 Jan 27 Dec
Sabaite Fathers	–	–	–	–	19 Mar	20 Mar	–	20 Mar 15 May	–	20 Mar

Theophany, since 13 January was also the end of the octave of Theophany.[329] Nevertheless, despite his connections to both the Monastery of Mar Sabas and the Monastery of Sinai, the new martyr monk ʿAbd al-Masīḥ, killed in Ramla on 9 March 857 according to Griffith and before 750 according to Binggeli, is not found either in Constantinopolitan calendars or in any Hagiopolite calendars other than in a few later Arabic Melkite synaxaria.[330] Since liturgical calendars were already quite developed by the seventh century, it is not surprising that New Martyrs are often missing from the sanctoral cycle of the Byzantine rite. Adding commemorations of new saints required someone or some important liturgical centre to promote their cult, which was often unknown outside of Palestine (see Table 4.13).

---

[329] Nikiforova, *Из истории Минеи в Византии*, 201–2.

[330] The Greek equivalent of ʿAbd al-Masīḥ is Χριστόδουλος. See Sauget, *Synaxaires Melkites*, 366–7. For his life, see Sidney H. Griffith, 'The Arabic Account of ʿAbd al-Masīḥ an-Nağrānī al-Ghassānī', Mus 98 (1985), 331–74; Mark N. Swanson, 'The Martyrdom of Abd al-Masīḥ, Superior of Mount Sinai (Qays al-Ghasānī)', in *Syrian Christians under Islam: The First Thousand Years*, ed. by David Thomas (Leiden: Brill, 2001), 107–29; John C. Lamoreaux, 'Hagiography', in Noble and Treiger, *The Orthodox Church in the Arab World*, 114–15 and 123–8. For a dating of his martyrdom to before 750, see André Binggeli, 'L'hagiographie du Sinaï en arabe d'après un recueil du IXe siècle (Sinaï arabe 542)', *Parole de l'Orient: revue semestrielle des études syriaques et arabes chrétiennes* 32 (2007), 163–80, esp. 175–7.

Sacred Objects, Places, and Events

The commemoration of sacred objects and places—rather than of holy people or events from salvation history—was common in Christianity from early times. Relics were venerated, transferred, deposed, and collected already from the fourth century, if not earlier.[331] Holy sites (ἅγιοι τόποι, *loci sancti*), sanctified by physical contact with the Saviour and the saints, were visited by pilgrims, and some sites eventually made their way into the liturgical calendar. A notable example is the Church of the Kathisma, built on a place associated with the apocryphal account of the Theotokos stopping on the way to Bethlehem, which was celebrated in the GL on 13 August and 3 December.[332] Among the sacred objects, places, and events examined in this section, particular attention will be paid to the relic of the Precious Cross, the Ark of the Covenant, the dedication of church buildings, and the commemoration of church councils.

The Precious Cross

Despite the Johannine and Pauline connection of the Cross with Jesus' glorification and with the sign of the Cross as an apotropaic rite in Christianity, the veneration of the Cross only developed after its finding in the fourth century.[333] This important relic was incorporated into various services in Jerusalem. Egeria mentions that processions to the Cross were held during daily services at the Church of the Anastasis.[334] On Holy Friday, the service at the sixth hour in the GL was held at Golgotha and included numerous prayers with genuflexion before the Cross, as well as a rite of washing and venerating the Cross.[335]

Apart from the particular veneration of the Cross during daily services and in the commemorations of the Passion of Christ during Holy Week, numerous other feasts of the Cross emerged, usually connected with some related

---

[331] Robert F. Taft and Alexander Kazhdan, 'Relics', ODB III, 1779–81. See also *Byzance et les reliques du Christ*, ed. by J. Durand and B. Flusin (Monographies 17, Paris: Centre de recherche d'Histoire et Civilisation de Byzance, 2004).

[332] GL § 1143; Gary Vikan, 'Locus sanctus', ODB II, 1244; Maraval, *Lieux saints*, 63–80 and 271–2.

[333] See BHG 396–451y, BHGna 396–451z; Gerhard Podskalsky, SJ, 'Cross: Theology of the Cross', ODB I, 549–50; Apostolos Karpozilos and Anthony Cutler, 'Cross: The Cross in Everyday Life', ODB I, 550–1; Robert F. Taft and Alexander Kazhdan, 'Cross, Cult of', ODB I, 551–3; Hansjörg Auf der Maur, 'Feiern im Rhythmus der Zeit. I: Herrenfeste in Woche und Jahr', in *Gottesdienst der Kirche: Handbuch der Liturgiewissenschaft*, vol. 5 (Regensburg: Verlag Friedrich Pustet, 1983), 186–9.

[334] Egeria, *Itinéraire*, §24.7 (= p. 240 Maraval). See Chapter 1, 'The *Itinerarium* of Egeria'.

[335] GL § 703 and GL Appendix I, § 115–62. See also Janeras, *Vendredi-Saint*, 279–90.

historical event that occurred after the life of Christ. The Exaltation of the Cross on 14 September was originally the second day of the Enkainia of the Anastasis in Jerusalem.[336] The origins of this feast are disputed, but are traditionally connected with the dedication of the Constantinian church complex around the Anastasis and the finding of the true Cross by St Helen.[337] The lifting up or 'exaltation' (ὕψωσις; აპყრობაჲ, *apqrobay*) of the Cross on 14 September is mentioned in Jerusalem in the GL and in Constantinople in the sixth-century account of the monk Alexander of Cyprus (527–65).[338] Al-Bīrūnī briefly describes the commemoration on 14 September, stating that it was the 'Feast of the Invention of the Cross by the Emperor Constantine and his mother Helen, which they tore from the hands of the Jews'.[339] This feast spread into all of Christendom and eclipsed the Hagiopolitan Enkainia feast of the Anastasis, perhaps due to the destruction and decline of the holy places.

Jerusalem and Constantinople also celebrated the appearance of the Cross over Golgotha in Jerusalem on 7 May 351, an event that is recounted by St Cyril of Jerusalem in a letter to Constantine and commemorated on this day in the AL and GL.[340] Several Georgian calendars, including the GL, the *Iadgari*, and Iovane Zosime's calendar, also indicate the commemoration of the apparition of the Cross to Constantine on 29 January.[341] The *oxitay* for the 7 May feast in the GL and *Iadgari* compares Constantine's vision of the Cross in a dream to its appearance in the sky to many faithful in Jerusalem.[342] Ironically, the commemoration, by Heraclius, of the return of the Cross to Jerusalem on Good Friday, 21 March 631—or on the third Sunday of Lent in the first days of March 630, depending on the tradition—was not widely celebrated in Jerusalem.[343] In Jerusalem, Egeria already notes a particular

[336] AL 363; GL (L) § 1240a.

[337] Louis van Tongeren, *Exaltation of the Cross: Toward the Origins of the Feast of the Cross and the Meaning of the Cross in Early Medieval Liturgy* (Liturgia Condenda 11, Leuven: Peeters, 2000), 17.

[338] GL (L) § 1240a; PG 87/3: 4072B.

[339] Al-Bīrūnī, *Fêtes des Melchites*, 312.

[340] AL, 332–5; GL § 957–63. For the letter of St Cyril, see BHG 413; PG 33: 1165–76; GL Appendix IIA, esp. § 13; E. Bihan, 'L'épitre de Cyrille de Jérusalem à Constance sur la vision de la croix (BHG^3 413)', *Byzantion* 43 (1973), 264–96.

[341] GL § 182; Garitte, *Calendrier palestino-géorgien*, 144–5 and 218; Stefano Parenti and Elena Velkovska, 'Two Leaves of a Calendar Written in "Mixed" Uncial of the Ninth Century', BBGG (terza serie) 7 (2010), 297–305, here 301.

[342] GL § 958; *Iadgari*, 236; Charles Renoux, 'Les hymnes du Iadgari pour la fête de la croix le 7 mai', *Studi sull'Oriente Cristiano* 4: 1 (2000), 93–102, here 100–1.

[343] Venance Grumel, 'La reposition de la vraie croix à Jérusalem par Héraclius: Le jour et l'année', *Byzantinische Forschungen* 1 (1966), 139–49; Cyril Mango, 'Deux études sur Byzance et la Perse sassanide. II: Héraclius, Šahrvaraz et la vraie croix', *Travaux et Mémoires* 9 (1985), 105–17; Michael van Esbroeck, 'L'invention de la croix sous l'empereur Héraclius', *Parole de l'Orient* 21 (1996), 21–46.

adoration of the Cross on Good Friday, although the first evidence of such a rite on Good Friday in Constantinople comes after 670, that is, after Heraclius.[344] A similar rite of the veneration of the Cross was practiced in Constantinople on the third Sunday of Lent.[345] Janeras has speculated that the March commemoration was not celebrated in Jerusalem because it fell during Lent, a time when liturgical feasts would be displaced by the Lenten cycle. Thus the 7 May commemoration was honoured with greater solemnity.[346] In Constantinople, the liturgical commemorations of the Lenten season absorbed the March commemoration of the return of the Cross instituted by Heraclius, and the feast was enshrined as the third Sunday of Lent in the Typikon of the Great Church as well as in the oldest Triodia—such as the oldest extant dated Greek manuscript from Mar Sabas Lavra, *Sinai Gr. 741* copied on 25 January 1099, which prescribes the veneration of the Cross on the third Sunday of Lent (τὴν Κυριακὴν τῆς γʹ ἑβδομάδας· εἰς τὴν προσκύνησις τοῦ τιμίου καὶ ζωοπιοῦ σταυροῦ).[347]

The importance of the Cross for Jerusalem can also be seen in homily collections such as *Sinai Gr. 493* (8th-9th cent.), which gather together various texts on the Cross along with homilies for feasts of saints of particular Hagiopolitan significance, such as James and Stephen.[348] Judging from the contents of lectionaries, there were more commemorations of the Cross in Jerusalem, since Hagiopolite lectionaries provide general readings for common celebrations that also took place on Wednesdays and Fridays every week, according to Iovane Zosime.

While there are no such general scriptural readings and hymns in early Constantinopolitan lectionaries, the Cross was closely associated with imperial rulers, which means that its cult was also important in Constantinople. With the arrival of the Cross and other relics of the Passion of Christ, such as the Lance and the Column of Flagellation of Christ, their veneration was incorporated into the cycle of services, especially on the days before the Exaltation of the Cross, during the fourth Week of Lent, and on Holy Thursday and Friday (see Table 4.14).[349]

---

[344] Egeria, *Itinéraire*, § 37: 1-3 (= pp. 284-7 Maraval); Janeras, *Vendredi-Saint*, 290-1.

[345] Mateos, *Typicon*, vol. 2, 38-46.   [346] Janeras, *Vendredi-Saint*, 298-9.

[347] 'Sunday of the third week, for the veneration of the precious and life-giving Cross', *Sinai Gr. 741* (25 January 1099), fol. 140r-146v; Mateos, *Typicon*, vol. 2, 38-9; Bertonière, *Sundays of Lent*, 69.

[348] Ehrhard, *Überlieferung*, vol. 1, 146-8. Ehrhard notes that many of the texts in this manuscript collection are unedited.

[349] Mateos, *Typicon*, vol. 1, 24-6;vol. 2, 38-46 and 72-82. See Bernard Flusin, 'Les cérémonies de l'exaltation de la croix à Constantinople au XIᵉ siècle d'après le Dresdenensis A 104', in *Byzance et les reliques du Christ*, ed. by Jannic Durand and Bernard Flusin (Monographies 17, Paris: Centre de recherche d'Histoire et Civilisation de Byzance, 2004), 61-89.

Table 4.14. The Precious Cross

	AL	GL	Sin. Geo. O.38 (979)	Sin. Syr. M52N (9th–10th cent.)	Sin. Geo. O.34 (10th cent.)	Vat. Syr. 19 (1030)	Al-Bīrūnī (11th cent.)	Sin. Gr. 1096 (12th cent.)	Typikon of the Great Church	Constantinople Praxapostolos (11th cent.)
Veneration	–	–	–	–	–	10–13 Sept	–	–	10–13 Sept	10–13 Sept
Exaltation	14 Sept	14 Sept	14 Sept	14 Sept	14 Sept	14 Sept	14 Sept	14 Sept	14 Sept	14 Sept
Apparition of the Cross	7 May	29 Jan 7 May	29 Jan 7 May	7 May	29 Jan 7 May	–	4 May	7 May	7 May	7 May
Discovery	–	–	–	–	–	–	–	–	6 Mar	–
Translation	–	–	–	–	–	–	–	–	1 May	–
Procession	–	–	–	–	–	–	–	–	1 Aug	31 July
Golgotha	–	–	–	15 Sept[350]	–	–	–	–	–	–
Wood of Life	–	20 Apr	–	–	–	–	–	–	–	–
Weekly	–	–	–	–	Wednesdays and Fridays	–	–	–	–	–

The Ark of the Covenant

The chest that contained the tablets of the Law (Exodus 40:18; Deuteronomy 10: 5) and was known as the Ark of the Covenant is mentioned in Hebrews 9:4 along with other sacred objects from the time of Moses, such as the golden vessel of manna (Exodus 16:34) and the rod of Aaron (Numbers 17:10). The Ark itself was constructed according to divine instructions and was to be the place whence God would speak to Israel (Exodus 25:10–22). After the fall of Jerusalem to the Babylonians in 587 BC, the location of the Ark became uncertain and, for patristic commentators, it became a symbol and prefiguration of the new law of Christ.[351]

Despite this new symbolic and typological approach to the Ark, a commemoration of the Ark of the Covenant was celebrated in the church of

---

[350] Commemoration of the 'life offered on Golgotha' (the title is *La vie offerte [sur] le Golgotha*). Philothée, *Nouveaux Manuscrits Syriaques*, 516.

[351] H. Lesêtre, 'Arche d'alliance', in *Dictionnaire de la Bible*, vol. 1, ed. by Fulcran Vigouroux (Paris: Letouzey et Ané, 1895), 912–23.

Jerusalem. Both the AL and GL place the feast of the Ark of the Law of the Lord on 2 July (კიდობნისა შჯულისა უფლისაო, *kidobnisa šjulisa uplisay*),[352] and in the GL this feast is followed the next day by the feast of the 'Raising of the Cup' (ბარძიმისა პოვნაჲ, *barzimisa povnay*),[353] presumably a celebration of the Holy Grail, the chalice of Christ from the Mystical Supper (Matthew 26:27, Mark 14:23, Luke 22:17 and 20). Commemorations of relics and objects from the Old Testament are quite rare in liturgical calendars. With regard to the Ark of the Covenant, the disappearance of this feast can perhaps be explained by the application of the typology of the Ark to the Theotokos, as the Ark of the Covenant that bore Christ. This is found throughout Byzantine Marian liturgical hymnography, in particular in the *akathistos* hymn: 'Rejoice, Tabernacle of God the Word. Rejoice, Holy one, holier than the Holies. Rejoice, Ark made golden by the Spirit' (Χαῖρε, σκηνὴ τοῦ Θεοῦ καὶ Λόγου· χαῖρε, Ἁγία Ἁγίων μείζων. Χαῖρε, κιβωτὲ χρυσωθεῖσα τῷ Πνεύματι).[354]

In Constantinople there was no commemoration of the Ark of the Covenant, although a commemoration of the laying of the Robe of the Theotokos at the Church of Blachernai was celebrated on 2 July.[355] While this connection is probably coincidental, it should be noted that the connection between the Ark and the Theotokos exists in the AL, which provides the same psalm verse for both the 2 July and the 15 August commemorations: 'Arise, Lord, in your rest, you and the ark of your sanctuary' (Psalm 131:8; see Table 4.15).

Table 4.15. The Ark of the Covenant

	AL	GL	Sin. Geo. O.38 (979)	Sin. Syr. M52N (9th–10th cent.)	Sin. Geo. O.34 (10th cent.)	Vat. Syr. 19 (1030)	Al-Bīrūnī (11th cent.)	Sin. Gr. 1096 (12th cent.)	Typikon of the Great Church	Constantinople Praxapostolos (11th cent.)
Ark of the Covenant	2 July	2 July	–	–	2 July	–	–	–	–	–

---

[352] AL, 34851; GL §§ 1069–73.

[353] GL § 1074–6. This is also found in *Sinai Geo. O. 34* (10th cent.) as the first commemoration. See Garitte, *Calendrier palestino-géorgien*, 76.

[354] Oikos 14, *The Service of the Akathist Hymn* (Boston, MA: Holy Transfiguration Monastery, 1991), 49; *fœderis arca* in Ambrose of Milan, *Sermo XLII*, PL 17: 689; Sophronios Eustratiades, Ἡ Θεοτόκος ἐν τῇ Ὑμνογραφίᾳ (Ἁγιορετικὴ Βιβλιοθήκη 6, Paris: Librairie Ancienne Honoré Champion, 1930), 35.

[355] τὰ καταθέσια τῆς τιμίας ἐσθῆτος ('the deposition of the precious vesture'). Mateos, *Typicon*, vol. 1, 328–30; Andreou, *Praxapostolos*, 376–7.

Church Buildings

The feast of the *enkainia* (ἐγκαίνια; საჲდგმაზრი, *satp'owri*), or dedication, of a church was very common in Hagiopolitan sources and is distinct from the commemoration of the foundation of a church.[356] Kekelidze states that these annual feasts of dedication, and not the annual commemoration of the saints to whom the church was dedicated, were the original patronal feasts of churches.[357] Over time, the Christocentric emphasis on the dedication of the church and its altar is lost, being completely replaced by the celebration of the saint.[358]

The GL commemorates at least eleven significant dedications in and around Jerusalem. The Church of St George in Lydda and the Church of the Nativity in Bethlehem, referred to as the Church of 'St Mary' in crusader sources, are known to have survived the Persians' and al-Ḥākim's devastation without significant damage, probably due to Muslim veneration of St George and the birth of Christ.[359] Less is known of the church of the Monastery of the Theotokos in Choziba and of the Church at the Probaitic (Sheep Pool), associated with the events surrounding the birth of the Theotokos.[360] The strong ties between Jerusalem and Sinai are revealed in the commemoration of the Enkainia of the Church of Sinai on 3 October in the GL, which Garitte speculates must be the principal church of the monastery dedicated to the Theotokos.[361] Al-Bīrūnī's calendar mentions a feast of the 'Renovation of the Temple' on 3 June but does not specify which one.[362]

With regard to the Church of the Kathisma, Garitte believes that the feast on 13 August was copied incorrectly in some sources. Rather than a dedication, he believes this is a synaxis, since the dedication is recorded on 2 or 3 December in other sources. Thus the 13 August celebration would have been a pre-festive one, connected with the Dormition of the Theotokos, rather

[356] Kekelidze, Канонарь, 173–5; Matthew Black, 'The Festival of Encaenia Ecclesiae in the Ancient Church with Special Reference to Palestine and Syria', *The Journal of Ecclesiastical History* 5 (1954), 78–85; Alexander Kazhdan, Anthony Cutler, and Robert F. Taft, 'Enkainia', ODB II, 699. See also Bernard Botte and Heinzgerd Brakmann, 'Kirchweihe', in *Reallexikon für Antike und Christentum*, vol. 20, ed. by Georg Schöllgen et al. (Stuttgart: Anton Hiersemann, 2001), 1139–69. For the most recent examination of this question, see Permiakov, *'Make This the Place Where Your Glory Dwells'*, 233–50. For more on the Feast of the Enkainia of the Anastasis, see 'Enkainia and the Exaltation of the Cross' in this chapter.
[357] Kekelidze, Канонарь, 174.
[358] Elena Velkovska, 'La celebrazione dei santi nel Typikon greco e slavo', in *Il tempo dei santi tra Oriente e Occidente: Liturgica e agiografia dal tardo antico al concilio di Trento: Atti del IV Convegno di studio dell'Associazione italiana per lo studio della santità, dei culti e dell'agiografia, Firenze, 26–28 ottobre 2000*, ed. by Anna Benvenuti and Marcello Garzaniti (Rome: Viella, 2005), 361–84, here 368.
[359] Pringle, *Churches of the Crusader Kingdom*, vol. 1, 137–56; vol. 2, 9–27.
[360] Sophronius of Jerusalem, Ἀνακρεόντεια 20: 81–94, PG 87.3: 3733–840, here 3821–4; Pringle, *Churches of the Crusader Kingdom*, vol. 1, 183–92; vol. 2, 389–97; Garitte, *Calendrier palestino-géorgien*, 246.
[361] Ibid., 348.   [362] Al-Bīrūnī, *Fêtes des Melchites*, 308.

than a feast of Enkainia.[363] The coincidence of the Enkainia of certain churches in early Hagiopolite calendars with commemorations of saints to which those churches were dedicated in later Hagiopolite or Constantinopolitan calendars is striking. For example, the Dedication, on 20 November, of the Nea Church—referred to as the 'Building of the God-loving King Justinian, the Church of the Theotokos' (დმრთოის მოყუარისა ისჯზნისა მეფისა მენებულსა. დმრთოისმშობდისა ეკლესიასა) in the GL—coincides with the Constantinopolitan feast of the Presentation of the Virgin Theotokos, celebrated on 21 November.[364] Nevertheless, not all dedications entered the liturgical calendar. For example, the consecration of the church of the Lavra of St Euthymius on 7 May 428 by Bishop Juvenal, mentioned in the Life of Euthymius did not enter the Hagiopolite calendar and was probably only commemorated locally in that monastery, if at all.[365]

General readings for dedications were copied in Hagiopolite lectionaries but are rare in Constantinopolitan lectionaries.[366] The Typikon of the Great Church includes a general service for Enkainia.[367] Occasionally such feasts are mentioned in other Constantinopolitan sources as well, for example the commemoration of the Enkainia of Theotokos in Chalkoprateia (ἐγκαίνια τῆς Θεοτόκου ἐν τοῖς Χαλκοπρατείοις) on 18 December,[368] the Opening of the Sacred Great Church (τὰ ἀνοίξια τῆς ἁγίας τοῦ Θεοῦ μεγάλης ἐκκλησίας) on 22 December,[369] the Enkainia of God's Sacred Great Church (τὰ ἐγκαίνια τῆς ἁγίας τοῦ Θεοῦ μεγάλης ἐκκλησίας) on 23 December,[370] the Enkainia of the Church of the Theotokos of Evergetis (τῶν ἐγκαινίων τῆς ὑπεραγίας Θεοτόκου τῆς Εὐεργέτιδος), listed as the second celebration, on 29 December, after that of the Holy Infants slaughtered by King Herod,[371] and the Enkainia of the Church of the Theotokos of the Spring (τὰ ἐγκαίνια τοῦ ναοῦ τῆς Θεοτόκου ἐν τῇ Πηγῇ) on 9 July.[372] The Enkainia of St George in Lydda is also mentioned in some Constantinopolitan synaxaria on 3 November, but is absent from Juan Mateos' edition of the Typikon of the Great Church (see Table 4.16).[373]

---

[363] Garitte, *Calendrier palestino-géorgien*, 301 and 401.

[364] GL §§ 1373–5; I. E. Anastasios, 'Εἰσόδια τῆς Θεοτόκου', *ΘΗΕ* 5, 451–4; Robert F. Taft and Annemarie Weyl Carr, 'Presentation of the Virgin', ODB III, 1715; Olkinuora, *Feast of the Entrance of the Theotokos*, 34–8.

[365] *Life of Euthymius*, Chapter 16, in Schwartz, *Cyril of Scythopolis*, 26.

[366] Mateos, *Typicon*, vol. 2, 290. For lections for general commemorations, see Chapter 5, 'General Commemorations'.

[367] See formula Τάξις γινομένη εἰς ἐγκαίνια ἐκκλησίας' ('order for the Enkainia of a church'), in Mateos, *Typicon*, vol. 2, 186.

[368] Andreou, *Praxapostolos*, 280.   [369] Ibid., 282.   [370] Ibid., 284.

[371] Dmitrievskii, *Описаниe* I, 364; Ehrhard, *Überlieferung*, vol. 1, 44.

[372] Mateos, *Typicon* I, 334; Andreou, *Praxapostolos*, 380. See also Cyril Mango and Nancy Patterson-Ševčenko, 'Pege', ODB III, 1616; 'Anonymous Miracles of the Pege', in *Miracle Tales from Byzantium*, ed. and trans. by Alice-Mary Talbot and Scott Fitzgerald Johnson (Dumbarton Oaks Medieval Library 12, Washington, DC: Harvard University Press, 2012), xiv–xviii, 205–97.

[373] Delehaye, *Synaxarium*, 191–2; Garitte, *Calendrier palestino-géorgien*, 374–5.

Table 4.16. Church buildings

	AL	GL	Sin. Geo. O.38 (979)	Sin. Syr. M52N (9th–10th cent.)	Sin. Geo. O.34 (10th cent.)	Vat. Syr. 19 (1030)	Al-Bīrūnī (11th cent.)	Sin. Gr. 1096 (12th cent.)	Typikon of the Great Church	Constantinople Praxapostolos (11th cent.)
Dedication of Anastasis	13 Sept AL (E): Sept 23	13 Sept	13 Sept	13 Sept	13 Sept	–	13 Sept	13 Sept	–	13 Sept
Dedication of Theotokos at Gethsemane	–	23 Oct	13 July	23 Oct	23/24 Oct	–	24 Sept	–	–	–
Dedication of St George at Lydda	–	10 Nov?	10 Nov	3 Nov	3 Nov	3 Nov	–	3 Nov	–	–
Dedication of Nea	–	16 Sept 20 Nov	–	20 Nov	20 Nov	–	–	–	–	–
Dedication of Theotokos of Choziba	–	18 Jan	18 Jan	16 Jan	16/18 Jan	–	–	–	–	–
Dedication of Sion	–	15 Sept?	–	15 Sept	14/16 Sept	–	–	–	–	–
Dedication of Theotokos Probaitic	–	9 June	–	–	9 June	–	–	–	–	–
Dedication of Theotokos of Spoudaioi	–	11 Aug	–	–	11 Aug	–	–	–	–	–
Dedication of Kathisma	–	13 Aug 3 Dec	13 Aug	–	13 Aug 3 Dec	–	–	–	–	–
Dedication of Bethlehem	–	31 May	–	–	18 Sept	–	–	–	–	–
Dedication of Sinai	–	3 Oct	–	–	3 Oct	–	–	–	–	–

Church Councils

Church councils were significant to the life of the church of Jerusalem, not only in resolving doctrinal issues but also in forming the identity of Hagiopolitan Christians. As already noted, many liturgical texts from Jerusalem, such as the diptychs of the anaphora of JAS, still make reference to the 'six synods' long after the eighth century, which suggests to Sidney Griffith that Melkite identity was grounded in this recognition and reception of only six ecumenical councils. The text of the diptychs of JAS, based as it is on the majority of Greek manuscripts up to the fourteenth century, is as follows:

Μνήσθητι, κύριε, τῶν ἁγίων μεγάλων καὶ οἰκουμενικῶν ἓξ συνόδων. Τῶν ἐν Νικαίᾳ τριακοσίων δέκα καὶ ὀκτὼ καὶ τῶν ἐν Κωνσταντίνου πόλει ἑκατὸν πεντήκοστα καὶ τῶν ἐν Ἐφέσῳ τὸ πρότερον διακοσίων καὶ τῶν ἐν Καλχηδόνι ἑξακοσίων τριάκοντα καὶ τῶν ἐν τῇ ἁγίᾳ πέμπτῃ συνόδῳ ἑκάτον ἑξήκοντα τεσσάρων καὶ τῶν εν τῇ ἁγίᾳ ἕκτῃ συνόδῳ διακοσίων ὀγδοήκοντα ἐννέα καὶ λοιπῶν ἁγίων συνόδων καὶ ἐπισκόπων, τῶν ἐν πάσῃ τῇ οἰκουμένῃ ὀρθοδόξως ὀρθοτομησάντων τὸν λόγον τῆς ἀληθείας.[374]	Remember, O Lord, the six holy, great, and ecumenical councils: the 318 [fathers] in Nicaea, the 150 [fathers] in Constantinople, the 200 [fathers] at the first [council] in Ephesus, the 630 [fathers] in Chalcedon, the 164 [fathers] at the holy fifth council, and the 289 [fathers] at the holy sixth council, and the remainder of the holy councils and bishops who throughout the inhabited world rightly proclaim the word of truth.

The Georgian text from *Sinai Geo. N. 58* (10th cent.) is virtually identical:

მოჲსჲენ, უფალო, წმიდანი და დიდთანი სოფლისა ექუსნი კრებანი: ნიკიას სამასათრვათექუთნი, კოსტანთინებპოლის ასორმეოცდაათნი, ეფესოს პირველად ორასნი, ქალკიდონს ექუსასოცდაათნი, მეხუთე კრებსა ასსამეოცდაოთხნი და მეექუსესა წმიდა კრებსა, მუნვე კოსტანტინებპოლის ორასომბეოცდაცხრანი, და ესე წმიდანი კრებანი. და ყოველთა ადგილთა ღირსნი მამანი ჩუენნი, რომელნი მართლმადიდებლობით ეპისკოპოზებს და რომელთა მართლ წარუმართებენ სიტყუასა იგი ჭეშმარიტებისასა.[375]	Remember, O Lord, the six holy and great ecumenical councils: at Nicaea— 318 [fathers], at Constantinople—150; at the first [council] in Ephesus—200, at Chalcedon—630, at the fifth holy council—164 and at the sixth holy council, again there, in Constantinople—289. And these are the holy councils; and our worthy fathers in all places who officiated in orthodoxy as bishops and who have rightly promoted the word of truth.

---

[374] Mercier, *Liturgie de Saint Jacques*, 216–18; Kazamias, Θεία Λειτουργία τοῦ Ἁγίου Ἰακώβου, 206.

[375] *Sinai Geo. N. 58* (10th cent.), fol. 29r–29v; *Liturgia ibero-graeca*, 96–7.

It is worth noting that the Georgian text seems better familiarized with the geography of the fifth and sixth ecumenical councils, indicating that they took place in Constantinople, whereas the Greek text refers to the fifth and sixth councils simply as 'holy'. In the Greek manuscripts of JAS, it is only after the fourteenth century that seven councils are commemorated in the diptychs, namely in the manuscripts *Sinai Gr. 1040* (14th cent.), *Koutloumoussiou 194* (14th cent.), and *Paris Suppl. Gr. 476* (15th cent.).

Not only were these councils commemorated in the diptychs of the anaphora of JAS, but they also entered liturgical calendars, to be celebrated during the year. The GL includes only one commemoration of four ecumenical councils on 26 September, once the octave of the Enkainia was complete.[376] Later Hagiopolite calendars, such as al-Bīrūnī's Melkite calendar, indicate that six ecumenical councils were commemorated on 21 or 22 April. Al-Bīrūnī also gives a detailed account of the councils' history, with numbers of participants similar to those of the diptychs, as well as with a summary of their major doctrinal disputes. A similar commemoration is repeated on 15 September, although it is unclear whether this refers to all six councils or only to the sixth, which is commemorated on 15 September in the synaxarion of Constantinople.[377] Unfortunately it is difficult to identify any commemorations of councils in *Sinai Geo. O. 38* (979) and *Vatican Syr. 19* (1030) because of either incomplete information or lacunae on the days when one would expect to find these commemorations.[378]

The synaxarion of Constantinople provides significant information on the commemoration of councils and shows that many were connected to the celebration of Saint Euphemia of Chalcedon (d. 16 September 303), whose relics featured prominently at the Council of Chalcedon, on 11 July and 16 September.[379] In both the calendar of Iovane Zosime and in various Greek Constantinopolitan sources, the fourth ecumenical Council of Chalcedon is often celebrated near the commemoration of Saint Euphemia, between 11 and 16 July, and the fifth ecumenical council on the Sunday after 16 July ('Τῇ μετ' αὐτῶν κυριακῇ τῶν ἁγίων πατέρων τῶν κατὰ Σεβῆρου τῆς ε΄ συνόδου').[380]

---

[376] GL § 1256f.

[377] See al-Bīrūnī, *Melkite Calendar*, 18–19 and 26; Mateos, *Typicon*, vol. 1, 34.

[378] See Binggeli, 'Calendrier melkite de Jérusalem', 184 for important corrections to *Sinai Syr. M52N*.

[379] Alexander Kazhdan and Nancy Patterson-Ševčenko, 'Euphemia of Chalcedon', ODB II, 747–8.

[380] 'On the following Sunday, the holy fathers of the fifth council, against Severus'. Garitte, *Calendrier palestino-géorgien*, 276; Delehaye, *Synaxarium*, 811–14 and 825–6; Séverien Salaville, AA, 'La fête du concile de Chalcédonie dans le rite byzantin', in *Das Konzil von Chalkedon: Geschichte und Gegenwart*, vol. 2: *Entscheidung um Chalkedon*, ed. by Aloys Grillmeier, SJ, and Heinrich Bacht, SJ (Würzburg: Echter Verlag, 1962), 677–95.

Table 4.17. Church councils

	AL	GL	Sinai Geo. O.38 (979)	Sinai Syr.M52N (9th–10th cent.)	Sinai Geo. O.34 (10th cent.)	Vatican Syr. 19 (1030)	Al-Bīrūnī (11th cent.)	Sinai Gr. 1096 (12th cent.)	Typikon of the Great Church	Constantinople Praxapostolos (11th cent.)
1st Council						(Sunday before Pentecost?)			29 May Sunday before Pentecost	Sunday before Pentecost
2nd Council									3 Aug	
3rd Council									9 Sept	
4th Council					17 Sept			11 July	11 July 16 July	11 July 16 July
5th Council									Sunday after 16 July July 25	Sunday after 16 July
6th Council				22 April			15 Sept		15 Sept	
7th Council									11 Oct	11 Oct
Four Councils		26 Sept								
Six Councils				26 Sept	22 April		21 April			
Seven Councils										

From what can be seen in Table 4.17, Hagiopolite calendars commemorated either the four or the six councils, while Constantinople did not group councils together, celebrating them instead individually, on their specific days, and favouring the first, the fourth, and the seventh ecumenical councils. None of the Hagiopolite calendars examined here commemorates more than six councils. In general, the local commemorations of councils that were once celebrated by a simple procession in Constantinople eventually became part of the universal Byzantine calendar.[381]

---

[381] Miguel Arranz, SJ, 'Les fêtes théologiques du calendrier byzantin', in *La liturgie, expression de la foi: Conférences Saint-Serge XXVᵉ semaine d'études liturgiques, Paris, 27–30 juin 1978*, ed. by A. M. Triacca and A. Pistoia (BELS 16, Rome: C. L. V. Edizioni liturgiche, 1979), 29–55. See also Ioannis M. Fountoulis, "Ἡ μνήμη τῶν Ἁγίων Πατέρων τῆς Β΄ Οἰκουμενκῆς Συνόδου στό Ἑορτολόγιο καὶ στήν Ὑμνογραφία', *Γρηγόριος ὁ Παλαμᾶς* (Thessalonike) 66 (1983), 61–79.

CONCLUSIONS

After perusing these case studies of liturgical commemorations from the calendars of Jerusalem and Constantinople, the reader will be able to confirm that the rich material that liturgical calendars contain can often be disorienting and overwhelming. The problems raised by the underdeveloped concepts of paired dating (*Gegendatierung*), concomitant feasts, and commemorations with discrepancies of one day across varying calendars remain unresolved.[382] Discrepancies of one day between the same commemorations in different calendars might be explained by various factors, such as leap years, confusion over the beginning of the day according to various modes of calculation, and incorrect transcriptions of dates in foreign calendars; but these hypotheses might explain only individual occurrences rather than the phenomenon as a whole. Nevertheless, the analysis of the chronological development of the liturgical commemorations in the above case studies allows us to classify manuscripts of liturgical calendars under three broad categories: authentic Hagiopolitan manuscripts reflecting the local Jerusalem tradition, transitional calendars giving a mixed tradition, and Constantinopolitan or highly Byzantinized manuscripts used in the Jerusalem patriarchate (see Table 4.18).

While *Sinai Geo. O. 34* (10th cent.) and al-Bīrūnī's eleventh-century Melkite calendar reflect aspects of both Jerusalem and Constantinople liturgical practices and are thus labelled 'transitional', calendars with the Hagiopolite or Constantinopolitan label do not always fit neatly into their respective categories. One should bear in mind that even the AL and GL offer variants and developments to the Hagiopolite liturgical tradition, just as there can be significant differences between Constantinopolitan synaxaria and Praxapostoloi. This clearly shows the variety of liturgical books and practice before standardization was possible—a process that culminates in the uniformity and reproduction made possible by the printing press. Thus even Byzantinized liturgical sources from Jerusalem do not reflect 'pure' Constantinopolitan usage. Further study of additional liturgical manuscripts described in Appendix 1 will fill out Table 4.8.

The following conclusions can be made on the basis of the material examined in this chapter:

1. Hagiopolite liturgical sources reveal a shift from a local calendar for city-wide celebrations to a universal calendar for local celebrations held in only one church. In other words, liturgical calendars were initially intended for the specific city or place in which they were to be used, and they included all the celebrations held throughout that city or place in different locations. These liturgical commemorations also had a

---

[382] See various examples of complications in Grumel, *Chronologie*, 166–80.

Table 4.18. Classification of liturgical calendars

	Hagiopolite	Transitional		Constantinopolitan
5th cent.	AL			
8th cent.	GL			
	Iadgari			
10th cent.	*Sinai Syr. M52N* (9th–10th cent.)			*Typikon of the Great Church*
	Sinai Geo. O. 38 (979)	*Sinai Geo. O. 34* (10th cent.)		
11th cent.			*Vatican Syr. 19* (1030)	
		Al-Bīrūnī (11th cent.)		*Constantinople Praxapostolos* (11th cent.)
12th cent.			*Sinai Gr. 1096* (12th cent.)	

strong local flavour. A shift occurs after the Arab conquest in the seventh century, when a calendar with saints from all of Christendom develops and is used for the whole church. Instead of the various commemorations throughout the city that had been held in Jerusalem and Constantinople during their stational liturgies, all the celebrations were held in individual churches, and people would no longer go to different locations in the city.

2. The generalization and universalization of the calendar coincides with the diffusion of the Sabaite Typikon and with liturgical Byzantinization. As Mikhail Skaballanovich (1871–1931) noted over a century ago, 'the Constantinopolitan type of calendar receives prevailing importance everywhere because, from its most ancient development, it strove evermore to smooth over its local colouring in order to become universal throughout the church'.[383] This conclusion agrees perfectly with Uspensky's observations concerning the diffusion of the Sabaite Typikon, which came into use on Athos in a period when the particularities and specificities of local liturgical practices began to disappear and the liturgy came under strong influence from Constantinople.[384]

3. Relics—rather than holy places, tombs of saints, or other aspects of sacred topography—begin to dictate the development of the liturgical calendar and determine the date of celebrating a saint during the period

---

[383] Skaballanovich, *Толковый Типиконъ*, vol. 1, 444. For more on Skaballanovich, see Peter Galadza, 'Baumstark's Kievan Contemporary, Mikhail Skaballanovich (1871–1931): A Biographical Sketch and Analysis of His Heortology', in *Liturgy Fifty Years after Baumstark*, 761–75.

[384] Uspensky, 'Чин всенощного бдения', 101.

of liturgical Byzantinization. Whereas the day of martyrdom or death of a certain saint once decided the date at which he or she was commemorated in the liturgical calendar, the importance of the transfer or deposition of relics—especially to Constantinople—dominates the calendar and Hagiopolitan dates for commemorations are replaced by Constantinopolitan dates. The terminology of liturgical calendars is also levelled or universalized, so that distinctions between death, martyrdom, and deposition or transfer of relics are generally ignored.

4. Since the manuscript sources for most of these commemorations come from lectionaries, synaxaria, or other liturgical calendars, the question of the calendar within the context of the so-called Stoudite and Sabaite synthesis cannot be grouped with that of the Euchologion or the Horologion, and must be addressed on its own.

5. The importance of hymnography for a study of the calendar cannot be overstated, since the calendar is a 'privileged bearer of scriptural exegesis'.[385] Questions of the displacement and transfer of hymnography in Hagiopolitan and Constantinopolitan sources are crucial to the study of Byzantinization and must be considered when examining and explaining the liturgical contexts, function, and use of hymnography.[386]

---

[385] Hannick, 'The Theotokos in Byzantine hymnography', 76.

[386] See 'Hagiography, Homilies, and Hymnography' in this chapter for references to the various catalogues and resources for the study of Byzantine hymnography.

5

The Lectionary of Jerusalem

Having examined the eucharistic liturgy and the calendar of the church of Jerusalem, it is now time to investigate the order of scriptural readings in Jerusalem's lectionary. A quick glance at the sources enumerated in Chapters 1 and 2 and in Appendix 1 reveals that liturgical manuscripts containing the lectionary are among the ones most securely attributable to the patriarchate of Jerusalem. This connection is established through the indication of stations within the city of Jerusalem and the outlying region, through the order of pericopes (περικοπή, plural περικοπαί: 'section', 'passage'), or through palaeographic evidence. But, even though the order of the pericopes of Hagiopolite lectionaries has been identified in Greek sources as distinct from the Byzantine order, its complete and precise structures have yet to be established, which means that its decline in favour of the Constantinopolitan order cannot yet be adequately explained. Certain periods of the year, such as Holy Week, have been studied by Gabriel Bertonière and Sebastià Janeras, who have made significant headway in establishing a Hagiopolite pericope order.[1] While my examination of the pericope order in the Jerusalem lectionary seeks to be thorough and representative, the dearth of complete post-eighth-century manuscripts that could offer a full picture of reading cycles makes this difficult. Most extant manuscripts are extremely fragmentary, some consisting of no more than a few folia.

The goal of the liturgical historian is to explain 'what is going on', and not just to present the sources.[2] For this reason it is necessary to understand the connections, if any, between the various readings cycles. As has been repeated many times in this book, the fragmentary nature of the sources makes a complete, synthetic account of the structure and nature of the Jerusalem lectionary very difficult. Likewise, there are few extant homilies from the period of the Byzantinization of Jerusalem that delve into the reading cycles or comment on particular Gospels or books of Scripture, since most are festal

---

[1] Bertonière, *Easter Vigil*; Janeras, *Vendredi-Saint*; Janeras, 'La Settimana Santa'; Janeras, 'Pericope evangeliche'.
[2] Taft, *Diptychs*, xxx.

homilies—and even these date from a period predating our manuscript testimonials for the Hagiopolite lectionary.

BIBLICAL TEXTUAL CRITICISM AND LECTIONARY STUDIES

The revival of biblical studies in the late nineteenth century also made an impact on the study of Byzantine liturgy. Studies of Greek New Testament manuscripts systematized the existing knowledge of the contents of these sources and provided indexes that have established the pericope order in the Byzantine church. The most notable works are those of two German theologians, Caspar René Gregory (1846–1917) and Kurt Aland (1915–94), who span the twentieth century.[3] Of all biblical scholars, Aland came closest to understanding the variations in the pericope order of Greek lectionaries and was the first to distinguish systematically between a Jerusalem pericope order and the pericope order of the Byzantine church.[4] Despite this achievement, Aland never explained the criteria he used to distinguish a lectionary of the Jerusalem pericope order. In some cases, it seems that this designation was simply used to indicate that the manuscript did not correspond to the known Byzantine order of pericopes.

The few monograph studies dedicated exclusively to the Jerusalem lectionary have also come from scholars in the German-speaking world. The study of Jerusalem's cathedral lectionary by Rolf Zerfass (b. 1934) compared early witnesses of Jerusalem's lectionary with other eastern lectionary traditions in order to discover their origins. Unfortunately, Zerfass limited his analysis to four sources that spanned the course of eight centuries, namely the *Itinerarium* of Egeria, the AL, the GL, and the Typikon of the Anastasis.[5] Hans-Michael Schneider focused more specifically on the feasts of the Incarnation of

---

[3] Gregory, *Textkritik*; Aland, *Kurzgefaßte Liste*. Aland's list has provided the framework for further resources for lectionary studies, such as Bruce M. Metzger, *Manuscripts of the Greek Bible: An Introduction to Greek Palaeography* (New York: Oxford University Press, 1991); James K. Elliott, *A Bibliography of Greek New Testament Manuscripts*, 2nd edn (New York: Cambridge University Press, 2000); Stefan Royé, 'The Cohesion between the Ammonian–Eusebian Apparatus and the Byzantine Liturgical Pericope System in Tetraevangelion Codices: Stages in the Creation, Establishment and Evolution of Byzantine Codex Forms' and Anatoly A. Alexeev, 'On Jerusalem Vestiges of the Byzantine Gospel Lectionary', both in *Catalogue of Byzantine Manuscripts in Their Liturgical Context: Subsidia 1*, ed. by Klaas Spronk, Gerard Rouwhorst, and Stefan Royé (Turnhout: Brepols, 2013), 55–116 and 173–82 respectively.
[4] *Jerusalemische Reihenfolge* and *Perikopenanordnung der byzantinischen Kirche*. See Kurt Aland, 'Erläuterungen und Abkürzungen', in idem, *Kurzgefaßte Liste*, xiii–xix. See also Galadza, 'Jerusalem Lectionary', 184–6.
[5] See Zerfass, *Schriftlesung*, 60.

Christ in sources of the Jerusalem lectionary, although he placed an emphasis on the hymnography found in the lectionaries and in the *Iadgari*.[6] Both employed the primary data provided by New Testament textual criticism towards understanding the structure and underlying theology of Jerusalem's lectionary.

The work of biblical scholars allowed liturgical scholars such as Cyril Korolevsky and Anton Baumstark to investigate the Jerusalem lectionary still further.[7] However, neither Korolevsky nor Baumstark ever succeeded in systematically describing the lectionary's distinct nature and structure. More recently, Sebastià Janeras (b. 1931) and Stéphane Verhelst have dedicated their attention to the liturgy of Jerusalem, always seeking to understand it in the larger context of the Byzantine rite.[8]

Similar studies on the lectionary have also been undertaken for the Byzantine rite, allowing a comparison between Hagiopolite and Constantinopolitan practices. The works of Yvonne Burns and Elena Velkovska are fundamental to an understanding of the structure and development of Byzantine lectionaries.[9] Recent editions of liturgical manuscripts containing the lectionary, such as the Praxapostolos and the Evangelion, also advance our knowledge of liturgical practice in a given period.[10] This enables us to rely on actual liturgical lectionaries rather than upon synaxaria or secondary sources that may not always be as faithful to the liturgical practice of their period.[11]

Although the study of the pericope order of lectionaries is crucial to liturgical studies, the majority of biblical studies have other methods and goals. One such method in the study of the lectionary is that of textual criticism. Popularized in the nineteenth and twentieth centuries, this method

---

[6] Schneider, *Lobpreis im rechten Glauben.*

[7] Charon, 'Le rite byzantin'; Charon, *History of the Melkite Patriarchates*; Anton Baumstark, 'Die melkitische Ordnung des syro-palästinensischen Lektionars', in idem, *Nichtevangelische Perikopenordnungen*, 131–72; Anton Baumstark, 'Die Sonntägliche Evangelienlesung im vorbyzantinischen Jerusalem', BZ 30 (1930), 350–9.

[8] See Janeras, 'Lectionnaires de Jérusalem'; Verhelst, *Lectionnaire de Jérusalem.*

[9] Yvonne Burns, 'The Greek Manuscripts Connected by Their Lection Systems with the Palestinian Syriac Gospel Lectionaries', in *Studia Biblica 1978*, vol. 2: *Papers on the Gospels, Sixth International Congress on Biblical Studies, Oxford 3–7 April 1978*, ed. by Yvonne Burns (Journal for the Study of the New Testament, Supplement Series 2, Sheffield: University of Sheffield, 1980), 13–28; Yvonne Burns, 'The Lectionary of the Patriarch of Constantinople', in *Studia Patristica 15*, Part I: *Papers presented to the Seventh International Conference on Patristic Studies held in Oxford 1975*, ed. by Elizabeth A. Livingstone (Berlin: Akademie-Verlag, 1984), 515–20. See also Yvonne Eileen Burns, *A Comparative Study of the Weekday Lection Systems Found in Some Greek and Early Slavonic Gospel Lectionaries* (Unpublished doctoral thesis, London: School of Slavonic and East European Studies, University of London, 1975); Velkovska, 'Lo studio dei lezionari bizantini'.

[10] Andreou, *Praxapostolos*; John Lowden, *The Jaharis Gospel Lectionary: The Story of a Byzantine Book* (New York: Metropolitan Museum of Art/Yale University Press, 2009).

[11] Mateos, *Typicon*; see also Delehaye, *Synaxarium*. For descriptions of these sources, see Chapter 1 here.

goes back to Origen (*c*.185–254), whose goal was to find, to the extent that this was possible, the exact text of the original writings of Scripture through a study of biblical texts in ancient manuscripts.[12] This involves gathering and organizing evidence, developing a methodology, and—perhaps most significantly for my study here—reconstructing the history of transmission.[13] In establishing the text's reliability from the perspective of the transmission history, one must deal with errors and deliberate changes in the text over the course of time.[14]

TEXTUAL VARIANTS AND THEOLOGICAL PROFILE

Although a textual analysis of the Jerusalem lectionary is beyond the focus of this study on liturgical Byzantinization, it is worth noting some significant variants by comparison with the standard critical editions of the Bible. Such departures include variant incipits and omissions of certain phrases. Among the most significant variants in Tarchnishvili's edition of the Jerusalem lectionary is a passage from Hebrews 11:32–40 read at the commemoration of St Anthony the Great on 17 January in the GL. Modern commentaries on Hebrews 11:32–40 in its received form state that, because the author of the Epistle names only some of the Old Testament heroes he is alluding to, 'it is impossible to know in all instances to whom the references apply'.[15] Patristic authors often quote Scripture in a similar way: often selectively, not always accurately, and occasionally with interpolations. In the case of Hebrews 11:32–40, however, no other Greek patristic commentaries associate the names interpolated here with this pericope. James Thompson Marshall's analysis of textual variants in Palestinian lectionaries does not mention this variant.[16] The same reading is also indicated in the GL for Prophet Jeremiah (1 May); Prophet Eliseus (14 June); Prophet Amos (17 June); the Nativity of John the

---

[12] Young, *Biblical Exegesis*, 21–7. See also John S. Kselman, SS, and Ronald D. Witherup, SS, 'Modern New Testament Criticism', in *New Jerome Biblical Commentary*, ed. by Raymond E. Brown, SS, Joseph A. Fitzmyer, SJ, and Roland E. Murphy, OCarm (Englewood Cliffs, NJ: Prentice Hall, 1990), 1130–45.

[13] Roger L. Omanson, *A Textual Guide to the Greek New Testament: An Adaptation of Bruce M. Metzger's Textual Commentary for the Needs of Translators* (Stuttgart: Deutsche Bibelgesellschaft, 2006), 11*.

[14] Arie Van der Kooij, 'Textual Criticism', in *The Oxford Handbook of Biblical Studies*, ed. by J. W. Rogerson and Judith M. Lieu (Oxford: Oxford University Press, 2006), 579–90.

[15] Myles M. Bourke, 'The Epistle to the Hebrews', in *New Jerome Biblical Commentary*, ed. by Raymond E. Brown, SS, Joseph A. Fitzmyer, SJ, and Roland E. Murphy, OCarm (Englewood Cliffs, NJ: Prentice Hall, 1990), 920–41, here 940.

[16] See James Thompson Marshall, 'Remarkable Readings in the Epistles Found in the Palestinian Lectionary', *JTS* 5 (1904), 437–45.

Baptist (24 June); the Maccabees (1 August); Prophet Samuel (20 August); the deposition of Isaiah, Prophet Zachariah, the Three Youths, and the Forty Martyrs (25 August); the Beheading of John the Baptist, and the Prophet Eliseus (29 August); and John the Baptist and Prophet Elias (29 September).[17] The text of the pericope preserved in Georgian translation in the GL runs as follows (the text given in italics indicates insertions into the text of Hebrews in the manuscript GL (P)):

თთუესა იანვარსა იზ̃: ჱსენებაჲ მაისა ჭუენისა ანტონისი.	*17 January: Commemoration of our father, Anthony.*
დ: საკითხავი: პავლჱ: ებრაელთაი: [32] და რაჲღამე ვიტქუათ რაჲმეთუ დამაკლებს ჭუენ ჟამი ესე მითხრობად მსაჯულთა თჳს. ბარაკის თჳს საფსონისთჳს. და იეფთაესათჳს: მეფეთა: დავითისათჳს და სამუელისთჳს და წინაასწარმეტყუელთა: აბრაჰამ: და მსაჯულნი [33] რომელნი სარწმუნოებით ერემდეს მეფეთა: აბრაჰამ: მოსჱ. ისუ. და ფინეეზ. იქმოდეს სიმართლესა: აბრაჰამ: ისუ და ქალებ: მიემთხუნეს აღთქუმასა: საფსონ. და დავით: და დანიელ. დაუყჳნეს პირნი ლომთანი: [34] *სამთა ყრმათა. ანანია. აზარია. და მისაელ. დაშრიტეს ალი ცეცხლისაჲ. ოვრია მიდელი და ელია წინასწარმეტყუელი. განჱრნეს პირსა მახჳლისასა. დავით მეფჱ: ეზეკია. ასა მეფჱ. განძრიელდეს უძრულობისაგან: <აბრაჰამ, ლოტ, მოსე და ისუ იქმნნეს ძლიერ მომძლასა შინა.> გედეონ. ბარაკ. საფსონ. და დავით. ბანაკები აოტეს უცხო* თესლთაჲ: [35] *სომანიტელმან მან და სარეფთელმან მოიყვანნეს დედათა აღდგომილნი მკუდარნი მათნი. მაკაბელნი შჳდნი ძმანი და დედაჲ და[P 6rb]თი: და სხუანი წინასწარმეტყუელნი: და სხუანი*	*Reading 4, Paul to the Hebrews:* [32] And what more can we say, for time would fail us in this description *of the judges*, of Barak, of Samson, and of Jephthah, *of the kings*, of David and Samuel and the prophets, *Abraham and the judges* [33] who through faith conquered kings; *Abraham, Moses, Joshua, and Phineas* administered justice, *Abraham, Joshua, and Caleb* received promises, *Samson and David and Daniel* shut the mouths of lions, [34] *the three youths Hananiah, Azariah, and Mishael* quenched raging fire, *Uriah, Mideli* [sic], *and Elias the Prophet* escaped the edge of the sword, *King David, Hezekiah, King Asa* won strength out of weakness, <*Abraham, Lot, Moses, and Joshua* became mighty in war,[18]> *Gideon, Barak, Samson, and David* put foreign armies to flight, [35] *the Shunammite* [*woman*] *and the* [*woman from*] *Sarepta* women received their dead by resurrection, *the seven Maccabee brothers and their mother and other prophets* were tortured, refusing to accept release, that they might rise again to a better life. [36] *Isaiah, Jeremiah, and Job* suffered mocking and scourging, *Jeremiah and Micah* were chained and imprisoned, [37] *Jeremiah and Naboth* were stoned, *Isaiah* was sawn in two, *Job and Zerubbabel* were tempted, *Micah,*

---

17 GL § 149, 947, 1029, 1040, 1059, 1120, 1162, 1180, 1191, 1263.
18 The text in angle brackets—including the phrase 'became mighty in war' in the received form of Hebrews—is absent from Tarchnishvili's edition. The variant names in Hebrews 11:34d are from *The Old Georgian Version of St Paul's Epistles (Redaction AB)*, ed. by Jost Gippert and Vaxtang Imnaishvili (Frankfurt am Main: Thesaurus Indogermanischer Text- und Sprachmaterialien, 1998–2007). At http://titus.uni-frankfurt.de/texte/etcs/cauc/ageo/nt/pavleni/pavle.htm (accessed on 3 December 2014).

მკრძალად ტანჯვითა აღესრულნეს და
არცა ღირს იქმნენ. [36] ესაია. იერემია.
და იობ: რომელ-ნიმე ტანჯვითა და
გუემითა განიცადნეს: იერემია და
მიქეა. ზორკილებათათა და საპყრობილ-
ებითა. [37] იერემია. და ნაბუთე. ქვითა
განიტჳნნეს. ესაია განიხერხა. იობ
ხორობაბელ განიცადნეს. მიქეა. ამოს.
ზაქარია მღდელი სიკუდილითა
მახჳლისათა მოწყდეს. იოვანე
ნათლისმცემელი. ელია. ელისჶ
იქცეოდეს ხალენებითა და თხის
ტყავებითა ნაკლულესანნი,
ჭირვეულნი, მძრ-ხილულნი [38]
სოფელი ესე: წინასწარმეტყუელნი
რომელთა ზრდი-და აბდია უდაბნოთა
ზედა. შეცთომილნი, მთათა, ქუაბთა და
ჯურელთა ქუეყნისათა [39] და ესე
ყოველნი იწამნეს სარწმუნოებითა და
არცა მოიღეს მათ აღნათქუემი იგი, [40]
რამეთუ ღმერთმან ჩუენთჳს უმჯობჶსი
წინასწარ განიგულა, რაათა არა
თჳნიერ ჩუენსა სრულ იქმნენ.[19]

A study of St Athanasius of Alexandria's quotation from the Epistle to the Hebrews reveals only minor textual variations from the received text and Athanasius' source is a faithful witness of the Alexandrian text type.[20] St Cyril of Jerusalem's quotations of Hebrews often contain variants that suggest that he was familiar with a passage similar to the one in GL (P) that contained glosses on the text. On three occasions, in the course of alluding to this passage from Hebrews, Cyril inserts the name of Isaiah as the one who was 'sawn in two' ($\dot{\epsilon}\pi\rho\acute{\iota}\sigma\theta\eta\sigma\alpha\nu$; განიხერხა, *ganixerxa*; Hebrews 11:37).[21] One author, however, comes very close in matching Old Testament figures with each allusion in the Epistle, namely St Ephrem the Syrian in his *Commentary*

Amos, and Zachariah the priest were killed by the sword, John the Baptist, Elias, and Eliseus went around in skins of sheep and goats, destitute, afflicted, ill-treated, [38] of whom the world was not worthy, *the prophet who nourished Obadiah*, wandered over deserts and mountains, and in dens and caves of the earth. [39] And all these, though well attested by their faith, did not receive what was promised, [40] since God had foreseen something better for us, that apart from us they should not be made perfect.

---

[19] Ibid., § 149.

[20] The designation of Athanasius' text as 'Alexandrian text type' is according to a group profile analysis. See Gerald J. Donker, *The Text of the Apostolos in Athanasius of Alexandria* (The New Testament in the Greek Fathers 8, Atlanta: Society of Biblical Literature, 2011), 187–8.

[21] Roderic Lynn Mullen, *Cyril of Jerusalem and the Text of the New Testament in Fourth-Century Palestine* (Unpublished doctoral thesis, Chapel Hill, NC: University of North Carolina at Chapel Hill, 1994), 254; Roderic Lynn Mullen, *The New Testament Text of Cyril of Jerusalem* (Atlanta: Scholars Press, 1997), 270. For other Patristic authors on Isaiah sawn in two, see Origen, *Letter to Africanus* 9, PG 11:65; Rowan A. Greer, *The Captain of our Salvation: A Study in the Patristic Exegesis of Hebrews* (Beiträge zur Geschichte der biblischen Exegese 15, Tübingen: Mohr Siebeck, 1973), 36.

on the Epistle to the Hebrews.[22] That this commentary is preserved in an Armenian translation suggests a connection between the text of the GL and early Armenian versions of the New Testament, which are characterized by their freedom to express the Greek idiomatically, in the style of Targum commentaries—a feature that Nikolai Marr has also noticed in Armenian translations of the Book of Chronicles noted for their fluid style.[23]

The interpolation of names of saints in this scriptural text immediately calls to mind other examples in Hagiopolite liturgy, such as the diaconal litanies that include various Old Testament and local saints ad libitum in the standard text.[24] A study of the parallels between Hagiopolite scriptural and Hagiopolite liturgical texts regarding the interpolation of names of local saints, along with greater reference to the Old Testament, remains to be done. Such a study would contribute to our understanding of the Melkite 'theological profile', as proposed by Sidney Griffith.[25] Similar studies may help in finding a theological criterion for determining the liturgical provenance of manuscripts. Furthermore, as Stefano Parenti notes, 'it would be interesting to verify, case by case, in a non-Byzantine source from the Middle East, if a prayer *common* to Euchologia of the periphery might effectively be ascribable to the Greek liturgical traditions of the Chalcedonian patriarchates of Alexandria and Antioch/Jerusalem'.[26] While both of these questions are beyond the immediate scope of the present book, it is hoped that the latter might contribute to the further investigation of these problems.[27]

STRUCTURES OF THE JERUSALEM LECTIONARY: GOSPEL CYCLES

The liturgical year can be divided into two cycles: (1) the fixed cycle, dependent upon the solar cycle and with commemorations on fixed days of

---

[22] *Commentary on the Epistle to the Hebrews: Works of Ephrem in Armenian*, trans. by Marco Conti (Ancient Christian Commentary on Scripture translation project), 226–7, cited in *Hebrews*, ed. by Erik M. Heen and Philip D. W. Krey (Downers Grove, IL: InterVarsity Press, 2005), 204–5.

[23] See N. Marr, 'Эчміадзинскій фрагментъ древне-грузинской версій Ветхаго Завѣта', *Христіанскій Востокъ* 2 (1913), 378–88, here 387; Metzger, *Early Versions of the New Testament*, 161–4. 'Ainsi leur traduction revêt-elle souvent la valeur d'un commentaire'. Stanilas Lyonnet, SJ, *Les versions arménienne et géorgienne du nouveau testament* (Paris: Gabalda, 1935), 7.

[24] See Chapter 4, 'Joint Commemorations of Old Testament Figures'.

[25] Griffith, 'The Church of Jerusalem and the "Melkites"', 191–7. See 'Melkites: A Subgroup?' in Chapter 2 here.

[26] *Certo sarebbe interessante verificare, caso per caso, in una fonte non bizantina del Medio-Oriente se una preghiera in comune agli eucologi periferici sia effetivamente riconducibile alle tradizioni liturgiche in Greco dei patriarcati calcedonesi di Alessandria e Antiochia/Gerusalemme.* Stefano Parenti, 'Preghiera della cattedra', 164.

[27] I have attempted to address this question in Galadza, 'Jerusalem Lectionary', 198–9.

the calendar year; and (2) the movable cycle, dependent upon the lunar cycle and with commemorations from Pascha onwards, throughout the whole year. This division is reflected in the lectionary. The fixed cycle prescribes scriptural readings for the Divine Liturgy and other services on days of commemorations such as those of St James the Brother of the Lord on 26 December, St Stephen on 27 December, or Sts Peter and Paul on 29 June. The movable cycle indicates readings for Pascha, Pentecost, Sundays throughout the year, and Lent.

Once the manuscript sources of lectionaries have been identified, the comparison of Hagiopolite lectionaries with Constantinopolitan usage is possible, although it is also challenging due to the fragmentary nature of many of the sources described in Chapters 1–2 and Appendix 1. Most of the pericopes from the movable Sunday Gospel cycles are either partially lost or completely absent in manuscripts of the Jerusalem lectionary. Of all the Hagiopolitan sources, *Sinai Geo. O. 38* (979) and *Sinai Ar. 116* (995/6) are the most complete with regard to the Sunday Gospel pericopes of the movable cycle. Although its fixed commemorations are quite complete and provide one commemoration for each day of the calendar year, the movable cycle in the GL has only the Lenten and paschal cycle and the very beginning of the Sundays of Matthew. In the Jerusalem lectionary, Gospel readings, as well as other lections from the Old and New Testaments, were appointed for JAS, and read at matins and at various other liturgical services—for example *lite* and vespers (λυχνικόν), as can be seen from the Gospel lectionary *Sinai Gr. 210* (861/2).

The Fixed Cycle of the Liturgical Year

As noted in the previous chapter, the concept of a 'liturgical year' expresses a modern phenomenon: back in late antiquity and the middle ages the various feasts and fasts celebrated throughout the year did not form a unity or a single entity.[28] Thus the apparent lack of a coherent cycle of scriptural readings for the various feasts of the Hagiopolite liturgical year is not a problem created by the fragmentary nature of our sources. There simply was no coherent cycle for the fixed feasts. This seems to be especially the case in Jerusalem, since the overarching principle of Hagiopolite liturgy was to read lections and hymns appropriate to the place and the day.[29] Generally speaking, the Jerusalem lectionary is topical and thematic, as suggested by Egeria's account already in the fourth century. Thus certain readings are selected simply because they mention the name of a saint or prophet or place being commemorated.

---

[28] Bradshaw and Johnson, *Origins of Feasts*, xiii. See the various subheadings under 'The Structure and Characteristics of the Hagiopolite Liturgical Year' in Chapter 4.

[29] Egeria, *Itinéraire* , § 25: 10, 29: 2, 47: 5.

Nevertheless, the earliest sources reveal certain discernible developments and patterns. In the AL, an Old Testament reading never immediately precedes the Gospel, so that there is always a reading from Acts or an Epistle between an Old Testament reading and the Gospel. The Gospel of Matthew is the text most frequently read from.[30] In the GL, Matthew falls into second place as the most frequently read Gospel, while Luke is read most frequently. This is due to the expansion of the sanctoral cycle so as to include more feasts from the early life of Christ and St John the Baptist.[31] Since the Gospel of Luke's initial chapters contain more accounts of events surrounding the conception and birth of both the Baptist and Christ, the Gospel of Luke is a natural choice for these feasts.

The Movable Cycle of the Liturgical Year

The movable cycle contains the readings for Great Lent, Pascha, Pentecost, and the weeks following Pentecost. The most complete lectionary, the GL, inserts the Lenten–paschal movable cycle into the fixed cycle between 31 March and 1 April.[32] The Greek Tropologion *Sinai Gr. N.E. ΜΓ 56* and *Sinai Gr. N.E. ΜΓ 5* (8th–9th cent.) includes the movable part of the liturgical year, from the Sunday of Meatfare (Κυριακὴ τῶν Ἀποκρεῶν) to Pentecost (ἡ ἅγια ν'), between 2 February and 1 June, although the fixed commemorations from April and May are interspersed between the movable commemorations after Easter.[33] The overlap between the two cycles in April and May in the Greek Tropologion is emblematic of how complex the organization of liturgical books and liturgical services in the period of Lent and Pentecost can be. Greek lectionaries, however, are either too fragmentary or not comprehensive enough to present a clear image of their original structure. What is clear, however, is that the Greek sources of the Jerusalem lectionary do not follow the Byzantine arrangement of the liturgical books. The latter separates the movable cycle—which is often called kanonarion (κανονάριον) or synaxarion (συναξάριον) and stretches from Pascha until Holy Saturday—from the fixed cycle—which is called synaxarion (συναξάριον) or menologion (μηνολόγιον) and stretches from 1 September until 31 August. The confusion or oscillation between these names reflects the fluid character of the terminology for the corresponding liturgical book types, which was not applied consistently and hence generated the duplication of certain terms.[34] The two cycles overlap throughout the whole year, each receiving great attention

---

[30] AL, 37.   [31] See the scriptural index of the GL (CSCO 205), 125–35.
[32] GL § 282–906.   [33] Nikiforova, *Из истории Минеи в Византии*, 207–33.
[34] For more on this problem, see Dmitrievskii, *Описаніе* I, 110, 172, 193; Kekelidze, *Канонарь*, 12–13; Noret, 'Ménologes, Synaxaires, Ménées'.

depending on the commemoration that falls on a certain day. For the sake of clarity, the following analysis of the Hagiopolite and Constantinopolitan lectionary cycles will follow the divisions of the Byzantine rite, since its structure and organization is more coherent and better studied.[35]

Gospel Readings for Pascha and Bright Week

The first movable Gospel cycle to consider is that of Pascha and Bright Week. Pascha (Πάσχα), the feast of the Resurrection of Christ, was celebrated for an octave that came to be called Bright Week or Renewal Week (ἡ ἑβδομὰς τῆς διακαινησίμου) in the Byzantine rite. In the Greek Tropologion, the hymnography of Pascha is repeated throughout the whole week.[36] The sources that contain readings for this period show a clear transition from the Hagiopolitan practice reflected in the GL to the Constantinopolitan practice reflected in the Typikon of the Great Church. The latter eventually became the tradition of the Byzantine rite (see Table 5.1).

Only the GL (L) contains readings for all of Bright Week, since the other GL manuscripts (P) and (S) are defective at this point. The bilingual Greek–Arabic Gospel *Sinai Ar. 116* (995/6) also has a peculiar reading that recounted the baptism of Jesus (Luke 3:21–2) 'on the same evening as the water blessing' (τῇ αὐτῇ ἑσπέρᾳ τὸν ἁγιασμὸν τὰ ὕδατα κατὰ Λούκαν, 1r–1v); this comes immediately after the defective reading for liturgy on the Saturday of Bright Week and immediately before the reading for liturgy on the second Sunday of Pascha (the latter was also called 'New Sunday', νέα Κυριακή).[37] In *Hagios Stavros Gr. 43* (1122), we already witness the combination of two distinct traditions as a result of dividing the readings associated with each tradition between the Divine Liturgy and matins—or across other services where a Gospel pericope could be read.

The most significant reading to note is that of the Divine Liturgy on the day of Pascha itself. Authentic Hagiopolitan practice prescribes Mark 16:1–8, while Byzantine practice has the prologue from John, which inaugurates a *lectio continua* from the Gospel of John during the following days. This *lectio continua* does not begin in Jerusalem until the prologue from John is read on New Sunday. Although the Byzantinized sources of *Vatican Syr. 19* (1030) and *Hagios Stavros Gr. 43* (1122) reveal a visible trend towards the adoption of

---

[35] For a basic summary of these cycles, see Gregory, *Textkritik*, 343–86; Ehrhard, *Überlieferung*, vol. 1, 35–53; Anatoly A. Alexeev, Библия в богослужении. Византуйско-славянский лекционарий (St Petersburg: Издательство «Нестор–История», 2008), 17–27; Job Getcha, *The Typikon Decoded: An Explanation of Byzantine Liturgical Practice*, trans. by Paul Meyendorff (Orthodox Liturgy Series 3, Yonkers, NY: St Vladimir's Seminary Press, 2012).
[36] Nikiforova, Из истории Минеи в Византии, 221.
[37] Garitte, 'Évangéliaire grec-arabe', 211. For more on this Sunday, see Vitaly Permiakov, 'The Historical Origins of the Feast of Antipascha', SVTQ 47.2 (2003), 155–82.

Table 5.1. Gospels for Bright Week

	GL (L) (8th cent.)	Sinai Gr. 210 (861/2)	Sinai Geo. O. 38 (979)	Sinai Ar. 116 (995/6)	Vatican Syr. 19 (1030)	Hag.Stav. Gr.43 (1122)	Typikon of the Great Church	Current Byzantine rite
Pascha								
Vigil	Mt 28:1–20		Mt 28:1–20			Mt 28:1–20	Mt 28:1–20	Mt 28:1–20
2nd Vigil	–					Jn 20:1–18		
Matins	Jn 20:1–18		Jn 20:1–18			Mk 16:1–	–	(Mk 16:1–8)
Liturgy	Mk 16:1–8		Mk 16:1–8		Jn 1:1–17	Jn 1:1–17	Jn 1:1–17	Jn 1:1–17
9th Hour	Lk 24:13–35				–		–	
Vespers	Jn 20:19–25	Jn 20:19–25	Jn 20:19–25		–	Jn 20:19–25	Jn 20:19–23	(Jn 20:19–23)
Monday Matins			Mt 28:1–20			Lk 24:1–12		
Liturgy	Lk 23:54–24:12		Lk 24:1–12		Jn 1:18–28	Jn 1:18–	Jn 1:18–28	Jn 1:18–28
Tuesday Matins			Mk 16:1–8			Mt 28:16–20		
Liturgy	Lk 24:36–40	Lk 24:36b–40	Lk 24:13–35		Lk 24:21–35	–	Lk 24:21–35	Lk 24:12–35
Wednesday Matins			Lk 24:1–12			Jn 20:1–10		
Liturgy	Lk 24:13–35		Lk 24:36–40		Jn 1:29–	–	Jn 1:25–52	Jn 1:35–51
Thursday Matins			Mt 28:1–20			Jn 20:11–18		
Liturgy	Mt 5:1–12		Mt 5:1–16		Jn 3:1–	–	Jn 3:1–16	Jn 3:1–15
Friday Matins			Jn 20:1–18			Jn 21:1–14		
Liturgy	Jn 21:1–14	Jn 21:1–14	Jn 21:1–14		Jn 2:12–	–	Jn 2:12–22	Jn 2:12–22
Saturday Matins			Mk 16:9–20			Jn 21:15–25		
Liturgy	Jn 21:15–25		Jn 21:15–25		Jn 3:22–	–	Jn 3:22–33	Jn 3:22–33
New Sunday Matins	–		Mt 28:1–20			–	–	Mt 28:16–20
Liturgy	Jn 1:1–17	Jn 1:1–17	Jn 1:1–17	Jn 1:1–17	Jn 20:19–31	–	Jn 20:19–31	Jn 20:19–31
Vespers	Jn 20:26–31	Jn 20:26–31	Jn 20:26–31	Jn 20:26–31	–	–	–	Jn 20:19–31

Table 5.2. Gospels for Bright Week and the resurrectional Gospels

	Sinai Geo. O. 38 (979)	Eleven Resurrectional Gospels of the Byzantine Rite	Typikon of the Great Church
Pascha			
Vigil	Mt 28:1–20	= First Gospel (Mt 28:16–20)	Mt 28:1–20
Matins	Jn 20:1–18	= Seventh Gospel (Jn 20:1–10) + Eighth Gospel (Jn 20:11–18)	–
Liturgy	Mk 16:1–8	= Second Gospel	Jn 1:1–17
Vespers	Jn 20:19–25	= Ninth Gospel	Jn 20:19–23
Monday			
Matins	Mt 28:1–20	= First Gospel (Mt 28:16–20)	–
Liturgy	Lk 24:1–12	= Fourth Gospel	Jn 1:18–28
Tuesday			
Matins	Mk 16:1–8	= Second Gospel	–
Liturgy	Lk 24:13–35	= Fifth Gospel	Lk 24:21–35
Wednesday			
Matins	Lk 24:1–12	= Fourth Gospel	–
Liturgy	Lk 24:36–40	= Sixth Gospel	Jn 1:25–52
Thursday			
Matins	Mt 28:1–20	= First Gospel (Mt 28:16–20)	–
Liturgy	Mt 5:1–16		Jn 3:1–16
Friday			
Matins	Jn 20:1–18	= Seventh Gospel (Jn 20:1–10) + Eighth Gospel (Jn 20:11–18)	–
Liturgy	Jn 21:1–14	= Tenth Gospel	Jn 2:12–22
Saturday			
Matins	Mk 16:9–20	= Third Gospel	–
Liturgy	Jn 21:15–25	= Eleventh	Jn 3:22–33

Constantinopolitan Johannine *lectio continua*, the readings for the various services of Bright Week according to the Hagiopolitan tradition—which is as early as the AL and the GL[38]—are actually retained in the Byzantine rite. These Hagiopolite Gospel pericopes from Bright Week eventually became the eleven resurrectional Gospels (εὐαγγέλια ἑωθινὰ ἀναστάσιμα) for Sunday matins throughout the year, which they were in the Byzantine rite by the tenth century.[39]

As the Table 5.2 indicates, the ten different Hagiopolite Gospel pericopes that recounted the Resurrection of Christ and were read at matins, in the liturgy, and at vespers throughout the seven days of Bright Week became the eleven pericopes read—the Hagiopolite pericope John 20:1–18 was divided into two to form the seventh (John 20:1–10) and eighth Gospel (John 20:11–18)—at Sunday matins in Constantinople. The pericope for the liturgy on the Thursday of Bright Week, which recounted the Beatitudes from the Sermon on the Mount from Matthew 5:1–16, seems out of place here. By the tenth century this series

[38] AL, 170–87; GL § 744–64. [39] For these pericopes, see Gregory, *Textkritik*, 364.

of Gospels had become the subject of hymnographic compositions, for example the resurrectional *idiomela* (ἑωθινὰ ἰδιόμελα ἀναστάσιμα) by Emperor Leo VI the Wise (866–912) and the resurrectional *exaposteilaria* (ἐξαποστειλάρια ἀναστάσιμα) by Emperor Constantine VII Porphyrogenitus (905–59).[40] Janeras has pointed out that this series of eleven Gospel pericopes inspired the formation of the series of eleven—ultimately twelve—'companion' Passion Gospels of matins on Holy Friday (ἀκολουθία τῶν παθῶν) in the Byzantine rite. Like the eleven resurrectional Gospels, the Passion Gospels were coupled with hymnography. Because twelve *idiomela* troparia had been composed for Holy Friday, a twelfth Gospel reading—the reading from Holy Saturday matins—was added as the last reading for the Passion Gospels, so that the number of Gospels would match the number of hymns.[41]

Another characteristic of *Hagios Stavros Gr. 43* (1122) is the absence of any Gospel pericopes prescribed for the Divine Liturgy from Tuesday until Saturday of Bright Week, where the manuscript ends. Although no Gospel reading is indicated, it appears that the pericope from the Constantinopolitan sources was read at the Divine Liturgy. In the services of Pascha and Bright Monday in *Hagios Stavros Gr. 43* (1122), the Jerusalem pericope for liturgy is prescribed to be read at matins and the Constantinopolitan pericope is read during liturgy instead. The same phenomenon—the transfer of the Jerusalem Divine Liturgy Gospel to matins—is apparent on Friday and Saturday; thus it can be assumed that on those days the Gospel reading in the Divine Liturgy was that of Constantinople. Consequently, by the twelfth century the Johannine *lectio continua* had taken its place in the Divine Liturgy during Bright Week in Jerusalem, most likely as a result of the association of resurrectional Gospel pericopes with Sunday matins, where the former had found their place in the Byzantine rite, so that they became the highpoint of that service.

The Sunday Gospel Cycles

As Sebastià Janeras has pointed out, the main difference between the Jerusalem and Constantinopolitan lectionary systems is the order in which the two traditions read the Gospels on Sundays throughout the liturgical year.[42] This broad outline can be summarized in Table 5.3.

---

[40] Alexander Kazhdan and Anthony Cutler, 'Leo VI', ODB II, 1210–11; Alexander Kazhdan and Anthony Cutler, 'Constantine VII Porphyrogennetos', ODB I, 502–3.

[41] See Janeras, *Vendredi-Saint*, 119–24; Sebastià Janeras, 'I vangeli domenicali della resurrezione nelle tradizioni liturgiche agiopolita e bizantina', in *Paschale Mysterium: Studi in memoria dell'Abate Prof. Salvatore Marsili (1910–1983)*, ed. by Giustino Farnedi (Studia Anselmiana 91, Rome: Pontificio Ateneo S. Anselmo, 1986), 55–69, especially 66–7, for more on the development of these series of Gospel readings.

[42] Janeras, 'Lectionnaires de Jérusalem', 83–5. *Hagios Stavros Gr. 43* (1122) ends with Bright Week and can provide no further information on the Sunday cycles.

Table 5.3. Comparative table of Sunday cycles

	Jerusalem	*Constantinople*
Pascha Divine Liturgy	Mark 16	John 1
Bright Week	Resurrection Gospels	John
New Sunday until Pentecost	John	John
Pentecost until Exaltation	Matthew	Matthew
After Exaltation	Mark	Luke
During Lent	Luke	Mark

Even where the order of the cycles is identical in Jerusalem and Constantinople—for example in the period between Pascha and the Exaltation of the Cross, when the Gospels of John and Matthew were read—the order and selection of pericopes is not. While Constantinopolitan Gospel and Epistle lectionaries often contain 'readings for Saturdays and Sundays of the whole movable cycle'[43] and, later on, 'readings for every day of the week',[44] this is not the case with lectionaries in Jerusalem. There are no extant lectionaries from Jerusalem that contain readings for every day of the year from the movable cycle and it is likely that weekday readings of the movable cycle never existed in Jerusalem. Such readings were never included in the Jerusalem lectionary before its eclipse.

The inclusion of weekday pericopes in the Byzantine lectionary dates back to the eighth or ninth century and is presumably the result of the reforms of St Theodore the Stoudite.[45] In the case of JAS served on weekdays, the lections read would have been for the saint or commemoration from the fixed cycle, which can be found in the GL. In Constantinople, weekday readings of the movable cycle appeared relatively late in liturgical practice. The earliest extant exemplar of a Gospel with pericopes for every day of the week is the fragmentary parchment manuscript *Leipzig Universitätsbibliothek Gr. 3* (8th cent.).[46] This type of Gospel book became more common in the tenth century. The need to provide weekday pericopes of the movable cycle coincides with the intensification of the practice of daily celebrations of the Divine Liturgy—a practice that seems to have been introduced at the Stoudios Monastery in Constantinople, where CHR was officiated on a daily basis.[47] The introduction of daily pericopes, however, did not affect the already established Sunday lections; rather it filled in the gaps between Sundays with a *lectio continua* from the particular evangelist read from during the liturgical season. Thus

---

[43] *Lesungen für die Wochentage zwischen Ostern und Pfingsten und die Sonnabende/Sonntage der anderen Wochen* ('Readings for weekdays between Easter and Pentecost, as well as the Saturdays/Sundays of other weeks'), abbreviated as 'ℓesk'. See Aland, *Kurzgefaßte Liste*, xv.

[44] *Lesungen für alle Wochentage* (ἑβδομάδες), abbreviated as 'ℓe'. Ibid., xv.

[45] Parenti, 'La "vittoria"', 45.   [46] ℓ 293: U-ℓe †. See Aland, *Kurzgefaßte Liste*, 236.

[47] See Velkovska, 'Lo studio dei lezionari bizantini', 258–9; Parenti, 'La "vittoria"', 45–6.

the conscious selection of a Sunday pericope in Jerusalem or Constantinople transmits a particular message that the anonymous compilers of the lectionary desired to express on a given Sunday. Where the Jerusalem lectionary selects different pericopes, one should also expect to find different hymnography associated with these days—and also a theological understanding different from that embodied in the Constantinopolitan pericopes of the Byzantine rite.

Because Saturday readings and weekday readings of the movable cycle are absent from the Jerusalem lectionary, I shall consider only the Sunday readings here in my examination of the Gospel cycles of John, Matthew, Mark, and Luke. For the movable cycle of the liturgical year, the two most complete periods in the manuscript sources of the Hagiopolite lectionary are Pascha and Great Lent. The paschal season has readings from the General Epistles, the Acts of the Apostles, and the Gospel of John. As noted above, although the Jerusalem and Constantinopolitan lectionaries read the Gospel of John during this liturgical season, the individual pericopes they prescribe differ for every Sunday. Great Lent in Jerusalem has readings from the Epistle to the Romans and from the Gospel of Luke (see Tables 5.8 and 5.12). The first Sunday's readings (Luke 15:1–10 and Romans 11:1–5) set the stage for the beginning of Lent, when God, who has not rejected his people (Romans 11:1) but has chosen them by grace (Romans 11:5), sets all aside to find the lost (Luke 15:4–7) and rejoices when they are found (Luke 15:10). The theme of 'lost and found' is repeated on the second Sunday of Lent through the reading of the prodigal son (Luke 15:11–32). On this day the Epistle instructs people how to live as Christians—not like the older son, who was envious and did not share the joy of his father (Luke 15:25–32), but rather by 'rejoicing with those who rejoice' (Romans 12:15) and by 'loving one another with brotherly affection' ($\tau\hat{\eta}$ φιλαδελφίᾳ εἰς ἀλλήλους φιλόστοργοι, Romans 12:10). The third Sunday of Lent preaches the importance of humility, entreating all to 'live in harmony with one another. Do not be haughty, but associate with the lowly' (Romans 12:16). This injunction is illustrated with the parable of the humble publican, who beats his breast and does not dare raise his eyes to heaven, and the Pharisee, who imagines himself to be better than his sinful neighbours (Luke 18:1–14). The fourth Sunday of Lent continues with the theme of loving one's neighbour through the parable of the Good Samaritan (Luke 10:25–37). The Epistle prepares people for the understanding of the Gospel through the reminder that 'love is the fulfilling of the law' (Romans 13:10), that the weak must be welcomed (Romans 14:1), and that 'salvation is nearer to us now than when we first believed' (Romans 13:11)—which is also a reminder of the approaching feast of Pascha. The readings of the fifth Sunday are connected in their allusion to coming events in the liturgical year: the raising of Lazarus on the following Saturday (Luke 16:19–31) and the Resurrection of Christ (Luke 16:30–1; Ephesians 4:30, 5:2).

Pentecost: The Gospel of John

The first Gospel cycle read after Pascha in both Jerusalem and Constantinople is that of the evangelist John the Theologian. The order of the Sundays in the Jerusalem lectionary is given according to the number born by the Sunday of a particular evangelist, in this case John. The Constantinopolitan order, however, is different: it counts the number of Sundays after Pascha. In this way the second Sunday of John in Jerusalem is equivalent to the third Sunday of Pascha in Constantinople (see Table 5.4).

Table 5.4 also reveals significant thematic differences between the Sunday readings. Whereas in Constantinople the third Sunday of Pascha is dedicated to Joseph of Arimathea and to the myrrhbearing women and includes an account of the Resurrection (Mark 15:43–16:8), the reading in Jerusalem for the second Sunday of John recounts Jesus' first sign at the wedding in Cana in Galilee (John 2:1–11). Within the Hagiopolitan cycle, the wedding at Cana was followed by Christ's encounter with the Samaritan woman (John 4:4–23). It is worth noting the differences between the Hagiopolite liturgical lectionaries on the fourth, fifth, and sixth Sundays of John. Differences are clear between the Georgian sources, specifically the GL and *Sinai Geo. O. 38*, and the Greek sources, namely *Sinai Gr. 210* and *Sinai Ar. 116*. The Georgian sources prescribe the healing of the official's son (John 4:43–54) on the fourth Sunday, Christ cleansing the Temple in Jerusalem (John 2:12–25) on the fifth, and the plot to kill Jesus (John 11:47–54) on the sixth Sunday, while the Greek sources prescribe Jesus' discourse on the bread of life on the fourth (John 6:27–40) and fifth (John 6:47–58) Sundays, followed by the discourse on Christ as the light of the world (John 8:12–20) on the sixth Sunday. On these three Sundays, the Georgian sources prefer Johannine narrative accounts for the Sundays of Pascha, while the Greek sources favour Christ's discourses.

Hagiopolite lectionaries from the Sinai 'new finds' do not clarify matters. The Hagiopolite lectionary *Sinai Gr. N.E. MΓ 11* (9th cent.) includes pericopes for all six Sundays of John. However, after the third Sunday the pericopes from this ninth-century Greek lectionary do not match any of the other Hagiopolitan sources; they prescribe lections for Sundays that are read on other days in the GL or in *Sinai Geo. O 38*.[48]

As shown in Table 5.4, the Constantinopolitan pericopes are completely different and include the accounts of Christ's healing of the paralytic (John 5:1–15) and the man born blind (John 9:1–38). In the Byzantine rite, the pericopes for the wedding at Cana and the discourse on the bread of life are read on weekdays—and not on Sundays, as found in the Jerusalem lectionary.

[48] Galadza, 'Two Sources of the Jerusalem Lectionary', 97–8.

Table 5.4. Gospels from the cycle of John

Sunday of John (Jerusalem)	GL (8th cent.)	Sinai Gr. 210 (861/2)	Sinai Geo. O. 38 (979)	Sinai Ar. 116 (995/6)	Vatican Syr. 19 (1030)	Typikon of the Great Church
2nd Sunday	Jn 2:1–11	Jn 2:1–11	Jn 2:1–11	Jn 2:1–11	Mk 15:43	Mk 15:43–16:8
3rd Sunday	Jn 4:4–23	Jn 4:4–42	Jn 4:4–42	Jn 4:4–42	Jn 5:1–	Jn 5:1–15
Mid-Pentecost	Jn 7:14–29	Jn 7:14–30	Jn 7:14–34	Jn 7:14–30	Jn 7:14–	Jn 7:14–30
4th Sunday	Jn 4:24[49]	Jn 6:27–40	Jn 4:43–54	Jn 6:27–40	Jn 4:5–	Jn 4:5–42
5th Sunday	Jn 2:12–25[50]	Jn 6:47b–58	Jn 2:12–25	Jn 6:47–58	Jn 9:1–	Jn 9:1–38
Ascension Matins	[defective]	–	Mk 16:9–20	–	Mk 16:9–20	
Liturgy	[defective]	Lk 24:41–	Lk 24:41–53	Lk 24:41–53	Lk 24:36–53	Lk 24:36–53
6th Sunday	[defective]	Jn 8:12b–20	Jn 11:47–54	Jn 8:12–20	Jn 17:1–	Jn 17:1–13
Pentecost Matins	–	–	Jn 14:25–29	–	–	–
Liturgy	Jn 14:15–19	Jn 14:15–	Jn 14:15–21	Jn 15:26–16:14	Jn 7:37–	Jn 7:37–8:12

[49] The manuscript sources of the GL are defective at this point. Only GL (L) suggests this incipit. See GL § 851.

[50] GL (P) is defective at this point. Only GL (L) suggests this incipit. See GL § 856.

Despite the seemingly arbitrary order of weekday Johannine pericopes,[51] the Hagiopolitan Sunday reading cycle—both in its Greek and in its Georgian forms—more faithfully maintains the *lectio continua* of John initiated on the Sunday after Pascha by reading pericopes sequentially and not jumping back and forth within the Gospel of John.

Three pericopes—for mid-Pentecost, Ascension, and Pentecost—fall outside the continued reading cycle of John in the Easter season. The mid-Pentecost reading is shared by both Hagiopolite and Constantinopolitan lectionaries, most likely because the Gospel account from John 7:14–30 takes place during 'the middle of the feast' (ἤδη δὲ τῆς ἑορτῆς μεσούσης, John 7:14). This also suggests that the pericope belongs to an ancient common tradition for mid-Pentecost.[52] The same can be said for the Gospel reading on Ascension. Both Hagiopolite and Constantinopolitan lectionaries prescribe Luke 24:41–53 for the Divine Liturgy, as opposed to the shorter account in Mark 16:9–20, which is prescribed at matins. The Gospel reading for Pentecost, however, reveals two distinct traditions: the Hagiopolitan tradition, which reads Christ's promise of the Holy Spirit (John 14:15–19), and the Constantinopolitan tradition, which prescribes Christ's discourse on living water (John 7:37–52, 8:12). It is worth noting that the passage on the woman caught in adultery (John 7:53–8:11) is omitted in all lectionaries, including all Greek and Georgian lectionary manuscripts, both Constantinopolitan and Hagiopolite.[53] The pericope in *Sinai Ar. 116* (995/6) focuses even more on the gift of the Holy Spirit (John 15:26–16:14), but is not prescribed by other Hagiopolite lectionaries. The choice of the Constantinopolitan pericope is most likely due to its mention of the 'last day of the feast' (ἐν δὲ τῇ ἐσχάτῃ ἡμέρᾳ τῇ μεγάλῃ τῆς ἑορτῆς, John 7:37). The feast mentioned here and at mid-Pentecost was, however, the feast of Tabernacles, which takes place on the fifteenth day of the Jewish month Tishri, between late September and late October. The connection of Pentecost to the feast of Tabernacles, however, does not agree with a chronological reckoning of Easter and Pentecost in late spring.[54] One could

[51] See, for example, *Tbilisi Central Historical Archive of Georgia 107* (9th cent.), fol. 191v–192r; Bernard Outtier, 'Un index inédit des lectures évangéliques du temps pascal selon le Lectionnaire géorgien de Jérusalem', in *ΣΥΝΑΞΙΣ ΚΑΘΟΛΙΚΗ* 2: 582–90.

[52] For more on Mid-Pentecost, see Anatoly A. Alexiev, 'On Jerusalem Vestiges of the Byzantine Gospel Lectionary', in *Catalogue of Byzantine Manuscripts in Their Liturgical Context: Subsidia 1*, ed. by Klaas Spronk, Gerard Rouwhorst, and Stefan Royé (Turnhout: Brepols, 2013), 173–82, here 175–7.

[53] For more on this pericope, see Maurice A. Robinson, 'Preliminary Observations Regarding the *Pericope Adulterae* Based upon Fresh Collation of Nearly All Continuous-Text Manuscripts and over One Hundred Lectionaries', *Filologia Neotestamentaria* 25/6 (2000), 35–59.

[54] Pheme Perkins, *The Gospel according to John: A Theological Commentary* (Chicago, IL: Franciscan Herald Press, 1978), 963–5; John J. Castelot and Aelred Cody, OSB, 'Religious Institutions of Israel', in *New Jerome Biblical Commentary*, ed. by Raymond E. Brown, SS, Joseph A. Fitzmyer, SJ, and Roland E. Murphy, OCarm (Englewood Cliffs, NJ: Prentice Hall, 1990), here 1279–80.

presume that Christians in Palestine would have had better knowledge of Jewish religious practices than Christians in Constantinople; nevertheless, this is only speculation and cannot be verified. Likewise, John's comment—that the Holy Spirit had not been sent because Christ had not yet been glorified ('οὔπω γὰρ ἦν πνεῦμα, ὅτι Ἰησοῦς οὐδέπω ἐδοξάσθη', John 7:39)—seems to break the post-Resurrection narrative of the lectionary readings from John, which emphasize the miracles and discourses of Christ, which his Apostles and followers understand in light of his Resurrection. These are, presumably, the reasons why the Hagiopolite lectionary avoids problems of biblical chronology or narrative continuity and focuses on the gift of the Holy Spirit on Pentecost.

Pentecost to Enkainia: The Gospel of Matthew

The first Gospel cycle read after Pentecost in both Jerusalem and Constantinople is that according to Matthew. The Gospel index in *Sinai Geo. O 38* (979) provides a heading for this period: 'Holy Gospels according to Matthew of Sunday for the Liturgy, from Pentecost until Enkainia' (წმიდათა კჳრიაკეთა სამხრაწ სახარებანი მათჱს თავისანი მარტჳლჳთა გან ვიდრე ენკენიაწმდე).[55] Here the feast of the Enkainia of the Anastasis on 13 September marks the end of the Gospel of Matthew in the Jerusalem lectionary. As previously mentioned, the Enkainia of the Anastasis was one of three major feasts that were followed by an octave in the Jerusalem lectionary and calendar.[56] However, the Gospel book *Sinai Ar. 116* (995/6) shows a change in this Hagiopolitan order, betraying the influence of Byzantinized practices. Here the heading for the same period of Matthew in both Greek and Arabic indicates that the end of the cycle of Matthew is the Exaltation of the Cross on 14 September, not Enkainia: 'from Pentecost until the [Exaltation of the] Cross' (ἀπὸ τῆς πεντηκοστῆς ἕως τοῦ σταυροῦ, fol. 23v).[57] This change in the lectionary rubrics is in keeping with the rise in prominence of the feast of the Exaltation of the Cross in Constantinople and the virtual absence of the commemoration of Enkainia from Constantinopolitan sources.[58] The GL gives the pericopes for the first three Sundays after Pentecost, but after this point all its manuscript sources are defective (see Table 5.5).[59]

Unlike the Johannine cycle, the pericopes from the cycle of Matthew in both the Greek and Georgian Hagiopolitan manuscripts show greater uniformity and no significant variants until the thirteenth Sunday of Matthew. This may be explained by the variable period of time between Pentecost in the spring and Enkainia/Exaltation in September. Thus the end of the Matthaean cycle

---

[55] Garitte, 'Index des lectures évangéliques', 386.   [56] See Chapter 4, 'Octaves'.

[57] Garitte, 'Évangéliaire grec-arabe', 212.

[58] See 'Enkainia and the Exaltation of the Cross' and 'The Precious Cross' in Chapter 4 here.

[59] See GL § 1693–6.

Table 5.5. Gospels from the cycle of Matthew

	GL (8th cent.)	Sinai Gr. 210 (861/2)	Sinai Geo. O. 38 (979)	Sinai Ar. 116 (995/6)	Vatican Syr. 19 (1030)	Typikon of the Great Church
1st Sunday	Mt 4:12–25	Mt 4:12–25	Mt 4:12–25	Mt 4:12–25	Mt 10:32–	Mt 10:32–33, 37–38; 19:27–30
2nd Sunday	[defective]	Mt 7:1–11	Mt 6:34–7:21	Mt 7:2–11	Mt 4:17–	Mt 4:18–23
3rd Sunday	–	Mt 8:1–13	Mt 8:1–13	Mt 8:1–13	Mt 6:22–	Mt 6:22–33
4th Sunday	–	Mt 8:14–27	Mt 8:14–27	Mt 8:14–27	Mt 8:5–	Mt 8:5–13
5th Sunday	–	Mt 8:28–9:8	Mt 8:28–9:8	Mt 8:28–9:8	Mt 8:28–	Mt 8:28–9:1
6th Sunday	–	Mt 9:9–17	Mt 9:9–17	Mt 9:9–17	Mt 9:1–	Mt 9:1–8
Athenogenes	Lk 10:1–20		Lk 10:1–20	–	–	–
7th Sunday	–	Mt 9:18–26	Mt 9:18–26	Mt 9:18–26	Mt 9:27–	Mt 9:27–35
8th Sunday	–	Mt 9:27–35	Mt 9:27–35	Mt 9:27–35	Mt 14:14–	Mt 14:14–22
9th Sunday	–	Mt 11:2–	Mt 11:1–15	Mt 11:2–15	Mt 14:22–	Mt 14:22–34
10th Sunday	–	Mt 12:9–23	Mt 12:9–23	Mt 12:9–23	Mt 17:14–	Mt 17:14–23
11th Sunday	–	Mt 14:14–21	Mt 14:13–21	Mt 14:14–21	Mt 18:23–	Mt 18:23–35
12th Sunday	–	Mt 14:22–36	Mt 14:22–36	Mt 14:22–36	Mt 19:16–	Mt 19:16–24
13th Sunday	–	Mt 15:21–31	Mt 15:21–31	Mt 15:21–31	Mt 21:33–	Mt 21:33–42
14th Sunday	–	Mt 15:32–	Mt 17:14–23	Mt 15:32–8	Mt 22:2–	Mt 22:2–14
15th Sunday	–	–	Mt 19:16–26	Mt 17:14–23	Mt 22:35–	Mt 22:35–46
16th Sunday	–	–	–	Mt 19:16–26	Mt 25:14–	Mt 25:14–30

depended on how early or how late the date of Easter fell in a particular year. Since the manuscript *Sinai Gr. 210* (861/2) is damaged at the fourteenth Sunday of Matthew (fol. 188v), it is impossible to know whether the manuscript also contained readings for the fifteenth and sixteenth Sundays. The Hagiopolite lectionary *Sinai Gr. N.E. MΓ 11* (9th cent.) includes five Sundays in the Sunday cycle of Matthew, namely the sixth, seventh, eighth, ninth, and twelfth Sundays, but very few of the pericopes match perfectly with other known pericopes for the Sundays of Matthew.[60] Apart from the fifth Sunday of Matthew (Matthew 8:28–9:1), there are no identical pericopes between the Hagiopolitan and Constantinopolitan cycles, although the common pericope here in both traditions is perhaps rather a coincidence.

In addition to the pericopes indicated above, certain manuscripts interrupt the movable cycle with commemorations inserted on the Sunday before or after a fixed feast. For example, in *Sinai Geo. O. 38* (979) the Sunday before the Nativity of John the Baptist (24 June) has a special Gospel from Luke (1:1–25) and the Sunday before his feast of beheading (29 August) has the Gospel from Matthew for the ninth Sunday (Matthew 11:1–15).[61] In both Georgian sources examined here, the seventh Sunday after Pentecost commemorates St Athenogenes (ათენაგენი, *at'enageni*). His feast day on 16 July was roughly the midpoint between Pentecost and Enkainia; hence it became a significant point of reference in Hagiopolitan Gospel reading cycles.[62] As already noted, the decline of the Jerusalem lectionary also brought about the decline in importance of Athenogenes' cult and presence in liturgical manuscripts.

From Enkainia to Theophany: The Gospel of Mark

The next Gospel cycle read in Jerusalem was from the Evangelist Mark. As with the cycle of Matthew, Hagiopolitan manuscripts from the tenth century have similar titles, which define the period in which the Gospel of Mark was read and reveal a change in the significance of certain feasts of the fixed cycle. The manuscript *Sinai Geo. O. 38* (979) indicates that the period runs from Enkainia until Theophany (შემდგომად ენკენიისა ზეთივისა ვიდრე განცხადებამდე),[63] while *Sinai Ar. 116* (995/6) specifies that the Gospel of Mark is read 'from the Exaltation of the Precious Cross until the Nativity [of Christ]' (ἀπὸ τῆς ὑψώσεως τοῦ τιμίου σταυροῦ ἕως τῶν γενεθλίων, fol. 48v).[64] The change in emphasis from the Enkainia of the Anastasis to the Exaltation at the end of the Matthaean cycle is also reflected here at the beginning of the

[60] Galadza, 'Two Sources of the Jerusalem Lectionary', 93.
[61] Garitte, 'Index des lectures évangéliques', 386–7.
[62] Kekelidze, *Канонарь*, 16. For more on St Athenogenes, see 'St Athenogenes' in Chapter 4.
[63] Garitte, 'Index des lectures évangéliques', 389.
[64] Garitte, 'Évangéliaire grec-arabe', 213.

Table 5.6. Gospels from the cycle of Mark

Jerusalem order	GL (8th cent.)	*Sinai Geo. O. 38* (979)	*Sinai Ar. 116* (995/6)	*Vatican Syr. 19* (1030)	*Typikon of the Great Church*	Constantinople order (after Pentecost)
1st Sunday	–	Mk 1:12–28	Mk 1:16–27	Lk 5:1–	Lk 5:1b–11	17th Sunday
2nd Sunday	–	Mk 1:29–45	Mk 1:29–45	Lk 6:31–	Lk 6:31–36	18th Sunday
3rd Sunday	–	Mk 2:1–12	Mk 2:1–12	Lk 7:11–	Lk 7:11–16	19th Sunday
4th Sunday	–	Mk 2:13–28	Mk 2:14–28	Lk 8:5–	Lk 8:5–8a	20th Sunday
5th Sunday	–	Mk 3:1–12	Mk 3:1–11	Lk 16:19–	Lk 16:19–31	21st Sunday
6th Sunday	–	Mk 4:35–41	Mk 4:35–41	Lk 8:26–	Lk 8:27–35, 38–39	22nd Sunday
7th Sunday	–	Mk 5:1–20	Mk 5:1–20	Lk 8:41–	Lk 8:41–56	23rd Sunday
8th Sunday	–	Mk 5:21–43	Mk 5:21–42	Lk 10:25–	Lk 10:25–37	24th Sunday
9th Sunday	–	Mk 6:34–44	Mk 6:34–44	Lk 12:16–	Lk 12:16–21, 14:35	25th Sunday
10th Sunday	–	Mk 6:45–56	Mk 6:45–56	Lk 13:11–	Lk 13:10–17	26th Sunday
11th Sunday	–	Mk 7:24–37	Mk 7:24–37	Lk 14:16–	Lk 14:16–24	27th Sunday
12th Sunday	–	Mk 8:1–9	Mk 8:1–9	Lk 17:11–	Lk 17:12–19	28th Sunday
13th Sunday	–	Mk 9:14–31	Mk 9:14–31	Lk 18:18–	Lk 18:18–27	29th Sunday
14th Sunday	–	Mk 10:17–27	Mk 10:17–24	Lk 18:35–	Lk 18:35–43	30th Sunday
15th Sunday	–	Mk 10:46–52	–	Lk 19:1–	Lk 19:1–10	31st Sunday
16th Sunday	–	–	–	Lk 18:10–	Mt 15:21–28	32nd Sunday

cycle of Mark.[65] The end of the Marcan cycle also shows a change in emphasis from the more ancient feast of Theophany on 6 January to the feast of the Nativity of Christ on 25 December, which was finally imposed on Jerusalem in the sixth century.[66]

As already noted, however, the Sundays were numbered in Constantinople according to their sequence after Pentecost and not according to the evangelist of the Gospel read on the particular Sunday (see Table 5.6).

Vatican Syr. 19 (1030) reveals a particular approach to ordering the Sundays. The first Saturday of the Constantinopolitan Lucan cycle is called 'First Saturday of Luke' and in the margin is written 'Second Saturday after the feast of the Cross'.[67] The numbering of the subsequent Sundays, although containing the readings of the Constantinopolitan order, follows the sequence in the cycle of Luke—and not the order of Sundays after Pentecost. The eleventh Sunday of Luke in the same source is also listed as being 'two Sundays before the Nativity'.[68] This is a clear example of the scribe attempting to present the Constantinopolitan pericope order to a reader more familiar with the Hagiopolitan liturgical tradition.

---

[65] See 'Pentecost to Enkainia: The Gospel of Matthew' in this chapter.
[66] See 'The Structure and Characteristics of the Hagiopolite Liturgical Year' in Chapter 4.
[67] *Vatican Syr. 19* (1030), fol. 55; Assemani, *Catalogus* II, 80.
[68] *Duabus Dominicis ante Nativitatem*, fol. 67 (margin). See Assemani, *Catalogus*, vol. 2, 82.

From Theophany to Palm Sunday: The Gospel of Luke

The Gospel of Luke was one of the more frequently read Gospels in the fixed commemorations of the Jerusalem lectionary and in the period after Christmas and Theophany in the movable cycle. While *Sinai Ar. 116* (995/6) defines the period of Luke from Theophany until Meatfare Sunday (ἀπὸ τῶν Θεοφανίων ἕως τῶν ἀπόκρεων, fol. 77v),[69] *Sinai Geo. O. 38* (979) indicates that it runs 'from Theophany until the [Sunday of] Palms' (თეთქუენასა განცხადებისა ვიდრე ბზობადმდე).[70] Thus the Hagiopolitan cycle of Luke after Theophany continues not just until the beginning of Lent but, as we shall see in what follows, all throughout Lent.

The Constantinopolitan Typikon of the Great Church and the Byzantinized *Vatican Syr. 19* (1030) have no specific Gospel cycle that begins after Theophany. Instead, the Gospel of Luke was read from the seventeenth until the thirty-second Sunday after Pentecost, when the Lenten cycle began with its own proper pericopes. The Hagiopolitan connection of the leave-taking (ἀπόδοσις) of Theophany on 13 January to the movable cycle and preparation for Lent is revealed by the monastic practice of the 'inter-hours', *mesoria* (μεσώρια)—'small hours' of prayer added between the first, third, sixth, and ninth hour of prayer on weekdays during fasting periods.[71] According to later redactions of the Typikon of St Sabas Lavra, the leave-taking of Theophany initiated the reading of the *mesoria* in church along with stricter ascetical practices.[72] Because there is no Constantinopolitan cycle that corresponds to this period of the liturgical year in Jerusalem, only pericopes of the Hagiopolitan sources are presented in Table 5.7.

A comparison of the Constantinople Lucan Sunday pericopes that run from the seventeenth to the thirty-first Sunday after Pentecost with those of the Jerusalem Lucan cycle shows that these two series do not correspond to each other. Pericopes from the first five chapters of Luke, which recount the birth and early ministry of John the Baptist and Jesus, were read in Constantinople mainly on the fixed feasts connected with those specific events or at the beginning of the Lucan *lectio continua* cycle.[73]

The rationale behind beginning the Lucan cycle immediately after Theophany in Jerusalem is clear from its first lection, Luke 4:1–15, which talks of

---

[69] Garitte, 'Évangéliaire grec-arabe', 215.

[70] Garitte, 'Index des lectures évangéliques', 391.

[71] Evgenii Diakovskii, *Послѣдованіе часовъ и изобразительныхъ. Историческое изслѣдованіе* (Kiev: Типографія Мейдлера, 1913), 104–18; Skaballanovich, *Толковый Типиконъ*, vol. 1, 422; Taft, *Hours*, 119.

[72] See Тѵпіконъ сіесть оуставъ (Moscow: Synodal Typography, 1904), 176v; Georgios Regas, *Τυπικόν* (Λειτουργικὰ Βλατάδων 1, Thessalonike: Πατριαρχικὸν Ἵδρυμα Πατερικῶν Μελετῶν, 1994), 432–3; Lutzka, *Die Kleinen Horen des byzantinischen Studengebetes*, 88–96.

[73] See the index in Mateos, *Typicon*, vol. 2, 225.

Table 5.7. Gospels from the cycle of Luke

	GL (8th cent.)	*Sinai Gr. 210 (861/2)*	*Sinai Geo. O. 38 (979)*	*Sinai Ar. 116 (995/6)*
1st Sunday	–	Lk 4:1–15	Lk 4:1–15	Lk 3:23–4:15
2nd Sunday	–	Lk 4:31–41	Lk 4:14–24	Lk 4:31–41[74]
3rd Sunday	–	Lk 4:42–5:11	Lk 4:31–41	Lk 4:42–5:11
4th Sunday	–	Lk 5:12–17	Lk 4:42–5:11	Lk 5:12–17
5th Sunday	–	Lk 5:18–26	Lk 5:12–17	Lk 5:18–26
6th Sunday	–	Lk 5:27–38	Lk 5:17–26	Lk 5:27–38
7th Sunday	–	–	Lk 5:27–38	–
8th Sunday	–	–	Lk 7:11–16	–

Jesus' temptation by the devil in the wilderness immediately after his baptism by John (Luke 3:21–22).

Gospel Readings for Great Lent

Fortunately more manuscripts of the Hagiopolite and Constantinopolitan lectionaries have preserved readings for the Sundays of Great Lent, which makes more extensive comparisons possible. Several Sundays of Great Lent have been treated in Gabriel Bertonière's study and I follow his conclusions here.[75] Differences exist between the numbering of the Sundays of Lent in Jerusalem and the numbering of the same in Constantinople. For the sake of simplicity I adopt Bertonière's approach and follow the Constantinopolitan numbering, which remains the current usage of the Byzantine rite today (see Table 5.8).[76]

The current Byzantine rite includes two preparatory Sundays before Meatfare Sunday: (1) that of the publican and the Pharisee (Luke 18:10–15), which is simply the thirty-third Sunday after Pentecost in the Constantinopolitan kanonarion–synaxarion (as edited by Mateos) but is indicated as the Sunday 'of the publican and the Pharisee' (τοῦ τελώνου καὶ τοῦ φαρισαίου) in the Constantinopolitan Praxapostolos *Moscow GIM Gr. Vladimir 21/Savva 4* (11th cent);[77] and (2) that of the prodigal son (Luke 15:11–32), which is called the Sunday 'before Meatfare' (πρὸ τῆς ἀπόκρεω) in the Constantinopolitan kanonarion–synaxarion and the Sunday 'of the prodigal [son]' (τοῦ ἀσώτου)

---

[74] κατὰ Μάρκον [sic]. Garitte, 'Évangéliaire grec-arabe', 215 (fol. 82r).
[75] Bertonière, *Sundays of Lent.*
[76] Ibid., 48 n. 4; I. Karabinov, *Постная Тріодь. Историческій обзоръ ея плана, состава, редакцій и славянскихъ переводовъ* (St Petersburg: Типографія В. Д. Смирнова, 1910), 25–6. For a discussion of the development of Lent and the calculation of forty days, see Bradshaw and Johnson, *Origins of Feasts*, 92–113.
[77] Mateos, *Typicon*, vol. 2, 166; Andreou, *Praxapostolos*, 183.

Table 5.8. Gospels for Great Lent

	GL (8th cent.)	Sinai Gr. 210 (61/2)	Sinai Geo. O. 38 (979)	Sinai Ar. 116 (995/6)	Vatican Syr. 19 (1030)	Hag.Stav.Gr.43 (1122)	Typikon of the Great Church
Meatfare							
Matins		(Meatfare)		–	–		
Liturgy	Mt 6:34–7:21	Mt 5:17–48	Mt 5:17–48	Lk 7:36–50 (1st Sunday)	Mt 25:31–		Mt 25:31–46
Cheesefare							
Matins		Lk 7:36–50 (1st Sunday)	Mt 6:34–7:21	–	–		–
Liturgy	Mt 6:1–33	Lk 12:32–40	Lk 12:32–41	Mt 6:16–33 (2nd Sunday)	Mt 6:14–		Mt 6:14–21
1st Sunday							
Matins		Mt 6:16–33 (2nd Sunday)	Mt 6:1–33	–	–		–
Liturgy	Lk 15:1–10	Mt 7:13–29	Mt 7:13–29	Mt 6:1–15 (3rd Sunday)	Jn 1:43–		Jn 1:44–52
2nd Sunday							
Matins		Mt 6:1–15 (3rd Sunday)	Lk 15:1–10	–	–		–
Liturgy	Lk 15:11–32	Mt 22:2–14	Mt 22:1–14	Lk 15:11–32 (4th Sunday)	Mk 2:1–		Mk 2:1–12
3rd Sunday							
Matins		Lk 15:11–32 (4th Sunday)	Lk 15:11–32	–	–		–
Liturgy	Lk 18:1–14	Mt 20:1–16	Mt 20:1–16	Lk 18:9–14 (5th Sunday)	Mk 8:34–		Mk 8:34–9:1
4th Sunday							
Matins		Lk 18:9–14 (5th Sunday)	Lk 18:1–14	–	–		–
Liturgy	Lk 10:25–37	Mt 21:33–46	Mt 21:33–46	Lk 10:25–37 (6th Sunday)	Mk 9:17–		Mk 9:17–31
5th Sunday							
Matins		Lk 10:25–37 (6th Sunday)	Lk 10:25–37	–	–		–
Liturgy	Lk 16:19–31	Mt 23:1–39	Mt 23:1–39	Lk 16:19–31	Mk 10:32–		Mk 2:14–17
Hyperthesis	Jn 10:11–16	Lk 16:19–31 and Jn 9:1–38	Lk 16:19–31	Jn 12:1–11	–	Jn 21:15–25	–
Lazarus Saturday	Jn 11:55–12:11	Jn 11:55–57	Jn 11:1–45	Jn 11:1–46	Mt 21:1–		Jn 11:1–45
Palm Sunday							
Vespers		Jn 11:1–45	Jn 11:55–12:11	–	–		–
Matins		Mk 11:1–11	Mk 11:1–11	–			–
Lite	1:Jn 12:12–22 / 2:Lk 19:29–38 / 3:Mk 11:1–10	Lk 19:29–40 / Jn 12:12–17	1:Jn 12:12–18 / 2:Lk 19:29–38 / 3:Mk 11:1–11	–		1:Mk 11:1–11 / 2:Lk 19:29–38 / 3:Jn 12:12–18 / 4:Mt 21:1–17	–
Liturgy	Mt 21:1–17	Mt 21:1–17	Mt 21:1–17	Mt 21:1–17	Jn 12:1–18	Jn 12:1–11	Jn 12:1–18

in the eleventh-century Constantinopolitan Praxapostolos.[78] The respective Lucan Gospel pericopes for these Sundays were the last readings of the Constantinopolitan cycle of Luke, which ended before Lent; they became fixed as readings that always preceded Great Lent and their themes were theologized as an appropriate preparation for the approaching Great Fast.[79] The Hagiopolite pericopes from Matthew for the preparatory Sundays—departing from the cycle of Luke, to which the Lenten season belonged in Jerusalem—can be explained by the simple fact that the Gospel of Luke does not include any passages with directives on how to fast. Thus the relevance of the appropriate pericopes from Matthew logically displaced the possible Lucan pericopes for those days. The aim was to give Christians guidance and encouragement from the Gospels on the approaching time of fasting.

A comparison between the Greek and the Georgian Hagiopolite pericopes reveals, again, two distinct traditions in the sequencing of Sundays. First, the Greek tradition, represented by *Sinai Gr. 210* (861/2) and *Sinai Ar. 116* (995/6), did not have a 'Cheesefare Sunday' but rather called this day the first Sunday of Lent. This meant that the Lenten week began on a Sunday and not on a Monday, which resulted in six Sundays of Lent, as opposed to five in the Georgian Hagiopolite and Constantinopolitan Greek lectionaries. The Hagiopolite Tropologion *Sinai Gr. N.E. ΜΓ 5* (8th–9th cent.) has no Cheesefare Sunday either but has six Sundays of Lent, in keeping with the Greek Hagiopolite lectionary tradition.[80]

Although the Constantinopolitan pericopes from Mark eventually became those of the synthesized Byzantine rite, the themes of Hagiopolite pericopes from Luke were retained in hymnography. This is why the theme of the Sunday hymnographic canons at matins on the second (Luke 15:11–32, prodigal son), the fourth (Luke 10:25–37, Samaritan woman), and the fifth (Luke 16:19–31, rich man and Lazarus) Sunday of Lent in the Byzantine rite does not match the theme of the Sunday Gospels from Mark read in the Divine Liturgy.[81] Moreover, some of these themes are found elsewhere in the Constantinopolitan lectionary and in the current Byzantine rite. The most notable pericope is that of the prodigal son during the preparatory Sundays. A similar process occurred in the case of Monday in Holy Week: the Byzantine rite adopted the Constantinopolitan pericope (Matthew 24:3–35) for vespers, but the primary hymnography of the day is based on the Hagiopolitan pericope (Matthew 20:17–28).[82]

[78] Mateos, *Typicon*, vol. 2, 2; Andreou, *Praxapostolos*, 185.
[79] Bertonière, *Sundays of Lent*, 31–2.
[80] Nikiforova, *Из истории Минеи в Византии*, 207–8 and 211.
[81] Bertonière, *Sundays of Lent*, 74, 97.
[82] Janeras, 'Pericope evangeliche', 34–6 and 49–50.

As has been shown so far, it is not uncommon for fixed commemorations to find their way into the movable cycle of lectionaries. This is the case in *Sinai Ar. 116* (995/6), where the Gospel of Luke for Annunciation (Luke 1:26–38) is indicated within the Lenten cycle.

The commemoration of a feast called *hyperthesis* (ὑπέρθεσις), indicated in Table 5.8, is particular to Jerusalem. This was the name for the conclusion of Great Lent on the Friday before Palm Sunday. On fol. 129v of the Gospel book *Sinai Ar. 116* (995/6), the Greek rubric before the pericope from John 12:1–11 reads εἰς ὑπέρθεσις ('for *hyperthesis*'), accompanied by an Arabic rubric explaining that the Gospel was 'read at the end of the fast'.[83] Apart from *Sinai Ar. 116*, Gérard Garitte indicates three other references to *hyperthesis*: in the Greek *Vita* of St Stephen the Sabaite (d. 794),[84] in the Arabic version of the same *Vita*,[85] and in *Sinai Gr. 210* (861/2).[86] A tenth-century manuscript containing the Greek *Vita* states that Lent ended 'on the fulfilment of the fortieth day, [which is] the day of *hyperthesis*' (τῆς τεσσαρακοστῆς πληρωθείσης ἐν τῇ ἡμέρᾳ τῆς ὑπερθέσεως) and a contemporary hand explains in a marginal note that in Jerusalem the 'preparation' day for Lazarus—that is, the Friday before Lazarus' celebration on Saturday—was called by the name *hyperthesis*.[87] The same day in the GL, however, has the fixed commemoration of two Hagiopolitan hierarchs connected with the construction of the Church of Sion: Archbishops John II (386–417), 'who first built Sion', and Modestus (d. 634), 'who built it second after the fire'.[88] In both Constantinople and Jerusalem, the raising of Lazarus and the entry of Christ into Jerusalem are commemorated on the following Saturday and Sunday, and similar Gospel pericopes in both lectionaries narrate the events leading up to Christ's passion and death during Holy Week.[89]

It is also worth noting that, for the Sundays of Great Lent, both Greek and Georgian Hagiopolitan sources prescribe specific matins Gospels. Most of the selected pericopes come from the end of the Gospel of Matthew and have a strong eschatological emphasis on the coming kingdom of God and on the

[83] Garitte, 'Évangéliaire grec-arabe', 219. For the Greek term, see Charles du Fresne du Cange, *Glossarium ad scriptores mediæ et infimæ Græcitatis* (Lyons: Anissonion, Posuel, and Rigaud, 1688), 1638; Lampe, *Patristic Greek Lexicon*, 1439. For more on this commemoration in Jerusalem, see Janeras, 'Vendredi avant le Dimanche des Palmes'.

[84] BHG 1670.

[85] *Sinai Ar. 505* (13th cent.), fol. 202v; Gérard Garitte, 'Le début de la vie de S. Étienne le Sabaïte retrouvé en arabe au Sinaï', AB 77 (1959), 338 n. 2.

[86] See fol. 64r. See Garitte, 'Évangéliaire grec-arabe', 219 n. 66.

[87] λέγουσι τὴν παρασκευὴν τοῦ Λαζάρου οἱ ἁγιοπολῖται ὑπέρθεσιν ('The Hagiopolitans call the Friday [before the raising] of Lazarus *hyperthesis*'). *Paris Coislin Gr. 303* (10th cent.); Garitte, 'Évangéliaire grec-arabe', 219 n. 66.

[88] GL § 565.

[89] For more on Lazarus Saturday and Palm Sunday, see Gaga Chourgaïa, *La tradizione liturgica del sabato di Lazzaro e della domenica delle palme nei manoscritti bizantini dei secoli XI–XII* (Excerpta ex Dissertatione ad Doctoratum, Rome: Pontificio Istituto Orientale, 1996).

conflict between Jesus and the Pharisees. This Hagiopolitan usage is significantly different from the practice of Constantinople, where no specific matins
Gospels are prescribed for these Sundays. In the current Byzantine rite, matins
Gospels during Lent are part of the normal eleven resurrectional Gospels read
at Sunday matins. Thus, while the Constantinopolitan pericopes focused
exclusively on the resurrectional character of Sunday matins, the matins
Gospels from Jerusalem addressed the liturgical season at hand and focused
on more eschatological themes during Lent.

Gospel Readings for Holy Week

Study of the development of Holy Week in the Byzantine rite is a world
unto itself and, as mentioned above, I rely on the works of previous scholars.[90]
For this reason I treat only the first four days, following the study of Janeras
(see Table 5.9).[91]

During the first three days of Holy Week, certain Gospel themes from
Jerusalem were adopted in Constantinople, particularly the readings for vespers on Tuesday about the Last Judgement (Matthew 24:3–26:2), and on
Wednesday about the woman who washes Jesus' feet (Matthew 26:6–16).
On Holy Thursday, after the patriarch of Constantinople washes the feet of
three subdeacons, three deacons, three priests, an archbishop, and two metropolitans, the Typikon of the Great Church has a composite reading for the
vesperal liturgy. This reading consists of Matthew 26:2–20, John 13:3–17,
Matthew 26:21–39, Luke 22:43–44, and Matthew 26:40–27:2.[92] The same
phenomenon occurs at vespers on Good Friday, where a composite pericope
made up of Matthew 27:1–38, Luke 23:39–44, Matthew 27:39–54, John 19:
31–37, and Matthew 27:55–61 is read. No such synthetic pericopes are known
in the Jerusalem lectionary. Janeras concludes that composite Gospel readings
are more common in Constantinople than in Jerusalem, where a single
pericope from one evangelist is read at both these services.[93] The practice of
synthesizing passages from different Gospels into one pericope spread in the
second century after Tatian's *Diatessaron*, whose synthesized readings were
even used as lectionaries in some Syriac churches. However, Irenaeus of Lyons
rejected such practices, emphasizing the authenticity of four separate Gospel
accounts.[94] The synthesized pericopes read in Constantinople seem to disre-
gard the unique perspective of each evangelist, giving an exegetical character
to the formation of Gospel pericopes rather than leaving the interpretation or
narrative development of a biblical event to other literary texts, such as

---

[90] See n. 1 in this chapter.   [91] Janeras, 'Pericope evangeliche'.
[92] Mateos, *Typicon*, vol. 2, 72–6.   [93] Janeras, 'Lectionnaires de Jérusalem', 89–90.
[94] Raymond E. Brown, *An Introduction to the New Testament* (New York: Doubleday, 1997),
13–14; W. L. Petersen, 'Diatessaron', GEDSH, 122–4; Young, *Biblical Exegesis*, 19–20.

Table 5.9. Gospels for Holy Week

	GL (8th cent.)	Sinai Gr. 210 (861/2)	Sinai Geo. O. 38 (979)	Sinai Ar. 116 (995/6)	Vatican Syr. 19 (1030)	Hag.Stav. Gr.43 (1122)	Typikon of the Great Church	Current Byzantine Rite[95]
Monday								
Matins	Mt 21:18–23	Mk 11:12–18	Mk 11:12–18	–	Mk 11:12–	Mt 21:18–22:14	–	Mt 21:18–43
Vespers	Mt 20:17–28	Mt 20:17–28	Mt 20:17–28	–	Mt 24:3–	Mt 20:17–28	Mt 24:3–35	Mt 24:3–35
Tuesday								
Matins	Jn 12:27–33	Lk 12:35–	Lk 12:35–39	–	Mt 22:15–	Mt 22:15–24:12	–	Mt 22:15–23:39
Vespers	Mt 24:3–26:2	Mt 24:43–26:2	Mt 24:1–26:2	Mt 24:3–26:2	Mt 24:36–	Mt 24:3–26:2	Mt 24:36–26:2	Mt 24:36–26:2
Wednesday								
Matins	Lk 13:31–35	Jn 12:20–50	Jn 12:20–50	–	Jn 12:17–	Jn 12:17–50	–	Jn 12:17–50
Vespers	Mt 26:3–16	Mt 26:14–16	Mt 26:2–16	–	Mt 26:6–	Mt 26:3–16	Mt 26:6–16	Mt 26:6–16
Thursday								
Matins	Lk 22:1–6	Lk 22:1–11	Lk 22:1–46	–	Lk 22:1–	Lk 22:1–39	–	Lk 22:1–39
3rd Hour	Lk 15:1–10							
Vesperal Lit.	Mt 26:20–24	Jn 12:1–11	Mt 26:17–30 Post-Comm.: Mk 14:12–26	Mt 26:17–30	Composite	Mk 14:12–26 Byzantine: Mt 26:1–27:2	Composite	Composite
Chrism	Mt 26:17–30					Mt 26:6–16	Composite	
Foot washing	Jn 13:3–30	Jn 13:1–17	Jn 13:1–30	–	Jn 13:1–	Jn 13:3–17	–	Jn 13:1–17; Composite

95 Based on Gregory, *Textkritik*, vol. 1, 362–3.

hymnography. Thus it is not surprising that the Jerusalem lectionary did not know the practice of synthesized pericopes, since it relied for exegesis more on hymnography, which was an integral part of the liturgical services. As noted above, the Gospel pericopes of Constantinople eventually emerged as those of the Byzantine rite, although with noticeable Hagiopolitan influence. Even if the Hagiopolitan pericopes were not accepted into the Byzantine lectionary, much of the hymnography adopted in the Lenten Triodion came from Jerusalem and is often connected thematically to the Hagiopolite lectionary.[96]

EPISTLE READINGS IN THE JERUSALEM LECTIONARY

Epistle readings have not received as much attention in liturgical studies as have Gospel cycles. This may be in part because very few sources with Epistle readings according to the Jerusalem pericope order exist. Baumstark echoes this same sentiment with regard to Syriac Melkite Epistle and Old Testament lectionaries when he gathers them under the convenient German label *Nichtevangelische Perikopenordnungen* ('non-Gospel pericope order'), stating that few manuscripts with readings in the Hagiopolitan pericope order are known to exist. One of the few examined Melkite Epistle manuscripts that Baumstark indicates is the Epistle book *Vatican Syr. 21* (31 October 1041) from Antioch.[97] While Hagiopolite Gospel books are relatively common, there is no extant Hagiopolite Praxapostolos, and those that do exist in Georgian translation, such as *Sinai Geo. O. 10* (11th cent.), already reflect the Byzantine pericope order.[98] Even among the manuscripts discovered in 1975 at St Catherine's Monastery on Mount Sinai, there are no witnesses of any separate Praxapostolos or Epistle book that follows the Jerusalem pericope order.

However, one reason why these books do not seem to exist may be that liturgical scholars have been looking in the wrong places. The older, comprehensive Jerusalem lectionary preserved in Armenian (AL) and Georgian (GL) contains all the readings for the liturgical year, both from the Old Testament and from the New Testament—and this of course covers the Epistles too. The Greek lectionary *Sinai Gr. N.E. MΓ 8* (10th cent.) is similar to the GL and contains hymnography as well as Old Testament and New Testament readings, some from Epistles. This Greek example is, however, quite rare. Extant Gospel books copied in the period after the GL, such as *Sinai Gr. 210* (861/2) and *Sinai Ar. 116* (995/6), were clearly copied for liturgical use. These separate,

---

[96] Janeras, 'Pericope evangeliche', 49–50.
[97] See Baumstark, *Nichtevangelische Perikopenordnungen*, 131; Assemani, *Catalogus*, vol. 1, 136–74; Nasrallah, 'Liturgie des patriarcats melchites', 169 and 178.
[98] See Chapter 2, 'Stoudite Monastic and Liturgical Reforms'; also Appendix 1.

larger format, sometimes more ornate Gospel books may have been intended to be read by more important clergy, sometimes even by the patriarch. For example, on Palm Sunday and Pascha *Hagios Stavros Gr. 43* (1122) specifically indicates who reads the Gospel but does not specify who reads the Epistle; it only says that the chanters sing the antiphons from the ambo.[99] Those reading from other books of Scripture, however, are usually not indicated or specified.[100] This is not to say that somehow the Epistles or other readings were less significant, or that they did not receive quite as much attention. But it seems reasonable to propose that the more important the reader, the more specified, customized, and ornamented the book may have been. So long as the pericope was known, the reader of the Epistle could read from a continuous text without difficulty. This remains a hypothesis requiring further confirmation from the manuscripts sources.

That the ornate Gospel books mentioned above are not matched by equivalent Epistle books for liturgical use is perhaps not surprising. There are a few examples of Gospel books that contain Epistle readings as a kind of appendix, namely *Sinai Gr. 212* (9th cent.) and *Sinai Gr. N.E. MΓ 11* (9th cent.), but these Epistles are usually for general commemorations and do not include readings for any kinds of cycles during the liturgical year. Whereas both manuscripts contain several Gospel cycles for Sundays, including resurrectional Gospels for the eight tones and Gospels for Sundays from all four evangelists, only *Sinai Gr. N.E. MΓ 11* gives one pericope for the Epistle of the first Sunday of Lent (2 Corinthians 6:2–10; this is the Epistle for Cheesefare Sunday in the GL).[101] The place where liturgical scholars may have more success is among continuous texts of the New Testament. Some examples of manuscripts of continuous New Testament texts that include the Epistles indicate pericopes in marginal notes. Such notes are quite clear in the bilingual Greek–Arabic lectionary *Sinai Gr. N.E. MΓ 2* (9th cent.), where the Epistle pericopes are mentioned in the margins. Many of the marginal notes perfectly match the Jerusalem lectionary, for example for Christmas and Palm Sunday, but the Epistle to the Hebrews is prescribed for Sundays of Lent, already revealing Constantinopolitan influence.[102] The Epistle book contained in *Sinai Geo. O. 58, Sinai Geo. O. 31, Sinai Geo. O. 60,* and *Sinai Geo. N. 8* (977) remains to be examined if one is to see whether marginal notes reveal

---

[99] See Papadopoulos-Kerameus, *Anastasis Typikon*, 24 and 201.

[100] See Janeras, 'Pericope evangeliche', 50–1. For more on the role of readers and chanters in Hagiopolite liturgy, see Longo, 'Narrazione', 254; Taft, 'The βηματίκιον', 677–9; Taft, 'Worship on Sinai', 152.'

[101] Galadza, 'Two Sources of the Jerusalem Lectionary', 83–90 and 92–102, especially 102. See GL § 325 for the Sunday Epistle pericope.

[102] See Nikolopoulos, *Νέα εὑρήματα*, 141 and table 1. My thanks to Father Justin Sinaites and Jack Tannous, who are preparing a study of this manuscript, for bringing this information to my attention.

any indications of pericopes according to the Hagiopolite or Constantinopolitan lectionary.[103]

While fragmentary sources of the Epistle make it difficult to speak definitively of the contents and nature of the Jerusalem lectionary, the comprehensive GL allows one at least to make general comments regarding the frequency of reading one book of the New Testament over another. Of all New Testament books other than the Gospels, Acts and Hebrews were the most frequently read. Whether this has to do with a connection to the local Palestinian topography mentioned in the Acts of the Apostles and to a continuity of Jewish traditions in the Jerusalem church is unclear and perhaps impossible to know. Also important to note is the absence of any readings from the Book of Revelation.[104] Despite its inclusion in the canon of the Greek Bible, in most eastern Christian traditions Revelation was not read liturgically or publicly.[105] The one exception in the current Byzantine rite is the Sabaite all-night vigil (ἀγρυπνία), where, depending on the liturgical season, any books of the New Testament—including Revelation—could be read during the 'Great Reading' between the end of vespers and the beginning of matins while the monks partake of the blessed bread and wine in the *artoklasia* at the *lite*.[106] This practice is first attested in Athonite liturgical Typika, but may have Palestinian Sabaite monastic origins.[107]

As stated above, the fragmentary nature of Hagiopolitan liturgical sources for Epistle readings makes it difficult to re-create the full set of readings from the movable cycle. Not even the GL contains a complete list of readings, as it does for the fixed cycle.

Epistle Readings for Pascha and Pentecost

Just like the Gospel cycle, the Hagiopolite Epistle cycle after Pascha shares certain similarities with the Byzantine lectionary. These readings are presented in Table 5.10.

Unfortunately only the GL provides a complete set of Hagiopolitan readings for the whole of Bright Week. Although *Hagios Stavros Gr. 43* (1122) includes hymns and lections for all of it, after Bright Monday there are no indications

---

[103] See Aleksidze et al., *Catalogue of Georgian Manuscripts*, 380; Frøyshov, 'The Georgian Witness', 267.

[104] See the scriptural index of the GL (CSCO 205), 125–35.

[105] Georg Kretschmar, *Die Offenbarung des Johannes: Die Geschichte ihrer Auslegung im 1. Jahrtausend* (Stuttgart: Calwer Verlag, 1985).

[106] Τυπικὸν τοῦ ὁσίου καὶ θεοφόρου πατρὸς ἡμῶν Σάββα τοῦ ἡγιασμένου, ed. Archimandrite Dositheos Kanellos (Athens: Ἱερὰ Σταυροπηγιακὴ Μονὴ Παναγίας Τατάρνης Εὐρυτανίας, 2010), 56 and 77 n. 83; Тѷпіко́нъ сіесть оўста́въ (Moscow: Synodal Typography, 1904), fol. 5v.

[107] Skaballanovich, *Толковый Типиконъ*, vol. 2, 189–94.

Table 5.10. Epistles for Pascha and Bright Week

	GL (L) (8th cent.)	*Typikon of the Great Church*		Sinai Geo. O. 10 (11th cent.)	*Vladimir 21/Savva 4* (11th cent.)	*Hag.Stav.Gr.* 43 (1122)
		Station	Great Church			
Pascha	Acts 1:1–18	Acts 1:1–8		Acts 1:1–12	Acts 1:1–8	Acts 1:1–8
Monday	Acts 2:22–28	Acts 1: 12–17, 21–26	Acts 2: 14–21	Acts 1:12–26	Acts 1:12–17, 21–26	Acts
Tuesday	Acts 2:29–30, 41–47 Jas 1:1–12	Acts 2:14–21		Acts 2:14–21	Acts 2:14–21	–
Wednesday	Acts 3:1–20 Jas 1:13–19	Acts 1: 12–14	Acts 2: 22–36	Acts 2:22–36	Acts 2:22–36	–
Thursday	Acts 1:1–12 Jas 2:1–13	Acts 2:38–43		Acts 2:38–43	Acts 2:38–43	–
Friday	Acts 8:29–40 Jas 2:14–23	Acts 3:1–8		Acts 3:1–8	Acts 3:1–8	–
Saturday	Acts 4:23–31 Jas 1:17–27	Acts 19:1–8	Acts 3: 11–16	Acts 3:11–16	Acts 3:11–16	–
New Sunday	Acts 5:34–42 1 Jn 1:1–7	Acts 5:12–20		Acts 5:12–20	Acts 5:12–20	–

for any Divine Liturgies, and thus no pericopes are given for Epistle readings. In Constantinople, a particularity of the Typikon of the Great Church is the prescription of two sets of readings: one at the Great Church and the other at stations where the patriarch served during Bright Week.[108] The remainder of the Sundays in the period after Easter are found in the GL:

> Pascha: Hosea 5:13–6:3, Zephaniah 3:6–13, Acts 1:1–18 (Mark 16:1–8)
> New Sunday: Acts 5:34–42, 1 John 1:1–7 (John 1:1–17)
> 2nd Sunday: Acts 3:13–?, 1 John 4:16–21 (John 2:1–11)
> 3rd Sunday: Acts 13:16–38, 1 Peter 1:13–25 (John 4:4–23)
> Mid-Pentecost: Acts 14:16–22, 1 Peter 2:1–10 (John 7:14–29)
> 4th Sunday: Acts 10:34–43, 1 Peter 2:21–25 (John 4:24–?)
> 5th Sunday: Acts 13:16–38, 1 Peter 3:17–22 (John 2:12–25)
> Ascension: Amos 9:5–6, Acts 1:1–12? [Luke 21:41–53]
> 6th Sunday: lacuna [John 8:12–20]
> Pentecost: Proverbs 14:27–15:4, Isaiah 63:14–15, Zephaniah 3:7–13, Acts 2:1–21, 1 Corinthians 12:1–14 (John 14:15–19)[109]

---

[108] Mateos, *Typicon*, vol. 2, 98.
[109] GL § 746–888. See Galadza, 'A Note on Hagiopolite Epistle Readings', 153–4.

The only other Hagiopolite lectionary to include Epistle readings for the period after Pascha is the Epistle lectionary *Sinai Gr. N.E. MΓ 73* (9th cent.), which covers the first three Sundays of Acts. It is important to note that the numbering of the Sundays of Acts corresponds to the numbering of the Sundays of John, even though Acts is prescribed at the Divine Liturgy on Pascha in the Hagiopolite lectionary.[110]

The most striking element of the Jerusalem lectionary is the reading of the General Epistle of James as the second reading during Bright Week. There was a *lectio continua* (or semi-*continua*) of the General Epistle of St James, along with readings from the Acts of the Apostles, at JAS during Bright Week in the GL. The reading from Acts always came first, being followed by a reading from the General Epistle.[111] Charles Renoux has speculated that the Epistle of James was read at this time in Jerusalem because of St James' martyrdom allegedly around Pascha in the year 62.[112] Thus, unlike Constantinople—which reserved the General Epistles for the end of the Epistle cycle before Great Lent, between the thirty-first and the thirty-sixth week after Pentecost[113]—Jerusalem read the General Epistles immediately after Pascha.

Sunday Epistle Cycles

Due to the fragmentary nature of the sources of the Jerusalem lectionary, it is impossible to re-create the Hagiopolite Sunday Epistle cycles outside the paschal and Lenten seasons. The sources of the Constantinopolitan lectionary show the order of the various Epistles and the sequence of their reading.[114] The Constantinopolitan Praxapostolos *Vladimir 21/Savva 4* (11th cent.) reveals the simplified scheme in Table 5.11:

---

[110] Ibid., 158–9.

[111] These readings begin at GL §758. See also Charles Renoux, 'Les lectionnaires arméniens', 53–74, and Bernard Outtier, 'Les lectionnaires géorgiens', 75–85, both in *La lecture liturgique des Épîtres catholiques dans l'Église ancienne*, ed. by Christian-Bernard Amphoux and Jean-Paul Bouhot (Histoire du Texte Biblique 1, Lausanne: Éditions du Zébre, 1996).

[112] Eusebius of Caesarea, Ἐκκλησιαστικῆς ἱστορίας, ed. by Gustave Bardy (SC 31, Paris: Éditions du Cerf, 1952), 2.23.18 (= pp. 87–8); Charles Renoux, 'La lecture biblique dans la liturgie de Jérusalem', in *Le monde grec ancien et la Bible*, ed. by Claude Mondésert (Paris: Éditions Beauchesne, 1984), 399–420, here 408–12. See Chapter 4, 'St James the Brother of the Lord'.

[113] Andreou, *Praxapostolos*, 178–89; Christian-Bernard Amphoux, 'Les lectionnaires grecs', in *La lecture liturgique des Épîtres catholiques dans l'Église ancienne*, ed. by Christian-Bernard Amphoux and Jean-Paul Bouhot (Histoire du Texte Biblique 1, Lausanne: Éditions du Zèbre, 1996), 19–46, esp. 28–30.

[114] For a study of the reading of the Epistle in the current Byzantine rite, see Ioannis M. Phountoulis, "Ὁ Ἀπόστολος Παῦλος στή θεία λατρεία', in idem, Τελετουργικά Θέματα, vol. 2 (Σειρά Λογική λατρεία 12, Athens: Apostoliki Diakonia, 2006), 25–40.

Table 5.11. Sunday Epistle cycles in Constantinople

Pascha to Pentecost	8 Sundays (7 weeks)	Acts
After Pentecost	6 Sundays (1st–7th Sunday)	Romans
Sunday of All Saints	*1 Sunday*	*Hebrews*
	6 Sundays (8th–13th Sunday)	1 Corinthians
	6 Sundays (14th–19th Sunday)	2 Corinthians
Exaltation of the Cross	*2 Sundays*	*Galatians*
	3 Sundays (20th–22nd Sunday)	Galatians[115]
	5 Sundays (23rd–27th Sunday)	Ephesians
Nativity of Christ	*1 Sunday (προπατόρων)*	*Colossians*
	1 Sunday (before Nativity)	*Hebrews*
	1 Sunday (after Nativity)	*Galatians*
Theophany	*1 Sunday (before Theophany)*	*2 Timothy*
	1 Sunday (after Theophany)	*Ephesians*
	3 Sunday (28th–30th Sunday)	Colossians
	1 Sunday (31st Sunday)	1 Timothy
	1 Sunday (32nd Sunday)	2 Timothy
Preparatory Sundays for Lent	1 Sunday (33rd Sunday, τοῦ τελώνου καὶ τοῦ φαρισαίου)	1 Thessalonians
	2 Sundays (34th Sunday, τοῦ ἀσώτου; 35th Sunday, τῆς ἀπόκρεω)	1 Corinthians
	1 Sunday (τῆς τυρηνῆς)	Romans
Great Lent	5 Sundays	Hebrews
Palm Sunday	1 Sunday (τῶν βαΐων)	Philippians

While the Epistles to Titus and the General Epistles are never read on Sundays, they are read on weekdays. Thus the Constantinopolitan lectionary reads every New Testament book, except for Philemon and Revelation, during the movable cycle every year. Neither Philemon nor Revelation are found in the fixed cycle of the GL. Their absence suggests that they may not have been read either as part of the movable Hagiopolite Epistle lectionary cycle.

Having seen the great differences elsewhere between Constantinopolitan and Jerusalem reading cycles, it is unwise to speculate further on the Hagiopolite Sunday cycles for Epistles on the basis of Constantinopolitan parallels.[116] Only through discovery of new, more complete manuscripts will one be able to address these questions more adequately. However, even the few newly found Epistle books from Sinai that have been examined often raise further questions. For example, the Epistle lectionary *Sinai Gr. N.E. MΓ 36* (9th cent.) provides a series of six pericopes from Romans, 2 Corinthians, and Ephesians,

---

[115] There appears to be an error in Andreou's transcription for the 21st Sunday after Pentecost. See Andreou, *Praxapostolos*, 164 (fol. 133r).

[116] This was the approach taken by John F. Baldovin, SJ, 'A Lenten Sunday Lectionary in Fourth Century Jerusalem', in *Time and Community: In Honor of Thomas Julian Talley*, ed. by J. Neil Alexander (NPM Studies in Church Music and Liturgy, Washington, DC: Pastoral Press, 1990), 115–22. For criticism of such a method, see Bertonière, *Sundays of Lent*, 37–38.

with rubrics that assign each of them to a Sunday. Whether they were read on consecutive Sundays is unclear.[117] It remains to liturgiologists to understand which New Testament manuscripts contain Epistles or rubrics for Epistle readings in marginal notes and to identify their reading cycles, as has been done for Gospel readings.

Epistle Readings for Great Lent

Of all Hagiopolite lectionaries, only the GL provides a complete set of Epistle readings for the Sundays of Great Lent (see Table 5.12).[118]

The only pericope in the Lenten cycle common to both Hagiopolite and Constantinopolitan lectionaries is Romans 13: 11–14: 4, which speaks of the need to be prepared for imminent salvation and discusses various fasting practices. While in Constantinople this pericope was read at the beginning of Lent on Cheesefare Sunday as an instruction on the behaviour of Christians in preparation for Pascha and as a guide to fasting, in Jerusalem it was read on

Table 5.12. Epistles for Great Lent

	GL (8th cent.)	*Typikon of the Great Church*	*Sinai Geo. O. 10* (11th cent.)	*Vladimir 21/Savva 4* (11th cent.)
Meatfare	Rom 14: 4–23, 16: 25–7	1 Cor 8:8–9:2	1 Cor 8:8–9:2	1 Cor 8:8–13, 9:1–2
Cheesefare	2 Cor 6:2–10	Rom 13:11–14:4	Rom 13:11–14:4	Rom 13:11–24, 14:1–4
1st Sunday	Rom 11:1–5	Heb 11:24–26, 32–40	Heb 11:24–40	Heb 11:24–6, 32–40
2nd Sunday	Rom 12:6–16	Heb 1:10–2:3	Heb 1:10–2:3	Heb 1:10–14, 2:1–3
3rd Sunday	Rom 12: 16–13:6	Heb 4:14–5:6	Heb 4:14–5:6	Heb 4:14–16, 5:1–6
4th Sunday	Rom 13: 10–14:6	Heb 6:13–20	Heb 6:13–20	Heb 6:13–20
5th Sunday	Eph 4:25–5:2	Heb 9:11–14	Heb 9:11–14	Heb 9:11–14
6th Sunday[a]	–	–	–	–
Annunciation	Phil 4:4–9	Heb 2:11–18 (= 26 Dec)	Heb 2:11–18 (= 26 Dec)	Heb 2:11–18
Hyperthesis	Eph 4:1–16	–	–	–
Lazarus Saturday	Eph 5:13–17	Heb 12:28–13:8	Heb 12:29–13:8	Heb 12:28–9, 13:1–8
Palm Sunday	Eph 1:3–14	Phil 4:4–9	Phil 4:4–9	Phil 4:4–9

[a] See Table 5.8 for the numbering of the Sundays of Lent

[117] Galadza, 'A Note on Hagiopolite Epistle Readings', 156–8.
[118] Bertonière, *Sundays of Lent*, 45.

the fourth Sunday of Lent, as part of other readings from Romans on Christian love and harmonious living.

The Gospel and Epistle lectionary *Sinai Gr. N.E. MΓ 11* (9th cent.) contains the reading from 2 Corinthians 6:2–10 shown above in the GL for Cheesefare Sunday, but prescribes it for the first Sunday of Lent (κυριακὴ αʹ τῶν ἁγίων νηστείων, fol. 124r). Although this is the last pericope and the remainder of the manuscript is lost, this variant numbering seems consistent with other Hagiopolite Gospel lectionaries, for instance *Sinai Gr. 210* (861/2) and *Sinai Ar. 116* (995/6) examined above, confirming two traditions for the naming and numbering of Lent Sundays, one Greek and one Georgian.

OLD TESTAMENT READINGS AT THE LITURGY OF ST JAMES AND THEIR DISAPPEARANCE

Readings from the Old Testament formed an integral part of the Liturgy of the Word in JAS in Jerusalem. Both the AL and the GL contain Old Testament readings. However, some later witnesses of the GL, while retaining the Jerusalem pericope order, omit all Old Testament readings for JAS. This is the case with most 'liturgical collections' such as *Sinai Geo. O. 54* (10th cent.), which contain JAS, various other prayers, and readings from the Hagiopolite lectionary for JAS.[119] While Armenian and Georgian manuscripts provide Old Testament readings for the Divine Liturgy, these are noticeably absent from Greek lectionary manuscripts, apart from the recently discovered manuscript *Sinai Gr. N.E. MΓ 8* (10th cent.)—the only known Greek manuscripts to contain an Old Testament reading for the Sunday eucharistic synaxis of the Divine Liturgy.[120]

As discussed before, various manuscript sources of JAS indicate the presence of an Old Testament reading during the Liturgy of the Word, and this is reflected in many sources of the Jerusalem lectionary.[121] The AL includes up to three scriptural readings during the Liturgy of the Word and the number of readings depended on the commemoration. Renoux has noted that commemorations of Old Testament figures had Old Testament readings that were always followed by a reading from Acts or from an Epistle. Figures from the New Testament, however, did not have an Old Testament reading except in a common commemoration of several New Testament figures.[122] According to this pattern, an Old Testament reading never immediately preceded the

---

[119] *Sinai Geo. O. 54* (10th cent.), fol. 66r–175v.
[120] *Sinai Gr. N.E. MΓ 8* (10th cent.), fol. 13v–18v; Galadza, 'Sinai Gr. N.E. MΓ 8', 225–6. See also Appendix 1.
[121] See Chapter 3, 'Lection(s)'.   [122] AL, 36–7.

Gospel, so that there was always a reading from Acts or an Epistle between an Old Testament reading and a Gospel one.[123] Similar patterns also apply to the GL, where there were between two and five readings from the Old Testament and New Testament.

The only Greek evidence for Old Testament readings in the Jerusalem lectionary for JAS comes from the fragmentary lectionary *Sinai Gr. N.E. MΓ 8* (10th cent.), which provides a complete set of readings with rubrics for the 'First Sunday of Lent' (α΄ κυριακὴ τῶν ἁγίων νηστίων εἰς σύναξιν, fol. 13v)—a day equivalent to Cheesefare Sunday. The service consists of readings from the Prophet Joel (Joel 2:15–27, fol. 15v–21r), the Epistle to the Romans (Romans 13:12–14:11, fol. 21v–25v), and the Gospel of Matthew (Matthew 6:16–24, fol. 26r–27v). This order of readings does not exactly match the GL, our only complete source of the Jerusalem lectionary on this Lenten Sunday. Nevertheless, the Gospel is consistent with the reading for Cheesefare Sunday in *Sinai Gr. 210* (861/2), while the Epistle is similar to the Constantinopolitan sources mentioned above. The reading from Joel is found in the GL as two separate pericopes on two different days: Joel 2:15–18 on the Friday before Cheesefare[124] and Joel 2:21–27 on the third Wednesday of Lent.[125] While the combination of these three readings points to great variability within the Jerusalem pericope order, even more importantly, it reveals the continued presence of Old Testament readings at the Sunday eucharistic synaxis.

The gradual disappearance of Old Testament readings at JAS in manuscripts of the Hagiopolite lectionary coincides with the period of Jerusalem's liturgical Byzantinization. In order to better understand this phenomenon, it is necessary to examine the presence of Old Testament readings in Constantinople at the eucharistic liturgy.

The earliest extant Constantinopolitan lectionaries do not provide Old Testament readings at the eucharistic synaxis. However, the Constantinopolitan Typikon of the Great Church does indicate other readings during the eucharistic synaxis. For example, on 15 September, in conjunction with the commemoration of the 'blessed fathers who gathered at the holy sixth ecumenical council in the God-protected and imperial city' (μακαρίων πατέρων τῶν συνελθόντων εἰς τὴν ἁγίαν καὶ οἰκουμενικὴν ς΄ σύνοδον ἐν τῇ θεοφυλάκτῳ καὶ βασιλίδι τῶν πόλεων), a rubric indicates: 'On this day the decree of the sixth ecumenical council is read before the Epistle reading'.[126] Thus the structure of the service allowed for the reading of other texts before the Epistle, such as the decree of a council, but we have no evidence that the reading was

---

[123] Ibid., 37.   [124] GL § 305.   [125] Ibid., § 416.

[126] Ἀναγινώσκεται δὲ πρὸ τοῦ ἀποστόλου κατὰ ταύτην τὴν ἡμέραν ὁ ὅρος τῆς ἁγίας καὶ οἰκουμενικῆς ς΄ συνόδου. Mateos, *Typicon*, vol. 1, 36.

from the Old Testament. The liturgical book known as the Prophetologion (προφητολόγιον) provides Old Testament readings only for the weekdays of Great Lent, at vespers on the eves of feasts, and as part of the vesperal liturgy on the eves of Christmas, Theophany, and Pascha, that is, on Holy Saturday.[127] Nevertheless, Juan Mateos believed that 'the Byzantine Church had three readings at the liturgy, as did the Roman, Milanese, Spanish, Gallican, and Armenian rites',[128] until the Old Testament reading was lost in the seventh century.[129] This theory was based on St Maximus Confessor's (*c*.580–662) reference to the 'Law and the Prophets' (ἐν νόμῳ καὶ προφήταις) and 'sacred readings from the inspired scriptures' (θείας τῶν πανιέρων βίβλων ἀναγνώσεις) as evidence of Old Testament lections in Constantinople.[130] Mateos also examined the structure of the vesperal liturgies, where Old Testament lections are present to this day. His analysis suggested that the presence of the last Old Testament reading and its distinct position after the Trisagion in the structure of eight readings at Christmas, thirteen at Theophany, and fifteen at Easter were signs of that final Old Testament reading's association with the actual eucharistic liturgy rather than with the preceding vigil service.[131] The fact that these examples only occur in connection with a vigil, both in the earliest liturgical sources and in the current Byzantine rite, is worth noting. Both Mateos and Taft believe that the absence of any reference to Old Testament lections in the mystagogy of Germanus of Constantinople (r. 715–30) indicates that these readings had disappeared by then.[132] It is worth noting that few of St John Chrysostom's homilies are dedicated to books in the Old Testament; John focuses primarily on New Testament books. This is quite different from the practice of other notable

---

[127] Carsten Hoeg and Günther Zuntz, 'Remarks on the Prophetologion', in *Quantulacumque: Studies Presented to Kirsopp Lake*, ed. by Robert P. Casey, Silva Lake, and Agnes K. Lake (London: Christophers, 1937), 189–226; James Miller, 'The Prophetologion: The Old Testament of Byzantine Christianity?', in *The Old Testament in Byzantium*, ed. by Paul Magdalino and Robert Nelson (Washington, DC: Dumbarton Oaks Research Library and Collection, 2010), 55–76; Robert F. Taft, SJ, 'Prophetologion', ODB II, 1737.

[128] *L'Église byzantine, en effet, possédait autrefois trois lectures à la Liturgie: prophétie, apôtre et évangile, tout comme les Églises romaine, milanaise, hispanique, gallicane et arménienne.* Mateos, *Parole*, 130.

[129] *Ce fut au cours du VIIe siècle que le cycle de lectures byzantines fut bouleversé et que la prophétie disparut* ('It was during the seventh century that the Byzantine cycle of readings was drastically changed and the [reading from the Old Testament] prophecies disappeared'). Ibid., 131.

[130] Boudignon, *Maximi Confessoris Mystagogia*, 51 and 39. Elsewhere St Maximus uses the term θεόπνευστος ('divinely inspired'). See also Lampe, *Patristic Greek Lexicon*, 630; Alexander Kazhdan, 'Maximos the Confessor', ODB II, 1323–4.

[131] Mateos, *Parole*, 131–2.

[132] St Germanus of Constantinople, *On the Divine Liturgy*, ed. and trans. by Paul Meyendorff (Crestwood, NY: St Vladimir's Seminary Press, 1984); Alexander Kazhdan, 'Germanos I', ODB I, 846–7; Taft, 'Old Testament Readings', 272; Taft, 'Maximus'.

scriptural commentators, for instance Origen, who commented on major parts of the Old Testament.[133]

The current expert on the Prophetologion, Sysse Engberg, has recently called into question the theory of Old Testament readings during the Divine Liturgy in Constantinople (a theory known as the 'triple lection theory').[134] Engberg believes that, although the Old Testament was read during the eucharistic synaxis in other regions that follow the Byzantine rite today, it was never read in Constantinople during an ordinary Sunday Divine Liturgy. In essence, her study attempted to examine the local character of liturgy from the perspective of the lectionary—something that Taft and Parenti have promoted for CHR, BAS, and other rites from the Euchologion.[135] Neither Mateos nor Taft was able to provide examples of the presence of the Old Testament during the regular Divine Liturgy in Constantinople; and Taft's last rebuttal of Engberg has not been able to prove that such readings existed. Rather it has confirmed that the current practice of Old Testament readings at the vesperal liturgy on the eves of the feasts mentioned above was already evident in Constantinople by the sixth century, if not earlier. There are indications of this in marginal notes in the biblical manuscript 'Codex B', *Vatican Gr. 1209* (4th cent.).[136] Thus there are sources that confirm the antiquity of certain Old Testament lections in the current Byzantine rite for vesperal eucharistic liturgies on the eves of Christmas, Theophany, and Pascha, but these same sources do not indicate any additional Old Testament readings during the Divine Liturgy beyond these three occasions; nor do they point to Old Testament readings from the Divine Liturgy that have since been lost. Taft's views have been adopted by Phillipe Raczka in his study of the lectionary in the time of St John Chrysostom, which seems to ignore Engberg's methodological approach, arguments, and conclusions.[137]

Regardless of the unresolved character of this question, it is clear that by the eighth century the Divine Liturgy in Constantinople had no Old Testament

---

[133] For more on this question, see Gerard Rouwhorst, 'The Liturgical Reading of the Bible in Early Eastern Christianity: The Protohistory of the Byzantine Lectionary', in *Catalogue of Byzantine Manuscripts in Their Liturgical Context: Subsidia 1*, ed. by Klaas Spronk, Gerard Rouwhorst, and Stefan Royé (Turnhout: Brepols, 2013), 155–72; Gerard Rouwhorst, 'The Reading of Scripture in Early Christian Liturgy', in *What Athens Has to do with Jerusalem: Essays on Classical, Jewish, and Early Christian Art and Archaeology in Honor of Gideon Foerster*, ed. by Leonard V. Rutgers (Interdisciplinary Studies in Ancient Culture and Religion 1, Leuven: Peeters, 2002), 305–31.

[134] See Sysse Gudrun Engberg, 'The Greek Old Testament Lectionary as a Liturgical Book', *Université de Copenhague, Cahiers de l'Institut du Moyen-âge grec et latin* 54 (1986), 39–48; Sysse Gudrun Engberg, 'Prophetologion Manuscripts in the "New Finds" of St Catherine's at Sinai', *Scriptorium* 57 (2003), 94–109.

[135] Sysse Gudrun Engberg, 'The Prophetologion and the Triple-Lection Theory: The Genesis of a Liturgical Book', BBGG (terza serie) 3 (2006), 67–92.

[136] See Taft, 'Old Testament Readings', 275–6.

[137] Raczka, *The Lectionary*, 50–88.

lection, while manuscript sources of the Jerusalem lectionary preserved Old Testament readings at the eucharistic liturgy alongside New Testament readings as late as the tenth century. In the tenth century the Great Church of Constantinople only read from the Old Testament at vespers, on weekdays during Great Lent and on the eves of sixteen major commemorations during the year.[138] Such a limited public reading shows that the Old Testament had less frequent liturgical use in Constantinople than it did elsewhere in Christendom, especially in Jerusalem. Whether or not the disappearance of the Old Testament in Jerusalem can be directly attributed to liturgical Byzantinization is unclear. What is clear, however, is that the disappearance of these readings occurred at the same time as Jerusalem's liturgical Byzantinization and was in keeping with the liturgical practice of Constantinople at that time.

Although my interest here is in the lectionary at the eucharistic liturgy of JAS, the Old Testament was also read during the hours in Jerusalem.[139] The GL provides extensive information on the Old Testament during the Liturgy of the Hours. During Great Lent, Old Testament readings were part of the daily Lenten services. From Monday of the fifth week of Lent, a new service, the third hour for the catechumens, was introduced into the GL, at which time two lections were read. Apart from these two lections, an instructional reading for catechumens was proclaimed at the gate of the church.[140] As mentioned above, the two readings could include the Pauline Epistles. None of the readings seems to follow a *lectio continua* and the selection of pericopes either followed a haphazard order or was done thematically. During the evening office three readings were normally read.

The Typikon of the Anastasis gives certain indications of Old Testament readings during matins. Towards the end of matins the Great Doxology ('Δόξα ἐν ὑψίστοις...') is divided into two, so that a Liturgy of the Word structure, with *prokeimena* and readings, was inserted between the verse 'those who know you' (τοῖς γινώσκουσί σε) and the verse 'Favour us, O Lord' (Καταξίωσον, Κύριε).[141] The order of this addition of a Liturgy of the Word during matins in Holy Week is shown in Table 5.13.

---

[138] Mateos, *Parole*, 133.

[139] Alfred Rahlfs, 'Die alttestamentlichen Lektionen der griechischen Kirche', in *Nachrichten der K. Gesellschaft der Wissenschaften zu Göttingen, philologisch-historische Klasse* (Berlin: Weidmannsche Buchhandlung, 1915), 28–136, here 59–67.

[140] GL § 478.

[141] For more on the Great Doxology, see Mateos, *Typicon*, vl. 1, 289; *Les Constitutions apostoliques, III: Livres VII et VIII*, ed. by Marcel Metzger (SC 336, Paris: Cerf, 1987), Book 7, Chapter 47 (= pp. 112–13); Taft, *Hours*, 393 ('Gloria in excelsis'); Papadopoulos-Kerameus, *Anastasis Typikon*, 211, 220, 227, 235, 244, 252; Follieri, *Initia hymnorum*, vol. 1, 320.

Table 5.13. Old Testament readings for Holy Week

	Monday[142]	Tuesday[143]	Wednesday[144]	Thursday[145]
Prokeimenon 1				
Reading 1	Genesis 1:1–13	Exodus 19:10–18	Proverbs 3:27–34	Genesis 22:1–19
Reading 2	Proverbs 1:20–33	Proverbs 2:13–22	Hosea 5:13–6:3	Acts 1:15–20
Reading 3	Isaiah 5:1–7	Hosea 4:1–6	–	–
Prokeimenon 2				
Gospel	Matthew 21:18–22:14	Matthew 22:15–24:12	John 12:17–50	Luke 22:1–39

This reflects the minimal information given by the GL, which also prescribes readings that should precede Καταξίωσον, Κύριε during the morning office.[146] A similar structure of readings is repeated for vespers.[147] The insertion of readings after the Great Doxology makes it similar in structure to the stational service on Palm Sunday, which also includes various hymns, *prokeimena*, and readings at locations around Jerusalem.[148] The Gospel book *Sinai Geo. O. 38* (979) included several pericopes for Holy Week and Bright Week that are to be read at matins, specifically after 'Glory to God in the highest' (გისკრაო, დიდებაა მაღალთასა შემდგომაო), presumably the Great Doxology.[149] The absence of any elaboration on the point at which these pericopes were to be read in conjunction with the Great Doxology suggests that the latter was a familiar point at which to insert scriptural readings in Jerusalem. The Euchologion *Sinai Gr. 973* (1153) also prescribes the matins Gospel to be read after the Great Doxology and not before the canon, as one might expect from Constantinopolitan practice.[150] However, the presence of this set of readings at the conclusion of matins points elsewhere. Rolf Zerfass suggests that the structure is an imitation of Holy Saturday, which is found in the AL.[151] That these readings are nestled between two forms of concluding petitions used in

[142] *Hagios Stavros Gr. 43* (1122), fol. 19r–21v. Papadopoulos-Kerameus, *Anastasis Typikon*, 40–1.
[143] *Hagios Stavros Gr. 43*, fol. 33v–36r. Papadopoulos-Kerameus, *Anastasis Typikon*, 58–9.
[144] *Hagios Stavros Gr. 43*, fol. 51v–53v. Papadopoulos-Kerameus, *Anastasis Typikon*, 74.
[145] *Hagios Stavros Gr. 43*, fol. 68r–70v. Papadopoulos-Kerameus, *Anastasis Typikon*, 94.
[146] GL § 599 and 624.
[147] For a comparison of the Typikon of the Anastasis and other sources for vespers readings, see Janeras, 'La Settimana Santa', 29–32.
[148] Papadopoulos-Kerameus, *Anastasis Typikon*, 16–22.
[149] Garitte, 'Index des lectures évangéliques', 353–5 and 359. See Appendix 1.
[150] Miguel Arranz, SJ, 'N. D. Uspensky: The Office of the All-Night Vigil in the Greek Church and in the Russian Church', SVTQ 24 (1980), here 112.
[151] AL, 294–5; Zerfass, *Schriftlesung*, 89.

monastic rites also suggests that they are a later addition.[152] Similarly, additional Old Testament readings are found at several points in *Sinai Gr. 1096* (12th cent.): apart from three Old Testament readings from Exodus for Prophet Moses on 4 September, the conclusion of matins and during the first hour on Holy Thursday indicates readings from Zachariah, Galatians, Isaiah, and Philippians, followed by readings from the Gospel of Matthew.[153] The placement of these readings at the end of the service is similar to that of the Constantinopolitan *proanagnosis* (προανάγνωσις) at the end of or before various services during the year. However, apart from the scriptural book or other text read, nothing is known about its structure and whether it had its own dismissal before the service it preceded.[154]

GENERAL COMMEMORATIONS

The most commonly found elements of the Jerusalem lectionary in liturgical manuscripts, present even in the appendices of some Euchologia, are the propers and the readings for general commemorations of saints and for weekdays. General services—including hymns, psalmody, and scriptural readings—for saints who did not have their own proper texts were used instead for their commemorations. As Olga Krasheninnikova has noted, elements of the weekday commemorations of the Oktoechos in the Byzantine rite derive from the most prominent or earliest commemoration of the respective category of saint as it appears in the liturgical year.[155] Thus, in the *Typografsky Ustav*, the reader who looks for a particular pericope is directed to search for the earliest appearance of a category of commemoration according to the order of the liturgical book. For example, the reader must look to the Miracle of the Archangel Michael at Colossae (6 September) for the general service for Angels and Bodiless Hosts and to the Nativity of the Theotokos (8 September) for the general service for the Theotokos, since the part of this liturgical book that deals with the calendar begins with September and these two feasts would be sequentially the first, for any angel or for the Theotokos.[156] Therefore the date to which a liturgical book directs the reader is of great importance.

---

[152] See 'Nota sul Salterio-*Horologion* del IX secolo Torino, Biblioteca Universitaria B.VII.30', in Parenti, *A oriente e occidente di Costantinopoli*, 103–13, here 112.

[153] See *Sinai Gr. 1096* (12th cent.), fol. 27r and 174v; Dmitrievskii, *Описаніе* III, 29 and 62. See Chapter 4, 'Joint Commemorations of New Testament Figures'.

[154] See Mateos, *Typicon*, vol. 2, 315.

[155] Krasheninnikova, 'Седмичные памяти октоиха', 265.

[156] *Типографский Устав: Устав с кондакарем конца XI–начала XII века*, 3 vols, ed. by B. A. Uspensky (Moscow: Языки славянских культур, 2006).

As has been seen with Gospel, Epistle, and Old Testament readings, the Hagiopolitan sources are quite diverse both in terms of their commemorations and in terms of the pericopes they indicate for the commemorations. Table 5.14 summarizes the readings for general commemorations of saints. The information in parentheses is found in each of the manuscripts, in rubrics.

Of these sources, three provide significant information on the readings for general commemorations. These are GL (L), *Sinai Gr. 212* (9th cent.), and *Sinai Ar. 116* (995/6). For the Theotokos, GL (L) prescribes the same readings and hymns from the feast of the Dormition of the Theotokos on 15 August. Similarly, for feasts of the Cross, readers are directed to the feast of the Appearance of the Cross in the Heavens on 7 May.[157] GL (L) also indicates the commemoration of the four Evangelists on June 12 as the primary celebration of the Apostles.[158] Surprisingly, the deposition of James the Brother of the Lord on 25 May serves as the primary celebration for prophets in the GL (L).[159] The themes of the readings are relevant to the celebration of prophets rather than to that of an apostle or a relative of Christ. The lectionary *Sinai Gr. 212* (9th cent.) stipulates that the common reading for dedications, also found in *St Petersburg Gr. RNB 44* (9th cent.), is the reading for the Enkainia of the Anastasis—the most significant celebration of the dedication of a church in the Jerusalem patriarchate.[160]

Marginal notes in other languages offer information not provided by the actual text of the manuscript. For example, the reading for the reposed in *Sinai Gr. 212* (9th cent.) is not indicated as such in Greek, but only in Arabic marginal notes. Similarly, the Arabic rubrics for both readings for angels in *Sinai Ar. 116* (995/6) are indicated as those for St Michael, while the Greek titles in the manuscript simply state 'for archangels' (εἰς ἀρχαγγέλους).[161] These are just two out of many examples showing how important Arabic marginal notes are for supplementing information from Greek liturgical manuscripts.

The Gospel lectionary *Sinai Ar. 116* (995/6) is also one of the few Hagiopolitan liturgical sources to provide readings for weekly commemorations. It is worth noting the presence of the Prophets Jonah and Elias in the cycle of weekly general commemorations, which shows the continued importance of Old Testament figures and local saints. The penitential theme of Monday and Tuesday and the commemoration of the Theotokos on Thursday all point to Sabaite practice, which is confirmed by a ninth-century Sabaite Horologion and by Iovane Zosime's calendar.[162]

[157] GL § 957–63.   [158] Ibid., § 1023.   [159] Ibid., § 989.
[160] *Sinai Gr. 212* (9th cent.), fol. 99r.
[161] Garitte, 'Évangéliaire grec-arabe', 219 and 222.
[162] Krasheninnikova, 'Седмичные памяти октоиха', 263; Mateos, 'Horologion', 62; Parenti, 'Fascicolo ritrovato', 355–6. For more on this question, see 'Octaves' in Chapter 4.

Table 5.14. Readings for general commemorations

	GL (L)[163]	Sinai Gr. 210 (861/2)	St Petersburg RNB Gr. 44 (9th cent.)	Sinai Gr. 212 (9th cent.)	Sinai Ar. 116 (995/6)	Typikon of the Great Church	Vladimir 21/Savva 4 (11th cent.)
Theotokos	Lk 1:39–56 (All of Aug 15)	–	–	Lk 10:38–42	–	–	See Sept 8 (Nativity; Phil 2:5–11) or Nov 21 (Entrance; Heb 9:1–7)
Cross	Mt 23:24–24:1 (All of 7 May)	–	–	–	–	8 options[164]	–
Apostles	1 Cor 4:6–14 Mt 9:35–10:15 (All of June 12)	Mt 19:27–29	1 Cor 4:9–15 Mt 10:1–10	1 Cor 4:9–15 Mt 10:1–15	Mt 10:1–15 *Other:* Lk 10:1–12	–	See June 30 (12 Apostles; 1 Cor 4:9–16)
Prophets	Rom 11:1–12	–	Heb 11:32	1 Cor 12:27–13:3	Mt 5:17–24 *Other:* Mt 5:1–16	–	See 17th Sat (1 Cor 14:20–25) or 23rd Fri (1 Thes 2:14–20)
	Mt 23:34–39 (All of May 25)	–	Mt 10:37–42	Mt 5:17–24 *Other:* Mt 5:13–16 *Other:* Mt 11:25–30			
Martyrs	Eph 6:10–18 Lk 21:12–19	Mt 10:16–[18]	Heb 11:34–37 Mt 10:16–21	Rom 5:1–5 Mt 10:16–22 *Other:* Mt 10:24–33	Mt 10:16–23 *Other:* Mt 10:24–33	–	See March 9 (Forty Martyrs of Sebaste; Heb 12:1–10)
Hierarchs	Col 1:23–2:2 Mt 28:15–20	–	Heb 4:14–5:6 Jn 10:1–10	Heb 4:14–5:6 Jn 10:11–16	Jn 10:1–16	Heb 5:4–6 Jn 10:9–16	See Sept 2 (Heb 7:26–8:2)[165]
Dedications	–	–	1 Cor 3:8–17 Mt 16:13–19	Heb 13:10–16 Mt 16:13–20 (Enkainia of Anastasis)	–	–	–

Angels	—	Heb 1:1–12 Mt 25:31–46	Heb 1:13–2:4 Mt 16:24–27 (Archangels)	Jn 1:43–51 *Other:* Mt 15:31	—	See Nov 8 (St Michael; Heb 2:2–10)
Women	—	2 Cor 4:7–12 Mt 25:1–13	2 Cor 4:7–12 Mt 25:1–13	Mt 25:1 (from Holy Tuesday)	Rom 8:14–21 Mt 8:14–18, 23	See 15th Thurs (Gal 3:23–4:5)
Venerables	—	Gal 5:22–26, 6:1–2 Mt 10:37–42	Mt 5:1–12a	Mt 10:37–42 *Other:* Mt 11:25–30	2 Cor 4:6–10 Jn 12:24–28	See July 16 (4th Council in Chalcedon; Heb 13:7–16)
Reposed	1 Thes 4:13–18 *Other:* 1 Cor 15:12–28 Jn 5:24–30	—	1 Thes 4:13–18 Jn 5:19–24	Jn 5:19–30	6 options[166]	6 options[167]

163 These readings from GL (L) are found in GL § 1437–543, especially in the notes among the variant readings.

164 Mateos, *Typicon*, vol. 2, 188–90. These are readings for the celebration of PRES or for the complete liturgy on Wednesdays and Fridays throughout the year: εἰς τὸν θέλοντα τετράδα καὶ παρασκευὴν λειτουργίας ἐπιτελεῖν, εἴτε καὶ προηγιασμένην εἴτε καὶ τελείας ('for those who would like to celebrate the liturgy, whether the presanctified or the complete liturgy, on Wednesday and Friday'). For more on this practice, see Alexopoulos, *Presanctified Liturgy*, 59–60.

165 This is the feast of St John the Faster, archbishop of Constantinople, and the first commemoration of a hierarch in the liturgical year starting on September 1. The rubric provides five other options. See Andreou, *Praxapostolos*, 407.

166 Mateos, *Typicon*, vol. 1, 194–6.

167 See Andreou, *Praxapostolos*, 404–5.

Table 5.15. Weekday readings

	Sinai Ar. 116 (995/6)		'Euchologium Sinaiticum' (11th cent.)	Contemporary Byzantine Rite Usage[168]
Monday, Tuesday, and Jonah	Lk 11:27–32	Monday	Eph 4:1–7 Mt 22:2–14	Heb 2:2–10 Mt 13:24–43 (Bodiless Powers)
–	–	Tuesday	Eph 5:6 Mk 10:32–45	Acts 13:25–32 Jn 1:29–34 (Forerunner)
Wednesday and Cross	Jn 3:13–21	Wednesday	2 Cor 6:16–7:1 Lk 6:1–10	Phil 2:5–11 Lk 10:38–42; 11: 27–28 (Theotokos)
Thursday and Theotokos	Lk 10:38–42	Thursday	Rm 12:1–3 Lk 11:1–13	1 Cor 4:9–16 Mt 10:1–8 (Apostles)
Friday	Jn 12:27–36	Friday	2 Cor 4:6–16 Mt 9:9–13	1 Cor 1:18–24 Jn 3:13–21 (Cross)
Prophet Elias	Lk 4:25–30	Saturday	Eph 5:8–20 Lk 12:32–40	1 Thes 4:5–17 Jn 5:24–31 (All Saints and Departed)

As Michael Wawryk and Stefano Parenti have pointed out, the weekday cycle found in the Euchologium Sinaiticum, contained in *Sinai Slav. 37 + Sinai Slav. 1/N* (11th cent.),[169] is none other than the octave following the monastic profession borrowed from *Barberini Gr. 336* (8th cent.), with a few minor changes (see Table 5.15).[170]

A comparison of the weekday cycles of *Sinai Ar. 116* with the general weekday readings in contemporary liturgical books of the Byzantine rite confirms what was said above regarding the development of weekly commemorations. This

---

[168] This cycle of pericopes is not found in Gregory, *Textkritik*, but it is found in the Church Slavonic Gospel and in the Epistle books. See Ст҃ое ѐѵⷩⷢ҇нгєлїе (Rome: Monastery of Grottaferrata, 1958), 740; Ап́остолъ (Rome: Monastery of Grottaferrata, 1955), 787–93.

[169] Rajko Nachtigal, *Euchologium sinaiticum: Starocerkvenoslovanski glagolski spomenik*, vol. 2: *Tekst s komentarjem* (Ljubljana: Slovenska akademija znanosti in umetnosti, 1942), 331–5; *Euchologium sinaiticum: Texte slave avec sources grecques et traduction française*, ed. by Jean Frček (PO 25.3, Turnhout: Brepols, 1989), 596–601; Ioannes C. Tarnanidis, *The Slavonic Manuscripts Discovered in 1975 at St Catherine's Monastery on Mount Sinai* (Thessaloniki: Hellenic Association for Slavic Studies, 1988), 79–82.

[170] Parenti and Velkovska, *Barberini 336*, 227–9 (§ 256); Michael Wawryk, 'The Offices of Monastic Initiation in the *Euchologium sinaiticum* and their Greek Sources', *Harvard Ukrainian Studies* 10: 1–2 (1986), 5–47, especially 42–4; Stefano Parenti, 'Il ciclo delle "letture quotidiane" nell'eucologio slavo del Sinai', BBGG (terza serie) 6 (2009), 313–16.

same comparison also reveals a sharp contrast between the weekday pericopes of the Euchologium Sinaiticum, which focus on the themes of following Christ and living the Christian life rather than on themes associated with the commemorations of each day of the week in the pericopes of *Sinai Ar. 116* and in current Byzantine rite usage.

MIXED CYCLES

Studying the connections between the various pericopes of the Jerusalem lectionary and their theological significance is further complicated by the presence of 'mixed cycles', or cycles of readings combined from different distinct traditions. Such 'mixed' rites are quite common during the period of Byzantinization in the liturgical calendars studied in the previous chapter and point to a 'transitional' rite in the process of transformation. This is also the case with the lectionary. A perfect example of this phenomenon is found in *Sinai Gr. 211* (9th cent.).[171] This manuscript contains a Greek uncial Gospel lectionary of 253 folios that contains readings for Saturdays and Sundays throughout the year. Unfortunately the colophon (fol. 250v) is undated and mentions only the patron of the manuscript, a certain Leontius (Λέωντι [sic]). For all intents and purposes, this source follows the standard Byzantine lectionary order and has been catalogued as such in Aland's *Kurzgefaßte Liste*. The opening rubric of the Gospel book (fol. 1r) confirms it:

εὐαγγέλιον σὺν Θ(ε)ῷ ἐκλογάδη τοῦ ἐνιαυτοῦ ὅλου. ἀρχόμενον ἀπὸ τὸ ἅγιον πάσχα, κατὰ Ἰωάννην...	The Gospel book of the whole year, with God, beginning from Holy Pascha, according to John...

Despite the seemingly standard content of the manuscript, there is a peculiar rubric on fol. 131v, which indicates that the order of pericopes follows the lectionary of Jerusalem for Holy Week:

δέον γινώσκειν· ὅτι ἀπὸ δὲ ἄρχεται τὰ εὐαγγέλια κατὰ τὸν κανόνα τῆς ἁγίας πόλεως· ἀπὸ τῶν βαΐων ἑσπέρας τοῦ σαββάτου· καὶ μέχρι τοῦ ἁγίου σαββάτου ἑσπέρας τῆς λειτουργί(ας).	It is necessary to know from whence begin the Gospels according to the canon of the Holy City: from the evening of the Saturday of Palms until Liturgy on the evening of Holy Saturday.

[171] See ℓ 845: U-ℓesk. Aland, *Kurzgefaßte Liste*, 269.

Hence the scriptural readings from the most solemn period of the year—Holy Week—were read according to the tradition of Jerusalem, where the events of Christ's entry into Jerusalem, passion, death, and Resurrection all took place. This illustrates the effect that solemn liturgical seasons often have in preserving certain aspects of liturgical practice.

Another example of mixed pericopes is found in the New Testament manuscript *Sinai Gr. N.E. МГ 2* (9th cent.).[172] In the marginal notes this manuscript indicates readings according to the Jerusalem pericope order for certain feasts, such as Palm Sunday (Ephesians 1:3, fol. 24r) and the Nativity of Christ (Hebrews 1:1, fol. 79r). However, a later hand has added marginal notes that prescribe Epistle readings from Hebrews for the Sundays of Lent (fol. 80v and 89r)—a clear sign of the intrusion of the Constantinopolitan pericope order.

CONCLUSIONS

Despite their limited and fragmentary nature, the sources of the Jerusalem lectionary provide a wealth of information for the study of Hagiopolite liturgy at the turn of the first millennium and shed much light on the process of liturgical Byzantinization in Jerusalem. On the basis of these sources I am able to make the following general conclusions:

1. The great diversity among the pericopes in Hagiopolite liturgical lectionaries makes it difficult to determine whether variations in the pericope order reflect authentic Jerusalem practices or some form of evolution, such as Byzantinization. For lack of a clear explanation for these variations, both Bernard Outtier and Charles Renoux have shown that, in its authentic form, Jerusalem's lectionary (and its liturgy in general) knew a higher level of plasticity and variability than in its later, Byzantinized form.[173] Despite this variability, it is nevertheless possible to separate distinct Greek and Georgian pericope orders within certain lectionary cycles. Whether these sources reflect two distinct, contemporaneous Hagiopolitan traditions or whether one preserves an older, unchanged pericope order is unknown. Kurt Aland's classification of all Greek manuscripts that did not match the Byzantine pericope order as 'Jerusalemite' suggests that the variability within what we call today the Hagiopolite lectionary may in fact be due to the conflation of several local traditions.

---

[172] See 'Structures of the Jerusalem Lectionary: Gospel Cycles' in this chapter.
[173] Outtier, 'Nouveau fragment oncial'; Renoux, 'La lecture biblique', 403.

2. Since individual Gospel and Epistle readings from the Jerusalem lectionary were part of reading cycles, the only way they could be abandoned or changed was through replacement: the whole Jerusalem lectionary could be replaced by the Constantinopolitan lectionary at once, or particular reading cycles could be replaced—such as the Johannine or Marcan cycles, or the readings for Holy Week and Pascha. In some cases the pericopes at the beginning or end of a particular cycle could be chipped away and the central elements retained at the core of that cycle. The observations gained from studying the transformation of the Jerusalem lectionary reveal that Gospel and Epistle cycles cannot be changed gradually, because they function as units. Removing one element would make the whole cycle collapse like a house of cards.

3. Although the Jerusalem pericope order was ultimately lost as a result of liturgical Byzantinization, some of its constitutive elements were preserved or adapted in other forms. This makes them similar to cobblestones, which can be pried out of their place and moved elsewhere. When they are moved around, they often have their edges removed; this makes them fit within a new space. In a similar way, Gospel cycles intended for one period or liturgical season in Jerusalem were adapted to another purpose and use in the synthesized Byzantine rite.

4. The disappearance of Old Testament readings in JAS in the Jerusalem lectionary can be seen as occurring alongside liturgical Byzantinization. Whether Byzantine influence was a causal factor in the loss of Old Testament readings in Jerusalem or was simply coincidental with that loss cannot be proven in the present state of our knowledge. Although the loss—or presence—of Old Testament readings in Constantinople in the Divine Liturgy cannot be conclusively proven, Hagiopolitan liturgical sources bear testimony to a gradual disappearance of Old Testament readings in JAS before the Jerusalem lectionary was completely lost.

Conclusion

Worship in Captivity

The church of Jerusalem experienced multiple captivities between the seventh and thirteenth centuries: first, political subjugation of the Byzantine province of Palestine to Arab caliphs and their Islamic forces from the seventh century on, then displacement of the Greek-praying Christians from the Holy Sepulchre by the western crusaders in the eleventh and twelfth centuries, and, finally, the loss of authentic Hagiopolitan liturgy in favour of a foreign, imperial liturgical tradition promoted by patriarchs from Constantinople in the thirteenth century—what would later be called 'the Byzantine rite'. All three 'captivities' are constituent elements of the phenomenon of the liturgical Byzantinization of the Orthodox patriarchate of Jerusalem. Focusing on the calendar and lectionary as identifying criteria instead of considering only Euchologia or liturgical books that contained the services for Holy Week has revealed numerous ignored, unexamined, or inedited Hagiopolitan liturgical sources. Their historical context shows that the devastating events of the Muslim Arab conquest in 638 and the destruction of the Anastasis in 1009 did not have as detrimental an effect on Hagiopolitan liturgy as scholars previously thought. Just as in other periods of Christian history, liturgical changes and trends were evolutionary and not revolutionary, which means that they were not suddenly instituted by influential individuals such as patriarchs or emperors, in response to the changed situation of the church imposed by caliphs after the Arab conquest.[1] Instead, the main protagonists in liturgical Byzantinization were scribes, often monks and priests, who copied liturgical books for the Hagiopolitan Christian communities. Many of these scribes were anonymous; few are known by name, and even fewer have left behind any information about themselves at all.

Nevertheless, the liturgical manuscripts they copied and their historical contexts confirm that the process of Byzantinization was gradual. JAS continued

---

[1] See Bradshaw, *Search for Origins*, 65–7.

to be served in Jerusalem into the twelfth century, although its structure had been affected over time by the rupture between its variable hymnography and the disappearing Hagiopolitan lectionary that inspired the themes of these hymns. Jerusalem's turbulent environment and changing topography were unable to provide the conditions for maintaining its indigenous liturgical tradition. Instead there was a trend towards the generalization and universalization of the calendar and lectionary, at the expense of their local character. Universal commemorations of Hagiopolitan origin were accepted into the calendar of Constantinople, which explains why Constantinopolitan liturgy has often been considered 'Jerusalemized' or 'Palestinized'. But lesser commemorations of saints in the universal calendar came to be celebrated almost invariably on dates connected to Constantinople. The liturgical commemorations of St John the Baptist and St James the Brother of the Lord are two of many examples. Because the universal Byzantine calendar that ultimately arrived in Jerusalem incorporated both Constantinopolitan and Hagiopolitan elements, the process of supressing local Hagiopolitan liturgical practice can rightly be called 'Byzantinization' rather than 'Constantinopolitanization'; and this reflects an awareness of the synthetic nature of the Byzantine rite. Certain scriptural reading cycles or hymns were also reused and recycled within the Byzantine rite in other forms, once more contributing to the synthetic nature of the Byzantine rite calendar and lectionary. All this reveals that the Byzantinization of the Jerusalem patriarchate was not consciously or systematically imposed by Constantinople upon Jerusalem and that the process was a gradual and spontaneous liturgical reform.

My focus on JAS, the liturgical calendar, and the lectionary of Jerusalem has been able to trace *what* changed in Jerusalem's liturgy and *when* it changed. For lack of any clear explanation of these liturgical changes by patriarchs of either Jerusalem or Constantinople, by Arab caliphs in control of Jerusalem, or by Byzantine emperors from Constantinople who defended Byzantine Orthodoxy, definitive answers to the question of *how* Byzantinization occurred remain speculative. The destruction of holy sites, the exile of Hagiopolitan patriarchs, the persecution of Christians in Palestine, and the prestige of Constantinople played a role in drawing the church of Jerusalem closer to Constantinople in its time of difficulty. The Byzantine imperial patronage of Manuel I Comnenus during the twelfth century was felt not only in the mosaics and adornment of the holy sites but also in liturgical books such as the Diakonikon *Sinai Gr. 1040*, which demonstrate that Byzantine emperors and Constantinopolitan patriarchs were commemorated in the diptychs of Hagiopolitan liturgies.[2] Even so, the decision to Byzantinize the liturgy of Jerusalem, to bring it in line with the liturgical practices of fellow Chalcedonian Christians in the Byzantine empire,

---

[2] See Appendix 1.

and to distinguish it from the practices of non-Chalcedonians in neighbouring Syria or Egypt was taken by local clergy and scribes at the Holy Sepulchre in Jerusalem, at Mar Saba Lavra in the Judean desert, at the monastery of Mount Sinai, and in the northern regions of the patriarchate in Palestinian Samaria, between the liturgical influence of Jerusalem and Antioch, as confirmed by liturgical manuscripts.

Further studies of the phenomenon of liturgical Byzantinization will find answers from the city of Antioch.[3] Jerusalem was definitively lost to the Byzantines in the seventh century; by contrast, Antioch's recapture in the tenth century put it on the front line of political contact with the eastern patriarchates and made it a bridge from which liturgical influence could spread southward, to Palestine and Jerusalem. Joseph-Marie Sauget realized that the centre of diffusion of a specifically Melkite calendar was Antioch, from where it eventually spread to Jerusalem and Alexandria.[4] This is apparent from liturgical manuscripts and their historical context. The mandate of Patriarch John of Antioch to 'bring order [*rattaba*] to the church of Cassian in Antioch, based on the model [*mithāl*] of St Sophia in Constantinople', shows how Byzantinization was imposed during the reign of Emperor Basil II at the end of the tenth century.[5] The exact way in which this calendar spread from Antioch to Jerusalem is unknown, but several manuscripts copied near Antioch in the eleventh century offer some clues. The Christian Palestinian Aramaic Gospel book in *Vatican Syr. 19* (1030), which Abbot Elias copied near Antioch and brought with him to his monastery in northern Palestine, reveals how books reflecting the liturgical changes imposed on Antioch travelled south—into the patriarchate of Jerusalem.[6] The region of Antioch was home to numerous monasteries where monks were able to observe first-hand the front line between Constantinopolitan and Hagiopolitan liturgical contact. Nicon of the Black Mountain sought to understand the differences between the two traditions but was disappointed to learn that even those who understood them—the monks of St Sabas Lavra—were unable to answer his questions and generally uninterested in the problems he pointed out to them.[7]

---

[3] Cyril Korolevsky, *Christian Antioch*, ed. by Bishop Nicholas Samra, trans. by John Collorafi (Fairfax, VA: Eastern Christian Publications, 2003); Todt, 'Griechisch-orthodoxe (Melkitische) Christen'; Todt, 'Region und griechisch-orthodoxes Patriarchat von Antiocheia'; Todt, 'Zwischen Kaiser und ökumenischem Patriarchen'; Wendy Mayer and Pauline Allen, *The Churches of Syrian Antioch (300–638 CE)* (Leuven: Peeters, 2012).

[4] Sauget, *Synaxaires Melkites*, 176.

[5] Yaḥyā al-Anṭakī, *History* II, 445–6. See Chapter 2, 'Byzantine Contact'.

[6] See Chapter 2, 'Byzantine Contact', and Appendix 1.

[7] *Das Taktikon des Nikon vom Schwarzen Berge*, 46–7. For other monasteries in the region of Antioch, see Wachtang Z. Djobadze, *Materials for the Study of Georgian Monasteries in the Western Environs of Antioch on the Orontes* (CSCO 372, Subsidia, Tomus 48, Louvain: Secrétariat du CorpusSCO, 1976).

This is, however, only one example of how Byzantinization occurred. How exactly the liturgical books of Constantinople found their way to Mar Saba and Mount Sinai at least fifty years earlier, where Iovane Zosime could consult them to compile his calendar, still remains to be explained.[8] One can presume that the multilingual monastic communities of Mar Saba and Mount Sinai, along with their connections to pilgrims from Constantinople, Mount Athos, and other parts of the Byzantine Empire, help to explain how the libraries of both monasteries came to possess numerous liturgical books that were not Hagiopolite, Sabaite, or Sinaitic, but often Constantinopolitan, Byzantine, or of yet other liturgical traditions. That Constantinopolitan and Byzantine books would have been used at Mar Saba is not surprising, if one considers the role of Palestinian monasticism at the service of Orthodox doctrine and the Byzantine church in the period after the Arab conquest. In the absence of virtually any information on Sabaite liturgical practices between the sixth-century hagiographies of Cyril of Scythopolis and the twelfth century, when we have the first extant copy of the Sabaite Typikon and Testament preserved in codex *Sinai Gr. 1096*, it is difficult to say more about Byzantinization at St Sabas Lavra—for example at the time of Iovane Zosime in the tenth century. In any case, the fact that the calendar of the Sabaite Typikon in the twelfth century bears hardly any traces of its Hagiopolitan origins suggests that Byzantinization had taken hold within Sabaite monasticism sooner than at the Holy Sepulchre in Jerusalem, where the copyist of the Typikon of the Anastasis, the monk Basil the Hagiopolite, had made significant efforts to preserve Jerusalemite liturgical practices.[9]

Nevertheless, examination of other liturgical manuscripts may provide new information, and new explanations may be found once these sources become more accessible through study. This problem will certainly be remedied through better editions and more detailed analyses, both of those texts known for centuries but never closely examined and of unedited manuscripts such as those described in Appendix 1. Once that is done, it will remain to analyse these texts with an awareness of the dynamic exchange and interaction between the local liturgies of Constantinople and Jerusalem in the formation of the Byzantine rite. The various languages and the interconnections between the various contents of these liturgical manuscripts will also be able to better elucidate the linguistic composition of the Jerusalem patriarchate, thereby shedding more light on what it meant to identify oneself as 'Byzantine' (Rūm), clarifying the use of the term 'Melkite' both self-referentially and in relation to others, and establishing what the criteria were for identifying someone as a native Hagiopolitan or Palestinian Christian familiar with the

---

[8] See Chapter 2, 'Georgian Monastic Liturgy', and Appendix 1.
[9] Patrich, *Sabaite Heritage*; Booth, *Crisis of Empire*. See Chapter 2, 'Hagiopolitan Patriarchs in Exile'; also Appendix 1.

local liturgical tradition or as a foreigner with his or her own expressions of Orthodox Christian worship. The identity-forming role that liturgy played in Byzantium generally, and in particular for those Hagiopolitan Christians who began praying in Jerusalem as the Byzantines did in Constantinople as a result of Byzantinization, has not received the attention it deserves.[10]

The exchange of one calendar and lectionary for another, which is at the heart of the phenomenon of Hagiopolite liturgical Byzantinization examined here, raises the question of a change of tradition and a change of theology. The change of one's liturgical tradition signals a crisis of identity and a loss of the necessary understanding of that tradition. Can such a crisis of tradition and a change of theology be traced in the liturgical sources? Is the change in theology of the lectionary comparable to the change in the theology of baptism around the fourth century, from the Johannine emphasis on new birth in the Spirit expressed in John 3 to the Pauline accent on dying with Christ in Romans 6?[11] The absence of a Hagiopolite liturgical commentary after the time of St Cyril of Jerusalem means that any answer is merely hypothetical. No theologian of the time noted this change or commented on its theological significance. Hence understanding it in the *theologia prima* (as David Fagerberg calls it)[12]—that is, in the meaning that resides in the structure of the liturgy rather than in its symbolic interpretation—is left to scholars who study the manuscripts of Jerusalem's extinct liturgical tradition.

While this question remains open, observing a theological change also depends upon perspective. A *sticheron* sung today in the Byzantine rite in connection with the Cross serves as an example:

Σήμερον τὸ προφητικὸν πεπλήρωται λόγιον, ἰδοὺ γὰρ προσκυνοῦμεν εἰς τὸν τόπον, οὗ ἔστησαν οἱ πόδες σου Κύριε, καὶ ξύλου σωτηρίας γευσάμενοι, τῶν ἐξ ἁμαρτίας παθῶν ἐλευθερίας ἐτύχομεν, πρεσβείαις τῆς Θεοτόκου, μόνε Φιλάνθρωπε.[13]	Today the words of the prophet have been fulfilled: behold, we worship at the place on which your feet have stood [cf. Psalm 131:7], Lord; and tasting from the tree of salvation, we have been delivered from our sinful passions at the prayers of the Mother of God, O only lover of mankind.

[10] See Angeliki E. Laiou, 'The Foreigner and the Stranger in 12th-Century Byzantium: Means of Propitiation and Acculturation', in *Fremde der Gesellschaft*, ed. by Marie Theres Fögen (Frankfurt: Klostermann, 1991), 71–97; Gill Page, *Being Byzantine: Greek Identity before the Ottomans* (Cambridge: Cambridge University Press, 2008); Averil Cameron, *Byzantine Matters* (Princeton, NJ: Princeton University Press, 2014), 87–111 (Chapter 5: 'The Very Model of Orthodoxy?').

[11] See Maxwell Johnson, 'Крещение и Миропомазание в египетской традиции III–IV веков', ПУЦТ, vol. 1, 234–56, here 255.

[12] David W. Fagerberg, *Theologia prima: What Is Liturgical Theology?* (Chicago, IL: Hillenbrand, 2004), 19.

[13] 'Tone 6, sessional hymn after the third ode of the canon at matins, third Sunday of Great Lent'. Follieri, *Initia hymnorum*, vol. 3, 495. This hymn is also found as the fourth troparion at

The paraphrase of Psalm 131:7[14] raises the question: Is the place where his feet stood the Cross, his footstool (ὑποπόδιον, cf. Psalm 109:1, Hebrews 1:13), or literally the place where Christ's feet stood (ὁ τόπος, οὗ ἔστησαν οἱ πόδες αὐτοῦ) in Jerusalem on Golgotha? Since Psalm 131, 'a hymn of ascent', was a pilgrimage song for pilgrims to the holy sites of Jerusalem[15] and is not used in the GL in connection with the Cross, both interpretations seem possible, depending on one's perspective. Patristic commentaries appear to be silent about this verse, allowing for both interpretations.[16] However, this, too, remains an open question and points to the problem that it is always possible to find that which one is seeking. On the basis of what has been presented in this book, it is hoped that at least the label of 'historicism' will cease to be applied to Hagiopolite liturgical practices, as has been done in the past.[17]

Should these conclusions affect liturgical practice today? Robert Taft's closing remarks in his detailed study of the Great Entrance insisted that 'all we have proposed is quite modest: *that the rites be restored to what they were always intended to be*'.[18] The question before me in this study was different, and one should not expect or hope for the full restoration or revival of the lost liturgical tradition of Jerusalem. Any such hopes would ignore the synthetic nature of the Byzantine rite of the Orthodox liturgical tradition, of which the Orthodox Church of Jerusalem is a crucial part. Such an expectation would, likewise, ignore the fact that liturgy is a living tradition of the church that cannot simply be reset to a particular point in history.

Nevertheless, it is worth relating the observations of this study to the contemporary practice of the Orthodox Church. I propose three observations to this effect. First, any celebration of JAS in today's Byzantine rite should avoid treating the Divine Liturgy as an exercise in exotic historical revivalism. Although this is not specified in any of the rubrics found in the manuscripts of JAS examined in Chapter 3, the liturgy today is often celebrated *versus*

---

matins for the Exaltation of the Cross in the Typikon of the Great Church. See Mateos, *Typicon*, vol. 1, 28.

[14] Εἰσελευσώμεθα εἰς τὰ σκηνώματα αὐτοῦ· προσκυνήσωμεν εἰς τὸν τόπον οὗ ἔστησαν οἱ πόδες αὐτοῦ. The Revised Standard Version (RSV) translates the verse as 'Let us go to his dwelling place; let us worship at his footstool'.

[15] John S. Ksleman, SS, and Michael L. Barré, SS, 'Psalms', in *New Jerome Biblical Commentary*, ed. by Raymond E. Brown, SS, Joseph A. Fitzmyer, SJ, and Roland E. Murphy, OCarm (Englewood Cliffs, NJ: Prentice Hall, 1990), 524.

[16] See *Psalms 51–150*, ed. by Quentin F. Wesselschmidt (Downers Grove, IL: InterVarsity Press, 2007), 365–8.

[17] For a corrective to the label of historicism often applied to Jerusalem's liturgy, see Taft, *Beyond East and West*, 44–5.

[18] Taft, *Great Entrance*, 428. Emphasis in the original. Since writing those words in 1975, Taft has changed his view and often referred to himself as a 'liturgical informer' rather than a 'liturgical reformer'. See Robert F. Taft, 'Response to the Berakah Award: Anamnesis', in id., *Beyond East and West*, 281–305; Robert F. Taft, 'Good Bye to All That: Swansong of an Old Academician', SVTQ 59.2 (2015), 129–61.

populum, that is, with the presider facing West behind the altar, in a way familiar to many western Christians after the liturgical reforms since the last third of the twentieth century. Likewise, anything the celebrants imagine to be accretions of an unspecified, later period—such as wearing mitres or baroque vestments, placing tabernacles on the altar, or using Communion spoons to distribute Communion to the faithful—is removed.[19] For the very same people, such innovations to the liturgical celebration of JAS would be unimaginable in the usual liturgies of CHR or BAS today. Nevertheless, they are considered acceptable or even proper when celebrating JAS. If, however, JAS is to be treated as an assimilated and Byzantinized Divine Liturgy of the Byzantine rite today, it should be celebrated according the formularies of BAS and CHR, but with the unique prayers of JAS. In today's practice both BAS and CHR share the same structure, which is familiar to the clergy and to the faithful alike. The only difference between the two lies in the different prayers recited by the presider and in the several hymns sung by the faithful. If this Divine Liturgy is to be treated as a Hagiopolite eucharistic liturgy, the proper hymnody, psalmody, and scriptural readings should be employed, especially since these sources are now known and accessible. The currently precarious position of JAS in the Orthodox Church requires greater reflection. Second, this study should raise awareness of the legitimacy of local liturgical practices, which the imposition of universal uniformity has often done away with. History teaches us that different ways of praying, reading scripture in the lectionary, and celebrating the memory of saints existed legitimately and contemporaneously. Third, and perhaps most importantly, people should become aware of the fact that churches can be Orthodox, adhering to Chalcedonian Christology and to the teachings of at least the first seven ecumenical councils without having to worship in a manner imposed on them from the outside or in keeping with the order and *taxis* of another, distant patriarchate. In other words, it is possible to be united by a universal, Orthodox faith and still worship in a varied manner, authentic to the local church. This should not be mistaken as a promotion of 'bi-ritualism' or as a relativistic approach to liturgical practice, but rather be understood as an expression of authentic unity in diversity. Such a conclusion arises from an honest examination of the historical sources: the Orthodox patriarchate of Jerusalem, faithful to Chalcedonian Christology and remaining in Communion with the patriarchate of Constantinople up to the present day, had its own authentic, uninterrupted, home-grown liturgical tradition, with a distinct eucharistic Divine Liturgy, a local calendar, and a unique lectionary— and it was still Orthodox. For Patriarch Theodore Balsamon in the twelfth century, the possibility that someone would pray according to a different rite

---

[19] For a study of the Greek nineteenth-century edition of JAS, see Brakmann and Chronz, 'Eine Blume der Levante'; Michael Zheltov, 'Литургия апостола Иакова', ПЭ 41: 244–53, esp. 251–3.

and yet be faithful to Chalcedonian Christology and defend communion with Constantinople was incomprehensible and unwelcome.[20] Such thinking accompanies a shift in emphasis from the canon of Scripture in the lectionaries read in the local stational liturgy of the church of Jerusalem to the canons and legislation of church councils—a shift perceptible in the mosaics of the Church of the Nativity in Bethlehem, where quotations from canonical texts line the walls of the basilica, rather than Old Testament prophecies or Gospel narratives of the birth of Christ.[21] The perspective of contemporary Orthodox theologians has since changed, and authentic liturgical diversity united in a common faith is understood, even if it is far from being lived and put into practice.[22]

As ruthless devastation, earthquakes, war, and foreign invasions progressively erased the landscape of the sacred and sanctified topography of Jerusalem—the place where Christ's feet stood—the scribes of the Holy City's Orthodox patriarchate rewrote the cycle of its feasts and commemorations like a palimpsest, superimposing the holy days of Constantinople, a city that had tried to emulate Jerusalem for centuries. Arab caliphs contributed to the destruction of the holy sites and to general instability, while Byzantine emperors and patriarchs in Constantinople observed from afar. Once the process of Byzantinization was complete, the Holy City—centre and birthplace of Christianity—lost its unique eucharistic liturgy, its distinct calendar of holy days, its unique lectionary for biblical readings, and its own liturgical theology and exegetical framework for understanding Scripture and became just another city of the Byzantine periphery.

---

[20] See Chapter 2, 'Theodore Balsamon and the Rite of Constantinople'.
[21] See Chapter 1, 'Stational Liturgy and the Topography of Jerusalem'.
[22] See Nicolas Lossky, 'Orthodoxie et diversités liturgiques', in *Liturgie et cultures: Conférences Saint-Serge, XLIIIe Semaine d'études liturgiques, Paris, 25–28 juin 1996*, ed. by Achille M. Triacca and Alessandro Pistoia (BELS 90, Rome: Edizioni Liturgiche, 1997), 137–41.

Liturgical Manuscripts

Writing of the liturgical historian's method, Anton Baumstark stated: 'the extant documents will always occupy the first place'.[1] This is especially true of the study of a liturgical tradition that no longer exists or is no longer celebrated, such as Jerusalem's liturgy during the Byzantine period. Delving into these texts makes the liturgical historian immediately aware of the numerous pitfalls accompanying the study of manuscripts. Some manuscripts without colophons naturally elicit concerns about dating and localization, drawing attention to the problems of giving more weight to criteria of palaeographic evaluation or to subjective impressions.[2] In addition to such concerns, scholars examining a liturgical manuscript must ask themselves how faithful the written text is as a witness of actual liturgical practice. Examples from contemporary liturgical services point to great disparities between theory—the way the service is intended to be celebrated according to the written text—and practice—the way the service is in reality celebrated, either by incorporating unwritten rites and texts that the celebrant and the faithful would be expected to know through handed down traditions, or by being abbreviated. Whether the scribe faithfully transmitted a liturgical text and rite as it was celebrated or copied an idealized or outdated model of a liturgical service is difficult (if not impossible) to confirm for many of the liturgical manuscripts presented in this Appendix. Although this is worth reflecting upon, it is not germane to this study to delve into such questions or to challenge the work of scholars competent in this field; all discussions of dating and localization will rely first on the codicological and palaeographic analysis carried out by specialists. Only then, in the context of this background information, will the liturgical content be examined and presented. Nevertheless, one should always be aware that older catalogues are not always reliable when examining the dating or the contents of liturgical manuscripts.

The last century has produced numerous resources for the study of manuscripts, especially for those that today find their home at the Monastery of St Catherine on Mount Sinai.[3] Due to its remote location and dry climate, the Sinai Monastery became a treasury and a repository of manuscripts, icons, and other precious articles that was able to withstand the ravages of time and marauding invaders. The collection of Greek

---

[1] Baumstark, *Comparative Liturgy*, 2.

[2] For more on the question of manuscript dating, see the comments of Guglielmo Cavallo, Paul Canart, Nigel G. Wilson, Ernst Gamillscheg, Jean Irigoin, and Giancarlo Prato as participants in a round table discussion at the fifth Colloquio Internazionale di Paleografia Greca held in Cremona, Italy, in 1998: 'Per la datazione e la localizzazione delle scritture greche: Tavola rotunda coordinata da Giancarlo Prato', in *Manoscritti greci*, vol. 2, 669–707.

[3] See Murad Kamil, *Catalogue of all manuscripts in the Monastery of St Catharine on Mount Sinai* (Wiesbaden: Otto Harrassowitz, 1970); *St Catherine's Monastery at Mount Sinai: Its Manuscripts and Their Conservation*, ed. by Cyril A. Mango and Marlia M. Mango (London: Saint Catherine Foundation, 2011).

manuscripts was catalogued several times and partially photographed in 1950 by an expedition of the Library of Congress in Washington, DC.[4] The 'new finds' of 1975 were catalogued under the direction of Panagiotes G. Nikolopoulos.[5]

Georgian manuscripts also form an important part of the Sinai collection and were catalogued extensively by scholars from the Georgian Academy of Sciences' Institute of Manuscripts in Tbilisi. Catalogues of the Georgian manuscripts on Sinai from the original collection are divided thematically into three volumes: the *Iadgari*, or Tropologion;[6] Athonite hymnals and Typika;[7] and lectionaries, hymnals, and other liturgical collections.[8] A catalogue of the Georgian 'new finds' has also appeared recently, along with catalogues of the Syriac and Arabic 'new finds'.[9] All these resources make it possible to study the liturgy of the multilingual environment of the Jerusalem patriarchate. These catalogues, however, give only part of the picture and cannot replace examination of the manuscripts themselves, which often reveal details beyond the interests of even the finest cataloguers.

[4] See, for example, Vladimir N. Beneshevich, Описаніе Греческихъ Рукописей монастыря Святой Екатерины на Синаѣ: *Catalogus codicum manuscriptorum graecorum qui in monasterio Sanctae Catharinae in monte Sina asservantur* (St Petersburg: Kirschbaum, 1911–17); Clark, *Sinai Checklist*; Kenneth W. Clark, 'Exploring the Manuscripts of Sinai and Jerusalem', *The Biblical Archaeologist* 16.2 (1953), 21–43. See also 'Online Resources' for digital access to many of these manuscripts.

[5] For an account of the discovery, see Nikolopoulos, Νέα εὑρήματα, 71–137. This catalogue should be considered along with Géhin and Frøshov, 'Nouvelles découvertes sinaïtiques'; Giuseppe de Gregorio, 'Materiali vecchi e nuovi per uno studio della minuscola greca fra VII e IX secolo', in *Manoscritti greci*, vol. 1, 83–151, esp. 149–51. See also Gregorios Sinaites, 'Τὸ ἀρχειακὸν ὑλικὸν τῶν εὑρημάτων τοῦ ἔτους 1975 εἰς τὴν Ἱ. Μονὴν Σινᾶ', in *Paleografia e codicologia greca: Atti del II Colloquio internazionale (Berlino-Wolfenbüttel, 17–21 ottobre 1983)*, vol. 1, ed. by Dieter Harlfinger and Giancarlo Prato (Turin: Edizioni dell'Orso, 1991), 571–7.

[6] *Description I: Sinai Geo. O.* 1, 14, 18, 20, 26, 34, 40, 41, 49, 59, 64, 65, and H2123.

[7] *Description II: Sinai Geo. O.* 5, 70, 75, 3, 13, 17, 21, 67, 96, 4, 61, 7/2, 9, 56, 69, 82, 92, 93, 94, and 95.

[8] *Description III: Sinai Geo. O.* 10, 12, 37, 47, 53, 54, 63, 66, 72, 73, 74, 76, 77, 83, 88, 89, 90, H1664, H2124, and 81 (Cagareli) add.

[9] Georgian: Aleksidze et al., *Catalogue of Georgian Manuscripts*. Those who intend to consult this trilingual Greek, Georgian, and English catalogue should be aware of crucial typographical errors. For example, *Sin. Geo. N.* 1, a copy of the eleventh-century Typikon of George Mt'acmideli (the Hagiorite), is incorrectly presented in English as a tenth-century manuscript (but correctly in Greek and Georgian). For further bibliography on Georgian liturgical and biblical texts, see Tinatin Chronz, 'Editionen georgischer liturgischer Texte', in *Bibel, Liturgie und Frömmigkeit in der Slavia Byzantina: Festgabe für Hans Rothe zum 80. Geburtstag*, ed. by Dagmar Christians, Dieter Stern, and Vittorio S. Tomelleri (Studies on Language and Culture in Central and Eastern Europe 3, München: Verlag Otto Sagner, 2009), 177–93; Metzger, *Early Versions of the New Testament*, 182–5; Frøshov, 'The Georgian Witness', 227–67. For Syriac manuscripts, see Sebastian P. Brock, *Catalogue of Syriac Fragments (New Finds) in the Library of the Monastery of Saint Catherine, Mount Sinai* (Athens: Mount Sinai Foundation, 1995); Philothée, *Nouveaux Manuscrits Syriaques*; Nasrallah, 'Liturgie des Patriarcats melchites'; and J. F. Coakley, 'Manuscripts', GEDSH, 262–4. For Arabic manuscripts see Yiannis E. Meimaris, Κατάλογος τῶν Νέων Ἀραβικῶν Χειρογράφων τῆς Ἱερᾶς Μονῆς τῆς Ἁγίας Αἰκατερίνης τοῦ Ὄρους Σινᾶ (Athens: Ἐθνικὸ Ἵδρυμα Ἐρευνῶν, 1985). See also Nasrallah, *Histoire* II.1, II.2, III.1.

Finally, as regards the structure of my review, all manuscripts considered in this section, regardless of their liturgical contents, are presented in chronological order. This facilitates subsequent diachronic analysis of the evolution of liturgical sources within particular language groups, as well as a synchronic analysis of specific liturgical elements, such as particular commemorations in the sanctoral or individual pericopes of the lectionary. This list of Hagiopolite liturgical manuscripts also follows the criteria established in Chapter 1, with particular attention to the liturgical calendar and lectionary, and does not pretend to be exhaustive.

Sinai Gr. N.E. ΜΓ 56 and *Sinai Gr. N.E. ΜΓ 5* (8th–9th cent.)

The two manuscripts *Sinai Gr. N.E. ΜΓ 56* and *Sinai Gr. N.E. ΜΓ 5* contain a Tropologion that follows the canon, or liturgical order, of the Church of the Anastasis in Jerusalem for all the feasts of the year: 'With God, the Tropologion of all the feasts of the saints for the whole year according to the canon of the Church of the Resurrection of Christ our God' ('*Σὺν Θεῷ τροπολόγιον πασῶν τῶν ἁγίων ἑορτῶν παντὸς τοῦ ἔτους κατὰ τὸν κανόνα τε τῆς Χριστοῦ τοῦ Θεοῦ ἡμῶν ἀναστάσεως*').[10] The two fragmentary codices were dated to the end of the eighth or beginning of the ninth century and confirmed to belong to one and the same Tropologion by Stig Frøyshov during a visit to Mount Sinai in April 2001.[11] Alexandra Nikiforova has subsequently studied and described the two manuscripts as part of a wider investigation of the evolution of the Menaion.[12] The extant five folios from *Sinai Gr. N.E. ΜΓ 56* begin with the canon of the pre-feast of the Nativity of Christ,[13] although the rubric itself does not indicate that it is for the pre-feast, but simply a *κανὼν ἁγίων γενεθλίων* ('canon of the holy Nativity', fol. 1r).[14] The service for Christmas itself continues in *Sinai Gr. N.E. ΜΓ 5*, which contains 240 folios. The remainder of the manuscript contains seventy-three commemorations, from the pre-feast of the Nativity of Christ to the commemoration of Joseph of Arimathea (12 June), at which point the manuscript is defective. The movable Lenten cycle is inserted between Hypapante (2 February) and the feast of the Great Martyr George (23 April). This manuscript includes 'hymns sung on Meatfare Sunday' (*τροπάρια ψαλλόμενα τῇ κυριακῇ τῶν ἀποκρέων*), through Holy Week and Pascha, until the Sunday of the Myrrhbearing Women.[15]

Sinai Gr. 210 [with additional fragments] (861/2)

My next source is a Gospel lectionary, *Sinai Gr. 210*, from the end of the ninth century. It is currently in four fragments written on parchment: *Sinai Gr. 210* (188 fol.); *Sinai*

---

[10] *Sinai Gr. N.E. ΜΓ 56*, fol. 1r. Nikolopoulos, *Νέα εὑρήματα*, 150 and table 11. For *Sinai Gr. N.E. ΜΓ 5*, see Nikolopoulos, *Νέα εὑρήματα*, 142 and table 49.

[11] See Frøyshov, *Horologe 'géorgien'*, 399.

[12] Nikiforova, 'Сокрытое сокровище'; Nikiforova, *Из истории Минеи в Византии*, 195–235; Nikiforova, 'The Oldest Greek Tropologion'.

[13] Incipit: *Ἔσωσε λαὸν θαυματουργῶν δεσπότης* ('The Old Master Who Works Wonders Saved a People'). Follieri, *Initia hymnorum*, vol. 1, 542.

[14] Nikiforova, 'Сокрытое сокровище', 9.

[15] For a description of the contents of these manuscripts, see Krivko, 'Гимнографические параллели', 87–8; Nikiforova, 'Сокрытое сокровище', 9–12.

Gr. N.E. Σπ. ΜΓ 12 (31 fol.);[16] *St Petersburg BAN K'pel 194* (4 fol.);[17] and *Sinai Gr. Harris Appendix* 16.22 (3 fol.).[18] Kurt Aland has classified it as a fragmentary uncial script selected Gospel lectionary (i.e. ἐκλογάδιον) according to the Jerusalem pericope order.[19] Both the manuscript's larger dimensions (approximately 350 by 210 mm) and its ink decoration[20] suggest that it was used for more solemn occasions in a prestigious locale. On one verso of *Sinai Gr. N.E. Σπ. ΜΓ 12* we find a damaged inscription, which reads:

εἰς δόξαν καὶ ἔπαινον τῆς ἁγίας ὁμ[ο]ουσίου ἀκτίστου κ[αὶ] ζωοποιοῦ τριάδος. [π](ατ)ρ(ὸ)ς καὶ υ(ἱο)ῦ καὶ ἁγίου πν(εύματο)ς· καὶ εἰς κόσμον καὶ εὐκλαιεῖαν τῆς ἁγιωτάτης ἐκκλησίας . . .	To the glory and praise of the holy, consubstantial, uncreated, and life-creating Trinity, Father and Son and Holy Spirit, and to the world and the glory of the most-holy church . . .
ἐγράφη καὶ ἐτελε[ι]ώθη τὸ ἱερὸν [καὶ ἅγιον] ἐκλογάδιν τ[ῶν ἁγίων] εὐαγγελίω[ν πασῶν] τῶν ἑορτ[ῶν ἅμα καὶ] κυριακῶν [τοῦ ὅλου] ἔτους· μη(νὸς) . . . ἔτους κόσμ[ου ἀπὸ ἀ]δὰμ ,[ςτ]ο· ἰ[ν]δ(ικτιῶνος) . . . σπουδῇ καὶ π[όνω καὶ] προθυμία· [. . . φιλο]χρίστου ἀδ[ελφοῦ καὶ] διακόνου [ναοῦ τῶν] πανευφήμ[ων ἀποστόλων] ἐγράφη ἐν τῇ μ[ονῇ τοῦ] ἁγίου π(ατ)ρ(ὸ)ς ἡμῶ[ν] . . .[21]	the sacred and holy selection [ἐκλογάδιν] of the holy Gospels of all the feasts along with Sundays of the whole year. [In the] month . . . [in the] year of the [creation of the] world from Adam, 6370 [861/2], of the Indiction . . . by the zeal and toil and will . . . of the beloved by Christ, brother and deacon of the church of the all-praised Apostles, written in the monastery of our holy father . . .

Politis suggests that the monastery mentioned may be that of St Sabas.[22] Dieter Harlfinger, Diether Roderich Reinsch, and Joseph A. M. Sonderkamp do not dismiss this suggestion, confirming that 'our Gospel lectionary not only represents the Palestinian textual tradition by its content . . . but also through its script and binding serves as an important witness of a larger group of Palestinian–Sinaitic codices written in inclined ogive uncial'.[23]

---

[16] Harlfinger, Reinsch, and Sonderkamp, *Specimina sinaitica*, 13, indicates 19 fols, while Aland, *Kurzgefaßte Liste*, 269, indicates 31 fols. Fragments are not indicated in Nikolopoulos, Νέα εὑρήματα.

[17] These fragments have been published in Описание Рукописного Отдела Библиотеки Академии Наук СССР, vol. 5, Греческие Рукописи, ed. by Irina N. Lebedeva (Leningrad: Наука, 1973), 19–20.

[18] The location of the 'Harris Appendix' is not altogether clear, as neither Aland, *Kurzgefaßte Liste*, nor the inventory of the Monastery of St Catherine on Mount Sinai provide further details.

[19] ℓ 844 + ℓ 1271 + ℓ 1273: U-ℓsel † (Jerusalem). Aland, *Kurzgefaßte Liste*, 269. See also Harlfinger, Reinsch, and Sonderkamp, *Specimina sinaitica*, 13–14, frontispiece, and tables 1–4; Ivan Karabinov, Постная Тріодъ: Историческій обзоръ ея плана, состава, редакцій и славянскихъ переводовъ (St Petersburg: Типографія В. Д. Смирнова, 1910), 25–6.

[20] Leslie Brubaker, 'Greek Manuscript Decoration in the Ninth and Tenth Centuries: Rethinking Centre and Periphery', in *Manoscritti greci*, vol. 2, 513–33, esp. 516–23.

[21] Transcription with proposed missing text from Harlfinger, Reinsch, and Sonderkamp, *Specimina sinaitica*, 13.

[22] Linos Politis, 'Nouveaux manuscrits grecs découverts au Mont Sinaï', *Scriptorium* 34 (1980), 5–17, here 10–11.

[23] [U]*nser Evangelienlektionar ist nicht nur inhaltlich ein Vertreter der palästinesischen Texttradition . . . sondern auch in Schrift und Buch ein wichtiger Zeuge einer größeren Gruppe von palästinensisch-sinaitischen Codices in rechtsgeneigter Spitzbogenmajuskel.* Harlfinger,

Because of the fragmentary nature of the additional folios, it is difficult to re-create the correct order of the manuscript as a whole without further examination of the original.[24] Nevertheless, *Sinai Gr. 210* contains Gospel readings beginning with the eve of Christmas until Theophany (fol. 1r–18r); then six Sundays of Luke (fol. 18r–25r); Hypapante and Lent (25r–64r); Saturday and Sunday of Palms (fol. 64v–75v); Holy Week (fol. 75v–146v); resurrectional Gospels (fol. 146v–155v); Pascha and Pentecost (fol. 155v–171v); and from Pentecost until the Exaltation of the Cross (fol. 171v–188v), at which point the manuscript is lost. Sebastià Janeras has studied this codex extensively, but the complete manuscript, along with the folios from the 'new finds', remains to be edited.[25]

Sinai Gr. 212 (9th cent.)

The lectionary in the ninth-century manuscript *Sinai Gr. 212* contains select Gospel and Epistle lections for the liturgical year according to the Jerusalem pericope order.[26] Despite the attention given to other lectionaries containing the Jerusalem pericope order, such as *Sinai Gr. 210* and *Sinai Ar. 116*, this manuscript has remained unexamined. This is surprising, considering that it contains both Gospel and Epistle readings. The lectionary's script is an uncial similar to that of *Sinai Gr. 210*, and it is written on parchment. Caspar René Gregory (1846–1917) identified it as a palimpsest with a lower layer from the fifth century containing the text of several psalms.[27] The smaller dimensions of the manuscript (approximately 145 by 117 mm) and the lack of any significant decoration do not help to locate it.

However, numerous marginal notes, both in Greek and in Arabic, suggest liturgical use within the Jerusalem patriarchate. Greek marginal notes, beginning with a Gospel reading for martyrs (εἰς μάρτυρας, Matthew 10:16–22, fol. 69r) that is consistent with the Jerusalem lectionary and continues until the end of the manuscript (fol. 114v), indicate responsorial psalm and Alleluia verses. Arabic marginalia, present from the eighth resurrectional Gospel reading for Tone 8 (John 21:1–14, fol. 44v) until the end of the manuscript, translate the Greek rubrics. But two margin notes are in Arabic alone. These two exceptions show the importance of Arabic marginalia in Sinaitic liturgical manuscripts. The marginal note at the Epistle reading for archangels (fol. 100v–102v) reads 'Michael' in Arabic, showing the clear connection of the general reading for archangels to the specific commemoration of the Archangel Michael. For the last pericope (1 Thessalonians 4:13–18, fol. 113r), the Greek rubric, written by a later hand, indicates only 'to the Thessalonians' (πρὸς Θεσαλλανηκής [sic]), while the Arabic marginal note gives the rubric 'concerning the dead and the Sabbath' (ʿala al-mawta wa-al-sabūt).[28]

Reinsch, and Sonderkamp, *Specimina sinaitica*, 14. For more on manuscripts of this script, see Perria, 'Scritture e codici orientali', especially 23–4.

[24] Harlfinger, Reinsch, and Sonderkamp, *Specimina sinaitica*, 13.

[25] Janeras, *Vendredi-Saint*, especially 39–40, 84–5, 201–2; Janeras, 'Lectionnaires de Jérusalem', especially 80.

[26] ℓ 846: U-ℓ+ᵃsel (Jerusalem). Aland, *Kurzgefaßte Liste*, 269; Galadza, 'Two Sources of the Jerusalem Lectionary', 81–90.

[27] Gregory, *Textkritik*, vol. 3, 1245.

[28] My thanks to Jack Tannous and Jeannette Rizk for a transcription and translation of the Arabic marginalia.

The actual contents of the lectionary begin with eight resurrectional Gospels according to the eight tones (fol. 1r–51v) and continue with Gospels at vespers for the Dormition of the Theotokos (fol. 51v–54r), for the Enkainia of the Anastasis (54r–57v), for prophets (fol. 57v–62v), for Apostles (fol. 62v–69r), two Gospels for martyrs (fol. 69r–72v and fol. 74r–78v), for Sts Stephen and John (fol. 78r–80r), another for prophets (fol. 80r–82v), for women virgins and martyrs (fol. 82v–87r), for venerable monks (ὅσιοι, fol. 87r–90r), for hierarchs (fol. 90r–92v), for archangels (fol. 92v–94r), for the deceased (fol. 94r–96v), and another for prophets (fol. 96v–98v). After half of an empty folio (fol. 98v), Epistle readings continue: for Enkainia (fol. 99r–100v), archangels (fol. 100v–102v), Apostles (fol. 102v–104v), prophets (fol. 104v–106v), martyrs (fol. 106v–108r), holy women (fol. 108r–110r), hierarchs (fol. 110r–113r), and for the deceased and Saturdays (fol. 113r–114v).

St Petersburg RNB Gr. 44 (9th cent.)

St Petersburg RNB Gr. 44 is a manuscript that contains propers for the Liturgy of the Word of JAS with ekphonetic musical notation.[29] The codex's script, decoration, and size (approximately 197 by 146 mm) suggested to Jean-Baptiste Thibaut that it was intended for use by a deacon or psalmist. Thibaut considered it to be of such value that he dubbed it 'Codex Sinaiticus L (liturgicus)' and asserted that it 'ranks among the most precious monuments of the liturgy and hymnography of the Greek church [*sic*]'.[30]

A note at the beginning of the Sunday services reads as follows:

Κ(ύρι)ε εὐλόγησον· ἐν ὀνόματῃ π(ατρό)ς καὶ υ(ἱο)ῦ καὶ ἁγίου πν(εύματο)ς νῦν·	Lord bless. In the name of the Father and of the Son and of the Holy Spirit now...

And then in Arabic: 'In the name of the Father and of the Son and of the Holy Spirit, one God. We begin with the help of God and write the Gospel, psalms, and Alleluia for the Sundays.'[31] Whether this is the initial blessing of the liturgy or the scribe's indication of a new section of the manuscript is unclear.[32] This does not seem to be the 'principal title' of the manuscript, as Thibaut suggests, especially since this phrase appears near the middle of the manuscript (fol. 19r).[33]

[29] ℓ 249: U-ℓ[+a]sel † (Jerusalem). Aland, *Kurzgefaßte Liste*, 233; Thibaut, *Monuments*, 17–30 and 3*–11* (edition of the text); Alexandra Nikiforova and Tinatin Chronz, 'The Codex Sinaiticus Liturgicus Revisited: A New Edition and Critical Assesment of the Text', OCP 82 (2017), 59–125.

[30] [L]e *codex Sinaiticus L prend place parmi les plus précieux monuments de la liturgie et de l'hymnographie de l'Église grecque*. Thibaut, *Monuments*, 17.

[31] Fol. 19r. Thibaut, *Monuments*, 19 table 13. The translation here is from the French provided by Thibaut: *Au nom du Père et du Fils et du St Esprit, Dieu unique. Nous commencerons avec l'aide de Dieu et écrirons l'évangile, les psaumes et l'alléluia pour le Dimanche.*

[32] See Vassa Larin, 'The Opening Formula of the Byzantine Divine Liturgy, "Blessed is the Kingdom," among Other Liturgical Beginnings', *Studia Liturgica* 43.2 (2013), 229–55.

[33] Thibaut, *Monuments*, 17.

The manuscript's extant sixty-nine folios contain sixteen services: eight for the Sundays after Pentecost (fol. 19r–27v, 37r–63r) and eight for various commemorations, including martyrs (fol. 1r–4r), prophets (fol. 4r–5v), venerable monks (ὅσιοι, fol. 5v–10v), hierarchs (fol. 10v–15v), Apostles (fol. 15v–18r), the Enkainia (fol. 18r–27v), and archangels (fol. 63r–69v). Each service contains a troparion; a Glory... Now... *theotokion*; a psalm with verse; an Epistle; an Alleluia with verse; Gospel; and hymns for hand washing and the gifts, accompanied by diaconal commands for the dismissal of the catechumens and the recitation of the Creed. Rubrical notes throughout the codex are indicated in Greek and Arabic and, according to Thibaut, certain characteristics in the Greek script betray the scribal hand of a foreigner, in other words a non-native speaker of Greek.[34]

Sinai Gr. N.E. ΜΓ 11 (9th cent.)

Sinai Gr. N.E. ΜΓ 11 is dated to the ninth century and consists of a lectionary. It contains selected Gospel readings (εὐαγγελιστάριον or ἐκλογάδιον εὐαγγελίων) and is fragmentary, with 125 folios in sixteen quires extant.[35] It is a manuscript of average size (approximately 228 by 165 mm) and was copied on parchment.[36] It contains general readings for the Theotokos (fol. 1r–4v) and for ascetics (fol. 5r–5v), then the sixth through to the ninth and twelfth Sundays of Matthew (fol. 6r–14r), several Sundays of Mark after Exaltation (fol. 14r–27v), Sundays of Luke after Theophany (fol. 27v–39v), Meatfare Sunday (fol. 39v–43r), six Sundays of Lent (fol. 43v–61r), and six Sundays of John after Pascha (fol. 62r–77v). Following this are pericopes for Enkainia (fol. 78r–79v), two for John the Baptist (fol. 79v–86v), and many readings for various categories of saints, the Saviour, and the deceased (fol. 86v–122r), including two Epistle readings for saints, prophets, and hierarchs (fol. 122r–124v) and for the first Sunday of Lent (fol. 124v–125v). Despite the absence of certain key liturgical seasons, such as Nativity, Theophany, Holy Week, and Pascha, the pericopes in this manuscript all conform to the Jerusalem lectionary order. Numerous Arabic marginal notes at the pericope headings suggest that the manuscript was used in an environment where Arabic was commonly spoken, such as the Jerusalem patriarchate.

Sinai Gr. N.E. ΜΓ 31 (9th cent.)

The Epistle lectionary *Sinai Gr. N.E. ΜΓ 31* was classified as a fragmentary uncial script lectionary by Aland and dated to the ninth century. The manuscript is extremely fragmentary and today consists of only one folio measuring 215 by 160 mm; it

---

[34] [Œ]*uvre d'un copiste allogène peu versé dans la connaissance de la langue greque* ('Work of a foreign copyist poorly versed in the knowledge of the Greek language'). Thibaut, *Monuments*, 17. For further analysis of this liturgical source, see also Taft, *Great Entrance*, 73–4, 97, 100–1.

[35] Nikolopoulos, Νέα εὑρήματα, 144. No photograph of this manuscript is provided.

[36] ℓ 2213: U-ℓsel (Jerus.). Aland, *Kurzgefaßte Liste*, 356; Galadza, 'Two Sources of the Jerusalem Lectionary', 90–102.

preserves only one pericope, Philippians 2: 5–2: 11, for the 'Tenth Sunday' (κυριακὴ ί πρὸς Φιλιππησίους) and for Transfiguration.[37]

Sinai Gr. N.E. ΜΓ 36 (9th cent.)

The ninth-century Epistle lectionary *Sinai Gr. N.E. ΜΓ 36* in uncial script is in the best condition of all Greek Epistle lectionaries from the Sinai 'new finds'. Today it contains seven folios measuring 225 by 165 mm with nine pericopes, mainly from Sundays from the cycle of the Epistle to the Romans.[38]

Sinai Gr. N.E. ΜΓ 73 (9th cent.)

The manuscript *Sinai Gr. N.E. ΜΓ 73* consists of six folios measuring 170 by 170 mm, as well as of several fragments of a seventh folio. Both Panagiotes Nikolopoulos and Kurt Aland have dated this manuscript to the ninth century on the basis of its script and material. Although this fragmentary codex is classified among the parchment manuscripts of the Sinai 'new finds' written in majuscule script, its material is actually paper. The seven folios contain three pericopes from Acts for the Sundays after Pascha.[39]

Sinai Syr. M52N (9th–10th cent.)

The earliest Syriac liturgical manuscript relevant to this study, *Sinai Syr. M52N*, is dated to the late ninth and early tenth century. It contains a complete calendar of fixed commemorations for the whole liturgical year (10 fol.) that closely follows the sanctoral of the Jerusalem lectionary and runs from 1 October (*Tishrīn I*) until 30 September (*Elul*), as well as a fragmentary lectionary (45 fol.).[40] Each day of the calendar includes one or at most two commemorations, for which it gives only the name of the saint or feast and, occasionally, an epithet. While this genre of Syriac calendar is exclusively Miaphysite according to all extant evidence from the seventh through to seventeenth centuries, the Syriac script in both parts of the manuscript is considered characteristically Melkite.[41] Likewise, similarities between the commemorations in this source and the calendar of *Sinai Geo. O. 34* (also described here) connect it with Jerusalem. André

---

[37] See ℓ 2214: U-ℓ^aP (Jerus.). Πραξαπόστολος Κυριακὴ ι΄, πρὸς Φιλιππησίους καὶ εἰς Μεταμόρφωσιν. Ἀρχ. Τοῦτο φρονείσθω ('Praxapostolos, 10th Sunday, to the Philippians and for Transfiguration. Beginning: "Have this mind"'). Nikolopoulos, *Νέα εὑρήματα*, 147; Aland, *Kurzgefaßte Liste*, 356; Galadza, 'A Note on Hagiopolite Epistle Readings', 156.

[38] See ℓ 2215: U-ℓ^aP (Jerus.). Πραξαπόστολος. Nikolopoulos, *Νέα εὑρήματα*, 147. No photograph of the manuscript is provided. See also Aland, *Kurzgefaßte Liste*, 356; Galadza, 'A Note on Hagiopolite Epistle Readings', 156–8.

[39] See ℓ 2216: U-ℓ^aP (Jerus.). Πραξαπόστολος Κυριακαὶ α΄-γ΄ Πράξεων ('Praxapostolos, 1st–3rd Sundays, Acts'). Nikolopoulos, *Νέα εὑρήματα*, 153 and table 87, where a photograph of fol. 1v–2r can be found. See also Aland, *Kurzgefaßte Liste*, 356; Galadza, 'A Note on Hagiopolite Epistle Readings', 158–9.

[40] Philothée du Sinaï, *Nouveaux Manuscrits Syriaques*, 501–20. This description should be read together with the article by Binggeli, 'Calendrier melkite de Jérusalem', which corrects Sister Philothée's numerous transcription errors. See also Grigory Kessel, 'Review of Philothée du Sinaï, *Nouveaux Manuscrits Syriaques du Sinaï* (Athens: Fondation du Mont Sinaï, 2008)', Богословские Труды 43–4 (2012), 625–34.

[41] Binggeli, 'Calendrier melkite de Jérusalem', 182.

Binggeli's preliminary study of this calendar has stressed its importance for the study of liturgy in Jerusalem between the integration of New Martyrs of the Arab conquest into the sanctoral and the ultimate liturgical Byzantinization of the Jerusalem patriarchate.[42] Binggeli himself emphasizes the need for a new, critical edition of this text.[43]

Sinai Geo. N. 58 (9th–10th cent.)

The ninth- or tenth-century manuscript *Sinai Geo. N. 58* consists of four different parts written by four different hands and is classified as a 'liturgical collection' due to its content and the small size (135 by 120 mm) of its 98 extant folios.[44] Although the binding is still intact, each of the four sections has missing folios. Only the first section of the manuscript, which contains the short version of JAS (fol. 1v–46v), is complete; and it is followed by scriptural readings according to the Jerusalem lectionary for various commemorations. A calendar of feasts for the liturgical year (fol. 59r–69r) is similar to that of Iovane Zosime found in *Sinai Geo. O. 34* (10th cent.), and Stéphane Verhelst has speculated that this calendar may be the 'Jerusalem' source used by Zosime for his own compilation calendar.[45] The last section of the manuscript contains prayers from the Euchologion, including a funeral rite and prayers for the dead 'according to the order [განგება, *gangeba*]' of St Sabas Lavra (fol. 69v–85v).[46]

Sinai Geo. O. 30 and Sinai Geo. O. 38 (979)

Two tenth-century Georgian manuscripts *Sinai Geo. O. 30* and *Sinai Geo. O. 38* were copied in the same year by two different hands, form one liturgical book of the four Gospels known as a Tetraevangelion. The first part, which contains the Gospels of Matthew and Mark, was copied by the scribe Ezra, while the second part, which contains the Gospels of Luke and John, was copied by Iovane Zosime.[47] At the end of *Sinai Geo. O. 38* (fol. 101r–115r) Iovane Zosime added a Gospel table or index of the Gospels for the whole year, which has been edited by Gérard Garitte.[48] The order follows the Jerusalem lectionary, beginning with Christmas on 25 December, then continuing through the months of January, February, and March, until the feast of the

---

[42] *Le principal intérêt de ce document réside donc dans le fait qu'il permet de remonter à un état du sanctoral de l'église Melkite d'avant la byzantinisation du rite dans le patriarcat de Jérusalem* ('The principal interest of this document resides in the fact that it permits one to return to the state of the sanctoral of the Melkite church before the Byzantinization of the rite in the patriarchate of Jerusalem'). Binggeli, 'Calendrier melkite de Jérusalem', 193.

[43] Ibid., 184.

[44] For more on the Georgian 'liturgical collection' book type, see Chapter 2, 'Georgian Monastic Liturgy'.

[45] Verhelst, *Lectionnaire de Jérusalem*, 231 and 233–45 (edition and translation). For *Sinai Geo. O. 34* (10th cent.), see Chapter 2, 'Georgian Monastic Liturgy'.

[46] Aleksidze et al., *Catalogue of Georgian Manuscripts*, 417–18; *Liturgia ibero-graeca*, 18–19 (= A in the apparatus of Khevsuriani et al.).

[47] Garitte, *Catalogue*, 69–71 and 144–52. For more on Iovane Zosime, see Chapter 2, 'Georgian Monastic Liturgy' on Georgian monasticism in Palestine.

[48] განგება და განწესება წმიდათა სახარებათა წელიწადისა დღეთა და დღესასწაულ-თა ('Order and Regulation of the Holy Gospels of the Days and Feasts of the Year'). Garitte, 'Index des lectures évangéliques', 341.

Annunciation on 25 March. Next comes the movable cycle of Lent, Holy Week, Easter, and Pentecost. The fixed cycle resumes with April and continues until December. Lections for feasts of the Theotokos, the cross, apostles, martyrs, other general commemorations, and Sunday matins Gospels follow. Until this point, the two manuscripts are in harmony with Tarchnishvili's edition of the GL. Note, however, that these two manuscripts do not provide readings for every day of the year, as does the GL.

The fragmentary nature of some of the manuscripts employed by Tarchnishvili for his edition of the GL makes manuscripts *Sinai Geo. O. 30* and *Sinai Geo. O. 38* invaluable for providing supplemental information on the pericope order of the Jerusalem lectionary. Iovane Zosime's Gospel table at the end of *Sinai Geo. O. 38* gives further indications for readings on all the Sundays of the year and for various services from the Euchologion such as marriage, monastic profession, ordinations, and burial.

Sinai Ar. 116 (995/6)

The bilingual Greek–Arabic Gospel book of codex *Sinai Ar. 116*, copied approximately sixteen years after the Georgian Tetraevangelion of Iovane Zosime examined in the previous section, contains readings according to the Jerusalem lectionary.[49] The scribe, John, son of Victor of Damietta, copied both the Greek and the Arabic text on Sinai while he was a priest in the monastery. He had previously entered the monastery and became a monk on Sinai in 984/5. The colophon (fol. 205v) is as follows:

Μνήσθητη κ(ύρι)ε τοῦ δούλου σοῦ Ἰω(άννου) πρεσβυτέρου ὁρύς Σινᾶ υ(ἰὸ)ς Βίκτωρος Ταμιαθέου ἀμὴν γένυτο [sic].
Latin translation of the Arabic:

Memento, o Domine, servi tui peccatoris Iohannis [yḥns] presbyteri in Monte Sina, filii Victoris [bṭqr] Blmla[50] Damiatensis; scripsit eum pro se ipso et pro (eis) qui legent in eo post eum; et ille rogat omnes qui legent in eo ut miserantur super eum. Et scripsit in anno trecentesimo octogesimo quito ex annis Arabum.

Et monachus-factus-est in hoc loco in anno trecentesimo septuagesimo quarto ex annis Arabum.[51]

Remember, Lord, your servant John, presbyter of Mount Sinai, son of Victor of Damietta. Amen. So be it.

Remember, Lord, your servant, the sinner John, presbyter of Mount Sinai, son of Victor Blmla of Damietta. He wrote it for himself and for those who read from it after him. And he prays that all who read from it may have mercy on him. And he wrote it in the year 385 [= 5 February 995 to 24 January 996].

And he became a monk in this place in the year 374 [= 4 July 984 to 23 May 985].

The peculiarities of the uncial script in presbyter John's Greek hand suggest that he was more familiar with Arabic.[52] The manuscript is of average size (approximately 208 by 150 mm) and written on bombax paper (*charta bombycina*).[53]

---

[49] *ℓ* 2211: U-ℓsel (Jerusalem, g-arb). Aland, *Kurzgefaßte Liste*, 356. See also Harlfinger, Reinsch, and Sonderkamp, *Specimina sinaitica*, 17–18 and tables 18–22.

[50] Or *tlmla, ṭlmla, nlmla,* or *ylmla*—a proper name.

[51] Greek text and Arabic translation into Latin from Garitte, 'Évangéliaire grec-arabe', 208–9.

[52] Ibid., 208.

[53] Aland, *Kurzgefaßte Liste*, 356; Harlfinger, Reinsch, and Sonderkamp, *Specimina sinaitica*, 17.

The manuscript's 207 folios begin with a reading for an evening water blessing (fol. 1r) and then pass to the Easter cycle, beginning with the first Sunday after Pascha, that is, New Sunday (fol. 2r). The Sunday cycle of John (fol. 2r–23r) then moves to the cycle of Matthew, from Pentecost until the Exaltation of the Cross (ἀπὸ τῆς πεντηκοστῆς ἕως τοῦ σταυροῦ, fol. 23v–48v). The next cycle, of Mark, begins after Exaltation and continues until Christmas (ἀπὸ τῆς ὑψώσεως τοῦ τιμίου σταυροῦ ἕως τῶν γενεθλίων, fol. 48–77v). Then the cycle of Luke continues from Theophany until Meatfare Sunday (ἀπὸ τῶν Θεοφανίων ἕως τῶν ἀποκρεῶν, fol. 77v–90v). Next come the fixed commemorations of the liturgical year, beginning with Christmas (fol. 93r–112r), followed by the Lenten cycle and Holy Week (fol. 112r–152r), and eight resurrectional Gospels (fol. 152r–166r). The Easter cycle concludes (fol. 166r–171r) and continues with fixed commemorations of June, August, and September (fol. 171r–183v). The remainder of the codex contains readings for various general commemorations (fol. 183v–205v).

Several other Arabic Tetraevangelia, such as *Sinai Ar. 72* (897), *Sinai Ar. 54* (9th cent.), *Sinai Ar. 74* (9th cent), *Sinai Ar. 70* (9th–10th cent), and *Sinai Ar. 97* (1123/4), follow the Jerusalem lectionary order and include names for the locations of Hagiopolitan liturgical stations.[54] Garitte has studied these manuscripts but did not edit them in their entirety. Thus only the information that Garitte provides can be incorporated into this study.

Sinai Gr. N.E. ΜΓ 8 (10th cent.)

The tenth-century Greek manuscript *Sinai Gr. N.E. ΜΓ 8*, along with fragments *Sinai Gr. Σπ. ΜΓ 22*, contains Epistle and Gospel readings, as well as hymnography and psalmody, for selected days of the year. The structure and contents of the liturgical services bear similarities to those of Georgian sources of the Jerusalem lectionary, such as the 'liturgical collections' that contain all hymnography and scriptural readings for a certain commemoration in one book.

Today the manuscript consists of forty-eight parchment folios written in characteristic Palestinian uncial script, with underwriting of a palimpsest in minuscule script that Nikolopoulos identified as Old Testament readings and troparia from a Prophetologion.[55] The text of the underwriting is in fact from the writings of Dorotheus of Gaza.[56] Despite its lacunary state, it is possible to recreate partially the order of the manuscript, which contains readings for feasts on 26, 27, and 28 December (fol. 48r, 45r–46v, 43r–44v, 8v–8r, 1r–3v, 6r–7v, 9v–9r, 4v–4r, 5v–5r),[57] Hypapante (fol. 35r–42v), Meatfare Sunday (fol. 10r–13v), the first Sunday of Lent (fol. 13v–25v), and the

[54] Garitte, 'Rubriques liturgiques'.

[55] ℓ 2212: U-ℓ⁺ᵃsel (Jerus.). Aland, *Kurzgefaßte Liste*, 356; Perria, 'Scritture e codici orientali', 25; Nikolopoulos, Νέα εὑρήματα, 142 and table 51; Galadza, 'Sinai Gr. N.E. ΜΓ 8'.

[56] See fol. 8v: οιονει δυναμιν παρ<εχει αυ>τω εις πλεον πολεμειν corresponds to Dorotheus of Gaza, *Epistle 5*, section 190, ii. 13–14. Similarly, fol. 34r reads τουτοις η οτι το μονασ<τηριον> which corresponds to *Didaskalia 2*, section 32, line 6. See *Dorothée de Gaza: Ouvres spirituelles*, ed. by Lucien Regnault and Jacques de Préville (SC 92, Paris: Cerf, 1963). I thank Giulia Rossetto for identifying this text.

[57] Folios of this manuscript were numbered in pencil before being correctly reordered. See Galadza, 'Sinai Gr. N.E. ΜΓ 8', 218.

third Sunday of Lent (fol. 26r–33v). Two liturgical rubrics in this manuscript deserve particular attention. First, an Old Testament reading (Joel 2: 15–27) is prescribed for the eucharistic synaxis on the first Sunday of Lent (fol. 13v–19r). To my knowledge, this is the only Greek liturgical manuscript to indicate an Old Testament reading during a Sunday Eucharist, as opposed to a festal vigil, where such readings have been retained until the present day in the Byzantine rite.[58] Second, in the days following Christmas, the *trisagion* is replaced by a hymn dedicated to the birth of Christ (fol. 7v), which is, to my knowledge, unprecedented.[59] Like certain lectionaries already discussed, this codex also contains Arabic notes to the rubrics; but these were copied by the scribe as part of the manuscript and not added later as marginal notes.

Sinai Geo. O. 34 (10th cent.)

The manuscript *Sinai Geo. O. 34* is an invaluable collection for the study of liturgy in Jerusalem. According to palaeographic data, the 210 folios that make up this codex are actually five different manuscripts of extremely diverse content.[60]

The first part of the manuscript contains an Horologion (fol. 1r–24v) copied by Iovane the Presbyter and revised by Iovane Zosime.[61] The section that is of the greatest interest to this study is the calendar (fol. 25r–33r), edited by Gérard Garitte.[62] The calendar is entitled 'Synaxes of the Months of the Year' (კრებაჲ თთუეთაჲ წელიწადისათაჲ) and its content reflects a mixed Hagiopolitan transitional liturgy. Garitte believes that this is not a liturgical calendar intended for actual use, but rather a kind of encyclopaedic synaxarion, which reveals the compiler's awareness of many sanctoral traditions that coexisted in his time.[63] Zosime himself identifies four sources for his collection: 'chiefly the canon [კანონი, *kanoni*], and also of the Greeks, and of Jerusalem, and of St Sabas'; and Garitte has made suggestions as to what these sources could have been. The canon (კანონისაჲთა, *kanonisayta*) would have been the Jerusalem lectionary;[64] a Greek model (საბერძნეთისაჲთა, *saberẓnetisayta*) was perhaps a synaxarion of Palestinian origin;[65] and the 'Jerusalem model' (იერუსალჱმისაჲთა, *ierusalēmisayta*) was something different from the Jerusalem lectionary, perhaps something like the hymnals or Menaia found in *Sinai Geo. O. 1, Sinai Geo. O. 59, Sinai Geo.*

[58] Galadza, 'Sinai Gr. N.E. MΓ 8', 216–18. For more on the question of Old Testament readings during the eucharistic liturgy, see Chapter 3, 'Lection(s)', and Chapter 5.

[59] Galadza, 'Sinai Gr. N.E. MΓ 8', 215 and 222; Galadza, 'Various Orthodoxies', 191–3 (Figure 9.1). For more on this hymn, see Chapter 3, 'The *Trisagion*'.

[60] For a codicological analysis of the manuscript, see Garitte, *Calendrier palestino-géorgien*, 15–19; Frøyshov, *Horologe 'géorgien'*, vol. 2, 195–7. See also Michel van Esbroeck, 'Le manuscrit géorgien Sinaïtique 34 et les publications de liturgie palestinienne', OCP 49 (1980), 125–41.

[61] For more information on Iovane Zosime, see Chapter 2.

[62] Garitte, *Calendrier palestino-géorgien*.

[63] *[L]e calendrier de Jean Zosime est un document hybride... Il ne semble pas qu'un tel document puisse être considéré comme un* ordo *destiné à régir réellement la vie liturgique d'une communauté* ('The calendar of John Zosime is a hybrid document... It does not seem that such a document could be considered to be an ordo intended to actually regulate the liturgical life of a community'). Garitte, *Calendrier palestino-géorgien*, 37 and 114.

[64] Garitte, *Calendrier palestino-géorgien*, 23–31.

[65] Ibid., 31–3.

O. 64, and *Sinai Geo. O. 65.*[66] There was also a contemporaneous Sabaitic model (საბაწმიდისაჲთა, *sabacmidisayta*), which Garitte does not identify.[67]

Other parts of the manuscript include the new *Iadgari* (fol. 34r–123r), the ancient *Iadgari* (fol. 123v–143r), the *Letters of Barsanuphius and John* (fol. 148r–195r), and lists of books of the Bible (fol. 202v–203v).[68]

Sinai Geo. O. 54 (10th cent.)

Codex *Sinai Geo. O. 54* is an acephalous 'liturgical collection' that begins with the litany before 'Our Father'[69] in JAS (fol. 1r–10v). Quire marks and the fragment *Sinai Geo. N. 33*, which forms part of *Sinai Geo. O. 54*, all suggest that JAS was the first liturgy in this manuscript. Following JAS are HagPRES (fol. 10v–13v), litanies (fol. 13v–28v), dismissals (fol. 29r–56v), prayers for blessing objects at various feasts of the year (fol. 56v–66r), and hymns, psalms, and New Testament lections for the liturgical year (fol. 66r–175v) that reflect the Jerusalem lectionary. The manuscript, originating in Palestine, is defective and ends with the rite for monastic tonsure.[70]

Sinai Geo. O. 63 (10th cent.)

The fragmentary, tenth-century manuscript *Sinai Geo. O. 63* contains a Gospel book according to the Jerusalem pericope order. Its fifty-seven folios begin with Christmas on 25 December (fol. 2v) and include Gospel readings for selected commemorations until the Annunciation on 25 March (fol. 23r). Then the readings pass to the movable cycle, beginning with the 'Sunday of Abstinence' or first Sunday of Lent (აღებასა პირველსა, fol. 24v), which is equivalent here to Cheesefare Sunday (τῆς ἀπόκρεως or τῆς τυροφάγου).[71] The manuscript ends with John 13:31, the first Gospel of the vigil of Holy Friday matins (fol. 53v). A marginal note in Arabic (fol. 2r) threatens with excommunication anyone who should remove the codex from Mount Sinai.[72]

Sinai Geo. O. 12 (10th–11th cent.)

Another 'liturgical collection', the acephalous manuscript *Sinai Geo. O. 12* begins with a short redaction of JAS at the presider's exclamation (*ekphonesis*), which

---

[66] Ibid., 33. For a description of these manuscripts, see Nikolai Marr, *Описание грузинских рукописей синайского монастыря* (Moscow: Академия Наук СССР, 1940), 99–107, 135–41, 141–52; *Description* I, 13–38 (*Sinai Geo. O. 1*), 162–86 (*Sinai Geo. O. 59*), 187–208 (*Sinai Geo. O. 64*), 208–9 (*Sinai Geo. O. 65*).

[67] Garitte, *Calendrier palestino-géorgien*, 35–7.

[68] The Greek version has been edited in Barsanouphios and John, *Questions and Answers*, ed. by Derwas James Chitty (PO 31.3, Paris: Firmin–Didot, 1966).

[69] *Liturgia ibero-graeca*, 102 (§97 line 24).

[70] *Description* III, 58–67; Outtier, 'Sinaï géorgien 54'; *Liturgia ibero-graeca*, 21.

[71] Garitte, *Calendrier palestino-géorgien*, 167; Garitte, 'Sin. geo. 63', 77. See Chapter 5 for an explanation of the variant numbering of the Sundays of Lent.

[72] *Liber evangelii. Excommunicatus qui amovebit eum a Monte Sina* ('Book of Gospels. Whoever will remove it from Mount Sinai will be excommunicated'). Garitte, 'Sin. geo. 63', 71.

introduces the 'Our Father'.[73] The difference between the short and long redactions of JAS is found in the prayers for Communion and at the conclusion of the liturgy: the long redaction contains more prayers and a longer dismissal and is generally found in manuscripts copied at the St Sabas Lavra in Palestine.[74] Both the short and the long redactions were regularly used side by side in the tenth and eleventh centuries.[75]

After JAS, this manuscript's 301 folios contain HagPRES, litanies (fol. 11r–34v), dismissals (fol. 35r–90r), blessings and sacraments, including baptism and marriage (fol. 90v–134r, 145v–168), prayers from the Liturgy of the Hours (fol. 135r–145v), as well as psalms and New Testament lections for the liturgical year and general commemorations (fol. 191r–286r). The manuscript ends (fol. 286v–301v) with a weekly chronological table (ქრონიკონი შუიდეოლი, *k'ronikoni šuideoli*) for the years 1 to 532 (781 to 1312) of the thirteenth cycle, copied by a later hand.[76] The cycle of 532 years, called the Kronikoni, was the 'result of multiplying the number of years in the full cycle of the sun (i.e. 28) by the number of years in the cycle of the moon (i.e. 19). According to this system, the same combination of the day of the month, the day of the week, and the phase of the moon is identical in every 532 years'.[77]

Vatican Syr. 19 (1030)

The eleventh-century Gospel book *Vatican Syr. 19* is written in Christian Palestinian Aramaic.[78] A very detailed colophon of the manuscript written in Garshuni gives the name of the scribe and various geographic references regarding the manuscript's origins and travels.[79] Another note (fol. 194v) indicates that the manuscript was completed on Wednesday 7 August 1030 near Antioch and brought to Samaria in Palestine. The text of the manuscript itself follows a structure similar to that of a Gospel book in the Byzantine rite. The kanonarion (fol. 1–147) follows the standard Byzantine order, beginning with the paschal season and the cycle of John, then continuing with Matthew, Luke, and Mark, the Sundays of Lent, Holy Week, and the eleven resurrectional Gospels. The synaxarion (fol. 148–194) begins with 1 September and ends with 31 August. The manuscript ends with additional readings for general commemorations. Although it claims to be written 'in accordance with the Syriac rite of Melkite Greeks' (*iuxta ritum syriacum graecorum melchitarum*), it follows the basic structure of a Byzantine Gospel book, according to Joseph and Stephanus Assemani.[80] Certain elements—such as the additional Gospel readings for vespers during Lent and the commemorations of some saints on days other than the standard Byzantine date—suggest that it still maintains elements of local usage. Gospel readings are also indicated at Vespers for every day of the first week of Lent (fol. 78–80).[81]

[73] *Liturgia ibero-graeca*, 106 (§ 98 line 4).   [74] Ibid., 31.
[75] Ibid., 32. See Chapter 3, 'The Long and Short Versions of the Liturgy of St James'.
[76] *Description* III, 33–47; Outtier, 'Sinaï géorgien 12'; *Liturgia ibero-graeca*, 25.
[77] See glossary in Aleksidze et al., *Catalogue of Georgian Manuscripts*, 481.
[78] For more on the language of this manuscript, see Christa Müller-Kessler, *Grammatik des Christlich-Palästinisch-Aramäischen*, vol. 1: *Schriftlehre, Lautlehre, Formenlehre* (Hildesheim: Georg Olms Verlag, 1991), esp. 23–4; Sebastian P. Brock, 'Christian Palestinian Aramaic', GEDSH, 96–7.
[79] See the colophon and discussion of the geographic information in Chapter 2, 'Byzantine Contact'.
[80] Assemani, *Catalogus*, vol. 2, 70–103.   [81] Ibid., 83.

Neither the GL nor Constantinopolitan sources such as the Typikon of the Great Church or the Stoudite Typikon indicate Gospel readings for PRES during this week.[82] Marginal notes written in Garshuni found throughout this manuscript explain and elaborate upon rubrics for pericopes. The fact that local usages reflect neither Hagiopolitan nor Constantinopolitan practices suggests that the book may contain evidence of Antiochene usage. This view is further strengthened by the history of the manuscript's journey from Antioch to Palestine. Thus *Vatican Syr. 19* is here considered as a Byzantinized liturgical manuscript of foreign provenance, later used within the Jerusalem patriarchate.

Sinai Geo. N. 12 (1075)

The manuscript *Sinai Geo. N. 12* is a Tetraevangelion dated to 1075 that contains the complete text of the four Gospels, with markings for readings throughout the whole liturgical year (fol. 1v–187v). The incipit is marked on the left margin with a *kancili* (კანწილი), a specific sign combining the initials for the words 'Christ' and 'holy' in Georgian uncial *asomtavruli* script,[83] while the desinit (i.e. the end) is marked with a cross on the right margin.[84] The colophon at the end of the Gospel of John (fol. 188r) indicates that the manuscript was copied on Sinai by Mikael in 1075 from the 'new translation' of George the Hagiorite, whose original is kept in the royal treasury in Constantinople together with the true Cross. Not only was this a new translation from a Greek model, but the index (fol. 189r–196v) also reflects the Greek rite. Its title reads as follows:

განგებაჲ ს[ახარებისაჲ ბერძუ]ლსა წეს-სა [ზედა, საძიე]ბელი რიცხვთა უ[ცთო]-მელი საწელიწდოდ, [ყოველნი] დღენი სრულიად და [მარ]ხვათა შაბათ-კჳრიაკენი და დღები.[85]	Order of the Gospel according to the Greek rite, infallible, index of numbers for the year, for all days completely, and for Saturdays and Sundays and days of Lent.[86]

The index breaks off at the fourth week of Lent. *Sinai Geo. N. 12* is almost identical to *Sinai Geo. O. 19*, another Tetraevangelion copied in 1074 by the same scribe Mikael.[87] The manuscript remains to be edited.

---

[82] Mateos, *Typicon*, vol. 2, 10–14. The Stoudite Typikon explicitly prescribes PRES for each day of Lent: ꙗко въ вьсь постъ на всѧкъ дьнь творѧть литѹргию постьноѹю ('throughout all of Lent on every day they serve the Lenten Liturgy'). Petras, *Typikon*, 42; Pentkovsky, *Типикон*, 239. See also Alexopoulos, *Presanctified Liturgy*, 62. For more on these sources, see Chapter 1, 'Early Constantinopolitan Liturgy'.

[83] ᲚᲚ (*kc*). See also the glossary in Aleksidze et al., *Catalogue of Georgian Manuscripts*, 480.

[84] Ibid., 382.   [85] Ibid., 256.   [86] Cf. ibid., 384.

[87] Ibid., 383–4. See also Garitte, *Catalogue*, 53–8. For more on the question of Georgian translations of the Bible and on the pre-Athonite and Athonite versions, see Chapter 2, 'Stoudite Monastic and Liturgical Reforms'.

Sinai Gr. 741 and *Sinai Gr. 742* (25 January 1099)

The two manuscripts *Sinai Gr. 741* and *Sinai Gr. 742* once formed a single Triodion copied at the monastery of St Sabas in Palestine.[88] Together, they are the oldest dated extant Greek liturgical manuscript copied at the St Sabas Lavra. The codex *Sinai Gr. 741* contains the first half of the Triodion, beginning with various introductory texts and continuing until the third Tuesday of Lent, and *Sinai Gr. 742* continues from the third Wednesday of Lent until Good Friday. The colophon reads:

ἐγράφη ἡ ἱερὰ αὕτη βίβλος τῶν τριῳδίων καὶ κανόνων καὶ λοιπῆς πάσης ἀκολουθ(ίας) τῆς ἁγίας τεσσαρακοστῆς. καὶ τῆς ἁγίας καὶ μεγάλης ἑβδομάδος τῶν ζωοποιῶν παθῶν τοῦ σ(ωτῆ)ρ(ο)ς ἡμῶν Ἰ(ησο)ῦ Χ(ριστο)ῦ τοῦ υἱοῦ τοῦ Θ(εο)ῦ καὶ Θ(εο)ῦ, ἐν τῇ σεβασμ(ίᾳ) λαύρᾳ τοῦ ἁγίου Σάβα τῆς ἐν Ἱεροσολύμοις. χειρὶ τοῦ εὐτελοῦς καὶ ἁμαρτωλοῦ Γερασίμου τοῦ ἀντιοχ(εί)τ(ου)· καὶ δευτερεύοντος τῶν πρεσβυτέρων τῶν ἐν Ἀσκά(λωνι) καθολικῆς καὶ ἀποστολικῆς ἐκκλη(σίας) κυ(ροῦ) Ἰωάννου· λόγῳ τοῦ σεβασμίου ναοῦ τοῦ ἐνδόξου μεγαλομ(ά)ρ(τυρος) Γεωργίου ἐν αὐτῇ τῇ Ἀσκά(λωνι) τὸ λεγόμενον κατὰ τὴν ἐγχώριον γλῶσσαν, τὸ χάδρα, ἀρχιεραρχοῦντος τῆς αὐτῆς πόλεως τοῦ ὁσιωτ(ά)τ(ου) καὶ παναγίου γέροντος κυ(ροῦ) Ἀντωνίου· μη(νὶ) ἰανουαρ(ίῳ) κε´· ἰνδικ(τιῶνος) ζ´· ἐν ἔτ(ει) ,ϛχζ´· οἱ ἐν αὐτῇ τῇ ἁγίᾳ βίβλῳ μελετῶντες καὶ εὐχόμενοι εὔξασθε διὰ τὸν Θ(εὸ)ν καὶ τὴν αὐτοῦ ἐντολὴν τοῦ γράψαντος εὑρεῖν αὐτὸν ἔλεος ἐν ἡμέρᾳ κρίσεως. ὁ θ(εὸ)ς συγώρη(σ)ον τῷ γράψαντι ταῦτα ὅσα σοι ἥμαρτεν, ἀμήν.[89]

This holy book of the Triodia and canons and the remainder of the services of holy Lent, and of Holy and Great Week, of the life-creating Passion of our Saviour Jesus Christ the Son of God and God, was copied in the venerable Lavra of Saint Sabas in Jerusalem, by the hand of the humble and sinful Gerasimus of Antioch, and by the eager zeal of the honourable monk and second priest in Ascalon of the catholic and apostolic Church, Lord John, for the venerable church of the glorious great-martyr George in Ascalon, called 'Green' according to the local language, during the episcopal rule of the city by the venerable and all-holy elder, Lord Anthony, on 25 January, seventh year of the indiction, in the year 6607 [= AD 1099]. Those studying and praying from this book: pray to God and his commandment that the copyist may find mercy in the day of judgement. God have mercy upon the copyist as much as he has sinned against you. Amen.

The manuscript was thus copied in the brief period of renewed Fatimid control over Jerusalem, after the Seljuks were driven out in August 1098 and before the crusaders captured the Holy City in June 1099. Gabriel Bertonière has studied this Triodion in his work on the Sundays of Lent,[90] but the content of the manuscripts has never been completely described.

The Triodion of *Sinai Gr. 741* actually begins on fol. 4r (ἀρχὴς σὺν Θεῷ τοῦ Τριωδίου τῆς ἁγίας μ´ καὶ μετὰ Χριστὸν τὸν Κύριον· ποίημα Ἰωσὴφ καὶ Θεοδώρου; 'Beginning with God of the Triodion of the holy forty [days] and with Christ the Lord. The composition of Joseph and Theodore') with the Sunday of the publican and the Pharisee, then continues with the Sunday of the prodigal son (fol. 7v), the Saturday for departed venerable monks (ὅσιοι, fol. 13v), Meatfare Sunday (fol. 20r), weekdays of Cheesefare

---

[88] Harlfinger, Reinsch, and Sonderkamp, *Specimina sinaitica*, 37–9, tables 83–7.

[89] Ibid., 37.   [90] Bertonière, *Sundays of Lent*, 162.

Week (fol. 29r–46v), the Saturday of departed ascetics (fol. 46v), Cheesefare Sunday (fol. 54v), the first week of Lent (fol. 60v–79r), and the Saturday of Theodore Teron (fol. 79r–86v). The first Sunday of Lent (fol. 86v–91r) is not identified as the 'Sunday of Orthodoxy' but retains the more ancient Constantinopolitan 'commemoration of the holy prophets Moses and Aaron and of the others' (μνήμη τῶν ἁγίων προφητῶν Μωϋσέως καὶ Ἀαρὼν καὶ τῶν λοιπῶν). Then follow the second week of Lent (fol. 91r–110r), second Saturday of Lent (fol. 110r), second Sunday of Lent (εἰς τὸν ἄσωτον written above the decorative band, fol. 114r–121r), third week of Lent (fol. 121r–136v), third Saturday of Lent (fol. 136v–139v), third Sunday of Lent (τὴν Κυριακὴν τῆς γ' ἑβδομάδος· εἰς τὴν προσκύνησιν τοῦ τιμίου καὶ ζωοποιοῦ σταυροῦ; 'Sunday of the third week, for the veneration of the precious and life-giving Cross', fol. 140r–146v), and the fourth week of Lent—not called 'fourth' (δ') but 'middle week' (τῆς μέσης ἑβδομάδος, fol. 147v–154v). Folios added to the end of the codex contain a canon for Theodore Teron at Pannychis on Friday evening (fol. 155–159v), for the venerable Mary of Egypt (fol. 159v–162r), and two canons for the second Sunday of Lent (fol. 162r–165r).[91]

The next codex comprising this Triodion begins immediately with the Wednesday of the fourth week. On the fourth Sunday of Lent (fol. 24r–27r), the canon 'I have become, O Christ, like one in the hands of thieves' (Ὡμοιώθην Χριστὲ τῷ ἐν χερσὶ τῶν λῃστῶν) is attributed to Elias the Hagiopolite.[92] The fifth week of Lent (fol. 27r–71r) includes the Great Canon of St Andrew of Crete, but the end of the sixth week (fol. 82v–102v) makes no mention of *hyperthesis*. The remainder of the Triodion continues with Lazarus Saturday (fol. 102v–114r), Palm Sunday (fol. 114r–121r), and ends with Holy Week.

The two manuscripts do not contain any scriptural readings, thereby strictly adhering to the liturgical book's type, Triodion. In other words, they contain primarily the hymnographic canons (with 'three odes') composed by Theodore Stoudite and later revised by Joseph the Hymnographer (d. *c*.886) and by Clement Stoudite (9th cent.).[93] The hymnography for each day is generally ordered according to its genre—*kathismata, stichera,* canons—so that the structure of the service within which the hymns were sung is unclear. Occasionally rubrics for some *stichera* prescribe them 'for the morning' (τῷ πρωΐ, i.e. for *orthros*). On Fridays, an exception is made to this order: the *sticheron* of the Triodion for vespers—presumably PRES—is included after the ninth ode of the canon, apart from the other *stichera*. *Kontakia* are not included in the canon after the sixth ode and troparia at 'The Lord is God' (Θεὸς Κύριος) are sometimes labelled '*kathismata* at "The Lord is God"' (καθίσματα εἰς τὸν Θεὸς Κύριος). Overall, the two manuscripts bear testimony to an early stage in the development of the Triodion book type, which is already highly Byzantinized.[94]

---

[91] For the incipits of these canons, see ibid., 83.

[92] See fol. 24v. See also Bertonière, *Sundays of Lent*, 87; Gabriel Bertonière, 'Four Liturgical Kanons of Elias II of Jerusalem', in *Crossroad of Cultures: Studies in Liturgy and Patristics in Honor of Gabriele Winkler*, ed. by Hans-Jürgen Feulner, Elena Velkovska, and Robert F. Taft, SJ (OCA 260, Rome: Pontifical Oriental Institute, 2000), 89–149.

[93] Alexander Kazhdan, Dimitri E. Conomos, and Nancy Patterson Ševčenko, 'Joseph the Hymnographer', ODB II, 1074. For more on Clement (Κλήμης) Stoudite, see PmbZ, 23705.

[94] Momina, 'О происхождении греческой триоди', 118.

Dumbarton Oaks MS 2 (11th cent.)

The eleventh-century codex *Dumbarton Oaks MS 2*, the only Georgian manuscript of
the Dumbarton Oaks Research Library and Collection, is a Menaion for the months of
December, January, and February that was part of a set of four manuscripts for the
whole fixed cycle of the liturgical year and is of extreme importance to the study of
liturgy in Jerusalem. The detailed colophon reads as follows:

სახელითა ღ(მრთისა)ჲთა: გამსრულდა:
ესეცა: წიგნი. სამი თთუჱ დეკემბერი
იანვარი და ფებერვალი: ბრძანებითა და
მოღუაწებითა ღ(მერ)თშემოსილისა:
მამისა: და მოღურისა: გ(იორგ)ი
პრობორე-სითა: ქ(რისტე)მან ამათ ყ(ოვე)
ლთა წ(მიდა)თა: მისთა თანა დ(იდე)ბ(უ)
ლ ყავნ: სული მათი: სასუფეველსა
ცათასა: ა(მე)ნ.

ლ(ო)ცვ(ა)სა მომიჴს(ე)ნ(ე)თ ც(ო)დვ(ი)
ლი უცბ(ა)დ მჩხრეკალი იოვანე დვალი წ
(მიდა)ნო მ(ა)მ(ა)ნო და რ(ომელ)ი
დამეკლოს შემინდვეთ ღ(მერთმა)ნ გარწმ
(უ)ნოს:

ვინ ესე წიგნი რა(ჲთა)ცა მიჰეზითა
მონასტერსა ჯ(უა)რისასა გამოაჴუას.
შემცაჩუენებულ არს: ვ(ითარც)ა უ(ოვე)
ლნი მწვალებელნი და სულნიმცა მისი
დააშჯილ არს ყ(ოვე)ლთა თანა რ(მრ)თისა
განმარისხებელთა.

შეიმოსა ჴელითა კ(უ)რთხ(ეუ)ლისა
ძმისა ნისთერეონისითა, ღ(მერთმა)ნ
აღუკუცენ(ინ) ყ(ოველ)ნი ბრ(ა)ლნი
მისნი ლ(ო)ცვ(ვ)ა ყ(ა)ვთ მის თჳს წ(მიდა)
ნო მ(ა)მ(ა)ნო.⁹⁵

In the name of God, this book is completed.
Three months, December, January, and February by the command and supervision of
the God-bearing father and teacher Giorgi
P'roxore. May Christ, with all his saints, make
his soul glorified in the kingdom of heaven.
Amen.

In your prayers, remember the sinful and
ignorant scribe Iovane Dvali, O holy fathers,
and in that which I have failed, forgive me.
May God convince you!

Whoever removes this book from the
Monastery of the Cross, no matter the reason,
may he be cursed like the heretics and his
soul be condemned as all those who infuriate
God.

[This book] was bound by the hands of the
blessed brother Nist'ereoni. May God destroy
all his iniquities. Pray for him, holy fathers!

Despite the absence of a date, the mention of the Abbot Giorgi P'roxore (d. 12
February 1066), of the monk Iovane Dvali, and of the 'blessed brother' Nist'ereoni in
the colophon of this and other manuscripts copied during the same period in Jerusalem helps to date the Dumbarton Oaks Menaion to the middle of the eleventh
century.⁹⁶ The 382 folios, with dimensions approximately 235 by 173 mm, are written
in clear *nuskhuri* script. The manuscript contains commemorations for every day of
the three months, except for 28 and 30 December and 8, 19, and 23 February.⁹⁷
Garitte's description of the manuscript gives us the name of the commemoration on
each day but does not transmit the hymnography indicated for the commemorations.
Nevertheless, an examination of the commemorations reveals a mixed calendar that is

---

⁹⁵ Garitte, 'Menée', 32.
⁹⁶ Tarchnishvili, *Geschichte*, 75; Sakvarelidze, 'Byzantinization of Georgian Liturgy', 284–90.
⁹⁷ Garitte, 'Menée', 31–2.

heavily Byzantinized but retains local commemorations such as the Enkainia (საჯღოჯჩო, *satp'owri*) of the Church of St Sabas (14 December) and Georgian saints such as St Abo (7 January) and St Nino (14 January). An edition of the Menaion's hymnography would indicate whether those commemorations that were common to both Jerusalem and Constantinople are fully Byzantinized by the presence of the Constantinopolitan hymns contained in this manuscript or still retain older Hagiopolitan hymns.

Messina Gr. 177 (11th cent.)

Of all the sources consulted by Mercier in the Greek edition of JAS, the one of greatest interest for this study is *Messina Gr. 177*, an eleventh-century parchment scroll.[98] It must be made clear from the start that Mercier never saw the actual scroll. He relied instead on Mondalini's edition in the *Codex liturgicus*.[99] *Messina Gr. 177* had been mutilated and Mercier filled in the missing parts with *Vatican Borgia Gr. 24* (17 March 1880), a nineteenth-century exact copy of the original scroll prepared by the southern Italian Greek priest and scholar Filippo Matranga (1822–88), which replicated the style and the various scripts of the original scroll, including several illuminations.[100]

Despite Mercier's dependence on the nineteenth-century *Vatican Borgia Gr. 24* copy, *Messina Gr. 177* is still of the utmost importance. The scroll's recto contains JAS,[101] while the Alexandrian Liturgy of St Mark is on the verso.[102] Jacob holds that both were intended for actual use, unlike another manuscript that contains both JAS and the Liturgy of St Mark, the Euchologion from Santa Maria di Patir, *Vatican Gr. 1970*.[103] The commemoration of the deceased in JAS from *Messina Gr. 177* are similar to that of *Sinai Gr. 1040*.[104] Several other references to Sinai in the text suggest that the manuscript was used on Sinai in the episcopal see of Pharan.[105] Jacob is cautious about the connection to Pharan but is certain of a Sinaitic origin for the manuscript's model.[106]

---

[98] For a description of the manuscript, see Mancini, *Codices monasterii Messanensis*, 243–4; Mercier, *Liturgie de Saint Jacques*, 135–6; Jacob, 'Messanensis gr. 177'; Stefano Parenti, 'L'originale dell'edizione di Assemani «ex antique mss. messanensi» della Liturgia di S. Giacomo', in *Mille anni di 'rito greco' alle porte di Roma. Raccolta di saggi sull tradizione liturgica del Monastero Italo-bizantino di Grottaferrata* (Ἀνάλεκτα Κρυπτοφέρρης 4, Grottaferrata: Monastero esarchico, 2004), 253–66.

[99] Assemani, *Missale Hierosolymitanum*, 68–99.

[100] See Mercier, *Liturgie de Saint Jacques*, 135–6 for the description of both manuscripts. See also Stefano Parenti, 'L'originale dell'edizione di Assemani "Ex antiquo mss. messanensi" della liturgia di S. Giacomo', in *Mille anni di 'rito greco' alle porte di Roma*, ed. by Stefano Parenti and Elena Velkovska (Ἀνάλεκτα Κρυπτοφέρρης 4, Grottaferrata: Monastero Esarchico, 2004), 253–66, here 257.

[101] *Condacium S. Iacobi*. Mancini, *Codices monasterii Messanensis*, 243; Brightman, *Eastern Liturgies*, xlviii–liv.

[102] ἡ θεία λειτουργία τοῦ ἁγίου Μά(ρκου) τοῦ ἀποστ(όλου καὶ εὐαγγελιστοῦ). Mancini, *Codices monasterii Messanensis*, 243.

[103] Jacob, 'Messanensis gr. 177', 123.

[104] Dmitrievskii, *Описание* II, 127–35. For a transcription of the text, see Brightman, *Eastern Liturgies*, 501–3.

[105] Mercier, *Liturgie de Saint Jacques*, 136.   [106] Jacob, 'Messanensis gr. 177', 122.

Mercier, following Assemani,[107] thought that the manuscript's *terminus post quem* was 984. He thought so on the basis of the names of the pope of Rome and patriarchs of Constantinople, Antioch, and Alexandria mentioned in the diptychs for the living.[108] The manuscript, however, does not give a name for the living patriarch of Jerusalem (τοῦ ἁγιοτάτου πατρὸς ἡμῶν καὶ πατριάρχου ὁ Δ τῆς ἁγίας Χριστοῦ τοῦ Θεοῦ ἡμῶν πόλεως) or for the archbishop of the city (καὶ ὁ Δ τοῦ ἀρχιεπισκόπου ἡμῶν).[109] Instead, the last patriarch of Jerusalem mentioned among the dead is Orestes.[110] According to the historian Yaḥyā al-Anṭakī, Patriarch Orestes accompanied an embassy to Constantinople around the year 1000 and died there four years later.[111] Following this authoritative historical source, which previous scholars had ignored, Jacob gives 1005 as the manuscript's *terminus post quem* and suggests that it was copied in the region of Rossano in southern Italy and based on a Sinaitic model.[112]

Sinai Geo. O. 10 (11th cent.)

The eleventh-century Epistle book (საწელიწდო სამოციქულო) *Sinai Geo. O. 10* follows the order of the Greek church (საკლესიოჲ ბერძულსა წესსა, fol. 1r).[113] Apart from Epistle readings for Sundays and weekdays of the movable cycle (fol. 1r–170r), the manuscript contains a calendar for all the months of the year, from 1 September until 31 August (fol. 170r–227v).[114] The remainder of the manuscript contains *prokeimena* (წარდგომანი, *cardgomani*) and Alleluia (ალელუანი, *aleluani*) verses and readings from the Catholic Epistles (fol. 234v–265v).

Sinai Gr. N.E. X 156 (11th cent.)

The sixty paper folios of eleventh-century codex *Sinai Gr. N.E. X 156* contain JAS in Greek. The title of the manuscript has been preserved and reads: 'The Divine Liturgy of Saint James the Apostle and Brother of the Lord'.[115] Despite the commemoration of only six ecumenical councils,[116] the commemoration of Patriarch Sophronius II (r. *c.*1059–64) among the living places the manuscript in the second half of the eleventh century, a date also confirmed by codicological analysis.[117] The manuscript contains numerous Arabic marginal notes.

---

[107] Assemani, *Missale Hierosolymitanum*, xxxix.
[108] Mercier, *Liturgie de Saint Jacques*, 220.   [109] Ibid.
[110] See the apparatus in Mercier, *Liturgie de Saint Jacques*, 188.
[111] Yaḥyā al-Anṭakī, *History* II, 461.
[112] See Jacob, 'Messanensis gr. 177', 116–18 and 124 for the reasoning behind his conclusion and previous attempts to date the manuscript.
[113] *Description* III, 8–33, here 8.   [114] Ibid., 12–31.
[115] 'Ἡ Θεία [Λει]τουργ[ία] τοῦ ἁγίου Ἰακώβου τοῦ ἀποστόλου καὶ [ἀ]δελφοῦ τοῦ Κυρίου'. Kazamias, Θεία Λειτουργία τοῦ Ἁγίου Ἰακώβου, 44–7, here 44; Nikolopoulos, Νέα εὑρήματα, 213 table 189.
[116] Μνήσθητι Κύριε τῶν ἁγίων μεγάλων καὶ οἰκουμενικῶν ἐξ συνόδων ('Remember, Lord, the holy, great, and ecumenical six councils'). Kazamias, Θεία Λειτουργία τοῦ Ἁγίου Ἰακώβου, 44. For more on the commemoration of Ecumenical Councils, see Chapter 4, ' Church Councils'.
[117] Kazamias, Θεία Λειτουργία τοῦ Ἁγίου Ἰακώβου, 44–5; Fedalto, *Hierarchia ecclesiastica orientalis*, vol. 2, 1003.

Tbilisi Geo. 193 (11th cent.)

The 300 folios of the eleventh-century manuscript *Tbilisi Geo. 193*, written in a combination of *asomtavruli* (ასომთავრული) uncial initials and *nusxuri* (ნუსხური) minuscule script called *huc'uri* (ჰუცური) script, contain a synaxarion (სვინაქსარი, *svinak'sari*) based on the model of George Mt'acmideli.[118] This highly Byzantinized source begins with the order for the fixed cycle, from 1 September to 31 August, and then passes to the movable cycle, beginning with Meatfare Sunday. The manuscript is defective, ending at the Friday of Cheesefare Week. Kornelii Kekelidze, who appended the remainder of the movable cycle from another, later manuscript, *Tbilisi Geo. 222* (12th cent.), published a detailed description of the text in 1908.[119] The text contains very specific liturgical indications for every day of the year, including the commemoration of the saint or feast, scriptural readings, hymnography, *prokeimena*, psalm verses, and Communion hymns. Unfortunately Kekelidze does not provide the original text, from which the reader may glean more than just the incipits of these diverse items. This source is useful to compare with other eleventh-century calendars in order to understand the state of Byzantinization of Georgian liturgical texts.[120]

Sinai Gr. N.E. M 35 (11th–12th cent.)

The selected Gospel lectionary (εὐαγγελιστάριον) in manuscript *Sinai Gr. N.E. M 35*, written in minuscule script, contains Gospel readings for the complete movable cycle, from Pascha to the resurrectional Gospel readings.[121] It is important to remember Aland's observation that these readings are in the order we encounter them in Jerusalem but contain the Byzantine pericopes.[122] First-hand examination of the manuscript clarifies Aland's statement. The pericopes match those of the Byzantine lectionary but the structure of the lectionary is extremely bare, as in *Sinai Gr. N.E. MΓ 8* (10th cent.). The order, however, is not that of the Jerusalem lectionary and it is unclear why Aland would have asserted that it was. The period of Pentecost, for example, contains the standard pericopes of the Byzantine lectionary and in the Byzantine order: the manuscript begins with the Sunday of Pascha (John 1:1–17, fol. 1r–4v), then goes on to the Sunday of Antipascha (John 20:19–31, fol. 4v–9r). The lection for Pentecost (John 7:37–8:12, fol. 13v–18r) is characteristic of Constantinople and not of Jerusalem. It appears that the sparse pericope order of the manuscript led Aland to question whether *Sinai Gr. N.E. M 35* could be considered a typical witness of a Byzantine lectionary. The folder for this manuscript in the archives of the Institute for New Testament Textual Research in Münster, Westphalia, confirms Aland's doubt: the manuscript is labelled as *misch Typ* ('mixed type') and not as *Jerusalemer* ('Jerusalemite'), as it has been identified in the second edition of Aland's *Kurzgefaßte*

---

[118] Kekelidze, *Литургическіе грузинскіе памятники*, 228–72.   [119] Ibid., 272–313.

[120] See Sakvarelidze, 'Byzantinization of Georgian Liturgy', 273–90.

[121] See *ℓ* 2218: *ℓ*[+a]sel. Aland, *Kurzgefaßte Liste*, 356; Nikolopoulos, Νέα εὑρήματα, 164. No photograph of this manuscript is provided.

[122] *Von πασχα bis εωθ. in jerus. Folge mit byzant. Texten* ('From Easter to resurrectional Gospels in Jerusalemite order with Byzantine texts'). Aland, *Kurzgefaßte Liste*, 356 n. 8.

Liste.[123] The codex also contains Epistle readings, but only for the Saturdays and Sundays of Lent. Its dimensions are small (120 by 105 mm) and it contains 155 parchment folios.

Sinai Gr. N.E. M 66 (11th–12th cent.)

Codex *Sinai Gr. N.E. M 66* is a lectionary of Gospel and Epistle readings (εὐαγγέλια· ἀπόστολοι) similar to the previous manuscript.[124] According to Aland, this manuscript's readings are delivered in the Hagiopolite pericope order but the text of readings is that of the Byzantine lectionary, just like *Sinai Gr. N.E. M 35*.[125] The extant fifty-seven folios of the parchment manuscript begin with Holy Thursday and continue through Easter until Pentecost. The last folios contain readings from the menologion from 6 August until 9 March. The format of the manuscript is small (125 by 105 mm).

Sinai Gr. NE X 87 (11th–12th cent.)

Labelled a Gospel book (εὐαγγελιστάριον) in Nikolopoulos' catalogue, the lectionary manuscript *Sinai Gr. NE X 87* is similar in its structure to *Sinai Gr. N.E. МГ 8* (10th cent.). The manuscript contains Gospel and Epistle readings, as well as some hymnography and psalmody for the eucharistic synaxis. Unlike *Sinai Gr. N.E. МГ 8* (10th cent.), this manuscript is written in minuscule script, on paper, and has no Arabic marginal notes, though it does contain one marginal note in Georgian.[126] What remains of it begins with six Sundays of Luke (fol. 1r–19r) after the feast of Theophany. This is followed by hymnography, psalmody, an Epistle, and a Gospel for the synaxis on the feast of Hypapante (fol. 19r–24v), and then by the matins Gospel and synaxis psalmody, Epistle, and Gospel readings for the Sunday of Meatfare (fol. 24r–39r). The manuscript is defective and ends with the Gospel for matins on the second Sunday of Lent (fol. 39v).

Sinai Gr. 257 (1101/2)

On the basis of information provided in its colophon, the Gospel lectionary in codex *Sinai Gr. 257* is, from all the manuscripts known to have been copied on Mount Sinai, the oldest extant one that is dated and exclusively Greek:[127]

---

[123] My thanks to Andreas Juckel and Matthias Schulz for helping me to access folder ℓ 2218 and many others during a visit to Münster on 4 September 2014.

[124] See ℓ 2219: ℓ[+a]sel. Aland, *Kurzgefaßte Liste*, 356; Nikolopoulos, *Νέα εὑρήματα*, 169. No photograph of this manuscript is provided.

[125] As he puts it, *in jerus. Reihenfolge, aber mit byzant. Lesungen*. Aland, *Kurzgefaßte Liste*, 356 n. 9.

[126] Nikolopoulos, *Νέα εὑρήματα*, 204 and table 173. The photograph provided in the catalogue is of fol. 14v–15r. Nikolopoulos' catalogue describes the manuscript as having forty folios in five quires, but when I viewed this manuscript at the library on Mount Sinai in July 2012 it had thirty-nine folios in four quires.

[127] Ševčenko, 'Manuscript Production', 240–1.

ἀρχ(ὴν) καὶ τέλος ποιοῦ Θ(εὸ)ν· ἀρχ(ὴν) ἀπάντων καὶ τέλος ἐτελιόθ(η) δ(ιὰ) χειρὸς ἐ[μοῦ] Πέτρου (μον)αχ(οῦ) καὶ πρε(σβυ)τ(έ)ρ(ου) ὁ τοῦ ἁγιοῦ ὄρους Σινᾶ ἔτους ͵ϛχι’ οἱ ἀναγηνόσκο(ντ)ες εὔχ(εσ)θ(έ) μοι δ(ιὰ) τὸν κ(ύριο)ν. ὢ Χ(ριστ)έ μου σῶσον μ(ε) ὡς μόνος ἐλεήμον τὸν Πέτρον.[128]	The beginning and the end were made by God. The beginning and the end of all [readings] was completed by the hand of me, Peter, monk and presbyter of the holy Mount Sinai, in the year 6610 [= AD 1101/2]. May those who read it pray for me to the Lord. O my Christ, save me as Peter, O only merciful one.

The Gospel follows the Byzantine pericope order and includes readings for every day between Pascha and Pentecost, and then only for Saturdays and Sundays in the movable cycle.[129] The manuscript also contains a list of Gospel pericopes for the commemorations of the fixed cycle of the liturgical calendar.[130] Arabic marginal notes are also found at various points in the manuscript.[131]

Hagios Stavros Gr. 43 and *St Petersburg RNB Gr. 359* (1122)

Known popularly as 'the Typikon of the Anastasis', codex *Hagios Stavros Gr. 43* and its missing folios in *St Petersburg RNB Gr. 359* present the liturgy of the Church of the Anastasis in Jerusalem during Holy Week, Pascha, and Bright Week.[132] The manuscript is acephalous; in its present state it begins with the services of vespers on the eve of Palm Sunday and ends with the service for the Saturday after Easter. Although it bears no title, it contains a lengthy colophon indicating that it was copied in 1122 by Basil the Hagiopolite, at the order of the *sakellios* and *skeuophylax* George, archon of the Holy City.[133] The manuscript has been edited by Athanasios Papadopoulos-Kerameus (1856–1912), who gave it the title 'Τυπικὸν τῆς ἐν Ἱεροσολύμοις ἐκκλησίας'. The codex provides complete texts of hymnography, scriptural readings, and rubrics for the services and has been studied by numerous scholars.[134]

[128] Harlfinger, Reinsch, and Sonderkamp, *Specimina sinaitica*, 40–1 and tables 91–4, here 40.
[129] See ℓ 891: ℓesk †. Aland, *Kurzgefaßte Liste*, 272.
[130] Harlfinger, Reinsch, and Sonderkamp, *Specimina sinaitica*, table 93.   [131] Ibid., 40.
[132] Διάταξις τῶν ἱερῶν ἀκολουθιῶν τῆς μεγάλης τῶν παθῶν ἑβδομάδος τοῦ κυρίου ἡμῶν Ἰησοῦ Χριστοῦ, κατὰ τὸ ἀρχαῖον τῆς ἐν Ἱεροσολύμοις ἐκκλησίας ἔθος, ἤτοι τὸ ἐν τῷ ναῷ τῆς Ἀναστάσεως ('Arrangement of the sacred services of the great week of the passion of our Lord Jesus Christ, according to the ancient customs of the church in Jerusalem, in the Church of the Resurrection'). Papadopoulos-Kerameus, *Anastasis Typikon*, 1; Dmitrievskii, *Древнѣйшіе Патріаршіе Типиконы*, esp. 41–59, for a list of corrections to the typographical errors in Papadopoulos-Kerameus' edition. For the St Petersburg folia, see Evgenia E. Granstrem, 'Каталог греческих рукописей ленинградских хранилищ, 4: Рукописи XII века', *Византийский Временник* 23 (1963), 171. See Chapter 2, 'Hagiopolitan Patriarchs in Exile'.
[133] Papadopoulos-Kerameus, *Anastasis Typikon*, 252–3.
[134] For a detailed description of this manuscript, see Chapter 2, 'Hagiopolitan Patriarchs in Exile'.

Sinai Gr. 1096 (12th cent.)

The manuscript *Sinai Gr. 1096* is a collection of various documents related to daily life at the Lavra of St Sabas in Palestine, south-east of Jerusalem.[135] The title of this codex is 'Typikon of the Ecclesiastical Service in Jerusalem of the Holy Lavra of Our Venerable and God-bearing Father Sabas' (Τυπικὸν τῆς ἐκκλησιαστικῆς ἀκολουθίας τῆς ἐν Ἱερουσαλύμοις εὐαγοῦς λαύρας τοῦ ὁσίου θεοφόρου πατρὸς ἡμῶν Σάββα).[136] The manuscript's 193 folios begin with a description of a liturgical office characteristic of Sabaite monasticism—the vigil (ἀγρυπνία, fol. 1r–10r). This description is followed by various chapters that regulate readings, times of services, and other aspects of liturgical and daily life at the monastery (fol. 10v–24v).

Of the greatest interest here is the calendar of the liturgical Typikon (fol. 25r–129r), from 1 September until 31 August, with commemorations for every day except 21 to 24 March.[137] The local character of this calendar is highlighted by the presence of numerous Sabaite saints; the constant addition of hymnography to St Sabas (Περὶ τῶν παρασκευῶν καὶ σαββάτων, fol. 19r),[138] even beyond his feast and the unique octave surrounding it (fol. 55r);[139] and the frequent processions to the tomb of St Sabas and other specific chapels of the Lavra during the all-night vigil at the end of vespers and matins.[140]

The remainder of the manuscript contains the service for the washing on Holy Thursday (ἀκολουθία τοῦ νιπτῆρος, fol. 129r–132r), an anonymous 'Letter of a Brother to an Elder' (Ἐπιστολὴ ἀδελφοῦ πρὸς γέροντα, fol. 132v–133r), an equally anonymous 'Synoptic Knowledge of the Response about the Points Investigated' (Εὐσύνοπτος εἴδησις τῆς ἀποκρίσεως περὶ τῶν ἐρωτηθέντων ὑποθέσεων, fol. 133v–147v), and 'The Form, Transmission, and Custom of the Venerable Lavra of St Sabas' (Τύπος καὶ παράδοσις καὶ νόμος τῆς σεβασμίας λαύρας τοῦ ἁγίου Σάββα, fol. 148r–149v), also known as the 'Founder's Typikon' of St Sabas. This last work was edited separately by Dmitrievskii and was later included in the Dumbarton Oaks series on monastic foundation documents.[141] The manuscript ends with the order of services from Great Lent (fol. 150r–175v), Holy Week (fol. 175v–183r), and Easter (183v–186r). As a result of damage to the manuscript, the folios after Thomas Sunday are difficult to read and the end of the codex is lost.

---

[135] This manuscript was not photographed during the 1950 Sinai expedition of the Library of Congress. See Clark, *Sinai Checklist*, 11. Dmitrievskii's description has been compared with the state of the manuscript in July 2012. The total number of extant folios observed in July 2012 was 193, as opposed to the 185 described Dmitrievskii. See Dmitrievskii, *Описание* III, 20–65.

[136] Ibid., 20.   [137] Ibid., 28–55.   [138] Ibid., 26.

[139] Ibid., 34–5.   [140] Ibid., 21–2 and 24–5.

[141] Edward Kurtz, 'Review of A. Dmitrijevskij, "Die Klosterregeln des hl. Sabbas" (russ.), Arbeiten (Trudy) des kiewischen Geistlichen Akademie (Januar 1890), 170–192', BZ 3 (1894), 168–70; Dmitrievskii, *Описание* I, 222–4; BMFD IV, 1311–18.

Sinai Gr. 1097 (1214)

Among extant manuscripts, the liturgical Typikon preserved in codex *Sinai Gr. 1097* is the second oldest dated Greek one known to have been produced on Sinai.[142] According to Dmitrievskii, it represents the Sinaitic redaction of the Typikon. Its colophon reads:

Τυπικὸν κατὰ τὸν τύπον τῆς λαύρας τοῦ ὁσίου πατρὸς ἡμῶν Σάββα τῆς ἐν Ἱεροσολύμοις μονῆς, οἰκονομηθὲν καὶ ἀφιερωθὲν τῇ πανσέπτῳ καὶ ἁγίᾳ μονῇ τῆς ὑπεραγίας Θεοτόκου, τῆς ἐν τῷ ἁγίῳ ὄρει Σινᾶ ἱδρυμένης, ἐν ᾗ τετίμηται καὶ ὁ θεόπτης μέγας προφήτης Μωϋσῆς, ἐπεκτίσθη δὲ ἐκ προστάξεως τοῦ ἐν ταύτῃ ἀρχιερατεύοντος τοῦ παναγιωτάτου καὶ οὐρανοπολίτου πατρὸς ἡμῶν μοναχοῦ κυροῦ Συμεών. Μηνὶ Θευρουαρίῳ ἰνδικτιῶνος β΄, ἔτους ‚ςψκβ΄.[143]	Typikon according to the model of the Lavra of our venerable father, Sabas, of the monastery in Jerusalem, intended for and dedicated to the all-sacred and holy monastery of the most holy Theotokos, established on the holy Mount Sinai, in which the great God-seeing Prophet Moses is also honoured. It was acquired at the behest of its bishop, our most holy father, citizen of heaven, monk, Lord Symeon. In the month of February, second indiction, the year 6722 [= AD 1214].[144]

The contents of the codex, as described by Dmitrievskii, have been examined by Nancy P. Ševčenko, although her comments are preliminary: they have been made in anticipation of a complete study of the entire manuscript.[145] The manuscript contains a 'Short Description of Church Order of the Monasteries in Jerusalem' (Ἔκφρασις ἐν ἐπιτομῇ ἐκκλησιαστικῆς διατάξεως τῶν ἐν Ἱεροσολύμοις μοναστηρίων, fol. 25v–33r), which is a description of how the psalter is read during various liturgical services.[146] A calendar for the year, entitled 'Service of the Ecclesiastical Psalmody of the Whole Year' (Ἀκολουθία τῆς ἐκκλησιαστικῆς ψαλμῳδίας τοῦ ὅλου ἐνιαυτοῦ, fol. 67r–138v), occupies the remainder of the manuscript.[147] Here the Typikon contains both Constantinopolitan commemorations that became universally accepted within the Byzantine rite and local commemorations proper to Sinai, such as the feasts of the Prophet Moses (4 September), of St Catherine (24 November), and of the martyred monks at Sinai and Raithou (14 January) and the earthquake of 1201 (1 May). Some of these commemorations, such as the feast of the Prophet Moses and the earthquake, were celebrated solemnly and had pre-feasts. Some services are described twice—once according to the Typikon of St Sabas (fol. 5r) and a second time according to the Typikon of St Theodosius the Cenobiarch (fol. 20r). The presence of two liturgical

---

[142] Ševčenko, 'Manuscript Production', 241.
[143] See fol. 5r; cf. Dmitrievskii, *Описание* III, 394.   [144] Cf. Ševčenko, 'Typikon', 275.
[145] Ševčenko, 'Typikon', 284; Ševčenko, 'Manuscript Production', 241.
[146] Dmitrievskii, *Описание* III, 394–419, here 403; Parpulov, *Byzantine Psalters*, 94–102. It should be noted that the folio numbering cited by Dmitrievskii does not match the current folio numbering in the manuscript, as shown in the microfilm at the Library of Congress.
[147] Dmitrievskii, *Описание* III, 408–19; Ševčenko, 'Typikon', 278–84. It must be noted that Nancy Patterson Ševčenko's translation of the reference to St John Climacus on 30 March requires correction. The note in Dmitrievskii says: '30 March. There is no service to John Climacus' (30 Марта. Службы Іоанну Лѣствичнику нѣтъ). See Dmitrievskii, *Описание* III, 414; Ševčenko, 'Typikon', 282.

rules side by side in the same book suggests that the monks of Sinai were praying according to a developing liturgical practice in transition.

Vatican Syr. 20 (1215)

This Syriac Gospel book from Mount Senir near Damascus was copied on 14 December 1215.[148] The colophon on fol. 218 reads as follows:

> The description of this Gospel is complete; this is 'The Separation of Gospel Readings according to the Greek Rite for Sundays, Saturdays, Weekdays, and Feasts of the Whole Year', by the hand of the needy, poor, wretched, worthless, and greatest of all sinners, Joseph the Deacon. Joseph, son of Masud, son of Daniel, to whose soul may God give rest, wrote this book in the God-protected village of Cautha, diocese of Zebedaea, from the province of Damascus, in Mount Senir. Completed by the same copyist in the month of December, on the fourteenth day, Monday, in the year 1527 according to King Alexander, son of Phillip [= AD 1215].[149]

At the end of the colophon, the copyist uses the common metaphor of the scribe arriving at the harbour through the completion of the manuscript.[150]

Although Baumstark believed that a similar source served as a model for the Melkite calendar copied by Arab polymath al-Bīrūnī (972/3–1050) in the eleventh century,[151] *Vatican Syr. 20* shows stronger signs of Constantinopolitan influence. The Evangelion is divided much like the Gospel books of the Byzantine rite, beginning with the kanonarion from Pascha and the cycle of John and continuing with Matthew, Luke, and Mark. Some of the peculiarities are alternative Gospel readings from Luke for the third, fourth, and fifth Sundays of Lent (fol. 90–92),[152] two Gospels for an additional supplicatory service on Palm Sunday (fol. 96–99),[153] and the celebration of PRES on Good Friday (fol. 149).[154] The synaxarion indicates that it follows the cycle of readings for the year according to the Greek rite (fol. 161), from 1 September until 31 August.[155] The calendar is peculiar in that it presents many saints twice, includes numerous feasts of Enkainia, and commemorates groups of saints, such as the four evangelists and the Old Testament patriarchs.

---

[148] Assemani, *Catalogus*, vol. 2, 103–36.

[149] *Absoluta est descriptio huius Evangelii, hoc est, Distinctionis Lectionum Evangelicarum iuxta Ritum Graecorum in Dominicas, Sabbatha, Ferias, et Festa totius anni, per manum inopis, pauperis, miseri, vilis, et peccatorum omnium maximi, Josephi, nomine tantum Diaconi. Scripsit hunc librum Josephus filius Masudi, filii Danielis, cuius animae requiem donet Deus, de pago a Deo custodito Cautha, diocesis Zebedaeae, e provincia Damasci, in monte Senir. Perfecta est autem eiusdem scriptio mense Canun priore, die 14. Feria 2. Anno 1527. Alexandri Regis filii Philippi.* Assemani, *Catalogus*, vol. 2, 135–6.

[150] Sebastian P. Brock, 'The Scribe Reaches Harbour', *Byzantinische Forschungen* 21 (1995), 195–202, here 197.

[151] Al-Bīrūnī, *Fêtes des Melchites*; Anton Baumstark, 'Ausstrahlungen des vorbyzantinischen Heiligenkalenders von Jerusalem', OCP 2 (1936): 129–44. For a description of this source, see Chapter 2.

[152] Assemani, *Catalogus*, vol. 2, 111–12.   [153] Ibid., 112.

[154] *Fer. 6. majori, ad consignationum calicis, idest, ad missam praesanctificatorum.* Ibid., 113.

[155] *Initium anni juxta ritum graecorum.* Ibid., 114, 136.

Sinai Gr. N.E. X 73 (13th cent.)

The fragmentary Gospel and Epistle lectionary (εὐαγγέλια καὶ ἀπόστολοι παρακλητηκῆς) in *Sinai Gr. N.E. X 73* is today composed of twenty paper folios of a small format (165 by 130 mm).[156] The manuscript's connection to Hagiopolite liturgy was noted by Kurt Aland, who stated that the manuscript 'follows Jerusalem's pericope order but contains the Byzantine readings'.[157] The manuscript contains readings from various points of the liturgical year, including Epistles and Gospels for weekdays, as well as seemingly arbitrary readings for the Transfiguration of Christ, St John Chrysostom, martyrs, St Thekla and St Marina, the third Sunday of Luke, and the Sunday of All Saints. As with *Sinai Gr. N.E. M 35* and *Sinai Gr. N.E. M 66*, there is little that is distinctly Hagiopolitan about *Sinai Gr. N.E. X 73*.

Sinai Gr. 1040 (14th cent.)

The codex *Sinai Gr. 1040* contains a service book for the deacon known as a Diakonikon (Διακονικόν). The frequently commemorated Archbishop Peter (9r, 16r, 19v, 33v, 37r, 47r, 47v, 73v) was identified as Archbishop Peter III of Sinai (r. *c.*1169–80?), a contemporary of Manuel I Comnenus (r. 1143–1180), but unidentified by Dmitrievskii.[158] Other names included in the diptychs of the living (fol. 9r–10r) and in litanies such as the prayers for the health of Emperor Manuel I Comnenus and his wife, Maria of Antioch (*c.*1140–82/3),[159] together with the commemoration of Patriarch Luke Chrysoberges of Constantinople (r. *c.*1157–70),[160] suggested to Dmitrievskii that the manuscript was copied during their lifetime, between 1156 and 1169. If, however, the dates for Archbishop Peter III are correct, the commemorations of the living point to 1169–70 as a possible date when the manuscript was copied. Dmitrievskii also believed that the script of the manuscript could be dated to the twelfth century.[161] Other palaeographers, however, suggested a later date. Victor Gardthausen (1843–1925), followed by André Jacob, Kamil Murad, and Alkiviades Kazamias, dated the manuscript to the fourteenth century.[162] Since the colophons at the end of the manuscript (fol. 76r) are themselves undated, the exact century when the manuscript

---

[156] ℓ 2220: ℓ+ᵃP. Aland, *Kurzgefaßte Liste*, 356; Nikolopoulos, Νέα εὑρήματα, 202. No photograph of this manuscript is provided.

[157] [W]ohl in jerus. Reihenfolge, aber mit byzant. Lesungen. Aland, *Kurzgefaßte Liste*, 356 n. 10.

[158] See Adrian Marinescu, *Mănăstirea Sf. Ecaterina de la Muntele Sinai și legăturile ei cu Țările Române: Perspectivă istorico-patristică* (Bucharest: Editura Sophia, 2009), 424–5. Peter is missing from Fedalto's list. See Fedalto, *Hierarchia ecclesiastica orientalis*, vol. 2, 1044–5.

[159] Charles M. Brand, Alexander Kazhdan, and Anthony Cutler, 'Manuel I Komnenos', ODB II, 1289–90; Charles M. Brand, 'Maria of Antioch', ODB II, 1298.

[160] Fedalto, *Hierarchia ecclesiastica orientalis*, vol. 1, 7.

[161] Dmitrievskii, Описаніе II, 127–8.

[162] Victor Gardthausen, *Catalogus codicum Graecorum Sinaiticorum* (Oxford: Clarendon, 1886), 219; Jacob, 'Une version géorgienne', 71–2; Kamil Murad, *Catalogue of All Manuscripts in the Monastery of St Catharine on Mount Sinai* (Wiesbaden: Otto Harrassowitz, 1970), 113 [ms. 1383]; Kazamias, Θεία Λειτουργία τοῦ Ἁγίου Ἰακώβου, 39 and 54–6. The manuscript is not listed in Clark, *Sinai Checklist*, and was not photographed by the Library of Congress. For the variety of opinions on the dating of this manuscript, see Stéphane Verhelst, 'La "kéryxie catholique" de la

was copied remains uncertain. Regardless of this unresolved question, I follow Taft, who claims that this is a fourteenth-century copy that transmits the liturgy of a twelfth-century original.[163]

The manuscript's seventy-seven folios contain the diaconal petitions from JAS (fol. 1r–19r) without any exclamations by the priest or chanters;[164] diaconal petitions from HagPRES (Διακονικὰ τῆς προηγιασμένης λειτουργίας τοῦ ἁγίου Ἰακώβου; 'Diaconal Litanies of the Presanctified Liturgy of St James', fol. 19r–32r); diaconal petitions for CHR (Διακονικὰ τῆς θείας λειτουργίας τοῦ ἐν ἁγίοις πατρὸς ἡμῶν Ἰωάννου τοῦ Χρυσοστόμου; 'Diaconal Litanies of the Divine Liturgy of Our Father among the Saints John Chrysostom', fol. 33r–53r), where Manuel I Comnenus and Maria of Antioch are commemorated among the living; diaconal petitions for PRES of St Basil (Διακονικὰ τῆς προηγιασμένης θείας λειτουργίας τοῦ ἁγίου Βασιλείου; 'Diaconal Litanies of the Presanctified Divine Liturgy of St Basil', fol. 53v–68v); the order of great vespers on Saturday evening (fol. 69r–74v); and the litany 'Save your people, O God' (Σῶσον, ὁ Θεός, τὸν λαόν σου, fol. 74v–75v).[165] Apart from the Hagiopolite liturgies of JAS and HagPRES, certain characteristically Hagiopolitan liturgical practices have found their way into CHR, such as the addition of saints into the petition 'Remembering the most holy, more pure' (Τῆς παναγίας, ἀχράντου, fol. 46v), the 'Prayer of those bringing offerings' (Εὐχὴ τῆς καρποφορίας, fol. 51r–52r),[166] and the diaconal command 'In the peace of Christ, sing' (Ἐν εἰρήνῃ Χριστοῦ ψάλατε, fol. 52r) before the Communion hymn.[167]

Sinai Gr. N.E. X 159 (14th–16th cent.)

The Praxapostolos (πραξαπόστολος) preserved in codex *Sinai Gr. N.E. X 159* was copied by Deacon Christodoulos.[168] Since the colophon provides no date or place of copying, the dating of the paper codex is disputed: Aland indicates that it is from the fourteenth century,[169] while Nikolopoulos prefers a later dating—the fifteenth or sixteenth century. Regardless of this uncertainty, the fourteenth century is already an extremely late date for any liturgical book to reflect the pericope order of the Jerusalem lectionary. Aland's brief description of the manuscript indicates that it contains Epistle readings from the first Sunday of Lent (κυρ. α´ νηστ) until Saturday of Bright Week (σαβ. διακιν.), then Saturday and Sunday readings, followed by the menologion, from 8 September until 29 August, and also Epistle readings for weekdays and resurrectional

---

liturgie de Jérusalem et le shemoneh 'esreh', *Questions Liturgiques* 81 (2000), 5–47, here 11; Verhelst, *Traditions judéo-chrétiennes*, 15.

[163] Taft, *Diptychs*, 13–14.

[164] The complete text is published in Dmitrievskii, Богослуженіе страсной и пасхальной седмицъ, 270–85.

[165] Dmitrievskii, Описаніе II, 127–35. Note that the page numbering in Dmitrievskii differs from the numbering in the manuscript as observed de visu in July 2012.

[166] Brakmann, 'Zur Εὐχὴ τῆς καρποφορίας'.

[167] Ibid., 134. See also Taft, *Precommunion Rites*, 253.

[168] The colophon reads 'Γράψαντα προστάξαντα Χριστόδουλος διάκονος'. Nikolopoulos, *Νέα εὑρήματα*, 213 and tab. 191.

[169] See ℓ 2221: ℓᵃP. Aland, *Kurzgefaßte Liste*, 356.

prokeimena (προκείμενα ἀναστάσιμα).[170] As in the case of the manuscripts *Sinai Gr. N.E. M 35*, *Sinai Gr. N.E. M 66*, and *Sinai Gr. N.E. X 73* (already discussed), Aland claims that this lectionary follows the Jerusalem order in structure but the content of the readings is that of the Byzantine order.[171] Closer inspection of the manuscript's eighty-eight extant folios indicates that the codex is a haphazard collection of Epistle readings used by a specific community for the Divine Liturgy on feasts of saints they particularly venerated. The presence of specific readings for St Thekla (fol. 38r–39r), Prophet Elias (fol. 62r–65r), and the Maccabean Martyrs (fol. 65r–67v) in such a sparse codex is unusual.

---

[170] See Nikolopoulos, *Νέα εὑρήματα*, table 191, where tones 1 to 3 are visible.

[171] [*W*]*ohl in jerus. Reihenfolge, aber mit byzant. Lesungen* ('Probably in Jerusalemite order, but with Byzantine readings'). Aland, *Kurzgefaßte Liste*, 356 n. 11.

APPENDIX 2

Maps and Plans

Plan of the Church of the Anastasis (4th, 11th, and 12th cent.)

Based on Pringle, *Churches of the Crusader Kingdom*, vol. 3, 8.

For other plans of the Anastasis Complex, see Corbo, *Il Santo Sepolcro di Gerusalemme*, vol. 2 (tavola 1); Pringle, *Churches of the Crusader Kingdom*, vol. 3, 39–40 and 49.

These three plans of the Church of the Anastasis show the state of the complex of buildings in the fourth, eleventh, and twelfth centuries. In each plan, the aedicule of the Anastasis remains constant in the rotunda, but the Martyrium and Golgotha are modified after the destruction in 1009: the Martyrium is lost and a new, smaller space replaces it, opening to the west, onto the aedicule of the Anastasis, rather than to the east, onto the main street (*cardo maximus*) of Jerusalem.

Map of the City of Jerusalem (4th–11th cent.)

Based on 'Jerusalem Baugeschichte, Karte III: Vom Wiederaufbau in hadrianischer Zeit bis zum Vorabend der Kreuzzüge (117–1099 n. Chr.)', in *Tübinger Bibelatlas: Auf Grunladge des Tübinger Atlas des Vordern Orients (TAVO)*, ed. by Siegfried Mittmann and Götz Schmitt (Stuttgart: Deutsche Bibelgesellschaft, 2001), B IV 7.

For other maps of the city of Jerusalem, see Abel, 'Jérusalem', 2304–5 (illustration 6175); Maraval, *Lieux saints*, 255; Verhelst, 'Lieux de station' I, 69; Pringle, *Churches of the Crusader Kingdom*, vol. 3, 477–81.

This map of the city of Jerusalem shows the main churches of Jerusalem's stational liturgy, as found in the AL and GL, as well as later buildings, added after 638. The network of the stational liturgy was centred on the Church of the Anastasis and included such churches as the Church of Sion and the Nea Church of the Theotokos inside the city walls, the Imbomon and the Apostoleion on the Mount of Olives outside the city walls, and the Kathisma Church and the Church of the Nativity in Bethlehem further afield.

Map of the Patriarchate of Jerusalem (4th–11th cent.)

Based on Yoram Tsafrir, Leah Di Segni and Judith Green, 'Churches in Byzantine Palestine', in *Tabula Imperii Romani: Iudaea, Palaestina: Eretz Israel in the Hellenistic, Roman and Byzantine Periods* (Jerusalem: Israel Academy of Sciences and Humanities, 1994); Levy-Rubin, 'The Reorganisation of the Patriarchate of Jerusalem', 225; 'Palästina in spätrömisch-byzantinischer Zeit (*c*.300–640 n. Chr.)', in *Tübinger Bibelatlas: Auf Grunladge des Tübinger Atlas des Vordern Orients (TAVO)*, ed. by Siegfried Mittmann and Götz Schmitt (Stuttgart: Deutsche Bibelgesellschaft, 2001), B VI 10.

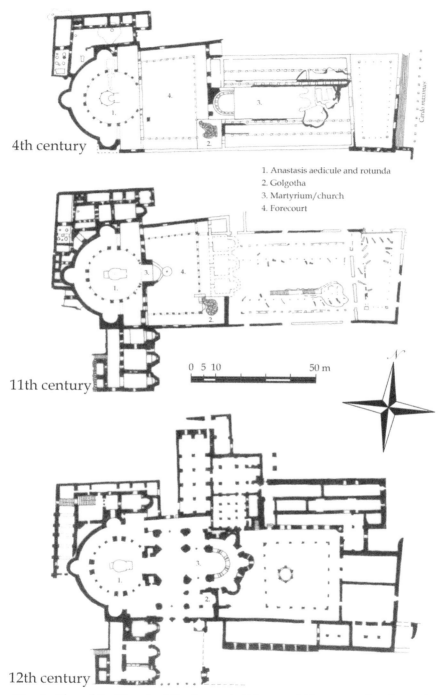

4th century

1. Anastasis aedicule and rotunda
2. Golgotha
3. Martyrium/church
4. Forecourt

0 5 10   50 m

11th century

12th century

Map 1. Plan of the Church of the Anastasis (4th cent., 11th cent., and 12th cent.)

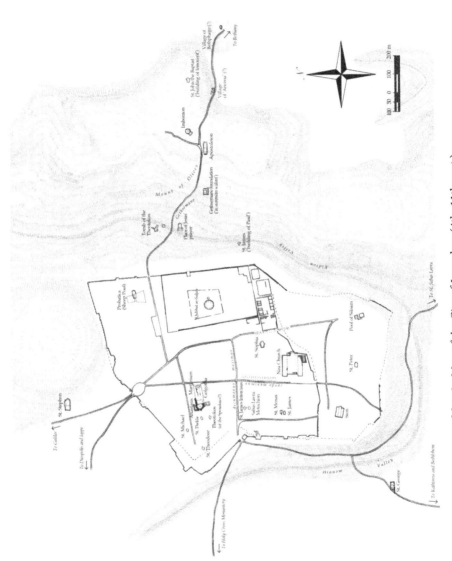

Map 2. Map of the City of Jerusalem (4th–11th cent.)

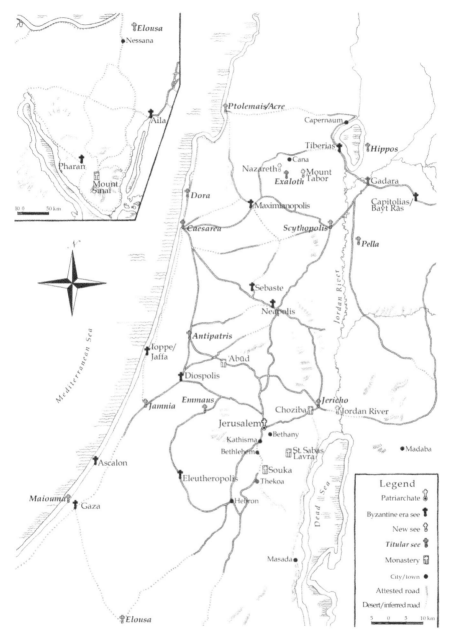

Map 3. Map of the Patriarchate of Jerusalem (4th–11th cent.)

This map of the patriarchate of Jerusalem, which consisted of the provinces of Palaestina I, Palaestina II, and Palaestina Salutaris/Palaestina III, including Sinai, shows the location of major episcopal sees between the fourth and eleventh centuries. Due to various factors, certain sees declined and became titular sees, while new sees arose after the Byzantine period in order to respond to the new situation of the patriarchate. Monasteries and other places of interest are also indicated on the map.

Glossary

Anaphora (ἀναφορά): the central prayer of the Divine Liturgy, which generally includes the initial dialogue between the presider and the assembly, the Sanctus, the institution narrative, epiclesis, and diptychs. See also Divine Liturgy.

Anastasis (ἀνάστασις): (a) 'resurrection', used to refer to the Resurrection of Christ and Pascha; (b) rotunda and aedicule over the tomb of Christ in Jerusalem, also known as the Holy Sepulchre.

Bright Week (διακαινήσιμος): the week from Pascha until the following Sunday, known as Thomas Sunday, New Sunday, or the Sunday of Antipascha. See also Pascha.

Chalcedonian: adjectival form used to denote followers of the decisions of the fourth Ecumenical Council in Chalcedon, Bithynia, in AD 451 on Christology. Those who did not accept this council's decisions are referred to as 'non-Chalcedonians'. See also Melkite.

Diakonikon (διακονικόν): (a) liturgical book containing the litanies, short petitions with brief responses by the singers, said by the deacon during the Divine Liturgy and the Liturgy of the Hours; (b) part of the church building, usually to the south of the altar, where sacred vessels or other objects may be kept and where the clergy prepare for liturgical services.

Divine Liturgy (θεία λειτουργία): the celebration of Eucharist, which includes the Liturgy of the Word, the transfer of the gifts, the anaphora, Communion, and the concluding rites. The prayers of the various Divine Liturgies, such as those of St James, St Basil the Great, or St John Chrysostom, are arranged according to their respective 'formulary', which contains the standard texts of the service, referred to as the 'ordinary'.

Enkainia (ἐγκαίνια): dedication or renewal, with reference to the dedication of a church. In Jerusalem, the term referred specifically to the annual commemoration of the Dedication of the Church of the Holy Sepulchre on 13 September, although it was also used to describe the commemoration of the dedication of other churches.

Euchologion (εὐχολόγιον): liturgical book of the presider at liturgical services; it contains the texts of prayers (εὐχαί) for the eucharistic Divine Liturgy, the Liturgy of the Hours, sacraments, and other blessings.

Feast (ἑορτή): the celebration or commemoration of a biblical event, such as Pascha, or of the death or martyrdom of a saint, such as the feast of St James. Liturgical services such as the synaxis or Divine Liturgy, or vespers and matins, were performed at feasts and included texts, for example pericopes and hymns, that were proper to the feast being celebrated.

Hagiopolite (ἁγιοπολίτης): adjective derived from the Greek phrase used to refer to Jerusalem, ἁγία πόλις (the 'Holy City). Although 'Hagiopolitan' would be the proper English form of a derivative of this type, 'Hagiopolite' has been used consistently in English language liturgical studies, likely under the influence of French (*hagiopolite*) and Italian (*agiopolita*) scholarship, and is followed here for the most part.

Holy Week (μεγάλη ἑβδομάς): the week before Pascha, from Holy Monday until Pascha. See also Pascha.

Horologion (ὡρολόγιον): liturgical book containing psalms, prayers, and hymns for the Liturgy of the Hours.

Iadgari (იადგარი): See Tropologion.

Introit: hymn sung during the entrance of the clergy into the church. The term derives from the Latin *introitus*, which meant 'entrance', and is equivalent to the Greek *eisodikon* (εἰσοδικόν) or the Georgian *oxitay* (ოხითაჲ).

Lectionary: liturgical book containing scriptural readings for liturgical services, particularly for the Divine Liturgy, usually arranged according to the order in which the pericopes are read during the liturgical year.

Liturgical calendar: list of all the commemorations of saints and feast days during the year. Such lists are often found at the end of the Praxapostolos, Tetraevangelion, or other liturgical lectionary.

Liturgy: the communal prayer of the church, but also, more specifically, the celebration of the Eucharist, i.e. the Divine Liturgy. See also Divine Liturgy.

Liturgy of the Hours: liturgical services and prayer at set points of the day, particularly in the morning (matins), in the evening (vespers), and at the various other hours of the day, such as the first, third, sixth, and ninth hours, according to the Byzantine reckoning of the hours of the day. The technical term is derived from the Latin phrase *liturgia horarum*. See also Horologion.

Liturgy of the Word: the first part of the Divine Liturgy, which contains introductory hymns and prayers and scriptural readings such as from the Epistle and the Gospel.

Matins: major service in the Liturgy of the Hours served in the morning and also known as Orthros (ὄρθρος). See also Liturgy of the Hours.

Melkite (*mălkāyā*): adjective used to refer to adherents of Chalcedonian Christology and members of the Orthodox Church in the eastern patriarchates of Alexandria, Antioch, and Jerusalem. The term comes from the Syriac word for 'royal' or 'imperial'.

Menaion (μηναῖον): liturgical book containing the variable hymnography for the movable feasts of the liturgical year, divided according to the twelve months (μήν, pl. μῆνες), from which the Greek name is derived. See also Liturgical calendar.

Oktoechos (ὀκτώηχος): liturgical book of hymnographic compositions for the Divine Liturgy and the Liturgy of the Hours according to the eight tones or modes.

Ordinary: fixed liturgical texts used during the Divine Liturgy and the Liturgy of the Hours that are constant, unlike the propers, which change according to the day or the specific commemoration. The texts of the ordinary provide the basic form and structure of their respective liturgical services. The term comes from the Latin technical use of *ordinarium*. See also Propers.

Pascha (*πάσχα*): Easter, the annual celebration of the Resurrection of Christ.

Pentecost (*πεντηκοστή*): (a) the commemoration of the descent of the Holy Spirit on the Apostles on the fiftieth day after Pascha; (b) the whole fifty-day period from Pascha until the commemoration of the descent of the Holy Spirit.

Pentekostarion (*πεντηκοστάριον*): liturgical book containing the liturgical hymns for Pascha, Bright Week, and the period of Pentecost. The book was once together with the Triodion, and older versions of the Pentekostarion still bear the name 'Triodion' in their titles. See also Pascha, Bright Week, Pentecost, Triodion.

Pericope: an excerpt from a scriptural text, to be read during a liturgical service. The length of each pericope can vary between a few verses and a whole chapter from a book of the Bible.

Praxapostolos (*πραξαπόστολος*): liturgical book containing New Testament readings other than the four Gospels, used at the Divine Liturgy; occasionally referred to as the 'non-Gospel' (*nichtevangelisch*) lectionary. The Greek name is derived from the name for the Acts of the Apostles (*Πράξεις τῶν Ἀποστόλων*) and Epistle (*ἀπόστολος*). See also Lectionary.

Propers: variable liturgical texts, such as scriptural readings, psalms, hymns, and prayers, used during the Divine Liturgy and the Liturgy of the Hours that depend on the day or the specific commemoration. The term is derived from the Latin technical term *proprium*. See also Ordinary.

Sabaite (*σαβαϊτικός, σαβαΐτης*): adjectival form referring to the Mar Saba Lavra, a monastery in Palestine south-east of Jerusalem, founded in the late fifth century by St Sabas the Sanctified.

Synaxis (*σύναξις*): (a) assembly, referring to the liturgical gathering, such as the eucharistic Divine Liturgy, but not exclusively; (b) category of celebration in the liturgical calendar, particularly 'concomitant feast' on the day after a major celebration of the liturgical year.

Tetraevangelion (*τετραευαγγέλιον*): liturgical lectionary of the four Gospels read at the Divine Liturgy and other liturgical services, particularly during matins.

Triodion (*τριῴδιον*): liturgical book containing hymns and scriptural readings, as well as prescriptions of patristic texts, to be read in the Divine Liturgy and the Liturgy of the Hours during the period of Great Lent and the preceding preparatory weeks. The name is derived from the three-ode hymnographic canon that is a particular feature of Great Lent in the Byzantine rite.

Tropologion (*τροπολόγιον*): liturgical book containing the various hymns for the liturgical year, generally in one volume. This book is the predecessor of the Menaion,

Triodion, Pentekostarion, and Oktoechos. The Georgian translation of this liturgical book is known as the *Iadgari* (იადგარი).

Typikon (τυπικόν): liturgical book regulating the various hymns, psalms, and scriptural readings for all the services of the liturgical year. The term has been used in liturgical scholarship to refer to both a regulatory book, as well as to books resembling a liturgical lectionary, Oktoechos, Menaion, Pentekostarion, and Triodion. See also Liturgical calendar.

Vespers (ἑσπερινός): major service in the Liturgy of the Hours served in the evening. See also Liturgy of the Hours.

Additional Byzantine liturgical terminology may be found in the following glossaries and dictionaries:

Archbishop Job Getcha, *The Typikon Decoded: An Explanation of Byzantine Liturgical Practice*, trans. by Paul Meyendorff (Orthodox Liturgy Series 3, Yonkers, NY: St Vladimir's Seminary Press, 2012), 287–300 (Glossary).
The Blackwell Dictionary of Eastern Christianity, ed. Ken Parry, David J. Melling, Dimitri Brady, Sidney H. Griffith, and John F. Healey (Oxford: Blackwell, 1999).
The Oxford Dictionary of Byzantium, 3 vols, ed. Alexander P. Kazhdan et al. (New York: Oxford University Press, 1991).
Православная Энциклопедия, vols 1–, ed. Sergei L. Kravets (Moscow: Церковно-научный центр «Православная Энциклопедия», 2000–).
Robert F. Taft, *Литургический лексикон* [Liturgical lexicon], ed. and trans. by Sergey V. Golovanov (Omsk: Амофра, 2013).
Θρησκευτικὴ καὶ Ἠθικὴ Ἐγκυκλοπαιδεία, 12 vols (Athens: Ath. Martinos, 1962–8).

Bibliography

Abel, 'Jérusalem' = Abel, Félix-Marie. 'Jérusalem'. DACL 7.2: 2304–74.

Abel, 'La sépulture de saint Jacques' = Abel, Félix-Marie. 'La sépulture de Saint Jacques le mineur'. *Revue Biblique* 28 (1919): 480–99.

Aland, *Kurzgefaßte Liste* = Aland, Kurt, ed. *Kurzgefaßte Liste der griechischen Handschriften des Neuen Testaments*, 2nd revised and expanded edn. Arbeiten zur neutestamentlichen Textforschung 1. Berlin: Walter de Gruyter, 1994.

al-Bīrūnī, *Fêtes des Melchites* = Al-Birouni, Abou Rîhân. *Les fêtes des Melchites*, ed. and trans. by Robert Griveau. PO 10.4: 292–312. Paris: Firmin-Didot, 1915.

Aleksidze et al., *Catalogue of Georgian Manuscripts* = Aleksidze, Zaza, Mzekala Shanidze, and Lily Khevsuriani. *Catalogue of Georgian Manuscripts Discovered in 1975 at St Catherine's Monastery on Mount Sinai*, trans. Mzekala Shanidze. Athens: Greek Ministry of Culture and Mount Sinai Foundation, 2005.

Alexopoulos, *Presanctified Liturgy* = Alexopoulos, Stefanos. *The Presanctified Liturgy in the Byzantine Rite: A Comparative Analysis of Its Origins, Evolution, and Structural Components*. Liturgia Condenda 21. Leuven: Peeters, 2009.

Andreou, *Praxapostolos* = Andreou, Georgios. *Il* Praxapostolos *bizantino dell'XI secolo: Vladimir 21/Savva 4 del Museo Storico di Mosca: Edizione e commento*. Unpublished doctoral dissertation. Rome: Pontifical Oriental Institute, 2008.

Arranz, 'Grandes étapes' = Arranz, Miguel, SJ. 'Les grandes étapes de la liturgie byzantine: Palestine—Byzance—Russie: Essai d'aperçu historique'. In *Liturgie de l'Église particulière et liturgie de l'église universelle*, 43–72. BELS 7. Rome: Edizioni Liturgiche, 1976.

Ashgate Companion to Byzantine Hagiography I = *The Ashgate Research Companion to Byzantine Hagiography*, vol. 1: *Periods and Places*, ed. by Stephanos Efthymiadis. Burlington, VT: Ashgate, 2011.

Ashgate Companion to Byzantine Hagiography II = *The Ashgate Research Companion to Byzantine Hagiography*, vol. 2: *Genres and Contexts*, ed. by Stephanos Efthymiadis. Burlington, VT: Ashgate, 2014.

Assemani, *Missale Hierosolymitanum* = Assemani, Joseph Aloysius. *Codex liturgicus ecclesiæ universæ*, vol. 5: *Missale Hierosolymitanum*. Rome: Hæredes Barbiellini, 1752.

Assemani, *Catalogus* = Assemani, Stephanus Evodius, and Joseph Simonius Assemani. *Bibliothecæ apostolicæ vaticanæ codicum manuscriptorum catalogus: in tres partes distributus in quarum prima orientales in altera graeci in tertia latini italici alorumque europaeorum idiomatum codices*, 3 vols. Paris: Librairie Orientale et Américaine, 1926 [1758].

Aubineau, *Hésychius de Jérusalem* = *Les Homélies festales d'Hésychius de Jérusalem*, 2 vols, ed. by Michel Aubineau. SH 58–9. Brussels: Société des Bollandistes, 1978–80.

Auzépy, 'De la Palestine à Constantinople' = Auzépy, Marie-France. 'De la Palestine à Constantinople (VIIIᵉ–IXᵉ siècles): Étienne le Sabaïte et Jean Damascène'. *Travaux et Mémoires* 12 (1994): 183–218.

Baldovin, *Liturgy in Ancient Jerusalem* = Baldovin, John F., SJ. *Liturgy in Ancient Jerusalem*. Grove Liturgical Study 57. Nottingham: Grove Books, 1989.

Baldovin, *Urban Character* = Baldovin, John F., SJ. *The Urban Character of Christian Worship: The Origins, Development, and Meaning of Stational Liturgy*. OCA 228. Rome: Pontifical Oriental Institute, 1987.

Balsamon, 'Λύσεις ἐπὶ ταῖς ἀπορίαις' = Θεοδώρου Ἀντιοχείας τοῦ Βαλσαμῶνος. 'Λύσεις ἐπὶ ταῖς ἀπορίαις τοῦ ἁγιωτάτου πατριάρχου Ἀλεξανδρείας κῦρ Μάρκου ἐξενεχθεῖσαι ἐπὶ τῆς πατριαρχείας τοῦ ἁγιωτάτου πατριάρχου Κωνσταντινοπόλεως κῦρ Γεωργίου τοῦ Ξιφιλίνου.' In Manouel I. Gedeon, ed., *Νέα βιβλιοθήκη ἐκκλησιαστικῶν συγγραφέων*, vol. 1.1: 135–60. Constantinople: *Πατριαρχικοῦ Τυπογραφείου*, 1903.

Baumstark, *Comparative Liturgy* = Baumstark, Anton. *Comparative Liturgy*, rev. edn, ed. by Bernard Botte, trans. by Frank L. Cross. Westminster, MD: Newman Press, 1958.

Baumstark, *Nichtevangelische Perikopenordnungen* = Baumstark, Anton. *Nichtevangelische syrische Perikopenordnungen des ersten Jahrtausends*. Liturgiegeschichtliche Forschungen 3. Münster: Aschendorff, 1921.

Bertonière, *Easter Vigil* = Bertonière, Gabriel, OCSO. *The Historical Development of the Easter Vigil and Related Services in the Greek Church*. OCA 193. Rome: Pontifical Oriental Institute, 1972.

Bertonière, *Sundays of Lent* = Bertonière, Gabriel, OCSO. *The Sundays of Lent in the Triodion: The Sundays without a Commemoration*. OCA 253. Rome: Pontifical Oriental Institute, 1997.

Bieberstein, 'Gesandtenaustausch' = Bieberstein, Klaus. 'Der Gesandtenaustausch zwischen Karl dem Grossen und Hārūn ar-Rašīd und seine Bedeutung für die Kirchen Jerusalems'. *Zeitschrift des Deutschen Palästina-Vereins* 109 (1993): 151–73.

Bieberstein, 'Sion' = Bieberstein, Klaus. 'Die Hagia Sion in Jerusalem: Zur Entwicklung ihrer Traditionen im Spiegel der Pilgerberichte'. In *Akten des XII. Internationales Kongresses für Christliche Archäologie, Bonn, 22.–28. September 1991*, ed. by Ernst Dassmann, Josef Engemann, and Josef Engemann, vol. 1, 543–51. Münster: Aschendorffsche Verlagsbuchhandlung, 1995.

Bieberstein, Klaus, and Hanswulf Bloedhorn. *Jerusalem: Grundzüge der Baugeschichte vom Chalkolithikum bis zur Frühzeit der osmanischen Herrschaft*, 3 vols. Beihefte zum Tübinger Atlas des Vorderen Orients, Reihe B (Geisteswissenschaften), Nr. 100/1–3. Wiesbaden: Dr. Ludwig Reichert Verlag, 1994.

Binggeli, 'Calendrier melkite de Jérusalem' = Binggeli, André. 'Un ancien calendrier melkite de Jérusalem (Sinaï syr. M52N)'. In *Sur les pas des Araméens chrétiens: Mélanges offerts à Alain Desreumaux*, ed. by Françoise Briquel Chatonnet, and Muriel Debié, 181–94. Paris: Geuthner, 2010.

Bitton-Ashkelony and Kofsky, 'Monasticism in the Holy Land' = Bitton-Ashkelony, Brouria, and Aryeh Kofsky. 'Monasticism in the Holy Land'. In *Christians and Christianity in the Holy Land: From the Origins to the Latin Kingdoms*, ed. by Ora Limor and Guy G. Stroumsa, 257–91. Turnhout: Brepols, 2006.

Booth, *Crisis of Empire* = Booth, Phil. *Crisis of Empire: Doctrine and Dissent at the End of Late Antiquity*. Transformation of the Classical Heritage 52. Berkeley, CA: University of California Press, 2014.

Bornert, *Commentaires* = Bornert, René, OSB. *Les commentaires byzantins de la Divine Liturgie du VIIe au XVe siècle.* Archives de l'Orient Chrétien 9. Paris: Institut français d'études byzantines, 1966.

Botte, *Les origines de la Noël et de l'Épiphanie* = Botte, Bernard, OSB. *Les origines de la Noël et de l'Épiphanie: Étude historique.* Textes et Études Liturgiques 1. Louvain: Abbaye du Mont César, 1932.

Boudignon, *Maximi Confessoris Mystagogia* = *Maximi Confessoris Mystagogia una cum Latina interpretatione Anastasii Bibliothecarii,* ed. by Christian Boudignon. CCSG 69. Turnhout: Brepols, 2011.

Bradshaw, *Search for the Origins* = Bradshaw, Paul F. *The Search for the Origins of Christian Worship,* 2nd edn. New York: Oxford University Press, 2002.

Bradshaw and Johnson, *Eucharistic Liturgies* = Bradshaw, Paul F., and Maxwell E. Johnson. *The Eucharistic Liturgies: Their Evolution and Interpretation.* Collegeville, MN: Liturgical Press, 2012.

Bradshaw and Johnson, *Origins of Feasts* = Bradshaw, Paul F., and Maxwell E. Johnson. *The Origins of Feasts, Fasts and Seasons in Early Christianity.* Alcuin Club Collections 86. Collegeville, MN: Liturgical Press, 2011.

Brakmann, 'Zur Εὐχὴ τῆς καρποφορίας' = Brakmann, Heinzgerd. 'Zur Εὐχὴ τῆς καρποφορίας in der melchitischen Markos-Liturgie'. *Ephemerides Liturgicae* 98 (1984): 75–80.

Brakmann and Chronz, 'Eine Blume der Levante' = Brakmann, Heinzgerd, and Tinatin Chronz. 'Eine Blume der Levante: Zu den Anfängen der modernen Jakobosliturgie'. In *Orientalia Christiana: Festschrift für Hubert Kaufhold zum 70. Gerburtstag,* ed. Peters Bruns and Hinez Otto Luthe, 85–107. Eichstätter Beiträge zum Christlichen Orient 3. Wiesbaden: Harrasowitz Verlag, 2013.

Brakmann and Chronz, 'Jerusalemer Euchologion' = Brakmann, Heinzgerd, and Tinatin Chronz. 'Ist das jerusalemer Euchologion noch zu retten?' *Archiv für Liturgiewissenschaft* 54 (2012): 1–28.

Brightman, *Eastern Liturgies* = *Liturgies Eastern and Western: Being the Texts Original or Translated of the Principal Liturgies of the Church,* vol. 1: *Eastern Liturgies,* ed. by Frank E. Brightman. Oxford: Clarendon, 1896.

Brock, 'Manuscrits liturgiques' = Brock, Sebastian P. 'Manuscrits liturgiques en syriaque'. In *Les liturgies syriaques,* ed. by François Cassingena-Trévedy and Izabella Jurasz, 267–83. Études syriaques 3. Paris: Geuthner, 2006.

Buchinger, 'Das jerusalemer Sanctorale' = Buchinger, Harald. 'Das Jerusalemer Sanctorale: Zu Stand und Aufgaben der Forschung'. In *A Cloud of Witnesses: The Cult of Saints in Past and Present,* ed. Marcel Barnard, Paulus Post, and Els Rose, 97–128. Liturgia condenda 18. Leuven: Peeters, 2005.

Buchinger, 'Origin and Development' = Buchinger, Harald. 'On the Origin and Development of the Liturgical Year: Tendencies, Results, and Desiderata of Heortological Research'. *Studia Liturgica* 40 (2010): 14–45.

Cabrol, *Les églises de Jérusalem* = Cabrol, Fernand. *Les églises de Jérusalem: La discipline et la liturgie au IVe siècle: Étude sur la Peregrinatio Silviæ.* Paris: Librairie religieuse H. Oudin, 1895.

Canard, 'La destruction de l'église de la Résurrection' = Canard, Marius. 'La destruction de l'église de la Résurrection par le Calife Ḥākim et l'histoire de la descente du feu sacré'. *Byzantion* 35 (1965): 16–43.

Charon, *History of the Melkite Patriarchates* = Charon, Cyrille [Korolevsky, Cyril, pseud.]. *History of the Melkite Patriarchates (Alexandria, Antioch, Jerusalem) from the Sixth Century Monophysite Schism to the Present (1910)*, 3 vols, trans. by John Collorafi and Bishop Nicholas Samra, ed. by Bishop Nicholas Samra. Fairfax, VA: Eastern Christian Publications, 1998–2001.

Charon, 'Le rite byzantin' = Charon, Cyrille [Korolevsky, Cyril, pseud.]. 'Le rite byzantin et la liturgie chrysostomienne dans les patriarcats melkites (Alexandrie—Antioche—Jérusalem)'. In *XPYΣOΣTOMIKA: Studi e ricerche intorno a S. Giovanni Crisostomo*, 473–718. Rome: Libreria Pustet, 1908.

Chitty, Derwas J. *The Desert A City: An Introduction to the Study of Egyptian and Palestinian Monasticism under the Christian Empire*. Oxford: Blackwell, 1966.

Christian Archaeology in the Holy Land = *Christian Archaeology in the Holy Land: New Discoveries: Essays in Honour of Virgilio C. Corbo, OFM*, ed. by Giovanni-Claudio Bottini, Leah de Segni, and Eguenio Alliata. Studium Biblicum Franciscanum, Collectio Maior 40. Jerusalem: Franciscan Printing Press, 1990.

Clark, *Sinai Checklist* = Clark, Kenneth W. *Checklist of Manuscripts in St Catherine's Monastery, Mount Sinai, Microfilmed for the Library of Congress, 1950*. Washington, DC: Library of Congress, 1952.

Conybeare and Maclean, *Rituale armenorum* = Conybeare, Frederick C. and Arthur J. Maclean. *Rituale armenorum: Being the Administration of the Sacraments and the Breviary Rites of the Armenian Church together with the Greek Rites of Baptism and Epiphany from the Oldest Mss. and the East Syrian Epiphany Rites*. Oxford: Clarendon, 1905.

Corbo, *Santo Sepolcro* = Corbo, Virgilio C., OFM. *Il Santo Sepolcro di Gerusalemme: Aspetti archeologici dalle origini al periodo crociato*, 3 vols. Studium Biblicum Franciscanum, Collectio Maior 29. Jerusalem: Franciscan Printing Press, 1981.

Cross, *Lectures on the Christian Sacraments* = Cyril of Jerusalem. *Lectures on the Christian Sacraments: The Procatechesis and the Five Mystagogical Catecheses*, 3rd edn, ed. by Frank L. Cross. Crestwood, NY: St Vladimir's Seminary Press, 1995.

Cuming, Geoffrey. 'Further Studies in the Liturgy of St James'. *Studia Liturgica* 18 (1988): 161–9.

Cuming, *Liturgy of St Mark* = Cuming, Geoffrey. *The Liturgy of St Mark*. OCA 234. Rome: Pontifical Oriental Institute, 1990.

Cuming, 'Missa Catechumenorum' = Cuming, Geoffrey. 'The Missa Catechumenorum of the Liturgy of St James'. *Studia Liturgica* 17 (1987): 62–71.

Dagron, 'L'immigration syrienne' = Dagron, Gilbert. 'Minorités ethniques et religieuses dans l'Orient byzantin à la fin du Xe et au XIe siècle: L'immigration syrienne'. *Travaux et Mémoires* 6 (1976): 177–216.

Dauphin, *La Palestine byzantine* = Dauphin, Claudine. *La Palestine byzantine: Peuplement et populations*, 3 vols. British Archaeological Reports International Series 726. Oxford: Archaeopress, 1998.

Delehaye, *Synaxarium* = Delehaye, Hippolyte. *Propylaeum ad Acta sanctorum novembris: Synaxarium ecclesiae constantinopolitanae*. Brussels: Société des Bollandistes, 1902.

Delouis, *Saint-Jean-Baptiste de Stoudios à Constantinople* = Delouis, Olivier. *Saint-Jean-Baptiste de Stoudios à Constantinople: La contribution d'un monastère à l'histoire de l'Empire byzantain (v. 454–1204)*, 2 vols. Unpublished doctoral thesis. Paris: Université Paris I–Panthéon Sorbonne, 2005.

Description I = Metreveli, Eleni, Caca Čankievi, Lili Xevsuriani, and L. Jǧamaia. ქართული ხელნაწერთა აღწერილობა. სინური კოლექცია [*Kartuli xelnacerta aġceriloba: Sinuri kolekc'ia / Description of Georgian Manuscripts: Sinai Collection*], vol. 1. Tbilisi: Metsniereba, 1978.

Description II = Čankievi, Caca, and L. Jǧamaia. ქართული ხელნაწერთა აღწერილობა. სინური კოლექცია [*Kartuli xelnacerta aġceriloba: Sinuri kolekc'ia / Description of Georgian Manuscripts: Sinai Collection*], vol. 2. Tbilisi: Metsniereba, 1979.

Description III = Gvaramia, R., Eleni Metreveli, Caca Čankievi, Lili Xevsuriani, and L. Jǧamaia. ქართული ხელნაწერთა აღწერილობა. სინური კოლექცია [*Kartuli xelnacerta aġceriloba: Sinuri kolekc'ia / Description of Georgian Manuscripts: Sinai Collection*], vol. 3. Tbilisi: Metsniereba, 1987.

Dmitrievskii, *Богослуженіе страсной и пасхальной седмицъ* = Dmitrievskii, Alexei A. *Богослуженіе страсной и пасхальной седмицъ во св. Іерусалимъ IX–X в.* Kazan: Типо-литографія Императорскаго Университета, 1894.

Dmitrievskii, *Описаніе* I = Dmitrievskii, Alexei A. *Описаніе литургическихъ рукописей, хранящихся въ библіотекахъ православнаго востока*, vol. 1: *Τυπικά*. Kiev: Типографія Г. Т. Корчакъ-Новицкаго, 1895.

Dmitrievskii, *Описаніе* II = Dmitrievskii, Alexei A. *Описаніе литургическихъ рукописей, хранящихся въ библіотекахъ православнаго востока*, vol. 2: *Εὐχολόγια*. Kiev: Типографія Г. Т. Корчакъ-Новицкаго, 1901.

Dmitrievskii, *Описаніе* III = Dmitrievskii, Alexei A. *Описаніе литургическихъ рукописей, хранящихся въ библіотекахъ православнаго востока*, vol. 3: *Τυπικά*. Petrograd: Типографія В. Ѳ. Киршбаума, 1917.

Dmitrievskii, *Древнѣйшіе Патріаршіе Типиконы* = Dmitrievskii, Alexei A. *Древнѣйшіе Патріаршіе Типиконы Святогробскій Іерусалимскій и Великой Константинопольской Церкви. Критико-библіографическое изслѣдованіе.* Kiev: Типографія И.И. Горбунова, 1907.

Egeria, *Itinéraire* = Égérie. *Journal de voyage (Itinéraire)*, ed. by Pierre Maraval. SC 296. Paris: Cerf, 1982.

Ehrhard, *Überlieferung* = Ehrhard, Albert. *Überlieferung und Bestand der hagiographischen und homiletischen Literatur der griechischen Kirche von den Anfängen bis zum Ende des 16. Jahrhunderts*, 3 vols. Texte und Untersuchungen 50–52. Leipzig: J. C. Hinrichs, 1936–44.

El Cheikh, Nadia Maria. *Byzantium Viewed by the Arabs.* Harvard Middle Eastern Monographs 36. Cambridge, MA: Harvard University Press, 2004.

Encyclopaedia of Islam = *Encyclopaedia of Islam*, 13 vols, new edn, ed. by Peri J. Bearman et al. Leiden: Brill, 1960–2009.

Esbroeck, 'Encore la lettre de Justinien' = Esbroeck, Michel van. 'Encore la lettre de Justinien: Sa date: 560 et non 561'. AB 87 (1969): 442–4.

Esbroeck, *Homéliaires géorgiens* = Esbroeck, Michel van. *Les plus anciens homéliaires géorgiens: Étude descriptive et historique.* Louvain-la-Neuve: Université Catholique de Louvain, 1975.

Esbroeck, 'La lettre de l'empereur Justinien' = Esbroeck, Michel van. 'La lettre de l'empereur Justinien sur l'Annonciation et la Noël en 561'. AB 86 (1968): 351–71.

Essays on Early Eastern Eucharistic Prayers = *Essays on Early Eastern Eucharistic Prayers*, ed. by Paul F. Bradshaw. Collegeville, MN: Liturgical Press, 1997.

Failler, 'Le séjour d'Athanase à Constantinople' = Failler, Albert. 'Le séjour d'Athanase II d'Alexandrie à Constantinople'. REB 35 (1977): 43–71.

Fassler, 'The First Marian Feast in Constantinople and Jerusalem' = Fassler, Margot. 'The First Marian Feast in Constantinople and Jerusalem: Chant Texts, Readings, and Homiletic Literature'. In *The Study of Medieval Chant*, ed. by Peter Jeffery, 26–87. Woodbridge, Suffolk: Boydell Press, 2001.

Fedalto, *Hierarchia ecclesiastica orientalis* = Fedalto, Giorgio. *Hierarchia ecclesiastica orientalis*, 3 vols. Padua: Edizioni Messagero, 1988.

Fedalto, 'Liste vescovili' = Fedalto, Giorgio. 'Liste vescovili del patriarcato di Gerusalemme'. OCP 49 (1983): 5–41, 261–83.

Fenwick, *Anaphoras of St Basil and St James* = Fenwick, John R. K. *The Anaphoras of St Basil and St James: An Investigation into Their Common Origin*. OCA 240. Rome: Pontifical Oriental Institute, 1992.

Findikyan, *Commentary* = Findikyan, Michael Daniel. *The Commentary on the Armenian Daily Office by Bishop Step'anos Siwnec'i († 735): Critical Edition and Translation with Textual and Liturgical Analysis*. OCA 270. Rome: Pontifical Oriental Institute, 2004.

Flusin, 'L'hagiographie palestinienne' = Flusin, Bernard. 'L'hagiographie palestinienne et la réception du concile du Chalcédoine'. In *ΛΕΙΜΩΝ: Studies Presented to L. Rydén on His Sixty-Fifth Birthday*, ed. by Jan Olaf Rosenqvist, 25–47. Uppsala: Uppsala Universitet, 1996.

Flusin, 'Palestinian Hagiography' = Flusin, Bernard. 'Palestinian Hagiography (Fourth–Eighth Centuries)'. In *The Ashgate Research Companion to Byzantine Hagiography*, vol. 1: *Periods and Places*, ed. by Stephanos Efthymiadis, 199–226. Burlington, VT: Ashgate, 2011.

Follieri, *Initia hymnorum* = Follieri, Enrica. *Initia hymnorum ecclesiae graecae*, 5 vols. ST 211–215. Vatican City: Biblioteca Apostolica Vaticana, 1960–1966.

Frøyshov, 'Early Development' = Frøyshov, Stig Symeon Ragnvald. 'The Early Development of the Liturgical Eight-Mode System in Jerusalem'. SVTQ 51.2/3 (2007): 139–78.

Frøyshov, 'The Georgian Witness' = Frøyshov, Stig Symeon R. 'The Georgian Witness to the Jerusalem Liturgy: New Sources and Studies'. In *Inquiries into Eastern Christian Worship: Selected Papers of the Second International Congress of the Society of Oriental Liturgy, Rome, 17–21 September 2008*, ed. by Bert Groen, Steven Hawkes-Teeples, and Stefanos Alexopoulos, 227–67. Eastern Christian Studies 12, Leuven: Peeters, 2012.

Frøyshov, *Horologe 'géorgien'* = Frøyshov, Stig Symeon R. *L'horologe 'géorgien' du Sinaiticus ibericus 34*, 2 vols. Unpublished doctoral thesis. Paris: Université de Paris-Sorbonne (Paris IV), Institut Catholique de Paris, and Institut de théologie orthodoxe Saint-Serge, 2004.

Galadza, Daniel. 'Sources for the Study of Liturgy in Post-Byzantine Jerusalem (638–1187 CE)'. DOP 67 (2013): 75–94.

Galadza, '"Les grandes étapes de la liturgie byzantine" de Miguel Arranz' = Galadza, Daniel. '"Les grandes étapes de la liturgie byzantine" de Miguel Arranz, quarante ans après'. In *60 semaines liturgiques à Saint-Serge: Bilans et perspectives nouvelles*, ed. by André Lossky and Goran Sekulovski, 295–310. Studia Oecumenica Friburgensia 71. Münster: Aschendorff Verlag, 2016.

Galadza, 'Jerusalem Lectionary' = Galadza, Daniel. 'The Jerusalem Lectionary and the Byzantine Rite'. In *Rites and Rituals of the Christian East: Proceedings of the Fourth International Congress of the Society of Oriental Liturgy, Lebanon, 10–15 July 2012*, ed. by Bert Groen, Daniel Galadza, Nina Glibetic, and Gabriel Radle, 181–99. Eastern Christian Studies 22. Leuven: Peeters, 2014.

Galadza, 'Melkite Calendar' = Galadza, Daniel. 'Liturgical Byzantinization in Jerusalem: Al-Bīrūnī's Melkite Calendar in Context'. BBGG (terza serie) 7 (2010): 69–85.

Galadza, 'A Note on Hagiopolite Epistle Readings' = Galadza, Daniel. 'A Note on Hagiopolite Epistle Readings in Three Greek Manuscripts from the Sinai New Finds'. In *Sion, Mère des Églises: Mélanges liturgiques offerts au Père Charles Athanase Renoux*, ed. by Michael Daniel Findikyan, Daniel Galadza, and André Lossky, 149–61. Semaines d'Études Liturgiques Saint-Serge, Supplément 1. Münster: Aschendorff Verlag, 2016.

Galadza, 'Sinai Gr. N.E. ΜΓ 8' = Galadza, Daniel. 'A Greek Source of the Jerusalem Lectionary: Sinai Gr. N.E. ΜΓ 8 (10th cent.)'. In *ΣΥΝΑΞΙΣ ΚΑΘΟΛΙΚΗ: Beiträge zu Gottesdienst und Geschichte der fünf altkirchlichen Patriarchate für Heinzgerd Brakmann zum 70. Geburtstag*, ed. by Diliana Atanassova and Tinatin Chronz, vol. 1: 213–28. Vienna: Lit Verlag, 2014.

Galadza, 'Two Sources of the Jerusalem Lectionary' = Galadza, Daniel. 'Two Greek, Ninth-Century Sources of the Jerusalem Lectionary: *Sinai Gr. 212* and *Sinai Gr. N. E. ΜΓ 11*'. BBGG (terza serie) 11 (2014): 79–111.

Galadza, 'Various Orthodoxies' = Galadza, Daniel. 'Various Orthodoxies: Feasts of the Incarnation of Christ in Jerusalem During the First Christian Millenium'. In *Prayer and Worship in Eastern Christianities, 5th to 11th Centuries*, ed. by Brouria Bitton-Ashkelony and Derek Krueger, 181–209. London: Routledge, 2017.

Garitte, *Calendrier palestino-géorgien* = Garitte, Gérard. *Le calendrier palestino-géorgien du Sinaiticus 34 (Xe siècle)*. SH 30. Brussels: Société des Bollandistes, 1958.

Garitte, *Catalogue* = Garitte, Gérard. *Catalogue des manuscrits géorgiens littéraires du Mont Sinaï*. CSCO 165. Louvain: Durbecq, 1956.

Garitte, 'Évangéliaire grec-arabe' = Garitte, Gérard. 'Un évangéliaire grec-arabe du Xᵉ siècle (cod. Sin. ar. 116)'. In *Studia Codicologica*, ed. by Kurt Treu, 207–25. Texte und Untersuchungen 124. Berlin: Akademie-Verlag, 1977.

Garitte, 'Index des lectures évangéliques' = Garitte, Gérard. 'Un index géorgien des lectures évangéliques selon l'ancien rite de Jérusalem'. Mus 85 (1972): 337–98.

Garitte, 'Menée' = Garitte, Gérard. 'Le Menée géorgien de Dumbarton Oaks'. Mus 77 (1964): 29–64.

Garitte, 'Rubriques liturgiques' = Garitte, Gérard. 'Les rubriques liturgiques de quelques anciens tétraévangiles arabes du Sinaï'. *Mélanges liturgiques offerts à Bernard Botte OSB de l'Abbaye du Mont César à l'occasion du 50. anniversaire de son ordination sacerdotale (4 Juin 1972)*, 151–66. Louvain: Abbaye du Mont César, 1972.

Garitte, 'Sin. geo. 63' = Garitte, Gérard. 'Un fragment d'évangéliare géorgien suivant l'ancien rite de Jérusalem (Cod. Sin. géo. 63)'. BK 32 (1974): 70–85.

Géhin and Frøyshov, 'Nouvelles découvertes sinaïtiques' = Géhin, Paul, and Stig Frøyshov. 'Nouvelles découvertes sinaïtiques: À propos de la parution de l'inventaire des manuscrits grecs'. REB 58 (2000): 167–84.

Gil, *History of Palestine* = Gil, Moshe. *A History of Palestine, 634–1099*, trans. by Ethel Broido. Cambridge: Cambridge University Press, 1997.

Gregory, *Textkritik* = Gregory, Caspar René. *Textkritik des Neuen Testamentes*, 3 vols. Leipzig: J. C. Hinrichs, 1900–9.

Griffith, 'The Church of Jerusalem and the "Melkites"' = Griffith, Sidney H. 'The Church of Jerusalem and the "Melkites": The Making of an "Arab Orthodox" Christian Identity in the World of Islam (750–1050 CE)'. In *Christians and Christianity in the Holy Land: From the Origins to the Latin Kingdoms*, ed. by Ora Limor and Guy G. Stroumsa, 175–204. Turnhout: Brepols, 2006.

Griffith, 'From Aramaic to Arabic' = Griffith, Sidney H. 'From Aramaic to Arabic: The Languages of the Monasteries of Palestine in the Byzantine and Early Islamic Periods'. DOP 51 (1997): 11–31.

Griffith, 'Holy Land in the Ninth Century' = Griffith, Sidney H. 'Byzantium and the Christians in the World of Islam: Constantinople and the Church in the Holy Land in the Ninth Century'. *Medieval Encounters* 3 (1997): 231–65.

Griffith, 'Neo-Martyrs' = Griffith, Sidney H. 'Christians, Muslims, and Neo-Martyrs: Saints' Lives and Holy Land History'. In *Sharing the Sacred: Religious Contacts and Conflicts in the Holy Land, First–Fifteenth Centuries CE*, ed. by Arieh Kofsky and Guy G. Stroumsa, 163–208. Jerusalem: Yad Izhak Ben Zvi, 1998.

Grumel, *Chronologie* = Grumel, Venance. *La chronologie*. Traité d'Études Byzantines 1. Paris: Presses Universitaires de France, 1958.

Grumel, *Regestes* I.2–3 = Grumel, Venance. *Les regestes des actes du patriarcat de Constantinople*, vol. 1: *Les actes des patriarches*, fasc. 2–3: *Les regestes de 715 à 1206*, ed. by Jean Darrouzès. Paris: Institut Français d'Études Byzantines, 1989.

Grumel, 'Les réponses canoniques' = Grumel, Venance. 'Les réponses canoniques à Marc d'Alexandrie, leur caractère officiel, leur double rédaction'. *Échos d'Orient* 38 (1939): 321–33.

Handbook for Liturgical Studies = *Handbook for Liturgical Studies*, 5 vols, ed. by Anscar J. Chupungco, OSB. Collegeville, MN: Liturgical Press, 1998.

Hänggi and Pahl, *Prex eucharistica* = Hänggi, Anton, and Irmgard Pahl. *Prex eucharistica: Textus e variis liturgiis antiquioribus selecti*. Fribourg: Éditions Universitaires Fribourg Suisse, 1968.

Hannick, Christian. 'Annexions et reconquêtes byzantines: Peut-on parler d'"uniatisme" byzantin?' *Irénikon* 66 (1993): 451–74.

Hannick, 'The Theotokos in Byzantine Hymnography' = Hannick, Christian. 'The Theotokos in Byzantine hymnography: Typology and allegory'. In *Images of the Mother of God: Perceptions of the Theotokos in Byzantium*, ed. by Maria Vassilaki, 69–76. Aldershot: Ashgate, 2005.

Harlfinger, Reinsch, and Sonderkamp, *Specimina sinaitica* = Harlfinger, Dieter, Diether Roderich Reinsch, and Joseph A. M. Sonderkamp, with Giancarlo Prato. *Specimina sinaitica: Die datierten griechischen Handschriften des Katharinen-Klosters auf dem Berge Sinai. 9. bis 12. Jahrhundert*. Berlin: Dietrich Reimer Verlag, 1983.

Horn and Phenix, *Lives* = *John Rufus: The Lives of Peter the Iberian, Theodosius of Jerusalem, and the Monk Romanus*, ed. and trans. by Cornelia B. Horn and Robert R. Phenix, Jr. Writings from the Greco-Roman World 24. Atlanta: Society of Biblical Literature, 2008.

Husmann, 'Hymnus und Troparion' = Husmann, Heinrich. 'Hymnus und Troparion: Studien zur Geschichte der musikalischen Gattungen von Horologion und

Tropologion'. In *Jahrbuch des Staatlichen Instituts für Musikforschung Preußischer Kulturbesitz*, 7–86. Berlin: Verlag Merseburger, 1971.

Iadgari = Metreveli, Elene, Caca Čankievi, and Lili Xevsuriani. უძველესი იადგარი [*Uzvelesi Iadgari / The Most Ancient Iadgari*]. Tbilisi: Metsniereba, 1980.

Jacob, *Formulaire* = Jacob, André. *Histoire du formulaire grec de la Liturgie de Saint Jean Chrysostome*. Unpublished doctoral thesis. Louvain: Université de Louvain, 1968.

Jacob, 'Messanensis gr. 177' = Jacob, André. 'La date, la patrie et le modèle d'un rouleau italo-grec (Messanensis gr. 177)'. *Helikon* 22/27 (1982/1987): 109–25.

Jacob, 'La tradition manuscrite' = Jacob, André. 'La tradition manuscrite de la Liturgie de Saint Jean Chrysostome (VIIIᵉ–XIIᵉ siècles)'. In *Eucharisties d'Orient et d'Occident: Semaine liturgique de l'Institut Saint-Serge II*, 109–38. Lex Orandi 47. Paris: Cerf, 1970.

Jacob, 'Une version géorgienne' = Jacob, André. 'Une version géorgienne inédite de la liturgie de Saint Jean Chrysostome'. Mus 77 (1964): 65–119.

Jammo, *La structure de la messe chaldéenne* = Jammo, Sarhad Y. Hermiz. *La structure de la messe chaldéenne du début jusqu'à l'anaphore: Étude historique*. OCA 207. Rome: Pontifical Oriental Institute, 1979.

Janeras, 'Lectionnaires de Jérusalem' = Janeras, Sebastià. 'Les lectionnaires de l'ancienne liturgie de Jérusalem'. *Collectanea Christiana Orientalia* 2 (2005): 71–92.

Janeras, 'Pericope evangeliche' = Janeras, Sebastià. 'Le pericope evangeliche dei tre primi giorni della Settimana Santa nelle tradizioni agiopolita e bizantina'. *Studi sull'Oriente Cristiano* 15.1 (2001): 29–52.

Janeras, 'La Settimana Santa' = Janeras, Sebastià. 'La Settimana Santa nell'antica liturgia di Gerusalemme'. In *Hebdomadae sanctae celebratio: Conspectus historicus comparativus*, ed. by Antonius Georgius Kollamparampil, 19–50. BELS 93. Rome: Edizioni Liturgiche, 1997.

Janeras, Sebastià. 'I vangeli domenicali della resurrezione nelle tradizioni liturgiche agiopolita e bizantina'. In *Paschale Mysterium: Studi in memoria dell'Abate Prof. Salvatore Marsili (1910–1983)*, ed. by Giustino Farnedi, 55–69. Studia Anselmiana 91. Rome: Pontificio Ateneo S. Anselmo, 1986.

Janeras, 'Vendredi avant le Dimanche des Palmes' = Janeras, Sebastià. 'Le vendredi avant le Dimanche des Palmes dans la tradition liturgique hagiopolite'. *Studi sull'Oriente Cristiano* 4.1 (2000): 59–86.

Janeras, *Vendredi-Saint* = Janeras, Sebastià. *Le Vendredi-Saint dans la tradition liturgique byzantine: Structure et histoire de ses offices*. Studia Anselmiana 99/Analecta Liturgica 13. Rome: Pontificio Ateneo S. Anselmo, 1988.

Janin, *Églises des grands centres byzantins* = Janin, Raymond, AA. *Les Églises des grands centres byzantins (Bithynie, Hellespont, Latros, Galèsios, Trébizonde, Athènes, Thessalonique)*. Paris: Institut Français d'Études Byzantines, 1975.

Janin, *Les églises et les monastères* = Janin, Raymond, AA. *La géographie ecclésiastique de l'Empire byzantin: Première partie: Le siège de Constantinople et le patriarcat œcuménique*, vol. 3: *Les églises et les monastères*, 2nd edn. Paris: Institut Français d'Études Byzantines, 1969.

Kaplan, 'Leontios' = Kaplan, Michel. 'Un patriarche byzantin dans le royaume latin de Jérusalem: Léontios'. In *Chemins d'outre mer: Études sur la Méditerranée médiévale offertes à Michel Balard*, ed. by Damien Coulon vol. 2, 475–88. Paris: Publications de la Sorbonne, 2004.

Kazamias, Θεία Λειτουργία τοῦ Ἁγίου Ἰακώβου = Kazamias, Alkiviades K. Ἡ Θεία Λειτουργία τοῦ Ἁγίου Ἰακώβου τοῦ Ἀδελφοθέου καὶ τὰ νέα σιναϊτικὰ χειρόγραφα. Thessalonike: Ἵδρυμα Ὄρους Σινᾶ, 2006.

Kekelidze, *Канонарь* = Kekelidze, Kornelii S. *Іерусалимскій Канонарь VII вѣка (Грузинская версія)*. Tbilisi: Лосаберидзе, 1912.

Kekelidze, *Литургическіе грузинскіе памятники* = Kekelidze, Kornelii S. *Литургическіе грузинскіе памятники въ отечественныхъ книгохранилищахъ и ихъ научное значеніе*. Tbilisi: Типографія "Братство", 1908.

Kongress für Christliche Archäologie = *Akten des XII. Internationales Kongresses für Christliche Archäologie, Bonn 22.–28. September 1991*, 2 vols, ed. by Ernst Dassmann, Klaus Thraede, and Josef Engemann. Jahrbuch für Antike und Christentum. Ergänzungsband 20.1. Münster: Aschendorffsche Verlagsbuchhandlung, 1995.

Korolevsky, *Christian Antioch* = Korolevsky, Cyril. *Christian Antioch*, ed. by Bishop Nicholas Samra, trans. by John Collorafi. Fairfax, VA: Eastern Christian Publications, 2003.

Krasheninnikova, 'Седмичные памяти октоиха' = Krasheninnikova, Olga Aleksandrovna. 'К истории формирования седмичных памятей октоиха'. *Богословские труды* 32 (1996): 260–8.

Krasnosel'tsev, 'Review' = Krasnosel'tsev, Nikolai. Review of A. A. Dmitrievskii, *Богослуженіе страсной и пасхальной седмицъ во св. Іерусалимъ IX–X в.* (Kazan, 1894). *Византийский Временник* 2 (1895): 632–55.

Krivko, 'Гимнографические параллели' = Krivko, Roman N. 'Синайско-славянские гимнографические параллели'. *Вестник ПСТГУ. III: Филология* 1.11 (2008): 56–102.

Külzer, *Peregrinatio* = Külzer, Andreas. *Peregrinatio graeca in Terram Sanctam: Studien zu Pilgerführern und Reisebeschreibungen über Syrien, Palästina und den Sinai aus byzantinischer und metabyzantinischer Zeit*. Studien und Texte zur Byzantinistik 2. Frankfurt am Main: Peter Lang, 1994.

Литургія св. Іакова (Ladomirova) = Божественнаѧ литургіа свѧтагѡ ап́остола Іа́кѡва бра́та Бож́їѧ ѿ пе́рвагѡ іера́рха Іеросалѵ́мскагѡ. Ladomirova: Бра́тство препод́обнагѡ Іѡва, Rome: Monastery of Grottaferrata, 1970 [1938].

Lampe, *Patristic Greek Lexicon* = Lampe, Geoffrey W. H. *A Patristic Greek Lexicon*. Oxford: Clarendon, 1961.

Leeb, *Die Gesänge* = Leeb, Helmut. *Die Gesänge im Gemeindegottesdienst von Jerusalem (vom 5. bis 8. Jahrhundert)*. Wiener Beiträge zur Theologie 28. Vienna: Herder, 1970.

Leeming, 'The Adoption of Arabic as a Liturgical Language' = Leeming, Kate. 'The Adoption of Arabic as a Liturgical Language by the Palestinian Melkites'. *ARAM* 15 (2003): 239–46.

Levy-Rubin, 'The Reorganisation of the Patriarchate of Jerusalem' = Levy-Rubin, Milka. 'The Reorganisation of the Patriarchate of Jerusalem'. *ARAM* 15 (2003): 197–226.

Liddell, Scott, and Jones, *Greek–English Lexicon* = Liddell, Henry George, and Robert Scott, *A Greek-English Lexicon*, rev. by Sir Henry Stuart Jones. Oxford: Clarendon, 1996.

Liturgia ibero-graeca = *Liturgia ibero-graeca sancti Iacobi: Editio, translatio, retroversio, commentarii*, part I: *The Old Georgian Version of the Liturgy of Saint James*, ed. by L. Khevsuriani, M. Shanidze, M. Kavtaria, and T. Tseradze; part II: S. Verhelst, *La Liturgie de Saint Jacques: Rétroversion grecque et commentaires*. Jerusalemer Theologisches Forum 17. Münster: Aschendorff Verlag, 2011.

Liturgy Fifty Years after Baumstark = *Acts of the International Congress Comparative Liturgy Fifty Years after Anton Baumstark (1872–1948), Rome, 25–29 September 1998*, ed. by Robert F. Taft, SJ, and Gabriele Winkler. OCA 265. Rome: Pontifical Oriental Institute, 2001.

Longo, 'Narrazione' = Longo, Augusta. 'Il testo integrale della "Narrazione degli abati Giovanni e Sofronio" attraverso le *"Ἑρμηνεῖαι"* di Nicone'. RSBN 12–13 (1965–6): 223–67.

Louth, *St John Damascene* = Louth, Andrew. *St John Damascene: Tradition and Originality in Byzantine Theology*. New York: Oxford University Press, 2002.

Lutzka, *Die Kleinen Horen des byzantinischen Studengebetes* = Lutzka, Carolina. *Die Kleinen Horen des byzantinischen Studengebetes und ihre geschichlitche Entwicklung*, 2nd edn. Forum Orthodoxe Theologie 7. Berlin: Lit Verlag, 2010.

Luzzi, 'Epoca di formazione del sinassario di Costantinopoli' = Luzzi, Andrea. 'Precisazioni sull'epoca di formazione del sinassario di Costantinopoli'. RSBN 36 (1999): 75–91.

MacEvitt, *Crusades and the Christian World of the East* = MacEvitt, Christopher. *The Crusades and the Christian World of the East: Rough Tolerance*. Philadelphia, PA: University of Pennsylvania Press, 2008.

Mancini, *Codices monasterii Messanensis* = Mancini, Augustus. *Codices graeci monasterii Messanensis S. Salvatoris*. Messine: Typis d'Amico, 1907.

Mango, 'Greek Culture in Palestine' = Mango, Cyril. 'Greek Culture in Palestine after the Arab Conquest'. In *Scritture, libri e testi delle aree provinciali di Bisanzio: Atti del Seminario di Erice, 18–25 settembre 1988*, ed. by Guglielmo Cavallo, Giuseppe De Gregorio, and Marilena Maniaci, 149–60. Spoleto: Centro Italiano di studi sull'alto medioevo, 1991.

Mango and Scott, *Chronicle of Theophanes* = *The Chronicle of Theophanes Confessor: Byzantine and Near Eastern History, AD 284–813*, trans. by Cyril Mango and Roger Scott, with the assistance of Geoffrey Greatrex. Oxford: Clarendon, 1997.

Manoscritti greci = *I manoscritti greci tra riflessione e dibattito: Atti del V Colloquio Internazionale di Paleografia Greca (Cremona, 4–10 ottobre 1998)*, 3 vols, ed. by Giancarlo Prato. Papyrologia Florentina 31. Florence: Edizioni Gonnelli, 2000.

Maraval, *Lieux saints* = Maraval, Pierre. *Lieux saints et pèlerinages d'orient: Histoire et géographie des origines à la conquête arabe*. Paris: Éditions du Cerf, 1985.

Mateos, 'Horologion' = Mateos, Juan, SJ. 'Un horologion inédit de Saint-Sabas: Le Codex sinaïtique grec 863 (IXe siècle)'. In *Mélanges Eugène Tisserant*, vol. 3, 47–76. ST 233. Vatican City: Biblioteca Apostolica Vaticana, 1964.

Mateos, *Parole* = Mateos, Juan, SJ. *La célébration de la parole dans la liturgie byzantine: Étude historique*. OCA 191. Rome: Pontifical Oriental Institute, 1971.

Mateos, *Typicon* = Mateos, Juan, SJ. *Le Typicon de la Grande Église: Ms. Sainte-Croix n° 40, Xe siècle*, 2 vols. OCA 165–6. Rome: Pontifical Oriental Institute, 1962–3.

McCauley and Stephenson, *Works of Saint Cyril of Jerusalem* = Cyril of Jerusalem. *The Works of Saint Cyril of Jerusalem*, 2 vols, trans. by Leo P. McCauley, SJ, and Anthony A. Stephenson. Washington, DC: Catholic University of America Press, 1969–70.

McCormick, *Survey of the Holy Land* = McCormick, Michael. *Charlemagne's Survey of the Holy Land. Wealth, Personnel, and Buildings of a Mediterranean Church between Antiquity and the Middle Ages*. Washington, DC: Dumbarton Oaks, 2011.

Mercier, *Liturgie de Saint Jacques* = Mercier, Basile-Charles, ed. *La Liturgie de Saint Jacques: Édition critique du texte grec avec traduction latine*. PO 26.2. Paris: Firmin-Didot, 1946.

Métrévéli, 'Manuscrits liturgiques géorgiens' = Métrévéli, Hélène. 'Les manuscrits liturgiques géorgiens des IXe–Xe siècles et leur importance pour l'étude de l'hymnographie byzantine'. BK 36 (1978): 43–8.

Métrévéli et al., 'Le plus ancien Tropologion géorgien' = Métrévéli, Hélène, Caca Tchankieva, and Lili Khevsouriani. 'Le plus ancien Tropologion géorgien'. BK 34 (1981): 54–62.

Metzger, *Early Versions of the New Testament* = Metzger, Bruce M. *The Early Versions of the New Testament: Their Origin, Transmission, and Limitations*. Oxford: Clarendon, 1977.

Michael the Syrian, *Chronicle* = *Chronique de Michel le Syrien*, 5 vols, ed. by Jean-Baptiste Chabot. Paris: Ernest Leroux, 1899–1924.

Mimouni, *Dormition et assomption de Marie* = Mimouni, Simon Claude. *Dormition et assomption de Marie: Histoire des traditions anciennes*. Théologie Historique 98. Paris: Beauchesne, 1995.

Momina, 'О происхождении греческой триоди' = Momina, Maiia A. 'О происхождении греческой триоди'. ПС 28 (91) (1986): 112–19.

Mystagogical Catecheses = Cyrille de Jérusalem. *Catéchèses mystagogiques*, ed. by Auguste Piédagnel, trans. by Pierre Paris. SC 126bis. Paris: Cerf, 1988.

Nasrallah, *Histoire* II.1 = Nasrallah, Joseph. *Histoire du mouvement littéraire dans l'Église Melchite du Ve au XXe siècle*, vol. 2.1 (634–750). Damascus: Institut Français de Damas, 1996.

Nasrallah, *Histoire* II.2 = Nasrallah, Joseph. *Histoire du mouvement littéraire dans l'Église Melchite du Ve au XXe siècle*, vol. 2.2 (750–X^e s). Louvain: Peeters, 1988.

Nasrallah, *Histoire* III.1 = Nasrallah, Joseph. *Histoire du mouvement littéraire dans l'Église Melchite du Ve au XXe siècle*, vol. 3.1 (969–1250). Louvain: Peeters, 1983.

Nasrallah, 'Liturgie des patriarcats melchites' = Nasrallah, Joseph. 'La liturgie des Patriarcats melchites de 969 à 1300'. OC 71 (1987): 156–81.

Nikiforova, 'Сокрытое сокровище' = Nikiforova, Alexandra. '"Сокровенное сокровище": Значение находок 1975 года на Синае для истории служебной Минеи'. *Гимнология*, vol. 6, 8–31. Moscow: Московская государственная консерватория, 2011.

Nikiforova, 'The Oldest Greek Tropologion' = Nikiforova, Alexandra. 'The Oldest Greek Tropologion Sin.Gr. МГ 56+5: A New Witness to the Liturgy of Jerusalem from Outside Jerusalem with First Edition of the Text'. OC 98 (2015): 138–73.

Nikiforova, *Из истории Минеи в Византии* = Nikiforova, Alexandra. *Из истории Минеи в Византии. Гимнографические памятники VIII–XI вв. из собрания монастыря святой Екатерины на Синае*. Moscow: Издетльство Православного Свято-Тихоновского Гуманитарного Университета, 2012.

Nikolopoulos, *Νέα εὑρήματα* = *Τὰ νέα εὑρήματα τοῦ Σινᾶ*, ed. by Panagiotes G. Nikolopoulos et al. Athens: ῎Ιδρυμα ῎Ορους Σινᾶ, 1998.

Noble and Treiger, *The Orthodox Church in the Arab World* = *The Orthodox Church in the Arab World, 700–1700: An Anthology of Sources*, ed. by Sam Noble and Alexander Treiger (with a foreword by Metropolitan Ephrem Kyriakos). DeKalb, IL: Northern Illinois University Press, 2014.

Noret, 'Ménologes, Synaxaires, Ménées' = Noret, Jacques. 'Ménologes, Synaxaires, Ménées: Essai de clarification d'une terminologie'. AB 86 (1968): 21–4.

Olkinuora, *Feast of the Entrance of the Theotokos* = Olkinuora, Jaakko. *Byzantine Hymnography for the Feast of the Entrance of the Theotokos: An Intermedial Approach*. Studia Patristica Fennica 4. Helsinki: Suomen Patristinen Seura, 2015.

Ostrogorsky, *History of the Byzantine State* = Ostrogorsky, George. *History of the Byzantine State*, trans. by Joan Hussey. New Brunswick, NJ: Rutgers University Press, 1969.

Ousterhout, 'Rebuilding the Temple' = Ousterhout, Robert. 'Rebuilding the Temple: Constantine Monomachus and the Holy Sepulchre'. *Journal of the Society of Architectural Historians* 48.1 (1989): 66–78.

Ousterhout, 'Sacred Geographies' = Ousterhout, Robert. 'Sacred Geographies and Holy Cities: Constantinople as Jerusalem'. In *Hierotopy: The Creation of Sacred Spaces in Byzantium and Medieval Russia*, ed. by Alexei Lidov, 98–109. Moscow: Indrik, 2006.

Outtier, 'Nouveau fragment oncial' = Outtier, Bernard. 'Un nouveau fragment oncial inédit du *lectionnaire* de Jérusalem en géorgien'. In *Pèlerinages et lieux saints dans l'Antiquité et le Moyen Âge: Mélanges offerts à Pierre Maraval*, ed. by Béatrice Caseau, Jean-Claude Cheynet, and Vincent Déroche, 323–8. Paris: Association des Amis du Centre d'Histoire et Civilisation de Byzance, 2006.

Outtier, 'Un nouveau témoin partiel' = Outtier, Bernard. 'Un nouveau témoin partiel du lectionnaire géorgien ancien (Sinaï géorgien 12)'. BK 41 (1983): 162–74.

Outtier, 'Sinaï géorgien 54' = Outtier, Bernard. 'Un témoin partiel du lectionnaire géorgien ancien (Sinaï géorgien 54)'. BK 39 (1981): 76–88.

Pachymérès, *Relations historiques* = Georges Pachymérès. *Relations historiques*, 5 vols, ed. by Albert Failler, trans. by Vitalien Laurent. Paris: Les belles lettres/Institut français d'études byzantines, 1984–2000.

Pahlitzsch, *Graeci und Suriani im Palästina der Kreuzfahrerzeit* = Pahlitzsch, Johannes. *Graeci und Suriani im Palästina der Kreuzfahrerzeit: Beiträge und Quellen zur Geschichte des griechisch-orthodoxen Patriarchats von Jerusalem*. Berliner Historische Studien 33. Berlin: Duncker und Humbolt, 2001.

Panchenko, *Arab Orthodox Christians* = Panchenko, Constantin A. *Arab Orthodox Christians under the Ottomans: 1516–1831* (with a foreword by His Beatitude Patriarch John X of Antioch and All the East), trans. by Brittany Pheiffer Noble and Samuel Noble. Jordanville, NY: Holy Trinity Seminary Press, 2016.

Papadopoulos-Kerameus, *Anastasis Typikon* = Papadopoulos-Kerameus, Athanasios. ῾Ι. *Τυπικὸν τῆς ἐν ῾Ιεροσολύμοις ἐκκλησίας*᾽. In *Ἀνάλεκτα ῾Ιεροσολυμητικῆς Σταχυολογίας*, vol. 2, 1–254. St. Petersburg: Kirschbaum, 1894.

Parenti, *A oriente e occidente di Costantinopoli* = Parenti, Stefano. *A Oriente e Occidente di Costantinopoli: Temi e problemi liturgici di ieri e di oggi*. Monumenta Studia Instrumenta Liturgica 54. Vatican City: Libreria Editrice Vaticana, 2010.

Parenti, 'Cathedral Rite' = Parenti, Stefano. 'The Cathedral Rite of Constantinople: Evolution of a Local Tradition'. OCP 77 (2011): 449–69.

Parenti, *L'eucologio slavo del Sinai* = Parenti, Stefano. *L'Eucologio slavo del Sinai nella storia dell'eucologio bizantino.* Seminario del Dipartimento di Studi Slavi e dell'Europa Centro-Orientale. Filologia Slava 2. Rome: Università di Roma 'La Sapienza', 1997.

Parenti, 'Fascicolo ritrovato' = Parenti, Stefano. 'Un fascicolo ritrovato dell'*horologion Sinai gr. 863* (IX secolo)'. OCP 75 (2009): 343–58.

Parenti, 'Preghiera della cattedra' = Parenti, Stefano. 'La preghiera della cattedra nell'eucologio Barberini gr. 336'. BBGG (terza serie) 8 (2011): 149–68.

Parenti, 'Σιγησάτω πᾶσα σάρξ' = Parenti, Stefano. 'Nota sull'impiego e l'origine dell'inno Σιγησάτω πᾶσα σὰρξ βροτεία'. Κυπριακαὶ Σπουδαί 64–5 (2000–1): 191–9.

Parenti, 'Towards a Regional History' = Parenti, Stefano. 'Towards a Regional History of the Byzantine Euchology of the Sacraments'. *Ecclesia Orans* 27 (2010): 109–21.

Parenti, 'La "vittoria"' = Parenti, Stefano. 'La "vittoria" nella Chiesa di Costantinopoli della Liturgia di Crisostomo sulla Liturgia di Basilio'. In Stefano Parenti, *A Oriente e Occidente di Costantinopoli: Temi e problemi liturgici di ieri e di oggi*, 27–47. Vatican City: Libreria Editrice Vaticana, 2010. [Originally printed in *Acts of the International Congress Comparative Liturgy Fifty Years after Baumstark (1872–1948), Rome, 25–29 September 1998*, ed. by Robert F. Taft, SJ, and Gabriele Winkler, 907–28. Rome: Pontifical Oriental Institute, 2001.]

Parenti and Velkovska, *Barberini 336* = *L'Eucologio Barberini gr. 336*, ed. by Stefano Parenti and Elena Velkovska, 2nd rev. edn. BELS 80. Rome: Edizioni Liturgiche, 2000.

Parenti and Velkovska, *Барберини гр. 336* = *Евхологий Барберини гр. 336. Издание текста, предисловие и примечания*, ed. by Stefano Parenti and Elena Velkovksa, trans. by Sergei Golovanov. Omsk: Golovanov, 2011.

Parpulov, *Byzantine Psalters* = Parpulov, Georgi R. *Toward a History of Byzantine Psalters ca. 850–1350 AD* [sic]. Plovdiv: n.p., 2014.

Patrich, *Sabaite Heritage* = *The Sabaite Heritage in the Orthodox Church from the Fifth Century to the Present*, ed. by Joseph Patrich. OLA 98. Leuven: Peeters, 2001.

Patrich, *Sabas* = Patrich, Joseph. *Sabas, Leader of Palestinian Monasticism: A Comparative Study in Eastern Monasticism, Fourth to Seventh Centuries.* Washington, DC: Dumbarton Oaks Research Library and Collection, 1995.

Patrich, 'Transfer of Gifts' = Patrich, Joseph. 'The Transfer of Gifts in the Early Christian Churches of Palestine: Archaeological and Literary Evidence for the Evolution of the "Great Entrance"'. In *Pèlerinages et lieux saints dans l'Antiquité et le Moyen Âge. Mélanges offerts à Pierre Maraval*, ed. by Béatrice Caseau, Jean-Claude Cheynet, and Vincent Déroche, 341–93. Paris: Association des Amis du Centre d'Histoire et Civilisation de Byzance, 2006.

Pentkovsky, 'Богослужебные уставы' = Pentkovsky, Aleksei. 'Константинопольский и иерусалимский богослужебные уставы'. Журнал Московской Патриархии (2001, April): 70–8.

Pentkovsky, *Типикон* = Pentkovsky, Aleksei. *Типикон патриарха Алексия Студита в Византии и на Руси.* Moscow: Издательство Московской Патриархии, 2001.

Peradse, 'Liturgiegeschichte Georgiens' = Peradse, Gregor. 'Ein Dokument aus der mittelalterlichen Liturgiegeschichte Georgiens'. *Kyrios: Vierteljahresschrift für Kirchen- und Geistesgeschichte Osteuropas* 1 (1936): 74–9.

Permiakov, 'Make This the Place Where Your Glory Dwells' = Permiakov, Vitaly. 'Make This the Place Where Your Glory Dwells': Origins and Evolution of the Byzantine Rite for the Consecration of a Church. Unpublished doctoral thesis. Notre Dame, IN: University of Notre Dame, 2012.

Perria, Repertorio = Perria, Lidia. Repertorio dei manoscritti greci di area orientale (palestino-sinaitica). Messina: n.p., 2000.

Perria, 'Scritture e codici orientali' = Perria, Lidia. 'Scritture e codici di origine orientale (Palestina, Sinai) dal IX al XIII secolo,' RSBN 36 (1999), 19–33.

Perria, Tra oriente e occidente = Tra oriente e occidente: Scritture e libri greci fra le regioni orientali di Bisanzio e l'Italia, ed. by Lidia Perria. Testi e Studi Bizantino-Neoellenici 14. Rome: Università di Roma La Sapienza, 2003.

Perrone, La chiesa di Palestina = Perrone, Lorenzo. La chiesa di Palestina e le controversie cristologiche: Dal concilio de Efeso (431) al secondo concilio di Costantinopoli (553). Testi e ricerche di Scienze religiose 18. Brescia: Paideia Editrice, 1980.

Perrone, 'Christian Holy Places' = Perrone, Lorenzo. 'Christian Holy Places and Pilgrimage in an Age of Dogmatic Conflicts: Popular Religion and Confessional Affiliation in Byzantine Palestine (Fifth to Seventh Centuries)'. POC 48 (1998): 5–37.

Perrone, 'Monasticism' = Perrone, Lorenzo. 'Monasticism as a Factor of Religious Interaction in the Holy Land during the Byzantine Period'. In Sharing the Sacred: Religious Contacts and Conflicts in the Holy Land: First–Fifteenth Centuries CE, ed. by Arieh Kofsky and Guy G. Stroumsa, 67–95. Jerusalem: Yad Izhak Ben Zvi, 1998.

Petras, David M. The Typicon of the Patriarch Alexis the Studite: Novgorod–St Sophia 1136. Cleveland: Star Printing, 1991.

Pétridès, 'Spoudæi' = Pétridès, Sophrone. 'Le monstère des Spoudæi à Jérusalem et les Spoudæi de Constantinople'. Échos d'Orient 4 (1900–1): 225–8.

Petrynko, Weihnachtskanon = Petrynko, Oleksandr. Der jambische Weihnachtskanon des Johannes von Damaskus: Einleitung, Text, Übersetzung, Kommentar. Jerusalemer Theologisches Forum 15. Münster: Aschendorff Verlag, 2010.

Philothée, Nouveaux manuscrits syriaques = Philothée du Sinaï. Nouveaux manuscrits syriaques du Sinaï. Athens: Fondation du Mont Sinaï, 2008.

Pott, Byzantine Liturgical Reform = Pott, Thomas. Byzantine Liturgical Reform: A Study of Liturgical Change in the Byzantine Tradition, trans. by Paul Meyendorff. Orthodox Liturgy Series 2. Crestwood, NY: St. Vladimir's Seminary Press, 2010.

Price and Gaddis, Acts = The Acts of the Council of Chalcedon, vol. 1. General Introduction: Documents before the Council, Session I, trans. by Richard Price and Michael Gaddis. Translated Texts for Historians 45. Liverpool: Liverpool University Press, 2005.

Pringle, Churches of the Crusader Kingdom = Pringle, Denys. The Churches of the Crusader Kingdom of Jerusalem: A Corpus, 4 vols. New York: Cambridge University Press, 1993–2009.

Raczka, The Lectionary = Raczka, Gary Philippe. The Lectionary at the Time of Saint John Chrysostom. Unpublished doctoral thesis. Notre Dame, IN: University of Notre Dame, 2015.

Radle, 'Liturgical Ties' = Radle, Gabriel. 'The Liturgical Ties between Egypt and Southern Italy: A Preliminary Investigation'. In ΣΥΝΑΞΙΣ ΚΑΘΟΛΙΚΗ: Beiträge *zu Gottesdienst und Geschichte der fünf altkirchlichen Patriarchate für Heinzgerd Brakmann zum 70. Geburtstag,* ed. by Diliana Atanassova and Tinatin Chronz, vol. 2: 617–31. Vienna: Lit Verlag, 2014.

Radle, 'Sinai Greek NE/MΓ 22' = Radle, Gabriel. 'Sinai Greek NE/MΓ 22: Late 9th/Early 10th Century Euchology Testimony of the Liturgy of St John Chrysostom and the Liturgy of the Presanctified Gifts in the Byzantine Tradition'. BBGG (terza serie) 8 (2011): 169–221.

Raes, 'La fête de l'Assomption en Orient' = Raes, Alphonse, SJ. 'Aux origines de la fête de l'Assomption en Orient'. OCP 12 (1946): 262–74.

Renoux, *Hymnaire de Saint-Sabas* = Renoux, Charles (Athanase), ed. *L'hymnaire de Saint-Sabas (V^e–VIIIe siècle): Le manuscrit géorgien H 2123,* vol. 1: *Du Samedi de Lazare à la Pentecôte.* PO 50.3. Turnhout: Brepols, 2008.

Renoux, *Hymnaire de Saint-Sabas* II = Renoux, Charles (Athanase), ed. *L'hymnaire de Saint-Sabas (V^e–VIIIe siècle): Le manuscrit géorgien H 2123,* vol. 2: *De la Nativité de Jean-Baptiste à la Liturgie des Défunts.* PO 53.3. Turnhout: Brepols, 2017.

Renoux, 'Hymne des saints dons' = Renoux, Charles (Athanase). 'L'hymne des saints dons dans l'Octoéchos géorgien ancien'. In Θυσία αἰνέσεως: *Mélanges liturgiques offerts à la mémoire de l'Archevêque Georges Wagner (1930–1993),* ed. by Job Getcha and André Lossky, 293–313. Paris: Presses S. Serge, Institut de théologie orthodoxe, 2005.

Renoux, *Hymnes de la résurrection* I = Renoux, Charles (Athanase). *Les hymnes de la résurrection,* vol. 1: *Hymnographie liturgique géorgienne: Textes du Sinaï 18.* Sources liturgiques. Paris: Cerf, 2000.

Renoux, *Hymnes de la résurrection* II = Renoux, Charles (Athanase). *Les hymnes de la résurrection,* vol. 2: *Hymnographie liturgique géorgienne: Textes des manuscrits Sinaï 40, 41 et 34.* PO 52.1. Turnhout: Brepols, 2012.

Renoux, *Hymnes de la résurrection* III = Renoux, Charles (Athanase). *Les hymnes de la résurrection,* vol. 3: *Hymnographie liturgique géorgienne: Introduction, traduction, annotation des manuscrits Sinaï 26 et 20 et index analytique des trois volumes.* PO 52.2. Turnhout: Brepols, 2012.

Renoux, *Introduction* = Renoux, Charles. *Le Codex Arménien Jérusalem 121,*vol. 1: *Introduction aux origines de la liturgie hiérosolymitaine: Lumières nouvelles.* PO 35.1. Turnhout: Brepols, 1969.

Renoux, 'La lecture biblique' = Renoux, Charles. 'La lecture biblique dans la liturgie de Jérusalem'. In *Le monde grec ancien et la Bible,* ed. by Claude Mondésert, 399–420. Paris: Éditions Beauchesne, 1984.

Rose, 'Saint Leontios' = Rose, Richard B. 'The Vita of Saint Leontios and Its Account of His Visit to Palestine During the Crusader Period'. POC 35 (1985): 238–57.

Sakvarelidze, 'Byzantinization of Georgian Liturgy' = Sakvarelidze, Nino. 'Some Aspects of the Byzantinization of the Georgian Liturgy: The Example of the Menaion'. In *Rites and Rituals of the Christian East: Proceedings of the Fourth International Congress of the Society of Oriental Liturgy, Lebanon, 10–15 July 2012,* ed. by Bert Groen, Daniel Galadza, Nina Glibetic, and Gabriel Radle. Eastern Christian Studies 22, 255–91. Leuven: Peeters, 2014.

Sardshweladse and Fähnrich, *Altgeorgisch-Deutsches Wörterbuch* = Sardshweladse, Surab, and Heinz Fähnrich. *Altgeorgisch-Deutsches Wörterbuch.* Handbook for Oriental Studies 12. Leiden: Brill, 2005.

Sauget, *Synaxaires Melkites* = Sauget, Joseph-Marie. *Premières recherches sur l'origine et les caractéristiques des synaxaires Melkites (XIe–XVIIe siècles)*. SH 45. Brussels: Société des Bollandistes, 1969.

Schick, *Christian Communities of Palestine* = Schick, Robert. *The Christian Communities of Palestine from Byzantine to Islamic Rule: A Historical and Archaeological Study*. Studies in Late Antiquity and Early Islam 2. Princeton, NJ: Darwin Press, 1995.

Schneider, *Lobpreis im rechten Glauben* = Schneider, Hans-Michael. *Lobpreis im rechten Glauben: Die Theologie der Hymnen an den Festen der Menschwerdung der alten Jerusalemer Liturgie im Georgischen* Udzvelesi Iadgari. Hereditas Studien zur Alten Kirchengeschichte 23. Bonn: Borengässer, 2004.

Schwartz, *Cyril of Scythopolis* = *Kyrillos von Skythopolis*, ed. by Eduard Schwartz. Texte und Untersuchungen zur Geschichte der altchristlichen Literatur 49, Heft 2. Leipzig: Hinrichs, 1939.

Ševčenko, 'Manuscript Production' = Ševčenko, Nancy P. 'Manuscript Production on Mount Sinai from the Tenth to the Thirteenth Century'. In *Approaching the Holy Mountain: Art and Liturgy at St Catherine's Monastery in the Sinai*, ed. by Sharon E. J. Gerstel and Robert S. Nelson, 233–58. Turnhout: Brepols, 2010.

Ševčenko, 'Typikon' = Ševčenko, Nancy P. 'The Liturgical Typikon of Symeon of Sinai'. In *Metaphrastes, or, Gained in translation: Essays and translations in honour of Robert H. Jordan*, ed. by Margaret Mullet, 274–86. Belfast Byzantine Texts and Translations 9. Belfast: Belfast Byzantine Enterprises, 2004.

Shalev-Hurvitz, *Holy Sites Encircled* = Shalev-Hurvitz, Vered. *Holy Sites Encircled: The Early Byzantine Concentric Churches of Jerusalem*. Oxford: Oxford University Press, 2015.

Skaballanovich, *Толковый Типиконъ* = Skaballanovich, Mikhail. *Толковый Типиконъ. Объяснительное изложеніе Типикона съ историческимъ введеніемъ*, 3 vols. Kiev: Типографія Императорскаго Университета Св. Владиміра, 1910–15.

Swainson, *Greek Liturgies* = Swainson, Charles Anthony. *The Greek Liturgies Chiefly from Original Authorities*. Cambridge: Cambridge University Press, 1884.

ΣΥΝΑΞΙΣ ΚΑΘΟΛΙΚΗ = *ΣΥΝΑΞΙΣ ΚΑΘΟΛΙΚΗ: Beiträge zu Gottesdienst und Geschichte der fünf altkirchlichen Patriarchate für Heinzgerd Brakmann zum 70. Geburtstag*, 2 vols, ed. by Diliana Atanassova and Tinatin Chronz. Orientalia, Patristica, Oecumenica 6.1. Vienna: Lit Verlag, 2014.

Taft, 'The βηματίκιον' = Taft, Robert F., SJ. 'The βηματίκιον in the 6/7th c. *Narration of the Abbots John and Sophronius* (BHGNA 1438w): An Exercise in Comparative Liturgy'. In *Crossroad of Cultures: Studies in Liturgy and Patristics in Honor of Gabriele Winkler*, ed. by Hans-Jürgen Feulner, Elena Velkovska, and Robert F. Taft, SJ, 675–92. OCA 260. Rome: Pontifical Oriental Institute, 2000.

Taft, *Beyond East and West* = Taft, Robert F., SJ. *Beyond East and West: Problems in Liturgical Understanding*, 2nd rev. and enlarged edn. Rome: Pontifical Oriental Institute, 2001.

Taft, *Byzantine Rite* = Taft, Robert F., SJ. *The Byzantine Rite: A Short History*. Collegeville, MN: Liturgical Press, 1992.

Taft, *Concluding Rites* = Taft, Robert F., SJ. *The Communion, Thanksgiving, and Concluding Rites*, vol. 6 of *A History of the Liturgy of St John Chrysostom*. OCA 281. Rome: Pontifical Oriental Institute, 2008.

Taft, *Diptychs* = Taft, Robert F., SJ. *The Diptychs*, vol. 4 of *A History of the Liturgy of St John Chrysostom*. OCA 238. Rome: Pontifical Oriental Institute, 1991.

Taft, *Great Entrance* = Taft, Robert F., SJ. *The Great Entrance: A History of the Transfer of the Gifts and Other Pre-Anaphoral Rites of the Liturgy of St John Chrysostom*, 4th edn. OCA 200. Rome: Pontifical Oriental Institute, 2004.

Taft, 'Holy Week' = Taft, Robert F. SJ. 'Holy Week in the Byzantine Tradition'. In *Hebdomadae sanctae celebratio: Conspectus historicus comparativus*, ed. by Antonius Georgius Kollamparampil, 67–91. BELS 93. Rome: Edizioni Liturgiche, 1997.

Taft, *Hours* = Taft, Robert F., SJ. *The Liturgy of the Hours in East and West: The Origins of the Divine Office and Its Meaning for Today*, 2nd rev. edn. Collegeville, MN: Liturgical Press, 1993.

Taft, 'Liturgy of the Great Church' = Taft, Robert F., SJ. 'The Liturgy of the Great Church: An Initial Synthesis of Structure and Interpretation on the Eve of Iconoclasm'. DOP 34/5 (1980–1): 45–75.

Taft, 'Maximus' = Taft, Robert F., SJ. 'Is the Liturgy Described in the Mystagogia of Maximus Confessor Byzantine, Palestinian, or Neither?' BBGG (terza serie) 7 (2010): 247–95.

Taft, 'Old Testament Readings' = Taft, Robert F., SJ. 'Were There Once Old Testament Readings in the Byzantine Divine Liturgy? Apropos of an Article by Sysse Gudrun Engberg'. BBGG (terza serie) 8 (2011): 271–311.

Taft, *Precommunion Rites* = Taft, Robert F., SJ. *The Precommunion Rites*, vol. 5 of *A History of the Liturgy of St John Chrysostom*. OCA 261. Rome: Pontifical Oriental Institute, 2000.

Taft, Robert F., SJ. 'Comparative Liturgy Fifty Years after Anton Baumstark (d. 1948): A Reply to Recent Critics'. *Worship* 73 (1999): 521–40.

Taft, Robert F., SJ. 'Mount Athos: A Late Chapter in the History of the Byzantine Rite'. DOP 42 (1988): 179–94.

Taft, 'Worship on Sinai' = Taft, Robert F., SJ. 'Worship on Sinai in the First Christian Millennium: Glimpses of a Lost World'. In *Approaching the Holy Mountain: Art and Liturgy at St Catherine's Monastery in the Sinai*, ed. by Sharon E. J. Gerstel and Robert S. Nelson, 143–77. Turnhout: Brepols, 2010.

Taft, *Through Their Own Eyes* = Taft, Robert F., SJ. *Through Their Own Eyes: Liturgy as the Byzantines Saw It*. Berkeley, CA: InterOrthodox Press, 2006.

Taft and Parenti, *Storia della liturgia di S. Giovanni Crisostomo* = Taft, Robert F., SJ, and Stefano Parenti. *Storia della liturgia di S. Giovanni Crisostomo: Il Grande Ingresso: Edizione italiana rivista, ampliata e aggiornata*. Ἀνάλεκτα Κρυπτοφέρρης 10. Grottaferrata: Monastero Esarchico, 2014.

Das Taktikon des Nikon vom Schwarzen Berge = *Das Taktikon des Nikon vom Schwarzen Berge: Griechischer Text und kirchenslavische Übersetzung des 14. Jahrhunderts*, ed. by Christian Hannick, Peter Plank, Carolina Lutzka, and Tat'jana I. Afanas'eva. Monumenta Linguae Slavicae Dialecti Veteris 62. Freiburg im Breisgau: Weiher Verlag, 2014.

Talley, *Liturgical Year* = Talley, Thomas J. *The Origins of the Liturgical Year*. New York: Pueblo, 1986.

Tarby, *Prière eucharistique* = Tarby, André. *La prière eucharistique de l'église de Jérusalem*. Théologie Historique 17. Paris: Beauchesne, 1972.

Tarchnishvili, 'Ecclesial Autocephaly of Georgia' = Tarchnishvili, Michael. 'The Origin and Development of the Ecclesial Autocephaly of Georgia'. *Greek Orthodox Theological Review* 46.1/2 (2001): 89–111.

Tarchnishvili, *Geschichte* = Tarchnishvili, Michael. *Geschichte der kirchlichen georgischen Literatur.* ST 185. Vatican City: Biblioteca Apostolica Vaticana, 1955.

Tarchnishvili, *Liturgiae ibericae antiquiores* = Tarchnishvili, Michael. *Liturgiae ibericae antiquiores*, 2 vols. CSCO 122–3. Louvain: Secrétariat du CSCO, 1950.

Taylor, *Christians and the Holy Places* = Taylor, Joan E. *Christians and the Holy Places: The Myth of Jewish–Christian Origins.* Oxford: Clarendon, 1993.

Theophanis Chronographia = *Theophanis Chronographia*, vol. 1, ed. by Carolus de Boor. Hildesheim: Georg Olms Verlag, 1980.

Thibaut, *Monuments* = Thibaut, Jean-Baptiste. *Monuments de la Notation Ekphoné-tique et Hagiopolite de l'Église Grecque: Exposé documentaire des manuscrits de Jérusalem du Sinaï et de l'Athos conservés à la Bibliothèque Impériale de Saint-Pétersbourg.* St Petersburg: Kügelgen, Glitsch & Cie, 1913.

Thomson, *Armenian History Attributed to Sebeos* = *The Armenian History attributed to Sebeos*, part I: *Translation and Notes*, trans. by Robert W. Thomson (with historical commentary by James Howard-Johnston and assistance from Tim Greenwood). Translated Texts for Historians 31. Liverpool: Liverpool University Press, 1999.

Todt, 'Griechisch-orthodoxe (Melkitische) Christen' = Todt, Klaus-Peter. 'Griechisch-orthodoxe (Melkitische) Christen im zentralen und südlichen Syrien: Die Periode von der arabischen Eroberung bis zur Verlegung der Patriarchenresidenz nach Damaskus (635–1365)'. Mus 119.1/2 (2006): 33–88.

Todt, 'Region und griechisch-orthodoxes Patriarchat von Antiocheia' = Todt, Klaus-Peter. 'Region und griechisch-orthodoxes Patriarchat von Antiocheia in mittelbyzantinischer Zeit (969–1084)'. BZ 94 (2001): 239–67.

Todt, 'Zwischen Kaiser und ökumenischem Patriarchen' = Todt, Klaus-Peter. 'Zwischen Kaiser und ökumenischem Patriarchen: Die Rolle der griechisch-orthodoxen Patriarchen von Antiocheia in den politischen und kirchlichen Ausei-nandersetzung des 11.–13. Jh. in Byzanz'. In *Zwei Sonnen am Goldenen Horn? Kaiserliche und patriarchale Macht im byzantinischen Mittelalter*, ed. by Michael Grünbart, Lutz Rickelt, and Martin Marko Vučetić, 137–76. Byzantinische Studien und Texte 3. Münster: Lit Verlag, 2011.

Trapp, *Lexikon zur byzantinischen Gräzität* = *Lexikon zur byzantinischen Gräzität besonders des 9.–12. Jahrhunderts*, vol. 1 (A–K), ed. by Erich Trapp et al. Vienna: Verlag der Österreichischen Akademie der Wissenschaften, 2001.

Tsougarakis, *Life of Leontios* = *The Life of Leontios Patriarch of Jerusalem*, ed. by Dimitris Tsougarakis. The Medieval Mediterranean 2. Leiden: Brill, 1993.

Uspensky, 'Чин всенощного бдения' = Uspensky, Nikolai D. 'Чин всенощного бдения (ἡ ἀγρυπνία) на православном Востоке и в Русской Церкви'. *Богословские Труды* 18 (1978): 5–117.

Vangeli dei popoli = *I vangeli dei popoli: La parola e l'immagine del Cristo nelle culture e nella storia*, ed. by Francesco D'Aiuto, Giovanni Morello, and Ambrogio M. Piazzoni. Vatican City: Biblioteca Apostolica Vaticana, 2000.

Velkovska, 'Lo studio dei lezionari bizantini' = Velkovska, Elena. 'Lo studio dei lezionari bizantini'. *Ecclesia Orans* 13 (1996): 253–71.

Verhelst, *Lectionnaire de Jérusalem* = Verhelst, Stéphane. *Le lectionnaire de Jérusalem: Ses traditions judéo-chrétiennes et son histoire suivant l'index des péricopes évangéliques, conclu par le sanctoral du* Sin. *géo. 58* novus. Spicilegii Friburgensis Subsidia 24. Freiburg: Academic Press Fribourg, 2012.

Verhelst, 'Lieux de station' I = Verhelst, Stéphane. 'Les lieux de station du lectionnaire de Jérusalem. Ière partie: Les villages et fondations'. POC 54 (2004): 13–70.

Verhelst, 'Lieux de station' II = Verhelst, Stéphane. 'Les lieux de station du lectionnaire de Jérusalem. IIème partie: Les lieux saints'. POC 54 (2004): 247–89.

Verhelst, 'Liturgie melkite de saint Jacques' = Verhelst, Stéphane. 'L'histoire de la liturgie melkite de saint Jacques: Interprétations anciennes et nouvelles'. POC 43 (1993): 229–72.

Verhelst, 'Liturgy of Jerusalem' = Verhelst, Stéphane. 'The Liturgy of Jerusalem in the Byzantine Period'. In *Christians and Christianity in the Holy Land: From the Origins to the Latin Kingdoms*, ed. by Ora Limor and Guy G. Stroumsa, 421–62. Turnhout: Brepols, 2006.

Verhelst, Stéphane. 'Les Présanctifiés de saint Jacques'. OCP 61 (1995): 381–405.

Verhelst, *Traditions judéo-chrétiennes* = Verhelst, Stéphane. *Les traditions judéo-chrétiennes dans la liturgie de Jérusalem, spécialement la liturgie de saint Jacques frère de Dieu*. Studies in Liturgy 18. Leuven: Peeters, 2003.

Viscuso, *Guide for a Church under Islām* = Viscuso, Patrick Demetrios. *Guide for a Church under Islām: The Sixty-Six Canonical Questions Attributed to Theodōros Balsamōn: A Translation of the Ecumenical Patriarchate's Twelfth-Century Guidance to the Patriarchate of Alexandria* (with foreword by Sidney H. Griffith). Brookline, MA: Holy Cross Orthodox Press, 2014.

Wade, 'The Oldest *Iadgari*' = Wade, Andrew. 'The Oldest *Iadgari*: The Jerusalem Tropologion, V–VIII c.'. OCP 50 (1984): 451–6.

Wilkinson, *Egeria's Travels* = Wilkinson, John. *Egeria's Travels*, 3rd edn. Warminster: Aris & Phillips, 1999.

Wilkinson, *Jerusalem Pilgrims* = Wilkinson, John. *Jerusalem Pilgrims Before the Crusades*, rev. edn. Warminster: Aris & Phillips, 2002.

Wilson, *Abbot Daniel* = *The Pilgrimage of the Russian Abbot Daniel in the Holy Land, 1106–1107* AD [*sic*], ed. by Charles W. Wilson. New York: AMS Press, 1971.

Winkler, 'Die Interzessionen I' = Winkler, Gabriele. 'Die Interzessionen der Chrysostomusanaphora in ihrer geschichtlichen Entwicklung (I. Teil)'. OCP 36 (1970): 301–36.

Winkler, 'Die Interzessionen II' = Winkler, Gabriele. 'Die Interzessionen der Chrysostomusanaphora in ihrer geschichtlichen Entwicklung (II. Teil)'. OCP 37 (1971): 333–83.

Witvliet, 'The Anaphora of St James' = Witvliet, John D. 'The Anaphora of St James'. In *Essays on Early Eastern Eucharistic Prayers*, ed. by Paul F. Bradshaw, 153–72. Collegeville, MN: Liturgical Press, 1997.

Xevsuriani, *Tropologion* = Xevsuriani, Lili M. *Структура древнейшего Тропология*. Unpublished doctoral thesis. Tbilisi: Институт рукописей им. К. С. Кекелидзе/ Академия наук Грузинской ССР, 1984.

Yaḥyā al-Anṭakī, *History* I = *Histoire de Yahya-ibn-Saʿīd d'Antioche, continuateur de Saʿīd-ibn-Bitriq*, fasc. V, ed. and trans. by Ignaty Kratchkovsky and Aleksandr Vasiliev. PO 18.5. Paris: Firmin-Didot, 1924.

Yaḥyā al-Anṭakī, *History* II = *Histoire de Yahya-ibn-Saʿīd d'Antioche, continuateur de Saʿīd-ibn-Bitriq*, fasc. II, ed. and trans. by Ignaty Kratchkovsky and Aleksandr Vasiliev. PO 23.3. Paris: Firmin-Didot, 1932.

Yaḥyā al-Anṭakī, *History* III = *Histoire de Yahya-ibn-Saʿīd d'Antioche: Édition critique du texte arabe*, ed. and trans. by Ignace Kratchkovsky, Françoise Michaeu, and Gérard Troupeau. PO 47.4. Turnhout: Brepols, 1997.

Yaḥyā al-Anṭakī, *Cronache* = Yaḥyā al-Anṭakī. *Cronache dell'Egitto fatimide e dell'impero Bizantino (937–1033)*, ed. and trans. by Bartolomeo Pirone. Patrimonio Culturale Arabo Cristiano 3. Milan: Jaca Book, 1998.

Young, *Biblical Exegesis* = Young, Frances M. *Biblical Exegesis and the Formation of Christian Culture*. Cambridge: Cambridge University Press, 1997.

Zerfass, *Schriftlesung* = Zerfass, Rolf. *Die Schriftlesung im Kathedraloffizium Jerusalems*. Liturgiewissenschaftliche Quellen und Forschungen 48. Münster Westfalen: Aschendorffsche Verlagsbuchhandlung, 1968.

Online Resources

Bombaxo: *Lectionaries Old and New*, ed. by Kevin P. Edgecomb. N.d. http://www.bombaxo.com/lectionaries.html

Galadza, Peter. 'Byzantine Christian Worship'. *Oxford Research Encyclopedia of Religion*. May 2016. http://religion.oxfordre.com/view/10.1093/acrefore/9780199340378.001.0001/acrefore-9780199340378-e-56

Institut de Recherche et d'histoire des textes. *Pinakes / Πίνακες*, ed. by Pierre Augustin, André Binggeli, and Matthieu Cassin. 2008–. http://pinakes.irht.cnrs.fr/

Institut für Neutestamentliche Textforschung. *New Testament Virtual Manuscript Room*. http://ntvmr.uni-muenster.de/liste

Library of Congress. 'Manuscripts in St. Catherine's Monastery, Mount Sinai'. *Library of Congress Digital Collections*. 2017. https://www.loc.gov/collections/manuscripts-in-st-catherines-monastery-mount-sinai/

Library of Congress. 'Manuscripts in the Libraries of the Greek and Armenian Patriarchates in Jerusalem'. *Library of Congress Digital Collections*. 2017. https://www.loc.gov/collections/greek-and-armenian-patriarchates-of-jerusalem/

Logike Latreia: Michael Zheltov's Liturgical Website, ed. by Michael Zheltov. 2006–17. http://www.mhzh.ru/en

Православная Энциклопедия, vols 1–, ed. by Sergei L. Kravets et al. Moscow: Церковно-научный центр 'Православная Энциклопедия', 2000–. http://www.pravenc.ru

syri.ac: An Annotated Bibliography of Syriac Resources Online, ed. by Jack Tannous and Scott F. Johnson. 2015. http://syri.ac

ThALES = *Thesaurus antiquorum lectionariorum ecclesiae synagogaeque*, ed. by Daniel Stoekl Ben Ezra. 2017. http://www.lectionary.eu

TITUS = Thesaurus indogermanischer Text- und Sprachmaterialien. *Old Georgian Lectionary*, ed. by Jost Gippert. 2004–7. http://titus.uni-frankfurt.de/texte/etcs/cauc/ageo/lekt/lektpar/lektp.htm

Index of Biblical References

Note: Page number followed by *t* indicates tables

Genesis
  1:1–13 341*t*
Exodus
  16:34 289
  19:10–18 341*t*
  25:10–22 289
  40:18 289
Numbers
  17:10 289
Deuteronomy
  10:5 289
1 Kingdoms (1 Samuel)
  17:1 104
2 Kingdoms (2 Samuel)
  5:1–10 257, 259
4 Kingdoms (2 Kings)
  2:1–15a 252
  5:9–15 243
1 Maccabees
  1:45 104 n. 203
  1:59 257
  6:7 104 n. 203
Psalms
  2:7 241
  2:8 241
  5:12a 265
  5:12b–13 265
  17:31 259
  17:51 259
  18:2 262
  18:5 262
  20:4–5 265
  20:4b 195*t*
  32:1 254
  33:9 42*t*, 212
  33:10 195*t*
  33:20 260
  36:18 260
  36:29 260
  36:30–2 253
  44:15 195*t*
  50 254
  63:1 254
  63:2 267

  63:6–7 254
  63:11 254, 267
  67:36 195*t*
  70:8 212
  86:5 85
  91:13 267
  92 189 n. 197
  94:1 196
  94:6 181
  96:10 195*t*
  96:11 254
  103:4 195*t*
  104:14 252
  104:15 195*t*, 252
  109:1 241, 257, 355
  110:9 267
  114 48*t*
  115 48*t*
  118 142, 235
  131 355
  131:1 257, 259
  131:2 259
  131:7 354, 355
  131:8 290
  131:9 262
  131:11 259
  132–6 48 n. 117
  148:1 212
Proverbs
  1:20–33 341*t*
  2:13–22 341*t*
  3:27–34 341*t*
  8:22–31 241
  14:27–15:4 332
  20:6–15 252
Hosea
  4:1–6 341*t*
  5:13–6:3 332, 341*t*
Amos
  9:5–6 332
Joel
  2:15–18 337
  2:15–27 337, 370
  2:21–27 337
  3:1–5 36

Zephaniah
  3:6–13 332
  3:7–13 332
Malachi
  4:5–6 252
Isaiah
  5:1–7 341*t*
  6:2–3 41*t*
  12:1–6 243
  53:7 162
  63:14–15 332
Ezekiel
  1:4–24 223 n. 17
Daniel
  2:34–35 241
  3 193
  9:27 104 n. 203
  11:31 104 n. 203
  12:11 104 n. 203
Matthew
  1:18–25 242
  2:1–23 241, 242
  2:13 261
  2:13–23 188
  4:12–25 319*t*
  4:18–23 319*t*
  5:1–12 310*t*, 345*t*
  5:1–16 310*t*, 311, 311*t*, 344*t*
  5:13–16 344*t*
  5:17–24 344*t*
  5:17–48 324*t*
  6 204
  6:1–15 324*t*
  6:1–33 203, 324*t*
  6:9–13 42*t*, 211
  6:14–21 324*t*
  6:16–24 337
  6:16–33 324*t*
  6:22–33 319*t*
  6:34–7:21 319*t*, 324*t*
  7:1–11 319*t*
  7:13–29 324*t*
  8:1–13 319*t*
  8:14–23 345*t*
  8:14–27 319*t*
  8:28–9:1 319*t*
  8:28–9:8 319*t*
  9:1–8 319*t*
  9:9–17 319*t*, 346*t*
  9:18–26 319*t*
  9:27–35 319*t*
  9:35–10:15 344*t*
  10:1–8 346*t*
  10:1–15 344*t*
  10:16–22 344*t*, 363
  10:24–33 344*t*

  10:37–42 344*t*, 345*t*
  11:1–15 319*t*, 320
  11:25–30 344*t*, 345*t*
  12:9–23 319*t*
  13:24–43 346*t*
  13:54–8 262 n. 223
  14:1–12 251, 253, 257
  14:13–22 319*t*
  14:22–34 319*t*
  14:22–36 319*t*
  15:21–31 319*t*, 321*t*
  15:32–8 319*t*, 345*t*
  16:13–20 344*t*
  16:24–27 345*t*
  17:14–23 319*t*
  18:23–35 319*t*
  19:16–24 319*t*
  19:16–26 319*t*
  19:27–29 344*t*
  20:1–16 324*t*
  20:17–28 325, 328*t*
  21:1–17 324*t*
  21:18–43 328*t*
  21:18–22:14 328*t*, 341*t*
  21:33–42 319*t*
  21:33–46 324*t*
  22:1–14 319*t*,
    324*t*, 346*t*
  22:15–23:39 328*t*
  22:15–24:12 328*t*, 341*t*
  22:35–46 319*t*
  22:41–6 257, 259
  23:1–39 324*t*
  23:24–24:1 344*t*
  23:34–24:1 260
  23:34–39 344*t*
  24:1–26:2 328*t*
  24:3–35 325, 328*t*
  24:3–26:2 327, 328*t*
  24:15 104 n. 203
  24:36–26:2 328*t*
  25:14–30 319*t*
  25:31–46 324*t*, 345*t*
  26:1–27:2 328*t*
  26:2–20 327, 328*t*
  26:6–16 327, 328*t*
  26:14–16 328*t*
  26:17–30 328*t*
  26:20–24 328*t*
  26:21–39 327
  26:27 290
  26:40–27:2 327
  27:1–38 327
  27:39–54 327
  27:55–61 327
  28:1–20 310*t*, 311*t*
  28:16–20 310*t*, 344*t*

Mark
1:12–28 321*t*
1:16–27 321*t*
1:29–45 321*t*
2:1–12 321*t*, 324*t*
2:13–28 321*t*
2:14–17 324*t*
3:1–12 321*t*
4:35–41 321*t*
5:1–20 321*t*
5:21–43 321*t*
6:1 262
6:14–30 254, 257
6:34–44 321*t*
6:45–56 321*t*
7:24–37 321*t*
8:1-9 321*t*
8:34–9:1 324*t*
9:14–31 321*t*
9:17–31 324*t*
10:17–27 321*t*
10:32 324*t*
10:32–45 346*t*
10:46–52 321*t*
11:1–11 324*t*
11:12–18 328*t*
14:12–26 328*t*
14:15 36
14:23 290
15:43–16:8 315, 316*t*
16 313
16:1–8 204, 309, 310*t*,
    311*t*, 332
16:9–20 310*t*, 311*t*, 316*t*, 317

Luke
1:39–56 344*t*
3:23–4:15 323*t*
4:1–15 323*t*
4:14–24 323*t*
4:25–30 346*t*
4:31–41 323*t*
4:42–5:11 323*t*
5:1–11 321*t*
5:12–17 323*t*
5:17–26 323*t*
5:27–38 323*t*
6:1–10 346*t*
6:31–36 321*t*
7:11–16 321*t*
7:36–50 324*t*
8:5–8 321*t*
8:26–35 321*t*
8:38–39 321*t*
8:41–56 321*t*
10:1–12 344*t*
10:1–20 319*t*
10:25–37 321*t*, 324*t*

10:38–42 344*t*, 346*t*
11:1–13 346*t*
11:27–32 346*t*
12:16–21 321*t*
12:32–41 324*t*, 346*t*
12:35–39 328*t*
13:10–17 321*t*
13:31–35 328*t*
14:35 321*t*
14:16–24 321*t*
15:1–10 324*t*, 328*t*
15:11–32 324*t*
16:19–31 321*t*, 324*t*
17:11–19 321*t*
18:1–14 324*t*
18:9–14 324*t*
18:10 321*t*
18:18–27 321*t*
18:35–43 321*t*
19:1–10 321*t*
19:29–38 324*t*
19:29–40 324*t*
21:12–19 344*t*
22:1–6 328*t*
22:1–11 328*t*
22:1–39 328*t*, 341*t*
22:1–46 328*t*
22:12 36
22:17–20 290
23:54–24:12 310*t*
24:1–12 310*t*, 311*t*
24:12–35 310*t*, 311*t*
24:21–35 310*t*, 311*t*
24:36–40 310*t*, 311*t*
24:37 24
24:41–53 316*t*
24:36–53 316*t*

John
1 313
1:1–17 310*t*, 311*t*,
    332, 379
1:18–28 310*t*, 311*t*
1:25–52 310*t*, 311*t*
1:29–34 346*t*
1:35–51 310*t*
1:44–52 324*t*, 345*t*
2:1–11 315, 316*t*, 332
2:12–22 310*t*, 311*t*
2:12–25 315, 316*t*, 332
3 354
3:1–16 310*t*, 311*t*
3:13–21 346*t*
3:22–33 310*t*, 311*t*
3:13–21 346*t*
4:4–23 315, 316*t*, 332
4:4–42 316*t*
4:5–42 316*t*

John (*cont.*)
  4:24 316*t*, 332
  4:43–54 315, 316*t*
  5:1–15 315, 316*t*
  5:19–24 345*t*
  5:24–30 345*t*, 346*t*
  6:27–40 315, 316*t*
  6:47–58 315, 316*t*
  7:1–13 316*t*
  7:14–30 316*t*
  7:37–8:12 316*t*, 379
  7:39 318
  8:12–20 315, 316*t*, 332
  9:1–38 315, 316*t*, 324*t*
  10:1–16 344*t*
  10:9–16 344*t*
  10:11–16 324*t*
  11:1–45 324*t*
  11:47–54 315, 316*t*
  11:55–57 324*t*
  11:55–12:11 324*t*
  12:1–11 324*t*, 326, 328*t*
  12:1–18 324*t*
  12:12–18 324*t*
  12:12–22 324*t*
  12:17–50 328*t*, 341*t*
  12:24–28 345*t*
  12:24–41 265
  12:27–33 328*t*
  12:27–36 346*t*
  13:1–17 328*t*
  13:1–30 328*t*
  13:3–17 327, 328*t*
  13:3–30 328*t*
  13:31 371
  14:15–19 316*t*, 332
  14:15–21 316*t*
  14:25–29 316*t*
  15:26–16:14 316*t*
  19:20 22
  19:31–37 327
  20:1–10 310*t*
  20:1–18 310*t*, 311*t*
  20:11–18 310*t*
  20:19–23 310*t*, 311*t*
  20:19–25 310*t*, 311*t*
  20:19–31 310*t*, 311*t*, 379
  20:26–31 310*t*
  21:1–14 310*t*, 311*t*, 363
  21:15–25 310*t*, 311*t*, 324*t*

Acts
  1:1–8 332, 332*t*
  1:1–12 332, 332*t*
  1:1–18 332*t*
  1:12–26 332*t*
  1:12–14 332*t*

1:13 36
1:15–20 341*t*
2:1–21 332
2:1–42 22
2:14–21 332*t*
2:22–28 332*t*
2:22–36 332*t*
2:29–47 332*t*
2:38–43 332*t*
3:1–8 332*t*
3:1–20 332*t*
3:11–16 332*t*
4:23–31 332*t*
5:12–20 332*t*
5:34–42 332*t*
6:5 264
6:8–7:60 264, 267
6:8–8:2 265
12:12 36
13:17–38 252
13:25–39 254, 346*t*
15:1–29 257
15:13–29 259, 260
19:1–8 332*t*

Romans
  5:1–15 344*t*
  6 354
  8:14–21 345*t*
  11:1–5 314, 335*t*
  11:1–12 344*t*
  12:1–3 346*t*
  12:6–16 314, 335*t*
  12:16–13:6 314, 335*t*
  13:10–14:6 314, 335*t*
  13:11–14:4 314, 335, 335*t*
  13:12–14:11 337
  14:1–23 314, 335*t*
  16:25–27 335*t*

1 Corinthians
  1:18–24 346*t*
  3:8–17 344*t*
  4:6–14 344*t*
  4:9–16 344*t*, 346*t*
  8:8–9:2 335*t*
  11:26 25
  12:1–14 332
  12:27–13:3 344*t*
  14:20–25 344*t*
  15:12–28 345*t*

2 Corinthians
  4:6–10 345*t*
  4:6–16 346*t*
  4:7–12 345*t*
  4:7–15 265
  6:2–10 330, 335*t*, 336
  6:16–7:1 346*t*

Galatians
3:23–4:5 345*t*
5:22–26 345*t*
6:1–2 345*t*

Ephesians
1:3–14 335*t*
4:1–16 335*t*, 346*t*
4:25–5:2 335*t*
5:6 346*t*
5:8–20 346*t*
5:13–17 335*t*
6:10–18 344*t*

Philippians
2:5–11 344*t*, 346*t*
4:4–9 335*t*

Colossians
1:23–2:2 344*t*

1 Thessalonians
2:14–20 344*t*
4:5–17 346*t*
4:13–18 345*t*, 363

Titus
2:11–15 243

Hebrews
1:1–12 345*t*
1:10–2:3 335*t*
1:13–2:4 345*t*
2:2–10 345*t*, 346*t*

2:11–18 335*t*
4:14–5:6 335*t*, 344*t*
5:4–6 344*t*
6:13–20 335*t*
7:26–8:2 344*t*
9:1–7 344*t*
9:11–14 335*t*
11:24–40 335*t*
11:32 344*t*
11:34–37 344*t*
12:1–10 344*t*
12:28–13:8 335*t*
13:7–16 345*t*
13:10–16 344*t*

James
1:1–12 332*t*
1:13–19 332*t*
1:17–27 332*t*
2:1–13 332*t*
2:14–23 332*t*

1 Peter
1:13–25 332
2:1–10 332
2:21–25 332
3:17–22 332

1 John
1:1–7 332, 332*t*
4:16–21 332

Index of Manuscript References

Note: Page number followed by *t* indicates tables

Alexandria
  Alexandria Gr. 288 (911) (16th–17th cent.)
  207
Athos
  Vatopedi Gr. 322 (956) (13th–14th cent.)
  63 n. 221
  Panteleimonos Gr. 86 (11th–12th cent.)
  262 n. 223
  Koutloumoussiou Gr. 194 (14th cent.) 82
Berlin
  Berlin Staatsbibliothek (Preußischer
  Kulturbesitz) Gr. 277 (Fol. 41) (12th cent.)
  226
  Berlin Or. Oct. 1019 (12th cent.) 271
Besançon
  Besançon Bibliothèque Municipale Gr. 42
  (13th cent.) 198
Cambridge, MA
  Harvard University Houghton Library Gr. 3
  (1105) 208
Charfet
  Charfet Fonds patriarcal 87 (19th cent.) 194
Dresden
  Dresden Sächsische LB Gr. A.104 (11th cent.)
  62, 63 n. 215
Florence
  Laurentian Gr. LIX, 13 (15th–16th cent.)
  216 n. 355
Graz
  Universitätsbibliothek Graz Pergament 27
  (7th cent.) 50
  Graz University Library Cod. No. 2058/4
  (985) 174, 177*t*
  Graz Geo. 5 (12th cent.) 172
Grottaferrata
  Grottaferrata Γ.α. I (1300) 186
  Grottaferrata Γ.β. IV (10th cent.) 213
  Grottaferrata Γ.β. VII (10th cent.) 213
  Grottaferrata Γ.β. X (11th cent.) 213
  Grottaferrata Δ.β. XVII (11th–12th cent.)
  198 n. 251
  Grottaferrata Δ.γ. XII (970) 54 n. 163
  Grottaferrata Z.δ. CXIX (13th cent.)
  176 n. 133

Jerusalem
  Jerusalem St James Monastery Arm. 121
  (1192 and 1318) 47
  Hagios Sabas Gr. 153 (1275) 144
  Hagios Sabas Gr. 412 (11th cent.) 68 n. 249
  Hagios Stavros Gr. 40 (10th–11th cent.) 61,
  62, 223
  Hagios Stavros Gr. 43 (1122) 13, 70, 140,
  144, 207 n. 297, 211, 212 n. 331, 218*t*,
  309, 312, 324*t*, 330, 331, 341*t*, 381
Leipzig
  Leipzig Universitätsbibliothek Gr. 3 (8th cent.)
  313
London
  British Museum Add. 12150 (411) 226
  British Museum Add. 14528 (6th cent.) 246
  British Museum Or. 4951 (12th cent.?) 168
Messina
  Messina Gr. 177 (11th cent.) 169, 176, 178*t*,
  192, 200–1, 207, 218*t*, 377–8
Mestia
  Mestia Historic-Ethnographic Museum 51
  (10th cent.) 50
Milan
  Milan Bibliotheca Ambrosiana Gr. C. 101
  Sup. (12th cent.) 227
Moscow
  Moscow GIM Gr. 129D (9th cent.) 64, 166
  Moscow GIM Gr. Vladimir 21/Savva 4 (11th
  cent.) 62–3, 226, 245, 323
  Moscow RGB Gr. 27 [Sevastianov 474]
  (10th cent.) 70
Oxford
  Bodleian MS. Arm. d. 2 (before 1359) 47
Paris
  Paris BNF Arm. 44 (10th cent.) 46–7
  Paris BNF Geo. 3 (10th–11th cent.) 50
  Paris BNF Gr. 216 (10th cent.) 151 n. 484
  Paris BNF Gr. 1538 (12th cent.) 151 n. 484
  Paris BNF Gr. 1587 (12th cent.) 227
  Paris BNF Gr. 1590 (1063) 245
  Paris Coislin Gr. 114 (14th–15th cent.)
  216 n. 355
  Paris Coislin Gr. 213 (1027) 262 n. 223
  Paris Coislin Gr. 303 (10th cent.) 326 n. 87

Paris (*cont.*)
Paris Suppl. Gr. 303 (16th cent.) 199
Paris Suppl. Gr. 476 (15th cent.) 82, 295
Patmos
Patmos Gr. 266 (9th cent.) 61–2
St Petersburg
St Petersburg RNB Gr. 44 (9th cent.) 165,
181, 187, 191, 199, 203, 207, 213, 343,
344*t*, 364–5
St Petersburg RNB Gr. 359 (1122) 381
St Petersburg RNB, Novgorod St Sophia 1136
(13th cent.) 63 n. 220
Sinai
Sinai Ar. 54 (9th cent.) 99, 369
Sinai Ar. 70 (9th–10th cent.) 99, 369
Sinai Ar. 72 (897) 99, 369
Sinai Ar. 74 (9th cent.) 99, 369
Sinai Ar. 97 (1123/4) 99, 369
Sinai Ar. 116 (995/6) 99, 188 n. 191, 225,
307, 309, 310*t*, 315, 316*t*, 317, 318, 319*t*,
320, 321*t*, 322, 323*t*, 324*t*, 325–6, 328*t*,
329, 336, 343, 344*t*, 346*t*, 347, 363, 368–9
Sinai Ar. 455 (12th cent.) 114 n. 266
Sinai Ar. 505 (13th cent.) 326 n. 85
Sinai Geo. O. 1 (10th cent.) 101, 370
Sinai Geo. O. 10 (11th cent.) 133, 329, 332*t*,
335*t*, 378
Sinai Geo. O. 12 (10th cent.) 69, 102, 174,
177*t*, 252 n. 168, 371–2
Sinai Geo. O. 18 (10th cent.) 55
Sinai Geo. O. 19 (1074) 373
Sinai Geo. O. 20 (987) 55
Sinai Geo. O. 26 (10th cent.) 55
Sinai Geo. O. 31 (977) 330
Sinai Geo. O. 30 (979) 367–8
Sinai Geo. O. 34 (10th cent.) 32, 53, 55, 69,
89, 90, 101, 123, 144, 222, 225, 229, 237*t*,
249, 255, 261, 275, 290, 296*t*, 297, 298*t*,
366, 367, 370–1
Sinai Geo. O. 35 (973) 101 n. 178
Sinai Geo. O. 37 (982) 50
Sinai Geo. O. 38 (979) 237*t*, 255, 275, 295,
296*t*, 298*t*, 307, 310*t*, 311*t*, 315, 316*t*, 319*t*,
320, 322, 323*t*, 324*t*, 328*t*, 341, 367–8
Sinai Geo. O. 40 (10th cent.) 55
Sinai Geo. O. 41 (10th cent.) 55
Sinai Geo. O. 53 (9th–10th cent.) 171,
173, 177*t*
Sinai Geo. O. 54 (10th cent.) 69, 102, 171,
174, 177*t*, 252 n. 168, 336, 371
Sinai Geo. O. 58 (977) 330
Sinai Geo. O. 59 (10th cent.) 101, 370
Sinai Geo. O. 60 (977) 330
Sinai Geo. O. 63 (10th cent.) 371
Sinai Geo. O. 64 (10th cent.) 101, 370

Sinai Geo. O. 65 (10th cent.) 101, 370
Sinai Geo. O. 89 (11th cent.) 172
Sinai Geo. N. 8 (977) 330
Sinai Geo. N. 12 (1075) 69, 373
Sinai Geo. N. 22 (10th cent.) 174, 177*t*, 199,
200, 252 n. 168
Sinai Geo. N. 23 (10th cent.) 90
Sinai Geo. N. 26 (9th–10th cent.) 171, 173,
177*t*, 252 n. 168
Sinai Geo. N. 31 (9th–10th cent.) 173, 177*t*
Sinai Geo. N. 33 (10th cent.) 174, 371
Sinai Geo. N. 53 (10th cent.) 174, 177*t*
Sinai Geo. N. 54 (10th cent.) 97, 175, 177*t*,
178, 179, 252 n. 168
Sinai Geo. N. 58 (9th–10th cent.) 85 n. 70,
102, 169, 173, 177*t*, 252 n. 168, 294, 367
Sinai Geo. N. 63 (10th cent.) 171, 175,
177*t*, 199
Sinai Geo. N. 65 (10th cent.) 175, 177*t*
Sinai Geo. N. 66 (10th cent.) 172
Sinai Geo. N. 70 (10th cent.) 175, 177*t*
Sinai Geo. N. 79 (10th cent.) 175, 177*t*
Sinai Geo. N. 81 (10th cent.) 175, 177*t*
Sinai Geo. N. 83 (10th cent.) 174, 177*t*
Sinai Gr. 14 (12th cent.) 208
Sinai Gr. 150 (10th–11th cent.) 63 n. 221,
186, 187–8
Sinai Gr. 210 (861/2) 69, 247, 307, 310*t*,
315, 316*t*, 319*t*, 320, 323*t*, 324*t*, 325–6,
328*t*, 329, 336–7, 344*t*, 361–3
Sinai Gr. 211 (9th cent.) 347
Sinai Gr. 212 (9th cent.) 113, 194, 195*t*,
199, 330, 343, 344*t*, 363
Sinai Gr. 213 (967) 71
Sinai Gr. 257 (1101/2) 380–1
Sinai Gr. 286 (12th cent.) 263
Sinai Gr. 287 (13th cent.) 263
Sinai Gr. 493 (8th–9th cent.) 288
Sinai Gr. 556 (11th cent.) 54 n. 163
Sinai Gr. 579 (11th cent.) 54 n. 163
Sinai Gr. 596 (9th–10th cent.) 132
Sinai Gr. 607 (9th–10th cent.) 54 n. 163, 132
Sinai Gr. 608 (9th–10th cent.) 132
Sinai Gr. 741 (25 January 1099) 132, 288,
374–5
Sinai Gr. 742 (25 January 1099) 132, 374–5
Sinai Gr. 759 (11th cent.) 54 n. 163
Sinai Gr. 777 (11th cent.) 54 n. 163
Sinai Gr. 784 (12th cent.) 54 n. 163
Sinai Gr. 789 (12th cent.) 54 n. 163
Sinai Gr. 863 (9th cent.) 90, 184 n. 171, 225
Sinai Gr. 973 (1153) 341
Sinai Gr. 1039 (13th cent.) 171, 176, 178*t*
Sinai Gr. 1040 (14th cent.) 82, 97, 177,
178*t*, 178–9, 200 n. 264, 203 n. 275, 207,
211, 270 n. 266, 295, 351, 377, 385–6

Sinai Gr. 1096 (12th cent.) 7 n. 26, 58 n. 189, 70, 89, 92, 94, 97, 98 n. 159, 126, 144, 161, 186, 224, 228–9, 237*t*, 243, 245, 257, 271, 274–5, 282–3, 296*t*, 298*t*, 342, 353, 382

Sinai Gr. 1097 (1214) 70, 89, 161–2, 186, 271, 383–4

Sinai Gr. 1500 (10th–11th cent.) 63 n. 220

Sinai Gr. 2095 (9th–10th cent.) 186

Sinai Gr. N.E. MΓ 2 (9th cent.) 330, 348

Sinai Gr. N.E. MΓ 5 (8th–9th cent.) 53, 132, 182, 183, 243, 246, 281, 284, 308, 325, 361

Sinai Gr. N.E. MΓ 8 (10th cent.) 50, 69, 113, 178, 187, 199, 242–3, 329, 336–7, 369–70, 379, 380

Sinai Gr. N.E. MΓ 11 (9th cent.) 113, 315, 320, 330, 336, 365

Sinai Gr. N.E. MΓ 22 (9th–10th cent.) 172

Sinai Gr. N.E. MΓ 28 (9th–10th cent.) 132

Sinai Gr. N.E. MΓ 31 (9th cent.) 365–6

Sinai Gr. N.E. MΓ 36 (9th cent.) 334, 366

Sinai Gr. N.E. MΓ 53 (8th–9th cent.) 168

Sinai Gr. N.E. MΓ 56 (8th–9th cent.) 132, 243, 246, 281, 284, 308, 361

Sinai Gr. N.E. MΓ 73 (9th cent.) 333, 366

Sinai Gr. N.E. MΓ 118 (8th–9th cent.) 173, 177*t*

Sinai Gr. N.E. M 35 (11th–12th cent.) 69, 379–80, 385, 387

Sinai Gr. N.E. M 66 (11th–12th cent.) 69, 380, 385, 387

Sinai Gr. N.E. M 151 (10th cent.) 174, 177*t*

Sinai Gr. N.E. E 24 (11th cent.) 175, 177*t*

Sinai Gr. N.E. E 59 (1070) 175, 177*t*

Sinai Gr. N.E. E 80 (11th cent.) 175, 177*t*

Sinai Gr. N.E. Σ 3 (11th cent.) 171, 175, 177*t*

Sinai Gr. N.E. Σπ. MΓ 22 (861/2) 247, 362

Sinai Gr. N.E. X 73 (13th cent.) 69, 385, 387

Sinai Gr. N.E. X 87 (11th–12th cent.) 380

Sinai Gr. N.E. X 156 (11th cent.) 75–176, 178*t*, 378

Sinai Gr. N.E. X 159 (14th–16th cent.) 69, 386–7

Sinai Gr. N.E. X 239 (12th–13th cent.) 98, 114

Sinai Slav. 37 (11th cent.) 346

Sinai Slav. 330 (11th cent.) 63 n. 220

Sinai Slav. 333 (11th cent.) 63 n. 220

Sinai Slav. 1/N (11th cent.) 346

Sinai Slav. 5/N (10th–11th cent.) 172 n. 102

Sinai Syr. M52N (9th–10th cent.) 98, 222, 225, 237*t*, 247–8, 255, 279, 295 n. 378, 296*t*, 298*t*, 366–7

Tbilisi

Tbilisi Centre of Manuscripts A-86 (11th cent.) 176, 178*t*, 199

Tbilisi Centre of Manuscripts H1741 (1048) 133

Tbilisi Centre of Manuscripts H2123 (9th–10th cent.) 55

Tbilisi Erovnuli Library 40 (10th cent.) 50

Tbilisi Geo. 193 (11th cent.) 379

Tbilisi Geo. 222 (12th cent.) 379

Tbilisi Geo. 1831 (8th cent.) 50

Vatican City

Vatican Barberini Gr. 319 (1039/1168) 70

Vatican Barberini Gr. 336 (8th cent.) 6 n. 22, 10 n. 44, 67, 110, 164, 179, 198, 210–11 n. 324, 346

Vatican Borgia Geo. 7 (13th–14th cent.) 176, 178*t*

Vatican Borgia Gr. 24 (17 March 1880) 377

Vatican Ar. 13 (9th cent.) 99

Vatican Ar. 76 (1068) 262

Vatican Gr. 112 (14th cent.) 216 n. 355

Vatican Gr. 771 (11th–12th cent.) 198 n. 251

Vatican Gr. 1209 (4th cent.) 339

Vatican Gr. 1970 (13th cent.) 165 n. 59, 176, 178*t*, 178, 181, 187, 194, 200, 207, 208, 210 n. 324, 377

Vatican Gr. 2281 (1209) 211

Vatican Gr. 2282 (9th cent.) 113, 173, 177*t*, 182, 213–14

Vatican Ottoboni Gr. 459 (15th cent.) 216 n. 355

Vatican Palatine Gr. 367 (13th cent.) 216 n. 355

Vatican Syr. 19 (1030) 69, 99, 111, 237*t*, 255, 298*t*, 295, 296*t*, 298*t*, 309, 310*t*, 316*t*, 319*t*, 321*t*, 321–2, 324*t*, 328*t*, 352, 372–3

Vatican Syr. 20 (1215) 69, 99, 255, 261, 384

Vatican Syr. 21 (31 October 1041) 329

Vatican Syr. 69 (1547) 262

Washington DC

Dumbarton Oaks MS 2 (11th cent.) 122, 376–7

Yerevan

Yerevan Matenadaran Arm. 985 (10th cent.) 47

General Index

Note: Page number followed by *t* indicates tables

Accacius of Caesarea 38
Aelia Capitolina 20-1
Agapius, patriarch of Antioch 110
Aland, Kurt 69, 71, 99, 198, 301, 313, 347,
 348, 362-8, 379-81, 385-7
al-Bīrūnī 75, 82-4, 144, 222, 237, 238*t*, 248,
 250*t*, 256*t*, 261, 266*t*, 272*t*, 274*t*, 277*t*,
 278*t*, 280*t*, 285*t*, 287, 289*t*, 290*t*, 293*t*,
 295, 296*t*, 298*t*, 384
Aleksidze, Zaza 16, 69, 80, 90, 97, 102, 105,
 169, 172, 174, 252, 260, 331, 360, 367,
 372, 373
Alexander III, pope of Rome 148
Alexandria 3, 11, 14-15, 19, 20, 21, 76, 83, 91,
 93, 109, 117, 129, 134, 136, 145, 149-51,
 157, 162, 165, 207, 306, 352, 377
Alexandrian text type 305
Alexius I Comnenus, emperor 125
Alexopoulos, Stefanos 159, 177, 193, 345, 373
al-Ḥākim, caliph 4, 13, 117-19, 122, 139-40,
 143, 277
Amos, prophet 303, 305; see also *Index of
 Biblical References*
Anastasis
 aedicule 17, 388-9, 394
 Church of 1, 4, 32-5, 39, 45, 49, 54, 59, 64,
 71, 352-3, 388-9, 393
 Enkainia of 38, 44, 222, 228, 238, 244-6,
 287, 343, 364-5, 377, 384, 393
 Typikon, *see* Typikon of the Anastasis
 see also *resurrection*
Anastasius the Persian, St 160
Andreou, Georgios 62-6, 184-6, 206, 226,
 245, 250, 255, 262-3, 267, 276, 279, 290,
 292, 302, 323, 325, 333-4, 345
Anna Comnene 112
Annunciation 23, 56, 91, 233, 238*t*, 240, 246,
 250*t*, 326, 335*t*, 368, 371
Anthony Rawḥ 106, 283-5
Antiba, Nicholas 19
Antioch 3, 11, 12, 14-15, 19-22, 43, 59, 69,
 76, 80, 83, 85, 91, 93, 99, 100, 103, 104,
 106, 109-15, 118, 123, 129, 134, 136, 143,
 145, 147-8, 150, 157, 162, 167, 186, 229,
 247, 306, 329, 352, 372-4, 378, 385-6,
 394, 400, 406, 409, 415-17
 Church of Cassian 111
 Great Church 111

Antiochus Strategus 103, 104, 115
antiphon 48, 64-5, 79, 142, 179-80, 185-7
apolytikion 213; *see also* dismissal hymn,
 troparion
Apostolic Constitutions 43, 46
Arab conquest (of Jerusalem) 4, 22, 29, 37, 48,
 74-5, 86, 89, 94, 103-7, 123, 128, 215,
 231, 268, 350, 353
Arabic
 language 22, 36, 80-3, 98-100, 111-15,
 120, 124, 140, 153, 222, 227, 255, 318,
 326, 360, 364, 368
 marginal notes 31, 113, 173, 343, 363, 365,
 378, 380, 381
Arabization 17, 112-15
Arianism 38, 76
Ark of the Covenant 289-91
Armenian
 language 20, 22, 211, 329
 lectionary 30, 31, 36, 37, 46-9, 51, 65, 67,
 69, 72, 77, 181, 185, 190, 198-201, 222-3,
 226-9, 237-40, 243-7, 249-51, 256-8,
 263-4, 266, 269-72, 274-5, 277-8, 280,
 284-5, 287-90, 293, 296-8, 301, 308, 311,
 329, 336, 341, 388
Arranz, Miguel 4, 13, 58, 62, 116, 117, 185-6,
 296, 341
Assemani, Joseph 111, 169, 176, 201, 207,
 250, 321, 372, 378
Assemani, Stephanus 111, 250, 321, 372
Athanasius II of Alexandria,
 patriarch 149-51
Athenogenes, St 233, 275-7, 319-20
Atticus, archbishop of Constantinople 262-3
Auzépy, Marie-France 81, 96, 97, 107,
 129, 189

Baldovin, John 30, 33-4, 36, 45-6, 49, 85, 88,
 142, 334
Balsamon, *see* Theodore Balsamon
Barsanuphius and John, *Letters* of 371
Basil II, emperor 110, 112, 352
Basil the Great, St 158, 160-1, 165, 171,
 275, 393
 Liturgy of 10, 18, 25, 66, 97, 99, 109, 131,
 136-7, 157-8, 160-1, 163-7, 171-2,
 175-9, 184, 202, 208-9, 213-14, 356, 393
Basil the Hagiopolite 141, 185, 353, 381

Baumstark, Anton 6, 8–10, 32, 73, 83, 89, 116, 187, 206, 220–1, 229, 231, 246–7, 251, 254, 257, 269, 271, 302, 329, 359, 384
Behr, John 24–5
bematikion 59
Benedictus 41, 210–11
Beneshevich, Vladimir 13, 360
Bertonière, Gabriel 13, 39, 52, 126, 142–3, 196–7, 208, 243, 288, 300, 323, 325, 334–5, 374–5
Bethlehem 36–7, 125, 240–1, 247, 286, 390, 391
    Church of the Nativity 36–7, 88, 127, 291, 293*t*, 357
Bickell, Gustav 14
Bieberstein, Klaus 35–6, 115
Binggeli, André 98, 279, 282, 285, 295, 366
Black, Matthew 168, 271, 291
Black Mountain 59, 100, 102, 112, 352
Botte, Bernard 9, 239–40, 273, 291
Bradshaw, Paul 30–1, 39, 158, 159, 222, 307, 323, 350
Brakmann, Heinzgerd 4, 14, 15, 18, 109, 143, 144, 160, 168, 169, 176, 211, 212, 240, 291, 356, 386, 399, 403, 412, 413
Brightman, Frank 82, 158, 169, 171, 197, 210, 292, 377
Brock, Sebastian 76, 80, 87, 98–100, 111–12, 138, 189, 194, 215, 360, 372, 384
Buchinger, Harald 39, 220–1, 226, 232, 240
Burns, Yvonne 302
Byzantinization 4–16, 19–22, 66–71, 162–7, 236–8, 350–7

Caesarea 20–1, 38, 110, 123, 391
canticle 64, 65*t*, 193
Capitolias 106, 283–5, 391
catechumens 39, 40, 41*t*, 157, 180*t*, 340, 365
Chalcedon, Council of 3, 20, 37, 75–9, 81, 86, 93–4, 166, 215, 231, 239, 294, 295, 345*t*, 393
Chalcedonian Orthodox, *see* Melkite
Chariton, Lavra of St 21, 91, 108, 142
Charon, Jean François Joseph, *see* Korolevsky, Cyril
cheroubikon 59, 64–5, 163, 165–7, 181, 204, 206–9, 218
Christian Palestinian Aramaic 22, 39, 78–9, 88, 98, 114, 352, 372
Christology 93, 244, 356–7, 393, 394
Chronicles, Book of 306
Chronz, Tinatin 18, 52, 168, 169, 356, 360, 364, 399, 403, 412, 413
Colosians, Epistle to the 334*t*; see also *Index of Biblical References*

Communion
    hymn 42*t*, 51*t*, 52, 59, 62, 65*t*, 163, 196, 201, 202*t*, 212–13, 379, 386
    prayer for 46, 170, 372
    reception of 18, 32, 42*t*, 45, 131, 160, 166, 196, 201, 208, 214, 231, 356, 393
    spoon 18, 160, 231, 356
Conybeare, Frederick Cornwallis 46–7, 104, 115
Constantine the Great, emperor 34–5, 117–18, 120, 123, 231, 268, 287
Constantine V Copronymus, emperor 129
Constantine VI, emperor 130
Constantine VII Porphyrogenitus, emperor 13, 227, 312
Constantine IX Monomachus, emperor 120, 131
Constantine Palaeocappa 199
Constantinople 120, 128–30, 133–8, 151–2
    First Council of 35, 294
    Great Church of, *see* Hagia Sophia
    patriarchate of 20–1, 124, 134–356
Coptic 20, 76, 81, 198, 211, 227, 271
Corinthians, Epistle to the 334*t*; see also *Index of Biblical References*
Cormack, Robin 120
Crusade
    First 29, 74, 123, 125–7
    Second 125–7
    Fourth 13
crusaders 4, 22, 81, 112, 116, 121, 125–8, 148, 269, 291, 350, 374
Cyprus 2, 70, 91, 108, 146–7, 150–1, 245, 287
Cyril of Jerusalem 29, 33–6, 38–40, 66, 72, 79, 87, 159–60, 168–9, 202, 278*t*, 287, 305, 354
Cyril of Scythopolis 37, 58, 78, 91, 96, 216, 231, 273, 353

Damianos, patriarch of Jerusalem 17
Daniel, abbot 92, 126, 283
Daniel, prophet 104, 270, 272*t*, 273, 304,
Day, Juliette 40
De Meester, Placide 11, 162–4, 167, 172
Delehaye, Hippolyte 62, 86, 128, 220–1, 227, 230–1, 245, 254, 262–4, 267–8, 271, 275, 284, 292, 295, 302
Didache 42
diptychs 42*t*, 65, 82, 85, 143, 145, 150, 163, 173, 174, 184, 201, 202, 210*t*, 211–12, 236–7, 294–5, 300, 351, 378, 385, 393
dismissal
    from the liturgy 42*t*, 45, 51*t*, 90, 107, 180*t*, 342, 365, 372
    hymn 52, 181, 202*t*, 213–14; see also *apolytikion*
    prayer 202*t*, 213–14

Dmitrievskii, Aleksei 12–14, 61, 82, 90, 92, 95, 196, 283, 381–3, 385–6

earthquakes 119, 123, 125, 161, 162, 277, 383
Edelby, Néophyte 19
Edessa 44, 81, 93, 100, 106, 108, 110, 282–3
Egeria 29, 32–3, 35–6, 43–6, 48, 67, 72, 78–9, 84, 87, 90, 95, 98, 114, 142, 159, 168, 197, 223, 226, 231, 234, 244, 286–8, 301, 307
eisodikon 163, 179, 181–2, 185, 189, 394; see also *introit*
Elias, abbot 111, 352
Elias, patriarch of Antioch 109
Elias, prophet 112, 147, 253–4, 270–2, 304–5, 343, 346*t*, 387
Elias of Crete, metropolitan 137–8
Elias I of Jerusalem, patriarch 90–1
Elias II of Jerusalem (the Hagiopolite), patriarch 375
Eliseus, prophet 252–4, 270–2, 303–5
Engberg, Sysse 339
Enkainia 228, 238*t*, 244–6, 276, 287, 291–2, 295, 318–20
Entrance of the Theotokos, see Presentation
epakouston 196–7, 218
Ephesians, Epistle to the 334*t*; see also *Index of Biblical References*
Ephesus, council of 240, 294
epiclesis 41t, 210*t*, 393
Epiphanius, archbishop of Jordan 17
Euchologion 5, 24, 49, 66–7, 69–70, 89, 102, 110, 131, 167–8, 174, 176–9, 198, 208, 218, 262, 299, 339, 341, 367–8, 377, 393
Eusebius of Caesarea 2, 23, 34, 284, 333
Exodus 271, 342; see also *Index of Biblical References*
Ezekiel, prophet 272*t*

Fagerberg, David 25, 354
Fedalto, Giorgio 71, 76, 117, 139, 143–4, 378, 385
Fenwick, John 159
Findikyan, Daniel 48, 179, 189, 198
Frøyshov, Stig 16, 21, 30, 53, 54, 55, 59, 64, 89, 90, 100–2, 105, 132, 169, 181, 234, 281, 331, 360, 361, 370

Galadza, Daniel 4, 50, 84, 113, 170, 187, 188, 195, 239, 257, 301, 306, 315, 320, 330, 332, 335, 336, 363, 365, 366, 369, 370
Galadza, Peter 6, 298
Galatians, Epistle to the 334*t*; see also *Index of Biblical References*
Galilee 20, 315
Garitte, Gérard 13, 50, 84, 99–102, 122, 145, 224, 228, 255, 261, 268, 275–6, 277, 281, 284, 287, 290, 291, 292, 295, 309, 318, 320, 322, 323, 326, 341, 343, 367, 368, 370, 371, 373, 376
Garshuni 111, 372, 373
Genesis 196; see also *Index of Biblical References*
George Pachymeres 149–51
Georgian
    language 15, 22, 33, 49, 53, 133, 304, 329,
    lectionary 9, 15, 30, 31, 36, 39, 49–52, 55–7, 67, 69, 77, 79, 88, 90, 94, 102, 116, 142, 145, 165, 181–9, 191–208, 212–13, 218–19, 222, 223, 225, 228–9, 237, 238, 240–53, 256–63, 265–70, 273–8, 280–1, 285–93, 295–8, 300–45, 355, 368, 373, 388
Gerontius 7, 195
Getcha, Job 309, 396
Gethsemane 35, 37, 132, 142, 247, 249, 293
Giorgi P'roxore 121–2, 376
Glibetic, Nina 179
Golgotha 33–4, 88, 91, 108, 121, 123, 142, 286, 287, 289, 355, 388–9
Greek
    language 1, 22, 73, 79, 123, 214, 365
    monasticism 95–7
Gregory Pacourianus 140
Griffith, Sidney 16, 60, 80–2, 86, 104, 106, 108, 113, 115, 134, 151, 152, 282, 283, 285, 306
Grumel, Venance 109–10, 136–7, 139, 140, 165, 222, 287, 297
Guy de Lusignan 127

Hadrian 20
Hagia Sophia 2, 5, 7, 52, 60, 62, 64, 66, 77, 107, 110, 121, 131, 137–8, 141, 149, 208, 216, 243, 245, 248, 263–4, 332, 340; see also *Typikon of the Great Church*
    Enkainia of 292
Halkin, François 151, 220, 226, 230
Hannick, Christian 135, 233, 299
Harris, Simon 191–3
Hawkes-Teeples, Steven 138, 164
Hebrew language 22
Hebrews, Epistle to the 334*t*; see also *Index of Biblical References*
Heraclius 93, 95, 115, 287–8
Hesychius 48, 215, 226, 232, 247, 257
Hikelia 37
Hintze, Gisa 190–4
Hohmann, Gregor 11
Holy, see Vatican
Holy Sepulchre, see Anastasis
Huculak, Laurence 6

hymn
  for hand washing 56, 166–7, 184, 202–5,
    209, 213, 217–18, 241, 252–3, 259, 266, 365
  of the holy gifts 163, 165, 167, 202, 204,
    205–9, 213, 217–18, 242
  see also *cheroubikon*, Communion hymn,
    introit, troparion, sticheron
Hypapante 44, 225, 229, 238–40, 361, 363,
    369, 380
hyperthesis 324, 326, 335, 375
hypopsalmon 194–6

Iadgari 31, 41*t*, 46, 52–6, 67, 79, 105, 183,
    185, 208, 225, 233, 241, 242, 243, 251,
    265, 269, 281, 287, 298*t*, 302, 360, 371,
    394, 396
iconoclasm 10, 60, 63, 67, 82, 94, 108, 128–9
introit 163–5, 167, 179, 180*t*, 180–5, 189, 190,
    205, 213, 217, 394; see also *eisodikon*,
    oxitay, troparion
Iovane Zosime 50, 55, 69, 84, 89, 100–2, 144,
    174, 224, 276, 288, 295, 353, 367, 368, 370
Irenaios, patriarch of Jerusalem 17
Isaiah
  Georgian saint 281
  prophet 228, 272*t*, 304–5, 342; see also
    Index of Biblical References
Italy, southern 2, 6, 67, 71, 109, 135, 186, 208,
    234, 378

Jacob, André 25, 109, 160, 164, 172, 176,
    214, 385
James, son of Zebedee 47, 162, 257–8
James the Brother of the Lord, St 10, 12,
    14–18, 22, 35, 41, 136–7, 160, 257–64,
    307, 343, 351
  Liturgy of 29, 41–3, 58, 59, 69, 82, 85, 97,
    102, 157–219, 235, 236, 240, 242–3, 257,
    264, 270, 294–5, 307, 313, 333, 336–7,
    340, 349, 350–1, 355–6, 364, 367, 371–2,
    377–8, 386
Jeremiah
  Lamentations of 139
  prophet 47, 138–9, 272*t*, 303, 304
Jerome, St 36, 160
Jerusalem 20–1, 29, 69, 77, 300, 388, 390
  Patriarchate 1–3, 16–18, 20, 75–103,
    123–5, 139–45, 178, 231, 277, 350
  patriarchs of 139–45
  Russian Ecclesiastical Mission 12
Job 304
Joel, prophet 337; see also *Index of Biblical
    References*
John, Gospel of 309, 313–18, 333, 347, 365,
    367, 369, 372, 373, 384; see also *Index of
    Biblical References*

John, monk and scribe on Sinai 99, 368
John, priest in Ascalon 374
John Cassian 33, 195
John Chrysostom, St 60, 114, 137, 226, 239,
    240, 280, 280*t*, 281, 338–9, 385,
  Liturgy of 10, 18, 25, 66, 97–9, 131, 136,
    157–8, 160–1, 164–5, 167, 171–2, 175–9,
    201–2, 209, 213–14, 247, 254, 269, 313,
    339, 356, 371, 386, 393
John Climacus, St 215, 274, 274*t*, 383
John Moschus 32, 58–9, 87–9, 94, 142, 180,
    182, 194, 197–8, 216, 279
John of Antioch, patriarch 110, 352
John of Bolnisi 233
John of Damascus, St 35, 81, 96, 128, 129,
    215, 229, 240, 274*t*, 283
John Philoponus 91
John Phocas 87, 126
John Rufus 35
John the Baptist, St 48, 51*t*, 84, 201, 223,
    226, 229, 235, 251–7, 260–1, 266, 270,
    271, 275, 303–4, 305, 308, 320, 322, 323,
    351, 365
John the Faster 345
John the Silentiary, St 283
John the Theologian, St 47, 61, 125, 162, 258,
    265, 269, 270*t*, 364
John I Tzimisces 110, 112
John II, archbishop of Jerusalem 36, 40, 47,
    232, 277, 278*t*, 326
John II Comnenus, emperor 147
John III, patriarch of Jerusalem 77
John VII, patriarch of Jerusalem 117
John XI Beccus 149
Johnson, Maxwell 39, 40, 158–9, 196, 222,
    307, 323, 354
Johnson, Scott 79, 292
Jonah, prophet 272*t*, 343, 346*t*
Jordan river 124, 125, 243, 283, 391
Joshua 304
Justinian I, emperor 37, 57, 96, 120, 165–6,
    239, 258, 292
Juvenal, patriarch of Jerusalem 37, 83, 85,
    239, 277, 292

Kapustin, Antonin 12, 246
Kathisma Church 37, 57, 286, 291, 293*t*, 388
Kazamias, Alkiviades 82, 164, 169–77, 180,
    187, 190, 192, 199, 202, 205, 207, 211,
    214, 237, 294, 378, 385
Kazhdan, Alexander 21, 59, 60, 61, 63, 96,
    124, 230, 282, 286, 312, 338, 375
Kekelidze, Kornelii 13, 49, 55, 60, 77, 80, 87,
    90, 132, 133, 176, 222, 233, 236, 251, 253,
    275, 276, 291, 308, 320, 379
kiss of peace 41*t*, 163, 209

Korolevsky, Cyril 14–15, 18, 21–2, 80, 83, 97, 112–13, 136–7, 262, 302, 352, 400, 406
Krasnosel'tsev, Nikolai 12, 61, 141, 142, 144
Kretschmar, Georg 34, 42, 43, 271, 331
Krueger, Derek 10

Larin, Vassa 145, 364
Latas, Dionysius 17–18, 169
Latin
  clergy 126, 127, 148
  Kingdom of Jerusalem 74, 126, 128
  language 21, 22, 74, 78, 97–8, 120, 148, 190, 368
Latinization 6, 19
lectionary 23–4, 46–52, 198–9, 200–1, 300–49
Leeb, Helmut 51–2, 159, 165, 181–5, 191–5, 200–8, 212, 236
Leeming, Kate 16, 98, 114–15
Lent 30, 39, 47–9, 51–3, 62–3, 78, 132, 161, 165, 166, 193, 204, 213, 222, 233, 276–8, 288, 307–8, 313–14, 322–9, 335–8, 340, 365, 368, 369–75, 380, 395
Leontius of Jerusalem, patriarch 145–8
Liturgy
  comparative method in 8–9, 116, 231
  Divine, *see* Liturgy of St Basil, Liturgy of St James, Liturgy of St John Chrysostom
  of the Eucharist 46, 201–14
  of the Hours 5, 13, 15, 24, 33, 90, 114, 131, 169, 185, 196, 340, 372, 394
  of the Presanctified Gifts 159, 161, 173–8, 198, 212, 214, 345, 371, 372, 373, 375, 384, 386
  of the Word 46, 179–200, 218, 336
  reform of 9–10, 19, 67, 130–3, 220, 313, 351, 355–6
  stational 33–7, 48, 56, 69, 72, 87–9, 94, 116, 200, 357
  study of 8–9, 13–16, 102, 172
Loseva, Olga V. 12
Lossky, Nicolas 357
Lüstraeten, Martin 115

Maccabees 248, 257, 304
Mango, Cyril 3, 81, 95, 104, 108, 121, 129, 145, 165, 227, 263, 284, 287, 292, 359
Manuel I Comnenus 127, 146–7, 351, 385–6
manuscripts 15–16, 21, 23, 30, 102, 126, 132, 152, 163, 167, 173, 217, 300, 352; *see also* *Appendix 1 and Index of Manuscript References*
Mark
  Gospel of 313–14, 320–1, 325, 365, 367, 369, 372, 384; *see also* *Index of Biblical References*

Liturgy of St 12, 136–7, 157, 165, 176, 177–8*t*, 198–9, 211, 377
  of Ephesus 160
  of Otranto 96
  III, patriarch of Alexandria 12, 136
Martin I, pope of Rome 76
Mateos, Juan 32, 45, 61–6, 77, 88, 90, 101, 141, 159, 166, 179–88, 190–1, 194–6, 198, 200–1, 206, 213, 222–5, 238, 244–5, 248, 254, 262, 267–9, 273, 276, 279, 288, 290, 292, 295, 302, 322–3, 325, 327, 332, 337–40, 342–3, 345, 355, 373, 407
Matthew
  Gospel of 48*t*, 51*t*, 201, 204, 226, 275, 307–8, 313–14, 318–20, 325–6, 342, 365, 367, 369, 372, 384; *see also* *Index of Biblical References*
Matthew of Edessa 110
Maximus Confessor 89, 94, 104, 215, 277, 338
Melania 7, 88, 196
Melkite 11, 19, 80–4, 172, 244, 248, 261, 351, 394
  Arab Christian identity 80–4
  Greek Catholic Church 11, 19, 80
Mercier, Basile-Charles 41, 82, 85, 157, 164–92, 200–14, 236, 270, 294, 377–8
mesodion 197–8, 218
Metreveli, Elene (Hélène Métréveli) 52, 53, 55, 56, 233
Micah, prophet 304
Michael, archangel 342, 363
Michael Psellus 120
Modestus, patriarch of Jerusalem 103, 115, 253, 277, 278, 326
monazontes 32, 90
Monoenergism 93–4
Monotheletism 76, 93–4, 104
Mount Athos 128, 132, 160, 262, 298, 353
Mount Carmel 20
Mount of Olives 7, 35, 98, 142, 195, 388
multilingualism 21, 22, 78–9, 95, 97–9, 113, 153, 353, 360
mystagogy 31, 66, 179, 214–17, 232, 338

Nasrallah, Joseph 14–15, 21–2, 76, 79, 95, 104, 105, 111, 113, 114, 136, 329
Nativity
  of Christ 23, 36, 52, 56, 64, 96, 127, 161, 187–8, 223, 226, 239–44, 247, 258, 261, 264, 267, 273, 320–1, 348
  of John the Baptist 255, 256*t*, 303–4, 320,
  of the Theotokos 182, 229, 250*t*, 342
Nea Church 37, 115, 292, 293*t*, 388
New Martyrs 99, 106, 282–5, 367

Nicaea
  First Council of 20–1, 240, 294
  Second Council of 82–3
Nicephorus I, patriarch of Jerusalem 139
Nicephorus II, patriarch of Jerusalem 146
Nicon of the Black Mountain 59, 102, 352
Nikiforova, Alexandra 53–4, 182, 183, 246,
  281, 285, 308, 309, 325, 361, 364
Nikolopoulos, Panagiotes 96, 98, 173–6, 216,
  249, 330, 360, 366, 369, 380, 386

ode 64, 185, 195, 197, 201, 354, 375, 395;
  see also canticles
Olkinuora, Jaakko (Damaskinos) 235,
  246, 292
Orestes, patriarch of Jerusalem 109–10, 117, 378
Ousterhout, Robert 72, 117, 119–22, 249
Outtier, Bernard 47, 55, 100, 102, 174, 200,
  270, 317, 333, 348, 371, 372
oxitay 51, 56, 165, 181–3, 189, 240–1, 251–2,
  258, 265, 287, 394

Palestine 20–1, 89–95, 230, 391
Papadopoulos-Kerameus, Athanasios 45, 90,
  104, 130, 141–4, 151, 161, 182, 185, 201,
  212, 227, 235, 341, 381
Parenti, Stefano 3, 24, 30, 59, 66, 67, 75, 83,
  84, 90, 95, 102, 109, 110, 131, 136, 137,
  160, 162, 164–6, 168, 172, 179, 184, 190,
  197, 206–8, 211, 213, 218–19, 223, 225,
  235, 287, 306, 313, 339, 342–3, 346, 377
Pascha 1, 12, 30, 39, 45, 49, 63, 114, 118, 140,
  142, 144, 161, 165, 181, 182, 185, 188–9,
  204, 206, 220, 222, 225–6, 235–6, 242,
  248, 280–1, 309–15, 330–5, 338–9, 347,
  349, 361, 363, 365–6, 369, 372, 379,
  381, 384, 393–5; *see also* Anastasis,
  resurrection of Christ, resurrectional
  Gospels
Patmos 61, 146
Patrich, Joseph 57, 87, 91, 95–7, 114, 126,
  208–9, 353
Patterson Ševčenko, Nancy 84, 91, 96, 132,
  162, 220, 230, 275, 383
Paul, St 268–70
pentarchy 3, 21, 280
Pentecost 1, 22, 30, 35, 36, 45, 56, 62, 65, 77,
  129, 183–4, 198, 222, 225, 238, 275–6,
  312–20, 331–4, 395
Pentkovsky, Aleksei 4, 7, 13, 24, 63, 117,
  186, 373
Permiakov, Vitaly 168, 244, 291, 309
Perria, Lidia 68, 99, 109, 112, 139, 232,
  363, 369
Persian, invasion of Jerusalem 4, 88, 95, 103,
  108, 253
Peter, St 268–70

Peter Apselamus, St 47, 284
Peter Aspebet 83
Peter the Iberian 7, 35, 80, 231, 261
Philemon, Epistle to 334
Philippians, Epistle to the 334*t*; see also *Index
  of Biblical References*
Piédagnel, Auguste 38, 40
pilgrimage 30, 70, 75, 86–7, 126, 128, 153,
  283, 355
Pitra, Jean-Baptiste 13
Pott, Thomas 5, 9–10, 130–1, 164
prayer
  for the dismissal 213–14, 372
  for those bringing offerings 143, 202*t*,
    211–12, 386
  Lord's (Our Father) 40, 42, 163, 166, 202*t*,
    204, 371, 372
  of incense 175, 180, 192, 205
  of thanksgiving 42*t*, 46
  of the cathedra 110
  of the enarxis 163, 179
  of the Gospel 163–4, 201
  of the *trisagion* 187
Presentation 249, 250*t*, 292
Pringle, Denys 35, 37, 87, 92, 116, 127, 253,
  268, 269, 291, 388
Procopius of Caesarea 37
propsalmon 59, 193–4
prokeimenon 59, 65, 190–3, 198, 218

Raczka, Gary Philippe 61, 339
Radle, Gabriel 83, 109, 165, 168, 172
Ray, Walter 29, 247
relics 34, 47, 72, 75, 118, 119, 125, 209, 228,
  229, 249, 258, 260, 262–4, 266–9, 275,
  280, 286, 288, 290, 295, 298–9
Renoux, Charles (Athanase) 46–9, 55–6, 79,
  100, 193, 200, 206, 208, 227, 235, 239,
  252–3, 264, 287, 333, 348
resurrection of Christ 23–5, 49, 111, 183, 188,
  210, 228, 242, 309, 393, 395; *see also* Pascha
resurrectional Gospels 311–12, 327, 330, 363,
  364, 369, 372, 379
Revelation, Book of 65, 331, 334; see also
  Index of Biblical References
Romans, Epistle to the 334*t*; see also *Index of
  Biblical References*
Romanus III Argyrus 119, 120, 134, 139
Romanus the Melodist 60, 255
Rome 3, 6, 7, 14, 33, 76, 80, 85, 96, 106, 137,
  148, 159, 269, 279
  pope of 6, 125, 129, 378

Sabas
  Lavra of St 2, 21, 50, 55, 89–103, 108, 132,
    284, 285, 352, 395
  St 91, 97, 188

Typikon of 70, 92, 97, 114, 126, 132, 322, 382, 383

Samuel, prophet 205, 270, 304; see also *Index of Biblical References*

Sanctus 41*t*, 42, 210*t*, 393

Sauget, Joseph-Marie 9, 162, 172, 221, 227, 233, 260, 283–5, 352

Severus ibn al-Muqaffaʿ, bishop 81

Shanidze, Akaki 55

Sinai
  Monastery of St Catherine 2, 16, 21, 64, 102, 150, 161, 174, 215, 293*t*
  'new finds' manuscripts 15–16, 53, 359–60

Sion 1, 35–6, 85, 142, 210
  Church of 36, 88, 249, 257–8, 265, 267, 293*t*, 326, 388, 390

Sophronius I, patriarch of Jerusalem 32, 58, 59, 87, 88, 94–5, 103–5, 142, 180, 182, 194, 197–8, 216–17, 232, 242, 264, 277, 278*t*

Sophronius II, patriarch of Jerusalem 216–17, 378

Spinks, Bryan 43, 211

spoudaioi 32, 54, 88, 90–1, 142, 293

Stephen, St 47, 195, 229, 264–8

Stephen the Sabaite 97, 129, 326

sticheron 182–4, 203–7, 228, 235–6, 242, 354, 375

Stoudios Monastery 2, 7, 63, 130, 254–5, 313

Symeon Metaphrastes 84

Symeon of Thessalonike 138

synaxarion 62–3, 101, 128, 227, 233, 245, 308

Syriac language 22, 211, 215, 217, 222, 226, 234, 248, 282, 360

Syrian monasticism 97–100

Taft, Robert F. 2–5, 8–10, 15, 21, 25, 30–2, 40, 42–3, 45, 51, 52, 54, 59, 61, 63, 66, 68, 71, 75, 83, 102, 116, 123, 128, 131–2, 143, 157–8, 160, 163–7, 172, 179–80, 182, 187, 191, 194, 196, 202, 205–9, 211–16, 221, 231–2, 235, 237, 240, 243, 251, 286, 291–2, 300, 322, 330, 338–40, 355, 365, 375, 386, 396, 407, 410, 413–14

Takala-Roszczenko, Maria 7

Tarchnishvili, Michael 15, 49, 169, 172, 176–7, 182, 202–5, 222, 232, 303–4, 368, 376

Theodore Abū Qurrah 81, 96, 106, 129, 215

Theodore Balsamon 12, 136–9, 218, 248, 356

Theodore Stoudite 128, 130–3, 243, 274–5, 375

Theophanes 107–8, 129, 145, 151, 283

Theophany 30, 44, 49, 56, 149–50, 161, 197, 220–3, 239–44, 285, 320–3, 334, 338

Theophilus I, patriarch of Jerusalem 139

Thessalonians, Epistle to 334*t*; see also *Index of Biblical References*

Thessalonike 121, 140, 171, 235

Timothy, Epistle to 334*t*; see also *Index of Biblical References*

Timothy I, patriarch of Constantinople 249

Timothy, patriarch of Jerusalem 16

trisagion 59, 65*t*, 163, 164, 166, 179, 180*t*, 181, 182, 185, 186, 187–90, 192, 197, 208, 242, 338, 370

troparion 54, 65, 142, 163, 179, 181, 182, 184–5, 188, 197, 201, 236, 243–4, 254, 255, 262, 267, 365; see also *apolytikion, eisodikon, introit*

Tropologion 52–6, 132, 141, 182–3, 234, 243, 246, 281, 284, 308–9, 325, 360–1, 395; see also Iadgari

Trullo, Council in 136–7, 159, 188, 248

Tsipras, Alexis 17

Typikon of the Anastasis 13, 45, 49, 70, 90–1, 107, 114, 122, 126, 140, 144, 161, 181–2, 186–7, 197, 201, 206, 209, 212, 235, 353, 381; see also *Hagios Stavros Gr. 43* in *Index of Manuscript References*

Typikon of the Great Church 61–6, 122, 185–6, 206, 224*t*, 237, 238*t*, 245, 248, 250*t*, 263*t*, 266*t*, 269, 270*t*, 272*t*, 274*t*, 275, 276, 277*t*, 278*t*, 280*t*, 285*t*, 288, 289*t*, 290*t*, 292, 293, 296, 298, 309, 322, 327, 332, 337, 373

Uspensky, Nikolai 58–9, 185, 298, 341, 415

Vatican 14, 16–18; see also *Index of Manuscript References*

Velkovska, Elena 5, 6, 54, 67, 83–4, 110, 162, 164, 168, 179, 190, 198, 211, 225, 287, 291, 302, 313

Verhelst, Stéphane 34–8, 46, 50, 57, 87–8, 94, 116, 136, 145, 164–5, 168–9, 200, 208, 214, 233, 247, 253, 260–1, 268, 270, 367, 385, 388, 407, 416

Victor of Damietta 99, 368

Wilkinson, John 34, 43, 44, 45, 86, 125

Winkler, Gabriele 8, 20, 169, 172, 189, 200, 202, 211, 240, 244, 247, 254, 269, 273

Xevsuriani, Lili (Lili Khevsuriani) 52, 53, 55, 169, 173–6, 367

Yahyā al-Anṭakī 36, 110, 378

Zachariah, father of John the Baptist 251, 260, 272*t*

Zachariah, prophet 304–5

Zakynthos 17

Zerfass, Rolf 45, 301, 341

Zosime, *see* Iovane Zosime

Printed and bound by CPI Group (UK) Ltd, Croydon, CR0 4YY